A Companion to Early Modern Women's Writing

Blackwell Companions to Literature and Culture

This series offers comprehensive, newly written surveys of key periods and movements, and certain major authors, in English literary culture and history. Extensive volumes provide new perspectives and positions on contexts and on canonical and post-canonical texts, orientating the beginning student in new fields of study and providing the experienced undergraduate and new graduate with current and new directions, as pioneered and developed by leading scholars in the field.

A COMPANION TO

EARLY MODERN
WOMEN'S WRITING

EDITED BY **ANITA PACHECO**

Blackwell
Publishing

Copyright © Blackwell Publishers Ltd 2002
Editorial matter, selection and arrangement copyright © Anita Pacheco 2002

Editorial Offices:
108 Cowley Road, Oxford OX4 1JF, UK
Tel: +44 (0)1865 791100
350 Main Street, Malden, MA 02148-5018, USA
Tel: +1 781 388 8250

First published 2002 by Blackwell Publishing Ltd, a Blackwell Publishing company

Library of Congress Cataloging-in-Publication Data has been applied for.

ISBN 0-631-21702-9 (hbk)

A catalogue record for this title is available from the British Library.

Set in 11 on 13 pt Garamond 3
by SNP Best-set Typesetter Ltd., Hong Kong
Printed and bound by MPG Books Ltd, Bodmin, Cornwall

For further information on
Blackwell Publishers, visit our website:
www.blackwellpublishers.co.uk

For my mother

Contents

Notes on Contributors

Elaine Beilin is Professor of English at Framingham State College. She is the author of *Redeeming Eve: Women Writers of the English Renaissance* and numerous articles on early modern women writers. She edited *The Examinations of Anne Askew* for the *Women Writers in English* series published by Oxford University Press. She is currently working on *Constructing the Commonwealth: Women Writing History* and *A Woman for All Seasons: A Cultural History of Anne Askew.*

Patricia Brace is Assistant Professor in the English Department at Laurentian University, Sudbury, Canada, where she teaches early modern and medieval literature. She has published articles on Isabella Whitney and Abraham Fleming and is working on a facsimile edition of Elizabeth Tyrwhit's *Morning and Euening Praiers* (1574). Her research is on sixteenth-century women writers, with a particular interest in their engagement with print and entry into the book market.

Kenneth Charlton is Emeritus Professor of the History of Education, University of London, King's College. He is author of *Education in Renaissance England* and *Women, Religion and Education in Early Modern England*. He is currently contributing to *The Cambridge History of Early Modern English Literature* and *The New Dictionary of National Biography*.

Rebecca De Haas is currently a graduate student working on her Ph.D. at the University of Georgia. Her research interests include seventeenth-century poetry and early modern women's literature, specifically the work of Katherine Philips.

Margaret J. M. Ezell is currently the John Paul Abbott Professor of Liberal Arts at Texas A&M University. She is the author of *The Patriarch's Wife: Literary Evidence and the History of the Family*, *Writing Women's Literary History* and *Social Authorship and the*

Advent of Print. Presently she is at work on volume five for the forthcoming *Oxford English Literary History* series.

Elizabeth H. Hageman, Professor of English at the University of New Hampshire, is currently Chair of the Executive Committee of the Brown University Women Writers Project and a member of the Executive Council of the Renaissance English Text Society. She is general editor of the series *English Women Writers, 1350–1850*, and co-editor for that series of the forthcoming volume of Katherine Philips's poetry, plays and letters.

Margo Hendricks is Associate Professor of Literature at the University of California at Santa Cruz. She is co-editor of *Women, Race, and Writing in the Early Modern Period*. She has published on Marlowe, Shakespeare, race and Renaissance culture, and Aphra Behn. She recently completed a study of race and Aphra Behn, and her current research explores race and Shakespeare. A future project will examine African women in Renaissance culture and feminist historiography.

Hilary Hinds teaches in the English Department at Lancaster University. Her previous publications include *God's Englishwomen: Seventeenth-Century Sectarian Writing and Feminist Criticism*, an edition of Anna Trapnel's prophecy *The Cry of a Stone*, and (co-edited with Elspeth Graham, Elaine Hobby and Helen Wilcox) *Her Own Life: Autobiographical Writings by Seventeenth-Century Englishwomen*.

Elaine Hobby is Professor of Seventeenth-Century Studies at Loughborough University. She has been researching women's writing from the period 1640–1700 since 1978, and finds it more fascinating as each year passes. Her publications include *Virtue of Necessity: English Women's Writing 1649–1688*, co-editorship of *Her Own Life: Autobiographical Writings by Seventeenth-Century Englishwomen* and *Jane Sharp, The Midwives Book*. She is currently working on a history of the early modern midwifery manual.

Sara H. Mendelson is Associate Professor in the Arts and Sciences Programme at McMaster University. She is the author of *The Mental World of Stuart Women: Three Studies, Women in Early Modern England 1550–1720* (with Patricia Crawford) and *Paper Bodies: A Margaret Cavendish Reader* (with Sylvia Bowerbank), as well as articles on Stuart women's diaries, early modern sexual identities (with Patricia Crawford) and women's civility in seventeenth-century England.

Naomi J. Miller is Associate Professor of English Literature and Women's Studies at the University of Arizona. Her publications include *Changing the Subject: Mary Wroth and Figurations of Gender in Early Modern England* as well as a collection of essays on Wroth, co-edited with Gary Waller, entitled *Reading Mary Wroth: Representing Alternatives in Early Modern England*. Most recently, she has been working on a book-length study of constructions of maternity, *Labor and Delivery: Working Mothers in Early Modern England*, and has co-edited, with Naomi Yavneh, an interdisciplinary collection of essays entitled *Maternal Measures: Figuring Caregiving in the Early Modern Period*.

Sheila Ottway gained her Ph.D. from the University of Groningen in the Netherlands in 1998, with a thesis entitled *Desiring Disencumbrance: The Representation of the Self in Autobiographical Writings by Seventeenth-Century Englishwomen*. She has published articles on women's writings from the early modern period, and is co-editor of *Betraying Ourselves: Forms of Self-Representation in Early Modern English Texts* and of *Writing the History of Women's Writing*. She now lives in Oxford.

Anita Pacheco is a Lecturer in the Department of Humanities at the University of Hertfordshire. She has published articles on Aphra Behn and is the editor of *Early Women Writers 1600–1720* and joint editor (with John Stachniewski) of *Grace Abounding and Other Spiritual Autobiographies*.

Bronwen Price is a Lecturer in English at Portsmouth University. She specializes in seventeenth-century literature and has published a range of essays on early modern women's writing and seventeenth-century poetry. She has just finished editing a volume of new essays entitled *Francis Bacon's New Atlantis* for Manchester University Press's *Texts in Culture* series.

Melinda Alliker Rabb is Associate Professor of English at Brown University where she teaches seventeenth- and eighteenth-century literature and serves on the Advisory Board of the Women Writers Project. Her publications include work on Jonathan Swift, Alexander Pope, Delarivier Manley, Laurence Sterne, Henry Fielding, Samuel Richardson, William Godwin and Sarah Scott. She is currently completing a book on Delarivier Manley and the satirical 'secret history'.

Debra K. Rienstra is Assistant Professor of English at Calvin College in Grand Rapids, Michigan. She received her Ph.D. from Rutgers University, where she began working in the area of early modern women and English religious poetry. Her previous publications include articles on Shakespeare, the Countess of Pembroke and Aemilia Lanyer. She is also a published poet.

Paul Salzman is a Senior Lecturer in English at La Trobe University, Melbourne, Australia. He has published widely in the area of early modern women's writing, and has edited *Early Modern Women's Writing: An Anthology 1560–1700* for Oxford World's Classics. He has just finished a book entitled *Writing 1621*, and is now working on a study of the reception and textual fortunes of the writing of six early modern women.

Patricia Springborg holds a chair in political theory in the Department of Government at the University of Sydney. She is the author of *The Problem of Human Needs and* *the Critique of Civilization, Royal Persons: Patriarchal Monarchy and the Feminine Princi- ple, Western Republicanism and the Oriental Prince*, and two editions of the writings of Mary Astell. She is currently a fellow of the Wissenschaftscolleg zu Berlin.

Tim Stretton is the author of *Women Waging Law in Elizabethan England*. He has taught at universities in Britain, New Zealand and Canada and held a three-year Research Fellowship at Clare Hall, Cambridge. He is currently an Assistant Profes- sor at Saint Mary's University in Halifax, Nova Scotia and is working on the history of married women and the law in England from 1536 to 1925.

Frances Teague is Professor of English at the University of Georgia. In addition to several books on Shakespeare and his contemporaries, she has published a biography of Bathsua Makin, a number of essays about Elizabeth I and a facsimile edition of seventeenth-century educational pamphlets.

Sophie Tomlinson is a Lecturer in English at the University of Auckland. She has published essays on Queen Henrietta Maria and female performance, and the dramatic writings of Margaret Cavendish and Katherine Philips. She is completing a book, *Women on Stage in Stuart Drama*, and is working on an edition of John Fletcher's comedy *The Wild-Goose Chase*.

Diane Willen is Professor and Chair of the Department of History at Georgia State University in Atlanta, Georgia. She is author of *John Russell, First Earl of Bedford, One of the King's Men*. She has published essays on women in early modern England, includ- ing articles on women and religion in the *Journal of Ecclesiastical History* and *Albion*. She served as executive secretary of the North American Conference on British Studies and as President of the Southern Conference on British Studies.

Gweno Williams is Senior Lecturer in Literature Studies at the College of Ripon and York St John. Drama by early modern women is one of her major research interests, particularly the plays of Margaret Cavendish. She has produced original film versions of a number of Cavendish's plays and is co-author, with Alison Findlay and Stephanie Hodgson-Wright, of *Women and Dramatic Production 1550–1700*.

Susanne Woods is Provost and Professor of English at Wheaton College and Adjunct Professor of English at Brown University, where she taught for many years and was founding director of the Women Writers Project. She has written *Lanyer: A Renais- sance Woman Poet* and edited *The Poems of Aemilia Lanyer* and, with Margaret P. Hannay, *Teaching Tudor and Stuart Women Writers*. She has also written numerous articles on Renaissance poetry and poetics, and a book on the development of English verse, *Natural Emphasis: English Versification from Chaucer to Dryden*.

Introduction

Anita Pacheco

The study of early modern women's writing is a relatively new academic field, and its emergence has been characterized by a sustained and rigorous examination of the premises of feminist literary history. In the 1970s, as poststructuralism became a force to be reckoned with in the academy, the early work on women's writing by critics like Ellen Moers, Elaine Showalter, Sandra Gilbert and Susan Gubar came under increasingly heavy fire. The charges levelled against them are by now familiar: in treating women writers as the coherent, controlling origins of textual meaning, these critics were peddling humanist conceptions of authorship and self-hood that were both outmoded and politically retrograde. How, it was asked, could academic feminism hope to profit from the adoption of a model of the author spawned by bourgeois patriarchy and instrumental in the creation of a male-dominated literary canon?

Poststructuralism, in accordance with Roland Barthes's claim that 'it is language that speaks, not the author' (Barthes 1977: 209), pronounced the author dead, and in so far as his demise signalled the weakening of an exclusionary canon, it could only be greeted with a sigh of relief by feminist critics. But the poststructuralist dismissal of authorial signature obviously posed problems for the study of women authors, which it seemed necessarily to discredit as an academic enterprise. Indeed, under the influence of poststructuralism and Lacanian psychoanalysis, some French feminist theorists called into question the political usefulness of privileging women's writing as an object of study; for if all language was inevitably tainted by patriarchy, what mattered was not the biological sex of the author but whether or not a piece of writing contained traces of the 'feminine': the pre-oedipal realm of infancy, dominated by the mother and repressed upon the child's entry into the symbolic order.

For feminist critics committed to the recovery and study of women's writing, the indifference of some French feminist theorists to female authors seemed at the very least politically complacent. As Janet Todd put it in 1988 in her book *Feminist Literary History*:

> The long tradition of actual female writing which it has been the business of American historical feminist criticism to recover is ignored. . . . French-influenced critics . . . make no effort to remake or shake the canon, and it appears that theory can substitute for reading female writers of the past; 'reading woman' takes over from reading women. (Todd 1988: 78)

Underneath Todd's exasperation with French feminism lay two related assumptions: that women and other social groups traditionally excluded from or marginalized by literary studies deserve a voice, and that to kill off the author is to ensure their continued silence. Todd had no truck with the naive humanism of some of the pioneers of feminist literary history, but neither did she want the history of women's writing to be consigned to oblivion at the very moment that it was beginning to make itself known. Many feminist critics of women's writing shared Todd's desire to preserve the author without reverting to liberal humanist notions of the free and self-determining individual on which it had hitherto been based. While accepting the poststructuralist dictum that there is no nature outside culture, these critics argued as well that the cultures that create us are 'neither seamless wholes nor swallowed whole' (Jones 1990: 2); that the tensions and instabilities built into them create the conditions for social struggle and change; that within the limits set by the dominant groups, there is room for manoeuvre and resistance by subordinate groups. The female author, by this account, would be read not as an autonomous 'great writer' but as a product of history who was also an agent, capable of negotiating her marginal position and of intervening creatively in a masculine discursive system.

Yet poststructuralist thought also raised searching questions about the nature of historical enquiry. Suddenly, the past seemed a very distant land, the lives and experiences of its inhabitants available to us only in the form of representations that we inevitably interpret through the filter of our own values and preconceptions. In the face of such limitations, it seemed wise at least to acknowledge the 'interestedness' of the stories we construct about the past, and the 1980s and 1990s witnessed a widespread interrogation of the critical agendas and historiographical assumptions that had shaped the study of women's writing. Much of the early work in the field had been either ahistorical, looking at women writers almost entirely in terms of their gender and so effectively detaching them from their social and cultural contexts, or had adapted a traditional linear model of history to its feminist ends, locating in the history of women's writing a steady progression of feminist sensibilities. As a guiding principle of women's literary history, this evolutionary feminism now seems ill-suited to pre-1700 women writers, who either looked unappealing alongside their more 'enlightened' successors or were airbrushed into early but reassuringly recognizable versions of ourselves. The point here is not that there are no critical perspectives on women's subordination in early modern women's texts, rather that readings of them need to be properly historicized. As Susanne Woods points out in her essay on Aemilia Lanyer in this volume, *Salve Deus Rex Judaeorum* (1611) offers a 'woman-centred' rewriting of Christ's passion, but the text's 'proto-feminism' should be seen in relation to the Jacobean patronage system and Lanyer's plea for 'the attention and favours of higher-born patronesses'.

Feminist literary historians were increasingly criticized for offering insufficiently historicized readings of early women's texts, for trying to establish 'continuities and identities between past and present that bully the past and its literature out of their specificity and materiality' (Todd 1988: 97). This critique led to the questioning of many of the most well-established historical 'facts' of women's writing before 1700: that there were few women writing during this period; that those who did were 'rare and eccentric creatures' (Ezell 1993: 42), usually of aristocratic or at least upper-class birth; and that the scarcity of women writers in early modern Britain was due to the overwhelmingly oppressive power of patriarchal ideologies. Thanks to the research of scholars and literary historians like Margaret J. M. Ezell, Elaine Hobby, Hilary Hinds, Wendy Wall, Margaret Ferguson and many others, we have been able significantly to revise this reconstruction of the past, and to recognize the extent to which it derived from notions of literature as a commercial enterprise and of the author as a professional who wrote for profit in the medium of print – notions that are far more appropriate to the nineteenth and twentieth centuries than to the sixteenth and seventeenth. This imposition of a modern conception of the author on to the early modern era obscured the characteristics of authorship in 'a pre-professional literary environment' where to publish was 'the exception for both men and women' (Ezell 1993: 34). Coupled with a narrow view of literature as the traditional canonical genres of poetry, drama and fiction, this preoccupation with publication and commercialism led feminist literary historians to overlook or ignore the significant numbers of women of different classes who were involved in coterie literature and manuscript circulation, and who wrote for an audience (though not for profit) in a wide variety of genres: letters, diaries, prophecies, advice books, religious treatises, as well as more traditional 'literary' genres.

In her essay in this volume on 'Women and Writing', Margaret J. M. Ezell delineates a vibrant pre-1700 literary culture that was based at least as much on social interaction as on solitary endeavour and that encompassed such disparate cultural practices as the reading and writing circles that formed an integral part of domestic life for elite women; the popular tradition of exchanging verses; the creation of commonplace books that often registered a plurality of hands and voices; and the political petitions and appeals compiled by Quaker women, as well as the professionalism that became more common in the latter half of the seventeenth century. This book aims to familiarize its readers with this lively, diverse and widespread female literary culture and to bring together the work of many of the literary critics and historians who have been instrumental in its recovery. It is designed to convey the remarkable extent of women's textual production in early modern England, as well as the generic variety of their writings. It also seeks to situate those writings in their social and cultural contexts and in so doing to provide accounts from different historical perspectives of women's participation in and contributions to early modern culture and society. On this level, Part One of the book, 'Contexts', reveals a broad consensus among literary, social and cultural historians of early modern women. In her essay, Margaret Ezell observes that while early modern England was unquestionably a patriarchal and hierarchical society, 'the oft-cited injunction that women should be chaste, silent and obedient and confine their creative work to needles and threads . . . can no longer be taken as an accurate delineation of women's participation in early modern literary culture'. The gap Ezell notes between patriarchal decrees and actual practice appears in varying forms in each of the 'Context' chapters. Kenneth Charlton's chapter on 'Women and Education' contrasts the limited educational opportunities available even to elite women with the extensive role upper- and middle-class women played as educators within the family. Diane Willen, looking at Puritan women of elite and middling status in pre-revolutionary England, finds that their Protestant faith simultaneously reinforced oppressive constructions of femininity and legitimized their adoption of active spiritual roles within their communities. In his chapter on 'Women, Property and Law' Tim Stretton points out that a legal system that seriously disadvantaged women and restricted their access to property did not in fact prevent them either from going to law 'in their thousands' or from owning and controlling considerably more property than has hitherto been recognized. Sara H. Mendelson traces the long, demanding and highly resourceful working lives conducted by poor, middling and elite women in a society which denied all women a professional work identity.

The aim of these social and cultural historians is not to question the existence of patriarchal oppression but to capture something of the complexity of women's position in a society where practice did not always adhere to prescription, where there might be substantial variation in women's experiences of male domination, and where women were able both to resist social pressures and constraints and to make the most of the limited opportunities their society often unwittingly afforded them.

Part Two, 'Readings', presents critical introductions to ten major texts by early modern women in a variety of genres: poetry, prose romance, tragic drama, comedy, autobiography, prophecy, political polemic, and translation. Part Three, 'Genres', provides extended coverage of autobiography, defences of women, prophecy, poetry, prose fiction and drama. This section is designed to give readers a clear sense of the number and range of women who were writing in England during the sixteenth and seventeenth centuries. The authors represented in Part Two are probably the best-known and most frequently studied figures in the field, and a significant number of them either belonged to the upper ranks of society or were royalists or both. While it is debatable whether any of them, with the exception of Aphra Behn, could be called 'canonical' writers, it is nonetheless important to supplement their texts with the work of less familiar but equally significant writers and to avoid perpetuating a narrow and exclusionary 'canon' that silences other women authors of this period, many of whom came from lower social ranks or held radical political beliefs. Many also wrote in non-canonical genres, and it is hoped that the genre chapters will serve to underline the need for a broader understanding of what constitutes 'literature' in the early modern period. As Elaine Hobby points out in her chapter on 'Prophecy', there were over 300 women prophets in England during the seventeenth century, which arguably makes prophecy 'the single most important genre for women in the early modern period'. The broad generic categories covered in this section in fact encompass numerous sub-genres. Sheila Ottway's chapter on 'Autobiography', for example, looks in some detail at diaries and mothers' advice books, both popular forms of writing for women in this period. Mothers' advice books in particular have recently attracted considerable scholarly interest; they figure prominently not only in Sheila Ottway's essay but also in Diane Willen's chapter on religion, where they exemplify the capacity of Christianity to create a space for women to construct and affirm their identities, in this instance by taking on responsibility for the spiritual education of their families.

Translation is generally recognized as playing a vital role in the establishment of early modern female literary culture. While there is not a separate chapter devoted to translation in this volume, it is the central focus of Debra Rienstra's essay on Mary Sidney's *Psalmes* in Part Two, and its importance is registered by numerous other contributors, including Kenneth Charlton, Bronwen Price, Sophie Tomlinson and Paul Salzman. Women's extensive involvement in translation, especially of biblical and religious texts, is often explained on the grounds that a mode of writing that was at once devotional and second hand would have been a 'safe' literary venture for women. Both Debra Rienstra and Bronwen Price suggest that translation's appeal for early modern women may be more complicated than this view allows. Rienstra reminds us that in a period in which imitation was a central principle of poetic composition, translation was highly valued as a form of artistic endeavour. Both critics also stress that Sidney's *Psalmes* are notable not for their decorous self-effacement but for their startling technical virtuosity.

In Part Four, 'Issues and Debates', readers will find in-depth consideration of two of the major challenges facing the field of early modern women's writing: the canon and feminist historiography. As we have seen, the canon has always posed problems for the study of women writers, and in her essay 'The Work of Women in the Age of Electronic Reproduction', Melinda Alliker Rabb presents a thought-provoking review of the difficulties that trouble both integrationist and separatist approaches. More worryingly, she concludes that early modern women's writing remains a marginal academic field due to 'the powerfully restrictive intellectual systems that govern postmodern interpretive communities'. In Rabb's view, so entrenched are 'the fixed systems of valuation and comprehension' deriving from the conventions of print culture, that they continue to devalue the texts produced in the largely pre-professional literary world documented in this book. Rabb is nonetheless optimistic about the future of the field. What we need are new ways of reading and responding to the written word, and these, she argues, may prove to be timely by-products of e-culture. Databases like *The Brown University Women Writers Project* and *The Perdita Project*, based at Nottingham Trent University, are already making early modern women's texts available in a form free of the interventions of anthology editors. Perhaps more importantly, the worldwide web may encourage modes of reading, writing and interpretation more akin to the practices of early modern manuscript culture.

Margo Hendricks also stresses the need for new ways of reading. Her chapter on 'Feminist Historiography' addresses a problem that has dogged feminist history, literary and otherwise, since its inception: the tendency to treat women of the past as if they belonged to a homogeneous subculture; as if they all shared precisely the same set of experiences regardless of other determinants of identity such as class, ethnicity and sexuality. This kind of historical writing works to privilege as 'normative' the experiences of the middle- and upper-class Englishwomen whose histories are most visible to us. While Hendricks acknowledges the progress feminist historians have made in recognizing and rejecting 'the universal woman model', she argues convincingly that there remain too many histories that portray early modern England as 'homogeneous and white' and that collapse women of different classes into the single category of 'Early Modern Woman'. She calls for more archival research in order to make visible the full range of women living in Britain in the sixteenth and seventeenth centuries, and urges that we read the archival records in ways that do not simply confirm our own preconceptions; that we ask not only what they reveal but also what they conceal and attempt to make sense of both.

It is hoped that this book will contribute to the development of a feminist historiography that is 'truly representative of "women's histories"' (Hendricks, this volume). Much more work needs to be done, of course, especially on the non-elite and non-European women who leave fewer traces in a historical record biased in favour of the gentry and aristocracy. But in the pages that follow readers will discover something of the diversity of women's lives and writings in early modern England. They will also encounter some of the opportunities for agency available to many women of the period. One of the major 'recurring themes' of the book is the enormous importance of religion in the lives of early modern women of different classes, for whom it offered not only spiritual consolation but also an entry into the public domain. Diane Willen's study of the Puritan community of Caroline England, Hilary Hinds's essay on *Anna Trapnel's Report and Plea* and Elaine Hobby's discussion of prophecy are just a few of the chapters that serve to remind us that in early modern England religion was a political issue. By serving God many Englishwomen adopted a political role as well; as Diane Willen succinctly puts it, 'godliness abetted politicization'. Numerous texts discussed in this volume register women's interventions in the political conflicts and debates of the period, often (though not always) from a religious perspective: from the Fifth Monarchist Anna Trapnel to the royalist Margaret Cavendish to the High Church Tory Mary Astell.

This book also helps to illuminate the close connection between women's writing and their reading. The popularity of the commonplace book during this period illustrates the extent to which reading and writing were inseparable activities for the small portion of the population who could write as well as read; women and men copied out and collected passages from their reading and in doing so created books of their own. Patricia Brace reads the non-aristocratic Isabella Whitney's *A Sweet Nosegay* as a poetic text rooted in this conception of reading as a kind of transformative gathering of textual fragments. Elaine Beilin reveals the intimate connection between the aristocratic Elizabeth Cary's reading and her writing by discussing *The Tragedy of Mariam* in relation to Lucy Cary's account, in *The Lady Falkland: Her Life* (1645), of her mother's extensive reading of history.

Much of women's reading and writing took place in social settings, and the contributors to this book offer us numerous glimpses of a range of early modern women in a variety of social literary environments: Mary Sidney reading and writing with her brother Philip before his death, and later circulating her translation of the *Psalmes* in manuscript among her Wilton coterie; Quaker women in the 1650s composing prophecies collectively, often from prison; upper-class women writing plays 'intended both for reading and performance within their families, or within circles defined by kinship and political alliances' (Tomlinson, this volume), to name but a few. These women, as Margaret Ezell emphasizes, did not seem to need 'a room of their own' in which to read and write and reflect, and this book reveals how fully they participated in their social and cultural world and the skill with which they located spaces in which their voices could be heard.

References and Further Reading

Barthes, Roland (1977). 'The death of the author.' In John Caughie (ed.), *Theories of Authorship: A Reader*. London: Routledge and Kegan Paul.

Ezell, Margaret J. M. (1993). *Writing Women's Literary History*. Baltimore, MD: Johns Hopkins University Press.

Ferguson, Margaret (1998). 'Renaissance concepts of the woman writer.' In Helen Wilcox (ed.), *Women and Literature in Britain 1500–1700* (pp. 143–68). Cambridge: Cambridge University Press.

Hinds, Hilary (1996). *God's Englishwomen: Seventeenth-Century Radical Sectarian Writing and Feminist Criticism*. Manchester: Manchester University Press.

Hobby, Elaine (1988). *Virtue of Necessity: English Women's Writing 1649–88*. London: Virago Press.

Jones, Anne Rosalind (1990). *The Currency of Eros: Women's Love Lyric in Europe, 1540–1620*. Bloomington and Indianapolis: Indiana University Press.

Todd, Janet (1988). *Feminist Literary History: A Defence*. Cambridge: Polity Press.

Wall, Wendy (1993). *The Imprint of Gender: Authorship and Publication in the English Renaissance*. Ithaca, NY: Cornell University Press.

PART ONE
Contexts

1
Women and Education
Kenneth Charlton

Introduction

When 'education' (of whomsoever) is discussed, first thoughts centre on what is to be taught, on the content of education, and then on the methods of teaching deemed appropriate to that content. The discussion may then move on to consider who should be the teachers, who the taught, when this education should take place and where. It is only when these at first sight eminently practical questions have been adumbrated and discussion is under way that we become aware that certain assumptions have been made as to whether this education should take place at all, and if so for what purposes – purposes which on occasion are taken to be so self-evidently agreed by all as not to require expression, least of all discussion. It becomes critical, therefore, to include in any description and discussion of the education of girls and women in early modern England (or any other group at any other time) – i.e. the what? the how? the by whom? the for whom? the where? the when? – an 'ought' variable, which recognizes at the same time that 'prescription' concerns itself not only with what should be the case in the future but also with what is seen to be the best of current and past practice, just as the flood of 'now-a-daies' complaint referred to the worst of such practice. Authors of prescriptive literature in the matter of education had to feel that their prescriptions were in some sense reasonable, not plucked out of some ideal world, incapable of being realized.

Anne Murray, who was born in 1623, recollected in her autobiographical memoirs that her widowed mother

> spared no expense in educating all her children . . . and paid masters for teaching my sister and me to write, speak French, play on the lute and virginalls, and dance, and kept a gentlewoman to teach us all kinds of needlework . . . but my mother's greatest care [was to ensure] that from even our infancy we were instructed never to neglect to begin and end the day in prayer and orderly every morning to read the Bible and ever to keep the church as often as there was occasion. (Loftis 1979: 10)

Reflecting on this, it becomes clear that it describes only part of a much wider picture, one which will require an inclusive rather than an exclusive use of the term 'education', and more particularly an avoidance of the equating of 'education' with 'schooling', if by that is meant what is transacted in the formal institution called 'school'. That other educative agency, the church, long pre-dated the school, and Osbert Sitwell's observation that he was 'educated during the vacations from Eton' reminds us that the family, pre-dating both church and school, continues to have a role in 'education'. Moreover, in the early modern period, John Milton expressed his own awareness that 'whatever thing we hear or see, sitting, walking, travelling or conversing, may fitly be called our book, and is of the same effect as writings are' (*Areopagitica*, 1644).

Plenty has been written about the 'learned ladies' of the past, but remarkably little about how far and in what ways they acquired their learning, and, equally important, whether and how they passed on their learning to their children. That some women in the early modern period were 'learned', 'educated' in the achievement sense, is not difficult to demonstrate, as the essays in Part Two of this volume will show. Precisely how they came to acquire that learning and the skill to express it is rather more difficult, and more so if we widen our enquiry to encompass the many as well as the few.

For our purpose here we shall distinguish between the few and the many by reference to their levels of literacy, at the same time noting the relatively greater importance of reading literacy, as contrasted with the ability to write (too often equated by historians with an ability to sign one's name at a particular time in a particular situation). By the turn of the sixteenth century most women in the upper and middle classes were able to read and write in a functional way. The vast majority of women, however, were quite illiterate in both senses. Their education, in our inclusive sense, was therefore based on their aural willingness to make use of an oral provision. Provided mainly in church and family, it was a provision which was directed, of course, to all classes of the population, and was primarily religious in content. It was in the parish church that literate and illiterate alike would, through the lessons of the Book of Common Prayer, become acquainted with the contents of the Bible, the readings being planned to cover the text of the Old Testament in the course of a year and that of the New Testament twice a year. In addition, the choosing of a biblical text and its explication was a function of the sermon preached by the parish priest or his curate. Despite the invention of movable type and the spread of the printed book, pamphlet and broadsheet, early modern England remained for a very large majority of women (and men) an essentially oral culture, and it was for this reason that Latimer reminded his congregation of Paul's words to the Romans: 'We cannot be saved without faith, and faith cometh from hearing the Word' (*Sermons*, ed. G. B. Corrie 1844: 200), and later, in his characteristic way, that John Donne reminded his that 'the ears are the acqueducts of the waters of life' (*Sermons*, ed. E. M. Simpson and G. R. Potter, 1953: V, 55).

In the early modern period it was well known that women constituted the larger part of the parish church's congregation, a fact attributed by contemporaries to their apparently 'natural piety'. There were, needless to say, plenty of men who found it desirable to attend more than one sermon in the week, but it was to women of like mind that the pejorative label 'gadders' was applied, as John Wing, for example, reported in his *The Crown Conjugall or The Spouse Royall* (1620):

> Nay (says many an impious and profane wretch) if she be a churchgoer, a gadder after sermons, let her go, I will have none of her. I cannot endure these precise dames who are all for religion and never well busied but are poring over their Bibles.

Oliver Heywood recalled with pride that his mother Alice

> hath in her time taken intolerable pains to hear sermons; scarce any public exercise, stated or occasional within many miles, but that she went to it; she was, as it were, the centre of news for knowing the time and place of weekday sermons. (J. H. Turner, ed., *Autobiography, Diaries . . .* 1883: I, 48)

Lucy Apsley, who was born in 1620, and who later married Colonel John Hutchinson, remembered that by the time she was four she was carried to sermons, and 'whilst I was very young could remember and repeat sermons exactly, and being caressed, the love of praise made me attend more heedfully' (Sutherland 1973: 288).

Reinforcement has ever been an essential part of education, and was never more enjoined and practised than with respect to the sermon. John Donne was repeating a common homely metaphor when he likened repetition – repeating the sermon to oneself or to one's family – to chewing the cud: 'The holy rumination, the daily consideration of his Christianity, is a good character of a Christian . . . all good resolutions . . . must pass a rumination, a chewing of the cud, a second examination' (*Sermons* IV, 36; VI, 52; VII, 327–9). In the 1590s Margaret Hoby noted in her diary, almost as a matter of course, that she 'talked with some of the house of the sermon'; 'after dinner I conferred of the sermon with the gentlewomen that were with me'; 'kept company with my friends talking somewhat of the sermon' (Moody 1998: *passim*). The preacher of Lady Anne Waller's funeral sermon reported in 1662 that

> Her custom was after the sermon both in the morning and the afternoon to retire to her chamber and call before her her maidservants and such boys as served in the house to give an account of what they had heard, helping their memories and wherein they failed clearing up the sense of what was delivered . . . exhorting and pressing them to be doers of the Word and not hearers only. (E. Calamy, *The Happiness of Those Who Sleep in Jesus*, 1662: 28)

In some cases attendance and repetition were further reinforced by the practice of taking notes either at the sermon itself or later at home. Margaret Hoby constantly wrote up her notes when she returned home. Before she married Robert Harley in 1623, Brilliana Conway kept a commonplace book in which she kept notes of sermons she had heard (Eales 1990: 48–9). John Barlow, who preached Lady Mary Strode's funeral sermon in 1619, reported that

> She was a notary and took down sermons which she heard by her own hand . . . She did this when as many much meaner than she come with their fans and feathers, whereas (me seems) goose quill would far better befit their fingers . . . Moreover, having taken her notes she did in her chamber repeat to her maidservants the sermons she had heard and penned. (*The True Guide to Glory*, 1619: 48)

In this way, then, the religious education of girls and women of all classes, begun in the church, was continued in the household, to be supplemented by prayers and psalm-singing. Moreover, in his *Book of Martyrs* John Foxe recorded that Bible-reading was undertaken in the households of the less affluent families. Foxe's book itself, especially in Timothy Bright's abridged version, was popular family reading throughout the early modern period, being recommended for that purpose in Thomas Salter's *Mirrhor Mete for all Mothers, Matrones and Maidens* (1579), by Philip Stubbes in his *Anatomie of Abuses* (1583), as well as in Thomas White's *Little Book for Little Children* (1674) and Benjamin Keach's *Instructions for Children* (1693). Margaret Hoby read it to members of her household, and Elizabeth Walker included it in her 'prudent choice of books of instruction and devotion' which she drew up for the benefit of her two daughters, Margaret and Elizabeth (Charlton 1999: 216–19).

It has to be remembered that religious education such as this was taking place in the context of a Protestant state church concerned to ensure the continuance of itself and its crowned head. The maintenance of orthodoxy, uniformity and conformity became the overriding concern of those in authority. Religious education, therefore, was suffused with a political education which entailed an induction not only into religious observance and doctrine, but also into the power structure of society, with obedience, deference and subordination receiving particular attention. It was not for nothing that there was an 'authorized' Bible (whether the Great Bible of 1539, or the Bishops's Bible of 1569 or eventually the Authorized Version, 'King James's Bible', of 1611), a Book of Common Prayer in which figured prayers for the sovereign and his or her ministers, and an authorized catechism which glossed the fifth commandment to include not only 'thy father and thy mother' but also 'my governors, teachers, spiritual pastors and masters, [and] to order myself lowly and reverently to all my betters . . . to do my duty in that state of life unto which it shall please God to call me'. Glosses on the fifth commandment in the form of sermon or commentary poured from the presses in increasing numbers. Yet whatever form of control was used – statute, royal proclamation, episcopal injunction, authorized Bible, Book of Common Prayer, catechism – the early modern state was relatively powerless to enforce attendance at church, to control what was said in the pulpit, and above all to monitor what religious and political education was engaged in inside the family. The result, therefore, was an extremely heterodox outcome, even within a godly family. Even in the matter of choice of marriage partner young women (and men) were enjoined in marriage sermons, 'Advices' and conduct books to marry only with the advice and consent of parents, with biblical proof-texts to substantiate the argument. A similar procedure was followed in the prescriptive literature about the suckling of infants (Charlton 1999: 29ff., 198–9). For some young women it was simply a Christian duty to follow such advice, though of course there were others, parents and children, who did not. Henry Parker alluded to the matter in his discussion of the relative rights of subjects and princes:

> In matrimony there is something divine . . . but is this any ground to infer that there is no humane consent or concurrence in it? Does the divine institution of marriage take away freedom of choice before, or conclude either party under an absolute degree of subjection after the solemnization? (*Jus Populi*, 1644: 4–5)

As always, social and moral codes were susceptible to interpretation by individuals, and therefore productive of a variety of prescription, attitude and behaviour.

This was nowhere more noticeable than in the constant reminders to girls and women alike that the virtuous woman should be 'chaste, silent and obedient', both before and after marriage. The prayer designed for wives which was included in the Edwardian Primer of 1552 was repetitively typical:

> Give me grace, I most entirely beseech thee, to walk worthy of my vocation, to knowledge my husband to be my head, to learn thy blessed word of him, to reverence him, to obey him, to please him, to be ruled by him, peaceably and quietly to live with him. (*Two Liturgies* AD *1549 and* AD 1552, ed. J. Ketley, 1844: 465)

But even in the prescriptive literature this was not the whole story. Ambiguous familial metaphors and analogies, and innumerable glosses frequently hedged injunction round with conditional clauses in an attempt to reconcile patriarchy with affectionate mutuality in marriage (Goldberg 1986). Some wives were willing to accept a subordinate position in the matter of decision-making. In 1632 Lady Mary Peyton, for example, advised her daughter, newly married to Henry Oxinden of Barham, 'withal to be careful that whatsoever you do to love, honour and obey your husband in all things that it is fitting for a reasonable creature', and in so doing to 'show yourself a virtuous wife whose price is not to be valued' (*The Oxinden Letters 1609–42*, ed. D. Gardiner, 1933: 97). Elizabeth Walker's advice to her daughters Margaret and Elizabeth could not have been more customary, citing Proverbs 12.4 and 31.7 as well as 1 Peter 3.1–6. Lucy Hutchinson was her own witness:

> Never man had a greater passion for a woman, nor a more honourable esteeme of a wife; yet he was not uxurious, nor remitted not that just rule which it was her honor to obey,

but manag'd the reines of government with such prudence and affection that she who
would not delight in such an honorable and advantageable subjection must have wanted
a reasonable soul. (Sutherland 1973: 10)

Yet for a variety of reasons other women did not subscribe to such 'advantageable
subjection'. Anne Askew, for example, left her husband of an arranged marriage when
(as John Bale reported): 'In the process of time by oft reading the sacred Bible, she
clearly fell from the old superstitions of papistry to a perfect belief in Jesus Christ . . .
whereupon she thought herself free from that uncomely kind of cloaked marriage by
this doctrine of St Paul, I Cor.6' (*Select Works of John Bale*, ed. H. Christmas, 1849:
199). Foxe celebrated the lives of other women contemporary with Askew, who held
fast to their reformed religion in the face of 'unbelieving' husbands. Other women
expressed their wish for a degree of independence by ignoring the customary injunction to marry only with the advice of friends and parents. Anne More, daughter of
Sir George More of Loseley near Guildford, resorted to secrecy in her marriage with
John Donne (R. C. Bald, *John Donne: A Life*, 1970: 128–90). Elizabeth Freke followed
a similar path in 1671 when she married her cousin Percy Freke (M. Carbery, *Mrs
Elizabeth Freke, Her Diary, 1671–1714*, 1931: 148). There were many others of
like mind.

In the Household of Another

Most of the education we have touched on so far took place either in the home of the
upper and middle levels of society, or, with the rest of society (at least those who
attended), in the church – of whichever denomination, for in the religious education
of girls and women there was remarkably little difference between the various religious groupings. However, following the medieval tradition of sending boys and girls
to spend their childhood in another, preferably socially superior, household, many
parents of high social standing sent their daughters to join another family where they
would be expected to receive the kind of education considered appropriate to their
class. It is important to recognize that this was but one method of socialization
amongst several for such girls. The plurality of method was itself expressed in the
public–private debate in education then current, a debate which recognized the reduc-
tiveness of the view that sending children away to this kind of education stemmed
simply from a lack of affection on the part of parents. As always in such cases, motivation varied from one family to the next and, as the records of individual families
show, was in some cases mixed.

Nicholas Orme has used the domestic correspondence of the mid- and late-fifteenth
century to show this practice at work (*From Childhood to Chivalry: The Education of
English Kings and Aristocracy 1066–1530*, 1984). The letters which passed between
Arthur Plantagenet and his second wife Honor Basset, in the early sixteenth century,
tell a similar story of the placing of their daughters, Bridget and Elizabeth Plantagenet and Catherine, Anne and Mary Basset. In Sir Thomas More's house we find

Anne Cresacre, Francis Staverton and Margaret Giggs. Catherine Hastings, wife of the 'puritan Earl' Henry, third Earl of Huntingdon, had in her household Margaret Dakins, later Lady Margaret Hoby, whose first husband was Walter Devereux, who, with his sisters Penelope and Dorothy, was also a resident member. In a postscript to a letter to Sir Julius Caesar in 1618, Lady Catherine quite justifiably claimed 'I think there will be none make question but I know how to breed and govern young gentlewomen', and as part of the 'breeding' process this deeply religious woman doubtless made it plain to her charges that she 'governed' in accordance with the fifth commandment (C. Cross, *The Puritan Earl*, 1966: 24–7, 57). On occasion, of course, a pious upbringing was not the only or indeed the prime reason for sending a daughter to another's household. Sir Edward Molineux, for example, sent his two daughters to the house of his cousin, to be brought up, as he said, 'in virtue, good manners and learning, to play the gentlewoman and good housewife, to dress meat and oversee their households'. Henry Thorndike was more tersely direct in sending his niece to live with the Isham family in Northamptonshire 'that she might find match by having the honour of being in your house' (Pollock 1989: 236).

The greatest household to which a girl could be sent was the royal court, an old chivalric tradition by which both girls and boys were sent to learn the appropriate mode of service to their elders, as well as to acquire courtly manners and to participate in the religious pattern of the royal household (Charlton 1999: 131–2). The practice continued virtually unchanged in the sixteenth and seventeenth centuries, and nowhere more so than in the pious ambience of the court of Henry VIII's queen Catherine of Aragon. It was to this place that in 1517 Catherine Parr's newly widowed mother Maud went as a 21-year-old lady-in-waiting to the queen, accompanied by her three young children, Catherine aged three, Anne aged two and the infant son William, there to be joined eventually by the young Princess Mary, with whom they were brought up alongside Katherine Willoughby and Joan Guildford, daughters of Catherine's other ladies-in-waiting. The court of Queen Elizabeth was also used as a 'school' for numerous other 'maids of honour'. In 1575, when she was 13, Mary Sidney, daughter of Sir Henry and Lady Mary Sidney and sister of Philip, was sent to Elizabeth's court where she became a lady-in-waiting, as had her mother before her. The household of Queen Henrietta Maria was of quite different religious orientation, but it was there that Margaret Lucas, later Duchess of Newcastle, was sent, following her mistress on the outbreak of war first to Oxford and then to France. Elizabeth Livingstone (later Delaval) was also at court aged 18, serving in the Privy Chamber of Queen Catherine, wife of Charles II.

Academies for the Daughters of Gentlemen

It was during the seventeenth century, however, that a new kind of provision became popular, the 'academies for the daughters of gentlemen' (Charlton 1999: 131–41), thus widening the debate as to whether boys should be educated at home by a private tutor or sent away to the increasing number of grammar schools which took in boarders. When John Batchiler printed his *The Virgins Pattern* in 1661, in which he memorialized 'the life and death of Mistress Susanna Perwich', he dedicated it 'To all the young ladies and gentlewomen of the several schools in and about the City of London and elsewhere'. His reason for doing so arises from the fact that Susanna was the daughter of Robert Perwich who had a school in Hackney, in which she finished her education and had then become a teacher. Hackney was at the time a salubrious suburban village to the north of the City of London, in which many prosperous middle- and upper-class people had taken residence, and in which were to be found several schools of a similar kind and clientele. One of the earliest to be mentioned was that run by a Mrs Winch, which became known in 1637 as a result of a notorious and well-reported abduction (Fraser 1984: 23–5). It was in the following year that the 8-year-old Katherine Fowler arrived in Hackney to attend the school of a Mrs Salmon; Fowler would later marry and, as Katherine Philips, make her name as a poet, 'the Matchless Orinda'. The two eldest daughters of Sir John Bramston were also sent to Mrs Salmon's academy on the death of their mother in 1648, and in his notebook Samuel Sainthill of Bradninch, north of Exeter in Devon, recorded his outgoings for the teaching and boarding there of his sister during the three years 1651–3. Mary Aubrey, a cousin of the antiquary, also attended the school, and in 1675 Ralph Josselin's two daughters Mary and Elizabeth arrived with their mother from Earls Colne in Essex.

The Hackney schools were plainly well supported over the years by the prosperous parents of young ladies, but no records of the schools themselves have survived. Similar schools were started in the villages which circled London in the seventeenth century. Evidence of such schools in the provinces is scattered and equally lacking in detail other than that of their existence. All that is known of the schooling of Margaret and Mary Kytson, daughters of Sir Thomas and Lady Elizabeth Kytson of Hengrave Hall in Suffolk, is derived from an account book entry which recorded expenditure 'For a drinking at Thetford and the children going to school at Norwich' in January 1573, Norwich lying about 30 miles to the east of their home.

Elementary Schools

It was in the seventeenth century, too, that a new kind of provision, an endowed elementary school, was made available for the children of the poor (Charlton 1999: 142–53). The early Protestant reformers had emphasized the need for all believers to learn to read (at least the Bible), 'so that they may better learn to believe, how to pray and how to live to God's pleasure', as the 1536 Royal Injunction put it. Thomas Becon called for the setting up of a nationwide system of schooling in his *New Catechisme* (1559), and such a comprehensive system continued to be called for, especially during the Commonwealth period. William Dell, for example, stipulated that 'in the villages no women be permitted to teach little children but such as are most sober and grave' (which suggests that women were already active in such a role), and that 'in these schools they first teach them to read in their native tongue, which they speak without teaching, and then presently as they understand, bring them to read the Holy Scriptures' (Dell, *The Right Reformation of Learning*, 1646, in *Several Sermons and Discourses of William Dell*, 1709: 643).

It was left to the task of philanthropy to attempt to provide funds for this level of education, the bulk of the evidence being found in wills, wherein the rents from donated lands or the interest from a capital sum were indicated to be put to the provision of education for the children of those 'sorts' of parents usually labelled 'poor', 'humble', 'labouring'. Unfortunately, most such testaments provide only the barest of detail – a sum of money or parcel of land, with the number and 'sort' of children to be provided for, as in the will (1562) of William Pepyn of Wenhaston in Suffolk, who left £20 to educate poor children of the village in 'learning, godliness and virtue'. Some benefactors provided a little more detail. In 1586, for example, George Whateley of Stratford-upon-Avon granted lands in Henley and other parts of Warwickshire, half the rents of which were to provide for a master to teach 30 children reading, writing and arithmetic in Henley-in-Arden. Anthony Walker, Rector of Fyfield in Essex, left by his will of 1687 (he died in 1692) houses and land to teach the poor children of Fyfield to read, write and cast accounts, and to say their catechism. The sum of £1 was allocated for the purchase of books and paper for the poorest children, plus £1 for Bibles.

Other benefactors were more generous. In 1611, for example, Marmaduke Longdale of Dowthorpe Hall, Skirlaugh in Yorkshire left £200 for a school. In 1634 William Smyth left £250 to purchase lands whose rents were to be used for a master to teach 'all youth rich and poor, female amd male' who had been born in West Chiltington in Sussex. Laurence Bathurst's 1651 bequest of £150 was for the poor of the parish of Staplehurst in Kent to be taught reading and writing, together with 'instruction in their duty to God and man', an initiative which was supplemented in 1655 by a subscription which raised the sum of £40. Some few will-makers were concerned to direct their bequests to the education of girls only, though examples of this occur only towards the end of the century, as in the 1683 will of Batholomew Hickling. Part of the monies accruing from the rent of lands was to be spent on the purchase of Bibles to be distributed to the children in the area round Loughborough. The rest was to be used to found a school for 20 poor girls from the town, with a mistress who would be paid £4 per annum to

> teach and instruct said girls in learning the English alphabet of letters and the true spelling and reading of the English tongue, in good manner and behaviour, and also in the grounds and principles of Christian religion. (B. E. Elliott, *History of Loughborough College School*, 1971: 12)

For the vast majority of these schools for the poor we have no evidence of their subsequent history. Some, however, became subsumed under eighteenth-century charity school provision, and surfaced later as elementary schools in the nineteenth century. Some few survived, in different guises, even later, as in the case of the Loughborough school and that founded in the village of Madeley in Staffordshire by the will of Sir John Offley (1645) (Charlton 1999: 150–2).

The evidence for the elementary education of girls is scattered and usually lacking in detail, and in almost every case lacking (as with the academies) any serial documentation such as is available for the male-only establishments, the grammar schools and universities. Even so, it is clear that at this educational and social level, schooling was provided by both men and women founders for girls to be taught by both masters and mistresses, sometimes alongside boys and sometimes on their own, and that the overriding aim of such education was a religious one – the fostering of a God-fearing and deferential clientele.

Accomplishments

Religious and political education were undoubtedly considered to be the most important part of the education of the younger generation – female and male – but not the whole. Young women of the upper and middle classes were expected, in addition, to acquire what were considered to be the social graces or 'accomplishments', much as Anne Murray had reported in her memoirs. Margaret Lucas, Lucy Apsley and Anne Harrison reported in similar vein.

As in the cases of these young ladies, music was a common feature in what might be called the upper-class curriculum, though none of them in their reports gives any detail as to who taught them to read music or play an instrument. The same was true of Margaret Hoby who recorded in her diary for 26 January 1600 that she 'played and sung to the alpherion [a stringed instrument] to refresh myself being dull' (Moody 1988: 56). Lady Mary Wroth, daughter of Sir Robert and Lady Barbara Sidney, niece of Philip and Mary, was brought up in a musical family. Her father was the dedicatee of Robert Jones's *First Booke of Songes or Ayres* (1600) and Robert Dowland's *A Musicall Banquet* (1610), whilst Mary herself was the dedicatee of Jones's *The Muses Gardin of Delight* (1610). In her portrait painted after her marriage to Sir Robert Wroth, she is shown standing with an archlute (a base lute with an extended, unfretted peg-box), which, if it was meant to have actual rather than symbolic significance, would certainly have required some form of tuition. Even so, no record of music tutors appears in the family papers. In her autobiography Alice Thornton, who was born in 1627, reported that among her other accomplishments her mother, Alice, was taught the 'Harpsicalls and lute', and that she herself received tuition in the lute and theorbo (a double-necked lute), this alongside a detailed religious education (Surtees Society, 62, 1875: 8). Nicholas Ferrar's nieces at Little Gidding found time from their extensive religious exercises to engage in lute playing (T. T. Carter, *Nicholas Ferrar: His Household and Friends*, 1892: 125). The madrigalist Henry Lawes was tutor to Alice and Mary Egerton, daughters of John, Earl of Bridgewater, and dedicatees of Lawes's *Book of Ayres and Dialogues* (1653) (I. Spink, *Henry Lawes: Cavalier Song Writer*, 2000: 5, 12). Sir Edward Dering recorded in his household book for 1 June 1649: 'Paid Mr Lawes a months teaching of my wife £1 10s', Lady Mary being the dedicatee of Lawes's *Second Booke of Ayres and Dialogues* (1655) (E. Rimbault, *Notes and Queries*, 1st Ser. 1859–60: 162). The extended Kytson family of Hengrave Hall were similarly involved with musicians (Lawes, John Dowland and Henry Wilbye) who, whilst in residence at the Hall, taught the children and dedicated their works to various members (Woodfill 1953: 252ff.). The household accounts of Sir William Petre of Ingatestone Hall, Essex, have numerous entries relating to the purchase and repair of musical instruments, as well as to visits by William Byrd and to resident musicians Richard Mico and John Oker. From 1558 to 1560 a Mr 'Persey' was paid 'for teaching the gentlewomen to play on the virginalls', presumably including the daughters of the household, Dorothy, Elizabeth, Thomasine and Catherine.

It should be noted that music (as well as dancing) was not universally deemed suitable for young girls and women; in the opinion of some, such as Thomas Salter in his *Mirrhor Mete for all Matrones* (1579) and Thomas Powell in his *Tom of All Trades* (1621), it encouraged lasciviousness and other vices. Those who approved of it, on the other hand, regarded it as the epitome of harmony, as well as providing opportunity for acceptable recreation, and as Margaret Hoby found, a remedy against 'dullness'. Some found it a useful mark of marriageableness, whilst others argued that for too many this was its only justification, taking up time which would be better spent reading godly books and meditating on one's ultimate end.

During the sixteenth century some families, notably those of Thomas More, Edward Seymour and Anthony Cooke, engaged their daughters in the study of Latin and Greek. By the turn of the century, however, such a practice was going out of fashion, and in any case, it was argued, had been rendered unnecessary due to a good deal of classical literature being available in translation. In the seventeenth century modern languages, and particularly French, had become part of the curriculum for young gentlewomen, though only because it was considered fashionable to converse in French, since translators were also making romances in French available in English (Charlton 1965: 109, 208–9, 227–34).

The 'accomplishment' which was universally accepted as an integral part of a young woman's education was housewifery. Manuals on cookery, needlework, medicine and midwifery, directly addressed to women, frequently appeared in print throughout the period. For the majority of girls such skills would be learned at the elbow of their mothers, by observation as much as by precept, in the certain knowledge that they themselves would be called upon to exercise these skills in their own households. At the same time, they would be constantly enjoined in church that it was their godly duty – their 'vocation' – to 'husband' the resources which had been gathered in by their 'better half' outside of the home. Even among the more affluent, we find an acceptance of the prescribed division of labour. Margaret Hoby's diary, for example, gives a detailed account of a woman of some substance 'busy in the kitchen . . . busy about the reckonings . . . busy preserving . . . busy in my garden all the day almost . . . all the day setting corn' and so on. Sir John Oglander acknowledged his indebtedness to his wife Frances, who 'was up every day before me, and oversaw all the outhouses; she would not trust her maids with directions, but would wet her shoes to see it done herself' (C. A. Oglander, *Nunwell Symphony*, 1945: 39). Sir Hugh Cholmley reported in similar vein about his wife Elizabeth, who 'went round her whole domain from hop-garth to hen-yard, from linen closet to larder' (Cholmley, *Memoirs*, 1870: 30). Plainly these were not simply pragmatic arrangements to meet exceptional circumstances, but in the minds of some a more reflective enactment of that principle of mutuality for which biblical texts provided a justification. For others, an informed oversight of servants was simply a matter of housekeeping economics or a reinforcement of social hierarchy.

Women as Agents

Thus far we have considered girls and women as recipients of education provided by others, usually men. The question now has to be asked how far and in what ways did women act as agents in their own and others' education. Women's diaries provide first-hand evidence of books women actually read. Anne Venn, daughter of the regicide Colonel John Venn, kept a diary 'written in her own hand and found in her closet after her death,' in which she noted:

> I got a book called Mr Rogers Evidences and another called The Touchstone of True Grace and another called None But Christ and divers others . . . read Mr Dod upon the Commandments . . . a little book called the Marrow of Modern Divinity . . . reading some sermons of Mr Marshalls and others . . . one of Mr Burrowes books and fifty sermons of Mr Knights . . . opened Mr Burroughs book which I read many daily hours together. (Venn, *A Wise Virgins Lamp Burning*, 1658: *passim*)

In the diary of Elianor Stockton (Dr Williams' Library, Modern Ms. 24.8, fols. 20–2) is found a record of 'short sentences that I have met with in my reading', including 'Caryl on Job 30.2 . . . The Christians Daily Wake . . . The Spirits Office Towards Believers . . . Mr Crow on the Lord's Supper . . . that small piece of Mr Flavell's entitled A Token for Mourners'. The reading of Mary Rich, Countess of Warwick, included Foxe's *Book of Martyrs*, the sermons and writings of Jeremy Taylor, the poems of George Herbert and Richard Baxter's *Crucifying of the World by the Cross of Christ*, her favourite book (Charlton 1999: 180–7). Lady Catherine Gell was a regular correspondent of Richard Baxter, and confessed to him in one of her letters 'many a time

I goe about my house among my servants when I had rather locke myself in a roome alone amongst my books. For meditation I never knew it my duty till I had read your *Saints Rest*, and then setting on it I found it very hard' (Keeble and Nuttall 1991, I: 249). Meditation in the privacy of their own closet was a further practice which enabled women to educate their minds and their emotions, Baxter's *Saints Everlasting Rest* (1650 and many editions) being one of the most popular among many expositions of the practice (Charlton 1999: 171–7).

Mary Rich was not the only reader of George Herbert's religious poetry, which was published posthumously in 1633 as *The Temple. Sacred Poems and Private Ejaculations*. Susanna Howard, Countess of Suffolk, died in 1649. In the funeral sermon preached by Edward Rainbowe, Bishop of Carlisle, he referred to her reading of

> divine poetry, in which kind she took excessive delight to be conversant in Mr Herbert's *Temple*, in which she found out such fit and significant elegancies that when she read or repeated them it was hard to determine whether the author or she made the sense, such innumerable descants would she make upon every single expression there. . . . Begin a religious ode of Mr Herbert's which she had read and she would ordinarily repeat the rest without sticking or missing'. (*A Sermon Preached at the Interring . . . of Susanna, Countess of Suffolk . . .* , 1649: 12–13)

Lady Mary Wharton died in 1674. In her funeral sermon reference was made to her wide reading of godly authors, including 'Mr Herbert's verses which she could repeat without book' (P. Watkinson, *Mary's Choice . . .* , 1674: 34). Mary Rich produced for George, Earl of Berkeley, at his request, a set of 'Rules for Holy Living', in which she urged him to 'remember that Mr Herbert in his excellent poem says "Game [i.e. gaming] is a civil gunpowder in peace / Blowing up houses with their whole increase"' (*Church Porch*, stanza 34) (C. Fell Smith, *Mary Rich Countess of Warwick*, 1901: 184). Berkeley himself (mis)quotes (from heart presumably) stanza 55 of the poem in his *Historical Applications and Occasional Meditations* (1666: 17), adding a couplet of his own which has distinct echoes of the opening stanza of Herbert's 'Constancie'.

Of course, women read other literature than godly books. If she could read at all, it seems, Sir Thomas Overbury's 'Chambermaid' would read romances: 'she reads Greene's works over and over, but is so carried away with the *Mirrour of Knighthood* that she is many times resolved to run out of herself and become a Ladie Errant' (*Characters*, 1614; in *The Overburian Characters*, ed. W. J. Paylor, Oxford, 1936: 43). But the chambermaid's mistress, too, was not averse to such reading. Margaret Cavendish, Duchess of Newcastle, complained

> The truth is, the chief study of our sex is romances, wherein reading, they fall in love with the feigned carpet-knights with whom their thoughts secretly commit adultery, and in their conversation and manner, or forms or phrases of speech, they imitate Romancy Ladies. (*Sociable Letters*, 1664: 39)

Mary Rich acknowledged that until she was married (1641) she spent her 'precious time in nothing else but reading romances and in reading and seeing plays' (T. C. Croker, ed., *Autobiography of Mary Countess of Warwick*, 1848: 21). Lady Elizabeth Delaval blamed her governess for encouraging her in such reading matter, concluding, when she came to write her memoirs, 'Thus vainely passed the blossom time of my life which should have been spent in laying a good foundation of what is to be learned in such books as teach us heavenly wisdom' (Surtees Society, 190, 1978: 32). Two kinds of 'romance' are being referred to here, one which might be termed the 'chivalric' romance and which included works such as *Morte d'Arthure*, *Amadis de Gaule*, *The Mirrour of Knighthood* and the long-popular tales of Robin Hood, the other being the new generation of romance, originating in France in the mid-seventeenth century and quickly being translated into English – the 'Cassander, the Great Cyrus, Cleopatra and Astrea' which Elizabeth Delaval had read. It should be said that men, too, read these works, Francis Kirkman, for example, who later translated part of *Amadis* and other romances, recollecting with pleasure his reading of them in his youth, when he 'wished myself squire to one of these knights'. John Milton, Richard Baxter and John Bunyan were not alone in regretting the time they 'wasted' in reading such literature (Charlton 1987: 467–9). Its existence, and the constant stream of criticism directed towards it and its authors, should serve to remind us that 'education' took place as much outside the classroom as in it, and it is, at the very least, a moot point (then as now) as to which kind of education, formal or informal, is the more influential in the upbringing or 'formation' (in the French sense of the term) of young and adult alike. As Sir Philip Sidney acknowledged in his *Apologie for Poetrie* (1595):

> Truely, I have known men, that even with reading *Amadis de Gaule* (which God knoweth wanteth much of a perfect poesie) have found their harts moved to the exercise of courtesie, liberalitie and especially courage. (Sig. E4 verso, F1 recto)

The same was true of the theatre-going public (as also, in the sixteenth century at least, of the open-air performing of the mystery plays), when the cathartic effect of vicarious humour and bawdy as well as adultery, murder and illicit passion, gave the wider audience a sense of sharing a range of basic emotions not only with their peers but also with their 'betters'.

If women were active in the process of self-education, so too did they contribute in no small measure as agents in the education of others. A first contribution to the education of those who could read only their native tongue would be the translations that women made of works in foreign languages. An early example would be Margaret Beaufort's translation of Book II of Thomas à Kempis's *Imitatio Christi*, which was published in 1504, and Margaret Roper's *Treatise upon the Pater Noster* (1525), which she translated from the Latin of Erasmus. As well as translating the French of Du Plessis Mornay and Robert Garnier and the Italian of Petrarch, Lady Mary Sidney completed her brother Philip's translation of the *Psalmes of David* from the Latin of the Vulgate. Ann (Prowse) Lok (or Locke) published her *Markes of the Children of God and Their Comforts in Afflictions* from the French of Jean Taffin in 1590, by which time she had married her second husband, Edward Dering. In her Epistle Dedicatorie she gave a detailed account of her purpose in the undertaking:

> First to admonish some . . . that they learne to applie unto themselves whatsoever they hear or reade of the triall of God his children. . . . Secondlie, to awake others abounding both in knowledge and other graces who notwithstanding Satan . . . hath so rockt asleepe that they seem almost . . . to have forgotten both themselves, their holy calling and profession. Last of all to comfort another sorte, whom it hath pleased God so to press down with sorrowes they can scarce receive the words of any comfort.

Elizabeth Cary, the Catholic Lady Falkland, was briefer but equally forthright when, in her translation *The Reply of the Most Illustrious Cardinall Perron to the Answeare of the Most Excellent King of Greate Britaine, the First Tome* (1630), she insisted

> I will not make use of that worn-out form of saying, I printed it against my will, moved by the importunity of friends; I was moved to it by my belief that it might make those English that understand not French, whereof there are many, even in our universities, read Perron. (*To the Reader*, sig. A2 verso)

– and, of course, to consider his religious arguments. When Margaret Tyler translated from the Spanish her *Mirrour of Princely Deedes and Knighthood* in 1578, on the other hand, she was more concerned to justify her intrusion into what was considered to be a male preserve.

By far the most important part played by women as agents in the education of others in the early modern period was their contribution to the education of their own children, which I have dealt with at length elsewhere (Charlton 1999: ch. 7). We have already noted here a kind of surrogate mothering in the practice of sending girls away from home to live with another family. When Bridget Plantagenet was sent, aged about 7, to the household of Sir Anthony and Lady Jane Windsor, Sir Anthony wrote to her father in 1538: 'she is very spare and hath need of cherishing, and she shall lack nothing in learning or otherwise that my wife can do for her' (M. Saint Clare Byrne, ed., *The Lisle Letters*, 1981: V, 219–20). Despite the stereotypical picture of the all-powerful husband and often possibly harsh patriarch, there was in the early modern period a common acceptance of the prime role of the mother as an agent in the education of her children, a role which continued well beyond the period of early infancy.

In the family setting direct attention was paid to the view that 'religious education' consisted not simply of 'religious knowledge' – of the Ten Commandments, the Lord's Prayer, the Creed and the contents of the Bible – but also of everyday behaviour, the Christian virtues which were expressed in the multitude of conduct books and 'Advices', and which were to be the immediate end-product of all public and private worship, prayer, reading and exhortation. Example, therefore, was considered to be a prime motivator in familial education. As R[oger] C[arr] put it, 'verbal instruction without example of good deedes is dead doctrine' (*A Godly Form of Householde Governement*, 1598: 260). William Gouge likewise insisted that 'Example is a real instruction and addeth a sharp edge to admonition' (*Of Domesticall Dueties*, 1600: 542). Parents' example was thus crucial in the formation of their children, though that provided by their servants was almost always cited as something to be shunned. Grace Mildmay, for example, reported that she had been warned by her parents to avoid the serving men of the household, 'whose ribald talk and idle gestures and evil suggestions were dangerous to our chaste ears and eyes to hear and behold' (Pollock 1993: 46). Elizabeth Walker was quick to see the danger, her husband recalling that she would 'strictly charge the servants not to teach her children foolish stories or teach them idle songs, which might tincture their fancies with vain or hurtful imaginations (A. Walker, *The Holy Life of Elizabeth Walker*, 1690: 90). As we have seen already, wives also paid attention to educating their servants in the Christian virtues (Charlton 1999: 234–7).

Of course, precept figured equally with example in mothers' efforts to educate their children. Advice books such as Dorothy Leigh's *The Mothers Blessing* (1616), Elizabeth Jocelin's *A Mothers Legacie to her Unborne Child* (1624) and Elizabeth Richardson's *A Ladies Legacy to her Daughters* (1645) figured largely in the advice literature of the period. When Lucy Hutchinson produced a more organized text in her *Principles of Christian Religion*, which she addressed to her newly married daughter Barbara, she started with a disclaimer:

> You may perhaps, when you have read these common principles and grounds which I have collected for you, thinke that I might have spard my payns and sent you a twopennie catechize which contains the substance of all this.

But she was convinced that this would not suffice:

> You will find it my duty [she continued] to exhort and admonish you according to the talent entrusted with me, and to watch over your soul, though now under another's authority . . . and advize you to exercise youre owne knowledge therein by instructing your children and servants. (5–7, 90–1; the text was not published until 1817)

In keeping with her last comment, her advice was thoroughly orthodox, as was that of Lady Anne Halkett in her *Instructions for Youth*, 'for the use of those young noblemen and gentlemen' whose education was committed to her. Letters from mothers to their children often included similar advice, alongside the usual news of family illness and good health and considerate enquiries about the health and behaviour of the recipient (Charlton 1999: 234–7).

Conclusion

Two final questions remain fundamental to any study of women writers and their work. First, how did they acquire the education which enabled them to engage in such an erudite activity? Second, who read their work and for what purpose, who benefited from reading it? These are questions not of production but of distribution and reception. Such questions are rarely asked, least of all in biographies and biographical chapters, and not surprisingly, since the evidence by which to answer them is rarely available. For example, how did Ann Lock acquire sufficient skill in French to be able to translate Jean Taffin's theological treatise? Or Margaret Tyler acquire skill in Spanish? Did they have a tutor or were they 'self-educated'? If the latter, what manuals did they use? Such manuals existed, but which particular one did they use? We know that Katherine Fowler Philips was educated at Mrs Salmon's academy in Hackney. It would be reasonable to suppose that she received an education similar to that of Susanna Perwich, which might have enabled her to undertake her translation of Corneille's *La Mort de Pompée. Tragédie* in 1663. But further than that we cannot go. We know that Margaret Roper received a classical education in the house of her father, Sir Thomas More, which presumably enabled her to translate Erasmus, but we have no precise details to reinforce the presumption. Damaris Masham was educated at home by her learned father, the Cambridge Platonist Ralph Cudworth, but again we have no precise details to indicate how she became the woman who later was able to correspond with the Revd John Norris on matters theological, a correspondence which resulted in Norris's *Reflections upon the Conduct of Human Life . . .* (1690). Mary Astell's correspondence with Norris was also published by him as *Letters Concerning the Love of God Between the Author of the Proposal to the Ladies and Rev John Norris* (1695). Before she left her native Newcastle-upon-Tyne for London in 1688 she was apparently tutored by her father's bachelor brother, Ralph Astell, who had been a pupil of Ralph Cudworth when the Cambridge Platonists were active in Cambridge, and had thus imbibed their views about the desirability of a rational consideration and justification of Christian faith, a view which we find in both the *Letters* and Astell's *Serious Proposal*, as well as her *Christian Religion as Profess'd by a Daughter of the Church* (1705). Yet Astell's biographer has to rely on 'according to tradition' as her evidence for the tutoring (Perry 1986: 46).

To conclude, then, it has to be remembered that in the matter of education in the early modern period women were as much agents as recipients – recipients at home, in church and at school, agents of both prescription and provision in the education of others, including their own children. Yet, even for the affluent, for the most part the content of education was limited and limiting, with most of it provided by men, leading Mary Astell, even at the end of the period, to complain 'so partial are men as to expect bricks where they afford no straw' (*Serious Proposal*, 1696: 24). Whilst for the majority, both affluent and poor, education was a matter of conforming to the social and cultural norms prescribed by those in authority, some few seized the opportunity to 'turn the world upside down', and to use their new-found ability, to read the Bible for instance, to challenge stereotypical views about the nature of masculinity and femininity and the purpose of 'nurture', well aware that, as Bathsua Makin put it, 'A learned woman is thought to be a comet, that bodes mischief whenever it appears' (*Essay to Revive the Antient Education of Gentlewomen*, 1673: A2 recto). Whilst those in authority looked for uniformity and conformity, the picture the historian finds is one of contradiction and doubt, a picture in other words of the untidiness of life. The history of women's education is not simply about women and girls, but about males and females and their inextricably bound interactions, and how these affected and were affected by conceptions such as virtue, obedience, citizenship and power, which could and often did produce behaviour and action very different from that intended.

See also RELIGION AND THE CONSTRUCTION OF THE FEMININE; AUTOBIOGRAPHY

REFERENCES AND FURTHER READING

Aughterson, K. (1995). *Renaissance Women: A Source Book: The Construction of Femininity in Early Modern England 1520–1660*. London: Routledge.

Charlton, K. (1965). *Education in Renaissance England*. London: Routledge.

——(1987). " 'False Fonde bookes, ballades and rimes': an aspect of informal education in early modern England.' *History of Education Quarterly*, 27, 449–71.

——(1999). *Women, Religion and Education in Early Modern England*. London: Routledge.

Eales, J. (1990). *Puritans and Roundheads: The Harleys of Brampton Bryan and the Outbreak of the English Civil War*. Cambridge: Cambridge University Press.

Fraser, A. (1984). *The Weaker Vessel: Woman's Lot in Seventeenth-Century England*. London: Weidenfeld and Nicolson.

Goldberg, J. (1986). 'Fatherly authority: the politics of Stuart family images', in M. W. Ferguson, et al. (eds), *Rewriting the Renaissance: the Discourses of Sexual Difference in Early Modern Europe*. Chicago: University of Chicago Press.

Grantley, D. (2000). *Wit's Pilgrimage: Drama and the Social Impact of Education in Early Modern England*. Aldershot: Ashgate.

Green, G., et al. (eds) (1988). *Kissing the Rod: An Anthology of Seventeenth-Century Women's Poetry*. London: Virago.

Green, I. (1996). *The Christian's ABC: Catechism and Catechizing in England c.1530–1740*. Oxford: Clarendon Press.

Hannay, M. P. (1990). *Philip's Phoenix: Mary Sidney, Countess of Pembroke*. New York: Oxford University Press.

Houlbrooke, R. A. (1984). *The English Family 1450–1700*. London: Longman.

Hufton, O. (1995). *The Prospect Before Her: A History of Women in Western Europe, Vol. 1, 1500–1800*. London: Harper Collins.

Jones, K. (1988). *A Glorious Fame: The Life of Margaret Cavendish, Duchess of Newcastle*. London: Bloomsbury Publishing.

Keeble, N. H. and Nuttall, G. F. (eds) (1991). *A Calendar of the Correspondence of Richard Baxter*, 2 vols. Oxford: Clarendon Press.

Laurence, A. (1994). *Women in England 1500–1760: A Social History.* London: Weidenfeld and Nicolson.

Loftis, J. (ed.) (1979). *The Memoirs of Anne, Lady Halkett and Anne, Lady Fanshawe.* Oxford: Clarendon Press.

Mendelson, S. and Crawford, P. (1998). *Women in Early Modern England 1550–1720.* Oxford: Clarendon Press.

Moody, J. (ed.) (1998). *The Private Life of an Elizabethan Lady: The Diary of Margaret Hoby 1599–1605.* Stroud: Sutton.

Morgan, P. (1989). 'Frances Wolfreston and "Hor Bouks": a seventeenth-century woman book-collector.' *The Library*, 6th Ser., XI, 197–219.

O'Day, R. (1982). *Education and Society 1500–1800.* London: Longman.

Perry, R. (1986). *The Celebrated Mary Astell: An Early English Feminist.* Chicago: Chicago University Press.

Pollock, L. (1989). '"Teach her to live under obedience": the making of women in the upper ranks of early modern England.' *Continuity and Change*, 4, 231–92.

——(ed.) (1993). *With Faith and Physic: The Life of a Tudor Gentlewoman: Lady Grace Mildmay 1552–1620.* London: Collins and Brown.

Price, D. C. (1981). *Patrons and Musicians of the English Renaissance.* Cambridge: Cambridge University Press.

Prior, M. (ed.) (1985). *Women in English Society 1500–1800.* London: Methuen.

Roberts, J. A. (1983). *The Poems of Lady Mary Wroth.* Baton Rouge: Louisiana State University Press.

Simon, J. (1966). *Education and Society in Tudor England.* Cambridge: Cambridge University Press.

Spufford, M. (1974). *Contrasting Communities: English Villagers in Cambridgeshire 1575–1700.* Cambridge: Cambridge University Press.

Sutherland, J. (ed.) (1973). *Memoirs of the Life of Colonel Hutchinson.* London: Oxford.

Watt, T. (1981). *Cheap Print and Popular Piety.* Cambridge: Cambridge University Press.

Woodfill, W. L. (1953). *Musicians in England from Elizabeth to Charles I.* Princeton, NJ: Princeton University Press.

2
Religion and the Construction of the Feminine
Diane Willen

Introduction

As our understanding of gender as an analytic category has evolved, we have also gained new insight into the complexity of religious practices in early modern England. Revisionist historians contest the notion of a singular Protestant Reformation whose irreversible success derived from the tradition of English anti-clericalism and the appeal of the vernacular Bible. They argue that instead of the Reformation in England, we should understand a process of reformation, initiated, reversed and finally consolidated by the state from above; below, in the population at large, while a minority embraced evangelical Protestantism, traditional Catholicism proved tenacious well into the Elizabethan period. According to Christopher Haigh, one of the foremost revisionists, the bibliocentric religion of Protestantism was not so much responsible for the growth of literacy (the older view) as it was dependent upon the spread of literacy for its final triumph (Haigh 1993: 276). The newer research has not replaced older views but has qualified them and made us more aware of the diversity of religious practices and the importance of regional studies.

If the process of Protestantization remains the central question in the historiography of the sixteenth century, the relationship between the Reformation and the Revolution remains a central issue for the seventeenth century. Here revisionist historians initially rejected the notion of a Puritan Revolution. Questioning the existence of an intrinsic radical impulse in parliament or in Puritanism, they see alternative dynamics at work: after 1625 the crown favoured Arminian clerics, who promoted notions of free will over Calvinist predestination, and thereby undermined the stability of the Elizabethan settlement. Yet the historiography of the past two decades has reaffirmed the importance of religious ideology as a motive in Stuart politics. We have not only gained greater appreciation of the appeal of the Elizabethan prayer book within the established church, but also greater understanding of

Puritanism and the spiritual imperatives within its godly community. Moreover, even as historians reject traditional Whig views of a politically progressive, ideological revolution, they have broadened our understanding of the process of politicization and the creation of political opinion beyond the ranks of parliament.

Scholarship on the Reformation and Revolution thus reaffirms the significance of religion and recognizes the role of the laity, including women, whether in resisting, advocating, accepting or even ignoring religious change in early modern England. In a tandem development, a new scholarship has emerged on issues of gender and religion in early modern England. Historians of gender recognize that religion played a prominent part in women's lives and culture; that women in turn must be part of the narrative of religious change (here explicitly integrating women into the ranks of the laity); and that religion was itself gendered, that is, experienced differently by men and women and expressed through gendered images or language. Not surprisingly, historians who focus on issues of gender have emphasized the importance of piety in the lives of women, especially women of the middling and elite classes for whom written evidence survives. Contemporaries believed women 'inclinable to holiness': piety was a virtue in which they could and should excel. Sanctioned with such legitimacy, women found solace and affirmation in the practice of piety. In theory and often in practice, the husband functioned as head of the religious household, the wife as 'yoke fellow,' a spiritual companion responsible for the religious education of their young children. Religion provided women a means to address the pain and fear attending childbirth as well as the emotional costs of infant mortality or unhappy marriage; it promised spiritual egalitarianism and, despite the patriarchal nature of church and society, piety could be a means of self-expression and a source of influence. Piety also provided women of various ranks with a platform on which to emerge on a public stage, especially in the mid-seventeenth century during the sectarian radicalism of the Civil War and Revolution.

In developing these new lines of enquiry, historians have moved away from any simplistic formula or consensus on how religion operated to construct femininity or feminine role models in early modern England. Certainly the prevailing ideology of gender appears straightforward. A misogynist tradition embedded in Christianity emphasized women's weakness and potential for corruption. The story of Eve demonstrated the ease with which woman might be seduced or led to disobedience. The image of the harlot represented unruly women of all ranks and persuasions, but it was also a metaphor that contemporaries of both sexes invoked against hostile forces, most commonly when Protestant writers denounced the Catholic church as the whore of Babylon. In this context, women by nature were inferior and therefore subordinate to their husbands. Whatever the impact of the Reformation on family, patriarchy and the spiritualized household, Catholics and Protestants agreed on the qualities that defined the virtuous woman. She should be chaste, obedient, silent, pious and humble, virtues which women themselves embraced and internalized.

Yet historians of gender recognize that perceptions of female attributes on the one hand, and the dominant construct for idealized feminine behaviour on the other, created a dynamic tension. Given women's weaknesses, how could men rely upon them to be either obedient or chaste? The perceived biological differences between the sexes, resting upon a precarious balance of bodily fluids, further threatened gender constructs. The danger was double-edged: on the one hand, men might slip into effeminacy; on the other, assertive, unruly women could threaten men's masculinity. Anthony Fletcher and others thus recognize an anxiety associated with seventeenth-century patriarchy, evident in literary sources and in the pamphlet warfare evoked by women who cross-dressed (Fletcher 1995: 3–43). Susan Amussen demonstrates a crisis in gender relations, evident in increased litigation against women and linked to attempts to contain social disorder (Amussen 1988: 122–3, 182–3). Religion, of course, deserves a special role in any discussion that focuses on the instabilities of patriarchy. Establishing idealized norms of behaviour, religion offered a prescriptive set of values that could channel women's activities and reinforce their subservient social roles. But religion also provided the legitimacy and authority for women to assert or express themselves, whatever their denominational or political persuasion.

We are left with no alternative but to acknowledge such ambiguities and contradictions. The work of Patricia Crawford, Phyllis Mack, Sara Mendelson, Merry Wiesner, Peter Lake, Patrick Collinson and Suzanne Trill recognizes these contradictions explicitly. Collinson argues that Protestant reformers, despite 'misogynistic chauvinism', also exhibit a 'gynophilia', especially in their descriptions of female martyrs and other remarkable women. 'The devout woman even became (as a type of the church) a kind of emblem for the representative and ideal Christian' (Collinson 1994: 126). Suzanne Trill argues that women involved in religion brought 'to the fore' the inherent 'instabilities' in the gendered category of woman (Trill 1996: 31). Anne Askew, a Protestant martyred in the 1540s, and Margaret Clitherow, an Elizabethan recusant, also martyred, each came to represent a model of religious activism, influence, courage and insight, far different from the model of passivity and obedience extolled in advice literature. The idealized construction of the patriarchal family in the early modern period mirrored similar ambiguities. The legacy of Christian humanism, derived from the Catholic tradition, and the Protestant emphasis on spiritual companionship and reciprocity, mitigated and complicated the practice of patriarchy.

I have argued elsewhere that it is futile to categorize the legacy of the Reformation as a negative or positive influence on the lives of women (Willen 1989: 158). Religious changes, interacting with a variety of intellectual, social and political forces, affected individual lives in a variety of ways that transcend any simple set of criteria. Historians who look at piety and its impact on gender note the similarity in Catholic and Protestant traditions. Yet even before the English Revolution and the rise of sectarianism, Protestantism exacerbated the tensions between practice and prescription. It eliminated some options for women but also provided women new opportunities through its promotion of vernacular scriptures, its emphasis on godly exemplars among the laity, and its tendency, however inadvertent, toward religious pluralism.

To understand how religion constructed gender, we must relinquish the notion of a sharp private–public dichotomy for the early modern era. Contemporaries perceived distinctions between private and public spheres and believed that women's sphere resided in the household. Hence the Puritan minister William Gouge, in his influential advice book *Of Domesticall Duties* (1622), explained that the office of the wife was 'to tarry at home'. Fellow-minister Nicholas Guy eulogized and praised Gouge's wife Elizabeth: 'she most prudently and prouidently ordered the affairs of her house, whereby hee [her husband] had the more leisure to attend his publike function' (*Pieties Pillar*, 1625). Such rhetoric, however, should not lead to the conclusion that women's piety was a private matter relegated to a separate sphere. In economic, political and religious terms the early modern family was integral to society and state. Indeed, the state mandated and enforced (at least intermittently) religious uniformity, and contemporaries saw the patriarchal household as an analogy for the hierarchical state. Furthermore religious practice was itself not confined to the household. Women's piety began with private devotions and household prayer, extended to the religious instruction of children and servants, and also looked outward to encompass charitable activities in the neighbourhood, and often participation in the godly community. Acting in arenas that extended beyond family, women might serve as patrons of the clergy, translators of religious texts, prophets and visionaries, sectarian figures, religious exemplars and lay teachers.

No essay can do justice to the multiple ways in which religion operated to construct feminine values and actual behaviour. This essay relies upon selected texts – some written about women but also personal texts written by women – to demonstrate how religion affected perceptions and behaviour in fundamental and diverse ways.

Refashioning Prescriptive Roles

Funeral sermons, subsequently printed to reach a wide audience, became an important genre in the first half of the seventeenth century. Especially popular among Puritans, the funeral sermon served multiple purposes: clergy expressed their respect or friendship for the deceased, they acknowledged patronage and, most significant for our purposes, they created a text for edification. The eulogy or biographical portrait in the sermon usually followed the explication of a biblical citation and often focused on the deathbed and the significant lessons to be derived from the death of one of the elect. Jeri McIntosh sees a gendered difference within the genre and suggests that women more often than men achieved exemplary deaths, a result that she attributes to virtues prescribed for female behaviour which facilitated a good death: humility, patience in suffering, subordination to higher powers (McIntosh 1990: 166–8). The argument is valid but does not exhaust the insights on gender that can be gleaned from these texts. On their deathbed and in their lives, women played an *active* spiritual role in the godly community, and funeral sermons provide evidence of how religion refashioned the very gender roles it also prescribed.

The gentlewoman Katherine Brettergh, 'by nature very humble and lowlie . . . very meeke, and milde', possessed virtues constructed to acknowledge feminine inferiority (William Harrison and William Leygh, *Deaths Advantage Little Regarded*, 1617). Feminine inferiority, however, made the virtue of any individual woman all the more remarkable. Eulogizing Lady Frances Roberts, Hanniball Gamon asserted 'the weaker her sex is, the more shee shall be commended' (*The Praise of a Godly Woman*, 1627). Preaching upon the death of Mrs Rebecca Crisp, the Puritan divine Thomas Gataker saw examples of the weaker sex 'the more effectuall' for shaming men and encouraging women (*Pauls Desire of Dissolution and Deaths Advantage*, 1620). Clergy exalted godly women as exemplars for both sexes, sons as well as daughters, and beyond the family, as models for members of the greater community. Saints, wrote Gamon, 'desire more the Imitation, than the Commendation of their virtues.'

Given examples of godliness or piety worthy of emulation, clergy chose texts and language that transcended gender. When John Carter preached the funeral sermon for Frances Egerton, Countess of Bridgewater in 1636, he selected as the text Psalm 37.37: 'Marke the perfect man, and Behould him upright'. With reference to the text, Carter advised his audience to dismiss any distinction in gender: 'Change but the sexe and make it woman, or take the word in its full latitude as it comprehends the woman'. Drawing upon male biblical models, the preacher went on to describe Lady Frances as an exemplar of the upright, pious man. As was customary to the genre, Carter's praise was strong. He compared the Countess to a light upon the hill, 'whose gracious Influence might draw the sublinary World to the like perfection.' He cast his own role as that of David mourning Saul. We learn little about Lady Frances beyond her piety, her respect for God's commandments, her attention to prayer and sermon, her instruction of her seven children 'both by precept and example', her charity to the poor. Such deeds complied perfectly with the idealized notion of a domestic sphere, but a manuscript elegy for Lady Frances urges readers to dismiss their 'private greife' and instead to 'bewaile a publike losse' (Huntington Library, Ellesmere 6883).

In 1620 Stephen Denison, a Puritan divine and London lecturer, eulogized Elizabeth Juxon, who died at the age of 27, the wife of a merchant-tailor. Denison dedicated Juxon's funeral sermon to her daughters for whom she was meant to serve as exemplar, but he also saw her as a model for the entire godly community. He described her piety: the care with which she read the scriptures not 'as many do in haste, but with serious consideration'; her acts of charity and clerical patronage; her observance of the Sabbath; her attendance of nine or ten sermons weekly, sometimes four on the Sabbath alone. He praised her submission to her husband, her sense of humility and her denial of self. Disparaging her own zeal and spiritual needs, 'she was brought to plain nothing in her own eyes'. Nonetheless, we learn that Juxon fashioned her own spiritual role. She questioned Denison about theology, consulted with several godly ministers, used her deathbed to exhort family and friends, chose her own text for her funeral sermon, and wrote devotional pieces, some of which Denison included in his published sermon for the edification of his readers. Gender distinctions at such moments become blurred in the sermon. Speaking as Juxon's chaplain for the last five years, Denison acknowledges that she was 'a most kind mother and nurse unto me'. Yet elsewhere he compares her to male as well as female biblical models and speaks of the zeal and love of god achieved by 'her inner man' (*The Monument or Tombe-stone*, 1620).

Social rank complicated the realities of gender. Aristocratic and gentry women, by virtue of their status, acted as patrons to the clergy, exercised authority over servants, and were treated deferentially in their local community. Historians of gender nevertheless have argued that gender created a cohesive woman's culture in the sixteenth and seventeenth centuries more effectively than differences in social rank divided women; that is, gender was more powerful than class in creating prescriptive roles. This essay takes a different tack, suggesting that if class complicated gender, religion could transcend it. In some cases social rank added to the stature of the lay saint. John Carter, for example, was well aware that the Countess of Bridgewater had been born Frances Stanley, daughter to the Earl of Derby. He acknowledged her aristocratic birth even as he sought to distinguish the nobility in her blood from the nobility of her soul. Mary Simpson, in contrast, was of humble status, but she too became a godly exemplar through her spiritual works and the power of her edifying words. John Collings, a Presbyterian minister, eulogized her as an 'Eminent preacher', who during three years of sickness, shared her spiritual experiences and directed others to the ways of God. Though not a pulpit preacher, Collings wrote, Simpson did more good than the ordained clergy. Like Carter and Denison earlier, Collings used rhetoric that seemed to ignore gender as he called Simpson 'a true Christian, a sight of him, in a Copy' (*Faith and Experience or, A short Narration of the holy Life and death of Mary Simpson*, 1647).

Piety was grounded in obedience, humility, patience and silence. Advice books enjoined women from all forms of public speech, whether preaching, public writing or forms of gossip. Yet, in what is surely an extreme case, Collings wished that his own 'tongue were so sanctified' as Simpson's. Moreover, as in the case of Denison and Juxon, Collings's text incorporates Simpson's words, giving her a platform to exhort the godly, a task in which she willingly engaged. She describes her struggle with scriptures, finally apprehended through God's grace, and her understanding of justification. She employs spousal imagery to depict her relationships with Christ:

> I lookt upon Christ as a husband, but yet as a husband going [on] a Journey, and hid
> behind a curtaine, so that my soule was the spouse, *restless* in looking out to *inquire* after
> him; but in time he send many love letters to me.

Such imagery was not unique, but this rhetoric suggests how Simpson used gender
to construct her own meaningful spiritual identity. She also used her spiritual relationship to overcome gender prohibitions. In her view God provided the affliction of
her illness not only to punish her sin and test her faith, but also to give her unusual
opportunity:

> that I might have *liberty* to take occasion to make a report to others what God hath done
> for my soule, that by this meanes, I might bring some honour to God . . . I *might be set*
> upon that *evangelicall work of setting forth the high praise of* God.

Simpson had witnessed the sectarianism of the 1640s and considered joining the Independents. But after examining scriptures she decided that Independency erred in its
interpretation of the covenant. Still a young woman when she died, she claimed that
Christ's intercession had led her to 'holy *boldness* and *confidence.*'

Women's Spiritual Identities

Internalizing traditional feminine virtues, women nonetheless managed to create their
own spiritual identities in ways that reflected their unique experiences, education,
family situations and circumstances. Much of the history of gender focuses on those
women who did so on a public stage, especially during the radicalism of the 1640s,
when censorship collapsed and new religious contexts allowed greater variation of
behaviour. But even in pre-revolutionary England evidence suggests that literate
women across the religious spectrum read and appropriated religious texts in ways
that gave their lives meaning and sanctity.

Literacy was of critical importance in the daily lives of many women renowned for
their piety. Even in London over 80 per cent of the female population in the mid-
seventeenth century remained illiterate, falling to just over 50 per cent by the end of
the century, but these statistics comprise women of all social ranks and rest upon the
ability to sign (writing) rather than the ability to read. Women in the upper ranks of
society generally could read in the seventeenth century; apologetic about their
writing, they usually wrote at a functioning level. Lady Margaret Hoby read not only
John Foxe but also such Puritan clerics as Thomas Cartwright, William Perkins and
Richard Greenham. The first Countess of Bridgewater had an extensive book collection that included plays and histories as well as devotional works (Huntington Library,
Ellesmere 6495). During her widowhood from 1629 to 1636, the Puritan matriarch
Lady Joan Barrington purchased several religious works, often multiple copies (for

example, Foxe's *Book of Martyrs*) which she clearly meant to give as gifts. For her own use she bought some books to serve practical household needs and others to feed her interest in contemporary and religious affairs (Essex RO, D/DBa A 15). Joan's daughter-in-law, Lady Judith Barrington, was eulogized by Thomas Goodwin as 'in the very upper Forme of Female-Scholars' (*A Fair Prospect*, 1658). Judith shared with her husband Thomas a commitment to godly Protestantism, an interest in ecclesiological issues and a great concern for the fate of continental Protestantism. It is reasonable to assume that she read among the books he regularly purchased, many of which followed religious and ecclesiological controversies. Lady Brilliana Harley of Hertfordshire shared a variety of books with her eldest child Ned when in 1638 at age 14 he began his studies at Oxford. As an adolescent, Brilliana had read Calvin's *Institutes* and throughout her lifetime continued to put her literacy to spiritual use. Ill in 1638 and with time on her hands, she chose to read some of Luther's writings and subsequently translated excerpts to send to Ned. She also requested and received copies of devotional books from her son, whose spiritual well-being was her highest priority.

Women read a variety of religious texts but, above all, the Bible. Philip Stubbes claimed that the Bible 'or some other good booke' was almost always in his wife's hand (*Cristal Glas for Christian Women*, 1592). Katherine Brettergh read godly books for instruction and eight chapters daily from the Bible. John Ley reported that Jane Ratcliffe 'was addicted with an incredible desire' to reading Holy Writ (*A Patterne of Pietie*, 1640). Critics, however, questioned women's ability to study the Bible, and as late as 1645 Samuel Torshell in *The Woman's Glory* upheld their right to do so. Torshell commends women for their 'constant and diligent' reading of the Bible and urges them not to allow 'popish envy' to deprive them of this privilege. While some biblical passages may be difficult to comprehend, Torshell reasons that men too cannot understand all they read. Turning the argument, Torshell concludes that if difficult to understand, scriptures should therefore be read 'the *oftener* and with the more *attention.*'

Women did in fact study and wrestle with scriptures, and in that process they found meanings to the text and derived their own authority on spiritual matters. A particularly telling example is found in the manuscript collections of Elizabeth Egerton, second Countess of Bridgewater, daughter-in-law to Lady Francis Egerton. A collection of devotional papers and prayers, transcribed after her death in 1663, reveal a conventional though intense preoccupation with spiritual matters (Huntington Library, Ellesmere 8376). Lady Elizabeth was well versed in scriptures, commented on prayer, communion and fasting, and spoke of Christ as bridegroom. Childbirth (whose danger and pain she describes as 'great torture') and motherhood (which brought joy and thanksgiving) were inseparable components of her spiritual identity; many of her devotional writings were prayers during specific pregnancies, or during labour, or during the illness of a child. Her marriage to John Egerton, then Viscount Brackley, was an affectionate one and undoubtedly reaffirmed her conventional views on wifely obedience. To esteem matrimony, she wrote, the wife should esteem the husband, value his judgement and yield to his counsel. If he be hasty, 'tis fitt she should be silent, giving him no cause to be angry'. She should, however, not stand in such awe of him that in private she refrains from speaking freely and 'if he have a reciprocall affection to his wife, it makes them both blest in one another'. A good marriage, resting upon fear of God and mutual love, she saw as a 'happy and blessed friendshipp'.

Egerton's piety thus reflects traditional views on gender roles. Yet evidence suggests that Elizabeth Egerton also created her own spiritual identity and could reinterpret fundamental assumptions on which gender prescriptions rested. In her prayers, Elizabeth Egerton identified and appropriated for use both male and female biblical models. In her extensive meditations on the Bible, chapter by chapter, she departed from some of the most traditional teachings of the church (Ellesmere 8374). Commenting on mankind's fall from grace, she holds Adam as guilty of sin as Eve, then emphasizes the blessing of children rather than the punitive pain of childbirth. Commenting on God's covenant with Abraham, she makes Sarah fundamental to the narrative: 'the Lord would chose her, she should bee a mother of nations, Kings should bee of her'. Commenting on the story of Jacob, Rachel and Leah, she focuses again on the blessing of children, in Leah's case as gifts from God to compensate for a marriage without amity. Elizabeth Egerton's success in creating her own biblical paradigms is all the more striking when compared to her husband's meditations and reflections. The second Earl cites verses from the New Testament to explicate chapters in Genesis and draws conclusions far different from his wife (Ellesmere 34 B 18). He notes that the serpent beguiled Eve (2 Corinthians 11.3) and concludes that Adam was not deceived 'but the woman being deceiued was in the transgression'. He sees conception and childbirth linked to punishment and sorrow, matrimony linked to patriarchy. He also treats far differently than does his wife the story of Abraham and Sarah and draws no conclusion from the story of Rachel and Leah. The comparison strongly suggests that the Earl and Countess of Bridgewater read the scriptures through gendered experience and reached gender-specific conclusions.

Women asserted their spiritual identity by assuming responsibility for edification: they willingly provided encouragement, spiritual advice, even religious instruction in the family. Catholic and Protestant humanists in the sixteenth century and Puritans in the seventeenth century were most vocal in emphasizing the mother's role in providing religious training, especially for young children. Pious women naturally took this responsibility very seriously and exercised it effectively. In recusant families, mothers transmitted Catholicism from generation to generation. Some like Margaret Clitherow harboured Catholic schoolmasters or sent their children abroad for Catholic education. Elizabeth Grymeston, a Catholic motivated by concern for her son's salvation, wrote a book of advice for his moral guidance. Elizabeth Joceline, a Protestant, wrote *The Mothers Legacie to her unborn Child* (1624) because she prophetically feared her own death in childbirth and she 'so exceedingly desired' to provide her child with religious instruction. Dorothy Leigh wrote *The Mothers Blessing* (1616) to entreat her sons to learn the Bible and in turn to teach their children 'be they Males or Females' to read the Bible 'in their owne mother tongue'. Brilliana Harley in 1629 requested a Bible for her son as soon as he began to read at age five, as that was the book she 'would haue him place his delight in'. Adult children of various religious persuasions frequently testified to the effectiveness of such teaching at the hands of their mothers.

Women remained concerned and involved with their children's moral and spiritual well-being far beyond the early years. Their letters often served as texts of advice, especially as children left home. Jacqueline Eales, biographer of the Harleys, suggests that Lady Brilliana's experiential view of religion as well as the Puritan emphasis on introspection and self-examination were important assumptions underlying the religious edification she offered her son (Eales 1990a: 51–2). Lady Brilliana in the 1630s went so far as to compose a small booklet of moral precepts and treasured teachings. Since her separation from Ned no longer allowed her opportunity to perform her 'duty' as often as she desired, she presented him this offering: 'let theas Linnes sometimes present to your Eyes, those things which I would speake to your Eares' (BL, Add. MS. 70118). In subsequent letters she continued to advise her son on matters ranging from diet, exercise and health to theology. Most of all, however, she was concerned with his moral well-being and his spiritual growth. Dorothy Hutton, a widow, wrote to her son Charles in 1653 in terms reminiscent of those earlier expressed by Brilliana Harley:

> Keep this paper secret but loose it not. When you are alone read it once or twice a weeke at least. Be very serious in perusing it and endeavor that your carriage may be in some measure suitable to this patterne I haue set before you. I have writt this because I know not whether ever I may see you. . . . But by the looking herin you may know what my desires are concerning you. (BL, Stow 744)

Citing the biblical model of Jacob, Hutton urged her son to embrace moderation, to avoid inordinate eating and drinking, to be prudent in giving his affections. 'Call understanding thy kinswoman', she advised, a telling choice of metaphor that challenged popular assumptions about gendered attributes.

As I have elsewhere demonstrated, the Puritan notion of the godly community or 'communion of the saints' provided an arena for women to practise edification (Willen 1995: 20ff.). Dorothy Hutton was sister to Sir Thomas Fairfax, and Dorothy and two of her sisters, Ellinor Selby and Frances Widdrington, wrote letters of advice and edification to a fourth sister, Mary Fairfax Arthington during the 1630s and 1640s. Widdrington's letters, 25 of which survive, are especially interesting. Many read like miniature sermons, for Widdrington sought to compensate for her sister's inability to find godly preaching. At one point Widdrington apologized for her ignorance on a specific issue, but both Widdrington and Hutton, despite their lack of formal training in theology, found confidence and authority in their knowledge of scriptures (Bodleian, Add. A. 119).

Caroline Walker Bynum, Phyllis Mack, Patricia Crawford and Amanda Porterfield have given us rich analyses of how both men and women appropriated gendered images and rhetoric in religious discourse. Not surprisingly women in their own writings turned to the same images that they heard in sermons and read in devotional or theological tracts. While the Presbyterian minister Samuel Rutherford wrote to a female correspondent about sucking comfort from the breast of Christ (*Letters* 1891: 81), such female imagery was highly atypical. Women saw divinity in male terms: God as the father, Christ as the bridegroom or heavenly husband. Spousal imagery could become erotic, and in her analysis of women's diaries, Sara Mendelson sees some evidence of 'erotic transference' (Mendelson 1985: 195). Women generally chose metaphors that reflected popular perceptions of gender, whether that imagery was negative (scold and whore) or positive (bride and spouse to Christ). They were comfortable with images of motherhood (the womb, fruitfulness), and a variety of pious women (Joan Barrington, Frances Widdrington, Lettice Falkland, and later, Quaker women) were themselves deemed 'mothers in Israel'.

Yet a close look at religious imagery and rhetoric also conveys what Patrick Collinson has called 'gender confusion' (Collinson 1994: 141). Godly ministers like Richard Sibbes, Thomas Gataker and Samuel Rutherford, as well as the young John Winthrop, described their own loving, subordinate relationship to Christ by assuming the feminine role and depicting Christ's love in erotic terms. Caroline Bynum's analysis of medieval imagery is relevant here: males embraced the feminine as a symbol of dependence on God. Bynum also argues that medieval religious women avoided 'metaphorical maleness' and relied instead on female images to describe their own relationships with God. She concludes that medieval women 'saw in their own female bodies . . . a symbol and a means of approach to the humanity of God' (Bynum 1987: 296). By the early modern era, however, women (like men on occasion) blurred distinctions in gender for their own spiritual purposes. Reminiscent of the gender blending – or transcendence of gender – seen in funeral sermons, a young Brilliana Conway, writing in her commonplace book before her marriage to Sir Robert Harley, identified herself with one of the adopted sons of God. Women appropriated male as well as female biblical models and employed rhetoric that emphasized militancy and combat. In a letter of edification Mary Blencow, for example, urged her sister to embrace a godly, chaste life but hardly a passive one. 'Read the Bible daily and hourly', she advised, 'that you may be able to kill all your enemies with the sword of the Spirit' (Bodleian, Rawlinson D. 273, 402). Brilliana Harley, Dorothy Hutton, Jane Ratcliffe and Mary Simpson also embraced military metaphors. Lady Elizabeth Brooke, in warfare against Satan, saw herself fighting not alone, but as part of 'a whole *Army* engaged in the Quarrel . . . the Saints *collectively* make War upon him'. Brooke's writings became public when printed as an appendix to her funeral sermon (Nathaniel Parkhurst, *The Faithful and Diligent Christian Described*, 1684). I would suggest that with such language these women were not reversing images of self but expanding their self-images beyond traditional gender constraints according to the spiritual imperatives imposed by their piety.

Integration of Public and Private

Religious teachings had multiple repercussions, affecting different women in different ways or affecting the same woman in different ways. Spiritual imperatives taught from the pulpit did not necessarily agree with gender prescriptions advocated in advice literature. The Puritans provide a striking example of the way that religion could expand gender roles, in this case encouraging women's participation in public issues. Puritanism here implies not an organized movement or a doctrinal programme but a style of piety, a form of spirituality with an emphasis on religious fervour, preaching, scriptures and the godly community.

Members of the godly community in Caroline England perceived Lady Joan Barrington as a spiritual exemplar. Men as well as women, indeed clergy as well as laity, acknowledged this Puritan matriarch as a 'lady elect', a spiritual authority in her own right. Widowed at about age 70, she presided over an influential gentry family in Essex. Her husband, Sir Francis Barrington, an experienced member of parliament, had been imprisoned when he refused to serve as collector of the forced loan levied by Charles I. His death in July 1628, the year after his release, deeply affected Lady Joan. She questioned her own election and during the 1630s experienced sustained periods of grief and even despair.

Strikingly, however, in the midst of her personal problems and anxieties, Lady Joan's family took for granted her abiding interest in national policy and politics. Members of her family, especially her sons as members of parliament, kept her informed of events in London as popery and Arminianism became central parliamentary issues. Her nephew, Sir Thomas Bourchier, sought her intervention on behalf of the commonwealth after the impasse between crown and Commons in March 1629. Blending gender distinctions, Bourchier described the practice of saints in times of peril to 'quitte thems selves like men'. Calling himself 'a worme and no man', he entreated his aunt to act through prayer for the public good:

> If . . . such pillars [as the saints] be awakened, how with a holye violence will yow wrastle with our father, not lettinge him reste til he againe looke with an amiable countenance upon this deformed and ingratefull nation. (*Barrington Family Letters*: 60)

Joan Barrington was a representative figure, one of several pious women within the self-fashioned Puritan community in Caroline England who integrated spiritual and political priorities to become politicized. Especially among the Puritans, where spiritual imperatives imposed their own agenda for protecting and extending the

Reformation, godliness abetted politicization. With no thought to challenge social and political conventions, Puritan women, like their menfolk, supported ministers, issues and spiritual initiatives that the crown found threatening. The women in this self-fashioned godly community, at least before the Civil War, expressed no aspiration to vote, nor to hold office, nor to make policy. Nonetheless, during the two decades preceding revolution, these women became politicized: that is, they developed a form of political consciousness and acted to influence political outcomes. In this case at least, the religious construction of gender, however inadvertently, led to participation in the political culture.

The one issue that most galvanized the political and spiritual concerns of Puritans in the early 1620s was the fate of continental Protestantism during the Thirty Years War. Seeing themselves in terms of an international Protestant community, the godly advocated a Protestant foreign policy. Neither geography, class nor gender inhibited their interest and comment. Personal ties and experiences among the godly reinforced their ideological commitment as sons or other relatives served in the English volunteer force for the Palatinate. Yet such personal ties were more symptom than cause of the Puritans' tendency to see the continental struggles in impassioned, even apocalyptic terms. In the parliaments of the 1620s Sir Robert Harley argued in Commons on religious grounds for war against Spain and, in the 1630s, Lady Brilliana Harley saw events in terms of the Lord's cause. Both would have agreed with the Puritan artisan Nehemiah Wallington, who according to Paul Seaver, saw the European wars as a struggle between Christ and Antichrist (Seaver 1985: 192). Lady Harley regularly supplied Ned at Oxford with newsbooks and, when available, corantos which detailed events on the Continent. She exhorted her son to be informed about local affairs while also expressing her desire that he 'keep awake in the knowledg of things abroode' (*Letters*: 32).

The Barrington correspondence demonstrates how this whole family, men and women, avidly followed the fortunes of their fellow Protestants on the Continent and shared domestic political gossip. Lady Joan Barrington relied upon her entire family network, including her granddaughter Joan St John, to keep her informed of the latest military campaigns. Lady Judith Barrington described battles and provided her mother-in-law with newsbooks and corantos. Her sons-in-law, Sir William Masham and Sir Gilbert Gerard, wrote to tell her which publication had been sent and when the next would be available.

Not able to speak or sit in parliament nor join armies, godly women still had avenues through which to engage the political and religious issues dominating their concerns. Godly women of the elite classes acted as patrons, benefactors and protectors of the clergy. During the 1620s Lady Mary Vere, a godly matron whose husband led the English volunteer forces for the Palatinate, interceded with her brother-in-law, Secretary of State Conway, to advance the claims of both John Davenport and James Usher. Davenport maintained a correspondence with Vere and in 1628 wrote both about the unhappy state of parliamentary affairs and his own likely problems at the hands of the new Bishop of London, William Laud. Supported by Richard Sibbes, Davenport urged Lady Vere to remain with her husband in Holland in order to serve the public or common good (BL, Add. MS. 4275, 160, 166).

Above all, women who sought to promote godliness at home and abroad had recourse to those spiritual strategies accessible to all members of the godly community. Their daily devotional practices, including reliance upon scripture and preaching, fostered personal piety, introspection and personal encounters with God. But marks of their religious fervour (for example, recourse to prayer and fasting) might equally serve the needs of the larger godly community. Prayer offered an especially important method of intercession and participation by the individual. The Puritan divine Stephen Geree, citing the biblical example of Hannah, saw no distinctions in terms of gender: 'The Prayers of faithfull women, as well as men *pierce the clouds, and pull downe Gods blessings*, upon themselves and others' (Geree, *The Ornament of Women*, 1639). Brilliana Harley recorded in her commonplace book that even without the holiness of biblical 'fathers and profets . . . yet if we belieuve . . . we haue as much assurance to be hard as they had' (Nottingham University Library, Portland MSS, 205).

Intent upon fighting the Antichrist in all its forms, women prayed for the nation, its parliament, its church, and its pursuit of godly politics. Hence the plea from Lady Joan Barrington's nephew that the saints wrestle with their heavenly father for the sake of the nation. Under such circumstances, as Paul Seaver argues, prayer itself became 'the ultimate political act' (Seaver 1985: 178). Writing of events in parliament and abroad in 1629, Robert Barrington informed his mother of the need of earnest prayers by all the godly. Brilliana Harley prayed for the fortunes of parliament in the 1620s and in May 1640, days before the dissolution of the Short Parliament, invoked prayers on its behalf (BL, Add. MS. 70110 and *The Letters*). Upon the death of Mrs Jane Ratcliffe, godly matron of Chester, her eulogizer, John Ley, lamented that the city sustained a great loss with her death and missed the support of her supplications.

Expectations surrounding the Long Parliament naturally heightened the political interests, rhetoric and passions of the godly. Anna Temple, member of a Puritan family in Sussex and sister to Viscount Say and Sele, wrote to her daughter Anna Busbridge in June 1640 about the hope of rooting out idolatry and superstitions:

> Altars begin to goe downe apace, and railes in many places, and yours must follow if it
> bee not downe already, let us laber to be thankefull and continue our prayers, hould up
> our hands that Israell may prevaile. (East Sussex RO, Dunn 51/54)

Hannah Brograve, aunt to the MP Simonds D'Ewes, described local petitioning campaigns in the autumn of 1640 and felt 'if eaver it is now a time to pray'. In the following March, Brograve exhorted D'Ewes to advance the sceptre of Christ on behalf of complete reformation, although she was prudent enough to warn against 'leaving us word then yea found us'. Brograve continued to follow events in parliament closely and in 1642 entreated D'Ewes to send his assessment of votes in the Lords against episcopacy (BL, Harleian MS. 384, 86ff.).

In the spring of 1644, when the Committee against Scandalous Ministers in Essex collected evidence against offending clerics, women and men alike provided testimony that integrated religious and political concerns. Susan Kent complained about John Jegon for his remark, 'twas Pitty that ever the Bible was translated into English; for now every Woman & beggarly Fellow thinke themselves able to dispute with reverend Divines' (BL, Add MS. 5829, 21–2). The outbreak of the Civil War led to the fragmentation of Puritanism, the rise of sectarianism and the acceleration of politicization among women at large. Patricia Crawford (1993) and Phyllis Mack (1992) provide narrative and analysis of the story in its complexities. Yet the radicalism of the mid-century should not obscure the earlier participation of godly women in political concerns, nor indeed the rationale behind John Jegon's remark.

Conclusion

Through their political concerns and interests, godly women in Caroline England developed a dynamic relationship to the state, one far more complex than traditional gender roles would suggest. Puritanism led them beyond introspective piety to a form of participation that integrated spiritual and political imperatives. A number of factors in early modern culture, namely women's lack of formal political power, the prescriptive legal and religious sources, women's internalization of societal values, and the spiritual context in which political issues operated, tend to obscure or disguise their politicization. Nonetheless, women found in godliness an ideology of sorts which inherently mixed public and private: they could be saints and affect the state in that capacity long before they were to become citizens.

During the Civil War women emerged more visibly on the public stage although they tended to be women of lower rank, participating in a variety of religious denominations and in religious prophecy. Patricia Crawford describes a type of 'sexual politics' as men and women competed with one another for control in many congregations (Crawford 1993: 140ff.). By the time of the Restoration, however, conventional gender roles had withstood the potential radicalism of the sects. Even among Nonconformists whose survival was tied to the participation of women, patriarchal norms prevailed. Phyllis Mack demonstrates how the Quakers confounded gender distinctions, yet within this community as well, women assumed more traditional roles by the end of the century (Mack 1992: 274–6). Women remained 'inclinable to piety', but politics and religion diverged. Religion continued to impose its prescriptive values, but the political, scientific and economic context would not remain static.

Perhaps no single figure better exemplifies the tensions between religious imperatives and gender prescriptions during the Restoration than Lucy Hutchinson. Writing
her husband's memoirs some twenty years after the Civil War, Hutchinson demonstrated anew the ambiguities that characterized expectations for and by women.
Colonel John Hutchinson died in prison, a discredited regicide, and his wife wrote to
vindicate his public career and the godly cause for which he had fought. Like her predecessors among the ranks of ladies elect, Hutchinson extolled the patriarchal values
of submission and obedience. Indeed, she blamed the origins of the English Civil
War at least in part on Queen Henrietta Maria, a powerful politicized female, who
had overturned the patriarchal norm. According to Hutchinson, the influence of
Henrietta Maria had been 'fatall to the kingdome, which never is any place happie
where the hands that are made only for distaffes affect the management of Sceptres'.
Hutchinson recognized that some of her readers would look back with fondness and
praise to the reign of another female monarch, Queen Elizabeth, but cautioned that
'the felicity' of that reign was the result of Elizabeth's 'submission to her masculine
and wise Councellors' (Hutchinson 1973: 48).

Paradoxically, Hutchinson's actions, indeed her very act of writing the *Memoirs*,
undermined the patriarchal ideal which she espoused. N. H. Keeble establishes the
inconsistencies and contradictions through his insightful analysis of Hutchinson's
work and the rhetorical strategies it employs. Referring to herself and her husband
in the third person, Lucy Hutchinson adopted the voice of a first-person narrator in
order to avoid assuming so assertive a role as the Colonel's wife. Keeble sees the irony
of the situation:

> Lucy Hutchinson's whole text is a gross impropriety. Its mere existence contradicts
> its own avowals. The text denies Lucy Hutchinson any being apart from John
> Hutchinson even as, without him, it confers on her an enduring identity. . . . Hands
> that should not grasp at sceptres had no more business grasping pens. (Keeble
> 1990: 235)

Hutchinson reveals herself in the text as highly politicized and highly partisan.
She relied on her own journals as well as other histories as sources for her narrative
of events. Her analysis, whatever its bias, confidently and skilfully draws upon
her own political knowledge and acumen, acquired and developed for over two
decades. According to Hutchinson's account of Charles's reign, any who had dared
to question the king's 'impositions in the worship of God' had been classified as
seditious, a disturber of the public peace. Those who had grieved at the dishonour
of the kingdom or objected to 'unjust oppressions of the subject', those who had
in fact represented the public interest, had been branded Puritan, 'and if Puritanes,
then enemies to the king and his government' (Hutchinson 1973: 43ff.). Under
such circumstances, Hutchinson saw the spiritual and political destinies of

England inextricably linked, reason enough to justify her own level of politicization.

This chapter thus ends as it began by emphasizing the contradictions and ambiguities inherent in the relationship between religion and gender. Religious values and assumptions provided the rationale not only to construct and defend conventional norms for feminine behaviour but also to transcend those same prescriptive norms. Although men and women acknowledged spiritual imperatives and religious teachings in order to expand gender roles and blur distinctions of gender, they rarely questioned or challenged the patriarchal ideal. Samuel Torshell's tract *The Woman's Glory* (1645) may serve as our final text. It originated as a sermon to commemorate the birth of King Charles I's second daughter. In the text Torshell defends women's right to read scripture, but expects women's silence in public except in extraordinary cases. He describes the state of grace as egalitarian: 'there is neither male nor female, no prefering of one sex before the other, but all one in Christ Jesus'. Yet he strongly defends the patriarchal norm: 'Even *Sarah* the mother of Believers, from whom *Kings* and *Nations* came, called her husband *Lord*.' The message was mixed enough to justify a rich variety of behaviours and perceptions within patriarchy.

See also WOMEN AND EDUCATION; WOMEN AND WRITING; AUTOBIOGRAPHY

ACKNOWLEDGEMENT

I wish to thank the Duke of Sutherland for permission to quote from the photocopy facsimile housed at the Huntington Library in San Marino, California: Elizabeth Egerton, Countess of Bridgewater, 'Meditations on the General Chapters of the Holy Bible', EL 8374, 35 C 16.

REFERENCES AND FURTHER READING

Amussen, S. D. (1988). *An Ordered Society: Gender and Class in Early Modern England*. Oxford: Blackwell Publishers.
Bynum, C. W. (1987). *Holy Feast and Holy Fast*. Berkeley: University of California Press.
Collinson, P. (1994). *Elizabethan Essays*. London: Hambledon Press.
Cope, E. S. (1992). *Handmaid of the Holy Spirit: Dame Eleanor Davies, Never Soe Mad a Ladie*. Ann Arbor: University of Michigan Press.
Crawford, P. (1993). *Women and Religion in England 1500–1720*. London: Routledge.
Eales, J. (1990a). *The Puritans and Roundheads: The Harleys of Brampton Bryan and the Outbreak of the English War*. Cambridge: Cambridge University Press.
——(1990b). 'Samuel Clarke and the "lives" of godly women in seventeenth-century England.' In W. J. Sheils and D. Wood (eds), *Women in the Church* (pp. 365–77). Studies in Church History, 27. Oxford: Blackwell Publishers.
Fletcher, A. (1995). *Gender, Sex and Subordination in England 1500–1800*. New Haven, CT: Yale University Press.

Haigh, C. (1993). *English Reformations: Religion, Politics and Society under the Tudors*. Oxford: Clarendon Press.

Harley, B. (1968). *Letters of the Lady Brilliana Harley*, ed. T. T. Lewis. New York: AMS Press.

Houlbrooke, R. (1998). *Death, Religion, and the Family in England, 1480–1750*. Oxford: Clarendon Press.

Hutchinson, L. (1973). *Memoirs of the Life of Colonel Hutchinson*, ed. J. Sutherland. Oxford: Oxford University Press.

Keeble, N. H. (1990). '"The Colonel's shadow": Lucy Hutchinson, women's writing and the Civil War.' In T. Healy and J. Sawday (eds), *Literature and the English Civil War* (pp. 227–47). Cambridge: Cambridge University Press.

Lake, P. (1987). 'Feminine piety and personal potency: the emancipation of Mrs Jane Ratcliffe.' *The Seventeenth Century*, 2, 143–65.

McIntosh, J. I. (1990). 'English funeral sermons, 1560–1640: the relationship between gender and death, dying and the after-life.' Masters thesis, Oxford.

Mack, P. (1992). *Visionary Women: Ecstatic Prophecy in Seventeenth-Century England*. Berkeley: University of California Press.

Mendelson, S. (1985). 'Stuart women's diaries and occasional memoirs.' In M. Prior (ed.), *Women in English Society, 1500–1800* (pp. 181–210). London: Methuen.

Mendelson, S. and Crawford, P. (1998). *Women in Early Modern England 1550–1720*. Oxford: Clarendon Press.

Porterfield, A. (1992). *Female Piety in Puritan New England: The Emergence of Religious Humanism*. Oxford: Oxford University Press.

Searle, A. (ed.) (1983). *Barrington Family Letters 1628–1632*. London: Camden Society, 4th series, no. 28.

Seaver, P. S. (1985). *Wallington's World: A Puritan Artisan in Seventeenth-Century London*. Stanford, CA: Stanford University Press.

Trill, S. (1996). 'Religion and the construction of femininity.' In H. Wilcox (ed.), *Women and Literature in Britain 1500–1700* (pp. 30–55). Cambridge: Cambridge University Press.

Wiesner, M. E. (1993). *Women and Gender in Early Modern Europe*. Cambridge: Cambridge University Press.

Willen, D. (1989). 'Women and religion in early modern England.' In S. Marshall (ed.), *Women in Reformation and Counter-Reformation Europe* (pp. 140–65). Bloomington: Indiana University Press.

——(1992). 'Godly women in early modern England: Puritanism and gender.' *Journal of Ecclesiastical History*, 43, 561–80.

——(1995). '"Communion of the saints": spiritual reciprocity and the godly community in early modern England.' *Albion*, 27, 20–41.

3
Women, Property and Law
Tim Stretton

Introduction

The clearest embodiment of the secondary status of early modern English women can be found in their restricted legal rights and limited access to property. Travellers to England regularly commented on English women's paucity of rights compared to their European neighbours, particularly if they were married. According to Dutchman Emanuel van Meteren, 'Wives in England are entirely in the power of their husbands, their lives only excepted'. However, these same travellers puzzled over the apparent freedoms English women enjoyed in practice. Van Meteren went on to note that despite the overwhelming power of husbands, English wives 'are not kept so strictly as they are in Spain and elsewhere'. A German observer agreed that English women 'have much more liberty than perhaps in any other place'. National stereotypes of this kind make dubious historical sources. However, the discrepancy these writers detected, between theoretical subjection and apparent liberty, provides a neat encapsulation of the complex and contradictory nature of women's rights in early modern England. For despite possessing fewer legal rights and opportunities than men, early modern English women went to law in their thousands, and while a myriad of different pressures acted to limit their access to property, examples can be found of women possessing or controlling large estates, borrowing and lending money and operating successful businesses.

The regularity with which practice parted company from theory in the realm of women's rights might suggest that the legal system was somehow out of step with the society it served – that the population at large found ways to ignore a patriarchal legal system they regarded as unnecessarily harsh. However, the true picture is clearly more complicated, for the period witnessed unprecedented levels of participation in the legal process. Furthermore, the divergence between laws and behaviour did not follow a consistent path, and practice was sometimes *harsher* than the law demanded.

It seems likely, therefore, that the slippage in the system stemmed not from its inefficiency but from its flexibility, a flexibility that helps explain how discriminatory laws and legal doctrines that attracted comments from defiant women as well as foreign visitors could operate, adapt and persist for so long without being seriously challenged. In terms of male bias and patriarchal values the distance between subjection and liberty in law and practice is a sign not of the weakness of the system but of its abiding strength.

Legal Status, Marriage and Identity

At the heart of many early modern English legal institutions lay a general belief in women's inferiority to men. On the basis of this belief women were prevented from voting in elections, sitting in parliament, acting as judges or lawyers or serving on juries (apart from specialist 'juries of matrons' who examined female victims and suspected criminals). In short, society denied women a role in the making and administering of the laws which bound them. Expressions of the belief in female inferiority could be condescending, viewing women as weak and incapable, or paternalistic, viewing women as weak and in need of protection. Sometimes the attitude was simply discriminatory and contemptuous, as when the Chancery judge Anthony Benn expressed his desire to ban all women from appearing in courtrooms 'for their wit is so little and their will so great that nothing is just with them but that which satisfieth them'. Regardless of the rationale or the intent behind each expression, women's underlying inferiority was rarely in doubt. Yet, while this premise might be said to be universal, its application was not. Time and again it was tempered or contradicted by other considerations, such as a belief in the need for equality before the law or more often an acknowledgement of the crucial importance of property ownership.

Many positions of public responsibility in early modern England were tied to the ownership of specific property, for example the right and duty to administer the customary courts attached to manors. To exclude female property owners from public office in such cases might satisfy feelings of male superiority, but inevitably risked undermining the power of property qualifications and inheritance. The dynastic concerns of the monarchy, for example, were sufficiently powerful to allow Mary I and Elizabeth I to sit on the throne, despite deeply held reservations about female rule. This was in contrast to France, where the Salic law prohibited female succession. In most cases, however, the result was a compromise: ladies of the manor kept the courts attached to their manors, but most did so through stewards rather than in person. By making or encouraging women to delegate power to male representatives, lawmakers and other authorities managed to prevent women from exercising direct authority while keeping the property qualification intact. What is interesting in this context is how rarely written laws or regulations specifically barred women from holding lesser offices or from voting in elections. And in the absence of such restrictions examples

can be found of women serving their communities as sextons, churchwardens, returning officers and in other positions of public influence. These exceptions are revealing,
but they were also extremely rare, thanks to the insidious influence of convention and
local prejudice.

As Hilda Smith has pointed out, a feature of this society was the frequency with
which lawyers, judges and civic or religious leaders interpreted ostensibly universal
terms, such as 'householders', 'property owners' or 'the people', as applying only to
men (Smith 1998: 329–30). Early in the seventeenth century, for example, the
eminent common lawyer Edward Coke asserted that copyholders (customary tenants)
could serve on the juries of manor courts, 'but this is meant of men and not women'.
In 1622 a lecturer at Gray's Inn argued that although the law did not exclude women
from being churchwardens or overseers of the poor, they were in fact 'uncapable' of
holding these offices because of the 'weakness of their sex' which made them 'unfit
to travel' and because they were 'for the most part uncapable of learning to direct
in matters of judicature'. In similar fashion, the religious writer Richard Hooker
applauded the tradition of giving away brides in marriage, because he believed 'it
putteth women in mind of a duty whereunto the very imbecility of their nature doth
bind them, namely to be always directed, guided and ordered by others, although our
positive laws do not tie them now as pupils'. It was habits of thought like Hooker's
and Coke's, as much as positive laws and explicit rules, that consistently kept women
away from power, and allowed observers and legal commentators to explain away the
few exceptional women who managed to wield power as just that: exceptional.

A practical reason why communities and authorities did not think it fitting for
women to serve in positions of authority was related directly to the law, and concerned
the very real incapacity that women suffered if they married. At the heart of the legal
system's view of women rested the long-standing legal principle of coverture, a set of
ideas built around the doctrine of 'unity of person'. Just as the Bible suggested that
a husband and wife were one flesh, the common law said they were one person: they
shared a single legal personality and that personality was the husband's. A married
woman was known as a *feme covert* because her legal identity was covered or over-
shadowed by her husband's. Because she lacked an independent personality, in theory
a married woman could not enter into contracts, sue or be sued or write a will. Worse
than that, she could not control property, which technically prevented her from personally accepting gifts or inheriting legacies. On marriage a woman's personal property (her moneys, belongings and personal effects, including the clothes she stood up
in) became her husband's outright, along with any gifts she received or monies she
earned during marriage. A woman's real property (her lands) also came under her
husband's control, although only for the duration of the marriage. This meant that a
husband could exploit his newly acquired real estate and keep the profits as his own,
but after his death the lands reverted to his wife or to her heirs. In theory he could
not sell or otherwise alienate lands he held 'in right of his wife' without her consent
(and mechanisms existed to examine married women separately from their husbands

to determine whether they gave this consent freely), but in practice husbands did sell their wives' interests in lands, and the restrictions of coverture made it difficult for wives to recover those interests while their husbands remained alive.

Most legal commentators couched justifications of coverture in positive rather than negative terms. Coverture was supposedly good for wives and supplied them with a protection unique in English law. The well-being of a marriage depended on unity, and pooling a husband's and wife's legal identities and property supposedly promoted that unity by removing potential subjects of dissension and assisting couples to present a united front to the world. Of course, when personalities clashed within real marriages the idealism of these justifications could quickly turn sour. The law gave vindictive husbands the right to use 'reasonable' force to discipline wives and the ability to sell their clothes and treasured possessions. What constituted 'reasonable' correction was a matter of spirited debate, and Susan Amussen and Elizabeth Foyster have demonstrated the social and cultural forces limiting the level of male violence that communities regarded as tolerable. It seems likely, for example, that domestic violence may have been more prevalent, or at least less policed, in the eighteenth century than in the sixteenth (Amussen 1994: 71–2, 82–4). Nevertheless, the fact remains that common law authorities placed the security of marriages above the security of women within marriages. In a society where moral and political philosophers regarded households as the essential building blocks of the state – as mini monarchies that nurtured and policed hierarchical bonds of respect, deference and obligation – public authority depended on domestic order. And to maintain an orderly household, writers argued, a patriarch had to have power not just over his children and servants but over his wife. Stark recognition of this belief can be found in the statutory penalties for domestic homicide, where a man convicted of killing his wife was guilty of murder and might hang, but a wife who killed her husband (in common with servants who killed their masters or children who killed their fathers) was guilty of petty treason, a crime against the state, and might be burned at the stake.

What made coverture such a potent force was women's effective inability to escape its bonds. Marriage once entered was for life, for throughout the early modern period divorce in the modern sense (the ending of a marriage permitting remarriage) was effectively impossible. With the exception of Henry VIII and a handful of aristocrats who could afford to divorce by private bills in parliament, for most couples the bonds of matrimony could be broken only by the death of either spouse. Despite repeated calls for reform by Protestant reformers from Thomas Cranmer in the sixteenth century to Milton in the seventeenth, this situation persisted until the passing of the Divorce Act in 1857. All a woman could hope for was that the church courts would grant her an annulment or a separation *a mensa et thoro* (from 'bed and board'). However, while the latter might remove a woman from the immediate danger posed by a violent husband, in most cases it did not free her from the restricting influence of coverture, and numerous husbands of separated women tried to assert ownership over property and income their wives had accumulated while living apart.

The theoretical limits of coverture were extreme, yet many married women went about their daily lives as if the concept did not exist. They provisioned their houses, played an active role in credit networks, bought and sold second-hand clothing and household items and treated personal possessions as their own, behaviour that only became a problem if their husbands or other interested parties raised objections. Many men and women did not fully understand the doctrine, like the Blackfriars parishioners who took 'much exception' to William Gouge's suggestion that wives could not dispose of family property without their husbands' consent, while others poked fun at the absurdity of the fiction that two people could become one. Nevertheless, it is important not to underestimate the ideological force of coverture. As the widow Blackacre in William Wycherley's Restoration comedy *The Plain Dealer* exclaims, 'marriage is worse than excommunication in depriving a woman of access to law'. In theoretical terms the doctrine undermined not just wives' but *all* women's capacity to hold positions of authority, because the potential (and in many instances the expectation) existed that single or widowed women might marry in the future and become legally subject to their new husbands. The dramatic changes in status coverture wrought also help explain the fixation of legal authorities with women's marital status, and why women in legal records were invariably identified not by their social rank, trade or profession, but as the daughters, wives or widows of named men.

By offering women certain rights and withholding others, and by linking legal status to marital status, laws helped to define female identity. At the same time the legal system established and maintained a general climate of bias in favour of men that regularly, but by no means always, worked to the detriment of women. In practice some individuals chose to enforce principles such as coverture to their limits, others circumvented or ignored them, still others found ways to exceed them, producing considerable variation in women's experiences of rights and law. This variation was compounded by the fact that the legal system was not a single, coherent, unified whole, but a jumble of overlapping and competing jurisdictions, each of which provided women (and men) with unique sets of rights, restrictions, obligations and remedies.

Common Law and Statute

The common law (judge-made laws and principles supplemented by statutes) is regarded by many historians as the single biggest impediment to women's freedom in the early modern period. It dealt with property, and in particular 'real property' or land, and as we have seen with coverture, it regularly put the interests of men ahead of the interests of women. Perhaps the best-known example is the common law principle of primogeniture, which channelled all of a dying man's lands to his eldest son. Under this principle daughters could inherit lands only in the absence of surviving sons, and in such cases the inheritance did not go to the eldest daughter, but was shared equally between daughters (coparceny). The original rationale for primogeniture, which worked to the detriment of younger sons as well as daughters, had its roots in feudal obligations, reflecting the desire of lord and monarch to keep landed estates intact for military purposes, to supply knights for combat. However, this does not explain why primogeniture outlived the system it was designed to sustain, persisting throughout and beyond the early modern period until its abolition in 1925.

The bias against women inherent in primogeniture is clear, but there are a number of things to note about the principle. First of all, it applied only to real property, and therefore did not affect the bulk of the population who possessed only personal property or lesser interests in land such as leases. Secondly, although it severely disadvantaged women, it did not exclude them altogether, in contrast to Italy, for example, where in certain jurisdictions a deceased man's brothers would inherit before his daughters. Thirdly, although it began as an automatic principle, by the early modern period it applied only to intestate succession, to individuals who died without making a will. Those individuals who did write wills, especially if they were below the level of the aristocracy or the affluent gentry, often went against the spirit of primogeniture and made sure that each of their children received a share of their estates – in fact this seems to have been a key incentive for writing a will. As Amy Erickson has shown, some testators (particularly in Yorkshire) ignored primogeniture altogether and left parcels of lands to daughters and younger sons, while many more sought to compensate these children in other ways (Erickson 1993: 61). Usually this meant leaving daughters and younger sons increased shares of personal property (and at a time when a bed could be worth as much as £2 and a house as little as £5, it was easier than today for those below the great landowning classes to divide their estates equitably). Alternatively, testators left all their lands to their eldest sons, but attached conditions stipulating that heirs provide for their siblings out of the revenues from these lands, whether by paying them an annual sum until they reached adulthood or providing them with a dowry or portion if they decided to marry. There was a strong tendency in both law and practice to deprive women of unfettered ownership or control of real property, but not to deny them resources of other kinds. As Erickson's researches reveal, in early modern England 'daughters inherited from their parents on a remarkably equitable basis with their brothers' and the level of resources parents needed to devote to raising girls and boys was commonly 'identical' (ibid.: 19).

As we have seen, the common law undeniably curtailed the legal rights of married women. Yet while the principle of coverture placed custody of wives' rights in the hands of their husbands, it did not remove those rights altogether. So, for example, while a wife technically could not participate in a lawsuit without her husband, she could participate *with* her husband, and it is revealing that the single largest grouping of female litigants in almost every court in the land (including common law courts) consisted of married women appearing, or at least named, alongside their husbands. Moreover, women who were not married – single women and widows –

possessed virtually the same rights under private law as men. In contrast to a married woman who was *feme covert*, an unmarried woman or widow was *feme sole* with a distinct legal identity and the freedom to sue and be sued, enter contracts, and buy, sell and own property.

In addition to providing unmarried women and widows with rights roughly equivalent to those enjoyed by men, the common law also provided widows with a positive right, the entitlement to dower. During the early modern period this amounted to a one-third interest for life in lands their husbands had held during marriage. This right applied regardless of the financial contribution women or their families made or did not make at the time of the marriage, in other words whether or not they had contributed a portion or dowry. Women did not receive the lands outright, but a right to control them and take the income, with which they were supposed to support themselves and maintain any dependent children. On one level a one-third interest seems miserly, especially when compared with the male equivalent of 'Curtesy', which gave husbands who outlived their wives a life interest in *all* of their wives' lands, as long as their marriage had produced a child (and therefore a potential heir). However, one third of a large landed estate could be considerable, and as we shall see, in the majority of cases one third of a man's lands represented a more generous right than the alternative arrangements many couples favoured in practice. The problem with dower was not so much its value, but the difficulties associated with claiming it. To begin with it applied only to land, and therefore meant little to the bulk of the population who owned other types of property. Worse than that, it applied only to freehold lands held in 'fee simple' and therefore did not apply to lands held by other means, such as leases or copyhold, or the huge proportion of lands tied up in 'uses' or trusts. And finally, there was the problem of determining which lands dower applied to, when multiple transactions throughout a marriage could make lands held 'at any time' during marriage an extremely difficult concept to define.

The common law and statute law often discriminated against women. However, where they did so they usually fixed the level of discrimination. Dower may have offered no more than a one-third interest, but it guaranteed no less than one third. Similarly, primogeniture permitted daughters to inherit real property only in the absence of sons, but it also guaranteed that they would inherit in such instances. And as we shall see, while other jurisdictions might exceed the common law in the generosity of rights and provisions for women, on many occasions they ended up offering women less.

Ecclesiastical Law

Ecclesiastical authorities oversaw an extensive jurisdiction concerned with the regulation of marriage and the moral and spiritual well-being of the nation. This jurisdiction suffered a number of blows over the course of the early modern period, as Henry VIII, parliaments and generations of common lawyers encroached on its traditional powers and undermined its authority. Despite these attacks, and a steady diminution of their power, the church courts continued to operate at a significant level throughout the early modern period, and their activities had a considerable impact on women.

First of all, the ecclesiastical courts played a key role in the administration of inheritance. They held a monopoly over probate matters and so dealt with the administration of wills, and they also had a monopoly over the distribution of personal property in cases of intestate succession where the deceased did not leave a will. As we have seen, the common law principle of primogeniture governed the division of freehold lands or real property in such cases, but it was the church courts that were responsible for dividing up and distributing that person's personal property (their chattels or moveable goods). Rather than favour eldest males, the church courts operated a system of property distribution built around equality rather than discrimination. A deceased man's widow, for example, was entitled to one third of his moveable goods, and his children shared the remaining two thirds equally between them; a deceased widow's goods were shared between her children, while the property of unmarried women or men was divided equally between their surviving sisters and brothers.

These entitlements were not only more egalitarian than their common law equivalents, but in practice the courts often exceeded them, favouring daughters, younger sons and widows at the expense of eldest sons or other heirs. Amy Erickson has analysed the distribution of moveable goods by ecclesiastical authorities in a number of English counties and discovered that equal division was observed in as few as one third of cases (Erickson 1993: 75). Time after time authorities increased the shares of daughters (and younger sons) and reduced the shares of eldest sons or heirs who were to receive real property under primogeniture or had received other 'advancements' such as apprenticeship indentures from the deceased before he or she died. They were also more generous to widows with children, allotting them on average almost twice their usual one-third share, and in some cases the whole of their husbands' estates in goods, because their children were still dependants or they were grown up and had left the household.

The church courts assisted women in another way in inheritance. In cases where a man wrote a will, the rules of intestate succession obviously did not apply and he was usually free to dispose of his personal property as he wished. However, in certain ecclesiastical provinces, most notably York, Wales and the City of London, the ecclesiastical authorities enforced a long-standing custom called 'reasonable parts' which limited the freedom of testators to dispose of their personal property. Under these customs a married testator could include only one third (if he had children) or one half of his moveable goods in his will. One third of the remaining goods went to his widow (or one half if the couple was childless) and another third was divided equally between his children. The right of widows and children to receive 'reasonable' parts of their husbands' and fathers' moveable goods persisted until the end of the seventeenth century in York and until the beginning of the eighteenth century in London, when statutes abolished them.

Unlike the courts of common law, the church courts did not observe the doctrine of coverture. They allowed married women to sue in their own names separate from their husbands. One result, as we have already seen, was that wives could petition the courts to gain orders of separation 'from bed and board'. Another result was that large numbers of married women from urban communities proved able to bring defamation (slander) suits against their neighbours to defend their reputations, and the reputations of their husbands and families, against a barrage of insults, sexual innuendo, gossip, rumour and verbal assault. Laura Gowing has made a study of these court battles over reputation in which women, especially married women, predominated both as plaintiffs and defendants, and she notes that 'at every level, the occasions involved in defamation made it a verbal and legal process that enabled women to stake some specific claims to authority in the household and the community' (Gowing 1994: 43).

The church courts, then, provided many women with an attractive alternative to the common law. However, this does not mean that the ecclesiastical authorities were somehow miraculously free from bias or discrimination: far from it. In their disciplinary or regulatory function, church courts regularly punished female offenders, usually single women, for sexual offences such as fornication, adultery and bastard bearing, and prosecuted women of every marital status for 'scolding', an offence for which a number of unfortunate women were 'cucked', 'ducked' or 'washed' in rivers on 'cucking' or 'ducking' stools. The prosecutions of women for sexual offences, when men often escaped free, suggest that the sexual double standard was alive and well, something which Elizabeth Foyster's examination of separation cases seems to confirm (Foyster 1999: 77–87). In theory, either spouse could request a church court sanctioned separation 'from bed and board' on the grounds of adultery or cruelty. In practice, however, men regularly gained separations for adultery alone, whereas women almost always had to establish cruelty as well.

Customary Law

For a large proportion of rural and urban dwellers, particularly at the beginning of the early modern period, the law which most affected their lives was not common law or ecclesiastical law, but customary law, the local custom of the manor, or the borough customs of town or city. The period 1550 to 1700 saw a steady decline in the amount of land held by customary tenures, particularly after the abolition of most of the last remaining feudal tenures late in the seventeenth century. However, copyhold (holding an interest in lands 'by copy of the court roll') remained common in many counties throughout the period, and women who lived on manors or had interests in copyhold lands found themselves subject to an alternative set of rules, rights and obligations. Customary law was by definition local, and customs varied from manor to manor, town to town, so it is difficult to generalize about customary rights. However, two customs in particular deserve mention, one that affected wives and another that affected widows.

In still another exception to coverture, it seems that certain urban communities in London and elsewhere allowed married women to enjoy status as *feme sole traders* if they were engaged in business, allowing them to buy and sell goods without constantly having to gain the consent of their husbands, and to bring and defend suits relating to their business activities in local borough courts. For widows, many manors observed customs called 'widow's estate' or 'freebench' which provided the widows of copyholders (men who held interests in copyhold lands) with a right to those interests during widowhood. On most manors this entitlement amounted to a half or often the *whole* of the copyhold interest, which was obviously more generous than the one third of common law dower. However, unlike dower, widow's estate was not always for life. On some manors it persisted only for the duration of widowhood and dissolved if a widow remarried or was found guilty of living an 'unchaste life'. The fact that remarriage might extinguish the right suggests that widow's estate was not intended solely for the benefit of women. It was a means of maintaining widows and allowing them to care for dependent children, but if a woman remarried then her new husband was expected to assume these responsibilities; male anxiety and jealousy, it seems, endured beyond the grave. It was also not uncommon for heirs to challenge individual widows' claims to widow's estate, but the right itself, and the idea that widows should retain an interest in the lands they had worked with their husbands, remained strong in popular consciousness wherever customary law persisted.

Equity

Equity, the body of principles developed and applied in the courts of Chancery, Requests and the equity side of Exchequer, looms large in all recent assessments of early modern women's rights. Many historians regard these courts, and their local equivalents, as women's most visible allies in matters of law and property, because of the relief they offered individual women from the worst excesses of the common law. The influence of equity is undoubtedly important, not simply in practical but also in symbolic and ideological terms, but recent research suggests that equity probably hindered more women than it helped.

Equity courts' favourable reputation stems from their treatment of married women and widows. For many women contemplating or experiencing widowhood, jointure offered an attractive alternative to common law dower. Jointure could take a number of forms, not all of them linked to equity jurisdictions, but in essence it involved making a clear arrangement for a woman's possible widowhood at the time of marriage or just after: one that specified the interest in lands she would inherit or the level of an annual money payment she would receive. These arrangements came into effect the moment a woman's husband died, in contrast to dower interests which could be difficult to identify, time-consuming to claim, and which, as we have seen, applied only to unencumbered freehold lands. And if someone contested a jointure claim, women could approach equity judges for a remedy.

The flexibility that equity judges showed in recognizing and enforcing jointures extended to their treatment of married women in general. These men acknowledged the principle of coverture, but they proved far more sensitive than common law judges when applying it, even to the point of allowing occasional exceptions. For example, they recognized the right of 'paraphernalia', which allowed wives to claim their clothes and personal effects as their own, rather than have them swallowed up within the estates of their husbands. In a tiny minority of instances these judges went further and permitted married women to sue their own husbands. These wives sued to gain protection from violent husbands, to protect the property interests they had brought to marriage and to request maintenance payments. In agreeing to hear these cases, equity judges recognized that the rules of coverture made little sense in marriages that had irrevocably broken down, and that unprincipled husbands were exploiting those rules to cause their wives physical and financial harm.

That equity judges allowed wives to sue their husbands is extraordinary; however, only a handful of married women benefited from this exceptional treatment. Far more took advantage of equitable devices such as the 'use' and later the 'trust', which allowed them to keep some or all of their property interests separate from their husbands. These devices operated by separating beneficial ownership of property from legal ownership. Before marriage a woman could transfer legal title of her property interests to a third party (a 'feoffee to uses' or a trustee), leaving her with nothing that could pass into her husband's hands. However, as the beneficiary of the use or trust, she retained rights to the property in equity and so might receive the income from it during marriage (although technically this income would immediately become her husband's) and more importantly, recover full ownership and control of the interest if she outlived her husband. The advantages that these equitable devices brought women could be significant, especially when wealthy, experienced widows chose to marry for a second or third time. Uses and trusts could be secret, or they could form part of the marriage negotiations, in which case couples often set them down in marriage settlements, the same documents which many individuals used to record the details of jointures. These settlements, in effect prenuptial contracts, could be used not only to specify the fate of a woman's property interests during and after marriage, but also to provide women with rights that coverture would otherwise deny them, such as the ability to make a will. Furthermore, they appear to have been relatively common and not restricted to aristocratic women or elite families.

The potential benefits to women from marriage settlements seem almost immeasurable, and they increased over the early modern period. However, euphoria over equity's role as the champion of wives and widows needs to be checked, for each of these apparent advances in fact disguises a darker side. Firstly, women had to make all of these arrangements, from jointures to trusts, in advance, usually near the time of their marriages, and this required knowledge and the means to instruct and pay lawyers. Most also required married women to rely on trustees and feoffees, who were usually men, and if these representatives misbehaved or were fraudulent, wives would have to enlist the support or co-operation of their husbands to sue them. More importantly, the level of benefit a settlement gave to a woman depended on her ability to negotiate, whether in person or through her family, and women's bargaining positions were rarely as strong as their husbands'. This imbalance of power, both in terms of negotiations and desired ends, manifested itself in settlements that could reduce as well as extend women's entitlements. By the close of the seventeenth century most members of the elites designed settlements with the primary purpose not of ensuring wives had rights and property, although many did that, but to limit female access to real property in the future. The authors of so-called 'strict' settlements used 'entails' to keep land in male hands for generations to come, by disinheriting daughters, granddaughters and great granddaughters in favour of male uncles, brothers or cousins to ensure the survival of the family name along with the family estate. It was equity courts, therefore, that oversaw the kinds of exclusions of females from inheriting estates that are so common in Jane Austen's novels. As Eileen Spring has pointed out, under primogeniture females should have inherited in the 20–25 per cent of marriages that produced daughters but no surviving sons. Yet elite heiresses in the seventeenth century actually inherited landed estates in only around 5 per cent of cases, due mainly to the operation of equitable settlements and trusts (Spring 1993: 14). Common law rules of succession may have been bad, but equity's willingness to enforce biased settlements was worse.

Finally, while jointures were preferable to dower for practical reasons, the value of jointures was a fraction of traditional dower entitlements. In place of one third of their husbands' lands, an increasing number of women received an annual money payment that was a percentage of the value of the dowry they had brought to marriage, commonly between one fifth and one tenth. A woman with a £100 dowry could expect to receive £10 to £20 a year during widowhood, which meant that she would have to outlive her husband by five or ten years just to recoup her original investment. The practical advantage of jointures was undeniable, but it would be a mistake to pretend that jointures were more valuable than dower in its original intended form, or that different legal systems were any worse or better than the litigants who made use of them.

Property and Litigation

Various forces in early modern England, then, from common law rules to the caprice of will-makers and the dynastic ambitions of the architects of strict settlements, conspired to limit women's access to independent control over interests in land. However, despite these efforts, a considerable amount of land found its way into female hands, even if only temporarily. The recipients included daughters whose parents died intestate without any sons, daughters whose parents left them land in wills and widows who succeeded in claiming dower or took over responsibility for their husbands' estates or businesses. Many more women possessed property of other kinds, such as money, moveable goods or leases, through inheritance, as the beneficiaries of trusts, or through the fruit of their labours. Estimates vary, but it seems that around 15–20 per cent of households were headed by women, and at any one time between 10–20 per cent of property was in female hands. The contrast between the desire to keep women away from property and power, and the recognition that temporary control was inevitable and often desirable, is reflected in two statistics. Only around one fifth of early modern will-makers were women, yet women acted as executors or administrators of other people's estates (alone or with others) in upwards of two thirds of cases. Women, in other words, were no strangers to earning, managing, investing and protecting property interests.

Ongoing research by historians such as Barbara Todd and Amy Froide is beginning to confirm how single women and widows in the middle and upper ranks of society were active in moneylending and investment circles, first in informal credit networks with kin and neighbours and later as participants in civic and crown loan schemes. Single women invested their wages and their portions or dowries, gaining interest until they decided to marry or to establish an independent household, while widows invested their own property and property they held as representatives of their deceased husbands' estates. And as we have seen, wives placed monies and other property in trust. It is impossible at present to declare with precision the levels of wealth women enjoyed, the types of property they controlled and how these varied between classes and over time, beyond the broad general patterns already outlined. It is possible, however, to estimate levels of female participation in litigation – in legal wrangles over money, debts, property, reputation and a host of other matters – which provide some indication at least of the effects of legal restrictions on women and of the numbers of women who were aware of their rights and had interests in property worth pursuing at law.

The proportion of women named as parties to civil court actions in early modern England varied greatly from court to court. Only a little over 8 per cent of plaintiffs in the prerogative Court of Star Chamber were women, whereas in London's church courts Laura Gowing has shown that the equivalent figure rose in the seventeenth century as high as 54 per cent (Gowing 1994: 33). In most jurisdictions, however, the range was less dramatic, usually falling between 10 and 15 per cent in central Westminster courts of common law, such as Common Pleas and King's Bench, and courts of equity, such as Chancery and the Court of Requests. What is striking is that women went to law not just over exclusively female matters such as dower and jointure, but over debts, bonds, wages, rents, trespass, defamation and a catalogue of other complaints that in many respects resembled the complaints that men took to court. In overall terms women's participation in litigation was low for a group that comprised half the population. Yet it was surprisingly high for a society and a legal system that restricted women not only in terms of the rights they might hold, but also the likelihood that they would possess property or interests worth taking to court. In other words, while their actual presence was modest, their symbolic presence was considerable.

In the late sixteenth and early seventeenth centuries a woman was named as plaintiff or defendant, alone or with others, in between one quarter and one third of all actions initiated in the largest common law and equity courts in the land, and upwards of one half of actions begun in the church courts. This meant that judges were accustomed to seeing a woman's name, a woman's lawyer or a woman herself in one in every two, three or four cases before them. Furthermore, the total number of women going to law was on the rise. Early modern England witnessed one of the most astonishing eruptions of litigation in history. According to recent estimates by Craig Muldrew, levels of litigation in national and local courts rose to as high as 1,102,000 actions a year by the end of the sixteenth century, at a time when the total population was less than 4,000,000 (Muldrew 1998: 236). Everyone, it seems, was suing everyone else, including tens of thousands or perhaps hundreds of thousands of women. At this time of rapid change, overcrowded court rooms, general confusion and jurisdictional rivalry, women appear to have played a more active role in lawsuits bearing their names than they did in the eighteenth and nineteenth centuries. This apparent independence attracted comment, first from irate judges like Anthony Benn and later from writers and playwrights who made litigating women the subject of satires and drama, as John Webster did in his play *The Devil's Law-Case: Or, When Women Go to Law The Devil is Full of Business.*

Changing Fortunes

Women in early modern England gained rights from and suffered male bias in a variety of jurisdictions. How women fared in the legal realm depended on where they lived, their social background, the types of property they owned, their knowledge of their rights and their access to different courts. It also depended to a large degree on the inclinations of the men around them, from fathers, brothers and husbands to trustees, lawyers and judges. Some women had few rights and suffered at the hands of unscrupulous and violent men; others faced the world from behind a wall of lawyers and protected or enhanced their wealth in campaigns of masterful litigation. The only common thread linking different women in early modern society, from the poorest widows to the Tudor queens, was a general disability and disadvantage compared to men of equivalent background, status or position.

The picture is a complex one, one that resists facile generalizations about whether every woman's legal rights and access to property either 'improved' over the course of the early modern period or 'worsened'. However, it is possible to speculate about some broad patterns of change affecting various different groupings of women. The increasing complexity of equitable devices such as trusts, for example, extended the theoretical possibilities for women seeking to protect their property and other interests during marriage, so that a single woman or widow contemplating marriage in 1750 had more options available than she would have had in 1550. Yet as we have seen, while a well-made marriage settlement could protect a woman's property and secure her right to make a will, an equally well-made settlement could restrict a woman to a jointure that was a fraction of her dowry and remove female children from future inheritances. The nature of this change is still significant, even if it benefited only the small percentage of independent women who could afford to pay their lawyers the spiralling costs for creating these increasingly elaborate legal and equitable devices. However, it is important to understand that women's ability to protect their property in these ways was not unbounded: equity judges regularly struck down trusts that married women had made without the knowledge of their unsuspecting husbands, arguing that this amounted to a disappointment of men's expectations in marriage.

While the theoretical possibilities for a few well-placed women expanded, other aspects of the law hardened or narrowed over the course of the period. As courts became more formalized and rule bound and published law reports made decisions more available for scrutiny, judges became less and less likely to make exceptions to general principles. It seems, for example, that central court judges enforced the doctrine of coverture more diligently in the seventeenth century than they had in the sixteenth, a tendency that increased in the eighteenth, nineteenth and early twentieth centuries. Yet the push for consistency in rulings was accompanied (in the wake of the Civil Wars and the beheading of Charles I) by more open and vigorous debate about the limits of married women's rights, both by the lawyers on the losing side in these cases and in the published opinions of minority judges. The same formalizing of the courts also pushed up the costs of litigation, especially in Westminster, limiting access for less well-off women. This tendency was made worse by the gradual reduction in the influence and extent of rival jurisdictions to common law and equity, such as custom and ecclesiastical law, which both declined during the seventeenth and eighteenth centuries, and with the disappearance of cheap equity courts such as Requests, which ceased to function in the turmoil of the 1640s and was never revived after the Restoration. Whether smaller local courts took up the slack remains to be seen.

A more profound change with implications for women's rights, one that is easier to sense than to chart precisely at any one moment, was the long slow move away from a conception of property based around personal relationships, best represented by feudal tenures, towards our modern sense of property as a marketable commodity. Throughout the early modern period, individuals' rights to alienate real and moveable property increased, as a result of the limiting of the application of primogeniture and measures like the Statute of Wills in the mid-sixteenth century, and the abolition of feudal tenures in the seventeenth. The growth of individual freedom was not even: as we have seen, entails and strict settlements, which gave extraordinary control to their makers, limited the rights and freedoms of future generations. Nevertheless, the direction of travel seems clear, and was accompanied by a shift from rights such as dower and widow's estate, that like primogeniture were once fixed and universal, towards negotiated and tailored arrangements such as jointures and trusts. All of these changes placed greater power in the hands of individuals, but not all individuals benefited equally. The individuals who benefited most were landowning heads of households, and 80–85 per cent of household heads were male.

As the early modern period came to a close, it seems that the actions of patriarchs, lawmakers and judges served to limit many women's access to land and to various types of political power. The latter had never been great, but fewer women appear to have slipped through the cracks to wield positions of authority in their communities. Yet at the same time, women's access to other kinds of property was considerable, and for an elite few, the means to manage and protect property interests, even during marriage, were growing. Contrasts and contradictions of this kind, between an enlargement of opportunities for some and a narrowing of opportunities for most, appear to have encouraged a growing awareness among educated women about the injustices of the legal system. Towards the end of the period female writers began to describe marriage as a form of 'slavery' for women, in which wives were little better than their husbands' 'chattels'. However, change of this kind took place against a backdrop of remarkable continuity. Throughout the early modern period male authorities and heads of households consistently denied women equality with men in virtually every area of legal rights and property ownership, but they could not, and did not seem to want to, exclude them altogether. Whether as battling litigants in courts, heads of households, moneylenders, investors, business women, wage earners, or owners or controllers of property, women consistently appear in the historical records, usually making up 10, 20 or 30 per cent of each of these categories. Many women had to fight hard for these levels of participation, but they succeeded in large part because they were members of families, and for rich and poor alike families lay at the heart of the economic, social and political nation.

REFERENCES AND FURTHER READING

Amussen, S. D. (1994). ' "Being stirred to much unquietness": violence and domestic violence in early modern England.' *Journal of Women's History,* 6: 2, 70–89.

Baker, J. H. (1990). *An Introduction to English Legal History,* 3rd edn. London: Butterworths.

Bennett, J. M. and Froide, A. M. (1999). *Single Women in the European Past, 1250–1800.* Philadelphia: University of Pennsylvania Press.

Capp, B. (1996). 'Separate domains? Women and authority in early modern England.' In P. Griffiths, A. Fox and S. Hindle (eds), *The Experience of Authority in Early Modern England* (pp. 117–45). Basingstoke: Macmillan.

Cavallo, S. and Warner, L. (1999). *Widowhood in Medieval and Early Modern Europe.* London: Longman.

Churches, C. (1998). 'Women and property in early modern England: a case study.' *Social History,* 23, 165–80.

Cioni, M. L. (1985). *Women and Law in Elizabethan England with Particular Reference to the Court of Chancery.* New York: Garland.

Dolan, F. E. (1994). *Dangerous Familiars: Representations of Domestic Crime in England 1550–1700.* Ithaca, NY: Cornell University Press.

Erickson, A. L. (1993). *Women and Property in Early Modern England,* London: Routledge.

Foyster, E. A. (1996). 'Male honour, social control and wife beating in late Stuart England.' *Transactions of the Royal Historical Society,* 6th series, 6, 215–24.

——(1999). *Manhood in Early Modern England: Honour, Sex, and Marriage.* London: Longman.

Gowing, L. (1994). 'Language, power and the law: women's slander litigation in early modern London.' In J. Kermode and G. Walker (eds), *Women, Crime and the Courts in Early Modern England* (pp. 26–47). London: UCL Press.

——(1996). *Domestic Dangers: Women, Words, and Sex in Early Modern London.* Oxford: Oxford University Press.

Ingram, M. (1987). *Church Courts, Sex and Marriage in England, 1570–1640.* Cambridge: Cambridge University Press.

Kermode, J. and Walker, G. (eds) (1994). *Women, Crime and the Courts in Early Modern England.* London: UCL Press.

Muldrew, C. (1998). *The Economy of Obligation: The Culture of Credit and Social Relations in Early Modern England.* Basingstoke: Macmillan.

Prest, W. R. (1991). 'Law and women's rights in early modern England.' *The Seventeenth Century,* 6, 169–87.

Prior, M. (ed.) (1991). *Women in English Society, 1500–1800.* London: Routledge.

Rye, W. (ed.) (1967). *England as Seen by Foreigners in the Days of Elizabeth I and James I.* New York: Benjamin Blom.

Smith, H. L. (1998). 'Women as sextons and electors: King's Bench and precedents for women's citizenship.' In H. L. Smith (ed.), *Women Writers and the Early Modern British Political Tradition* (pp. 324–42). Cambridge: Cambridge University Press.

Sommerville, M. (1995). *Sex and Subjection: Attitudes to Women in Early-Modern Society.* London: Arnold.

Spring, E. (1993). *Law, Land and Family: Aristocratic Inheritance in England, 1300 to 1800.* Chapel Hill: University of North Carolina Press.

Staves, S. (1979). *Players' Scepters: Fictions of Authority in the Restoration.* Lincoln: University of Nebraska Press.

——(1990). *Married Women's Separate Property in England, 1660–1833.* Cambridge, MA: Harvard University Press.

Stretton, T. (1998). *Women Waging Law in Elizabethan England.* Cambridge: Cambridge University Press.

Todd, B. J. (1990). 'Freebench and free enterprise: widows and their property in two Berkshire villages.' In J. Chartres and D. Hey (eds), *English Rural Society 500–1800: Essays in Honour of Joan Thirsk* (pp. 175–200). Cambridge: Cambridge University Press.

——(1998). ' "To be some body": married women and *The Hardships of the English Laws.*' In H. L. Smith (ed.), *Women Writers and the Early Modern British Political Tradition* (pp. 343–61). Cambridge: Cambridge University Press.

4

Women and Work

Sara H. Mendelson

Introduction

Much of women's work in the early modern period has been hidden from historians, partly because of the widely held contemporary belief that women lacked a professional work identity. This presumption was enshrined in the legal system and was everywhere reflected in early modern records. Although officials noted men's occupations as a matter of course, they routinely classified women by marital status – as maid, wife or widow – rather than by occupation. And while marital status did not affect a man's choice of career, a woman's matrimonial condition might limit the kind of work she was officially allowed to perform. As a *feme covert* a married woman had no legal identity of her own in the eyes of the common law: man and wife were one person, and that person was the husband. Consequently a wife was barred by law from carrying on a trade or business in her own right, except in a few localities like the city of London where a married woman was permitted to trade as if she were a *feme sole* or single woman.

Women's traditional household routine was taken for granted by the larger society, not usually distinguished with the term 'work'. Childbearing, childrearing and housewifery were not considered real occupations, but were merely the things that women did. Moreover, the character of a woman's work identity was apt to change over a lifetime, as she married and bore children. Employed as a maidservant, a young woman performed household chores for wages; but on becoming a wife she worked at the same tasks without wages as she laboured within her own family. Compared with the fixed single occupation of the male artisan or lawyer, women's work roles were perceived as nebulous and disjointed.

Yet if we extend our investigation of women's working lives to determine what they actually did with their waking hours, we discover that most women in this period worked long and hard from a very early age until they were too old and weak to labour any longer. The majority poured their energies into an eclectic amalgam of trades and occupations rather than a single profession, constantly devising new expedients as their own circumstances changed, or in response to fluctuations in the economic climate.

Although most women were denied the opportunity to pursue the equivalent of a male professional career, they fabricated their own occupational patchwork quilt: over a lifetime, women constructed vocational identities which combined traditional feminine skills with a host of innovative economic strategies. As a reward for strenuous effort, some women succeeded in earning a comfortable subsistence – sometimes even turning a profit – for themselves and their families.

Because early modern England was a patriarchal society, the work women did reflected divisions of both gender and class. Work was highly gendered: some kinds of work were considered appropriate only for women, and would have been thought demeaning if performed by a man. All women (but no men) were expected to be occupied in childbearing, childrearing and housewifery, whatever their position in the social or economic hierarchy. Conversely, many occupations and professions were categorized as men's work, vocations from which women were excluded through institutional and informal constraints. At the same time, class divisions also defined the work women did. Manual labour was a mark of humble status, performed only by those at the lower end of the social spectrum, whether female or male.

At the lowest economic level, women deployed an assortment of creative strategies in order to maintain themselves and their families, pitting their energy and wit against an economic system that imposed double disabilities on them because they were both poor and female. Those at the middling level of society were most likely to pursue what we would call a profession, a single trade or business in which a woman was occupied full-time for most of her working hours. Although we tend to think of members of the female elite as a leisure class, women of the gentry and aristocracy also laboured during this period, not only as hard-working supervisors of large and complex households, but also as officeholders at court, and as capable administrators of medical and charitable institutions.

The Working Lives of Ordinary Women

In this survey of women's work we shall begin with the working life of ordinary women. Early modern England was a hierarchical society, with the bulk of the population situated at the bottom of the social and economic pyramid. Those women we can classify as 'poor' fall, roughly speaking, into two groups. The first group succeeded in maintaining themselves at or above subsistence level. They did not earn enough to be obliged to pay rates or taxes, but were not so destitute that they were dependent on the parish or other institutional authorities for poor relief.

The other group was made up of women living in absolute poverty, those whose resources were insufficient to provide them with a basic subsistence. Although such women may or may not have been receiving poor relief, they needed help with rudimentary subsistence needs: food, clothing and lodging. Over a lifetime, women's circumstances tended to decline as they grew older and less capable of labour. Marriage and children, the death of a spouse, illness or incapacity or old age could easily precipitate a woman from a comfortable subsistence to poverty and dependence.

These two groups of poor women, those living in relative or in absolute poverty, formed the majority of the female populace, making up somewhere between a half and two thirds of the population. The contemporary statistician Gregory King calculated that the poor – cottagers, labourers, servants and vagrants – were about two thirds of England's population toward the end of the seventeenth century (Mendelson and Crawford 1998: 261). Moreover, all such calculations of the proportion of indigent households may underestimate the poverty of the female sex as a group, since women could be relatively poor compared to other members of the household. Family resources were sometimes distributed unequally, with women taking for themselves a smaller share of food and other subsistence needs.

Women as a group were also more vulnerable to poverty than men at the same social level. They earned lower wages (including a smaller allowance for food) than men for the same work – typically one half to two thirds of the wages and other benefits men earned. Women had access to fewer occupations than their male counterparts, so those who worked for their own sustenance were crowded into the most ill-paid and labour-intensive jobs. Moreover, society assumed that wives and daughters would be dependent on men for their subsistence, an assumption which was not always borne out by women's actual circumstances. Widows and deserted wives frequently found themselves struggling to support their families on wages that would hardly provide a bare subsistence for a single person.

The work of poor women, the majority of the female populace, has been described by Olwen Hufton (1975) as the 'economy of makeshift'. Barred by lack of education and financial resources from pursuing a recognized profession, such women forged a 'subsistence identity' by combining a patchwork of part-time occupations, while developing a host of supplementary strategies in their efforts to put together an adequate livelihood (Mendelson and Crawford 1998: 260–98). At various times the occupations and other expedients that made up their working lives might include service, marriage, day-labour, a range of by-employments, and the receipt of institutional or informal charity, as well as gleaning, scavenging and begging. In some cases, women survived personal financial crises or the fluctuations of an erratic market economy by resorting to illegal occupations such as prostitution and theft.

The working life of poor women began very young. Those from destitute or vagrant families, girls who were orphaned, and illegitimate children might be taken from their families and put out to service or apprenticeship from age seven or even earlier. In dealing with young people under their care, authorities were chiefly concerned to prevent the cost of maintenance of poor children from becoming a drain on the poor rates. Consequently, the apprenticeship of poor girls was more often designed to shift financial responsibility for their subsistence away from the parish than to train them in a profession. Frequently, young girls were apprenticed to learn housewifery or husbandry, where they were set to work at menial chores rather than acquiring skills that would enable them to earn their own living. Even the trades that poor girls learned were apt to provide only a bare subsistence rather than a professional identity. Girls were routinely apprenticed to lacemaking, spinning or knitting, all labour-intensive and extremely low-paid crafts. A woman working full-time at any of these by-employments could gain at most a meagre subsistence for herself, with nothing left over for her family.

The vast majority of young unmarried women chose to work as servants as a temporary occupation during adolescence; those who had not yet married by their mid-twenties often continued in service as a permanent lifetime vocation. In any case, young single women who did not choose to go into service could be forced into it by law. By the provisions of the 1563 Statute of Artificers, any unmarried woman between the ages of 12 and 40 could be compelled by the courts to find a place as a servant, or else be ordered into service by local officials for whatever wages and conditions they thought fit. If a woman refused, she could be committed to prison 'until she shall be bounden to serve'. In practice, women of the gentry and aristocracy did not have to submit to the constraints of the Statute of Artificers. But young women of the labouring classes were frequently cited by the courts and ordered to be imprisoned for living out of service.

Young plebeian women living independently in households lacking a male authority figure were especially vulnerable to punishment under the 1563 Statute, even if they were successfully maintaining themselves with another occupation. Elizabeth Barber, reported to be 'living at her own hand', was one of many poor unmarried women who were ordered to Bridewell (the local house of correction) by the Norwich Mayoral Court for failing to find a berth as a servant within a specified time period (Mendelson and Crawford 1998: 96–7). Thus the Statute of Artificers was used as an effective weapon in local officials' efforts to ensure that all young women lived under the patriarchal discipline of a male-headed household.

All maidservants were expected to work at the multitude of chores entailed by early modern housewifery. In addition, they might perform other tasks as well, depending on the size of the household, the occupation of its master or mistress, and its location in town or countryside. In general, the nature and specialization of female servants' duties were directly proportional to the size and wealth of the establishment: the larger and more affluent the household, the more complex and specialized were the division and organization of female servants' labour.

In large noble establishments female staff were highly specialized, with separate servants employed in personal service, cooking, cleaning, laundry, kitchen work, childcare and a host of other specific tasks. In the countryside female servants on large estates assisted in the complex processes associated with baking, brewing, dairying and other chores entailed by the provisioning and maintenance of the household. Families in the middle ranks required fewer female servants than their aristocratic counterparts, with two or fewer maidservants per household the norm at this social level. Poor families typically kept only one female servant who served as the maid-of-all-work for the household, performing the most menial and labour-intensive chores while assisting in housewifery, childcare and whatever trade or by-employments family members pursued as an occupation.

Young women encountered very varied life experiences working as servants, with diverse conditions of employment depending on the character and occupation of the master and mistress of the household. As a minimum, servants earned their subsistence and lodging. Women's wages were very low in both absolute and relative terms, being typically one half to two thirds that of their male counterparts. But in addition to her wages, a servant might earn a range of perquisites if she managed to gain the respect and affection of her mistress. In the course of service a valued maidservant might obtain cast-off clothing and other material goods, assistance with the costs of her wedding when she left service to get married, and sometimes a legacy at the death of her mistress. Servants usually tried to save their wages and other perquisites towards marriage, since women of the plebeian classes were expected to contribute their share to the setting up of the new household. Some mistresses felt a sense of maternal responsibility for the future careers of maidservants under their charge. This might entail arranging for an advantageous marriage for a favourite maidservant, or planning for her promotion in the service hierarchy.

While it offered potential benefits, service also held particular hazards for young women. In addition to the kinds of mistreatment servants of either sex might suffer at the hands of a bad master or mistress, female servants were particularly vulnerable to sexual abuse by a master or other male members of the household, including fellow servants. Early modern court records are full of dismal tales of maidservants who had been raped or otherwise forced into a sexual relationship, made pregnant, and then summarily dismissed from the household. Having lost her reputation for 'honesty', a pregnant maidservant was rendered virtually unemployable, and often found her only option for survival was a life of vagrancy and prostitution.

Partly because there were so few vocational prospects for ordinary women, marriage as an occupation was by default one of their more attractive options. Marriage as a subsistence partnership appears to have been fairly common among the very poor, as we can infer from the number of married couples of widely disparate ages recorded in such sources as the Norwich Census of the Poor (Pound 1971). Yet marriage could also lead to greater poverty if either partner became incapacitated, or if the couple had more children than they were able to support. In her childbearing years a wife found her opportunities for gainful employment reduced at the same time that the additional mouths to be fed increased the financial burden on family resources, for a wife with young children could no longer seek employment as a day-labourer.

Women's work in marriage was similar to the work they had performed as household servants, except that wives added childbearing and childrearing to their extensive round of household duties. Although specific tasks might vary from one locale to another, housewifery was labour-intensive and time-consuming at every social level. In poor households women fetched water, gathered firewood and other fuel, and lit fires, in addition to cooking, cleaning, caring for children, making and mending clothes for the household, and scavenging for food and other necessities.

For poor women, access to a small piece of land and the ownership of a cow could make the difference between a comfortable subsistence and the descent into penury. Women who possessed sufficient land raised vegetables and legumes, or grains and medicinal herbs; those with grazing rights kept poultry and other small livestock. They processed dairy products to feed their families, or brought their eggs and butter to market; alternatively, they sold their produce to wealthier households for the cash which was needed to pay for rent, fuel and other expenses. Using linen made from home-grown flax and feathers from ducks and geese, wives even produced their own sheets and bedding. Women worked at textile by-employments such as spinning, knitting and lacemaking to fulfil a similar dual function: a wife's industry furnished clothes and linens for her own household, or she might sell the output of her labour for needed cash.

Textiles and clothing were very important in the subsistence economy of poor women. Clothes were treated by the poor virtually as a cash equivalent: items of clothing, linens and other textiles were bought and sold, begged or scavenged, or pawned in case of need. Wealthy women often bestowed worn or cast-off clothing as perquisites to their maidservants and their other female acquaintances among the poor, or gave specific items of clothing as legacies. In urban centres like London, women ran a thriving market in second-hand clothing, where the poor could trade clothing for cash (Lemire 1987).

Poor women often sold their labour to wealthier households, especially to large rural estates which were dependent on supplementary female help for a wide range of seasonal and miscellaneous tasks. Hired by their more prosperous neighbours, local women did laundry work and kitchen chores such as scouring and food preparation. They weeded gardens and fields, worked in the dairy and henhouse and brewhouse, assisted in preparations for Christmas and helped with family celebrations such as weddings. Their labour was also very important in harvesting and haymaking and other urgent seasonal tasks. Such work fell under the penumbra of paternalism: wives were customarily hired for supplementary labour only if they or other family members were already working on the estate. For poor women, casual part-time labour in town and countryside was as much a perquisite as it was a subsistence strategy, much like gleaning and begging, which also fell within a paternalistic framework.

Women in the countryside were also engaged in supplying foodstuffs and other miscellaneous provisions to large wealthy households. Early modern estate accounts frequently note payments to the milk-woman, the herb-woman, and to other local wives and widows who had brought such foodstuffs as butter, eggs, chickens, peas and other legumes, fruit, wildfowl and shellfish. Sometimes women sold their own produce; at other times they acted as petty chapwomen, hawking such miscellaneous commodities as soap and pins.

In both countryside and towns the female poor worked at a diverse array of by-employments. Most commonly, women spent their time at various textile crafts, including spinning, stocking knitting, lacemaking, silkwinding and needlework. But the by-employments open to women varied from one locality to another according to the predominant type of agriculture and available natural resources. In some regions women specialized in metalwork, including nailmaking and pinmaking, or engaged in subsidiary processes associated with coal mining. In other localities they made up a subsistence by working at several different occupations, for example combining dairying with textile crafts. In Devon in the seventeenth century a large 'spinster sub-culture' of unmarried women managed to subsist through a combination of dairying and lacemaking (Sharpe 1991).

The makeshift economy of poor women led to a good deal of mobility between town and countryside. Country wives brought their surplus foodstuffs and other produce into market towns to be sold. Those women at the bottom of the economic hierarchy might spend their summers in the countryside, a more favourable environment for seeking work, as well as for begging and scavenging foodstuffs. In winter, poor women could find lodgings and clothes more easily in the towns. Throughout the seventeenth and eighteenth centuries the relative success and prosperity of different industries such as the wool trade fluctuated a good deal from one region to another in both urban and rural districts, leading women to move away from areas of industrial decline to settle in localities where new proto-industrial occupations were on the rise.

As an overall trend, much of the movement of the female population was from the countryside to cities and towns, as women increasingly migrated to urban areas to seek opportunities for work. In most localities by the end of the early modern period there was considerably more work available for women in the towns than in rural districts. One of the most important of these sources of employment for women was the growing demand for maidservants in urban households. During the sixteenth and seventeenth centuries, middling as well as elite families in towns and cities increasingly hired a greater number and proportion of female servants, reversing the medieval practice by which the majority of servants in great noble households had been male.

At the same time, a surge in population in London and other large urban centres throughout the seventeenth century led to an exponential growth in all the service industries, notably the provision of food, drink and lodging. Since these were domestic skills which women had already acquired 'naturally' as part of their training in housewifery, they were quick to adapt their expertise in these trades to commercial purposes. In seventeenth-century London, where new housing could not keep pace with population growth from migration into the city, women set up lodging-houses which offered a range of accommodation for every income level. Women from the middling ranks kept elegant lodgings for the wealthy urban elite, while others who were poor let rooms to those who were in even greater poverty than themselves. Some women became innkeepers, supplying food and drink as well as lodgings to travellers.

An enterprising woman who kept a respectable lodging-house or a popular inn could earn a comfortable livelihood, and even save enough for old age. But the business of providing lodgings could lead to danger as well as profit. Women who let rooms to poor families risked prosecution under various municipal ordinances aimed at limiting the number of indigent people living in towns, for fear they would become a burden on the poor rates. Sometimes those who provided lodgings for unmarried women were prosecuted for keeping a bawdy house, because civic officials were always highly suspicious of women who lived on their own, independent of male authority.

Women were very prominent in the provisioning trades which supplied food and drink and a variety of other consumer goods for a burgeoning urban population. Many women brought small amounts of home-produced foodstuffs such as eggs or butter to sell at town and city markets. Others purchased perishable foods like fish and soft fruit from wholesale dealers, or came to the city on foot carrying fresh produce from market gardens in the countryside. Women then sold these perishable goods at retail city markets or in the streets as itinerant vendors, usually for a very small profit margin. Some women prepared the early modern equivalent of 'fast foods' which they then hawked about the city streets. Female street vendors offered an enormous variety of consumer goods, peddling not only raw foodstuffs and prepared food, but such diverse items as fresh flowers, brooms, stationery supplies and fireplace implements.

Because of their expertise in brewing ale, beer, cider and cordials for home consumption, many women earned their living by making and selling ale and other brewed beverages. One of the most common female occupations at this period was that of alewife. Although according to the law all alehouses were to be licensed by local authorities, many wives and widows sold home-brewed ale in their own houses, with or without benefit of a licence, setting up a front room or part of a room as a drinking parlour. The seventeenth-century blackletter ballad 'Joan's ale is new' recounted how local artisans and tradesmen spent half a crown apiece to drink up

Joan's freshly brewed ale, and 'promised Jone again to come / when she had brew'd anew', giving us some idea of the popularity and potential profitability of such small-scale private alehouses.

In the towns as well as the countryside most women combined multiple occupations in order to earn a subsistence. Female witnesses in London court cases who were asked to describe how they earned a living were likely to name two or more occupations or by-employments. Isabel Dodd, a 31-year-old London widow, mentioned four different occupations by which she earned a subsistence: 'she winds silk and knits and washes [laundry] and scours [pots and pans] whereby she maintains herself' (Mendelson and Crawford 1998: 278).

Although poor women did not mention gleaning and scavenging as regular occupations, we can infer from references to disputes over gleaning and scavenging rights in court records that many women in both town and country augmented their subsistence in this way. To supplement the family diet, women scavenged for foodstuffs in the countryside or begged for leftover food, skim milk, inferior fruit, bread too burnt to be sold, and other unwanted commodities from neighbours and tradesmen. In both urban and rural areas they deployed great skill and creativity in retrieving and utilizing foodstuffs, raw materials and consumer goods which had been abandoned or donated by others, using their labour to add value to what their wealthier neighbours dismissed as worthless or at least not worth the trouble of salvaging and processing.

Through established common rights women claimed the privilege of gleaning for grain and other crops after harvest; that is, of gathering what had been left in the fields by the harvesters. They also collected other foodstuffs such as windfall apples or other inferior fruit unwanted by landowners. Suits for the recovery of tithes sometimes mention fruit and nuts which were of too small a value to be tithed; their owners had not bothered to harvest these crops, but had left them on the trees to be gathered by poor women and children. Women even 'gleaned' textile raw materials such as inferior wool which had been discarded during the sheep-shearing process. In practice, the salvaging activities of poor women included a whole spectrum ranging from gleaning through scavenging to begging, sometimes even shading into opportunistic theft. Because poor women specialized in seeking commodities which they assumed others did not want, landowners and authorities frequently had trouble drawing the line between women's legal and illegal foraging activities. A pair of Oxfordshire women accused by a landowner of illegally gleaning wheat from his field replied that they had not been stealing his grain, but gathering the mustard which grew alongside it (Mendelson and Crawford 1998: 293).

When a woman failed to earn a livelihood despite her endeavours at a multitude of part-time occupations and other expedients, she could be reduced to absolute poverty. The official attitude to such women was that the bestowal of poor relief by the parish or other institutions was the last resort, to be granted only after all other avenues had been exhausted. First, authorities tried to set the poor to work, so that they could provide for themselves and their relations. If this was not feasible, then parochial and other officials were willing to grant maintenance to the 'worthy' poor, those women with immaculate reputations for hard work and sexual propriety, who had fallen into penury through no fault of their own. Official poor relief was for the sick, the very young, the very old and incapacitated: in other words, those who had shown themselves willing to labour but were physically unable to do so.

Employment was the first form of institutional poor relief to which indigent women had access. For those who were still capable of working, the parish and other civic authorities offered women a range of paid labour as a substitute for cash subsidies. Many of women's roles as medical helpers and caregivers were financed by parish funds, thus providing medical 'poor relief' for those who could not pay for it, while at the same time offering a supplemental income to the women who did the work.

Parish accounts frequently list payments to female caregivers, including foster mothers and those who looked after the sick and the infirm. Poor women tended old people who could no longer care for themselves, acted as 'keepers' of women in childbed, and nursed infants who fell under the supervision of parochial authorities. An indigent mother might even be paid for nursing her own children, since this entailed less expense to the parish than granting her a cash stipend while at the same time paying another woman to act as nurse. By the end of the seventeenth century a number of civic charitable institutions offered employment for women at various levels, as matrons, nurses and menial workers. The poor also earned a supplemental income by providing board and lodging for each other in their own homes.

Midwives' labour might also be subsidized, either directly by the authorities, or indirectly by allowing poor women to practise their profession without the requisite licence if this was their only source of income. Although churchwardens were charged with presenting unlicensed midwives to the bishops' courts, we find numerous instances of parochial authorities requesting that poor midwives in their parish be excused from purchasing a licence, especially if their activities included charitable help in childbed to other indigent women. In a Norfolk parish, churchwardens asked that a poor widow be allowed to continue practising midwifery without a licence because she had 'seven small children to maintain, and hitherto she out of her midwifery has provided for her said children without being chargeable to our said parish' (Mendelson and Crawford 1998: 284). Female schoolteachers, too, might be excused from the licensing requirement if they were too poor to pay the fee, especially if their income from teaching was their only source of sustenance keeping them off the poor relief rolls.

Women who were employed by the parish or who benefited from parochial assistance were expected to do whatever work was asked of them, including hazardous and unpleasant chores, or tasks associated with pariah occupations. Many of those who were deputed by civic authorities to be searchers – whose job was to examine dead bodies and determine the cause of death – were women of the plebeian classes who were already receiving some form of parochial aid. In times of plague or smallpox epidemics such work could be exceedingly dangerous. Poor women were also set to various forms of drudgery by civic officials, including spinning, processing hemp, cleaning the parish church and other menial tasks.

Women's activities might border on the illegal or even the criminal when lawful occupations and expedients proved insufficient in the quest for subsistence. Some professions were illegal for their practitioners merely because the women were too poor to pay for the necessary licence or permission to trade legally. Unlicensed alesellers and alewives appear to have been extremely common in the early modern period, although it is difficult to estimate their numbers because they made every effort to conceal their activities from the authorities. Partly because of the clandestine nature of unlicensed alehouses, they became linked in the official mind with a range of other illegal activities. Alewives who kept unlicensed premises were routinely accused of other crimes as well, including receiving stolen goods and keeping a bawdy house.

Contemporary court records show women being indicted for engaging in a range of petty criminal activities, chiefly the opportunistic theft of food and foodstuffs, firewood and other fuel, clothing and linens, and other items of relatively small value. Casual theft was widespread in the countryside, as was shoplifting in the towns. Women snatched linens drying on their neighbours' hedges, gathered fruit and nuts from orchards, and grain and vegetables from fields and barns; they milked other women's cows and took their straying poultry. Maidservants working in prosperous households believed they were entitled to take small amounts of leftover food and supplies as perquisites to bestow on their friends and family, or to give as alms to poor women begging at the door. Henry Best, a successful Yorkshire farmer, warned that landowners should hire maidservants who lived far away rather than nearby, otherwise servants would be tempted to smuggle food from their master's household to give to their own family and friends (Best 1984: 140).

By-employments and other occupations also provided poor women with opportunities for petty theft. Pilfering was rife in the textile trades, since it was difficult for employers to keep track of the exact quantity of raw materials they had supplied to female workers to be spun or otherwise prepared. In 1656 the Devon Quarter Sessions heard the case of a married woman who had been given a quantity of wool to be spun, and according to her employer, a yeoman farmer, 'did very much abuse us therein by withholding much of the yarn'. She was further accused of having sold yarn of the same colour (Mendelson and Crawford 1998: 294).

Prostitution in a diversity of forms provided a livelihood or an income supplement for women at every social level, from the mistress of a nobleman or king, who was granted titles and honours in addition to 'earning' an immense yearly stipend, down to the starving vagrant woman for whom the sale of sex offered her best chance for a meal. In rural areas sex was bartered for food or goods or small amounts of cash. One poor widow who was sentenced to death for infanticide told the court how she had become pregnant by engaging in a sexual liaison with her neighbour in order to buy food for her children (ibid.: 295).

Although casual opportunistic sex in exchange for small cash payments or favours was common in both city and countryside, prostitution as a recognized (although illegal) profession was more organized and more profitable in large urban areas like London, where upscale brothels catered to an elite clientele (Griffiths 1993). Both men and women served as keepers of bawdy houses, sometimes as husband-and-wife teams. The profits from brothel-keeping could be substantial: one London wife was said to have earned £300 over a period of three years 'by bawdrye' (Mendelson and Crawford 1998: 336).

The hazards of prostitution, however, almost invariably outweighed the financial gains. Women were vulnerable to infection from syphilis and gonorrhoea, and subject to harsh punishment if they were caught by civil or ecclesiastical authorities. In 1582 a York woman was ordered to be punished for 'misuseinge of her bodie' in the following manner: she was to sit on a barrel in the open market for an hour, with a paper describing her offence affixed to her head. Afterwards her head was to be shaved and she was to be whipped out of the city (ibid.: 296). Moreover, a woman's sexual reputation was crucial in her quest for legal employment. Those who appeared before the courts for sexual offences often found themselves barred thereafter from any respectable means of earning a livelihood.

The Working Lives of Women of the Middling and Upper Ranks

If we compare the working lives of more prosperous women with their counterparts among the poor, we can point to similarities and differences. Like plebeian women, those of the middling and upper ranks were expected to be concerned above all with the manifold tasks of housewifery, childbearing and childrearing. Indeed, wives of the aristocracy were made to feel it was their main role in life to produce healthy offspring, preferably of the male sex, to perpetuate the family lineage. Like their less prosperous sisters, elite women were limited by their sex in their choice of a salaried occupation or profession, and when they married they were subject to the same legal disabilities as the wives of poor men.

In fact there was probably more differentiation in men's and women's occupational identities at the top of the social and economic hierarchy than at the bottom. Elite women (along with the rest of the female sex) were excluded from practising law or serving in the ecclesiastical hierarchy, and professional female physicians were increasingly persecuted by their male counterparts during this period. At the apex of society even the wealthiest educated noblewomen were barred from formal political office because of their sex, with the sole exception of the reigning queen. At the other end of the social spectrum, in contrast, poor women as well as men worked at a range of unskilled agricultural tasks, were employed in mending roads and other heavy menial labour, or engaged in such 'masculine' occupations as nailmaking.

Despite their shared disabilities as members of the female sex, however, women of the wealthier classes had many more resources available to them to promote their advancement in a career. Women at this social level might have access to education, surplus capital to invest in a trade or business, or patronage connections through male relations which could lead to employment opportunities. Those women in the middling ranks of society were the group most likely to utilize their personal and financial resources to acquire an occupational or professional identity. While single women and widows in this group were freer than their married counterparts to practise a recognized profession, married women of the middling ranks were also likely to be fully employed at this period, even if they did not earn a salary in their own right.

Although rarely recognized as such, housewifery was itself a skilled, time-consuming and labour-intensive occupation during this period. Among the elite, wives governed large complex households, often running more than one establishment in different localities. Wives also managed the family estates while their husbands were away on business or attending parliament. Housewifery was more complicated and specialized at higher social levels, not only because establishments were on a much larger scale, but also because wealthy households had valuable consumer goods to be maintained and cared for, such as fine linens and delicate lace. Although the mistress of an aristocratic household did none of the manual labour herself, she directed the numerous staff who performed menial chores. As hostesses, elite women were concerned with hospitality and provisioning for a whole community of family members, guests, and servants and outside workers. Large farming households were likely to be close to self-sufficiency, as wives supervised the production of food, drink, clothing and linens for family members and servants, while converting surplus produce from their textile work, dairying and market gardens into cash profits.

At middling and upper levels, women were closely involved in the care and instruction of children, especially daughters. Godly women devoted themselves to the guidance and education of their maidservants in literacy and piety as well as the skills of housewifery. In general, wives whose husbands practised a trade or craft were responsible for providing the board and lodging and overseeing the good conduct of servants, apprentices and other labourers in the household.

Voluntary philanthropic work was another important vocational role developed by women of middling and elite status. Women worked actively as donors and administrators of institutional charities, as helpers of their neighbours in childbirth and sickness, and as amateur physicians and pharmacists dispensing medical charity to the poor. As patrons of the clergy, some women took on quasi-political roles, promoting their own favoured causes while establishing an informal power base in the local community. Lady Joan Barrington, who patronized the East Anglian Puritan clergy during the years preceding the English Civil War, was recognized as a commanding political influence by her male friends and relations (Mendelson and Crawford 1998: 312). At the upper end of the social spectrum, women's private roles as dispensers of charity and hospitality thus merged imperceptibly into more public roles as civic or community leaders.

Among the middling ranks in particular, we can point to numerous examples of women who established a professional career, despite the fact that professional salaried work identities were comparatively rare for early modern women as a group. Women at the middling level practised midwifery and other medical vocations, including specialized skills such as surgery; they served as salaried administrators in charitable and medical institutions; they earned a livelihood as schoolteachers, governesses and private tutors, or launched their own educational establishments; they managed shops, ran wholesale and retail businesses, and provided a vast array of services in the provisioning and lodging trades. Some worked as partners in tandem with their husbands, while others carried on their own independent trades, professions and businesses even after they were married.

As we saw earlier, one of the most common professions practised by women at this period was medicine. Although female practitioners were under increasing attack by male professional organizations, female medical workers and caregivers of varying social status are still plentifully scattered throughout contemporary records. Parochial and institutional accounts note frequent payments to female employees for nursing, healing the sick, and giving diverse kinds of medical care and treatment. Nursing, which was traditionally considered a wife's duty as part of her family responsibilities, became an important source of salaried employment for women of the middling ranks during this period.

There was a wide variation in proficiency, status and earnings among women in medical practice. Some female doctors of middling rank enjoyed a reputation for highly skilled professionalism comparable to that of their male colleagues, with salaries to match. Female physicians were retained by hospitals and other institutions to attend to particular medical skills such as surgical operations or the cure of specific ailments. Other female 'chirurgeons' and doctors had extensive private practices. Although such women were respected and well paid for their expertise, the field of medicine also included a host of amateur and plebeian practitioners, including 'wise women' and herbalists, who relied on their own experience and a female inheritance of popular lore rather than on formal medical training. Plebeian female healers had their partisans even among the educated elite – the philosopher Thomas Hobbes claimed he would rather 'have the advice, or take Physique [medicine] from an experienced old Woman, that had been at many sick people's Bed-sides, then from the learnedst but unexperienced Physitian' (Aubrey 1972: 314). But unlicensed female healers were viewed as unqualified competitors by male medical professionals, and many were prosecuted during this period by the Royal College of Physicians.

The fact that women from every social class practised medicine as a form of charity further weakened female physicians' sense of a professional identity. The plebeian artisan Leonard Wheatcroft wrote an elegy celebrating his mother's medical and surgical skills, which she had freely offered to all and sundry:

> Who e're was hurt, if this ould matron knew
> Haste would she make, and presently them view
> Either in head or foot, or armes, or shoulder;
> A rare Chirurgeon and the poores' upholder.
> All that she did was done for charitee:
> Come poor or rich, they all to her were free.

The popularity of amateur healers like Anne Wheatcroft reinforced the idea that women should practise medicine only as a philanthropic duty, never as a paid occupation.

Of all types of female medical practitioner, midwives sustained the strongest sense of a vocational identity. Through a system of apprenticeship, training and licensing, experienced midwives transmitted their skills to their younger colleagues, often handing down their expertise to daughters and other female relatives. During the seventeenth century, prominent practitioners like Elizabeth Cellier attempted to bolster midwives' professional standing by proposing the creation of formal institutional structures for midwives' training and qualification. Yet during this period there was a decline rather than an improvement in midwives' sense of a corporate professional identity.

Like other female medical practitioners, midwives confronted growing antagonism and competition from male physicians and man-midwives. Although most women still shared the belief that delivering babies was properly a woman's job, by the early eighteenth century some elite families were beginning to display a preference for male midwives. Moreover, women were accustomed to helping their female acquaintances in childbirth, viewing midwifery as a neighbourly duty rather than an occupation, thus weakening the professional claims of those who gained their livelihood by charging a fee. Finally, there are hints that women's elite status in eighteenth-century society was becoming increasingly defined in terms of membership in a leisured class; that is, a woman with pretensions to gentry status risked forfeiting her claim to gentility if she earned her living as a midwife or medical worker.

During the early modern period, teaching as a career was a growing source of paid employment for women of the middling and upper ranks. As with medicine and midwifery, there was a great variation in salaries and working conditions in the teaching profession. At the bottom of the hierarchy, poor women served as low-paid instructors in dame schools or taught local children on a casual part-time basis. But in contrast to medicine, education as a female profession was on the rise during the seventeenth and eighteenth centuries, as the growth of girls' schools and charitable institutions created an urgent need for female teachers. By the early eighteenth century, instructors at the top of the female hierarchy in the charity schools were earning as much as £25 a year, five to ten times the yearly income of a domestic servant. Women from the middling and upper ranks who taught daughters of elite families or who ran successful girls' schools were able to command even higher salaries: during the 1640s, Bathsua Makin received a stipend of £40 per annum while she was tutor to Princess Elizabeth.

Although women of the gentry were excluded from training in the higher professions such as law, they made use of a liberal education to forge careers in literature and the arts. We can trace an exponential growth in women's publications from the mid-seventeenth century onwards, as female authors branched out from religious and domestic subjects to produce novels, poetry and plays. Aphra Behn, who published more than twenty plays during the 1670s and 1680s, was one of the first English women to earn her living by her pen. There were also successful female artists, like the portraitist Mary Beale, who trained her two sons in her craft. Musicians like the court singer and lutenist Arabella Hunt were active in both performance and teaching. For her services as court musician and music tutor to Queen Mary II, Hunt was awarded a pension of £100 per annum during the 1690s.

Of all early modern women, those belonging to the middling ranks were most likely to be involved in a craft, trade or business. Although female apprenticeships to guild crafts had declined since the Middle Ages, we can still point to an impressive array of 'masculine' trades to which girls were apprenticed in this period: capper, weaver, plumber, whittawer [saddler], cordwainer, baker, fringemaker, sievemaker and housepainter, to give a few examples. Because it did not usually require a formal apprenticeship, retail trading was even more widespread as a female occupation, although married women were barred from running a business in their own right unless they lived in special localities like London, where, as mentioned earlier, custom permitted a *feme covert* to trade as if she were a *feme sole*.

The number and variety of trades pursued by women of the middling ranks appear almost unlimited. Women ran businesses as plumbers, plasterers, housepainters and coachmakers; they were prominent in the textile and clothing industries, working as milliners, mantua-makers, needleworkers and seamstresses. Some dealt in second-hand clothing, while others were wholesale cloth brokers, like Katharine Chidley, who supplied textiles to Cromwell's army. Women dominated the service industries, preparing and retailing food, drink and accommodation, working as victuallers, innkeepers, brewers and alewives; they also traded as wholesale dealers in grain, beer, coal and other commodities. Widows were permitted to work as printers or to follow other restricted guild crafts; some widows and single women ran businesses as pawn-brokers and moneylenders. Although women did not necessarily perform the manual tasks themselves in such businesses as the building trades, they were responsible for directing the enterprise and supplying the necessary workers, and it was they who kept the profits.

For middling and elite women, one of the most significant (and profitable) sources of paid employment was public office at court or in one of the medical or charitable institutions. During the reign of a female monarch the royal court was serviced by a vast retinue of female officeholders. Each royal appointee swore an oath of office to the crown, performed a specific set of duties and responsibilities, and received in reward a small fixed salary, with the potential for lucrative perquisites and other advantages. Like ordinary maidservants, royal servants could hope for gifts and other benefits from their mistress. For example, Princess Anne contributed a wedding gift of £5,000 when Henrietta Churchill, the eldest daughter of Anne's friend Sarah, Duchess of Marlborough, was married to Sidney Godolphin in 1698 (Harris 1991: 78–9). Because of their access to the monarch, female courtiers also enjoyed extensive opportunities for dispensing as well as receiving patronage, often accounting for the bulk of their profits from court office. In the reign of a male monarch, royal mistresses might be appointed to salaried court office as a sinecure. With their proximity to the king, they, too, were well-placed to dispense patronage for profit.

In addition to the royal court, various civic bodies and institutions hired women of elite or middling status to perform administrative and supervisory duties. Hospi-tals and other civic and charitable institutions employed a matron whose salary and other benefits were scaled in proportion to her social rank and her administrative responsibilities. Women also served as keepers of gaols and houses of correction and as overseers of workhouses and charitable foundations. In many civic posts in which a man was formally appointed to a salaried position, it was assumed that his wife was part of the team and that she would carry out a full set of duties and responsibilities associated with her husband's job.

If we search for trends in the working lives of women over the early modern period we find little alteration in the work patterns of those at the extreme ends of the social spectrum. Like their mothers and grandmothers, girls who were born poor were likely to remain poor, struggling to maintain themselves with a lifetime of low-paid, labour-intensive toil. At the top of the economic ladder, noblewomen continued to supervise large complex establishments and to hold office at court, much like their female ances-tors. It was at the middling level of society that women experienced the greatest number of choices and the most dramatic changes in their working lives, whether for good or ill. While medicine as a female career was in decline, other vocations like the teaching profession, literature and the arts, and the urban service industries offered profitable new occupational roles. As we watch increasing numbers of women exploiting these fresh opportunities to forge successful careers, we can glimpse a future in which a female work identity will no longer be a rarity, but rather a typical aspect of ordinary women's lives.

REFERENCES AND FURTHER READING

Aubrey, J. (1972). *Aubrey's Brief Lives*, ed. O. L. Dick. Harmondsworth: Penguin Books.

Ben-Amos, I. K. (1991). 'Women apprentices in the trades and crafts of early modern Bristol.' *Continuity and Change*, 6, 227–63.

Berg, M. (1988). 'Women's work, mechanization and the early phases of industrialization in England.' In R. E. Pahl (ed.), *On Work: Historical, Comparative and Theoretical Approaches* (pp. 61–94). Oxford: Blackwell Publishers.

Best, H. (1984). *The Farming and Memorandum Books of Henry Best of Elmsewell, 1642*, ed. D. Woodward. London: Oxford University Press for the British Academy.

Charles, L. and Duffin, L. (eds) (1985). *Women and Work in Pre-Industrial England*. London: Croom Helm.

Crawford, P. (1984). 'Printed advertisements for women medical practitioners in London, 1670–1710.' *Society for the Social History of Medicine, Bulletin*, 35, 66–70.

Earle, P. (1989). 'The female labour market in London in the late seventeenth and early eighteenth centuries.' *Economic History Review*, 2nd series, 42, 328–53.

Frith, V. (ed.) (1995). *Women and History: Voices of Early Modern England*. Toronto: Coach House Press.

Griffiths, P. (1993). 'The structure of prostitution in Elizabethan London.' *Continuity and Change*, 8, 39–63.

Harris, F. (1991). *A Passion for Government: The Life of Sarah, Duchess of Marlborough*. Oxford: Clarendon Press.

Hufton, O. (1975). 'Women and the family economy in eighteenth-century France.' *French Historical Studies*, 9, 1–22.

Kermode, J. and Walker, G. (eds) (1994). *Women, Crime and the Courts in Early Modern England*. London: UCL Press.

Laurence, A. (1994). *Women in England 1500–1760: A Social History*. New York: St Martin's Press.

Lemire, B. (1987). 'Consumerism in pre-industrial and early industrial England: the trade in second-hand clothes.' *Journal of British Studies*, 27, 1–24.

Marland, H. (ed.) (1993). *The Art of Midwifery: Early Modern Midwives in Europe*. London: Routledge.

Mendelson, S. H. (1987). *The Mental World of Stuart Women: Three Studies*. Brighton: Harvester.

Mendelson, S. H. and Crawford, P. (1998). *Women in Early Modern England 1550–1720*. Oxford: Clarendon Press.

Pelling, M. (1985). 'Healing the sick poor: social policy and disability in Norwich 1550–1640.' *Medical History*, 29, 115–37.

Pelling, M. and Webster, C. (1979). 'Medical practitioners.' In C. Webster (ed.), *Health, Medicine and Mortality in the Sixteenth Century* (pp. 165–235). Cambridge: Cambridge University Press.

Pound, J. F. (ed.) (1971). *The Norwich Census of the Poor, 1570*. Norfolk Record Society, 40.

Prior, M. (ed.) (1985). *Women in English Society 1500–1800*. London: Methuen.

Sharpe, P. (1991). 'Literally spinsters: a new interpretation of local economy and demography in Colyton in the seventeenth and eighteenth centuries.' *Economic History Review*, 44, 46–65.

Wales, T. (1984). 'Poverty, poor relief and the life-cycle: some evidence from seventeenth-century
    Norfolk.' In R. M. Smith (ed.), *Land, Kinship and Life-Cycle* (pp. 351–404). Cambridge: Cambridge
    University Press.
Wright, P. (1987). 'A change in direction: the ramifications of a female household, 1558–1603.' In D.
    Starkey (ed.), *The English Court from the Wars of the Roses to the Civil War* (pp. 147–72). London:
    Longman.

5

Women and Writing

Margaret J. M. Ezell

> But, why not women write, I pray?
> Sarah Jinner, 'To the Reader',
> *An Almanack or Prognostication of Women (1658)*

If this essay were being composed in the 1920s or 1930s the task would have been at once harder and simpler. It would have been harder in that the topic of early modern women writers had not been defined as an area suitable for intellectual enquiry beyond obscure antiquarian or genealogical interests. During that period, too, the dominant metaphor for literary history was of the literary past as a landscape and the historian's job was to provide a map or tour guide through its major points of attraction, defined by genre or monumental figures. The literary critic's task was to point out both the particular and the characteristic beauties of a region and also to warn the reader away from any deceptive shifting sands or literary fens.

In this version of literary history the territory occupied by writing women was largely populated by nineteenth-century novelists. Earlier female authors could be pointed out as interesting examples of rare creatures; typically mentioned in passing were Katherine Philips and Anne Finch, who dwelt in the realm of feminine sentimental or melancholy verse, or Margaret Cavendish, who occupied the isolated mansion of aristocratic, eccentric scribblers. Those readers game for a more robust tour of the literary past might encounter the bawdy Restoration dramatist Aphra Behn but none of her female contemporaries, respectable or not.

This topographical understanding of literary history, however, also made the task easier. The numbers of individuals to be discussed was small and the regions, or genres, in which to search for them clearly defined, either poetry or fiction. Using this approach, the critical questions to be answered about early modern women writers would have been why did not more women write and why were there no great women writers to rival their male contemporaries, apart from a handful of later women novelists.

While a recent literary historian will start with the same premise that a 1920s or 1930s one would, that early modern women writers existed within a conventionally patriarchal and hierarchical social structure, the oft-cited injunction that women should be chaste, silent and obedient and confine their creative work to needles and threads rather than pen and paper can no longer be taken as an accurate delineation of women's participation in early modern literary culture. Likewise, the traditional assumption that one reason why so few women wrote was because so very few were literate has also come under fire during the last few decades. As Margaret W. Ferguson has observed in her article examining Renaissance concepts of the 'woman writer', it is important to recognize still that we 'know little about how many women might have merited the label "writer" in any of that term's various senses', and that the 'concept of the "woman writer" in the early modern period signifies a shifting mix of illusion and empowerment; the consequences of women's emergence as writers were equally complex' (Ferguson 1991: 149, 163). What has changed between the 1920s and recent modes of thinking about women writers is not only the ways in which literacy is assessed but also the development of an appreciation of what is encompassed by the term 'authorship', the layers of issues involved in assessing connections between early modern women who wrote and women who read in terms of how texts were created, reproduced, circulated and preserved.

Since the 1970s, literary historians have recovered significant numbers of women's texts in both manuscript and print form. In addition to making rare individual items more widely available through the ESTC microfilm project, other groups such as the Brown University Women Writers Project, the Renaissance Women Writers Online, and the Perdita Project have worked to include such texts in electronic databases. Simultaneously, the last twenty years have seen an explosion of printed anthologies and editions, from Angeline Goreau's early collection *The Whole Duty of a Woman: Female Writers in Seventeenth-Century England* (1985), Germaine Greer et al.'s *Kissing the Rod: An Anthology of 17th Century Women's Verse* (1988), Roger Lonsdale's *Oxford Book of Eighteenth-Century Women Poets* (1989), to the most recent *Oxford Book of Early Modern Women Poets* (2001), edited by Jane Stevenson and Peter Davidson. Along with such anthologies, facsimile reprint series such as the Ashgate Library of Essential Writings by Early Modern English Women headed by Betty Travitsky and Patrick Cullen continue to call attention to the wide range of texts by early modern women which were in circulation among their contemporary readers.

Helen Wilcox has noted the paradox about early modern women that 'the centuries in question were thrilling ones in terms of new achievements by women writers . . . [however, their accomplishments] have always to be set against the backdrop of women's severely constrained social and legal position. In law, women had no status whatsoever but were only daughters, wives or widows of men' (Wilcox 1991: 4). Clearly, our earlier assumptions (shaped in part by Virginia Woolf's fictitious Judith Shakespeare in *A Room of One's Own*) that these conditions absolutely prevented women from writing, were misleading. Indeed, Jane Stevenson states that in the preparation of *The Oxford Book of Early Modern Women Poets* the editors determined that 'there were in the region of fifty English and Scottish women who wrote some kind of verse before 1600 which still survives in some form or other (and also a number of women composing in Welsh, Scottish Gaelic, or Irish, whose work falls outside this discussion). Of these fifty, about half printed at least some of what they wrote' (Stevenson 2000: 1). To explore more fully these rediscovered texts by women who lived and wrote within such social and legal constraints, we need to consider several issues in a larger context of literary culture and the dynamics of textual production and circulation. We need to think about not only women who wrote and published and got paid for doing so, but also about women who wrote and circulated texts socially, women who compiled volumes and managed the preservation and transmission of texts by themselves and by others, women who patronized and supported other writers through their writings, and even those early modern women who owned books and who interwove their own writing into others' texts.

Sites of Writing, Scenarios of Authorship

> I turned it into English in a roome where my children practiz'd the severall qualities they were taught, with their Tutors, & I numbred the syllables of my translation by the threds of the canvas I wrought in & sett them downe with a pen & inke that stood by me. (Lucy Hutchinson, dedication of her translation of Lucretius' *De rerum natura*)

Traditionally, when thinking about women and writing, the first question asked has been *what* a woman wrote, in terms of genre: did she write poetry? Fiction? Drama? A diary? Perhaps a more revealing way of rethinking the literary culture of early modern women might be to ask *where* did she write and *why*. Virginia Woolf imagined the early modern woman writing secretively, hiding her activity, yet her ultimate goal was to achieve public recognition and money. For Woolf, one essential requirement for being an author was the possession of private physical space for writing, a room of one's own, with a lock on the door, enabling the woman writer to close out the distractions of everyday domestic life as well as her society's definitions and expectations of her as a woman. Given the recovery of a much wider range of early modern women's texts than Woolf had access to in shaping her story of women and writing, what other scenarios can we imagine for an early modern woman writing? What types of questions can we raise for exploration of her writing and her reading as part of a larger picture of literary culture? Did some have a 'room of her own', some female domestic space, or was this, indeed, even viewed as a necessary prerequisite for authorship in early modern literary culture?

Let us begin with familiar images of women writing. Certainly, during the early modern period there were women writing in solitude and isolation as Woolf imagined them. Most, however, sought no immediate readership other than themselves and their God, and they wrote not for the financial reward which Woolf felt validated the act of writing for women, but for personal profits. Elizabeth Burnet (1661–1709), who wrote extensively and published her *Method of Devotion* (1708), observed that for the purpose of serious meditation a crowded household should still be able to provide 'little rooms or closets' in which to retreat. Sometimes used as a dismissive adjective of women's writing, such 'closet writing' needs to be reconsidered. The importance of the closet as a feminine site of authorship is combined with the fact that it also served multiple social functions in the household in addition to private devotional ones, from the preparation of medicinal concoctions to a place of private reflection and storage of books and writing materials.

It was in this type of domestic space, for example, that Anne, Lady Halkett (1623–99) retired to both read and write. At her death she left behind 21 folio and quarto manuscript volumes, composed between 1644 and the late 1690s, which are now housed in the National Library of Scotland, in addition to what her contemporary biographer described as 'about thirty stitched Books, some in Folio, some in 4tc. Most of them of 10 or 12 sheets, all containing occasional Meditations' ('S.C.', *Life*: 64). Her biographer 'S.C.' explained that Halkett regularly set aside five hours a day for devotion, 'from 5 to 7 in the Morning, from one in the afternoon to two, from 6 to 7, and from 9 to 10, together with nine [hours] for Business', and 'ten for necessary refreshment' (ibid.: 55). Clearly, for Anne Halkett, the act of writing down her meditations on the texts she read, her analysis of her dreams, her hopes for her children, and her autobiography were a vital part of her daily domestic devotions. As she herself observed in one of the volumes begun in 1676, 'It is naturall for all persons to please themselves in pursuing what is most suitable to there inclination. & to aime att an eminency in what ever profession there Genius lead them to, from wch many have arived to Great Knowledge in Severall Arts and Sciences' (National Library of Scotland MS 6494, f.1). Anne Halkett, as did other early modern women, wrote extensively and wrote for pleasure, but it was for her spiritual, not worldly, profit.

Examples of domestic devotional writing by women throughout the seventeenth and eighteenth centuries span numerous social classes and settings, from mothers recording spiritual advice for children (Dorothy Leigh, *The Mother's Blessing: Or the Godly Counsaile of a Gentlewoman not long since deceased, left behind for her children*, 1616; Elizabeth Clinton, Countess of Lincoln, *The Countess of Lincoln's Nurser*, 1622; Elizabeth Richardson, *A Ladies Legacie to her Daughters*, 1645), to women recording private prayers and meditations and keeping diaries or journals. Many of the volumes of this type of women's writing were published as historical records during the nineteenth and early twentieth centuries, but many still remain in manuscript copies. A brief survey of only a representative few suggests the appeal of diary and journal writing for early modern women of a variety of social backgrounds, religious persuasions and political positions: Lady Elizabeth Brackley, Countess of Bridgewater (1626–63), who wrote pastorals, occasional verse, and masques with her sister Lady Jane Cavendish, which will be discussed later, left behind a manuscript collection of *Meditations on the*

Several Chapters of the Holy Bible; a maid of honour in Catharine Braganza's court, Elizabeth Livingstone Delaval (1649–1717), created an elaborate memoir intertwining pious devotions and prayers with her romantic misadventures; the businesswoman Alice Thornton (1626–1707) wrote down her prayers as well as her fears over childbirth and poverty in her *Diaries*; Elizabeth, Vicountess Mordaunt (1632/3–79) carefully recorded wasting her time reading plays as well as the arrest of her husband for treason against the commonwealth in 1658; the parliamentarian paymaster's wife Mary Carey (1609/12–80) shared the pages of her meditations and verses with those of her second husband, George Payler, as they moved from town to town with the army.

Elizabeth Bury (1644–1720) offers an extended example of this type of women's writing. Born into a comfortable but not aristocratic family, Bury devoted her life to study, 'of almost every Thing . . . taking continual Pleasure in Reading and Conversation' (5). Her husband had portions of her diary printed after her death, noting that during her life, she had maintained an extensive correspondence on philosophical, historical, and spiritual subjects: 'in Writing of Letters, she had a great Aptness and Felicity of Expression; and was always so close and pertinent, and full to the Purpose; and withal, so Serious, Spiritual, and Pungent, that her Correspondence was greatly valued, by some of the brightest Minds, even in very distant Countries' (ibid.). This same talent for expression, Mr Bury maintains, shines through her diaries, begun when she was between 18 and 20 years of age and kept continuously until the end of her life; he was only able to publish the portions written after 1690, when she changed from recording her thoughts in shorthand with 'many peculiar Characters and Abbreviations of her own' (ibid.: 11). In her diaries, in which she wrote both in the morning and evening, 'with a very great Liberty and happy Variety of Expression', she recorded daily events, including providential acts of God towards herself and her family, 'the solemn transactions betwixt GOD and her own Soul, in her Closet, in her Family, in the Assembly, and in her daily Walk and Conversation with others; the Substance of what she had Read or Heard' (ibid.: 11–12). In short, Elizabeth Bury used writing to record, interpret and create a spiritual narrative of the events of the everyday life of a clergyman's wife in late seventeenth-century Suffolk.

For Englishwomen living abroad as part of religious houses, writing, too, was an integral part of their religious avocation and the convent house. Such separate devotional communities, including the Anglican community of Little Gidding, have remained a very little appreciated site of female participation in the creation, preservation and circulation of texts, as a site of communal authorship and vital supporting roles in maintaining a literary culture. The English nuns residing at the Benedictine community at Cambrai, founded in 1623 by Dame Gertrude More, produced meditations and prayers as part of their daily spiritual practice. Heather Wolfe stresses the importance of both reading and writing in these women's lives, pointing out that 'there was a particular emphasis on reading during Lent' in this community and that 'death notices' or biographies of fellow nuns were important texts as 'an example to posteritie' (Wolfe 2000: 206). At a nun's death, Wolfe notes, her 'loose papers' frequently were placed in the convent's library, bound together in a titled volume, such as 'a little book of Dame Mary Watsons Collections' or 'Eight Collection Bookes of . . . Mothere Clementia Cary'. Wolfe argues that the *Life of Lady Falkland* is an example of such convent-created texts. Other texts by the nuns, including the prayers and meditations of Gertrude More, for example, were occasionally published later for a general readership.

There are scenarios of women writing in solitude to consider other than religious retreat; some women had solitude imposed on their practice of writing because of their particular personal circumstances. Elaine Hobby has called such writers women who were 'making a virtue of necessity'. Hobby discusses at length the examples of Elizabeth Major and An Collins as 'celebration[s] of women's writings' where an authorial voice is created out of bodily distress and spiritual trials (Hobby 1989: 61–6). Elizabeth Major tells her readers that after having led a secular life wedded to 'earthen pleasures', 'God was pleased to visit me with lameness. . . . Then I was forc't to repair home to my Father again'. As part of her repentance, Major created *Honey on the Rod: Or a comfortable Contemplation for one in Affliction* (1656), detailing in prose and verse how her illness, 'I / In prime arrested, here I in prison lie', forced her to analyse the narrative of her past life as part of seeking future salvation and to organize and communicate her findings poetically (Greer et al. 1988: 183, 184).

Likewise An Collins, who published her *Divine Songs and Meditacions* (1653), was kept housebound by her illnesses and offers her poetry as 'the offspring of my mind' since her body will not have children. For Collins, her apparently sickly childhood created a scenario of authorship as a means of overcoming those 'Clouds of Melancholy over-cast / My heart' and writing formed part of her recreation: 'I became affected to Poetry, insomuch that I proceeded to practise the same; and though the helps I had therein were small, yet the thing it self appeared unto me so amiable, as that it enflamed my faculties, to put forth themselves, in a practise so pleasing' (Collins 1653: Sig. A1). Through writing, Collins continues in 'The Preface', 'sorrow serv'd but as springing raine / To ripen fruits, indowments of the minde, / Who thereby did abillitie attaine / To send forth flowers' and, although her circumstances dictate solitude while writing, she is determined to 'publish . . . those Truths' and to 'tell what God still for my Soule hath wrought'.

Thus far we have looked at scenarios of women writing which are not far removed from our modern expectations of the requirements of authorship: solitude, leisure and private domestic space. What other scenarios are revealed when one examines texts by early modern women writers? *Lady Falkland: Her Life* (1645), written (as Heather Wolfe has convincingly argued) by her daughter Lucy while a member of the convent at Cambrai, offers glimpses of some unexpected circumstances under which an early modern woman might conduct her reading and writing. We are told that as a child Elizabeth Cary, Lady Falkland (1586–1639) 'spent her whole time in reading;

to which she gave herself so much that she frequently read all night; so as her mother was fain to forbid her servants to let her have candles' (Weller and Ferguson 1994: 187). Married at age 15 to Sir Henry Cary, the young bride fell out with her mother-in-law who 'used her very hardly, so far, as at last, to confine her to her chamber; which seeing she little cared for, but entertained herself with reading'; when her mother-in-law had all the books removed from Elizabeth Cary's room, 'then she set herself to make verses' (ibid.: 189). Life improved with the return of her husband and

> he grew better acquainted with her and esteemed her more. From this time she writ
> many things for her private reaction, on several subjects, and occasions, all in verse (out
> of which she scarce ever writ anything that was not translations). One of them was after
> stolen out of that sister-in-law's (her friend's) chamber and printed, but by her own pro-
> curement was called in. Of all she then writ, that which was said to be the best was the
> life of Tamberline in verse. (Ibid.: 189–90)

In addition to the solitude imposed on her by her mother-in-law, Elizabeth Cary supposedly was able to compose under rather more distracting circumstances: she cared little about her appearance except to satisfy her husband's wishes and 'her women were fain to walk round the room after her (which was her custom) while she was seriously thinking on some other business, and pin on her things and braid her hair; and while she writ or read, curl her hair and dress her head' (ibid.: 194).

Throughout her subsequent conversion to Catholicism and her estrangement from most of her family and friends, Elizabeth Cary continued to write. Her environment was drastically changed, but her literary output continued even in conditions represented as being far removed from the comfort of her previous life. During this period of her life, waiting ladies did not follow her from room to room as she wrote, but instead she was reduced to living with a single servant, her room only furnished with a bed on the ground and 'an old hamper which served her for a table, and a wooden stool'; according to her daughter, here is where she composed in verse the lives of 'St Mary Magdalene, St Agnes Martyr, and St Elizabeth of Portingall . . . and of many other saints' (ibid.: 213–14).

Elizabeth Cary might seem to be an anomalous example of an early modern woman writing in extreme situations, but a closer look at the elements which characterize her sites of writing – her writing spaces, her scenarios of authorship, and her readers and the nature of the production of her texts – suggests further possibilities for exploring the literary activities of other women. Clearly, for Elizabeth Cary, the possession of a special space for writing was not central to her endeavours as an author. Nor do we see the scenario of the writer as the self-imposed social exile because of her literary pursuits, nor the woman hiding her identity as an author. As Margaret W. Ferguson points out in the preface to Cary's translation of *The Reply to the Most Illustrious*

Cardinall of Perron (1630), 'she not only used her own name but explicitly mentioned her refusal to "make use of the worne-out forme of saying I printed it against my will, moved by the importunitie of Friends"' (Weller and Ferguson 1994: 158).

The close connection between Elizabeth Cary's reading and writing habits is a key element in Barbara Kiefer Lewalski's assessment of the literary activities of other aristocratic women writing during the Jacobean period. Lewalski examines the accumulated writings of Lady Anne Clifford (1590–1676), including her histories of her parents as well as her own. Writing about her mother, Margaret Clifford, Anne noted that 'for though she had no language but her own, yet was there few books of worth translated into English but she read them, whereby that excellent mind of hers was much enriched' (Lewalski 1993: 134). In addition to her habit of studious reading, Margaret Clifford was also 'a lover of the study and practice of alchemy, by which she found out excellent medicines that did much good to many', which she, like many early modern women, recorded in a manuscript volume. Lewalski notes that in the 'Great Picture' of the Clifford family Margaret is painted with all the elements of her reading and writing practices defining the nature of her domestic space, 'holding the Psalms of David; the Bible, and English translation of Seneca, and (her own) hand-written book of alchemical distillations and medicines are on a shelf over her head' (ibid.: 373, n. 43).

Cary's example also invites a reconsideration of how and why women were writing. The scenario of Cary surrounded by her waiting women as she both read and wrote, for example, is one which Louise Schleiner has called a 'reading formation', a social situation consisting of aristocratic women and their waiting ladies, 'circles of women encompassing two or three social classes liv[ing] in daily association, reading and often making music together' (Schleiner 1994: 3). The practice of reading as part of a female circle, Schleiner maintains, 'might inspire various urges to write, up and down its encompassed social spectrum' and, she argues, is mirrored in the way in which women poets such as Aemilia Lanyer and Isabella Whitney use paratexts to celebrate the relationship between the waiting woman and her aristocratic female reader or, as in Whitney's situation, to lament its loss (ibid.: 4, 23, 25). Examples such as these cause us to ponder the scenario of a woman writing for an audience of women readers, perhaps even doing such writing in their company: in this scenario, rather than the isolated individual writing in solitude and not daring to seek an audience, we have instead the performance of reading and writing among women as part of their domestic life and an accepted elite social practice.

The female reading circles discussed by Schleiner and those women loosely associated with Queen Anne's court between 1605 and 1609 at Hampton Court and Somerset (Denmark) House, the Countess of Bedford, Cecily Bulstrode, Lady Ann Southwell (more of whom later in this essay) and Lady Mary Wroth also suggest that we can look for women writing as part of intricate social interactions as well as for moral or medicinal improvement. Leeds Barroll places Anne of Denmark at the centre of a 'rich and hospitable climate' for the arts, surrounding herself with literate and literary women and female patrons of contemporary male writers (Barroll 1998: 55). Mary Ellen Lamb likewise points to the importance of 'poetic numbers' for early modern women writers: for Lady Mary Wroth in particular, the numerous women writers in the Sidney family as well as the Vere family provided a ' "safe house" in which women could write' ambitious literary projects (Lamb 1990: 150). On a more casual level, as Jane Stevenson has observed, surviving textual evidence suggests that 'a number of women of the rank of gentlewoman or above participated in the writing of ephemeral poetry as a social activity' (Stevenson 2000: 4). Lewalski (1993) notes that some of the prose 'inventions' by Bulstrode and Southwell ended up being included in Sir Thomas Overbury's collection of miscellaneous pieces, *Sir Thomas Overbury His Wife* (1611), and Stevenson points to George Gascoigne's even earlier *Hundred Sundrie Flowers* (1573) containing several examples of witty exchanges of verses between gentlewomen and their male admirers (Stevenson 2000: 5–7).

Later in the seventeenth and early eighteenth century, the titles of women's poems found in published volumes often reveal both the connection between a woman's reading and her writing and the social or coterie origins of her verse. Writing at the end of the seventeenth century, the poet, novelist and medicinal writer Jane Barker (1652–c.1727) participated in a number of literary exchanges throughout her life. Kathryn R. King describes Barker's first appearance in print, *Poetical Recreations* (1688), as an example of a 'sociable text'; 51 of the 109 poems are by Barker and the rest are by 'Gentlemen of the Universities, and Others' (King 1994: 552). The titles of the poems reflect the occasions of their composition and their function as a type of social performance. This same pattern of linked verses where one poet writes in response to another's verse, typically written to record social occasions from weddings and deaths to broken friendships and flirtations, is not infrequently found in posthumous collections of poetry by women writers, such as Anne Killigrew's *Poems* (1686) and Mary Monck's *Marinda* (1716). Such posthumous volumes serve as a type of blueprint of the patterns of social verse exchange among women and their friends, both male and female: Killigrew's volume includes, for example, 'To My Lord Colrane, In Answer to his Complemental Verses sent me under the Name of Cleanor', while Mary Monck's volume includes 11 poems addressed to her as 'Marinda', as well as one entitled 'Upon an Impromptu of Marinda's, in answer to a Copy of Verses'.

This practice of the exchange of verses as part of a social pastime is clearly continued throughout the seventeenth and eighteenth centuries, and was not restricted to highly placed courtiers and aristocrats. At some times, too, the composition, compilation and preservation of manuscript volumes by women also act as a means of confirming religious or political loyalties within the woman's literary circle. Constance Aston Fowler organized her family and friends to contribute verses to her compilations in the 1630s and 1640s, and her correspondence contains several references to her compilations and to her family's lively literary life (Ezell 1999: 25–8). Fowler's manuscript miscellany reveals both her reading and writing practices: in addition to collecting poems by her father, her brother Herbert Aston (whose wife later assembled a separate manuscript volume of his verse), her brother-in-law Sir William Pershall, her sister-in-law Katherine Thimelby, her friend Lady Dorothy Shirley, and possibly herself, Constance Fowler also included verses by Ben Jonson, John Donne, Richard Fanshawe and Aurelian Townshend. Victoria Burke has described this as 'a clearly definable literary network', tying together a diverse group bound by their 'embattled Catholic faith', ranging from 'her blood relatives, to her relatives by marriage, to her friends in the Catholic faith, to diplomatic friends of her father's, to the people who were the means by which popular poetry circulating in manuscript reached her' (Burke 1997: 139).

The same practice of literary compilation and collaboration among family members rather than the scenario of the isolated artist is found in the manuscript volumes compiled by Lady Jane Cavendish (1621–69) and Lady Elizabeth Brackley (1626–63), the daughters of the Duke of Newcastle by his first wife. As with the Aston family circle, the manuscript volume, *Poems Songs and a Pastoral*, also reveals how literary exchanges were used to cement social bonds during times of duress. The two sisters were at Welbeck when it was besieged by parliamentary troops, and several of the verses reflect the women's concerns for their absent relatives fighting for the king in the Civil War, while the play *The Concealed Fansyes* features scenes of witches overturning natural order and harmony to create civil strife. As preserved miscellanies and family papers show us, the Duke of Newcastle encouraged his children from an early age to write and to compose little social verses; their surviving manuscript volumes embody their continuing literary activities as young women, wives and mothers (Ezell 1998: 256–7).

The social aspect of women's writing can also be seen in the practice of writers sharing space on the page itself. The Cavendish sisters, for example, intermingled their poems, not dividing them into separate author sections. Manuscript volumes often reflect multiple generations of women readers and writers at work, and such volumes often display their multiple functions within the family and household. Anna Cromwell Williams assembled *A Booke of Several Devotions collected from good men* (1656, 1660), whose inscription declares it to have been a gift between sisters. Williams also embellished the good men's devotions with her own verses; in the same volume other hands recorded poems on family events, such as the death of Bettina Cromwell (British Library Harl. Ms. 2311).

The shared commonplace book of Lady Anne Southwell (1573–1636) and her second husband, Captain Henry Sibthorpe, likewise displays multiple hands, voices, agendas and genres of writing. Lady Anne's original verses are mingled with copies of her letters, one to Cicely MacWilliams on the superiority of verse to prose, and one to Elizabeth Cary's husband on his return to England. The same volume also contains the hand of her father-in-law, John Sibthorpe, prosaically recording his account of receipts for moneys spent during the Dutch war, as well as Ann Johnson and Mary Phillips signing receipts for rents. As Jean Klene notes, this remarkable collection also includes Henry Sibthorpe's tribute to his departed wife, 'the pattern of conjugall love and obedience', and Klene views the preservation of manuscript text with all its hands and purposes as a husband's monument to his remarkable spouse (Klene 1998: 165).

Still other women joined together to write collaboratively for pressing political reasons. By far the largest single group of women publishing their writings during the Restoration period were Quakers, who wrote not only to record their individual spiritual journeys for the assistance of their fellow travellers, but who also turned out accounts of persecutions, trials and incarceration where the authorship of a single document is the work of several hands, carrying several signatures. They sent petitions and appeals with over 100 women's signatures attached to plead their causes. Such use of the press to present a public appeal can be seen as a continuation of the practices of other women petitioners during the 1640s and during the Civil War years. In 1642 the 'Gentlemen and Tradesmens Wives, In and About the City of London' petitioned parliament to protect its citizens against the dangers of papistry and false prelates (Archbishop Laud), citing as their precedent for writing Esther's petition to King Ahasuerus on behalf of the church. During the war years women associated with the Leveller movement petitioned for the release of John Lilburne in 1649, and in 1653 a group of some 6,000 women petitioned parliament to stop his trial. The Quaker Mary Forster (*c*.1620–87) explained 'To the Reader' in a petition presented in May 1659 arguing against tithes that the 7,000 women who attached their names to the petition do so in order to be the 'weak means to bring to pass his mighty work'.

Better known than such examples of multiple women writers combining to create a single female public voice are individual women such as Katherine Chidley (believed to have participated in the Leveller group petitions), who used pamphlet writing to explain her political opposition to a national church and to argue for the right of women to preach. Other women turned to printed pamphlets and broadsides to map out their visions of England's future: Mary Cary (*c*.1621–53) wrote petitions explaining to parliament the plans to build God's kingdom on earth, *A New and Exact Mappe or Description of New Jerusalems* (1651), and in *Twelve Humble Proposals* (1653) she, like Chidley and the 1659 women petitioners, recommended the abolition of tithes as a first step. In the 1680s and 1690s Elinor James (fl. 1675–1715), in contrast, used broadsides to support the established church and the Stuart monarchy, the titles of her broadsides clearly displaying her loyalties; for example, 'Mrs. James's Defence of the Church of England in a short answer to the canting Address: with a word or two concerning a Quakers good advice to the Church of England' (1687) and 'Mrs. James's letter of thanks to the Q—n and both houses of Parliament for the deliverance of Dr. Sacheverell' (1710).

We also find individual women making their private writing public in response to legal cases involving their families. During the war years individual women such as Elizabeth Lilliburne petitioned on behalf of their imprisoned husbands. During the

Restoration women such as Mary Love approached parliament with numerous petitions to spare the life of her husband Christopher; the unsuccessful petitions were subsequently published, along with letters between the husband and wife in a volume called *Love's Name Lives* (1663). Rachel, Lady Russell (1636–1723) took the notes at her husband's trial for high treason that were used as part of his defence; like Mary Love, she unsuccessfully pleaded for his life and as with the letters of Love, Lady Russell's letters to her husband and to her spiritual advisers were subsequently published.

Still another group of women whose writings begin appearing as printed volumes during the period following the Restoration were motivated by a desire to improve the status of the female sex as a whole and to respond to male writers' representation of women's roles and natures. Polemical writers such as Judith Drake (fl. 1696), Bathsua Makin (*c*.1600–?) and Mary Astell (1666–1731) argued strenuously for the education of middle- and upper-class women as rational rather than ornamental creatures. Others such as Sarah Fyge Egerton (1669–1722) turned to satire, publishing *The Female Advocate* (1686) to rebut Robert Gould's attack; Mary, Lady Chudleigh (1656–1710) was sufficiently provoked by the Revd John Sprint's advice to brides to reply with *The Ladies Defense* (1701). All of these women share the view that while men had rejected the notion of absolutism in national politics, they had strenuously preserved it in the domestic realm. For these women, writing and reading were the keys to middle-class women's improvement of their lives, and they argued for a system of education for women which paralleled that offered to men of that station.

Finally, the scenario of authorship most familiar to us, the commercial, professional woman writer, also begins to be performed more frequently during the latter part of the seventeenth century. As Janet Todd has observed, 'the Restoration and early eighteenth century is the first period when women as a group began writing for money clearly and openly' (Todd 1989: 37). With the reopening of the theatres, the expansion of commercial publishing, as well as the development of new types of literary genres such as periodicals, earning money by writing became more of a possibility for middle-class women in search of an income. The theatres were hungry for new materials to present, and women dramatists such as Aphra Behn (*c*.1640–89), Delarivier Manley (*c*.1663–1724), Catherine Trotter (1679–1749), Eliza Haywood (1693–1756) and Mary Pix (1666–1729) provided comedies and tragedies for the new theatre companies at a considerable rate. Jacqueline Pearson's study of women dramatists of the period credits Behn with over 20 plays, Manley 6, Pix 13 and Susanna Centlivre (?–1723) with 19 (Pearson 1988: 288–91). While Trotter produced fewer dramas, only five, she was widely known for her attempts to write for a 'reformed' stage, although she, along with Pix and Manley, was satirized in *The Female Wits* (1696). As unpleasant as the caricatures of these women dramatists are, it does suggest that women commercial writers as a group posed a sufficient, visible competition to provoke defensive measures from concerned professional rivals.

Although professional women writers drew attacks from male professionals, it is also clear that women writers were frequently supportive of the literary activities of their peers. Todd notes that during the later part of the seventeenth century 'there was . . . a sense of a female writing community, which in many ways looked towards the Bluestocking groupings of the last half of the eighteenth century' (Todd 1989: 40). Sometimes the public, printed endorsement of another woman's writing was simply a continuation of a literary relationship begun as part of a social literary exchange: Elizabeth Thomas wrote enthusiastic letters and poems to Mary Chudleigh which she later published; Chudleigh and Mary Astell knew and endorsed each other's works and opinions in verse as well as prose; and Chudleigh introduced Thomas to Astell's circle. Women dramatists provided prefaces and commendatory verses for other women's plays. Aphra Behn included verses by other women, such as 'Mrs. Taylor', in her verse miscellanies. In *Nine Muses, or Poems written by as many Ladies Upon the Death of the Late Famous John Dryden Esq* (1700) Manley assembled poems by herself and her female acquaintances, including Egerton, Trotter, Pix, and Trotter's patron, Lady Sarah Piers.

The self-representations of this generation of women writers we see in their printed texts are remarkably similar to the various masks of authorship assumed by their male contemporaries. Elizabeth Singer Rowe (1674–1737) jauntily rejected the advice of a friend 'Who Persuades me to leave the Muses' on the grounds that her literary pursuits harm no one:

> Forego the charming Muses! No, in spite
> Of your ill-natur'd prophecy I'll write;
> And for the future paint my thoughts at large,
> I waste no paper at the hundred's charge:
> I rob no neighbouring geese of quills, nor slink
> For a collection, to the church for ink:
>
> Yet I'm so naturally inclined to rhyming,
> That undesigned, my thoughts burst out a chiming;
> My active genius will by no means sleep,
> Pray let it then its proper channel keep.
> I've told you, and you may believe me too,
> That I must this, or greater mischief do:
> And let the world think me inspired, or mad,
> I'll surely write whilst paper's to be had.
> *Poems on Several Occasions, Written by Philomena*, 1696
> (Goreau 1985: 291–2)

In her poem 'The Liberty' Sarah Fyge Egerton voiced even more strongly her commitment to her pen in her role as the defender of the female sex. She rejects the model of a woman's writing as being confined to 'lofty Themes of useful Houswifery, / Transcribing old Receipts of Cookery': for Egerton, 'My daring Pen, will bolder Sallies

make / And like myself, an uncheck'd freedom take' (Greer et al. 1988: 347). Elizabeth Tipper (fl. 1690s), on the other hand, considers and rejects the role of satirist for
herself: 'Where's then my Muse? Does my Poetick Vein! / Want Skill or Courage for
this useful strain? / . . . / I find no Moment where I need explore / The Faults of others,
but my own deplore' ('The Pilgrim's Viaticum', 1698; ibid.: 71–2).

Although, as we have seen, the genres of women's texts varied widely and most
wrote in more than one, there are some recurrent metaphors used by women for
writing which transcend both period and geographical location. While the metaphor
of a poem or a book as the author's child is a common one for both male and female
writers during the early modern period, it seems important to look at the particulars
when considering how early modern women viewed their writing. While male authors
such as Dudley, 4th Lord North, tended to dwell upon the image of poetic creation
as involving labour and birth pains – 'a burden of perplexed thoughts, the very being
delivered (a terme well known to you Ladyes)' (Ezell 1999: 35) – the use of the image
by women more typically focuses on the pleasure of the creation and the subsequent
fond pride in the literary 'offspring'. This characterization of writing by women as
giving birth and the writers' affection for their productions crosses the social classes
of those women who wrote about writing. Margaret Cavendish, Duchess of Newcastle (1623–73), in 'An excuse for so much write upon my Verses', pleads: 'Condemme
me not for making such a coyle / About my Book, alas it is my Childe' (*Poems, and
Fancies*, 1653, Sig. A8v). A year before her volume appeared, 'Eliza' published *Eliza's
Babes: or The Virgin's Offspring* (1652), describing, as did An Collins, the pleasure of
writing; her poems, 'my Babes . . . were obtained by vertue, borne with ease and pleasure' through divine inspiration (Sig. A3). In a more exasperated use of the metaphor,
in the American colonies, Anne Bradstreet (1612–72) described her collection of
verses as 'my rambling brat' when she remarked on their publication in England under
the title *The Tenth Muse*: 'Thou ill-form'd offspring of my feeble brain, / Who after
birth didst'st by my side remain, / Till snatcht from thence by friends, less wise then
true' ('The Author to her Book', *Several Poems*, 1678). For such women, writing was
a natural process of generation from the woman's self and a process over which nature,
not the individual will, had the final say about production.

Early modern women also shared with contemporary male writers reasons to write
other than God's command or the urging of friends. In her 'Preface' to her *Miscellany
Poems* (1713) Anne Finch, Countess of Winchilsea (1661–1720) quotes from Beaumont's verse to Fletcher: 'no more can he, whose mind / Joys in the Muses, hold from
that delight / When nature, and his full thoughts, bid him write'; adding 'I not only
find true by my own experience, but have also to many witnesses of it against me,
under my own hand in the following poems'. She concludes, sounding rather like her
friend Alexander Pope, that it was 'an irresistible impulse' which is her primary reason
for writing. Occasional dramatist, coffee-house keeper, and novelist Mary Davys
(1674–1732) used the preface to her *Works* (1725) to assure her readers that 'idleness

has so long been an excuse for writing, that I am almost ashamed to tell the world it was that, and that only, which produced the following sheets'. She concludes by hoping that 'my pen is at the service of the public, and if it can but make some impression upon the young unthinking minds of some of my own sex, I shall bless my labour and reap an unspeakable satisfaction'. Writing for women was variously presented as childbirth, as an irresistible compulsion, a divine channelling, and an amusing pastime, and the wide variety of metaphors employed suggests to us the wide variety of scenarios of authorship.

Conclusion: Why Write?

Surveying the different materials written by early modern women as a whole, we find that by the end of the seventeenth century into the early part of the eighteenth, we are looking at a collage of various overlapping sites and scenarios of women writing rather than a map giving us individual landmarks and clearly defined territories. For example, the practice of keeping diaries and journals for private spiritual improvement feeds into the developing forms of fiction for profit; the mother writing for her children seems related to the woman writing for the improvement of her sex; the woman sitting with her waiting ladies or sending her poems to her friends in letters seems reflected in the links between the growing numbers of professional women writers praising and contributing to each other's works.

How did early women themselves describe their desires to write? As we have seen, many felt compelled to share with others their experiences of God and salvation, pain and hope. Tudor women, Margaret P. Hannay suggests, found a means to 'find their own voices through their proclamations of the Word of God' as translators and devotional writers (Hannay 1985: 14). During the Civil War years and Restoration period, women prophets from diverse social backgrounds such as the Quaker Ester Biddle (c.1629–96) and aristocratic Lady Eleanor Douglas (1590–1652) felt compelled to publish their warnings and prophecies for the good of England. Other women were clearly motivated by a compelling combination of contemporary politics and profit. As Paula McDowell has suggested in her study of the women writers, printers and booksellers occupying Grub Street during the years after the Restoration, 'religious and religio-political works' formed the 'largest category of women's (and men's) writings' (McDowell 1998: 18), but these are markedly different from the books of private devotions or solitary prophecy from the start of the century. The period following the Civil Wars, as she notes, was remarkable for the simultaneous 'birth of the modern literary marketplace . . . concurrent with women's emergence in significant numbers as publishing authors' (ibid.: 5). We are most familiar with women's participation in commercial literary culture as authors, but, in the same way that we have tended to overlook women's participation in the production and dissemination of manuscript texts, McDowell draws our attention to the activities of women 'working in *all* aspects of material literary production, and doing so for pay' (ibid.).

Where were early modern women writing and why? As their surviving manuscripts and volumes reveal, writing for women and men was a social activity as well as a means of private consolation. Once we leave behind the notion of authorship as an act defined by solitary alienation and the text as an isolated literary landmark, we start to see a much livelier literary landscape for early modern women. While looking at the diversity of texts they created and which have recently been recovered, we now can see them more clearly at their writing – alone, in groups, in the closet, in the courtroom – and for whom they wrote – for themselves, God, their friends, their children, parliament and for future readers. For many early modern women, writing was an essential part of their devotional life, as much a part of daily domestic life as prayer; while historians are right to remind us about the separation of the teaching of reading and writing skills, it is well to remember the role that reading played in inspiring many such women to write their own thoughts in response to what they read. For other women, writing was a means to reinforce family and social ties, often in manuscript volumes compiled by women and passed through generations of family readers and contributors. Writing women also created collections and compilations of others' works and added their annotations to printed books in their libraries. Separately printed broadsides and pamphlets permitted individual women such as Anna Trapnel, Lady Eleanor Douglas and Jane Lead to share their prophetic visions of God's wishes for England, while petitions gave groups of women a means of making written statements on political events which they were legally barred from participating in directly.

For early modern women, writing could be both a private pleasure and a means of public performance. Writing could be a response to a particular life crisis or a sustained life-long practice. When we imagine scenarios of authorship for these women, we need to remember that writing could function as an act of creation, a bid for fame, an affirmation of allegiances, and a part of a prayer, and that a woman who wrote probably did so in a variety of genres for a variety of audiences. In this expanded sense of the literary stage for early modern women – in her closet, in the children's schoolroom, in the sickroom, in the kitchen, in the great hall, in the courtroom, in prison and in the parlour – wherever one looks, the possibility is there that one will find women writing and that, indeed, there are more early modern women writers still waiting for us to see them.

See also RELIGION AND THE CONSTRUCTION OF THE FEMININE; ELIZABETH CARY, *THE TRAGEDY OF MARIAM*; AUTOBIOGRAPHY; DEFENCES OF WOMEN; POETRY; DRAMA; THE WORK OF WOMEN IN THE AGE OF ELECTRONIC REPRODUCTION

REFERENCES AND FURTHER READING

Barroll, Leeds (1998). 'The arts at the English court of Anna of Denmark.' In S. P. Cerasano and Marion Wynne-Davies (eds), *Readings in Renaissance Women's Drama: Criticism, History and Performance 1594–1998* (pp. 47–59). London: Routledge.

Beilin, Elaine V. (1987). *Redeeming Eve: Women Writers of the English Renaissance.* Princeton, NJ: Princeton University Press.

Blaine, Virginia, Grundy, Isobel and Clements, Patricia (eds) (1990). *The Feminist Companion to Literature in English.* New Haven, CT: Yale University Press.

Burke, Victoria (1997). 'Women and early seventeenth-century manuscript culture: four Miscellanies.' *The Seventeenth Century*, 12, 135–50.

Collins, An (1653). *Divine Songs and Meditacions.* London.

Ezell, Margaret J. M. (1998). '"To be your daughter in your pen": the social functions of literature in the writings of Lady Elizabeth Brackley and Lady Jane Cavendish.' In S. P. Cerasano and Marion Wynne-Davies (eds), *Readings in Renaissance Women's Drama: Criticism, History and Performance 1594–1998* (pp. 246–58). London: Routledge.

——(1999). *Social Authorship and the Advent of Print.* Baltimore, MD: Johns Hopkins University Press.

Ferguson, Margaret W. (1991). 'Renaissance concepts of the "woman writer".' In Helen Wilcox (ed.), *Women and Literature in Britain 1500–1700* (pp. 143–68). Cambridge: Cambridge University Press.

Goreau, Angeline (1985). *The Whole Duty of a Woman: Female Writers in Seventeenth-Century England.* Garden City, NY: Dial Press.

Greer, Germaine, Medoff, Jeslyn, Sansone, Melinda and Hastings, Susan (eds) (1988). *Kissing the Rod: An Anthology of 17th Century Women's Verse.* London: Virago Press.

Hannay, Margaret P. (1985). 'Introduction.' In M. P. Hannay (ed.), *Silent But for the Word: Tudor Women as Patrons, Translators, and Writers of Religious Works* (pp. 1–14). Kent, OH: Kent State University Press.

Hobby, Elaine (1989). *Virtue of Necessity: English Women's Writing 1649–88.* Ann Arbor: University of Michigan Press.

King, Kathryn R. (1994). 'Jane Barker, *Poetical Creations*, and the social text.' *English Literary History*, 61, 551–70.

Klene, Jean (1998). 'Introduction.' In J. Klene (ed.), *The Southwell–Sibthorpe Commonplace Book, Folger MS V.b.198* (pp. xi–xliii). Tempe, AZ: Medieval and Renaissance Texts and Studies.

——(2000). '"Monument of an Endless affection": Folger MS V.b.198 and Lady Anne Southwell.' In Peter Beal and Margaret J. M. Ezell (eds), *English Manuscript Studies 1100–1700*, vol. 9 (pp. 165–86). London: British Library.

Lamb, Mary Ellen (1990). *Gender and Authorship in the Sidney Circle.* Madison: University of Wisconsin Press.

Lewalski, Barbara K. (1993). *Writing Women in Jacobean England.* Cambridge, MA: Harvard University Press.

McDowell, Paula (1998). *The Women of Grub Street: Press, Politics, and Gender in the London Literary Marketplace, 1678–1730.* Oxford: Clarendon Press.

Pearson, Jacqueline (1988). *The Prostituted Muse: Images of Women and Women Dramatists 1642–1737.* New York: St Martin's Press.

Prior, Mary (ed.) (1985). *Women in English Society, 1500–1800.* London: Methuen.

'S.C.' (1701). *The Life of Lady Halkett.* Edinburgh.

Schleiner, Louise (1994). *Tudor and Stuart Women Writers.* Bloomington: University of Indiana Press.

Stevenson, Jane (2000). 'Women, writing and scribal publication in the sixteenth century.' In Peter Beal and Margaret J. M. Ezell (eds), *English Manuscript Studies 1100–1700*, vol. 9 (pp. 1–32). London: British Library.

Todd, Janet (1989). *The Sign of Angellica: Women, Writing and Fiction, 1660–1800.* London: Virago Press.

Weller, Barry and Ferguson, Margaret W. (eds) (1994). Elizabeth Cary. *The Tragedy of Mariam The Fair Queen of Jewry with The Lady Falkland Her Life.* Los Angeles: University of California Press.

Wilcox, Helen (1991). 'Introduction.' In Helen Wilcox (ed.), *Women and Literature in Britain 1500–1700* (pp. 1–6). Cambridge: Cambridge University Press.

Wolfe, Heather (2000). 'The scribal hands and dating of *Lady Falkland Her Life.*' In Peter Beal and Margaret J. M. Ezell (eds), *English Manuscript Studies 1100–1700*, vol. 9 (pp. 187–217). London: British Library.

PART TWO
Readings

6
Isabella Whitney,
A Sweet Nosegay
Patricia Brace

In the British Library a slim volume with 'Isabella Whitney *Poems*' on the spine contains a copy of her *A Sweet Nosegay, or Pleasant Posye*, published in 1573 by Richard Jones. This work is the second of two by a figure who may be able to claim title as the first professional woman writer in England; for Whitney appears to have produced both *The copie of a letter, lately written in meeter, by a yonge gentilwoman: to her unconstant louer* (1567) and *A sweet nosegay*, a verse redaction of Hugh Plat's prose *Floures of philosophie* (1572), in an attempt to ameliorate financial distress. Certainly, her printer was known for his output of lucrative cheap print, such as ballads and popular sensational material. Up to this point, the women whose writings we know of belong to various intellectual and social elites: Margaret Roper and Mary Basset to the humanist circle of Thomas More; Margaret Beaufort, Katherine Parr, the youthful Elizabeth Tudor and Anne Cooke Bacon to aristocratic humanist and Reformist networks; Anne Askew and Ann Lok more tangentially to the same. In neither social nor literary terms does Whitney fit easily into this immediate tradition. She was in service, uses humanist rhetorical strategies and tropes without a display of erudition, shows broad familiarity with liturgy, but not with details of Reformist theology, and deals with matters of social concern but through an unmediated first-person speaker. This essay will argue that in *A sweet nosegay* Whitney uses her discursive practice to combat her low social status. While she emphasizes her desire for the text to generate revenue, Whitney gathers textual fragments in order to create symbolic wealth and then shapes this material into a demonstration of her alliance with the existing social order. Thus, while Whitney acknowledges her marginal social position, she uses her poems to transform it into literary authority.

While biographical information about Isabella Whitney is limited to suggestive traces within her work, she was likely raised in Smithfield (Schleiner 1994: 7), although perhaps born in Cheshire (Plat 1982: xviii). Her brother was Geoffrey Whitney, whose collection of emblems has received substantial critical attention. She certainly worked as a gentlewoman-in-waiting to a lady near London in her early adulthood, where 'her way of life was little different from that of literate merchants' daughters who might serve a high-ranking lady' (Schleiner 1994: 7). All of these details situate Whitney in a context in which economic issues are central, for Smithfield was the site of a market that figures prominently in late sixteenth- and early seventeenth-century city comedies, including Middleton and Dekker's *The Roaring Girl* and Jonson's *Epicoene* and *Bartholomew Fair*, which address relationships between gender and economics. Since Whitney appears to have lost her job as a result of malicious gossip by another servant (Jones 1990: 30; Schleiner 1994: 4), the publication of *A sweet nosegay* seems to have had a double purpose – to make some money from its sale to Richard Jones and to regain her employment – for she selects and orders Plat's aphorisms in such a way as 'to present an indirect plea for the restoration of her post' (Schleiner 1994: 4). The probable occasion for *The copie of a letter* was the jilting of Whitney by a fiancé because of an insufficient dowry (Beilin 1987: 91), an event that looks like a failed bid to cross a class boundary. However, Whitney's poems appeared in only a single edition each and were not reprinted until 1906, when *The copie of a letter* appeared in volume 8 of Edward Arber's *An English Garner.*

Whitney's negotiation of the uneasy relationship between gender and the economics of print emerges immediately in the prefatory material to *A sweet nosegay*, which serves both to 'frame' the main text by directing its interpretation and to position the author in relation to both the text and the print market. As a humanist strategy for both textual production and moral education, framing has, at its core, an interpretive and transformative impulse that makes it available to Whitney as a metaphor for authorship as a productive process; it also positions that authorship in relation to a literary marketplace beginning to identify labour as a component of the commodified book. As a process of creating meaning through gathered fragments of material by selecting, arranging and assimilating them so that 'the authority of the source is maintained while the production of new texts is made possible' (Crane 1993: 17), framing situates the author within the bounds of a group of precursor texts, a position that implies guidance by those forebears. Indeed, a principle behind this element of humanist education is that the act of gathering textual fragments facilitates absorption of their moral content, so that the student's moral fibre is shaped or framed by this active reading (Halpern 1991: 38, 78). In accounts of humanist education, the achievement of framing textual fragments so that they produce a new and coherent whole marks the success of the moral programme. On the other hand, reliance on gathering and framing as the basis for composition grants the same kind of formative power to the contemporary author (Crane 1993: 22) and extends beyond the domain of textual production to a broader notion of agency as the capacity to engage in transformative labour. This kind of agency is embodied in the student's facility with persuasive speech and writing, whose practical application lies in the achievement of a position in the world of politics and government (Halpern

1991: 23; Crane 1993: 13). Transformative labour, then, is represented as a kind of currency that can be used to construct a relationship with a patron or with an audience.

However, the potential offered by framing as a means to establish agency is certainly not unproblematic for women; there are very real tensions between, on the one hand, humanist agency and a rigidly stratified social structure and, on the other, between the humanist emphasis on the power of speech and gender ideologies that require women to be 'chaste, silent and obedient' (Hull 1982: 143). Humanist education offered the potential for its students to rise socially by their own efforts and earning power, a freedom of social movement that was greeted with anxiety and legislative efforts at containment. For example, sumptuary laws designated the types of cloth and styles of clothing permissible for wear by people of different classes, while other legislation criminalized vagrancy in an effort to prevent the migration of 'masterless men' from the countryside to the city. The basis for humanist upward mobility is the eloquence developed through a programme of reading. However, the link between labour and political and economic agency is suppressed in humanist accounts of education for women. Reading 'became a means of occupying women's weak and wandering minds with wholesome thoughts' (Wayne 1985: 20). For example, in his preface to Margaret More Roper's translation, *A Devout Treatise on the Pater Noster* (1526), Richard Hyrde argues that 'redyng and studyeng of bokes so occupieth the mynde that it can haue no leyser to muse or delyte in other fantasies whan in all handy werkes that men saye be more mete for a woman the body may be busy in one place and the mynde walkyng in another' (Roper 1526: Aivr).

Whitney expresses these tensions in her prefatory epistle to George Mainwaring in *A sweet nosegay.* In her account of the process of the production of her text, Whitney uses the organic metaphor of the garden as the source of her material in order to reposition herself as an author in a literary marketplace. She begins in the feminized domain of the household, noting that

> When I . . . had made this simple Nosegaye: I was in mind to bestow the same on som dere frend. . . . But wayting with myselfe, that although the Flowers bound in the same were good: yet so little of my labour was in them that they were not (as I wysh they should) to be exteemed [*sic*] as recompense. (Aiiiir)

Since Whitney identifies gathering as the initial step in production ('the Flowers bound in the same were good'), the opportunity for agency is located in this intervention. However, collecting in itself is inadequate without the work of shaping or framing that presents gathered material in a changed form. For Whitney, as for humanist theorists of the period, the labour exerted on the raw material is the element that turns it into something new. Also like the humanists, she attaches economic worth to transformative labour, here through a shift from a domestic and organic frame of reference to a mercantile one. Whitney reconceives the garden as a storehouse of material when she argues that 'though they be of an others growing, yet considering they be of mine owne gathering and making up: respect my labour and regard my good wil' (Aiiiiv). Her new product accrues value explicitly through her labour. Later in the letter to Mainwaring, Whitney uses a pun on 'slip' to link the horticultural trope to literary practice. She enjoins Mainwaring to 'savor to these SLIPS in which I trust you shal find safety: And if you take pleasure in them, I shall not only be occasioned to endeavor myself to make a further viage [voyage] for a more daintier thing' (Avr). As well as belonging to the domain of horticultural labour, the slips here are also paper – the pages of quatrains that, bound together, make up Whitney's 'nosegay'. The final step in the movement to a mercantile world occurs when Whitney indicates that the highly feminized and domestic act of arranging flowers will work according to the laws of the market: if her audience indicates a demand, she will undertake the work to supply further goods of the same type.

Whitney's mercantile discourse extends into the representation of her relationships with Mainwaring as patron and with her audience. She makes an explicit plea for patronage as a relationship of exchange, although located within the domain of friendship. Whitney initiates the exchange and controls the object that passes between them, while the book functions as a token of exchange to discharge debts in the past. She says:

> I come to present you like the porre man which hauing no goods, came with his hands full of water to reuere the Persian Prince withal, who . . . did not disdayne his simple Guift: . . . I being willinge to bestowe some Present on you, by the same thinking to make part of amendes for the much that you haue merited. (Aiiiiv)

Whitney makes an interesting equivocation in this passage. Although she here asserts the book's valuelessness and inadequacy as currency, in the rest of the letter she makes frequent reference to the value of her labour, embodied by the book, and insists on its status as currency when she says 'accept this my labour, for recompence of al that which you are unrecompenced for' (Avr). This ambivalence shows Whitney backing away from the boldness of constructing a non-familial and secular patronage situation but still not closing it off entirely.

Whitney's prefatory poem to *A sweet nosegay* is especially interesting because of the way in which she yokes humanist methods of textual production to real market concerns through the trope of the garden, which functions as a space for both leisure and work. Whitney figures her visit to the garden as a leisure activity, for the woman has 'reposed one howre . . . Amongst those Beds so bravely decked, / with every goodly Flower: / And Banks and Borders finely framed' and once a day has 'viewd that braue prospect' (Aviv). At the end of the epistle to the reader Whitney notes that, if one goes to 'Plat his Plot', one should 'take heed it is a Maze' (180). While pointing out the garden's complexity, she also implies a moneyed world of leisure in which people explore mazes created from shrubs. As it does for the ideal humanist lady, learning occupies Whitney's time and keeps her from harm. However, Whitney resists the script for the female humanist subject; for, after marking the garden as a place of repose, she notes that she has had to leave it because she 'leisure lacked, / and business bade me hie' (65–6). The economic world impinges on the privacy and safe containment of the garden. Conversely, her teacher, Fortune, is female and while she directs Whitney to this particular source, Whitney chooses how often she returns, noting that she is able 'to come when as I wyll' (90) and that her will controls the gathering of the material, for she may 'chuse all of his Flowers / which may my fancy fill' (91–2). She claims agency based on her ability to accept, reject and select her material.

The poem contains a narrative description of her sources, an account that links her use of the image of the garden to other humanist tropes for literary borrowing. The Bible, Virgil, Ovid, Mantuan and history books function as locations that Whitney occupies, in which she attempts to educate herself and from which she absorbs material, leaving them when Fortune guides her to her major source, Hugh Plat's *Floures of philosophie* ('Plat his Plot'). The central motif she uses is of the 'slip', commenting that 'A slip I took to smell unto' (71). This image yokes the practice of borrowing from a literary source with the metaphor of the garden and belongs to the tradition of representations of transformative literary imitation, especially metaphors in which the precursor texts are left intact, while the successor uses material drawn from them to create a new and different work (Greene 1982: 192; Pigman 1980: 4). Whitney is careful to mark her borrowing as non-aggressive as she directs others:

> . . . such as will with order get,
>   may gather whilst they list.
> Then pity were it to destroy,
>   what he with pain did plant.
>   (83–6)

Whitney reinforces her understanding of this form of borrowing as the ideal when, toward the end of the poem, she warns,

> For though he make no spare of them,
>   to such as have good skill:
> To slip, to shear, or get in time,
>   and not his branches kill:
> Yet bars he out, such greedy guts,
>   as come with spite to toot [pry].
> And without skill, both Herb and Flower
>   pluck rashly by the root.
>   (153–60)

This use of the image of slipping constructs transformative labour as the element that gives texts their value, for to refuse the agency of transformation indicates greed, spite, ineptitude and rashness.

In her 'Farewell to the Reader', which forms the other half of the paratextual frame, Whitney justifies her position in the literary marketplace, and thus her authorial agency, on the basis of her transformative labour. In the face of mixed response to her work, she comments, 'my mind is fully satisfied' (35). What she desires is for the text, whose parts 'the which to get some pain I took, / and travailed many hours' (3–4), to circulate:

> I must request you spoil them not,
>   nor do in pieces tear them:
> But if thyself do loathe the scent,
>   give others leave to wear them.
> I shall no whit be discontent,
>   for nothing is so pure:
> But one, or other will mislike
>   thereof we may be sure. (11.5–12)

The fact of Whitney's labour bestows value on a work that deserves to circulate in its own right.

In the treatment of Hugh Plat's aphorisms that forms the core of the volume, Whitney practises a version of humanist gathering and framing by selecting, ordering and rephrasing his quasi-philosophic statements to suit her central concerns: loyalty, economic misfortune and self-restraint. Her groupings of stanzas concentrate overwhelmingly on power, the regulation of social behaviour and ranging from the value and treatment of friends to the danger of ambition and the powerlessness of the poor in a legal system determined by wealth. What is most interesting is that, while Whitney advocates careful consideration of the sources of accusations against others (stanzas 10–16), wariness of ambition (stanzas 47–51) and treating neighbours well (stanzas 89–100), the advice is directed to the socially powerful and requires their self-regulation because, as a woman without employment, Whitney is not in a position to enforce these rules of conduct. For the weak, Whitney also prescribes self-control in warning against, for example, the dangers of despair (stanzas 45–6) and suicide (stanza 87) and loose tongues (stanzas 105–9). Rather than arguing for radical social change, Whitney favours a more benevolent version of the status quo, concluding, in 'A sovereign receipt', with a message of self-preservation that exhorts her readers 'the juice of all these Flowers take, / and make thee a conserve: / And use it first and last: / and it will safely thee preserve' (1–4). While she invokes humanist practice here by encouraging her readers to engage in the gathering of textual fragments, her goal is conservative in that they are to use the product of their gathering to shape and contain themselves.

Whitney recommends a similarly conservative approach to order in the poems that conclude the volume, 'An Order Prescribed' and the 'Wyll and Testament'. In the preceding verse epistles to her brothers, Geoffrey and Brooke, and to her cousin, F. W., Whitney shifts the focus from a general concern for the less powerful to the theme of the social and economic instability of her position by pointing out that she has lost contact with her family. In the poems to the brothers she suggests that she does not know 'how to send: / Or where to hearken of your health' ('G. W.' 5–6) and 'none can tell, if you be well, / nor where you do sojourn' ('B. W.' 3–4). These statements justify the appearance of the letters in a printed volume, rather than as private correspondence, but also show Whitney's isolation from a household. To both brothers, she emphasizes the vagaries of 'fortune' as the cause of her fiscal distress, which might be alleviated by appealing to friends or 'next our Parents dear' ('G. W.' 13–14). However, having represented herself as divorced from households of both birth and service, she recuperates her position. Whitney tells Geoffrey Whitney that the *Nosegay* is for 'a virtuous Lady, which / till death I honor will: / The loss I had of service hers, / I languish for it still' ('G. W.' 29–32). Because ties to her mistress transcend money and work, Whitney, despite her unemployment, is really still in service.

In the epistle to her sister, Anne, who has a husband and children, Whitney frames her position slightly differently by de-emphasizing her financial problems and the role of fortune, but retains her emphasis on the stability of her bonds of loyalty to social superiors. As with Whitney's former mistress, the relationship with Anne is figured as an exchange, but simultaneously as necessary and natural: 'nature did you bind: / To do me good: and to requite, / hath nature me inclined' ('A. B.' 8–10). As the sister securely established in an appropriate female milieu, Anne occupies the same kind of position as Whitney's former mistress, the 'virtuous Lady'. Similarly, the ties of this relationship lie beyond the control of either party, and Whitney represents herself as one innately inclined toward the bonds of community. The poem concludes with a statement that Whitney's engagement in writing is an interim measure, for 'Had I a Husband, or a house, / and all that 'longs thereto / Myself could frame about to rouse, / as other women do: / But till some household cares me tie, / My books and Pen I will apply' ('A. B.' 37–42). Whitney repositions herself within a household order, tacit acknowledgement that her writing, the result of losing a position that would likely have constituted an interim step toward marriage for a young woman (Sharpe 1987: 210–11; Phillippy 1998: 446), may represent deviation from this ideal. Thus, in the verse epistles to her brothers and older sister, Whitney uses the medium of print – which marks the instability of her economic position and the potential for disorder that she, as a masterless woman, represents – to place herself on the side of authority and order by pointing out her adherence to social norms.

In 'An Order Prescribed', a verse epistle to her two younger sisters, both in service in London, Whitney uses the act of writing and her tenuous economic position to produce an authoritative discourse based on its insistence, at all levels, on adherence to order. Like the aphorisms that precede it, the poem takes the form of a set of rules (possibly playing on the 'rule' governing a religious order) that deal sententiously with morning prayers, doing one's work well, not engaging in gossip, keeping secrets, honouring one's betters, and evening prayers. These regulations give the poem a legalistic tone and structure. At the same time as the poem organizes a day in the life of a maidservant, the bracketing of those details with morning and evening prayers moves the poem from a heavenly to an earthly domain and back again. This hierarchical ordering of earth and heaven is reinforced by the phrase 'To live to die, to die to live' (19) in the first 'rule'. Here Whitney's chiasmic phrase creates a rhetorical loop that renders a spiritual progression from earth to heaven inevitable.

Reinforcing this double frame of 'order' as both hierarchy and law is the imperative mood that characterizes the narrative voice. Whitney's speaker commands her audience: 'Peruse these lines, observe the rules' (3); 'forget not to commend' (10); 'Then justly do such deeds, / as are to you assigned: / All wanton toys, good sisters now / exile out of your mind' (21–4). Each stanza opens with a command that serves to locate the sisters within a hierarchy and to exhort them to approved behaviours. Grammatical authority belongs to Whitney as the speaker of the regulations, and she takes on the role of arbiter of female behaviour from a position outside her sisters' situation as servants. The sisters are 'subject' in two ways, for they are both the grammatical subjects, the enactors of each rule, and subjected to the speaker of the imperatives.

In terms of social expectations of class and gender, Whitney comes out firmly on the side of a hierarchical 'order'. In the instructions for her sisters' morning prayers, the speaker places the sisters within multiple social hierarchies as they are to pray (in this order) for themselves, their parents, friends, teachers and governors (13–15). In the same stanza their work is figured in terms of the moral necessity of service, for they are to 'justly do such deeds, / as are to you assigned' (21–2). Here the multiple meanings of 'just' (full, complete, right) imply an obligation to meet the standard required by the assigner. This sense of 'justice' also appears in stanza 5, when Whitney comments:

> And sith that virtue guides,
>   where both of you do dwell:
> Give thanks to God, and painful be
>   to please your rulers well.
>   (61–4)

Whitney appears committed to an order that, from God through the nobility to the servant class, is held together by reciprocal vertical ties. In keeping with this sense of a vertically integrated order, Whitney exhorts her sister-servants to 'see that their

Plate be safe, / and that no Spoon do lack, / See Doors and Windows bolted fast / for fear of any wrack' (81–4). Their job is to defend against the threat of disorder.

Whitney indeed frames herself as an arm of the social order; her words are to be taken seriously because she represents herself as empowered to oversee her sisters:

> All wanton toys, good sisters now
>   exile out of your mind,
> I hope you give no cause,
>   whereby I sould suspect:
>   (23–6)

In this passage Whitney invokes the idea that women's minds naturally wander even if their bodies are busy with tasks. Here, however, the speaker functions as a surveyor concerned not only with what the sisters do but also with what they think. This move specifies the function she attributes to the text at the beginning of the poem, when she notes that its purpose is to stand in for her 'when I / shall further from you dwell' (1–2) and later that 'Henceforth my life as well as Pen / shall your examples frame' (75–6). Her text is to work as a form of social control.

The weakness of the sisters' position here generates a powerful discursive position for Whitney as speaker. Not only does she appropriate the voice of the dominant ideology and engage in surveillance; she also uses her awareness of the danger and weakness of her sisters' position to ground and justify the disruption to gender ideologies posed by her writing when she argues: 'If God do not prevent, / or with his grace expel: / I cannot speak, or write too much, / because I love you well' (29–32). Indirectly here, Whitney gestures toward the silence that her writing and its circulation might violate, but by showing awareness of the potential for transgression and justifying it, she locates herself on the side of ideology.

Finally, in her instructions to her sisters, Whitney addresses directly the problem posed for women in service by the contending views of women's silence. Loose speech, presumably the cause for Whitney's unemployment, is dangerous, and she orders her sisters to

> See that you secrets seal,
>   tread trifles underground:
> If to rehearsal oft you come,
>   it will your quiet wound.
>   (45–8)

On the other hand, this quiet and self-containment, which echoes, in its reference to 'trifles' which must be hidden, Whitney's earlier exhortation to put 'wanton toys' out of mind, has its own dangers. A woman must maintain a careful balance and

Of laughter be not much,
    nor over solemn seem:
For then be sure they'll compt you light
    or proud will you esteem.

(49–52)

To display too much to the audience invokes the link between female speech and
sexual availability or waywardness, but to offer too little, to be too successful in the
containment of speech, brings with it the danger of being unknowable. Thus, while
Whitney appears to embrace the discourse of feminine silence and use it to a significant extent as the model for her 'order' and the ground for her own discursive
authority, she also points out the problems attached to it.

Whitney's complex establishment of authority by pointing out both her social
impotence and her internalized sense of order is rendered in more forceful terms in
the 'Wyll and Testament' that appears at the end of the volume. Preceding the 'Wyll
and Testament' is 'A Communication Which The Author Had To London Before She
Made Her Will'. Here Whitney begins her address to the personified London and lays
the cause of her distress at the feet of the city, for 'Thou never wouldst credit give /
To board me for a year, / Nor with any apparel me relieve / Except thou payed were'
(21–4). Whitney answers this failure on the part of the city as an institution by literally ordering it to permit her to restore what she sees as an appropriate social order:
'Now stand aside and give me leave / To write my latest will, / And see that
none you do deceive / Of that I leave them till' (33–6). Her invocation of the will,
as Wendy Wall argues, presents Whitney with a nearly unassailable, albeit ironic,
position of authority. She speaks with the authority of the liminal moment of death,
but is of course very much alive ('whole in body and in mind, / But very weak in
purse') and has nothing to bequeath, but is about to give away an entire city (Wall
1991: 35).

The disruption here is curious. Whitney inserts herself into a legal and economic sphere in which, as a young, unmarried woman, she has no standing and
which her fiscal distress denies her, but again recuperates her position by adhering
very closely to rules – of form and of social structure. That is, she reframes herself
by gathering and framing the fragments that make up her city. Throughout, the
poem follows the pattern of the will in that beneficiaries are named and specific
bequests made, with the imperatives that typify such statements. Her account of
various areas of London orders the city both topographically and socially by placing
different trades in locations in which the commerce that links merchant and gentry
classes takes place.

The focus of the second half of the poem is on the poor, who are seen as most potentially disorderly in contemporary pamphlet literature and other forms of social
writing. While Whitney enumerates the institutions that contain the poor and maintain order – Counter, Newgate and Fleet prisons, St Bartholemew's, Bedlam and

Bridewell hospitals – she points out their failure. Whitney comments that she had intended to reserve Ludgate, a debtor's prison, for herself, but

> I am not now in case to lie,
>   Here is no place of jest;
> I did reserve that for myself
>   If I my health possessed
> And ever came in credit so
>   A debtor for to be.
>   (177–82)

The problem is that no one will give Whitney credit enough to become a debtor (183–90), and she is too virtuous to wind up in Bridewell. The social order thus fails her.

However, Whitney's economic catastrophe forms the basis for her knowledge of the real workings of external forces for order and the necessity for self-regulation in the face of their inadequacy. While she leaves the buildings, streets and people to London and outlines the functions of the various hospitals and prisons, Whitney is the one who actually looks after the citizens, by bequeathing various necessities (food, clothing, money) to the people in the streets. She notes:

> For salt, oatmeal, candles, soap,
>   Or what you else do want,
> In many places shops are full;
>   I left you nothing scant.
> If they that keep what I you leave
>   Ask money when they sell it,
> At Mint there is such store it is
>   Unpossible to tell it.
>   (105–12)

Whitney thus becomes the centre of a reordering of the social and economic world in which she has lived, a function enabled by the imperative mood of the will. Her final address to London at the end of the poem reinforces this sense. Whitney insists: 'When I am gone, with conscience / Let them disbursed be' (259–60). Her echo of the divine fiat presents London with an inescapable task that carries moral weight because the disbursement must be done 'with conscience'. As in 'An Order Prescribed' Whitney derives authority from a position outside the economic order through the delineation of an internalized moral order that accords with the demands of gender and class.

Throughout *A sweet nosegay* Isabella Whitney engages in a complex negotiation of gender, class and print. Her economic motivation for producing her texts shows her actions to be transformative, as attempts either to call attention to or rectify her financially catastrophic situation. In her works she points out and attempts to rewrite in economic terms the gendered ideological scripts that are acted out to her disadvantage. Whitney's orientation is clearly toward both labour and print markets, as her use of framing as a process of discursive production shows, but her awareness of the gendered boundaries of these discursive and material practices results in an equivocal representation of her agency as she invokes ideological norms that she acknowledges herself breaking, uses discourse to repair those disruptions, indicates the instability of her social position and assumes an authoritative discursive stance. Ultimately, through the multiple potentials offered by 'order' as a version of framing she reshapes the experience of social impotence into literary authority.

See also WOMEN'S POETRY 1550–1700

REFERENCES AND FURTHER READING

Arber, Edward E. (ed.) (1906). *An English Garner. Ingatherings from our history and literature*, vol. 8. London: A. Constable.
Beilin, Elaine (1987). *Redeeming Eve: Women Writers of the English Renaissance*. Princeton, NJ: Princeton University Press.
Crane, Mary Thomas (1993). *Framing Authority: Sayings, Self, and Society in Sixteenth-Century England*. Princeton, NJ: Princeton University Press.
Greene, Thomas (1982). *The Light in Troy: Imitation and Discovery in Renaissance Poetry*. New Haven, CT: Yale University Press.
Halpern, Richard (1991). *The Poetics of Primitive Accumulation: English Renaissance Culture and the Genealogy of Capitalism*. Ithaca, NY: Cornell University Press.
Hull, Suzanne (1982). *Chaste, Silent and Obedient: English Books for Women, 1475–1640*. San Marino, CA: Huntington Library.
Jones, Ann Rosalind (1990). *The Currency of Eros: Women's Love Lyric in Europe, 1540–1620*. Bloomington: Indiana University Press.
Phillippy, Patricia (1998). 'The maid's lawful liberty: service, the household, and "Mother B" in Isabella Whitney's *A Sweet Nosegay*.' *Modern Philology*, 95, 439–62.
Pigman, G. W., III (1980). 'Versions of imitation in the Renaissance.' *Renaissance Quarterly*, 23, 1–32.
Plat, Hugh (1982). *The Floures of Philosophie (1572)*, ed. R. Panofsky. Delmar: Scholars' Facsimiles and Reprints.
Roberts, Michael (1990). 'Women and work in sixteenth-century English towns.' In P. J. Corfield and D. Keene (eds), *Work in Towns 850–1850* (pp. 86–102). Leicester: Leicester University Press.
Roper, Margaret (trans.) (1526). *A Devout Treatise on the Pater Noster*. STC 10477.
Schleiner, Louise (1994). *Tudor and Stuart Women Writers*. Bloomington: Indiana University Press.
Sharpe, J. A. (1987). *Early Modern England: A Social History 1550–1760*. London: Edward Arnold.
Travitsky, Betty (1980). 'The "Wyll and Testament" of Isabella Whitney.' *English Literary Renaissance*, 10, 76–94.
Wall, Wendy (1991). 'Isabella Whitney and the female legacy.' *English Literary History*, 58, 35–62.
——(1993). *The Imprint of Gender: Authorship and Publication in the English Renaissance*. Ithaca, NY: Cornell University Press.

Wayne, Valerie (1985). 'Some sad sentence: Vives' *Instruction of a Christian Woman.'* In M. P. Hannay (ed.), *Silent But For the Word: Tudor Women as Patrons, Translators and Writers of Religious Works.* Kent, OH: Kent State University Press.

Whitney, Isabella (1567). *The Copie of a Letter, Lately Written in Meeter, By a Yonge Gentilwoman: To her Unconstant Louer.* STC 25439.

——(1573). *A Sweet nosgay, or pleasant posye: contayning a hundred and ten Phylosophicall Flowers.* STC 25440.

Woods, Susanne (ed.) (2000). *The Poets: Isabella Whitney, Anne Dowriche, Aemilia Lanyer, Rachel Speght and Diana Primrose.* Aldershot: Ashgate/Scolar Press.

7

Mary Sidney, Countess of Pembroke, *Psalmes*

Debra K. Rienstra

The Countess of Pembroke makes an attractive and fascinating member of the small cohort current scholars piece together as 'early modern women writers'. But she herself would probably have identified with others of her class and religion before others of her gender. Both her Protestantism and her class helped shape a cultural space in which she could write, but her position as a countess in particular set her apart from many other writing women in the period. Her parents, Henry Sidney and Mary Dudley, were each members of influential Protestant families raised to prominence during the reign of Henry VIII, and when she married Henry Herbert at age 15, she married into an even more powerful Protestant family. Such a birth and marriage came with some advantages: she received an exceptional education under the supervision of private tutors, and she had access to books and intellectual conversation to further that education on her own. Moreover, cultural norms proscribing female speech and urging silence and humility as the ideal for women did not always apply as stringently to a countess as to someone of a lesser class position. An aristocratic woman might be honoured for her learning – provided her learning contributed to that most important of feminine qualities: virtue. Aristocratic Protestant women, especially, such as Ann Lok, Anne Cooke Bacon and Lady Jane Grey, had, by the late sixteenth century, created a small tradition of exercising virtuous learning by speaking out or writing for the Protestant cause. Lady Jane Grey, Mary Sidney's aunt, was featured in Foxe's *Actes and Monuments*, and the others had translated Protestant sermons, commentaries and treatises. So Mary Sidney's class and religion provided the resources and a limited cultural endorsement for literary activity not available to many women.

Mary Sidney – usually referred to as 'Pembroke' – had one other enormous advantage over other writing women of the period: her brother Sir Philip Sidney. By all contemporary accounts, Sidney was an extraordinary person: brilliant, charming, a rising star among Protestant aristocrats and intellectuals in England and on the

Continent. Among his other ambitions, Sidney hoped to improve what he considered the dismal state of English literature, an ambition he comments on famously in his *Defence of Poesy*. Wilton, the country estate in Wiltshire over which his sister presided after her marriage, served for several critical years as a home base for Sidney's own writing and for gatherings of literary-minded friends. Pembroke's level of participation in the literary discussions in this period is unknown, but she certainly enjoyed an affectionate and collegial relationship with her brother. His dedication to her of his prose romance *Arcadia* indicates that he wrote it for her (and their friends): 'You desired me to doe it', he wrote, 'and your desire to my heart is an absolute commandment. Now, it is done onely for you, only to you'. Sidney also evidently considered his sister a discerning reader and critic, indicating that *Arcadia* was written 'in loose sheetes of paper, most of it in your presence, the rest, by sheets, sent unto you as fast as they were done'.

When Sidney died in 1586 at age 32 of a wound received defending the Protestant cause in the Netherlands, Pembroke entered a period of deep mourning, one already initiated by the death of her small daughter in 1584 and both her parents earlier in 1586. During his life, Sidney provided Pembroke with inspiration and companionship in writing and reading. But his death, terrible as it was, opened to her even greater opportunity. She carefully nurtured his legacy as a writer, crafting that legacy into an invitation for her to adopt a more public role as writer and patron. Wilton continued to thrive during the 1590s as a centre of literary activity, now under her supervision. The writers who gathered there, and the members of the household who took up writing with her encouragement, acknowledged Pembroke as Sidney's heir, his phoenix, even a sort of reincarnation of him. While this might seem a way of eclipsing her own literary skill – always the moon to Sidney's sun – in fact Pembroke used the association with her brother to great advantage. The image she helped create for her brother and the space she carved for herself as a writer testify to Pembroke's courage, shrewdness, intelligence and poetic skill.

In the last century, until recently, Pembroke appeared in literary scholarship, if at all, as a footnote to her traditionally canonical brother. During the early period of feminist literary scholarship in the 1970s and 1980s, as part of a broad 'recovery' movement, scholars began to reinvestigate Pembroke's life and to study her work on its own merits. Margaret Hannay's (1990) biography of Pembroke, based on extensive new research, provides a fuller picture of this extraordinary writing woman, reestablishing in particular the place of cultural prominence she enjoyed during her lifetime.

Most fascinating to today's scholars is Pembroke's ability to negotiate the assumptions and proscriptions of her day about writing, publishing and gender. After Sidney's death, Pembroke took it upon herself to publish his works. She probably did so, in part, to establish authoritative editions of works that other of Sidney's associates also wished to publish. She sponsored publication of the 1593 edition of his *Arcadia*, and in 1598 authorized an edition of several of her brother's works. In securing Sidney's legacy as a writer, Pembroke made use of the fairly new medium of print, a medium often considered too public and vulgar a display for aristocratic writers. Shepherding his works into print helped make her own projects appear as natural continuations of what he had begun. She mourned her brother in verse along with his other poet-peers, and took up his translation projects, including the *Psalmes*. Even more remarkable for the 1590s, she published her own works. One of these, *A Discourse of Life and Death*, was a translation of a work by the French theologian Philippe de Mornay. This work falls into the category of Protestant devotional translations, that relatively safe enterprise for writing women of the period. However, Sidney and several of his friends on the Continent had been working on a series of Mornay translations; Pembroke was not seeking a safely feminine pastime, probably, so much as participating with a group of male peers. Moreover, Pembroke did not limit herself to devotional works. Her closet drama *Antonius*, a translation of a French play, went through two printings (*Discourse* was reprinted three times and reissued once), and influenced Samuel Daniel, Shakespeare and Elizabeth Cary. Finally, Pembroke's poem in praise of Elizabeth, 'A Dialogue betweene two shepheards, *Thenot* and *Piers*, in praise of *Astrea*', was printed in an anthology praising Queen Elizabeth. Pembroke, in sum, wrote and even published without apologizing for her gender or even mentioning it; instead, her activities between 1588 and 1601 indicate that she took on a leadership role in a group of writers among whom she was the ranking peer. If Pembroke sustained criticism for her literary initiatives, we have no record of it. Instead, the many references in dedications indicate that poets who knew her respected her not only as a patron but also a fellow writer. One of the most gifted of those who enjoyed her patronage, Samuel Daniel, wrote that her poetry would outlast Wilton House itself. 'By this', he wrote, speaking of Pembroke's *Psalmes*, '[Great Lady], thou must then be knowne, / When Wilton lyes low leuell'd with the ground'. And indeed, Wilton House succumbed to a fire in 1647, while Pembroke's poetry, 400 years later, is enjoying its largest readership ever.

'My Praises Uttmost Skill'

The particular work that Daniel admired most, the *Psalmes*, represents Pembroke's most voluminous and significant literary accomplishment. The *Psalmes* began as one of Sidney's several endeavours to improve English letters. The English tradition had produced numerous clusters of metrical psalms of varying quality, as well as two whole psalters suitable for singing. The most important of these, the Sternhold–Hopkins Psalter, had become the standard songbook in the churches shortly after its introduction in 1562, and young Philip and Mary had grown up singing from it. In this psalter all the psalms are rendered in ballad metre, which was the norm for metrical psalms in English, with the exception of a few other simple metrical variants. The

French psalter, however, which Philip and Mary also knew from childhood, made use of 110 different metrical forms, an artistic accomplishment which Sidney apparently intended to best. He took the more supple use of metre, imagery and lyric subjectivity developing in English love lyric and applied it to poetry imitating the 'unconceivable excellencies of God', the 'chief' kind of poetry according to the *Defence*. In translating the psalms into metre, however, Sidney did not attempt to create a singable psalter. Instead, he apparently wished to create a kind of art piece, a poetic showcase. Before his death Sidney completed his adaptation of the first 43 psalms, each of them rendered in a different metrical form. Pembroke then adopted this project, completed it after many years of effort, composed two dedicatory poems to accompany it (extant in only one manuscript), and circulated it in professionally prepared manuscript form. Because she contributed the bulk of the poems and was responsible for sending it out to readers as a complete unit, the *Psalmes* came to be associated more with Pembroke than with her brother. She herself seems to have valued it as her most important accomplishment, as she chose to be portrayed holding a copy of 'Davids Psalmes' in the 1618 portrait by Simon van de Passe.

The *Psalmes*, or Sidney–Pembroke Psalter, is a fascinatingly unique work: a brother–sister collaboration, a translation, a paraphrase, a scholarly meditation, an artist's sketchbook of poetic forms, a theological–aesthetic proposal and an intensely personal devotional exercise. Perhaps its very strangeness, its defiance of usual literary categories, is the main reason few have studied it until very recently. It was published in 1823 in a limited edition, and several psalms appeared scattered here and there in nineteenth-century anthologies. Between these appearances and J. C. A. Rathmell's 1963 edition, Pembroke's psalms were almost completely ignored, while Sidney's 43 psalms were sometimes included in editions of his collected works. Since Rathmell's edition, studies have appeared on Pembroke's psalms, most notably in the indispensable recent edition of Pembroke's *Complete Works*. But the *Psalmes* circulated in its own day, not as two pieces belonging to two authors, but as a single, complete work. Some of the insights it can provide into literature of the period depend on considering it whole.

For instance, recent studies of early modern writers sometimes consider translated works less interesting or important than 'original works'. Today we tend to prize innovation and novelty above all. This is a prejudice sixteenth-century writers would find puzzling if not foolish. Prevailing notions of art centred on *imitatio*, the idea that the artist is always imitating, whether the subject is nature or tradition; at the same time, the artist adds something unique to the effort. A product of both imitation and inspiration, as we might put it, art was seen as always both old and new, with the balance of imitation to inspiration varying greatly. So, in the sixteenth century, a fine translation was highly prized as an artistic accomplishment.

To propose, then, that Pembroke's psalms, as a translation of religious material, might represent a submerging of her subjectivity or a pious ventriloquism, would not only ignore Sidney's partnership in the project but also oversimplify the nature of translation. It is true that translating religious works was considered a safer activity for a woman than writing love lyrics, for instance, because the nature of the material was thought to keep her 'undisciplined' mind from ranging freely into improper territory. But in fact translation is a freeing-enough enterprise to be full of dangers, especially when the original is a text considered divinely inspired. One of the most difficult things for modern readers to register about the *Psalmes* is the complexity and seriousness, for these writers, of manipulating biblical texts. What does it mean to manipulate an inspired text and still call it a psalm? Does artistic variation represent an assertion of the self before the text, a transposition of the relationship of authority from text-over-reader to reader-over-text? These questions might not occur immediately to the modern reader, but they were primary questions for these poets. Studying the *Psalmes*, therefore, raises issues that require an understanding of sixteenth-century views of scriptural inspiration and the role of art in the devotional life.

Because Protestant scholars considered their work vital in educating the public in scripture and true doctrine, in any of their translation endeavours it was 'perillous to erre', as Thomas Norton put it. Obviously they felt the weight of responsibility most keenly when translating scripture. On the other hand, Protestant admonitions to learn scripture by heart, apply it to one's particular situation, and meditate devotionally upon the text gave adherents a certain freedom with the words of the Bible. This freedom is reflected in Protestant devotional literature of the 1580s and later, in which one sees verses from different psalms, for example, stitched together into prayers for this or that occasion. Metrical psalms nicely demonstrate this tension between faithful transmission of the text and freedom with it. Metrical psalmists had to shuffle words around, substitute a rhyming synonym for the word used in the translation, and so on, in order to get the psalm to fit the metre; but overall, an aesthetic of plain, transparent transmission applied. To present the text of scripture in fancy dress was considered dangerously inappropriate. For one thing, scripture was supremely beautiful, and needed no decoration. Moreover, any fanciness would draw attention to the skill of the poet, distracting the reader (or singer) from the text itself. The poet was supposed to acknowledge the authority of the text over himself and his readers, and choose poetic strategies that reflected that clear relationship.

In the *Psalmes*, however, Sidney and Pembroke rather emphatically reject this aesthetic of plainness, of transparent transmission, and affirm the Protestant validation of the individual's voice in response to scripture. That both poets took that principle further than their predecessors reflects Sidney's insistence, expressed in the *Defence*, upon the value of human inventiveness, the creating human reflecting the image of the Creator God. Pembroke took this basic approach further than Sidney, more liberally rearranging and expanding upon her material, creating speakers who exuberantly celebrate 'uttmost skill' and originality in the singing of divine song. Pembroke's translation of Psalm 111, for example, seems to drape her own passion for the work on the psalmist's basic framework:

At home, abroad most willingly I will
Bestow on god my praises uttmost skill:
Chaunting his workes, workes of unmatched might,
Deem'd so by them, who in their search delight.

(ll. 1–4)

Instead of effacing herself before the sacred original, deliberately subsuming artistry to the 'matter' as previous metrical psalmists did, Pembroke's poetic subjectivity operates in collaboration with the authoritative text; she asserts her own stylistic ingenuity and meditative idiosyncrasies upon and even against non-metrical translations.

This is not to say that either of the Sidneys approached their task with frivolous disregard for the authority of their scriptural source. On the contrary, to discern the spirit of the texts and re-speak them required study and meditation upon each psalm. Neither Sidney nor Pembroke explicitly Christianizes the Psalms or places interpretive overlays upon them in which, for instance, Geneva becomes Zion and the psalmists' enemies Roman Catholics – as some metrical psalmists did, and as the marginal notes to the Geneva Bible frequently do. Instead, they transpose each psalm's thought structure and emotive landscape into a sophisticated Elizabethan idiom while retaining (for the most part) the original psalmists' non-systematic, pre-Christian attitudes about God, the world and human beings. To inform this process both Sidney and Pembroke sought authoritative help. They based their poems mainly on the two most authoritative translations available: the Geneva Bible and Coverdale's Book of Common Prayer translation, also considering a Latin translation and the French psalter, among other sources. Pembroke's psalms especially reveal that she consulted the latest and best Protestant commentaries translated by her own associates, including John Calvin's commentaries on the Psalms, translated by Arthur Golding, and Theodore Beza's commentaries, translated by Anthony Gilby. In 25 cases early drafts are extant, allowing readers to note Pembroke's characteristic progress from an early version fairly close to the Common Prayer or Geneva translation to a finished version reflecting a stronger interpretive slant, more dramatic speech, and more skilful use of formal elements. The *Psalmes* can be considered a 'School of English versification', as Hallett Smith wrote of them in 1946, but also the tracings of highly personal, meditative study.

While the *Psalmes* can sometimes seem quaint or overwrought on a first reading, they do reward careful study, particularly when examined alongside the Geneva or Common Prayer Psalms. For the original readers of the poems, for whom the English (and perhaps Latin or French) translations of the Psalms were deeply familiar, echoes of phrasing or imagery in the *Psalmes* were immediately recognizable. For most readers today, gaining the pleasure both of familiarity and surprise in these poems requires more deliberate comparison and analysis. To guide that process in the study of Pembroke's psalms, readers can observe several characteristics of her style, taking note of the marked difference between her translation method and that of contemporary

English metrical psalmists. The elaborately varied metrical forms are the most readily noticeable feature; but Pembroke also moulded complex grammatical structures from the simple proximities of Hebrew style, added rhetorical figures, and intensified already bold and earthy images to create the particular effects of the poems. Finally, the way she handles difficult material and the boldness of the speaker's stance before the divine also set these poems apart from previous efforts to naturalize the Psalms to the English tongue.

'Measured by Melodious Eare' (Psalm 49.5)

Pembroke followed Sidney's lead in rendering each psalm in a unique metrical form. Since Sidney died with 107 psalms left to transpose, Pembroke invented by far the greater number of forms. In fact, earlier drafts display still more variants than in the most finished version of the psalter, so that Pembroke's psalms alone exhibit a total of 118 different metrical forms. These forms, like Sidney's, are all based on variations in line length, rhyme scheme, type of rhyme (masculine, feminine and even triple-rhymes) and stanza length. In addition to this, the best manuscripts contain a series of eight psalms, Psalms 120–7, in quantitative metre, reflecting the Sidney circle's experimentation with adapting Latin and Greek poetic forms to English.

The *Psalmes* exhibit a kind of jubilant play with these forms: an echo poem (Psalm 13), an acrostic (Psalm 117) and some clear attempts at rhyming *tours de force* (49, 55, 76). One example of an ingenious metrical form, Psalm 140, displays what might be called a wrap-around rhyme scheme. Each stanza has six lines of five feet each. The final syllable of the second foot rhymes with the final syllable of the last foot of the previous line, although the last line is adjusted to create a couplet with the penultimate line. The rhyme scheme is thus:

(f)   a
(a)   b
(b)   c
(c)   d
(d)   e
(f)   e

(The internal rhyme sound in the first and last lines remains the same throughout the five stanzas, while the others vary.) The result is a subtle music, lending dignity to the angered pleadings of this psalm:

> But yeeld ô Lord, that ev'n the head of those
> that me enclose, of this their hott pursute
> may tast the frute: with deadly venome stong

of their owne tongue, loe, loe, I see they shall,
yea coales shall fall, yea flames shall fling them low,
ay unrestor'd, to drown in deepest wo.

(ll. 19–24)

Whereas in the original the speaker in this passage remains in the imperative, requesting God's punishment upon his enemies, Pembroke's speaker draws the confident declarations from the end of the psalm into this earlier passage. The transition from making the request to witnessing its fulfilment, 'loe, loe', occurs after the caesura, creating the effect of surprise. The 'yea' and 'ay' in the next lines contribute as well to the dramatic effect of the speaker responding to events in process even as the lines are spinning out. The feelings of the speaker here do not exemplify a pious mercy for one's enemies, but they are true to the text and enhanced by a metrical form which propels the poem forward across the rhymes.

Psalm 92 demonstrates that Pembroke did not randomly apply metrical forms to psalmic material, but attended to the mimetic qualities of the forms. In this psalm each stanza is a series of three expanding tercets, linked by the a-rhyme in the first line of each, so that the syllable count and rhyme scheme create a pattern like this: 4a6b8b 4a6c8c 4a6d8d. The psalm is one of rejoicing and flourishing in the presence of the Lord. Pembroke accents and expands throughout upon the grass and tree metaphors in the text, so that the expanding metre is fittingly suggestive of growth. Even the rhyme scheme 'expands' through the stanza into new sounds, rather than closing with a repeated sound. The first stanza adds the suggestion of spring to prepare for the growth metaphors in the rest of the psalm:

> O lovly thing
> to sing and praises frame
> to thee, ô lord, and thy high name;
> with early spring
> thy bounty to display,
> thy truth when night hathe vanquisht day:
> yea soe to sing,
> that ten string'd instrument
> with lute, and harp, and voice consent.

(ll. 1–9)

While the mimetic potential of metrical forms is an important expressive tool, the purpose of creating so many metrical variants can only be surmised. Rivalry with the French psalter may be one reason Sidney set himself such a task. Expanding the possibilities for and testing the limits of English poetry was undoubtedly another. Pembroke persevered in it for these reasons, but also, perhaps, as an emerging artist's self-discipline. Moreover, the different metres reflect the varied nature of the Psalms themselves. Collected over hundreds of years, assembled from pieces dating from

different periods of Israel's history, taken from a variety of cultic traditions and settings, edited, modified, and finally canonized, the Psalms as a group do not exhibit
the kind of unity that late-sixteenth-century sonnet sequences or other poetry collections valued. The different metrical forms reflect that variety, while the limited scope
of the variants unifies the psalter as an Elizabethan sequence.

Partly as a result of their complex origins, and partly as a result of Hebrew language and style, individual psalms often seem like patchworks of loosely related
thoughts. Connections between verses and sections can often be inferred, but sometimes remain perplexingly elusive. Versifiers of this period typically let these mysteries rest in place, but Pembroke seems always to be seeking ways to mould each
psalm into a unified lyric. This might mean creating a flowing Elizabethan sentence
out of a grab-bag of Hebraic thoughts, subtly explaining shifts in voice or mood, or
otherwise adding structural elements to smooth over the gaps. Psalm 93 illustrates
this characteristic process. Pembroke takes verses 1 and 2,

> The Lord reigneth, & is clothed with maiestie: the Lord is clothed, & girded
> with power: the worlde also shalbe established, that it can not be moued.
>   Thy throne is established of olde: thou art from euerlasting.
> [Geneva]

and creates this complex sentence, with its anaphoric clauses:

> Cloth'd with state and girt with might,
>   Monark-like Jehova raignes:
> he who Earthes foundation pight,
>   pight at first, and yet sustaines.
>   he whose stable throne disdaines
> Motions shock, and ages flight:
>   he who endles one remaines,
> one, the same, in changlesse plight.
>   (ll. 1–8)

The figures of repetition in this and other examples also point to Pembroke's skill
with rhetorical strategies, either for decoration or to provide a framework for the poetic
movement. This rhetorical sophistication – expressive of the Renaissance impulse for
order, rationality, precision and play – distinguishes the *Psalmes* from other metrical
psalms of the period.

While the biblical psalms soar to heights of elegance and beauty in portraying the
excellencies of God, they just as often feature the homely, earthy, even gruesome side
of spiritual experience. Neither Sidney nor Pembroke rid their psalms of the indecorous or rough-edged image; Pembroke, in fact, tends to expand or intensify images

found or suggested in the text. Her typical method is to arrange for an image already in the text to strike her reader more forcefully. Psalm 64.3, for example, uses favourite psalmic images for slanderous enemies:

> Which haue whet their tongue like a sworde, and shot for their arrowes
> bitter wordes. [Geneva]

Pembroke emphasizes this image and enhances the mood of angry protest by allowing her speaker to be more conscious of it, coming up with the image, apparently, even as she speaks:

> For tongues they beare, not tongues, but swordes,
>   so piercing sharp they have them ground:
> and words deliver, shaftes, not words,
>   with bitter dint soe deepe they wound.
>   (ll. 9–12)

Pembroke draws the reader into the image with the speaker's expression of how the enemies' slanders feel – they feel sharp and they wound deeply. The images, in fact, actually arise from those feelings in Pembroke's version. With this example, an extant earlier draft allows us to see how this final version developed from a much less vivid initial effort:

> For their sharp tongues such edg do bear
> As fretted stones give whetted swords
> They levell so with bitter words
> As if not words but shafts they were.
>   (ll. 8–11)

The words 'whetted' and 'bitter' indicate that her first attempt was closer to the language of the Geneva (and Common Prayer) texts. The final line points to the image-in-process direction Pembroke decided to follow in her revision.

   Homely, violent or confusing images are not the only bumps to ride over in versifying psalms. There are related theological obstacles as well. Psalm 137, for instance, a song of mourning in remembrance of the Babylonian captivity, concludes with one of the most sickening passages in the Psalms. The psalmist anticipates God's vengeance on his people's captors, declaring: 'Blessed shal he be that taketh & dasheth thy children against the stones'. This hardly reflects the Christian law of love and therefore poses a problem for any interpreter after Christ. Pembroke, in her version, subtly acknowledges this problem, yet lets the psalm continue to speak in its own, more ancient voice. She draws out the thought of the previous verse, 'blessed shal he be that rewardeth thee [Babylon], as thou hast serued vs', and emphasizes that the psalmist is here only asking that the Babylonians experience the same woes that they have inflicted on Israel:

> And Babilon, that didst us wast,
>   thy self shalt one daie wasted be:
> and happy he, who what thou hast
>   unto us donne, shall do to thee,
> like bitternes shall make thee tast,
>   like wofull objects cause thee see:
>   yea happy who thy little ones
>   shall take and dash against the stones.
>   (ll. 33–40)

Pembroke by no means brings the passage into conformity with Jesus's New Testament exhortation to love one's enemies; but at least she tempers the shock of the last image by bringing to the foreground the unspeakable grief which has prompted the psalmist to express such a thought.

If Pembroke's method of composition represents an audaciously artistic approach to the sacred texts, some of that audacity is reflected in the tone of the speakers she creates for many psalms. Everywhere she sought ways to make the psalms more lyric-like, more clearly spoken by an individual voice. As Barbara Lewalski puts it, the psalmist is 'transfigured as an Elizabethan poet', a new David (or Deborah perhaps) (Lewalski 1979: 241). To do this was in keeping with emerging Protestant theories about the use of scripture: one was to find in scripture one's own voice, to speak from one's own heart in the words of the text.

In Psalm 143, for instance, Pembroke renders the posture of penitence, not with abject humility and self-effacement, but with a more confident petitioning. From a fairly conventional opening,

> Heare my praier, o Lord, & hearken vnto my supplicacion: answer me in thy trueth & in thy righteousnes [Geneva]

Pembroke creates this bold imperative:

> Heare my entreaty Lord, the suite, I send,
> with heed attend.
>   and as my hope and trust is
>   reposed whole in thee:
>   so in thy truth and justice
>   yeeld audience to me.
>   (ll. 1–6)

Here Pembroke has enhanced the latent bargaining tone of the psalm; the speaker clearly offers her trust in God as her side of a mutual agreement, which God will surely honour out of his 'truth and justice'. The careful attention demanded in the opening lines and the term 'yeeld' add an even bolder note.

'Those High Tons'

Was this exuberant playfulness and studied particularizing an appropriate approach to the holy texts? To paraphrase Herbert, as he would later put it in wrestling with his own anxieties over the theological implications of verse style, did the Sidneys weave themselves into the sense too much? Pembroke was evidently aware of this aesthetic and theological problem. In the poem she composed dedicating a copy of the *Psalmes* to Queen Elizabeth, 'Even now that Care', she terms her psalms a 'liverie robe' suitable for royal presentation. She knew very well that her psalms were no 'thred-bare cote', as William Hunnis described his 1583 psalms. Yet, in her poem dedicating the psalms to Sidney, 'To the Angell spirit of the most excellent Sir Phillip Sidney', Pembroke immediately insists that God will find in them no significant alteration. They are devised so

> That heaven's King may daigne his own transform'd
>   in substance no, but superficiall tire
>   by thee put on; to praise, not to aspire
> To, those high Tons, so in themselves adorn'd,
>   which Angells sing in their celestiall Quire.
>   (ll. 8–12)

Pembroke carefully figures the text–reader relationship represented by her volume. She here voices the common contemporary idea that the scriptures are sufficiently adorned in themselves. Yet her psalms embody a proposal about religious poetry, one that affirms the permissibility of applying one's 'uttmost skill' to the praises of God, even exercising an interpretive authority in co-operation with scripture. Her gesture of humility here is meant to set her and Sidney's intentions under the unobjectionable rubric of praise.

Pembroke's subtle strategy in presenting the implied theological–aesthetic proposal of her psalms is the most important strategy she had to devise, though it is rarely noted in scholarly treatments of the *Psalmes*. Instead, scholars tend to focus on negotiations made because of her gender, which also interestingly display her shrewd ability to create just the right public balance (e.g. Hannay 1985; Wall 1993). The passage above from 'Angell Spirit' pointedly neglects to include any apology for undertaking this task as a woman – a rare lacuna in women's writing in this period. However, this dedicatory poem presents the entire project as a gesture of mourning:

> To which theise dearest offrings of my hart
>   dissolv'd to Inke, while penns impressions move
>   the bleeding veines of never dying love:
> I render here: these wounding lynes of smart
>   sadd Characters indeed of simple love
>   not Art nor skill which abler wits doe prove,
> Of my full soule receive the meanest part.
>
> (ll. 78–84)

Pembroke places the psalter in the mode of elegiac utterance, an acceptable means of entry into writing for women. This is not to suggest that Pembroke's sentiments here are merely an elaborate invoking of conventions for the purpose of excusing her work on the *Psalmes*. In fact, Pembroke may indeed have turned to this project as a way of working through her grief. Studying and translating psalms was a traditional means of comforting oneself – her uncles, the sons of Northumberland, did it in the Tower, for instance, as did Sir Thomas Wyatt and many others – for good reason. Many of the psalms give voice to the blackest depths of distress or grief, and testify to the faithfulness of God even when circumstances seem desperate.

While the pernicious associations of publishing with unchastity for women are well documented, it seems unlikely, given her other publishing activities, that Pembroke refrained from publishing the *Psalmes* because of her gender. Instead, it seems that here again Pembroke was wisely navigating among her various options. Rather than sending the *Psalmes* into print, a medium associated with public display, the outcome of which could not be controlled, Pembroke chose to have the *Psalmes* prepared for presentation as beautifully scripted and bound manuscripts. By retaining the *Psalmes* for manuscript circulation only, Pembroke gained several advantages. First, knowing that her free renderings of the psalms might, for some people, push the boundaries of scriptural mediation too far, she appeared to assert nothing about the public use of her psalms. The more private mode of scribal publication implied an intention for a more private devotional use. Second, during this period manuscripts were still perceived as a more prestigious means of circulation, so that she preserved the unique dignity of this work. Third, with only a few copies available, Pembroke could more easily control who read them.

By this means the *Psalmes* circulated among some critical poetic minds of the period, including John Donne, Aemilia Lanyer and, it seems evident, George Herbert. For Lanyer, Pembroke provided a crucial precedent of a woman exegeting scripture, adapting the prophetic 'I' of the Psalms to a female voice. For Donne and Herbert, the *Psalmes* provided an authoritative precedent for rhetorically sophisticated depictions of thought processes and inner states arising from the speaker's contemplation of self in relation to God. In his poem praising the *Psalmes*, Donne declares that Sidney and Pembroke 'in formes of joy and art do re-reveale' the Psalms, a remarkable claim that lends the *Psalmes* a quasi-inspired status. Careful study of Herbert's poetry suggests that he learned much from the metrical experiments in the *Psalmes*, and struggled to reach his own peace about the *Psalmes'* implicit affirmation of artistic self-assertion before God. Thus, it is fair to say that Pembroke, immersed in scripture as were her contemporaries, initiated the emergence of the great English religious lyric of the early seventeenth century: original, meditative poetry, soaked with scriptural influence but ardently reflective of the individual poet's imagination and temperament.

See also WOMEN'S POETRY 1550–1770

REFERENCES AND FURTHER READING

Brennan, Michael (1988). *Literary Patronage in the English Renaissance: The Pembroke Family.* London: Routledge.

Hannay, Margaret Patterson (ed.) (1985). *Silent But for the Word: Tudor Women as Patrons, Translators, and Writers of Religious Works.* Kent, OH: Kent State University Press.

——(1989). ' "Princes you as men must dy": Genevan advice to monarchs in the *Psalmes* of Mary Sidney.' *English Literary Renaissance*, 19, 22–41.

——(1990). *Philip's Phoenix: Mary Sidney, Countess of Pembroke.* Oxford: Oxford University Press.

——(1991). ' "Wisdome the wordes": psalm translation and Elizabethan women's spirituality.' *Religion and Literature*, 23, 65–82.

——(1994a). ' "House-confinéd maids": the presentation of woman's role in the *Psalmes* of the Countess of Pembroke.' *English Literary Renaissance*, 24, 20–35.

——(1994b). ' "O daughter heare": reconstructing the lives of aristocratic Englishwomen.' In Betty Travitsky and Adele Seeff (eds), *Attending to Women in Early Modern England* (pp. 35–63). Newark: University of Delaware Press.

——(1999). ' "Most wordes her owne": sixteenth-century women's psalm translations.' In Barbara Smith and Ursula Appelt (eds), *Write or Be Written: Early Modern Women Poets and Cultural Constraints.* Brookfield, VT: Ashgate.

——(2000a). ' "Bearing the livery of your name": the Countess of Pembroke's agency in print and scribal publication.' *Sidney Journal*, 18, 7–42.

——(2000b). ' "When riches growes": class perspective in Pembroke's Psalmes.' In Mary Burke, Jane Donawerth, Linda L. Dove and Karen Nelson (eds), *Women, Writing, and the Reproduction of Culture in Tudor and Stuart Britain* (pp. 77–97). Syracuse, NY: Syracuse University Press.

Kinnamon, Noel J. (1990). 'The Sidney psalms: the Penshurst and Tixall manuscripts.' *English Manuscript Studies 1100–1700*, 2, 139–61.

Lamb, Mary Ellen (1982). 'The Countess of Pembroke's patronage.' *English Literary Renaissance*, 12, 162–79.

——(1990). *Gender and Authorship in the Sidney Circle.* Madison: University of Wisconsin Press.

Lewalski, Barbara K. (1979). *Protestant Poetics and the Seventeenth-Century Religious Lyric.* Princeton, NJ: Princeton University Press.

Pembroke, Mary Sidney Herbert, Countess of (1998). *Collected Works of Mary Sidney Herbert, Countess of Pembroke*, ed. Margaret P. Hannay, Noel J. Kinnamon and Michael G. Brennan. New York: Oxford–Clarendon.

Pembroke, Mary Sidney Herbert, Countess of, and Philip Sidney (1963). *The Psalms of Sir Philip Sidney and the Countess of Pembroke*, ed. J. C. A. Rathmell. Garden City, NY: Anchor–Doubleday.

Rienstra, Debra K. and Kinnamon, Noel J. (1999). 'Revisioning the sacred text.' *Sidney Journal*, 17.1, 51–74.

Roberts, Josephine (1984). 'Recent studies in women writers of Tudor England: Mary Sidney, Countess of Pembroke.' *English Literary Renaissance,* 14, 426–39.

Rohr-Sauer, Philipp von (1938). *English Metrical Psalms from 1600 to 1660: A Study of the Religious and Aesthetic Tendencies of the Period*. Freiburg: Universittsdruckerei Poppen and Ortman.

Smith, Hallett (1946). 'English metrical psalms in the sixteenth century and their literary significance.' *Huntington Library Quarterly*, 9, 249–71.

Wall, Wendy (1993). *The Imprint of Gender: Authorship and Publication in the English Renaissance*. Ithaca, NY: Cornell University Press.

Waller, Gary F. (1974). '"This matching of contraries": Calvinism and courtly philosophy in the Sidney psalms.' *English Studies*, 55, 22–31.

——(1979). *Mary Sidney, Countess of Pembroke: A Critical Study of her Writings and Literary Milieu*. Salzburg: Institut fur Anglistik und Amerikanistik, Universitat Salzburg.

Zim, Rivkah (1987). *English Metrical Psalms: Poetry as Praise and Prayer: 1535–1601*. Cambridge: Cambridge University Press.

8

Aemilia Lanyer, *Salve Deus Rex Judaeorum*

Susanne Woods

Aemilia Bassano Lanyer (1569–1645) published her only extant book of poems, *Salve Deus Rex Judaeorum* ('Hail, God, King of the Jews'), in 1611, the year the King James Bible appeared and John Donne published his *First Anniversary*. Her book is the first clear attempt by a woman writing in English to seek professional standing as a poet. It transforms gestures from the Jacobean patronage system into the language of an ambitious woman who seeks the attention and favours of higher-born patronesses. In praising these women in terms of their piety and learning, Lanyer also transforms contemporary Christianity from its misogynist assumptions to a critique of sinful men and a sensuous female gaze on Christ the Bridegroom. In the process, Lanyer shifts the focus of Petrarchan language, presents a version of Christ's passion that challenges patriarchal religion, and portrays a woman-centred Edenic society in which social class dissolves in bonds of affectionate friendship that centre the natural world and mirror a spiritual one (Lewalski 1993: 213–41).

Her life is a remarkable tale of sadness, success, ambition and obscurity (Woods 1999: 7–33). Lanyer was the daughter of Baptista Bassano, a court musician born in Venice who migrated with five brothers to England during the reign of Henry VIII, and Margaret Johnson, who may have been related to another family of court musicians. We know little of Lanyer's upbringing, except that her parents had connections with the reform Protestant movement and at some point she was educated in the household of Susan Bertie, the Dowager Duchess of Kent, the daughter of a Protestant heroine, Catherine Brandon Bertie, the Dowager Duchess of Suffolk. Lanyer's older sister, Angela, was already married when their father died in 1576 and was deceased by the time their mother died in 1587. At that point 18-year-old Aemilia Bassano inherited a small living consistent with her parents' lives among the minor gentry, but her fortune was elevated, probably not long after her mother's death, by her connection with Queen Elizabeth's cousin and Lord Chamberlain, Henry Cary, Lord Hunsdon.

We know something of her time at court and her relationship with the Lord Chamberlain from her reports to the fashionable astrologer Simon Forman, whom she visited several times between May and September 1597. His casebooks report that she described herself as having been 'paramour' to 'the old Lord Chamberlain' who 'maintained [her] in great pomp'. Forman's entry on 2 September 1597 summarizes Lanyer's life in Queen Elizabeth's court between about 1588 and 1592: 'She hath been favored much of her majesty and of many noblemen, and hath had great gifts and been much made of, and a nobleman that is dead [i.e. Lord Hunsdon, who died in 1596] hath loved her well and kept her and did maintain her long'. Forman's reports also tell us that when Aemilia Bassano became pregnant by the Lord Chamberlain she was married to 'a minstrel', the court musician Alfonso Lanyer. Independent records confirm their marriage in October 1592, and the birth of a son, Henry, in early 1593.

Lanyer's reports to Forman indicate discontent with the decline in her fortunes. She misses her access to Elizabeth's court and complains that her husband has dissipated the wealth she accrued during her time as the Lord Chamberlain's mistress. Nonetheless, her two reasons for visiting Forman are both connected to Alfonso: she is having some difficulty carrying to term (Forman reports that she hath 'many false conceptions' and she comes to him with pain from what appears to precede a miscarriage), and she is anxious to know whether Alfonso's signing up with the Earl of Essex for what would eventually be known as the Islands' Voyage of 1597 will advance the family fortunes. Lanyer, who is 'high-minded' and had been 'very brave [i.e. showy] in youth', wants to know whether or not Alfonso will be knighted and she, therefore, will be a lady. Despite whatever disappointments she feels, then, she is here struggling to make a life with Alfonso and to promote and hope for his advancement. Unfortunately, Alfonso never was knighted, and the one child they had together, Odillya, died in less than 18 months. Alfonso nonetheless made some important connections in his soldiering, including Henry Wriothesley, Earl of Southampton, and Sir Robert Cecil, and Henry Lanyer grew up to follow his putative father into a career as a court musician.

Aemilia and Alfonso apparently lived amicably but mostly apart after 1600, and for at least some portion of that time she was in the household of her most important patron, Margaret Russell Clifford, Countess of Cumberland. Presumably Aemilia had begun to write poetry much earlier (it may have been one of the skills she brought to her relationship with the old Lord Chamberlain), but she credits the Countess of Cumberland with inspiring and fostering her poetic talent along with her religious growth. According to 'The Description of Cookham', the last poem in her volume, Lanyer had enjoyed a summer of talks, readings, songs and happy companionship with the Countess and her daughter, Anne Clifford, who became Countess of Dorset in 1609. The Countess of Cumberland, who numbered Edmund Spenser and Samuel Daniel among the poets she patronized, apparently accepted a role as Aemilia Lanyer's patron as well. We know, for example, that the Countess gave a copy of

Lanyer's volume (less some of the more controversial dedicatory poems) to Henry, Prince of Wales (the copy is in the Dyce collection at the Victoria and Albert Museum).

Alfonso died in 1613, the Countess of Cumberland in 1616, and in 1617 Lanyer 'for her maintenance and relief . . . was compelled to teach and educate the children of divers persons of wealth and understanding'. The enterprise lasted until 1619, when legal wrangling with her landlord (from which our description comes) ended it. The rest of her life is mostly obscure, although we know that she had legal disputes with Alfonso's cousins over a hay and grain patent he had been granted for his service to King James, and that she spent the latter part of her life with her son Henry and his family. When she was buried at St James Clerkenwell on 3 April 3 1645 she was listed as a 'pensioner', or someone with a regular income.

The portrait that emerges is of an attractive, strong-willed and ambitious woman who tried many things to reconnect with the world of power that she felt she lost with her marriage to Alfonso. Central to that effort, and at least somewhat successful in achieving it, was her poetry. Although the title page of *Salve Deus Rex Judaeorum* describes the author in terms of husband and king ('Wife to Captain Alfonso Lanyer, Servant to the King's Majesty'), the book is by a woman, dedicated to women and in praise of women. The student of English poetry will immediately recognize many of its features, but a closer look will show a complex and transgressive vision that challenges many of the conventions Lanyer employs.

The book is in three parts: dedications, the long title poem on Christ's passion, and 'The Description of Cookham'. The first part consists of eleven dedicatory pieces, nine to women patronesses, one to 'All Virtuous Ladies in General' and one 'To the Virtuous Reader'. This latter, along with the dedicatory piece to her principal patron, the Countess of Cumberland, is in prose; the rest are in pentameter verse, mostly the six-line 'ballade' stanza or the seven-line 'rhyme royal', but with the longest and most complex poem, to the Countess of Pembroke, in quatrains. The strophic construction is conservative, going back beyond Chaucer, and of the sort praised specifically by George Gascoigne in his 'Certain Notes of Instruction Concerning the Making of Verse or Rhyme in English' (1575). The versification is competent and sometimes affecting, though not as practised and easy as some of her male contemporaries. Her language, stance and wit show her to be knowledgeable about Latin (and possibly Greek) models of epideictic verse and familiar with her immediate English tradition, particularly with the work of Spenser, Sir Philip Sidney, his sister, the Countess of Pembroke, Samuel Daniel and Michael Drayton.

The series of dedicatory pieces begins, appropriately, with a praise of Queen Anne, the highest social rank among her noble dedicatees. Anne (or Anna), James I's Danish-born consort, kept her own court and sponsored a number of poets and musicians, including those such as Daniel, Ben Jonson, Alfonso Ferrabosco and Nicholas Lanier, who helped create the masques for which her court was famous. Nicholas Lanier was

Alfonso Lanyer's nephew, and Ferrabosco was his brother-in-law, married to his sister Ellen in 1610. These connections, along with Alfonso's own continuing status as a court musician, probably assured Aemilia's acquaintance with the queen, if not the intimacy of patronage that the poet clearly desired.

A close look at 'To the Queen's Most Excellent Majesty' reveals the tone and several themes of the volume as a whole. Women's virtues and men's perfidy are among these themes, while feasts and mirrors are common images in the dedicatory pieces (McGrath 1991). In each of them Lanyer invites the dedicatee to enjoy the feast of the book's long poem, the 'Salve Deus Rex Judaeorum' itself, and to see their own virtues reflected in the 'glass' or mirror of Christ's virtues. So in this first poem Lanyer points to the 'Apology' for Eve she makes in the 'Salve Deus' poem (more on that shortly), 'which I have writ in honor of your sex',

> And do refer unto your Majesty,
> To judge if it agree not with the Text;
> And if it do, why are poor women blamed,
> Or by more faulty men so much defamed?
>
> (ll. 74–7)

Eve, portrayed 'in all her richest ornaments of honor' by Lanyer (l. 80), welcomes Queen Anne to 'this Feast' of the 'Salve Deus' poem, which is Lanyer's 'Paschal lamb', or passion story:

> This precious Passover feed upon, O Queen,
> Let your fair virtues in my glass be seen.
>
> (ll. 89–90)

The queen becomes the ideal reader, joining the world's first queen, an Eve redeemed by a woman author, whose book in turn holds up the mirror of virtue to the nature of Queen Anne's grace. Together, author and reader transgress patriarchal religion in the common cause of redeeming their gender.

This initial poem also negotiates the difficulties of 'that which is seldom seen, / A woman's writing of divinest things' (ll. 3–4). The terms of the patronage system, by which the lowly receives inspiration from the higher-born, is Lanyer's first step to authority: 'Your excellence can grace both it [the poem] and me' (l. 6). Her pious topic is another. A witty rendering of the traditional association of women with the natural world accomplishes the rest. She asks the queen's pardon for attempting what 'so many better can' and insists she is not trying to

> . . . compare with any man,
> But as they are scholars, and by art do write,
> So nature gives my soul a sad [i.e. serious] delight.
>
> (ll. 148–50)

But since all art comes from nature, she argues, why shouldn't nature, the 'mother of perfection', have a special care for a woman poet:

> Why should not she now grace my barren muse,
> And in a woman all defects excuse?
>
> (ll. 155–6)

'Grace' is one of the key terms throughout the volume. It not only signifies the relationship between patron and poet, and between God and humankind; it is also the term male poets traditionally applied to the blessings the inspiring woman bestowed on the lover. Lanyer reconnects these meanings – social, religious and Petrarchan – into a conflation of female virtue which mirrors Christ's sacrifice, orders the natural world, and leads to a woman's own poetic art. Lanyer establishes these meanings in this first dedication, when she asks for the queen's particular attention to her work, since there is no one greater in 'estate' or 'virtue':

> That so these rude unpolished lines of mine,
> Graced by you, may seem the more divine.
>
> (ll. 35–6)

Virtue is another key term throughout the volume. Originally a reference to manly power (from Latin *vir*), in English it comes to mean moral power or excellence, and, when applied to women, specifically signals chastity among other moral excellencies. So the male Renaissance poets make much of the relation between beauty and virtue, partly on the neo-Platonic assumption that the beautiful woman is closer to the ideal and therefore to moral good, and partly in recognition of the presumed power that a chaste woman possesses. Spenser's 'Hymn in Honour of Beauty', for example, makes the point that beauty represents a heavenly purity, so that a beautiful woman 'doth hold / A beauteous soul' which in turn is 'Fit to receive the seeds of virtue', because 'all that fair is, is by nature good' (ll. 135–9). The order is important here, and typical of the male poets in the period: beauty represents virtue. In the Petrarchan scheme (and in Castiglione's famous progression of 'Bembo's ladder of love' in Book IV of *The Courtier*) the male gaze begins by being drawn to female beauty and learns from it to admire the chaste virtue it signifies and that compels, in turn, virtuous action.

Lanyer's poetry reverses, and therefore denies, this progression. Of the six occasions when versions of the words 'beauty' and 'virtue' appear within ten words of each other, for example, 'virtue' always comes first. Beauty is a great danger to women, as Lanyer explains in an important digression in the 'Salve Deus' itself, but virtues themselves are 'fair', as she announces to Queen Anne. The volume's third poem (after a short tribute to Princess Elizabeth as worthy of her namesake, the late queen), 'To All Virtuous Ladies in General', underscores the point by describing Queen Anne's courtiers as

> Each blessed lady that in virtue spends
> Your precious time to beautify your souls.
>
> (ll. 1–2)

A reader tracing just the two words, 'grace' and 'virtue', will find in Lanyer's volume a powerful, woman-centred critique of Renaissance values as they were commonly expressed by the male poets.

The remaining dedicatory pieces are: 'To the Lady Arabella' (Arabella Stuart, James's cousin, famous for her learning); 'To the Lady Susan, Countess Dowager of Kent, and Daughter to the Duchess of Suffolk' (Lanyer's 'Mistress of my youth / The noble guide of my unbridled days', praised for her own virtues and her mother's famous escape to the Continent during the days of Catholic Queen Mary); 'The Author's Dream, to the Lady Mary, the Countess Dowager of Pembroke' (the most learned and complex of all the dedicatory poems, praising the Countess most particularly for her poems based on the Psalms); 'To the Lady Lucie, Countess of Bedford' (the most famous woman patron of her day, also much admired for her learning, and the queen's closest friend); 'To the Lady Margaret, Countess Dowager of Cumberland' (Lanyer's principal patron and the dedicatee of the 'Salve Deus' poem itself); 'To the Lady Katherine, Countess of Suffolk' (the only dedicatee Lanyer has not met, possibly chosen because of receptions she was known to have given at Cambridge when her husband was chancellor of the university, possibly because Lanyer may have met the husband, Lord Admiral Thomas Howard, during her years at the Elizabethan court); 'To the Lady Anne, Countess of Dorset' (the Countess of Cumberland's daughter and a formidable woman herself, holding on to her right to inherit as the only child of her father despite opposition from the king and her own husband); and 'To the Virtuous Reader' (a prose denunciation of those who disparage women).

The central poem, 'Salve Deus Rex Judaeorum', provides many avenues into a woman's perspective on Jacobean culture, including an attack on the dangers of 'outward beauty' (ll. 185–240), proto-feminist readings of biblical stories, and the assertion of a female authorial voice. The poem begins with acknowledgement and praise of the late Queen Elizabeth, suggesting that this poem would have sought the glory of her patronage, but now 'she gives glory unto God alone' (l. 8). Lanyer therefore turns to the Countess of Cumberland, 'that when to heaven thy blessed soul shall fly / These lines on earth record thy reverend name' (ll. 11–12). The author is, conventionally, unworthy to write, but the inspiration of the Countess and of God make possible strength out of weakness. Although the poem's great task is to show the passion of Christ, its stated purpose is to fulfil the author's vocation to glorify the Countess:

> And know, when first into this world I came,
> This charge was given me by th' Eternal powers,
> The everlasting trophy of thy fame

> To build and deck it with the sweetest flowers
> That virtue yields. . . .
>
> (ll. 1457–61)

Of the poem's 1840 lines (in *ottava rima* stanzas), roughly half are directly or indirectly in praise of the Countess of Cumberland, mostly framing the story of Christ's passion which is the central and ostensible subject. Margaret Clifford is the poet's inspiration, the model of contemplative piety in a distracting world, the epitome of that virtue which is true beauty, and the exemplary bride of Christ. Lanyer alludes to the Countess's suffering because of her late husband's notorious infidelities, and to the continuing tension with the king and the Clifford family over the rights of her daughter, Anne, to inherit the Cumberland title and lands. These sufferings, and Margaret's own religious nature, give her a special relationship with Christ and, over the course of the poem, translate her into a figure for the perfect church for whom Christ the bridegroom has performed his sacrifice and translation of suffering into triumph (ll. 1325–44).

Lanyer's Christ is a silent, feminized man who understands and is understood by women throughout the poem (Mueller 1994). His physical beauty, portrayed in language drawn from the Psalms and the Song of Songs, is subject to the desiring female gaze:

> This is that bridegroom that appears so fair,
> So sweet, so lovely in his spouse's sight,
> That unto snow we may his face compare,
> His cheeks like scarlet, and his eyes so bright
> As purest doves that in the rivers are
> Washed with milk, to give the more delight.
>
> (ll. 1305–10)

His story is told entirely from women's points of view: the Countess's 'eye of faith' (l. 1169), the tears of the daughters of Jerusalem (ll. 968–1000), the suffering of the Virgin Mary (ll. 1009–96) and, most surprisingly, the admonition of Pilate's wife.

Lanyer takes on the traditional *querelle des femmes*, or controversy about women, by placing a defence of Eve in the voice of Pilate's wife (the *tour de force* to which she referred Queen Anne in the first poem of the volume). Expanding on a single verse in Matthew (27.19), Pilate's wife in Lanyer's story elaborates her warning to her husband to have nothing to do with Jesus, into a praise of women and condemnation of men. Poor Eve gets blamed for eating the fruit and causing all our pain, the wife notes,

> But she (poor soul) by cunning was deceived,
> No hurt therein her harmless heart intended.
>
> (ll. 775–6)

The fall was really Adam's fault, she continues, following one of the standard responses to the attack on Eve, since 'what weakness offered, strength might have refused' (l. 779). It was Adam, fully conscious of what he was doing, that brought 'us all in danger and disgrace':

> And then to lay the fault on Patience back,
> That we (poor women) must endure it all!
> (ll. 792–3)

Yet even if Eve could be justly blamed (which the wife never concedes), her offence is nothing compared to what Pilate and other men are about to do to Jesus,

> Whom, if unjustly you condemn to die,
> Her sin was small, to what you do commit.
> (ll. 817–18)

In the most astonishing assertion of female independence on record from this period, the wife's conclusion goes well beyond the defence of women in the *querelle* tradition:

> Then let us have our liberty again,
> And challenge to yourselves no sovereignty.
> You came not into the world without our pain;
> Make that a bar unto your cruelty.
> Your fault being greater, why should you disdain
> Our being your equals, free from tyranny?
>   If one weak woman simply [i.e. ignorantly] did offend,
>   This sin of yours hath no excuse, nor end.
> (ll. 825–32)

This recognition of gender 'tyranny' seems surprisingly ahead of its time, yet Lanyer pointed specifically to it in her dedication to Queen Anne. The 'Salve Deus' is a pious poem filled with transgressions (Keohane 1997) that she expected even her queen to admire.

The volume's concluding work, 'The Description of Cookham', is the first 'country house poem' published in English. Ben Jonson's 'To Penshurst' has traditionally been so credited, but his was published in 1616, though presumably written before Prince Henry's unexpected death in November 1612 (he is mentioned in the poem as out hunting with his father, King James). Whatever their sequence, the two poems, both written in iambic pentameter couplets, provide an excellent set of comparisons between the worlds of men and women in the early seventeenth century. Both use the emblem of a country estate to signify the ordering presence of a noble patron. Lanyer's poem describes a lost world of egalitarian perfection. Jonson's celebrates an ongoing masculine hierarchy.

Sometime during the first decade of the seventeenth century Lanyer apparently spent at least a summer and early autumn with Margaret and Anne Clifford at Cookham, a crown property leased to Margaret's brother, Lord Russell of Thornaugh. She portrays the sojourn as idyllic, suggesting that she may have written the 'Salve Deus' there under the influence of the Countess's piety and encouragement. Lanyer describes the three women taking walks, reading scripture together under a particularly favoured oak tree, enjoying the view and singing. All of nature celebrates the Countess and mourns when she and her daughter leave, an inevitable displacement blamed on the transience of Edenic perfection (ll. 13–14) and on 'occasions', which 'called you so away / That nothing there had power to make you stay' (ll. 147–8).

There are many points of comparison between 'Cookham' and 'Penshurst', but one of the most interesting is their respective presentations of social class. Jonson accepts it completely as the proper ordering of nature, though he notes happily that he, though of low birth, was treated as well as the king when he was entertained at Penshurst. Lanyer, on the other hand, mourns the class differences that separate her from her higher-born friends:

> Unconstant Fortune, thou art most to blame,
> Who casts us down into so low a frame
> Where our great friends we cannot daily see,
> So great a difference is there in degree.
>
> (ll. 103–6)

Jonson has the confidence of a public poet in a man's world; Lanyer seeks the role of poet in the more restricted realm of women's lives. Her book as a whole shows her aware of, and not entirely accepting, the differences in privilege and liberty effected by gender and class. Her response is a fascinating balance between continuing aspiration, pious acceptance and sly wit.

Since Barbara K. Lewalski and the idiosyncratic historian A. L. Rowse variously resurfaced Lanyer's work in the 1970s, critics of Renaissance poetry have increasingly included Lanyer as a worthy figure in the early flourishing of the seventeenth-century lyric. She sits well among the other lyricists, including Jonson and Donne, and shows interesting affinities with Spenser, who was probably at the Elizabethan court at the same time as she and whose work seems to have had a substantial influence on hers. The variety of recent critical studies of Lanyer has served to raise as many interesting questions about a woman's situation in Jacobean poetic culture as it answers (see, for example, the essays in Grossman 1998). The unfolding richness of her work assures her canonical status for the foreseeable future.

Rowse was convinced that Lanyer was the 'dark lady' of Shakespeare's sonnets, but there has never been any evidence for this, even assuming that there was a real woman behind Shakespeare's invention. Rowse's conviction was based on an ignorance of Renaissance sonneteering conventions and imaginative readings (and misreadings) of a few biographical facts about Lanyer (Woods 1999: 90–8; Bevington, in Grossman 1998: 10–28). More interesting is the suggestion that the Bassano family may have had Jewish origins (a suggestion picked up by one of Rowse's disciples, Roger Prior, to try to argue that Lanyer might have been 'dark'). There were Jews in the Italian town of Bassano, from which the family originally came, and some English court musicians were of Jewish origin. There is no direct evidence, however, and by the time of Aemilia's birth her father's family had been practising Christians for at least two generations. Lanyer's Johnson heritage, from her mother's side, also limits any assurance that Lanyer had dark hair or eyes, but the possibility of a Jewish background on her father's side remains an interesting speculation.

See also DEFENCES OF WOMEN; WOMEN'S POETRY 1550–1700

REFERENCES AND FURTHER READING

Beilin, Elaine B. (1987). *Redeeming Eve: Women Writers of the English Renaissance.* Princeton, NJ: Princeton University Press.

Grossman, Marshall (ed.) (1998). *Aemilia Lanyer: Gender, Genre, Canon.* Lexington: University of Kentucky Press. (An essential collection that includes essays by David Bevington, Leeds Barroll, Barbara K. Lewalski, Katri Boyd McBride, Susanne Woods, Janel Mueller, Marshall Grossman, Naomi J. Miller, Michael Morgan Holmes, Achsah Guibbory and Boyd Berry, and an annotated bibliography by Karen Nelson.)

Keohane, Catherine (1997). '"That blindest weaknesses be not over-bold": Aemilia Lanyer's radical unfolding of the passion.' *English Literary History*, 64, 359–90.

Krontiris, Tina (1992). *Oppositional Voices: Women as Writers and Translators of Literature in the English Renaissance.* London: Routledge.

Lamb, Mary Ellen (1998). 'Patronage and class in Aemilia Lanyer's *Salve Deus Rex Judaeorum*.' In Mary Burke, Jane Donawerth, Linda Dove and Karen Nelson (eds), *Women, Writing, and the Reproduction of Culture in Tudor and Stuart England.* Syracuse, NY: Syracuse University Press.

Lasocki, David (1995). *The Bassanos: Venetian Musicians and Instrument Makers in England, 1531–1665.* With Roger Prior. Aldershot: Scolar Press.

Lewalski, Barbara K. (1985). 'Of God and good women: the poems of Aemilia Lanyer'. In Margaret P. Hannay (ed.), *Silent but for the Word: Tudor Women as Patrons, Translators, and Writers of Religious Works.* Kent, OH: Kent State University Press.

——(1989). 'The lady of the country house poem.' In Gervase Jackson-Stops, Gordon J. Schochet, Lena Cowen Orlin and Elisabeth Blair MacDougall (eds), *The Fashioning and Functioning of the British Country House.* Hanover, NH: National Gallery of Art.

——(1991). 'Rewriting patriarchy and patronage: Margaret Clifford, Anne Clifford and Aemilia Lanyer'. *The Yearbook of English Studies*, 21, 87–106.

——(1993). *Writing Women in Jacobean England.* Cambridge, MA: Harvard University Press.

McGrath, Lynette (1991). 'Metaphoric subversions: feasts and mirrors in Amelia Lanier's *Salve Deus Rex Judaeorum*.' *LIT: Literature-Interpretation-Theory*, 3, 101–13.

——(1992). 'Let us have our liberty again: Amelia Lanier's seventeenth-century feminist voice.' *Women's Studies*, 10, 331–48.

Mueller, Janel (1994). 'The feminist poetics of Aemilia Lanyer's *Salve Deus Rex Judaeorum*'. In Lynn Keller and Cristianne Miller (eds), *Feminist Measures: Sounding in Poetry and Theory.* Ann Arbor: University of Michigan Press.

Prior, Roger (1983). 'Jewish musicians at the Tudor court.' *Musical Quarterly,* 69, 253–65.

Purkiss, Diane (1994). *Renaissance Women: The Plays of Elizabeth Cary, the Poems of Aemilia Lanyer.* London: William Pickering.

Rowse, A. L. (1974). *Simon Forman: Sex and Society in Shakespeare's Age.* London: Weidenfeld and Nicolson.

Schleiner, Louise (1994). *Tudor and Stuart Women Writers.* Bloomington: University of Indiana Press.

Schnell, Lisa (1996). '"So great a difference is there in degree": Aemilia Lanyer and the aims of feminist criticism.' *Modern Language Quarterly,* 57, 23–35.

Wall, Wendy (1993). *The Imprint of Gender: Authorship and Publication in the English Renaissance.* Ithaca, NY: Cornell University Press.

Woods, Susanne (ed. and intro.) (1993). *The Poems of Aemilia Lanyer: Salve Deus Rex Judaeorum.* New York: Oxford University Press.

——(1994). 'Aemilia Lanyer and Ben Jonson: patronage, authority, and gender.' *The Ben Jonson Journal,* 1, 15–30.

——(1999). *Lanyer: A Renaissance Woman Poet.* New York: Oxford University Press.

9

Elizabeth Cary, *The Tragedy of Mariam* and History

Elaine Beilin

For who does not know history's first law to be that an author must not dare to tell anything but the truth? And its second that he must make bold to tell the whole truth?

Cicero, *De oratore* 2.15.62

In the opening lines of Elizabeth Cary's *The Tragedy of Mariam*, the title character, the 'fair queen of Jewry', turns to the past to find a precedent and a mirror for the present. Surprised by her present grief for her husband, Herod, who has supposedly been executed by Octavius Caesar, Mariam apostrophizes Julius Caesar. She finds that Caesar's tears for the death of his enemy, Pompey, exemplify contradictory yet genuine emotions:

> How oft have I with public voice run on
> To censure Rome's last hero for deceit:
> Because he wept when Pompey's life was gone,
> Yet when he liv'd, he thought his name too great.
> But now I do recant, and, Roman lord,
> Excuse too rash a judgement in a woman . . .
>
> (I.i.1–6)

Contemplating Caesar, she feels confirmed in her own experience that 'One object yields both grief and joy' (10). In her own case, Herod tyrannically restrained her liberty, murdered her brother and her grandfather, yet involuntarily, her tears flow as she also remembers his love for her, 'the deepest love that ever yet was seen' (56). Simultaneously using the past as a mirror for the present and as the source of a historical exemplar to illuminate her situation, Mariam introduces Roman history into the discourse of the play, invoking Julius Caesar as 'Rome's last hero'. Yet the reference to Roman heroism is immediately compromised by its historical context: this is Rome rent by civil war, an unstable world where friends become rivals for power and fight to the death.

Initially, Mariam's opening allusion to Caesar and Pompey appears to be an odd framework for an emotional appraisal of her marriage. But in these lines Cary is establishing the discursive foundation of her play. In the first decade of the seventeenth century this Roman rivalry carried moral and political implications made familiar in histories, plays and poems; it is adumbrated, for example, in the first scene of Shakespeare's *Julius Caesar* (1599) where the tribunes silence the people for celebrating Caesar's victory: 'you hard hearts, you cruel men of Rome. / Knew you not Pompey?' (1.1.36–7). As Mariam rapidly recounts Herod's murder of her angelic brother and her 'worthy grandsire' to consolidate his own power as king, his planned execution of her own self, and the struggle over succession to the kingdom of Judea, she indicates that the Roman propensities for betrayal and shifting allegiances appear to be thriving in an unstable, dangerous Judea (cf. Rebhorn 1990; Kahn 1997). In this opening scene, Cary pointedly creates a context for the play's domestic concerns at the historically momentous time of Octavius's victory over all his rivals, the time also of Herod's consolidation of power in Judea; the former was often interpreted as ushering in an era of peace and order, the latter as forerunning the advent of Christianity. Cary, however, signals the essential ambiguities which will multiply throughout her history play. If Julius Caesar is 'Rome's last hero', then Octavius belongs to a post-heroic age, and if Herod is a legendary villain, he is also a lover and a husband. With great historic identities so unstable, Mariam can assert her own significance in a comparison to Caesar and introduce a play where historical unknowns wrest the telling of history from the usual suspects.

As a history play, *The Tragedy of Mariam* does not resemble the epic or episodic plays of the 1590s, nor the large-scale providential and political history provided by her main source, Lodge's translation of Josephus's *Antiquities of the Jews*; rather, Cary represents Judea under Roman rule predominantly through the voices of those who are persecuted, repressed, hidden and resistant. It is thus a multivocal history in which no one voice dominates but in which Cary brings the times to life by the intertwining narratives and commentaries of various male and female characters struggling to survive in Herod's kingdom. Interestingly, although Mariam is the titular character, she will speak a scant 11 per cent of the play's lines, while 64 per cent will be devoted to diverse elements such as Salome's attack on Jewish law and morality; Constabarus's attack on women; Alexandra's *realpolitik*; Doris's maternal passion and vengefulness; the Sons of Babas' history lesson; and the views of the Chorus. Herod, who does not appear until Act 4, does speak a full 25 per cent of the play's lines, yet by then his voice can only be heard in the context of previous speakers, and he himself delivers a final account of his reign that ultimately confirms the highly critical opinions of the characters who have previously anatomized it.

If we were to ask why in the first decade of the seventeenth century Cary chose to write an account of the Hasmonean and Herodian families and the kingdom of Judea in 29 BCE, Mariam's first soliloquy points to some striking answers. Her invocation of the ambiguous images of Caesar triumphing and weeping, of Augustan Rome both victorious and declining, and of a desacralized Jerusalem may situate the play among many contemporary writings concerned with the succession question, the arrival of James I, the ensuing court factionalism, and conflicts over absolute rule. In an essay arguing for the influence of Tacitus on such political analyses from 1590 to 1630, Malcolm Smuts's view of Jonson, for instance, is that 'the interplay of praise and polemical attack is especially marked in three works produced around the time of James I's accession', where Jonson evokes 'a predatory style of politics, which destroys its victims through informers, false charges, corrupt judges and laws framed to serve tyranny' (Smuts 1993: 31–2). These very political elements abound in *The Tragedy of Mariam*, as Smuts argues they do in Jonson's *Sejanus* (1603), 'A Panegyre, on the Happie Entrance of James' (1603), and verses on James's entry into London (1604). In addition, as Goldberg shows, James I clearly appropriated Augustan iconography (Goldberg 1983: 46–50; Smuts 1993: 38). Cary, then, joins a discussion already in progress, writing a history that signals from its first lines a contemporary political subtext. In this regard, earlier criticism of the play has convincingly established the play's participation in 'the direct exposition of political ideas' expected of closet drama (Gutierrez 1991: 237); its reappropriation 'for the disempowered female [of] the political power of stoic heroism as an effective means of redress' (Straznicky 1994: 124); and its 'critique of patriarchal absolutism' (Raber 1995: 335). Accordingly, this essay will not revisit the play's Jacobean politics, but will examine the experiments with history writing that actually enabled Cary's political commentary on the Jacobean commonwealth.

Cary's own preparation to write a history play on the ancient world at so culturally complex a moment is documented in *The Lady Falkland: Her Life*, written in 1645 by her daughter, Lucy Cary, who became Dame Magdalena, a nun in the English Benedictine house at Cambrai (Wolfe 1999). Near the end of the *Life*, when Lucy surveys Elizabeth Cary's lifelong reading habits, she places poetry and history firmly at the head of the list. Particularly emphasizing the depth and breadth of Elizabeth Cary's interest in history, her daughter writes that

> She had read very exceeding much: poetry of all kinds, ancient and modern, in several languages, all that ever she could meet; history very universally, especially all ancient Greek and Roman historians, and chroniclers whatsoever of her own country; and the French histories very thoroughly, of most other countries something, though not so universally; of the ecclesiastical history very much, most especially concerning its chief pastors. (Cary 1994: 268)

Although we may not be able to date accurately the moment when Elizabeth Cary read any particular work, Lucy does write that until her mother was about 'twenty year old' her reading was 'for the most part poetry and history, except Seneca, and some other such, whose Epistles it is probable she translated afore she left her father's house' (ibid.: 190). Allowing for the possibility that Lucy may exaggerate her mother's youthful attainments, we may still assume that Cary had read substantial amounts of history by 1606 when she was 20 years old.

Cary's reading history 'universally' is surely suggestive when matched with the historical bent of Cary's writing. The *Life* reveals that before age 20, 'Of all she then writ, that which was said to be the best was the life of Tamberlaine in verse' (ibid.: 190) – a historical work, now apparently lost. At some time before 1612, when it was noted by John Davies, Cary wrote the historical work in verse that her daughter does not mention, *The Tragedy of Mariam* (printed 1613). In his dedication to *The Muses Sacrifice* (1612), Davies alludes to *Mariam* and another lost political, historical work: 'Thou mak'st Melpomen proud, and my heart great / of such a pupil, who, in buskin fine, / With feet of state, dost make thy Muse to meet / the scenes of Syracuse and Palestine' (Cerasano and Wynne-Davies 1998: 13). In addition, the prose history *Edward II*, '*Written by E. F. in the year 1627*' has been attributed to Cary (Lewalski 1993); her daughter also mentions another kind of history, saints' lives, now apparently lost, written around 1629 when Elizabeth Cary's mother died (Cary 1994: 213).

The historical discourses available to Cary in the first decade of the seventeenth century appeared in chronicles, poems, plays, treatises, narratives and translations, from the 'closet' drama of the Countess of Pembroke's coterie in which Gutierrez, Straznicky and Raber have situated *Mariam*, to a dozen Roman plays; from those humanist historiographers who argue for the use of history as the source of examples and as a mirror for the political present, to the providential history of Foxe. Interestingly, although Cary could learn many historiographic theories from her wide reading of ancient and modern history, she would find many of them conveniently articulated in the prefatory material to her sources for *The Tragedy of Mariam*. A discussion of the uses of history precedes both the main source for *Mariam*, Lodge's 1602 translation of Josephus's *Antiquities of the Jews*, and also a possible source, *A Compendious and moste marveylous History of the latter times of the Jewes commune weale*, translated by Peter Morwyng (ten editions, 1558–1608).

In his dedication of Josephus's *Antiquities of the Jews* to Charles Lord Howard, Lodge articulates the view that history provides examples of virtue to emulate:

and as *Themistocles* was animated to noble actions by beholding *Miltiades* Trophies, and *Alexander* in seeing *Achilles* tombe, did grievously sigh with an honourable emulation: so let the zeale, magnanimitie, and admirable constancie which everie where affronteth you in this booke . . . so settle your honourable love and affection to emulate the same, that as for glories in armes; so for preserving and protecting artes, you may outstrip your competitors, and amaisse to curious expectation.

In Lodge's view of history the reader is an independent agent, capable of shaping his actions in relation to good and bad examples and contributing his virtues to the commonwealth. As Arthur Kinney has argued, Lodge's view of history was influenced by his humanist reading of Plutarch, Polybius and Livy, and his own play, *The Wounds of Civill War*, reveals his 'sense of Roman history as parable, easily translated into a story of the rewards of good and evil' (Kinney 1986: 388).

Besides historical exemplarity, Cary would also have found providentialism in Josephus, whose Jewish history begins with the creation of the world. Josephus underlines the lesson from scripture 'that all things fall out happily, and beyond their expectation to those men, who observe the will of God, and are afraid to transgresse the lawes of his commandments; and that God hath prepared for such the crowne and reward of felicitie' (Lodge 1602: 2). Similarly, God's punishments await transgressors. Another possible source for *Mariam* is *A Compendious and moste marveylous History of the latter times of the Jewes commune weale*, which contains the detail not found in Josephus that Mariam was beheaded. Whether or not Cary used the work, 'The Epistle to the Reader' presents cultural commonplaces about history, demonstrating how exemplarity and providentialism often worked together in historical writing:

> Every man delyghteth to beholde the pictures of auncient persons, as of Hercules, Hector, Julius Caesar, Arthur, & reverenceth them as though they were halfe Gods: howe much more pleasure shoulde it be to behold the lively images of their mindes which appeare in their actes and dedes whyle they were here in this lyfe, whereby we shoulde learne to know good from evyll, & by the applying of their deedes unto our maners, with consideryng the event and successe they had of their actions, we maye take eyther an example, or some admonicion, or occasion to amend our lives, wherin besides pleasure, is also profite. As when thou seest the Jewes here afflicted with divers kindes of miserie, because they fell from God: then maist thou be admonished hereby to se the better to thine owne wayes, least the like calamities light upon thee . . . (v^v–vi)

History thus provides a wide spectrum of examples for emulation or avoidance. The very number of plural nouns in this passage suggests the multiplicity of models, whether the 'lively images' of heroic minds or the 'divers kindes of miserie' from God's punishments. Like these predecessors, Cary represents history both as the provider of virtuous and vicious examples relevant to public action, and as a demonstration of God's providential oversight. However, throughout the play, the moral and spiritual certitude often associated with exemplarity or providentialism is undercut. Specific characters articulate these historical perspectives, but their words never go unchallenged and their values are inevitably undermined. The multiplicity of views undermines the very concepts of historical mirrors, exemplars or providential order.

What Cary ultimately constructs is less the tragedy of Mariam alone and more the voices that compose the simultaneous decadence of the classical world of Rome and the tragic failure of the Old Testament world of Judea. As we remember the apocalyptic voices at the end of 1999, we may perhaps gather a hint of the end-of-a-world thinking that Cary embedded in her play set at the close of pagan times.

Cary's particular construction of history may be further illuminated by recalling Paul Dean's and Frank V. Cespedes's analyses of Shakespeare's English and Roman histories. Dean's examination of the humanist treatment of Roman history indicates that from medieval times, Rome is consistently depicted at exactly that time during the 'transition from paganism to Christianity', so that a significant aspect of Rome for English readers is the representation of

> a culture in the melting-pot, *a juxtaposition of diverse and apparently irreconcilable viewpoints* which may have prompted the eclecticism of the 'renaissance of the twelfth century' . . . and may even have helped to form the similar character of English Renaissance classicism. (Dean 1988: 85; italics mine)

Citing the cultural and political significance of this historical moment, Dean counts 11 plays on the Rome of the Caesars between 1599 and 1611, plays which are, by definition, also about civil war. He does not include the five Roman plays that belong to the group associated with the Countess of Pembroke's coterie, perhaps Cary's own literary circle (ibid.: 108; Gutierrez 1991; Straznicky 1994). Given Cary's immersion in classical and ecclesiastical history and the popularity of Roman plays, Lodge's translation of Josephus, where Rome and Judea appear in a cataclysmic confrontation, might have deeply engaged her interest. Although Rome is always offstage, Cary ensures that it is a continual verbal presence as she creates an archetypal historical moment when 'diverse and apparently irreconcilable viewpoints' illuminate the condition of the world immediately before the Incarnation.

Shakespeare's last history play, *Henry VIII* (1613), provides a parallel case of multivocal history which includes a critique of historiography. Dean argues that the play is a 'frieze in which a number of characters are systematically compared and contrasted. Since no single character is indispensable, the dramatist is freed to explore the larger movements of history to which all are subject' (Dean 1986: 178). Similarly, Cespedes argues that *Henry VIII* interrogates 'the optimistic principle of providential history' embodied in the play's progression towards Elizabeth's birth by showing the 'uncertainties of history in order to question the availability of an "omniscient" perspective on historical events' (Cespedes 1980: 417). Like *Henry VIII*, *The Tragedy of Mariam* may be read as an anatomy of historical interpretation, relying on the juxtaposition of perspectives and ideologies to complicate the construction of a historical moment from multiple 'truths'.

In Josephus's story of Mariam and Herod, Cary found a historical narrative that could be used to interrogate humanist assumptions about history. Readers of the play who have found ambiguities and irresolution at its heart have recognized the crucial indeterminacy required in such an endeavour. Nancy Gutierrez (1991), for example, characterizes closet drama as 'inquiry or debate' (ibid.: 239) and argues that the play 'leaves the audience with an ambiguous representation of the character of the hero and of the meaning of her actions' (ibid.: 246). Underlining Mariam's 'dilemma' rather than her character, Laurie Shannon (1994) argues that 'Cary addresses the impossibility of moral stability or purity when an authority creates laws whose "justice" operates to the detriment of those to whom the law applies' (ibid.: 136). Karen Raber (1995) reads the ways in which the play exposes 'the fissures, inconsistencies, and repressions of domestic patriarchy' (ibid.: 334), which, when transferred to the state, 'generates rather than resolves instability in its subjects' (ibid.: 340). Boyd Berry (1995) suggests that 'this is a play which cries out for simultaneous, multiple readings', including both comic and tragic Herods (ibid.: 270). Naomi Miller's (1997) analysis of the play's representation of maternal conflict, 'the swelling dissonance of maternal voices' (ibid.: 367), clarifies 'the simultaneous subjection and subjectivity of women' (ibid.: 368). Such analysis allows us to recognize the decentred, multivocal quality of the play and Cary's strategy of establishing successive historical discourses only to undermine and supplant them. Articulating and then supplanting exemplarity, providentialism and political mirror, the play proceeds to its inevitable open end.

Exemplarity appears to be most clearly articulated in the play by the Chorus, a 'company of Jews' that concludes each Act with generalizations based on its view of the characters' dialogue. The Chorus's main function, indeed, appears to be to draw useful moral lessons – according to their lights – from the historical characters' words and deeds. At the end of Act 1, for instance, they follow immediately after Salome's attack on her husband, Constabarus, with stanzas that would appear at first to condemn Salome's disobedience:

> Yet oft we see that some in humble state,
> Are cheerful, pleasant, happy, and content:
> When those indeed that are of higher state,
> With vain additions do their thoughts torment.
>> Th' one would to his mind his fortune bind,
>> Th' other to his fortune frames his mind.
>
> (505–10)

They continue: 'That man is only happy in his fate / That is delighted in a settled state' (515–16). A few more lines reveal, however, that their example of unsettled longing for change is Mariam, and they offer no criticism of Salome as an example of bad behaviour at all (Straznicky 1994: 127). As other readers have noted, the Chorus's relations to the rest of the play are consistently problematic (Belsey 1985: 174; Ferguson 1988: 107–9; 1991a: 51–3; Raber 1995: 328–9). Similarly, at the end of Act 3, the Chorus holds Mariam up as an example of the erring wife who speaks publicly to a man not her husband. But since it is Salome who has just been plotting to divorce her husband and marry her lover, Silleus, the reader's experience of the play appears to be quite different from that of the Chorus, calling into question the accuracy or even the possibility of exemplarity, at least as articulated by the voice of the community.

If other exemplars offer themselves in the play, they might be the apparent binary opposites, Graphina and Salome, who, as Ferguson (1991a: 47) notes, 'At first glance . . . seem to come from a medieval morality play'. But as Ferguson argues, Salome's resemblance to a plotting, fleshly Vice and Graphina's silent, obedient chastity do not produce a simply understood 'ethical opposition', since Salome also speaks resound-ingly against the inequalities of Jewish law and Graphina, becoming 'more opaque the more one studies her brief appearance', also introduces the possibility of mutual love and 'safe' feminine discourse (ibid.: 47–8).

Just as exemplarity is both present and problematic in the play, so is a providen-tial framework. Constabarus is most often the voice of providential belief, looking back in Act 1 to the days of Moses when God 'did work his wonders in the land of Ham' (1.6.446) and in Act 4 to the punishment of Eve, which is, according to him, 'Cham's servile curse', or slavery. Arguably, however, Constabarus's historical view that God will punish wrongdoers is compromised by Cary's locating its source in his anger at Salome's betrayal. His history sounds increasingly like uncontrolled ranting. More-over, providence appears to be seriously malfunctioning in the play, since Salome not only survives her brother's reign of terror, but also engineers the execution of the com-paratively innocent Mariam and the Sons of Babas. Whatever Cary's own religious faith was in the first decade of the seventeenth century, her play offers no clear message that God's punishments and rewards are visible in historic events. As I have argued elsewhere, Mariam's martyrdom does possess Christological echoes, and so might be taken as an element of providential history (Beilin 1987: 171–2; Ferguson 1991a: 55); however, Cary also foregrounds the politics of the historical moment, for Mariam's death ends the possibility that she and her family, the Hasmoneans, will exert any influence over Herod, whose rule they consolidated.

Herod's reign of terror is, of course, made possible by Roman military might; the Romans made Herod king of Judea and he needs their continued support to rule. Thus, he is absent for three acts seeking Octavius's pardon for having supported Antony in the recent wars. Yet throughout the play references to Rome are ambigu-ous, accentuating both an idealized version of its greatness and virtue and the dimin-ishment and corruption of its present days. When Herod returns to Jerusalem his eagerness to see Mariam is expressed in a comparison to the wonders of Rome, the 'world-commanding city, Europe's grace' (4.1.21). But if Rome is thought to be the standard of greatness, Herod reveals its inadequacy:

> I all your Roman beauties have beheld,
> And seen the shows your ediles did prepare;
> I saw the sum of what in you excell'd,
> Yet saw no miracle like Mariam rare.
>
> (4.1.25–9)

'No miracle' is loaded here with the connotations that will ultimately separate Rome from Judea after the birth of Christ, but more immediately it also undercuts the primacy of the Roman state, making Rome the lesser city. Similarly, Herod's ensuing sonnet comparing 'the fair and famous Livia, Caesar's love, / The world's commanding mistress' to a superior Mariam diminishes his patron's wife; moreover, the sonnet itself implodes in its bathetic final couplet and comic rhyme when, expecting Mariam's entrance, Herod discovers, 'Oh no, it is Pheroras. Welcome brother. / Now for a while I must my passion smother.' Both the idea of Rome as the seat of feminine excellence and Herod's amorousness dissolve. As Nancy Gutierrez has argued, Mariam's unwillingness to be the sonnet lady when she first sees her husband in Act 4, scene 3, refusing 'to fit herself to Herod's expectations' (Gutierrez 1991: 240), empties the sonnet form of its social and literary significance, taking down Livia and Rome with it.

Mariam's own view of Rome comes much earlier in her argument with her mother, Alexandra, in Act 1. Alexandra is perhaps the play's most political creature, even more so than Salome, because she lusts for power alone. Having ambitiously sent the pictures of both her children, Mariam and Aristobolus, to Antony, Alexandra dreams that Mariam might have won Antony, who would kill Herod, desert Cleopatra, and 'Then Mariam in a Roman's chariot set', presumably in a triumphal procession. These fantasies of Roman grandeur are immediately squashed by her daughter, who implies both the corruption of Rome and her own virtue:

> Not to be empress of aspiring Rome,
> Would Mariam like to Cleopatra live:
> With purest body will I press my tomb,
> And wish no favors Anthony could give.
> (1.2.199–202)

These Roman references suggest that Cary's approach to Rome is sceptical, perhaps even satirical; her sketch of Judea is just as critical, but differs in its tragic overtones.

The single most voluble voice in Judea is that of the tyrant Herod himself, but his cruelty and oppression are the theme for all the other voices who speak their versions of Judean history under his rule. The female characters are the primary historians in the play, and in turn, Mariam, Alexandra, Doris, and even Salome contribute their views. After Mariam's introductory references to Caesar and Pompey, her mother, Alexandra, takes up the narrative of recent Judean history by rehearsing the significance of Herod's murder of her son, Aristobolus, and father, Hircanus. She traces their Hasmonean lineage back to Jacob, and excoriates Herod as the descendant of 'damned Esau' who sold his birthright to his brother: 'What kingdom's right could cruel Herod claim, / Was he not Esau's issue, heir of hell? / Then what succession can he have but shame?' (1.2.100–3). It is Mariam herself who has inherited 'David's chair' from her father, Alexander, and it is her succession that should be passed on to her son, Alexander. According to Alexandra, Herod's usurpation of the throne of Judea has both broken the link between the Hasmoneans and the Hebrew patriarchs and delivered the throne to a king who 'ever thirsts for blood' (1.2.106) and demonstrates 'raging lunacy' (1.2.124).

In Act 2 Doris, the wife whom Herod put aside to marry Mariam, continues the historical narrative, providing a completely opposing view of the Hasmonean dynasty and Queen Mariam. To her, Herod is a 'false monarch' for marrying Mariam, and her only recourse is revenge against her rival. She has clearly schooled her son Antipater well in his history, for he eagerly anticipates 'some subtle hidden plot' to murder the adulterous Mariam's 'bastards'. Returning in Act 4 to confront the condemned Mariam, Doris continues her wrathful tirade. Speaking less as the discarded wife and more as a mother (Miller 1997: 365), she continues to emphasize the issue of succession by insisting on the illegitimacy of Mariam's sons. Mariam's concern for her children, expressed in her begging Doris to 'Curse not mine infants' (4.8.606) is prophetic, and Doris's blood-curdling curses will be in part historically fulfilled: if her son, Antipater, will not quite 'come to be the death' of Mariam's sons (624), he at least contributes notably to their father's hatred of them. Reading on in the *Antiquities*, Cary would find Josephus's account of the continued enmity between Mariam's sons and Antipater, Salome and Pheroras, until their volatile relationship with their father concluded with Herod's ordering their executions in 7 BCE (Book XVI).

By giving the narration of Judean history to the opposing voices of Mariam, Alexandra, Doris and even Antipater, Cary disallows an official history, an establishment view, or an uncontested perspective. Mariam cannot be merely a historical exemplar of female virtue in the context of her mother's machinations and her (perhaps sympathetic) enemy's accusations. The internal dissension and insane politics of Judea obscure the providential sweep of Mosaic law and patriarchal succession. Two small scenes, Act 2, scene 2 and Act 4, scene 6, featuring Constabarus and the Sons of Babas, provide a final rationale for Cary's treatment of the fall of Rome and Judea. The Sons of Babas have lived both in Julius Caesar's Rome and Herod's Judea, thus bridging the two worlds of the play.

It is worth pausing over Josephus's narrative of Babas's sons because he strikes the key themes of succession and historical change. Josephus introduces them after Mariam's execution, at the moment when Salome sends an illegal 'libell of divorse' against her husband, Constabarus, because, she claims, he is part of a plot against Herod with Antipater, Lysimachus and Dositheus. As evidence, she tells Herod that Constabarus has hidden Babas's sons for 12 years. Josephus then explains 'the cause of this enmitie and hatred' that Herod feels for them. In the days of Antigonus, the last Hasmonean king, when Herod was besieging Jerusalem in an attempt to assume the throne of Judea, Babas's sons

being in authoritie, and besides that, attended by a great number of men, persevered in their faithfull observation of *Antigonus*, and blamed *Herod* continually, encouraging the inhabitants to continue the kingdome in those to whom it appertained by discent: and they themselves followed that course, which in their opinion was most profitably for the commonweale. (400)

Constabarus, newly appointed governor of Idumaea, decides that it might be politically useful to protect the popular sons, so that he hides them for 12 years and swears to Herod that he does not know their whereabouts. Once betrayed by Salome, however, Babas's sons are murdered, 'so that no one of *Hircanus* kindred was now left alive, but all of them being slaine, who excelled in nobilitie and dignitie . . .' (401). Although Josephus does not clarify the sons' relationship to Hircanus (and modern historians do not comment on it), it thus appears that the sons of Babas are Mariam's relatives, since Hircanus was her grandfather. Perhaps anticipating the death of Mariam's sons before their father, Josephus represents Judea at the end of the Hasmonean succession, as does Cary.

But Josephus continues his analysis of the significance of this execution for Herod and for Judea, for with the Hasmoneans' extinction, Herod

> did what himselfe listed without any contradiction or controulement: for which cause he by little and little forsooke the ceremonies and ordinances of his countrey, and corrupted the decrees and institutions of their ancestors, which he ought to have kept inviolable, by his new and strange inventions. In whose time there was a very great change and alteration of the auncient and good manner of living; for all fell from bad to worse, and the politike order, whereby the people ought to be governed and kept within compasse of their duetie, went to decay. (401)

Here, Herod typifies absolutism and its worst possible effects, the destruction of 'the politike order'. Responding to Josephus's commentary, in Act 2, scene 2, Cary associates Constabarus and the Sons of Babas with an 'auncient and good manner of living'. Babas's two sons are characterized first by their gratitude to Constabarus for preserving them from Herod at risk of his own life. The First Son's language is both political ('lives and liberties', 'tyrant's sword') and religious ('redeem'd', 'sav'd', 'grace', 'noble spirit'), suggesting that their discourse opposes both Herod's absolutism and his demonic cruelty. Constabarus calls the First Son a 'valiant youth' and a 'noble youth', rhyming 'youth' both times with 'truth'. Their friendship summons a past ideal world:

> With friends there is not such a word as 'debt':
> Where amity is tied with bond of truth,
> All benefits are there in common set.
> Then is the golden age with them renew'd,
> All names of properties are banish'd quite:
> Division, and distinction, are eschew'd:
> Each hath to what belongs to others right.
>
> (2.2.100–6)

Perhaps remembering Montaigne, Cary links the Sons through friendship to 'the golden age', and Constabarus proposes the ancient biblical exemplum of David and Jonathan, which he glosses as a virtuous friendship that overcomes the 'hate' of both father and sovereign.

As they discuss whether Herod is alive or dead, Constabarus argues that Octavius would be an 'idiot' to let Herod, Antony's friend, live. At this point, the Second Son gives Constabarus a history lesson, based on his own observation and experience of Rome in his 'boyish age'. Calling on an idealized version of Rome's past, the Son describes Octavius as a boy, as Julius Caesar's page: 'Methought I saw such mildness in his face, / And such a sweetness in his looks did grow, / Withal, commix'd with so majestic grace, / His phys'nomy his fortune did foreshow': Octavius appears here as the antitype to Herod because that boyish 'love to clemency' will conquer the 'choler' of the grown man and ruler. However, the irony runs deep, for that ideal of Roman *virtus*, the sweet boy who grows into the merciful ruler, is translated in the world of *realpolitik* into the supreme ruler Octavius's permitting the tyrant Herod to live on and persecute his enemies.

By Act 4, scene 6, after Salome has betrayed the three friends to Herod, and they are on their way to execution, Constabarus and the Sons of Babas have lost their golden age and their idealism, and can speak only of the corruption of the state and the world. After all, they are sandwiched between scene 5 featuring the Butler, the false witness about to hang himself in the throes of his guilt for incriminating Mariam; and scene 7, Salome's devilish convincing of Herod that Mariam must be executed. If they began as possible examples of virtue, Constabarus and the Sons of Babas end as political casualties, and even their exemplarity is undermined by their political naivety and by Cary's writing for Constabarus a vituperative attack on women instead of a noble and dignified exit to execution. He bids farewell to Jerusalem: 'fair city, never more / Shall I behold your beauty shining bright' (307–8). This significantly elegiac mode for the old city and the world evaporates, however, and Constabarus launches into his assault on the 'commonwealth' of women, spewing forth his collection of terms from misogynist texts. Motivated by his rage at Salome, Constabarus attacks all women and articulates an end-of-time scenario: 'I do the sottishness of men bewail, / That do with following you enhance your pride: / 'Twere better that the human race should fail, / Than be by such a mischief multiplied' (336–9). Between 2.2 and 4.6 the action of the play represents the corruption of the world. The possibility of Eden has been succeeded by 'the way to death' which Constabarus and the Sons of Babas must now follow; Jerusalem is lost and belongs fully to Herod. Perhaps even more disturbing than Constabarus's cynicism and hatred are the words of the young, impressionable Second Son, who all too eagerly subscribes to the misogynist's tirade. If he were to live, he exits saying, 'I would forever lead a single life, / And never venture on a devilish wife'. In Herod's Judea, the Son's education seems to lead only to the blind following the angry.

The short, sad story of the Sons of Babas is Cary's historical parable of the fall, of innocence corrupted, a paradigm for both Rome and Judea. Their life and death illustrate, in Josephus's words, how 'the politike order, whereby the people ought to be governed and kept within compasse of their duetie, went to decay'. Perhaps Cary was addressing an audience who worried about the 'fall' of England in the new century as the old Tudor order ceded to the new Stuart regime. But perhaps she also saw herself as a historian writing about the end of a world order without revelation: the secular power of Rome and the sacred power of Judea are both *in extremis* as the years advance toward the Incarnation. The way Cary writes such a history is to short-circuit all the reassurances, all the order that history itself might be expected to offer. Instead, she creates a succession of conflicting, desiring and hysterical voices just short of cacophony, rounding out the parade with a lunatic Herod longing for annihilation. The final Chorus of the play tells us that 'This day alone, our sagest Hebrews shall / In after times the school of wisdom call'. Cary invites her readers to look at this history play to find wisdom, but implies that only if all its voices are heard will the whole truth emerge.

See also WOMEN AND WRITING; DRAMA

ACKNOWLEDGEMENTS

I am particularly indebted to the seminar on Reading and Writing Late Medieval and Early Modern Women, taught by Carolyn Collette and Arlyn Dimond at the Massachusetts Center for Renaissance Studies. I am grateful to Heather R. Wolfe, who kindly permitted me to cite 'The Scribal Hands and Dating of *Lady Falkland: Her Life*' before publication.

REFERENCES AND FURTHER READING

Beilin, E. (1987). *Redeeming Eve: Women Writers of the English Renaissance.* Princeton, NJ: Princeton University Press.

Belsey, C. (1985). *The Subject of Tragedy: Identity and Difference in Renaissance Drama.* London: Methuen.

Berry, B. M. (1995). 'Feminine construction of patriarchy; or what's comic in *The Tragedy of Mariam.*' *Medieval and Renaissance Drama in England*, 7, 257–74.

Callaghan, D. (1994). 'Rereading Elizabeth Cary's *The Tragedie of Mariam, the Faire Queene of Jewry.*' In M. Hendricks and P. Parker (eds), *Women, 'Race', Writing in the Early Modern Period* (pp. 163–77). London: Routledge.

Cary, E. (1994). *The Tragedy of Mariam, the Fair Queen of Jewry with The Lady Falkland Her Life By One of Her Daughters*, ed. B. Weller and M. W. Ferguson. Berkeley: University of California Press. (Original work published 1613.)

Cary, L. (1994) [*c.*1645]. *The Lady Falkland: Her Life.* In B. Weller and M. W. Ferguson (eds), *The Tragedy of Mariam the Fair Queen of Jewry with The Lady Falkland Her Life By One of Her Daughters.* Berkeley: University of California Press.

Cerasano, S. P. and Wynne-Davies, M. (eds) (1998). *Readings in Renaissance Women's Drama: Criticism, History, and Performance 1594–1998.* London: Routledge.

Cespedes, F. R. (1980). '"We are one in fortunes": the sense of history in *Henry VIII.' English Literary Renaissance*, 10, 413–38.

Cicero (1942). *De Oratore*, trans. E. W. Sutton. Cambridge, MA: Harvard University Press.

Dean, P. (1986). 'Dramatic mode and historical vision in *Henry VIII.' Shakespeare Quarterly*, 37, 175–89.

——(1988). 'Tudor humanism and the Roman past: a background to Shakespeare.' *Renaissance Quarterly*, 41, 84–111.

Ferguson, M. (1988). 'A room not their own: Renaissance women as readers and writers.' In C. Koelb and S. Noakes (eds), *The Comparative Perspective on Literature: Approaches to Theory and Practice* (pp. 93–116). Ithaca, NY: Cornell University Press.

——(1991a). '"Running on with almost public voice": the case of E.C.' In Florence Howe (ed.), *Tradition and the Talents of Women* (pp. 37–67). Urbana: University of Illinois Press.

——(1991b). 'The spectre of resistance.' In D. Kastan and P. Stalleybrass (eds), *Staging the Renaissance: Reinterpretations of Elizabethan and Jacobean Drama* (pp. 235–50). London: Routledge.

Goldberg, J. (1983). *James I and the Politics of Literature: Jonson, Shakespeare, Donne and their Contemporaries.* Baltimore, MD: Johns Hopkins University Press.

Gutierrez, N. A. (1991). 'Valuing *Mariam*: genre study and feminist analysis.' *Tulsa Studies in Women's Literature*, 10, 233–51.

Helgerson, R. 'Murder in Faversham: Holinshed's impertinent history.' In D. R. Kelley and D. H. Sacks (eds), *The Historical Imagination in Early Modern Britain: History, Rhetoric, and Fiction, 1500–1800* (pp. 133–58). Cambridge: Cambridge University Press and Woodrow Wilson Center Press.

Kahn, C. (1997). *Roman Shakespeare: Warriors, Wounds, and Women.* London: Routledge.

Kinney, A. (1986). *Humanist Poetics: Thought, Rhetoric, and Fiction in Sixteenth-Century England.* Amherst: University of Massachusetts Press.

Lewalski, B. (1993). *Writing Women in Jacobean England.* Cambridge, MA: Harvard University Press.

Lodge, T. (1602). *The Famous and Memorable Workes of Josephus.* London: G. Bishop, S. Waterson, P. Short and T. Adams.

Miller, N. (1997). 'Domestic politics in Elizabeth Cary's *Tragedie of Mariam.' Studies in English Literature*, 37, 353–69.

Morwyng, P. (trans.) (1558). *A Compendious and Most Marveilous History of the Latter Tymes of the Jewes Commune Weale* [from Abraham ben David's abstract in Book 3 of *Sefer ha-Kabalah*].

Raber, K. L. (1995). 'Gender and the political subject in *The Tragedie of Mariam.' Studies in English Literature*, 35, 321–43.

Rebhorn, W. (1990). 'The crisis of the aristocracy in *Julius Caesar.' Renaissance Quarterly*, 43, 75–111.

Shannon, L. J. (1994). '*The Tragedie of Mariam*: Cary's critique of the terms of founding social discourses.' *English Literary Renaissance*, 24, 135–53.

Smuts, M. (1993). 'Court-centered politics and the uses of Roman historians, *c*.1590–1630.' In K. Sharpe and P. Lake (eds), *Culture and Politics in Early Stuart England* (pp. 21–43). Stanford, CA: Stanford University Press.

Straznicky, M. (1994). '"Profane Stoical Paradoxes": *The Tragedie of Mariam* and Sidnean closet drama.' *English Literary Renaissance*, 24, 104–34.

Wolfe, H. R. (1999). 'The scribal hands and dating of *Lady Falkland: Her Life.' English Manuscript Studies*, 9.

10

Mary Wroth, *The Countess of Montgomery's Urania*

Naomi J. Miller

Mary Wroth was born Mary Sidney in 1587, the first child of Robert Sidney (later Viscount de L'Isle and Earl of Leicester) and his wife, Barbara Gamage. Wroth was niece to both Sir Philip Sidney, the well-known Renaissance poet–courtier (author of *Astrophel and Stella* and *Arcadia*), and Mary Sidney, the Countess of Pembroke (a poet and patron of aspiring authors). Mary Wroth wrote the first sonnet sequence in English by a woman, *Pamphilia to Amphilanthus* (1621), one of the first plays by a woman, *Love's Victory* (printed for the first time in 1988), and the first published work of fiction by an English woman, *The Countess of Mountgomeries Urania* (1621; first modern editions published in 1995 and 1999). Wroth is noteworthy not simply for her gender as a woman writer in a period dominated by male voices, but for the range of her authorship as well: whereas other English women writers at that time, such as Aemilia Lanyer or Elizabeth Cary, are known for single texts or for their work in single genres, the volume and diversity of Wroth's texts attest to her extraordinary voice as an author.

Wroth spent her childhood at Penshurst, the Sidney family estate, and came to court in the late years of Queen Elizabeth's reign. Following her marriage to Sir Robert Wroth in 1605, Wroth maintained an active presence in court circles. She gave birth to a son, James, one month before her husband's death in 1614. When her son died two years later, the estate reverted to her husband's uncle, leaving Mary Wroth to face her husband's debts. Subsequently, she engaged in an affair with her cousin, William Herbert, third Earl of Pembroke, bearing two illegitimate children, William and Catherine, and maintaining ties with her circle of friends despite her reduced standing at court. The first portion of *Urania* was likely composed during these years, and was published in 1621 with her lyric sequence *Pamphilia to Amphilanthus*. Her play *Love's Victory* and the unpublished manuscript of the second portion of *Urania* were probably written in the early 1620s. Wroth raised her children with support from both the Sidney and Pembroke families, and lived until 1653.

The publication of the first portion of *Urania* in 1621 occasioned a court furore, when the objections of King James's male courtiers to the book's satirical references to their private lives forced Mary Wroth to withdraw *Urania* from sale only six months after its publication. Her primary attacker, Edward, Lord Denny, specifically chose to make Wroth's gender an issue, lambasting her not only for her allegedly topical references to his life, but just as scathingly for her effrontery as a woman in presuming to write secular fiction and poetry, by contrast to the more pious femininity associated with her aunt, the Countess of Pembroke's translations of religious poetry.

In two hostile letters Denny charged that Wroth had slandered his family in her fictional account of Seralius and his father-in-law. Denny's attack included a poem, entitled 'To Pamphilia from the father-in-law of Seralius', which comprises a compendium of many of the misogynist figurations of gender marking the Jacobean court. Addressing Wroth in his poem as a 'Hermophradite in show, in deed a monster', Denny advised her to 'leave idle books alone / For wiser and worthyer women have writte none'. The image of a 'Hermophradite in show' echoes the language of the cultural debate over transvestism which had reached a climax just the previous year, with the publication in 1620 of *Hic Mulier; or, The Man-Woman* and *HaecVir; or, the Womanish Man*. *Hic Mulier*'s attack on the 'Female-Masculine' of 'these new Hermaphrodites' revealed men's fear and loathing of women whose cross-dressing disrupted the visual boundaries of sexual difference. Denny's use of the label of 'Hermophradite' betrays a similar fear and loathing, elicited in his case not simply by the 'show' of female appearance, but by the 'deed' of female language as well.

Although Lady Mary Wroth assured the Duke of Buckingham that she had stopped the sale of her books, she responded directly to Denny's attack with a scathing letter and counter-poem of her own. The opening line of Wroth's poem – addressing Denny as a 'Hirmophradite in sense, in Art a monster' – immediately replaces Denny's attack on the 'body' of her work (and by extension on her own female body, construed as a 'Hermophradite in show') with her attack on the 'sense' of his language, and on the deformation of his 'Art'. Responding, Arachne-like, to Denny's characterization of her discourse as a spun 'Thrid', Wroth spins a web of language around Denny that recasts him as a supremely incompetent author ('a Thrid but of your owne all wordes worse spunn'), whose 'railing rimes' at once expose and deflate his 'brains swolne tide'. In a further exchange of letters, Wroth reminds Denny that she is, after all, not Pamphilia but rather 'the author of the booke', and concludes: 'be assured you shall find mee; what my blood calls mee to be, and what my words have said mee to be' (letters reprinted in Wroth 1988: 32–5, 233–45). As both flesh-and-blood woman and as 'the author' of her own book, Mary Wroth claims a position of agency as a speaking subject who cannot be silenced.

Nevertheless, the immediate suppression of Wroth's text had long-range consequences: only a few copies of the 1621 published *Urania* and only one copy of her unpublished continuation of the romance survive today; the first modern edition of the published 1621 portion of her romance did not appear until 1995, while the first published edition of the manuscript continuation appeared in 1999. In the three centuries following the attempted erasure of Wroth's text from the public record, critical silence ensued. In the first half of the twentieth century, Wroth earned only brief and usually dismissive mention in studies of the English novel or in surveys of women writers. The first modern edition of *Pamphilia to Amphilanthus*, edited by Gary Waller, appeared in 1977, followed by Josephine Roberts's edition of the complete poems in 1983, and Michael Brennan's edition of Wroth's play in 1988. The 1980s witnessed the appearance of numerous articles on Wroth, while the 1990s marked the publication of the first collection of essays devoted to Wroth, edited by Naomi Miller and Gary Waller (1991), and the book-length studies by Mary Ellen Lamb (1990), Gary Waller (1993) and Naomi Miller (1996), which devote significant attention to Wroth's works.

Many scholars have called attention to the social and rhetorical obstacles confronting Renaissance women who attempted to write within genres structured by male categories and dominated by masculine discourse. Faced with these obstacles, some writers, such as the authors of the feminist pamphlets of the period, adopt a defensive stance in seeking to refute the stereotypes presented by misogynistic treatises. Mary Wroth, however, chose not to portray women only reactively, in relation to patriarchal norms, but rather to explore, in her fictions, the possibilities encoded within a culture defined by women's voices as well.

On one level, Wroth changes the subject of Renaissance representations of desire through her treatment of women's approaches to questions of identity and sexual difference, emphasizing bonds between women at once in relation to and in contradistinction from the bondage of passion often imposed upon women by husbands and lovers, fathers and brothers. On another level, by contrast to male-authored depictions of woman-as-object, Wroth changes 'the subject' by re-presenting women as subject to patriarchal authority and yet working to claim positions as speaking subjects with independent existences as well. Mary Wroth represents women-as-subjects not according to a single model of feminine identity, which would indicate simply reverse stereotyping in response to dominant contemporary definitions of womanhood, but rather through multiple examples of identity formation.

Where many of Wroth's male literary predecessors construct their fictions of desire upon extremes of romantic conflict, placing unremitting emphasis upon struggles between the sexes, Wroth highlights complex connections among women which predate, coexist with and outlast the continually changing examples of conflict between men and women. At notable moments Wroth's works re-present the potential resilience of female discourse in a world where fluctuations in romantic fortune may be determined by male lovers, but possibilities for subjectivity are forged in the bonds between women. For example, in *Urania* Wroth reconfigures the 'heroine/confidante' pattern governing the presentation of female bonds in both native and continental literary antecedents, to establish more equality of voice and role in her representations of ties between women. Here her emphasis on mutuality rather than hierarchy in female friendship intersects with the writings of other Jacobean noblewomen: surviving letters and diaries written by women of the period attest to close and complex personal friendships among women of the courtly class to which Wroth belonged.

Evidence of such bonds among women can be found in the diaries of Lady Margaret Hoby and Lady Anne Clifford, the latter of which includes several references to conversations with 'Lady Worth', or Mary Wroth, as well as with Wroth's mother, Lady Lisle, Wroth's sister, Barbara Sidney, and Wroth's sister-in-law, Dorothy Sidney, Countess of Leicester (August, October 1617). In Mary Wroth's immediate family circle, surviving letters documenting the relation between Wroth's sister-in-law, Dorothy Sidney, and Dorothy Sidney's own sister, Lucy, Countess of Carlisle, suggest that the Sidney family women relied upon each other for political news and advice where the affairs of the court were concerned, as well as for emotional support (1639–40, De L'Isle MSS, U1475, C129).

Wroth's bold juxtapositions of vocal, confident female characters with equally compelling examples of silently victimized or passively obedient women allow her to explore a spectrum of women's roles and identities. In Wroth's *Urania* in particular, chastity offers some women opportunities for social freedom even as it imposes patriarchal constraints upon others. Likewise, while some of Wroth's mothers accede to the voice of fatherly authority in the family, others speak out. And while some of Wroth's female characters relinquish their agency under the bonds of matrimony, others locate in the constancy of female friendship an opportunity to assert boundaries of selfhood beyond the control of inconstant husbands or lovers.

The present essay focuses on Wroth's exploration, in *Urania,* of different conceptions of female identity, viewed particularly in relation to bonds of heterosexual desire, of maternity, and of female affinity and friendship. The aim of this essay is to offer an introductory assessment of the diversity of Wroth's representations of women as speakers and spoken for, actors and audience, victims and agents, in a fictional world that at once intersects with and illuminates the parameters of Wroth's own early modern society.

Identity and Desire

In her prose romance *The Countess of Montgomery's Urania* Wroth vastly expands her treatment of the lover/beloved relationship beyond the boundaries defining the dynamics of desire in *Pamphilia to Amphilanthus* and *Love's Victory.* Not only does Wroth prepare a much broader canvas of characters and action for *Urania* than for her play and lyric sequence, but she treats a range of sexual relations across a significantly expanded time frame, which distinguishes her romance not only from her other texts but also from the romances of her male predecessors, whether in prose, verse or drama. Unlike the primarily youthful protagonists created by Sidney and Spenser, Montemayor and d'Urfe, for example, Wroth's characters grow from youth to maturity, with three generations represented, enabling a consideration of the continuity of relationships over time. Wroth thus explores the issue of constancy and inconstancy in love, so central to the romance tradition, in a temporal framework that extends beyond the immediate formation and dissolution of bonds among the protagonists.

Wroth further alters generic conventions in order to represent the problematics of female subjectivity through the voice of a woman. Whereas Montemayor's *Diana* and d'Urfe's *Astree* open with the laments of faithful male lovers rejected by the eponymous female characters, and Sidney's *New Arcadia* commences with the mourning of Strephon and Claius over the departure of their beloved Urania, Wroth's narrative opens with Urania herself mourning not for love of a man, as does Spenser's Britomart after confronting the image of Arthegall in the mirror, but rather over the question of her identity *as a woman*. Unlike Sidney's Urania, Wroth's protagonist is no absent ideal, but a very noticeable female presence. Having just discovered that the shepherds who raised her are not her real parents, and that her origins are unknown, Urania cries out to herself: 'Of any miserie that can befall woman, is not this the most and greatest which thou art falne into? Can there be any neare the unhappinesse of being ignorant, and that in the highest kind, not being certaine of mine owne estate or birth?' (1). The plight of Urania, and of another of Wroth's 'lost shepherdesses', Veralinda, can be linked more directly to Shakespeare's Perdita than to the lamenting male shepherds of the prose romance tradition, yet Wroth heightens the tension of unknown identity beyond the example of *The Winter's Tale* by insisting upon the relevance of gender. For a woman to lack knowledge of her family origins in a patriarchal society is to lack a social identity. Without the patriarchal parameters of 'estate or birth' to define identity, Urania must locate a separate position both from which to speak and from which to identify her kindred.

Having assumed the security of her identity through 'the love of those [she] tooke for parents', Urania grieves to learn 'the contrary, and by that knowledge not to know my selfe' (1). Her complaint on the one hand addresses her lack of 'identity' in the sense of 'essential sameness or oneness' with others – in this case her parents – while at the same time providing a starting point for the construction of an individual subjectivity through her interaction with others separate from herself. Urania's awareness of her loss indeed initiates her discovery of her subjectivity through a process of social interaction rather than cultural victimization. By positioning Urania's lament at the beginning of her narrative, Wroth establishes both the power of gender to shape discourse and the importance of self-awareness as a starting point for female constructions of identity.

Far more frequently than Urania, the other leading female protagonist in Wroth's romance, Pamphilia, must endure the isolation of several 'enchantments' in the process of defining her identity within the courtship relation. These enchantments culminate in the 'hell of deceit' episodes near the end of the 1621 *Urania,* where Pamphilia and her lover Amphilanthus are separated and encounter visions of the other being tortured for love. Searching for her lover in the forest where they have lost each other, Pamphilia comes upon a 'Crowne of mighty stones' and pulls open a door in the greatest stone to discover a tableau vivant 'as in the hell of deceit', in which Amphilanthus stands bound before one of Pamphilia's rivals for his love, Musalina, who is preparing to raze the name of Pamphilia from his exposed heart (493). Amphilanthus meanwhile encounters a similarly illusory vision in the forest, revealing Pamphilia lying dead with her breast cut open and his name engraved in burning flames upon her heart (554).

In both instances, when the lovers attempt to break into the tableaux they are cast out and awaken from trances to find the vision vanished and the entrance closed. This double enchantment recalls the tableau in Book III of *The Faerie Queene* where Britomart observes Busyrane torturing Amoret by carving characters in 'living blood' upon her exposed heart. However, in Spenser's text the male enacts the enchantment while the women suffer or watch, whereas in Wroth's text, both male and female lovers are subject to enchantment and potential objectification through separation, and must determine their own courses of action in response.

In the manuscript continuation of *Urania* the tensions of courtship between Pamphilia and Amphilanthus modulate into the further complications of a secret marriage. Pamphilia and Amphilanthus engage in a secret wedding ceremony before several witnesses, including Urania, which is performed 'nott as an absolute mariage though as perfect as that, beeing onely an outtward Serimony of the church, this as absolute beefore God and as fast a tiing, for such a contract can nott bee broken by any cause whatsoever' (I: fol. 14v). In fact, this type of *de praesenti* marriage contract was considered as binding as a church wedding in early modern England. The not uncommon occurrence of such contracts can be gathered both from the fact that Mary Wroth's brother, Robert Sidney, was secretly married to Lady Dorothy Percy in 1616, and from a reference in a letter from Dorothy to Robert, twenty years later, concerning a secret marriage between two lovers without the knowledge or consent of their parents (13 April 1637, De L'Isle MSS, U1475, C82/24).

In covert terms, then, Pamphilia and Amphilanthus experience the transition from courtship to marriage which marks the maturation process of all the major protagonists in the romance. Unlike the other characters, however, their marriage remains secret, and is later violated by Amphilanthus's public wedding to the Queen of Candia when he mistakenly believes Pamphilia to be unfaithful. Although Pamphilia subsequently agrees to a public marriage with Rodomandro, the king of Tartaria, the lasting significance of the original contract between herself and Amphilanthus is recalled by scattered references throughout the narrative, such as Urania's description of Pamphilia as Amphilanthus's 'truest wife' (II: fol. 51).

While the courtship and marriage relation provide one context for Pamphilia's social identity, Wroth moves beyond the Petrarchan trope of the female beloved as a voiceless object of desire to indicate that Pamphilia's emergent sense of self is predicated upon her growing ability to fashion a voice for her desire. By defining her constancy in relation to her love, rather than in defensive response to a jealous lover, Pamphilia, as a speaking subject, decentres the repeated absences of that lover through an increasingly empowering revision of her own subjection to love. Even as Wroth's friend and contemporary, Lady Anne Clifford, preserved her subjectivity in the face of the punitive absences of her husband by maintaining the privately resolute discourse of her diary entries, so Wroth's fictional protagonist Pamphilia safeguards the continuity of her discourse from the instability of changeable male response by resolving to maintain her constancy, whether in the presence or absence of Amphilanthus.

At the same time, significantly, Wroth provides more than one articulation of women's relation to love, counterpointing Pamphilia's dedication to constancy with Urania's emphasis on female agency. Thus Urania actually criticizes Pamphilia's 'bondage' to love, asserting that women must not let 'want of courage and judgement make us [love's] slaves', and advising Pamphilia that even the virtue of constancy is not absolute, but rather culturally constructed with 'limits to hold it in' (399–400). In Wroth's narrative the presence of two women produces two voices, not a single 'female' perspective on love. In many senses Urania and Pamphilia serve as polarized representations of female desire throughout much of the romance, even as they forge developing conceptions of their identities based increasingly on affinities with other women rather than on social conventions of female sexuality.

Identity and Maternity

The nascent maternal subjectivity which underlies *Pamphilia to Amphilanthus*, and emerges into the open in *Love's Victory*, finds extended expression in the shared linguistic practices of mothers and daughters, aunts and nieces, in *Urania*. Published the year that Wroth's mother died, and alluding on its title page to Wroth's bond with her author aunt, Mary Sidney, the Countess of Pembroke, Wroth's *Urania* offers many compelling examples not simply of paternal tyranny but also of maternal power. Urania's opening lament over her lack of knowledge of her family origins signals, as discussed earlier, both the difficulty and the potential empowerment that can attend a woman's attempt to fashion a position from which to speak outside the standard definitional lines of estate or birth.

After initially mourning the absence of parents whose identities could stabilize her own, Urania particularizes her lament to the absence of the female parent, in comparing herself to her lambs: 'Miserable Urania, worse art thou now then these thy Lambs; for they know their dams, while thou liue unknowne of any' (1). Subsequently, when she comes upon a lamb wandering lost, she returns to the subject of her own desire for a mother:

Poor Lambe, said she, what moane thou mak'st for losse of thy deare dam? what tor-
ments do I then suffer, which never knew my mother? thy misse is great, yet thou a
beast may'st be brought up, and soone contented hauing food; but what food can bee
giuen me, who feede on nothing but Despaire, can that sustaine me? No, want of knowledge starves me, while other things are plentifull. (16)

Like the authors of early modern mothers' advice books, such as Elizabeth Joceline
and Dorothy Leigh, Wroth privileges maternal nurturance over physical nourishment
in giving voice to Urania's longing for her mother. Urania's recognition of the
importance of mothering to the development of 'knowledge' of oneself shapes her
subsequent mothering of her own children, as well as her ability to help other
female characters to define feminine parameters of self-fashioning throughout the
narrative.

Pamphilia, on the other hand, inhabits an over-determined familial identity, not
only as a royal patriarch's daughter, but also as the King of Pamphilia's 'Neece, who
by his gift was to enjoy that kingdome after his decease, and therefore bore that name
likewise given by him' (82). Far from experiencing Urania's problem of not knowing
her parents, Pamphilia finds herself flanked by a strong father and a strong uncle –
family bonds not unlike those of Mary Wroth – while being courted by the most
heroic of princes. Wroth further acknowledges her own familial heritage by forming
Pamphilia's name from a combination of syllables that echoes the names of Sidney's
Pamela and Philoclea. Small wonder, then, that Wroth represents Pamphilia's concern
with asserting and preserving autonomy as a lover and ruler.

Pamphilia's construction of her sovereignty in relation to her familial heritage
emerges in a conversation with one suitor named Leandrus, when she responds to his
question: 'are you not soveraigne of your selfe by judgement, yeares and authoritie,
unlimited by fortunes, by government, and the love of your Parents', with the answer:
'these still are but the threads that tie my dutie' (279–80). Her sovereignty of herself,
then, is located not in a condition of isolation, but rather in the context of her acceptance of ties that bind. Even as Queen Elizabeth I asserted publicly that 'I have known
what it is to be a subject, and I now know what it is to be a sovereign' ('Reply to the
Petition Urging Execution of Mary, Queen of Scots', 1588), so Pamphilia can be said
to know what it is to be a sovereign because she has known what it is to be a subject.

On the other hand, in wrestling with her subjectivity as a lover, Pamphilia demands
of herself: 'Can thy great spirit permit thee to bee bound . . . ? Scorne such servilitie,
where subjects soveraignize; never let so meane a thing ore-rule thy greatest power;
either command like thy self, or fall downe vassall in despaire' (198). Her condition
– 'though great as any, yet in love was as much subject as the meanest borne' (198)
– validates rather than undermines her subjectivity, because her capacity to 'command
like [her]self' stems from her ability to govern her own actions even when another is
'Monarch of her heart' (481). At once sovereign and subject, Pamphilia is only eventually enabled to move beyond fluctuating experiences of political empowerment and

romantic victimization by relying upon the kinship advice of other women, including the maternal figure of her own aunt, the Queen of Naples, who is supportive of the relationship between her niece and her son Amphilanthus.

Throughout *Urania*, at the same time, Wroth exposes the problematic gendering of authority and subjectivity within many familial structures. One male character takes care to distinguish between the sexes, for example, in commenting upon the admirable self-control of a lady following the death of her beloved: 'O women how excellent are you, when you take the right way? else, I must confesse, you are the children of men, and like them fault-full' (36). This judgement of course depends upon a male conception of 'the right way' in the first place, and assumes a masculine capability to evaluate the faults of women as fathered by men. On the other hand, when another male character inveighs against women's lightness and jealousy, having lost the favour of his own beloved, it is Urania's future husband, Steriamus, who reminds him that 'your mother was a woman, and you must be favour'd by an other, to be blessed with brave posterity' (159). Such a reminder balances the earlier perspective of women as 'the children of men' with a recognition of the engendering role of women as mothers. In effect, Wroth shifts the focus from the mother's body as a fortuitous conjunction of womb and breasts to the mother's role as author of posterity. Furthermore, Wroth's distinction between the reproductive agency of mothers and the limitations associated with 'the children of men' underscores her own capacity to move beyond the characterizations of her male predecessors in the romance tradition, transforming those 'children of men' through her representation of relationships not only between the sexes, but also within the family structure itself.

By juxtaposing oppressive instances of fatherly authority with the frequently liberating effects of maternal presence, in figures ranging from the Queen of Naples to Urania herself, Mary Wroth re-presents the absent, dead, malevolent or merely incompetent mothers who haunt the texts of her paternal forebears as speaking subjects in their own right, whose maternal authority is able to empower shared female discourse. In some instances of maternal discourse Wroth moves beyond the purview of her female contemporaries as well, in conjoining a private rhetoric of authority within the family with a public vocabulary of nurture and desire within the state.

The centrality of Urania's role in particular, not only as the title character of the romance, but also as a maternal model of authority and subjectivity, becomes evident when her children as well as her nieces and nephews reflect upon her position in determining their own. Writing against the dominant example of Shakespeare, Wroth borrows the names of characters from *The Winter's Tale*, only to revise radically the operative familial dynamics of Shakespeare's plot. The betrothal of the 'shepherdess' daughter of the ruler Leonius and the young prince Floristello thus recalls the betrothal of the 'shepherdess' daughter of Shakespeare's Leontes and the young prince Florizel. In Wroth's romance, however, it is the present friendship of the young lovers' mothers which contextualizes their bond, by contrast to the past rivalry of the lovers' fathers which contextualizes the bond in *The Winter's Tale*. Wroth's 'lost shepherdess',

Lindavera, is the daughter not only of Leonius but more significantly of Veralinda, whose name as well as identity complement those of her daughter, while the prince Floristello is the son of Urania. The friendship between these two female protagonists influences their children, as well as other characters, far more directly than do the roles played by their husbands.

Floristello, for example, reflects upon the pastoral appearance of his beloved in relation to the example of his mother, observing: 'yett why may she oh why may shee nott bee other, her spiritt is as high as an Emperess; was nott my mother a sheapherdes, yes, and the fairest, loveliest Urania' (I: fol. 32). With further reference to his mother, Floristello resolves to love this seeming shepherdess apart from her potential to 'bee other' than she appears, even as Urania was first loved for her worth rather than for her class or family position. At the same time, Lindavera justifies her right to give voice to her love for Floristello, despite her humble appearance, by considering that 'Urania, the beautie and wonder of the world for worthe, was butt a shepherdese as I ame in showe when Steriamus first loved her, when Parselius first loved her . . . I may bee as great as shee' (I: fol. 37). As ruling mothers, then, Wroth's major female protagonists inhabit a state of maternity which, far from being restricted to sexual reproduction, works to authorize the emergent subjectivity of each successive generation.

Identity and Affinity

Wroth's prose romance encompasses more voices than her lyric sequence, and represents more bonds among women both in connection with and apart from men than her play. While the lyric sequence, the play and the prose romance are all framed by the dynamics of heterosexual desire, Wroth develops the relationships among the characters in *Urania* not only before but also after marriage, so that her narrative patterns are not cut off by the traditional terminus of heterosexual couplings so common to many of the male-authored literary texts of the period. Furthermore, because Wroth does not always match up her male and female characters in pairs, avoiding the 'Noah's ark' convention which defines many romances in particular, she is able to expand her characterizations of female homosocial bonds without necessarily subordinating them to parallel examples of male friendship. To an even greater extent in *Urania* than in her other two works, Wroth explores the nature not of a female 'subculture', but of a female culture, to create the sound not simply of women's voices in a man's world, but of a world of women's voices which sometimes intersect with, sometimes subvert, and sometimes even override or outlast the voices of men. At the same time, at the heart of Wroth's narrative in all three of her texts can be located not only the potentially disabling effects of romantic desire upon women, but the potentially enabling force of female affinity as well.

As the narrative progresses, Wroth highlights the growing bonds among her female characters, often locating those bonds in triangulated contrast to fluctuations of romantic fortune between the sexes, as when Urania and Pamphilia discuss their differing relations to Amphilanthus as sister and lover, by contrast to their ties with one another as cousins and friends. Refusing to leave Pamphilia in solitary silence, Urania confronts her friend on the assumption that she has been mourning the inconstancy of her still publicly unidentified beloved, 'a thing familiar with men', and advises her to 'hate that humour by your owne worthy constancy, . . . and let not so uncertaine a qualitie hurt you', concluding: 'This I advise as my selfe would be advised if in such extremity, and this I say to you my dearest Cosin, and would say, though I knew it were my owne brother caused this mischiefe' (398–9). Urania's advice reveals at once her capacity for identification with her friend and her unerring perspicuity about the nature of the relationship involved. Although Pamphilia maintains the constancy of her desire, her revealing choice of superlatives in naming Urania her 'onely friend and dearest Cosin' (399) suggests for the first time that her 'other' cousin, Amphilanthus, no longer so exclusively dominates her affections. Indeed, Urania's characteristic frankness initiates a probing exchange between the cousins on the respective merits of constancy and love which includes Urania's discourse on the 'limits' of constancy (400), and which leads not to any simple resolution of the challenges to be faced, but rather to an opening of the lines of communication between the women.

The friendship between Urania, Pamphilia and Veralinda in particular endures many changes in their respective situations, from adolescent virginity to marriage, from motherhood to widowhood. When Wroth's female protagonists confront the transforming power of desire, bonding in friendship often relieves bondage to passion. It is only once Pamphilia learns from friends like Urania and Veralinda to recognize the regenerative potential of change over stasis, for example, that she can begin to accept the dynamic potential of constancy to inform bonds not only between lovers, but also between women.

Particularly in the manuscript continuation of *Urania*, conversations between the women serve to interrogate gender-specific assumptions concerning the dynamics of heterosexual bonding. Pamphilia and Veralinda, for example, engage in a heated exchange over the implications of Amphilanthus's inconstancy:

> Those days are past, my deere Veralinda, cride Pamphilia, and hee is changed, and proved a man; hee was ever thought soe, sayd Veralinda, but when hee shall see you againe, bee assured hee will bee, nay hee can bee noe other then as truly, ore att least as passionately loving you as ever; what care I for passion, lett mee have truthe, cride shee; I, that is best, sayd the delicate Veralinda, butt you were, and are the discreetest of your sex, yett you would have impossibilities; you say Amphilanthus is a man, why did you ever know any man, especially any brave man, continue constant to the end? . . . all men are

faulty, I would nott my self have my Lord Constant, for feare of a miracle . . . say he hath left you, lett him goe in his owne pathe, tread nott in itt, an other is more straite, follow that, and bee the Emperess of the world, comaunding the Empire of your owne minde. (I: fols 40–40v)

Veralinda's wry distinction between 'passion' and 'truth' exposes the limitations of the masculine subject even as her emphasis on the faultiness of all men encodes her refusal to idealize the object of her own or any other woman's desire. Veralinda points Pamphilia to another path instead, leading away from feminine subjection and passivity in the face of male inconstancy toward the potential empowerment of female agency: 'bee the Emperess of the world, comaunding the Empire of your owne minde'. Rather than constructing women's roles in relation to men's faults, Wroth's Veralinda asserts the possibility that women may choose a path of their own. With the encouragement of female friends such as Urania and Veralinda, Pamphilia moves beyond the dependency of her 'first loving' (II: fol. 57v) to realize her capability, as a woman, to command her mind's 'Empire' and to claim the authority of her own discourse.

By depicting female affinities that do not depend upon a 'primary' context of heterosexual desire or a 'parallel' context of male friendship, Wroth rewrites the gender hierarchies which govern the romances of her predecessors. By contrast to many male-authored lyric sequences, plays and prose romances, where examples of female friendship are either non-existent or repeatedly subordinated to representations of male bonding or the gendered hierarchies of heterosexual desire, each of Wroth's texts works to render bonds between women not only viable, but also eminently visible. Most particularly in the complex and capacious frame of her prose romance, Wroth's female characters voice differences of perspective in the company of other women which can expand our appreciation of the otherwise partial glimpses of female bonding to be found in such cultural texts as the diary of Wroth's friend, Lady Anne Clifford, and the correspondence of her sisters-in-law, the Countesses of Leicester and Carlisle, as well as in female-authored polemical texts and mothers' advice books.

In *Urania* Mary Wroth represents bonds between women as sometimes troubled and yet enduring, at once potentially restrictive and liberating. In foregrounding female bonds across a spectrum of social positions, from virginity and marriage to motherhood and widowhood, Wroth succeeds in representing complex networks of affinity with the power to foster female agency as well as identity. While not attempting to disguise or idealize the suffering often attendant upon heterosexual desire for women in early modern England, Wroth dares to represent the simultaneous existence of an alternative network of affection, connection and communication between women.

By defining the roles of individual women in her lyric sequence, play and prose romance not solely, or even necessarily, in relation to husbands and lovers, but also in relation to a larger community of parents and children, siblings and cousins, neighbours and friends, Lady Mary Wroth refashions the emphasis of her culture's governing constructions of femininity. By illuminating female bonding and representing mutuality rather than hierarchy as a viable basis for communication in friendship and love, Wroth feminizes the discourses of 'romance' across generic boundaries. She translates the 'subculture' of gossips' networks and male-authored representations of female bonds into a governing force in her texts, reforming the focus on patriarchal tensions to be found in the texts of her male literary predecessors in particular with her own emphasis on matrilineal bonds and shared women's speech.

The multiplicity and variety of women's voices in Wroth's works resist an essentialist interpretation of the nature of femininity in early modern England, inviting rather our renewed awareness of the constructed nature of every voice. Mary Wroth's narrative of 'the woman's part' in *The Countess of Montgomery's Urania* conveys the potential for women – as daughters and mothers, friends and lovers – to find not one but many voices of their own.

See also WOMEN'S POETRY 1550–1700; PROSE FICTION

REFERENCES AND FURTHER READING

Beilin, Elaine (1987). 'Heroic virtue: Mary Wroth's *Urania* and *Pamphilia to Amphilanthus*. In *Redeeming Eve: Women Writers of the English Renaissance* (pp. 208–43). Princeton, NJ: Princeton University Press.

——(1999). 'Winning "the harts of the people".' In Sigrid King (ed.), *Pilgrimage for Love: Essays in Early Modern Literature in Honor of Josephine A. Roberts* (pp. 1–17). Tempe, AZ: Medieval and Renaissance Texts and Studies.

Carrell, Jennifer (1994). 'Attack of lies in a looking glass: Lady Mary Wroth's *Urania* and the magic mirror of romance.' *Studies in English Literature*, 34, 79–107.

Cavanagh, Sheila (forthcoming). *Cherished Torment: The Emotional Geography of Lady Mary Wroth's Urania.* Pittsburgh, PA: Duquesne University Press.

Clifford, Lady Anne (1991). *The Diaries of Lady Clifford*, ed. D. J. H. Clifford. Wolfeboro Falls, NH: Alan Sutton.

De L'Isle Manuscript Collection. Kent County Archives Office, Maidstone, England. Esp. the Sidney family letters, U1475 and U1500.

Gaines, James F. and Roberts, Josephine A. (1993). 'The geography of love in seventeenth-century women's fiction.' In James Grantham Turner (ed.), *Sexuality and Gender in Early Modern Europe: Institutions, Texts, Images* (pp. 289–309). Cambridge: Cambridge University Press.

Hackett, Helen (1992). '"Yet tell me some such fiction": Lady Mary Wroth's *Urania* and the "femininity" of romance.' In Diane Purkiss and Clare Brant (eds), *Women, Texts, and Histories, 1575–1760* (pp. 39–68). London: Routledge.

Hall, Kim F. (1994). '"I rather would wish to be a black-moor": beauty, race, and rank in Lady Mary Wroth's *Urania.*' In Margo Hendricks and Patricia Parker (eds), *Women, 'Race', and Writing in the Early Modern Period* (pp. 178–94). London: Routledge.

——(1995). 'Blackness and status in the *Urania*.' In *Things of Darkness: Economies of Race and Gender in Early Modern England* (pp. 187–210). Ithaca, NY: Cornell University Press.

Lamb, Mary Ellen (1990). *Gender and Authorship in the Sidney Circle*. Madison: University of Wisconsin Press.

——(1991). 'Women readers in Mary Wroth's *Urania*.' In Naomi J. Miller and Gary Waller (eds), *Reading Mary Wroth: Representing Alternatives in Early Modern England* (pp. 210–27). Knoxville: University of Tennessee Press.

Lewalski, Barbara (1992). 'Revising genres and claiming the woman's part: Mary Wroth's *oeuvre*.' In *Writing Women in Jacobean England*. Cambridge, MA: Harvard University Press.

Miller, Naomi J. (1989) ' "Not much to be marked": narrative of the woman's part in Lady Mary Wroth's *Urania*.' *Studies in English Literature*, 29, 121–37.

——(1991). 'Engendering discourse: women's voices in Wroth's *Urania* and Shakespeare's plays.' In Naomi J. Miller and Gary Waller (eds), *Reading Mary Wroth: Representing Alternatives in Early Modern England* (pp. 154–72). Knoxville: University of Tennessee Press.

——(1996). *Changing the Subject: Mary Wroth and Figurations of Gender in Early Modern England*. Lexington: University Press of Kentucky.

Miller, Naomi J. and Waller, Gary (eds) (1991). *Reading Mary Wroth: Representing Alternatives in Early Modern England*. Knoxville: University of Tennessee Press.

Quilligan, Maureen (1989). 'Lady Mary Wroth: female authority and the family romance.' In George M. Logan and Gordon Teskey (eds), *Unfolded Tales: Essays on Renaissance Romance* (pp. 257–80). Ithaca, NY: Cornell University Press.

——(1990). 'The constant subject: instability and female authority in Wroth's *Urania* poems.' In Elizabeth D. Harvey and Katherine Eisaman Maus (eds), *Soliciting Interpretation: Literary Theory and Seventeenth-Century Poetry* (pp. 307–35). Chicago: University of Chicago Press.

Roberts, Josephine A. (1990). 'Radigund revisited: perspectives on women rulers in Lady Mary Wroth's *Urania*.' In Anne Haselkorn and Betty Travitsky (eds), *The Renaissance Englishwoman in Print: Counterbalancing the Canon* (pp. 187–207). Amherst: University of Massachussetts Press.

——(1991). ' "The knott never to bee untide": the controversy regarding marriage in Mary Wroth's *Urania*.' In Naomi J. Miller and Gary Waller (eds), *Reading Mary Wroth: Representing Alternatives in Early Modern England* (pp. 109–32). Knoxville: University of Tennessee Press.

Salzman, Paul (1985). '*Urania* and the tyranny of love.' In *English Prose Fiction, 1558–1700: A Critical History* (pp. 138–44). Oxford: Oxford University Press.

Shaver, Anne (1999). 'Agency and marriage in the fictions of Lady Mary Wroth and Margaret Cavendish, Duchess of Newcastle.' In Sigrid King (ed.), *Pilgrimage for Love: Essays in Early Modern Literature in Honor of Josephine A. Roberts* (pp. 177–90). Tempe, AZ: Medieval and Renaissance Texts and Studies.

Swift, Carolyn Ruth (1984). 'Feminine identity in Lady Mary Wroth's romance *Urania*.' *English Literary Renaissance*, 14, 328–46.

Waller, Gary (1993). *The Sidney Family Romance: Mary Wroth, William Herbert, and the Early Modern Construction of Gender*. Detroit, MI: Wayne State University Press.

Weidemann, Heather L. (1991). 'Theatricality and female identity in Mary Wroth's *Urania*.' In Naomi J. Miller and Gary Waller (eds), *Reading Mary Wroth: Representing Alternatives in Early Modern England* (pp. 191–209). Knoxville: University of Tennessee Press.

Wroth, Mary (1983). *The Poems of Lady Mary Wroth*, ed. and critical introduction by Josephine A. Roberts. Baton Rouge: Louisiana State University Press.

——(1988). *Lady Mary Wroth's Love's Victory*: The Penshurst Manuscript, ed. and introduction by Michael G. Brennan. London: Roxburghe Club.

——(1995). *The First Part of the Countess of Montgomery's Urania* by Lady Mary Wroth, ed. and critical introduction by Josephine A. Roberts. Binghamton, NY: Medieval and Renaissance Texts and Studies. [Citations from the first part of *Urania* in this essay refer by page number to the original 1621 edition.]

——(1999). *The Second Part of the Countess of Montgomery's Urania* by Lady Mary Wroth, ed. Josephine A. Roberts, textual introduction by Suzanne Gossett and Janel Mueller. Tempe: Arizona Center for Medieval and Renaissance Texts and Studies. [Citations from the second part of *Urania* in this essay refer by book and folio number to the sole surviving ms. copy in the Newberry Library, Chicago.]

11

Margaret Cavendish,
A True Relation of My Birth, Breeding and Life
Gweno Williams

The literary achievement of Margaret (Lucas) Cavendish, Duchess of Newcastle (1623–73) is distinguished by the remarkably ambitious scope of her personally orchestrated publishing career, unique among early modern women writers. Her first published work, *Poems and Fancies*, appeared in print in 1653, while she was in London to petition for her exiled husband's estates; thereafter she published virtually everything that she wrote. Her literary *oeuvre* is extensive and wide-ranging, comprising single and multiple editions of works in almost every contemporary literary genre: poetry, romance, autobiography, philosophy, science, drama, letters and biography. She moved readily and confidently between fictional and non-fictional genres.

Cavendish was an attentive and unusually interventionist author, supervising and funding publication in London, even from continental exile; highly critical of printers' errors in original and revised editions of her various works. Indeed, she changed printers several times during her publishing career. In accordance with her often-stated desire for fame, folio rapidly became her preferred publication format, the most expensive and ostentatious available. Numerous prefaces to her readers, addenda, handwritten corrections, and her frequent habit of including an internal advertisement for future volumes indicate an informed authorial awareness of the conventions and impact of publication. In the latter part of her career, Cavendish carefully revised her earlier works, sometimes into three editions. Her books were sold commercially and she also donated copies to prestigious libraries, particularly Oxford and Cambridge colleges, as well as sending them as gifts to individuals. Since the works of many early modern women writers either remained in manuscript or were published by male relatives or connections, Cavendish's personal and attentive engagement with publication stands out as remarkable. The forthcoming publication of Shirley Stacey's important and extensive research into Cavendish's publishing practices will illuminate many of these issues.

Cavendish's brief prose autobiography, *A True Relation of my Birth, Breeding and Life*, has a unique and enigmatic status within her publishing career, as the only text which she actively withdrew from print. It appeared early in her career as the final text in the first edition of her fifth published work, *Natures Pictures drawn by Fancies Pencill to the Life* (1656), a substantial collection of prose and verse narratives. It was subsequently omitted without explanation from the second, heavily revised edition of *Natures Pictures* (1671). Cavendish's publishing pattern changed significantly after her return to England at the Restoration. From political exile she had published only new works, often two per year, but from 1663 onwards she systematically balanced original works with the publication of new, often revised, editions of her early works. It was usual for Cavendish to make significant alterations to different editions of a text; of all her works, the second edition of *Natures Pictures* is arguably the most extensively revised (Fitzmaurice 1997: 359–64), and the most striking change is the silent omission of *A True Relation*.

Cavendish wrote *A True Relation* at a time when many women were engaging in different forms of reflective life-writing. Yet she is exceptional among her female contemporaries who wrote secular autobiographies, such as Lucy Hutchinson, Alice Thornton, Anne Clifford, Ann Fanshawe or Ann Halkett, because she actively published *A True Relation* within her own lifetime. Her initial publication of her autobiography in a handsome and expensive folio format is clear evidence of its intended public status, as is the fact that Cavendish personally presented copies of the first edition of *Natures Pictures* to the city of Antwerp, where she and her husband were living as prominent citizens at the time of publication. Two possibly rebound composite volumes of Cavendish's complete early works to 1656, including *A True Relation*, have survived in Antwerp Staatsbibliothek, both carrying the handwritten inscription 'Ex Dono Scripticis'. One also carries the handwritten date 1656, and a separate inscription in English: 'Guift of the Authoresse the thrice Noble, Illustrious, & excellent princess Lady Marchionesse of Newcastle & presented this Library in Antwerp 1656'. Additionally, her careful definition of London in *A True Relation* as 'the Metropolitan City of England' (45) is clear evidence of an intended local continental readership.

By 1671, however, Cavendish's attitude to her autobiographical memoir had undoubtedly changed. This essay explores possible reasons for the silent excision of *A True Relation* from Cavendish's *oeuvre* by examining notable aspects of the text, in particular its preoccupation with autobiographical 'truth' and its representation of the Civil War. *A True Relation* will also be located within Cavendish's broader autobiographical project in an effort to throw light on its unusual publication history.

'True Relation' or 'Partial Register'?

A True Relation is an extremely appealing example of early modern women's lifewriting, written in an immediate, accessible and direct style. In approximately thirty pages Cavendish provides a candid and roughly chronological account of her experiences until about the age of 32. She covers her upbringing as Margaret Lucas in her well-to-do royalist birth family in Colchester, describing the lives and values of the household in some detail. She recounts her bold and life-changing decision to serve as a maid of honour to Queen Henrietta Maria at the exiled court in Oxford, despite the reservations of some family members. A brief account of her subsequent marriage in Paris to the disgraced royalist Civil War general, William Cavendish, then Marquis of Newcastle, is followed by a description of their life and fortunes in political exile in Antwerp, and the beginnings of her publishing career.

Although the text is presented as a continuous and undifferentiated narrative, it is clearly structured to fulfil the promise of Cavendish's title by describing her 'Birth' briefly, and her 'Breeding' and her 'Life' at greater length. In addition, she idiosyncratically includes a further final section of lively, detailed and engaging self-analysis – 'I think it fit, I should speak something of my Humour, particular Practise and Disposition' (59) – in which she characterizes herself in detail, both as an individual and as a writer. The strong emphasis on individuality throughout her memoir is reminiscent of Montaigne, and highly unusual among early modern women writers. The text offers a remarkable amount of frank self-analysis, as Cavendish discusses in some detail her temperament, her fears, her health, her diet, her moods, her handwriting, her occupations and her ambitions, making her memoir one of the most self-revelatory pieces of life-writing produced by any woman of the period.

One of the most striking features of *A True Relation* is Cavendish's marked emphasis on the veracity of her text. It is prefaced by an 'Epistle to the Reader' which concludes: 'for the sake of After-Ages, which I hope will be more just to me than the present, I will write the true Relation of my birth, breeding and to this part of my Life, not regarding carping Tongues, or malicious Censurers, for I despise them' (Cavendish 1656: Aaa4r). Cavendish defines her autobiography as a form of self-vindication, a textual defence against the imprecisely defined, negative forces of 'censure'. Even her title insists upon the accuracy of the narrative; an insistence maintained throughout the text with at least twenty internal usages of 'Truth' (both upper and lower case), ''tis true' and 'in truth'. Arguing further that 'my life hath been ruled with Honesty, attended by Modesty, and directed by Truth' (59), *A True Relation* concludes with a manifesto: 'neither did I intend this piece for to delight, but to divulge, not to please the fancy, but to tell the truth' (63).

A True Relation's position within the volume *Natures Pictures* seems significant in this regard. *Natures Pictures* signals that it belongs to an established genre by drawing on the discursive literary and entirely fictional model of Chaucer's *Canterbury Tales*, or Boccaccio's *Decameron*. It consists of a series of prose and verse stories, ostensibly told by a group of Ladies and Gentlemen sitting round a fire. Cavendish's distinctive amendment to the generic model is to complement the various fictions with her own autobiography, setting up a crucial, and apparently simple, binary opposition between 'feigning' and 'truth' from the earliest pages of the volume. She introduces the first edition of *Natures Pictures* as composed of 'several feigned Stories of Natural

Descriptions . . . and a true Story at the latter end, wherein there is no Feignings'
(Cavendish 1656: 8).

Yet this apparently simple opposition is undermined from the start. The full title
of the volume – *Natures Pictures drawn by Fancies Pencill to the Life* – complicates and
interrogates the aesthetic and theoretical relationship between fact and fiction,
through the metaphor of the pictorial artist. It invokes the complex negotiations
between life and art so characteristic of Cavendish's style and subject matter. Is
'Nature' or 'Fancy' the artist? As 'Natures Pictures' these are presumably realistic and
lifelike. They are also an artistic product of the creative imagination, Fancy, drawn in
'Pencill', which is both an artist's sketching tool and provisional. Yet they also claim
to be as exact and accurate as possible, since they are drawn from live models 'to the
Life', and the volume concludes with a first-person textual 'Life'.

The tensions in the title of the volume encourage a sceptical approach to
Cavendish's truth-claims from the outset. Paul John Eakin has suggested that
'autobiographical truth is not a fixed but an evolving content in an intricate process
of self-discovery and self-creation, and, further, that the self that is the centre of
all autobiographical narrative is necessarily a fictive structure' (Eakin 1985: 3). He
refers to 'the play of the autobiographical act itself' (ibid.: 5). Cavendish's later
works, particularly her plays, include numerous allusions to the self as performance,
and several feminist critics have noted the fictionality of the self that appears in
A True Relation, most obviously in the contradiction between Cavendish's startling
self-assertiveness and her affirmations of feminine shyness and modesty. The editors
of *Her Own Life* describe the self presented in the autobiography as 'a shifting image, bold and yet shy' (89), Sidonie Smith discusses the tension between
Cavendish's 'self-asserting and self-effacing representations' (Smith 1998: 126),
and Elaine Hobby considers the 'conflicting demands' of Cavendish's desire for fame
and her need to align herself with contemporary ideals of femininity (Hobby 1988:
83–4).

If aspects of Cavendish's self-presentation in *A True Relation* can so readily be perceived as a construction rather than as 'truth', the whole question of truth in this text
would seem to require interrogation. Cavendish protests too much; her repeated insistence on the absolute veracity of her narrative may betray an awareness that the relationship between fact and fiction is rather more complicated than she is willing to
admit. She was certainly unconvinced of the truth of life-writing in general, referring
wittily in *Sociable Letters* (1666) to '*Plutarch's Lives* or as some call them Plutarch's lies'
(Fitzmaurice et al. 1997: 154).

Cavendish's direct addresses to her readers in *A True Relation* seem to register her
awareness of the vulnerability of her truth-claims. One reference appears early in the
text as part of Cavendish's description of the impressive physical attributes of her birth
family: 'eight children . . . every ways proportionable, likewise well featured, cleer
complexions, brown hair . . . sound teeth, sweet breaths, plain speeches, tunable
voices'. She concludes her detailed catalogue of her siblings' advantages with the

defence: 'I hope this Truth will not offend my Readers, and lest they should think I am a partiall Register, I dare not commend my Sisters, as to say they were handsome, although many would say they were very handsome' (49).

The concept of *A True Relation* as a 'partiall Register' is a telling one: Cavendish's account *is* 'partial', both in the sense of incomplete and politically partisan. On one level, the text's incompleteness, its omissions and silences, relate to questions of gender that have been examined by feminist critics of the work. In *A True Relation* Cavendish ostensibly defines herself principally within and by patriarchal family structures. As Smith, Hobby and the editors of *Her Own Life* have pointed out, the 'I' of the text is framed by her relationship to male authority, starting with her father, and concluding with her husband. These references also frame *A True Relation* temporally, demonstrating that Cavendish defines her own historic existence within a patriarchal chronology. The text begins in the past before her birth, with the opening words: 'My father was a Gentleman' (41), and concludes with an imagined possible future beyond her own death: 'lest after-Ages should mistake . . . especially if I should dye, and my Lord Marry again' (63). Her social self is defined throughout the text by the status of her father, brothers and husband.

Cavendish's shaping textual deference to male authority is 'partial', however, in so far as it obscures the fact that she actually seems to have lived almost all her life prior to marriage under strong female government. The Lucas household was effectively matriarchal, headed from Margaret's infancy by her widowed mother, whom she idealizes in *A True Relation.* Cavendish largely occludes the evidence for her mother's self-assertiveness and independence, describing her instead as a model of wifely and widowed fidelity (48). Yet Lady Lucas appears to have been an exceptionally strong character who bore an illegitimate son to her husband before their marriage, and managed the family estates and finances effectively after his death. Cavendish notably omits any reference to her eldest brother Thomas's illegitimacy and also obscures the way that her mother seems to have overridden the dispositions of her husband's will and achieved a remarkable measure of legal and economic control over the estate. Cavendish explains her mother's retention of significant administrative authority in widowhood in almost euphemistic terms: 'by reason she and her children agreed with a mutual consent' (42).

A short section of *A True Relation* deals with her life between her birth family and marriage, when she became a maid of honour at Henrietta Maria's feminocentric court in exile (46–7). She indicates that this ambitious initiative was supported by her mother, despite the opposition of the older siblings, including, by implication, her brother John, the nominal head of the family, 'as it were the Father to take care of us all' (44). Cavendish's convoluted account of her own highly ambivalent responses to court life emphasizes her mother's pivotal role in her remaining there. Lady Lucas's authoritative interventions in her daughter's future appear to have been shrewdly judged, since Margaret Lucas's presence at the exiled court eventually secured her significant social advancement through her prestigious marriage to William Cavendish.

Cavendish's private unpublished courtship letters reveal the queen's strong opposition to the marriage (Battigelli 1998: 119–32), yet *A True Relation* omits all reference to her own challenges to and negotiations with the queen's authority. So Cavendish's memoir combines apparent deference to patriarchy and established authority with interestingly occluded evidence of her mother's and her own determined legal and economic manoeuvrings to secure their own independence and choices. Cavendish seeks to disguise female self-assertiveness in deference to the gender norms of the period.

'These Unhappy Wars'

If Cavendish's insistently labelled 'true relation' contains omissions and evasions regarding her gender role, its curious incompleteness applies equally to her account of the Civil War. Major and decisive political events are either omitted or registered with surprising brevity. The execution of Charles I, for example, is referred to only obliquely in her detailed account of her mother's wartime sufferings, in an imprecise execration of 'Barbarous people [who] would have pulled God out of Heaven . . . as they did Royaltie out of his Throne' (48). This brief and solitary allusion to the climactic event of the Civil War might be interpreted as registering the traumatic impact of the king's execution as an apparent point of no return for royalists, particularly for those who, like Cavendish, were in exile.

The other meaning of 'partial' in Cavendish's phrase 'partiall Register' is political: *A True Relation* is a politically partisan, royalist text. The opening lines of her autobiography obliquely foreshadow the crisis of 'these unhappy Wars' (48) in her nostalgic description of her father's times: 'the Kingdome being in a happy Peace with all other Nations and it self' (41). The royalist experience of the war permeates the text, registered in emotive terms of greed and loss: 'plundered', 'sequestered', 'lost', 'banished', 'ruined'. The word 'ruin' carries a double meaning for Cavendish in her memoir. Its Shakespearian resonances of natural decay are deployed in an extended compliment to Cavendish's mother: 'her beauty was beyond the ruin of time' (48); 'time making suddener ruin in their faces than in hers' (49). It also denotes the specific royalist political experience of unnatural and undeserved disaster: she refers to William Cavendish's 'ruined fortunes' (51), and sums up her families' experiences as follows: 'not onely the Family I am linkt to is ruin'd but the Family from which I sprung, by these unhappy Wars, which ruine my Mother lived to see, and then died' (48). Both meanings coalesce most resonantly in her understated reference to the several deaths which signal the disintegration of her birth family: 'my Mother lived to see the ruin of her children, in which was her ruin, and then dyed' (49).

The crisis of civil war, defeat and exile seems to create cracks and fissures in the text. In particular, it fractures the idealized portraits of self and family that litter the narrative and seek to present a positive, affirmative picture of the royalist cause. *A True Relation* is ostensibly about Cavendish herself, yet she devotes a substantial proportion of the text to family members, indulging in particular in an elevated rhetoric of praise for her mother and for Charles Cavendish, her brother-in-law. This rhetoric and the idealized portraits it produces have a political aim. Cavendish repeatedly strives to glorify herself and her family, and through them the royalist cause they espoused, through association with particular, usually stereotypically upper-class, royalist qualities such as loyalty, contemplation, honour, virtue and (for the women) bashfulness. (Many of these affirmative qualities resurface in her plays of the 1660s as allegorical names for her protagonists.) Her individual and collective compliments to her birth family are numerous and repeated, but they are also troubled by the motifs of bereavement, transition and loss. The most public and politically traumatic Lucas death recorded in *A True Relation* is the controversial summary execution of her brother Charles Lucas at the siege of Colchester, her birthplace. This is at once understated and valorized by Cavendish: 'my brother Sir *Charles Lucas . . .* being shot to death for his Loyall Service, for he was most constantly Loyall and Couragiously active, indeed he had a superfluity of courage' (49). The repetition of key descriptors here – 'loyal', 'courage' – is characteristic of Cavendish's emphasis on the virtues to which royalists laid claim.

Like her oblique allusion to the execution of Charles I, this rather evasive account of her brother's death seems all the more emotionally charged for being so brief. Her description of her brother's execution also points to her tendency in *A True Relation* to personalize the tragedy of the Civil War around her own family: the wrongful execution of the king which she can hardly bring herself to mention is here localized in the figure of her brother Charles.

This personalizing impulse appears strongly when Cavendish draws on the Old Testament Book of Job. Unlike the majority of women writers of the period, Cavendish is a predominantly secular writer who rarely invokes the Bible as intertext. It is therefore noteworthy when she does so. At first sight *A True Relation* appears to contain only a single and rather oddly chosen reference to the Book of Job, one which continues the idealization of family, ostensibly affirming and celebrating the extreme closeness and intimacy of her siblings even when married and living apart. 'But when they were at London, they were dispersed into several houses of their own, yet for the most part they met every day, feasting each other like Job's children' (45). However, a reference to Job would have been unequivocally symbolic of loss, destruction and despair in this period, and the Book of Job clearly identifies such familial conviviality as the narrative prelude to unexpected and unmerited disaster:

> there came also another, and said, Thy sons and thy daughters were eating and drinking wine in their eldest brother's house: And behold there came a great wind from the wilderness, and smote the four corners of the house, and it fell upon the young men, and they are dead; and I only am escaped alone to tell thee. (Job 1.18–19)

Cavendish's reference to Job introduces a brief but intensely apocalyptic description of the impact of the Civil War on her family, almost precisely mirroring the tempestuous imagery and disaster of the biblical narrative: 'But this unnatural war came like a whirlwind, which felled down their houses, where some in the wars were crushed to death, as my youngest brother Sir Charles Lucas and my brother Sir Thomas Lucas' (45). The whirlwind image is taken directly from the Book of Job – 'Out of the south cometh the whirlwind: and cold out of the north' (Job 37.9); 'Then the Lord answered Job out of the whirlwind' (Job 38.1) – and it communicates Cavendish's horror at what she sees as the undeserved suffering experienced by royalists in the period. Again, she personalizes this, describing the war in terms of its impact on the Lucas and Cavendish family fortunes. Cavendish identifies her husband and herself as survivors in her memoir: 'yet, Heaven hitherto hath kept us, and though Fortune hath been cross, yet we do submit, and are both content with what is, and cannot be mended' (54). But her implicit association of her family with the experience of Job undermines such statements of resignation, drawing attention to the darker subtext of her autobiography with its intimations of the traumatic intensity of the Civil War experience.

Cavendish's preoccupation with 'Fame' in *A True Relation* may be in part a strategy to defend against the individual losses and defeats of the war: 'I am very ambitious, yet 'tis neither for Beauty, Wit, Titles, Wealth or Power, but as they are steps to raise me to Fames Tower, which is to live by remembrance in after-ages' (61–2). The same strategy certainly informs the account of the execution of Charles Cavendish in an anonymous contemporary play based on popular pamphlet sources. *The Famous Tragedie of Charles I* (1649) has a subplot based on newsbook reports of the parliamentary siege of Colchester, culminating in the politically sensitive execution of Charles Lucas. William and Margaret Cavendish's shared personal and political commitment to both Charles I and Charles Lucas, and their interest in drama, make it highly likely that they knew of and read this play. *The Famous Tragedie* idealizes Charles Lucas, emphasizing his noble rhetoric, in which he anticipates posthumous fame as compensation for present adversity:

> let us provide us fame when we are dead, that the next Age, when they shall read the Story of this unnaturall, uncivill Warre, and amongst a crowd of Warriors find our Names filed with those that durst passe through all horrors by death and vengeance for their King and Soveraigne:
> They may sing Peans to our valiant Acts,
> And yeild us a kind plaudit for our facts. (Anon 1650: C3r–v)

This typically royalist idiom runs through Cavendish's text, characterizing the war as 'unnatural' (45) and finding consolation for defeat and suffering in the promise of posthumous glory. Other contemporary women writers formulate religious consolations in response to disaster (see Anne Bradstreet 'Upon the burning of our house', or Katherine Philips's 'EPITAPH. On her Son H.P. at St. Syth's Church where her body also lies Interred', for example), but Cavendish, resolutely secular, eschews religion, turning instead to standard royalist tropes in order to affirm the importance and power of memory and fame to counteract vicissitudes. In doing so, she claims for herself a privilege traditionally restricted to upper-class men.

A True Relation suggests interesting connections with another contemporary printed genre, one which raises again the question of Cavendish's almost obsessive preoccupation with establishing the truth of her narrative. Cavendish's choice of title is an unusual one for a personal memoir: in the mid-seventeenth century, both 'Relation' and 'True Relation' were labels much more commonly employed in the newly emerging, uncensored genre of newsbook or reportage, detailing political or sensational news from a number of highly partisan political perspectives (Raymond 1993: 1–25).

The term 'relation' occurs in the titles of a number of contemporary pamphlet accounts of the crucial royalist defeat at the battle of Marston Moor, in which Charles Lucas and William Cavendish participated. These include Colonel James Somerville's *A full Relation of the Victory at Marstam-Moor* (1644) and Simeon Ashe's *A true Relation of the late fight between the Parliamentary Forces and Prince Rupert* (1644). Margaret Lucas is likely to have read these reports for news of her brother Charles. (It is often overlooked that Charles Lucas was the initial point of contact between Margaret and William Cavendish, since William was Charles's commander at Marston Moor.) Once she had married William Cavendish in exile in 1645, the frequent satirical remarks about him that appeared in newsbooks from at least 1644 onwards (Trease 1979: 143, 154; Wenham 1970: 190–1) must also have concerned her, perhaps prompting a desire to set records straight in print through her own *True Relation*. There are also significant parallels with the titles of reports of the siege of Colchester at which Charles Lucas was summarily executed in 1648, such as *A True and Perfect Relation of the Condition of these Noblemen and Gentlemen in Colchester and of their Reason in Yielding up the Said Town to the Lord Fairfax* (1648) or *A True and Exact Relation sent in a Letter From an Officer in the Army to a Member of the House of Commons* (1648).

In Antwerp, where Cavendish's *True Relation* was composed, newsbooks and pamphlets from England were an obvious staple source of 'report' for details of the progress of the Civil War at home (Trease 1979: 166). The pamphlet-style title of *A True Relation* indicates that it is, in a sense, her war document from exile. Patricia Crawford has stressed the importance of the English Civil War as a catalyst for the emergence of women's writing in the period (Crawford 1991: 213–14). Significantly, Margaret Cavendish, who had written since childhood (Bowerbank and Mendelson 2000: 9), only began to *publish* during the war's disruptions, specifically the petitioning trip to England contingent upon her marriage. The fractures, strains and omissions in *A True Relation* indicate how profoundly Cavendish was affected by the experience of civil war. Her memoir is clearly a politically partisan work, dedicated in part to a vindication of herself, her family and the royalist cause. It is not surprising, given this political agenda, that Cavendish should insist so vehemently upon the absolute truth and objectivity of her narrative, seeking to represent it as another 'True Relation' of the war years.

Margaret Cavendish's Autobiographical Selves

To return to the question with which this essay began, there would seem to be a number of possible reasons for the suppression of *A True Relation* in 1671. As an adversarial war document it would have outlived its usefulness after the Restoration. Margaret and William Cavendish had returned to England from exile, and newsbooks and pamphlets were no longer published as sources of 'report' and 'censure'. I would also argue that Cavendish realized that her carefully developed early opposition between truth and feigning, fact and fiction, was ultimately unworkable; her references to her readers certainly suggest some kind of preliminary recognition of the slipperiness of truth in *A True Relation* in 1656.

By the 1660s she had moved away from an insistence upon self-vindication and 'truth' to the construction of stylized fictional selves. *A True Relation* has often been treated critically as Cavendish's sole idiosyncratic autobiographical work. It has not been widely recognized that life-writing in different genres is an extensive and persistent feature of her *oeuvre*. An important key to the puzzle of Margaret Cavendish's suppression of *A True Relation* in 1671 may lie in the recognition of the multiple autobiographical strategies which she deployed throughout her publishing career. She produced a series of texts in which autobiographical material is contained within a fictional frame, in different genres. These include: the verse 'fancy' *Fantasm's Mask* (in *Poems and Fancies* 1653, revised 1664 and 1668), a number of poems and elegies in *Poems and Fancies* (1653) and *Natures Pictures* (1653/1671), and key sections of her prose romance *The Blazing World* (1666). Autobiographical elements also appear in *Sociable Letters* (1664) and the plays *The Presence* (1668) and 'Scenes from *the Presence*' (1668). All of these remained in print, or were republished.

Cavendish also published a biography of her husband in 1667, in which she features as a shadowy presence. Within the seventeenth-century female autobiographical tradition, it was not unusual to produce more than one version of a memoir, as both Alice Thornton's and Lucy Hutchinson's writings show, though their texts remained unpublished in their lifetimes. Cavendish is distinctive, however, in her move from direct unmediated first-person narrative in *A True Relation*, to elaborate fictionalized versions of self in later works.

It is instructive to conclude by comparing the work which might be termed Cavendish's fantastic autobiography with her early suppressed memoir. Rather than attempting to distinguish between truth and fiction, her utopian fantasy *The Blazing World* (1666) mixes them freely in describing a friendship between the fictional empress of this imaginary world and 'the Duchess of Newcastle', clearly identified as Margaret Cavendish herself. The boundaries of fiction are ingeniously collapsed as the author is invoked as a character in her own text. Cavendish's third-person characterization of 'the Duchess' is sophisticated and stylized. She is talented, resourceful and happily settled back in her husband's estates, recovered after the Restoration. She mentions the material losses of the war in passing (221–2), as she describes her present life to the empress, but without direct reference to past traumas of ruin or bereavement. Significantly, she identifies herself solely in relation to her husband, rather than her birth family. The past may be obliquely present in the text's overarching political aim of vindicating absolutism as the sole guarantee of social stability. Nevertheless, a distinctive feature of this autobiographical fiction is its privileging of possible futures, symbolized by the infinite number of new worlds which can be created by any individual imagination. 'The Duchess' is characterized as forward-looking, eagerly participating in the empress's project of constructing new worlds. The fiction concludes with a self-reflexive paratext in the first person: 'The Epilogue to the Reader' (250–1). Here, Cavendish wittily complicates textuality still further by placing herself simultaneously inside and outside the fictional frame, figuring herself as both character and author, whose 'ambition is not onely to be Emperess, but Authoress of a whole World' (250). She refers back to the Civil War in summarizing the politics of her imaginary world: 'though I have made my *Blazing-world*, a Peaceable World . . . yet could I make another World, as full of Factions, Divisions, and Wars, as this is of Peace and Tranquility' (251). She firmly rejects war, personified by a roll call of military heroes from antiquity, opting instead for her own self-creation: 'I esteeming Peace before War . . . chose rather the figure of Honest *Margaret Newcastle*, which now I would not change for all this terrestrial World' (251). Cavendish's fluid Restoration fiction concludes by affirming peace over war, the future over the past, and creative generic experimentation over any effort to fix autobiographical truth.

See also AUTOBIOGRAPHY; PROSE FICTION

ACKNOWLEDGEMENTS

Particular thanks are due to Anita Pacheco and Sara Mendelson. I would also like to thank Oliver Pickering, Judy Giles and Carol Breakstone.

REFERENCES AND FURTHER READING

Anon (1650). *The Famous Tragedie of Charles I.* London.
Battigelli, Anna (1998). *Margaret Cavendish and the Exiles of the Mind.* Lexington: University Press of Kentucky.
Bowerbank, Sylvia and Mendelson, Sara (eds) (2000). *Paper Bodies: A Margaret Cavendish Reader.* Peterborough, Ontario: Broadview Press.

Cavendish, Margaret (1656). *Natures Pictures drawn by Fancies Pencill to the Life.* London.

——(1667). *The Life of William Cavendish, First Duke of Newcastle.* London.

——(2000a). *A True Relation of my Birth, Breeding and Life.* In Sylvia Bowerbank and Sara Mendelson (eds), *Paper Bodies: A Margaret Cavendish Reader* (pp. 41–63). Peterborough, Ontario: Broadview Press.

——(2000b). *The Blazing World.* In Sylvia Bowerbank and Sara Mendelson (eds), *Paper Bodies: A Margaret Cavendish Reader* (pp. 151–251). Peterborough, Ontario: Broadview Press.

Crawford, Patricia (1991). 'Women's published writings 1600–1700.' In Mary Prior (ed.), *Women in English Society 1500–1800* (pp. 211–67). London: Routledge.

Eakin, Paul John (1985). *Fictions in Autobiography: Studies in the Art of Self-Invention.* Princeton, NJ: Princeton University Press.

Fitzmaurice, James (1997). 'Front matter and physical make-up of *Nature's Pictures*.' *Women's Writing,* 4, 353–67.

Fitzmaurice, James, Roberts, Josephine, Barash, Carol, Cunnar, Eugene and Gutierrez, Nancy (eds) (1997). *Major Women Writers of Seventeenth-Century England.* Ann Arbor: University of Michigan Press.

Graham, Elspeth (1996). 'Women's writing and the self.' In Helen Wilcox (ed.), *Women and Literature in Britain 1500–1700* (pp. 209–33). Cambridge: Cambridge University Press.

Graham, Elspeth, Hinds, Hilary, Hobby, Elaine and Wilcox, Helen (eds) (1989). *Her Own Life: Autobiographical Writings by Seventeenth-Century Englishwomen.* London: Routledge.

Hobby, Elaine (1988). *Virtue of Necessity: English Women's Writing 1649–1688.* London: Virago Press.

Mendelson, Sara Heller (1991). 'Stuart women's diaries and occasional memoirs.' In Mary Prior (ed.), *Women in English Society 1500–1800* (pp. 181–210). London: Routledge.

Pacheco, Anita (ed.) (1998). *Early Women Writers 1600–1720.* London: Longman.

Plowden, Alison (1998). *Women all on Fire: The Women of the English Civil War.* Stroud: Sutton Publishing.

Raymond, Joad (ed.) (1993). *Making the News: An Anthology of the Newsbooks of Revolutionary England.* Moreton-in-the-Marsh: Windrush Press.

Rose, Mary Beth (1986). 'Gender, genre and history: seventeenth-century English women and the art of autobiography.' In Mary Beth Rose (ed.), *Women in the Middle Ages and the Renaissance* (pp. 245–78). Syracuse, NY: Syracuse University Press.

Smith, Sidonie (1998). ' "The ragged rout of self": Margaret Cavendish's *True Relation* and the heroics of self-disclosure.' In Anita Pacheco (ed.), *Early Women Writers 1600–1720* (pp. 111–32). London: Longman.

Thomas, Peter (1991). 'The impact on literature.' In John Morrill (ed.), *The Impact of the English Civil War.* London: Collins and Brown.

Trease, Geoffrey (1979). *Portrait of a Cavalier.* London: Macmillan.

Wenham, Peter (1970). *The Great and Close Siege of York, 1644.* Kineton: Roundwood Press.

Wilcox, Helen (1992). 'Private writing and public function: autobiographical texts by Renaissance Englishwomen.' In S. P. Cerasano and Marion Wynne-Davies (eds), *Gloriana's Face: Women, Public and Private in the English Renaissance* (pp. 47–62). Detroit, MI: Wayne State University Press.

12

Anna Trapnel, *Anna Trapnel's Report and Plea*

Hilary Hinds

England's Rulers and Clergie do judge the Lords hand-maid to be mad, and under the adminstration of evil angels, and a witch, and many other evil terms they raise up to make me odious, and abhorr'd in the hearts of good and bad, that do not know me.

Trapnel, 'To the Reader', *Report and Plea*

Anna Trapnel's catalogue of the kinds of hostile reception she received is an apt starting point for a consideration of one of the four texts published by and about her in 1654, the year in which she was most consistently in the public eye, for it serves as a reminder that in order to begin to make sense of her writings (and other activities) we need to take account of the context in which she was writing – a context variously hostile (as here) and sympathetic, but, for a while at least, unfailingly fascinated by her.

Trapnel was just one of the many women who participated in and shaped the radical Puritan sects that proliferated in the 1640s and 1650s, during the turmoil, instability, excitement, anticipation and fear (depending on one's political, social or religious position) generated by the events of the English civil wars, commonwealth and ensuing protectorate of Oliver Cromwell. These sectarian groupings were diverse and ever-changing, each with a distinct perspective and programme, but they had in common a sense that the 'revolution' being enacted by those in power (namely, parliament and the army) was not fundamental enough in its bid to eradicate ungodliness and corruption from church and state. Trapnel's particular alignment was as a Particular Baptist and a Fifth Monarchist: that is, she had a Calvinist belief in the predestined and unchangeable election of those who were to experience God's salvation, and she had a millenarian belief in the imminent destruction of the corruptions of this world and their replacement with the establishment on earth of the New Jerusalem (the 'Fifth Monarchy') and the second coming of Jesus, as ruler of this new order.

Trapnel's Calvinism was neither unusual nor seen as subversive; indeed, it had been the prevailing orthodoxy within the Church of England since late the previous century. Rather, it was her Fifth Monarchist beliefs that generated the kind of hostility that she details in the opening quotation, for it was these beliefs that had implications for, or impinged directly on, the institutions and systems of power in place at the time: as she says, it is the 'Rulers and Clergie' who inveighed most vigorously against her, and it is indeed their interests and privileges that her religious (and therefore social and political) programme most insistently and uncompromisingly challenged.

It was not, however, only Trapnel's millenarianism, with its attendant antipathy to the established church, tithes, the legal system, the universities, and (as the Fifth Monarchists saw it) the backsliding and betrayal of the previously sympathetic Cromwell, that troubled her audience; it was also the manner in which her beliefs and ideas were articulated: namely, in the form of prophecies, delivered by her in a state of (she claimed) God-given trance. It was in such a state of prophetic trance, indeed, that Trapnel first became known to a public broader than that of her own congregation, friends and family. In January 1654 she fell into a trance while she was at White-hall to attend the examination by the Council of State (the main executive body since the execution of the king in 1649) of a fellow Fifth Monarchist, Vavasor Powell, who had been arrested for preaching against the government. Friends took her to a nearby inn, where she stayed in her trance state for 12 days, eating and drinking almost nothing, and prophesying in extemporary verse as well as prose on the subject, by and large, of Cromwell's betrayal of the Fifth Monarchist cause. She had a diverse audience throughout the 12 days, including current and ex-MPs and well-known clergymen, and, from the fifth day onwards, her words were recorded by an anonymous 'relator'. Two accounts of this were soon published: the short *Strange and Wonderful Newes from White-hall* and the longer (some 75 pages) *The Cry of a Stone*, which includes, as well as a third-person account of the trance and a first-person account of Trapnel's earlier life and prophecies, the relator's transcription of the Whitehall prophecies themselves. The fact that one of Cromwell's most loyal and influential informers, Marchamont Nedham, sent a report on Trapnel to the Protector gives a sense of the kind of furore created by the prophecies and by the prospect of their subsequent dissemination in print. It was following the Whitehall trance and the resulting publicity that she was invited by friends to travel to Cornwall to continue her prophesying work. It is this journey that forms the basis of the narrative of her *Report and Plea*.

This brief excursion into the context and circumstances of production of the *Report and Plea* goes some way towards explaining the hostility that Trapnel and her work encountered. Not only was she a woman unapologetically staking her claim to a place in the overwhelmingly masculine world of the public domain; she was also voicing a series of radical ideas explicitly hostile to those in positions of social, political and religious power, expressed in such a way that to disregard her words was tantamount, her rhetoric suggested, to ignoring the words of God himself. Trapnel was acutely aware of the hostility generated by her activities, as well she might be: she wrote (or, more likely, dictated) the *Report and Plea* whilst in Bridewell, London's infamous House of Correction, where she was imprisoned for eight weeks following her arrest in Cornwall for 'aspersing the government' – that is, sedition. These details alone confirm that her characterization of others' responses to her was not exaggerated – indeed, the six months or so leading up to this moment, since her Whitehall prophecies brought her so much public attention, seem to have consisted of one series of accusations after another.

If this was the kind of response that Trapnel encountered, or expected to encounter, the question then arises as to the impact this expectation had on the texts that she produced. Certainly, she makes explicit reference to such reactions and accusations repeatedly in the text; that which opens this chapter is only one of many. This, however, is only one of several ways in which this text might be said to be explicitly in dialogue with Trapnel's detractors. In the rest of this chapter I aim to trace the discursive strategies in the *Report and Plea* working to pre-empt and disarm such opposition: in what ways does the text contrive to refute these accusations, and what complications do these strategies bring with them for the argument that Trapnel seeks to make? First, however, it is necessary briefly to describe the scope, structure and range of address of the *Report and Plea*, for, like so much seventeenth-century radical sectarian writing, the text is not easily accessible to readers now. Whilst some nine pages of the overall 62 are available in a collection of seventeenth-century autobiographical writings by women (Graham et al. 1989), the text is otherwise only open to those able to consult the original in a few research libraries. The following brief overview will, I hope, serve both to situate the anthologized extract and to encourage readers to turn to the full text wherever possible (see 'Textual Note' below).

Anna Trapnel's Report and Plea announces itself on the title page, in more ways than one, as a composite or multiple text:

Anna Trapnel's
Report and Plea.
Or, A
NARRATIVE
of her Journey from London into Cornwal, the
occasion of it, the Lord's encouragements to it,
and signal presence with her in it.

Proclaiming the rage and strivings of the People a-
gainst the comings forth of the Lord Jesus to reign . . .

Whereto is annexed
A DEFIANCE
Against all the reproachful, vile, horrid,
abusive, and scandalous reports, raised out

> of the bottomless pit against her, by the pro-
> phane generation, prompted thereunto by Professors
> and Clergie, both in Citie and Country, *who
> have a form of godliness, but deny the power* . . .

This first, narrative section comprises Trapnel's account of the request she received from friends to travel to Cornwall with them, the reaction and ultimate encouragement of her congregation, Trapnel's attempt to resist God's call to go, and her reconciliation to it; then follow the journey to Cornwall, accounts of her trances and prophecies, her arrest and hearing before the Justices of the Peace, her rearrest and journey under guard back to London, and her imprisonment in Bridewell. The second section, 'A Defiance', is a detailed enumeration and refutation of the various accusations she has encountered: witch, impostor, vagabond, whore and 'dangerous seditious Person, . . . devising and maliciously intending the peace, tranquillity and felicity of the good people of this Commonwealth of *England* to disturb, . . . to move, stir up, and raise discord, rebellion and insurrection' (p. 52). The juxtaposition of the 'Narrative' and the 'Defiance' raises interesting questions of the relationship between them: in what ways might the two sections be said to be in dialogue with each other, as well as with their readership? One way of thinking about this is to consider the narrative as constitutive of the 'report' – the factual, chronological recounting of events – whilst the 'defiance' forms the 'plea' – the polemical appeal to her readership to refute, with her, the accusations of her detractors. If this is the case, then the 'plea' might be said to be in excess of the narrative section, a final impassioned diatribe that rescues the overall text from the uncharacteristically (for Trapnel) *unprophetic*, moderate and measured tones of the narrative section.

Whilst the layout, and particularly the punctuation, of the title page allows for the separation of the 'report' from the 'plea' in this way, it is also possible to read the title page as announcing a rather different kind of 'multiple text'. As I have suggested elsewhere (Graham et al. 1989: 73–4), the narrative section *alone* can be seen to be constitutive of both report and plea; by this account, the 'Defiance' becomes a much more independent text, 'annexed' to the narrative section but separate from it. Not only does the layout of the title page allow this reading, but the rhetoric of the narrative itself, I think, encourages it. Early in the text, Trapnel makes explicit her aim in writing the narrative:

> I go not about to vindicate my self, but Truth; which indeed stands in no need of mine or any ones vindication; but I would shew love and respect to it, in opposition to those, who with spades and shovels dig up mire and rubbish to throw upon it. ('To the Reader')

In characteristic style, doubling back on and reinflecting her every statement, Trapnel here sets up 'Truth' and 'self' as incompatible. In order to vindicate the truth – God's truth – the self, a carnal impediment to divine revelation, must be kept at bay. 'Vindication', however, is perhaps too worldly an aim, as it suggests the vulnerability of God's truth to human opposition, so this initial aim is reworked (not entirely revoked, as it still stands in the text) as a desire to 'shew love and respect' to the truth – a much more deferential and subject-like position to take up in relation to it. This self-denying stance is reiterated at other points, but increasingly seems to exist in tension with a 'self' that refuses to vacate the text and a 'truth' that is much more complicated than the inviolable and free-standing truth of the initial declaration:

> though I fail in an orderly penning down these things, yet not in a true Relation, of as much as I remember, and what is expedient to be written; I could not have related so much from the shallow memory I have naturally, but through often relating these things, they become as a written book, spread open before me, and after which I write. (p. 34)

'A true Relation' is here clearly distinguished from 'an orderly penning down' or exact chronological account, and is seen instead to be the outcome of processes of memory, expediency and repetition. However, in this the self seems again to be too perilously close to intruding into the picture, particularly in the form of those all-too-human attributes of memory and expediency. Again, though, the text doubles back on itself, away from such dangers, by relocating the moment of composition as always elsewhere and always prior, so that in effect Trapnel becomes no more than her own amanuensis, copying her own words from a pre-existing 'written book' that has been produced by a more-than-natural (or other-than-natural) memory brought into being by the previous recounting of the events in question.

In the light of these kinds of textual manoeuvres, where the self can be seen manifesting and removing itself at so many levels in the text, it becomes increasingly difficult to maintain any rigid textual distinction between 'report' and 'plea'. If the report aims to vindicate or praise God's truth, and the plea is intended to clear Trapnel's name, then the latter aim can be seen to be achieved as much by the 'Narrative' as by the 'Defiance': for if the recording 'self' of the narrative is not as unblemished and unassailable – indeed, as transparent, as absent – as she claims, then the 'truth' of God's word will inevitably be called into question, and what she claims as such will have to be reread as carnal vainglory or the work of the devil. The plea for self-vindication thus comes to be an integral part of the establishing of her own prophetic bona fides, and, conversely, the report of God's word will inevitably work to vindicate Trapnel's reputation. A virtuous circle of report, plea, self, text, truth and God is thus set in train, whereby the multiple character of the text is the result of the imbrication of these elements rather than their juxtaposition, and where the success of the whole rhetorical and polemical enterprise stands or falls with each of these diverse elements.

This level of textual investment in tying in 'self' to godliness suggests a high —
and, as we have already seen, not inappropriate — level of anxiety about the ways in
which she and her prophecies are going to be read. There are many ways to make
sense of this insistent tone: a practical response to the hostility she had already experienced, as suggested above; a zeal for the establishment and communication of her
own particular spiritual and political programme; but also, as a number of critics have
recently pointed out, a recognition of and response to the complexity and vulnerability of the position that she found herself in, as a woman prophet of religio-
political ideas. The signifiers of prophecy and possession with which, necessarily, she
found herself working were profoundly opaque and open to contestation: her body,
with its ecstatic trances accompanied by tears and fasting, and the language associated with these bodily conditions in the prophecies themselves, had no commonly
(either culturally or religiously) agreed meanings. They could not simply be dismissed
out of hand as signs of melancholy or madness, for, as Michael MacDonald put it,

> Many godly Protestants believed that the Lord might directly inspire His prophets with
> visions of the future or doctrinal truths. . . . But when allegedly inspired prophets were
> not plausible instruments of God's purpose, either because they were sectarians or simply
> unworthy, many thought them insane . . . [A]s long as the possibility for inspiration
> remained widely accepted, only *individual* prophets could be debunked as madmen.
> (MacDonald 1981: 156–7)

MacDonald's final point is the key one here: as long as the possibility of direct inspiration or revelation from God was generally admitted, then a prophet might be castigated not on the grounds of the impossibility of their claim, but because of flaws
in the person of the prophet or in their doctrine — 'flaws' of politics ('they were sectarians') or of personal unworthiness (which might include such things as immodesty,
vainglory or a misplaced sense of revelation). Therefore each claim to direct divine
revelation had to have its claims to authenticity rigorously interrogated, for 'some
doubt always remained that strange perceptions might be genuine glimpses of the
unseen world, whose immediate and potent presence was assumed by almost everyone' (ibid.: 170). Moreover, there was not only the distinction between madness and
genuine possession to be made, but between godly and diabolic possession, all of
which manifested themselves in remarkably similar ways: as Phyllis Mack suggested,
'A person who was possessed might be experiencing a heavenly vision, an attack of
lunacy or a diabolical fit' (Mack 1984: 221). Gender added yet another dimension to
this configuration, for, as Mack argued, whilst women were on the one hand seen as
more likely to be chosen by God as conduits of his word because of their inherent
passivity, irrationality and passion, on the other hand these same traits rendered them
more open, too, to diabolic possession, and also reinforced the widespread cultural
association of femininity with hysteria and irrationality: 'Outrageous behaviour by a
woman, whatever her motives or the source of her inspiration, must have invited more

intense scrutiny than that by men' (ibid.: 222). For Trapnel, and other women prophets, this scrutiny was of both body and words, and of the complex relationship between the two.

The *Report and Plea* bears witness repeatedly to the vulnerability to misinterpretation of her bodily states and of her words. When, for example, Trapnel is incarcerated in Bridewell, she tells us that she is made ill by the dampness and stench of her cell. Nonetheless,

> the Matron urged me with the first day of the week to go hear their Minister at *Bridewell*, but I told her, I was very ill, she said, she thought I dissembled at the first, but afterward she thought it was a Judgement from the Lord, my sicknesse, because I was unwilling, she said, to hear their Minister: and she said, she saw by my high colour, that I was not well, and indeed I was much in a feaver that day only . . .
> But that second day in the night, I was pleading with the Lord, and asked of the Lord a removall of that sicknes, and saying, Lord, its very grievous to ly sick in this place; the Lord answered me, and said, I have taken away thy sicknesse, thou shalt be sick no more, while thou art here in *Bridewell*, for I will fill thee with more triumph here, than ever thou hadst in thy life . . . and I spake by way of prayer and singing from morning till night, and felt no sicknesse nor pain, nor faintnesse, not all that day, nor at night when I came to my self, to be capable of a body; for truly, all that day I was wrapt up, so that I could not tell, whether I was in the body or out . . . (pp. 41–2)

Clearly, the meaning of Trapnel's illness is in dispute here; the matron argues first that it is a marker of her duplicity, and then that it is divine punishment for refusing to go to listen to the minister, whilst for Trapnel it becomes a means by which God can once again demonstrate his love for her and a place where she can experience 'more triumph . . . than ever thou hadst in thy life'. In order to establish that it is indeed a sign of godliness rather than godlessness, however, Trapnel has to resort to evidence that is, in its turn, highly contested in meaning: namely, an instance of the trance state that accompanies her recovery, which, as always, removes her from any sense of her own body, its situation or its sensations: in other words, she can only turn to other opaque signifiers to attempt to confirm her reading of the one in question. Repeatedly, Trapnel attempts to fix the meanings of various bodily conditions, whether tears ('I weep not for sorrow, but my tears flow from apprehensions of communion with the Lord, and those glorified Saints there' (p. 30)), fasting ('coming into my ordinary capacity, I rose and had strength of body, though I could not eat the day before, nor ate this night, thus speaking so much; yet I was not dry, neither could I take any creature-refreshing' (p. 6)) or the trances themselves ('the Lord carried me in singing & prayer after they were gone two hours, as I was told, and then I came to my self . . . I said, *Have I lain alone all this day? I have had a sweet day:* she replied, and said *did not I hear the Justices there, and the uproar that was in my chamber?* I said, *No.*' (p. 22)). This insistence on her own readings of her body argues for both the significance and the power to signify of the prophetic body, and necessitates the recognition of an added dimension to Trapnel's repeated assertion that the self is a hindrance to the apprehension of the divine will: the 'transparency' of self that Trapnel seeks to secure is not that of a disembodied subject, but, on the contrary, that of an unselved body, commandeered by God, emptied of *social* meaning and marked out instead for *spiritual* meaning.

Like the body itself, the words that emanate from it are also vulnerable to misapprehension and abuse. Ensign Owen, for example, one of her guards while she is being transported back to London under arrest, 'indeavoured to catch my words, and to ensnare me, putting his own sense upon them, but the Lord kept me out of his ensnarements' (p. 33); likewise, Mr Hughes, a minister, said that 'he had read my book, and he from that drew that I was an impostor and he called the book nonsense' (p. 33). The impression is that, for Trapnel, words are signifiers as malleable, as opaque and as open to contestation as the body itself is, and need to be used with caution in order to try to control others' misconstruction of them. In her account of the behaviour of the JPs in court, for example, Trapnel writes:

> they were in a hurry and confusion, and sometimes would speak all together, that I was going to say, *What are you like women, all speakers and no hearers?* but I said thus, *What[,] do you speak all at a time? I cannot answer all, when speaking at once.* (p. 26a)

Not surprisingly, Trapnel cannot trust here that her words would not be turned back on her, and she thus chooses to rephrase her verbal parry in such a way as to make it work more straightforwardly to her own advantage.

If the JPs cannot be relied upon to interpret her words 'correctly', how then are we, as readers, to be persuaded to produce the desired interpretation of the words on the page? One answer to this question is that the text repeatedly re-enacts moments of conviction such as she seeks to secure in her reader; it works, in other words, through exemplification of the power of witness. Trapnel invokes her own bodily presence as a guarantee of her own prophetic status, by recounting time and time again the power of both her 'ordinary' and 'extraordinary' (ecstatic) bodily states to convince others of her version of herself. Her account of her court hearing, for example, is framed by the following two passages:

> as I went along the street, I had followed me abundance of all manner of people, men and women, boyes and girls, which crowded after me; and some pull'd me by the arm, and stared me in the face, making wry faces at me, & saying, *How do you now: how is it with you now?* and thus they mocked and derided at me. (p. 23)

> And as I went in the croud, many strangers were very loving and careful to help me out of the croud: and the rude multitude said, *Sure this woman is no witch, for she speaks many good words, which the witches could not.* And thus the Lord made the rude rabble to justifie his appearance. (p. 28a)

The text enacts for us, then, the process which it is seeking to induce in its reader-ship: the conversion of hostile sceptics to loving supporters. Unable to witness for ourselves the powers of conviction of the physical presence of Trapnel herself, we are shown, again and again, how (for all but 'Rulers and Clergy' such as the JPs) the mere *sight* of Trapnel combines with the power of her words to convince even the most scep-tical (as here) of the truth of her account. One of the false witnesses procured to speak against her (p. 27); Lieutenant Lark at Plymouth Fort (p. 32); the sailors on the ship from Plymouth (p. 35) – in each case, *seeing* her allows her words to have the power that God intended them to have. Trapnel herself sums up this process in the opening paragraph of the 'Defiance':

> some have said, they thought I had been a Monster, or some ill-shaped Creature, before they *came and saw*, who then said, they must change their thoughts, for I was a woman like others, that were modest and civil. (p. 49; my italics)

The textual enactment of such moments, however, cannot in itself be trusted to produce the requisite conviction of truth, for such representations are dependent on the still unreliable, because human and therefore carnal and corrupt, power of words. In other words, in her written text Trapnel is necessarily deploying in her own (or God's) defence (or praise) one of the sign systems that has in the first place been opening her up to accusations of fraud, witchcraft, immodesty and sedition: namely, language. Her trance state is justified by the words that she speaks, her words by the trance state in which she utters them: she is caught in a situation in which all attempts to confirm the godliness of her words or her condition can only be enacted by reference to yet more words and conditions that are open to dispute and misreading.

One way to break out of this loop, however, is to turn to the only language that is *not* subject to such carnal fallibility: that is, the undisputed word of God himself, as found in the Bible. This is precisely what happens in this text, through a process of what we might call 'self-inscripturation': the writing-in of herself, her text and her life to the scriptures. The most straightforward way in which she does this is by apply-ing passages from the scriptures to the circumstances she finds herself in – a well-established and uncontroversial Puritan practice that asks believers to judge their own and others' behaviour according to biblical standards:

> I prayed them that derided, that they would have a care, and that they therein would consider the saying of Christ in the 25. of *Matthew*, who said, what they did to his, they did to him, though I be one of the worst of Christs little ones, yet said I, he will own me. (p. 28)

Secondly, Trapnel makes direct comparisons between herself and her situation with figures and events from the Bible:

I can say with *Paul*, Through grace I am what I am; and I live, yet not I, but Christ lives in me; and the life that I live, is by the faith of the Son of God, who dies, and gave himself for a weak handmaid, as well as for a strong *Paul*. ('To the Reader')

These comparisons extend even to Christ himself: as Trapnel walks to the courthouse, she describes herself as 'in such a blessed self-denying lambe-like frame of Spirit . . . I had such lovely apprehensions of Christ's suffering, and of that Scripture which saith, *He went as a sheep, dumbe before the sheerers . . .*' (pp. 23–4); similar parallels are drawn between Trapnel's and Christ's trials and punishments throughout (see too, for example, p. 27a). Thirdly, these *explicit* comparisons are reinforced by *implicit* allusions to biblical events and tropes. This might be just at the level of an unattributed phrase, such as her description of her friends' behaviour in court as 'seasoned with the salt of grace', words which appear in Colossians 4.6. But the most sustained example of this is in the repeated recording that Trapnel communicated most directly with God whilst walking in gardens (see pp. 5, 11–13, 23, 25). This can be seen as an echo both of the *hortus conclusus* motif of the Song of Solomon (an ambiguous image in a book whose meaning has been long contested within Christianity, but which has in the past often been taken as describing the love of Christ for his church) and of Christ's communication with God in the garden of Gethsemane on the night prior to his crucifixion – a particularly potent allusion, given Trapnel's own circumstances.

Together, these modes of self-inscripturation have the effect, to some extent at least, of removing the text from the realm of fallible human language and realigning it with the revealed, scriptural word of God. Removing her prophecies (and herself) in this way from the problematic and vulnerable realm of opaque and contested signifiers, whether bodily or linguistic, is thus part of a rhetorical strategy to persuade her readership of the godliness of her prophecies and thereby to deflect or answer the kinds of accusations and persecutions she details in the *Report and Plea*. Whilst readers today might find themselves assessing the text on rather different grounds from those of Trapnel's contemporaries – we are perhaps less concerned with the 'truth' of her words, and more interested in the politics and rhetoric of her discourse – we still find ourselves in an actively discriminating and dialogic relationship with the writing. What we make of this unfamiliar, part-autobiographical, part-prophetic and part-polemical text is still in question. What I have tried to do in this chapter is offer some contextual and textual pointers towards a reading of it; however, it is still up to each new reader to 'well observe the ensuing Discourse' ('To the Reader') for themselves, to analyse its textual modes and strategies, and to consider the place in the history of women's writing of what seems, to this reader at least, to be an extraordinary piece of linguistic, rhetorical and polemical dexterity.

See also AUTOBIOGRAPHY; PROPHECY

Textual Note

A list of libraries holding *Anna Trapnel's Report and Plea* (1654) can be found in Wing (1994–8). For this essay, I consulted the edition held at Friends' Library: shelfmark 010 [Qm1/1]. The pagination of this edition is erroneous, running from 1–28, then 25–59. In this chapter, a reference to 'p. 26a', for instance, is to the first page 26.

References and Further Reading

Burrage, Champlin (1911). 'Anna Trapnel's prophecies.' *English Historical Review,* 26, 526–35.

Capp, B. S. (1972). *The Fifth Monarchy Men: A Study in Seventeenth-Century English Millenarianism.* London: Faber and Faber.

Chedgzoy, Kate (1996). 'Female prophecy in the seventeenth century: the instance of Anna Trapnel.' In William Zunder and Suzanne Trill (eds), *Writing and the English Renaissance* (pp. 238–54). London: Longman.

Graham, Elspeth, Hinds, Hilary, Hobby, Elaine and Wilcox, Helen (eds) (1989). *Her Own Life: Autobiographical Writings by Seventeenth-Century Englishwomen.* London: Routledge.

Hinds, Hilary (1996). *God's Englishwomen: Seventeenth-Century Radical Sectarian Writing and Feminist Criticism.* Manchester: Manchester University Press.

Hobby, Elaine (1988). *Virtue of Necessity: English Women's Writing 1649–1680.* London: Virago Press.

Ludlow, Dorothy (1985). 'Shaking patriarchy's foundations: sectarian women in England, 1641–1700.' In Richard L. Greaves (ed.), *Triumph over Silence: Women in Protestant History* (pp. 93–123). Westport, CT: Greenwood Press.

MacDonald, Michael (1981). *Mystical Bedlam: Madness, Anxiety and Healing in Seventeenth-Century England.* Cambridge: Cambridge University Press.

Mack, Phyllis (1984). 'Women as prophets during the English civil war.' In Margaret Jacob and James Jacob (eds), *The Origins of Anglo-American Radicalism* (pp. 214–30). London: George Allen and Unwin.

——(1988). 'The prophet and her audience: gender and knowledge in the world turned upside down.' In Geoff Eley and William Hunt (eds), *Reviving the English Revolution: Reflections and Elaborations on the Work of Christopher Hill* (pp. 139–52). London: Verso.

——(1992). *Visionary Women: Ecstatic Prophecy in Seventeenth-Century England.* Berkeley: University of California Press.

Prineas, Matthew (1997). 'The discourse of love and the rhetoric of apocalypse in Anna Trapnel's folio songs.' *Comitatus,* 28, 90–110.

Purkiss, Diane (1992). 'Producing the voice, consuming the body: women prophets of the seventeenth century.' In Isobel Grundy and Susan Wiseman (eds), *Women, Writing, History 1640–1740* (pp. 139–58). Athens, GA: University of Georgia Press.

Smith, Nigel (1989). *Perfection Proclaimed: Language and Literature in English Radical Religion 1640–1660.* Oxford: Clarendon Press.

Trapnel, Anna (1654a). *Anna Trapnel's Report and Plea.* London.

——(1654b) [2000]. *The Cry of a Stone,* ed. and intro. Hilary Hinds. Medieval and Renaissance Texts and Studies series. Tempe, AZ: Arizona Center for Medieval and Renaissance Studies.

Trubowitz, Rachel (1992). 'Female preachers and male wives: gender and authority in civil war England.' In James Holstun (ed.), *Pamphlet Wars: Prose in the English Revolution* (pp. 112–33). London: Frank Cass.

Wing, Donald (1994–8). *Short-Title Catalogue of Books Printed in England, Scotland, Wales and British America, and of English Books Printed in Other Countries, 1641–1700,* 2nd edn. New York: Modern Language Association of America.

Wiseman, Susan (1992). 'Unsilent instruments and the devil's cushions: authority in seventeenth-century women's prophetic discourse.' In Isobel Armstrong (ed.), *New Feminist Discourses: Critical Essays on Theories and Texts* (pp. 176–96). London: Routledge.

Woolrych, Austin (1982). *Commonwealth to Protectorate.* Oxford: Clarendon Press.

Worden, Blair (1985). 'Providence and politics in Cromwell's England.' *Past and Present,* 109, 55–99.

13

Katherine Philips, *Poems*

Elizabeth H. Hageman

She's the queen of poets, whosoer's the king.

Sir William Temple, 1664

The glory of our Sex, envy of men.

Philo-Philippa, 1667

In her own lifetime, Katherine Philips (1632–64) was a well-known member of the British literary 'scene'. When she was 19 a poem by her was printed as the first of 54 prefatory poems in William Cartwright's *Comedies, Tragi-Comedies, With other Poems . . . The Ayres and Songs set by Mr. Henry Lawes* (1651). In the same year her fellow Welsh poet Henry Vaughan included in his *Olor Iscanus* a poem 'To the most Excellently accomplish'd Mrs. K. Philips', in which he asserts that 'No Lawrel growes, but for [her] Brow' (l. 44). After the Restoration Philips's writing began to appear in print with some regularity. In 1662 her poem welcoming Catherine of Braganza to England, 'To the Queens Majesty on her Happy Arrival', was published on a broadside by the London bookseller Henry Herringman. Her translation of Pierre Corneille's heroic drama *Pompey* was performed at John Ogilby's Theatre Royal in Smock Alley, Dublin, in February 1663 and printed twice that spring – both times by John Crooke, king's printer in Dublin. In March 1663 Crooke printed a quarto edition for Samuel Dancer, who had a bookshop on Dublin's Castle Street, and in May he reprinted the play for sale at his own bookshop in St Paul's Churchyard in London. That spring, three of Philips's poems were published in *Poems, by Several Persons*, a collection also printed by Crooke for Dancer's bookshop, and in January 1664 an unauthorized octavo edition of 75 of her poems was printed in London by John Grismond for the publisher Richard Marriott. In the six months between that date and the date of her death, Philips apparently worked on two projects: a corrected edition of the poems and a translation of Corneille's *Horace*. When she died, she had almost finished the fourth act of *Horace*; the amount of progress she had made on an authorized edition of the poetry is not now known.

Poems by Philips also circulated in manuscript copies, many of which survive today in archives such as the Bridgewater Collection at the Huntington Library, the Evelyn Papers in the British Library, and the National Library of Wales. Some are extant in musical settings by musicians such as Henry Lawes and Henry Purcell, and one – an epitaph she wrote for her sister-in-law's husband John Lloyd – survives on his funeral monument in Cilgerran, Cardiganshire. Philips's *oeuvre* is a remarkable body of work, especially impressive when one remembers how short was her writing career. In addition to *Pompey* and most of *Horace*, she translated four French poems and one Italian song. Her original work includes poems on public topics such as the restoration and coronation of Charles II; philosophical poems on topics such as 'The World', 'Death' and 'Friendship'; social poems such as elegies, epitaphs and epithalamia; and a variety of more personal poems on love, marriage and friendship.

Family and friends figure prominently in Philips's work. Her extant writing includes poems on the deaths of her young son Hector; her mother-in-law, Anne Philips; her stepdaughter, Frances; and her third stepfather, Philip Skippon, whom she addresses as 'my truly honoured Publius Scipio'. In a number of surviving letters Philips plays on her brother-in-law's name Hector as she calls him 'the Trojan'. Similarly, she uses the Greek names Antenor for her husband and Cassandra for her sister-in-law Cicily. Others of her friends bear traditional pastoral sobriquets or names from contemporary plays and prose romances: Dering is Silvander; Frances Finch, Palaemon; Mary (Aubrey) Montague, Rosania; Anne Owen, Lucasia. Sir Charles Cotterell is the Poliarchus to whom Philips wrote letters printed after her death as *Letters from Orinda to Poliarchus*; Philips herself is Orinda.

In most respects, what is said above suggests that Katherine Philips's life and career were much like those of other well-known seventeenth-century poets and that her poetry would fit nicely into any standard literary history of the period. The daughter of a prosperous London merchant and the wife of a member of the Welsh gentry, Philips was an elite woman. Although she did not attend a university and apparently did not read Latin or Greek, she was fluent in French and knew at least some Italian. She was an active theatre-goer and well-read in seventeenth-century English and continental literature. She married a man of political significance (James Philips was in 1653, for example, a member of Cromwell's Nominated Parliament) and considerable fortune. A cousin by marriage to John Dryden, Katherine Philips was born in the same year as he. Like Dryden, she was 10 when the civil wars began, 17 when Charles I was executed, 28 when the monarchy was restored to England. As a result of family and school connections, she was acquainted with a large circle of prominent poets and politicians – both parliamentarians (as were many members of her own family) and royalists (as Philips herself tended to be). Although Philips's social class put her on an equal footing with many of the contemporaries she addresses in her poems, she uses the rhetoric of patronage poetry to address social superiors such as Alice, Countess of Carberry; Elizabeth Boyle, Countess of Cork; the Duchess of York; Charles II and Catherine of Braganza. Philips herself was never at court, but her friend Cotterell was master of ceremonies to Charles II and presented copies of her poems and of *Pompey* to members of the royal family. She was praised in print by Dryden; Wentworth Dillon, Earl of Roscommon; and Roger Boyle, Earl of Orrery; and her death was lamented in verse by men as prominent as Sir William Temple and Abraham Cowley. And yet there was of course a key difference between Katherine Philips and the other poets mentioned thus far in this essay: Philips was a woman writer.

In 1667 a posthumous volume of Philips's writing was published by Herringman. It includes 117 original poems and the translations mentioned above. A handsome folio, it is introduced by a series of telling documents. The frontispiece image by the important engraver William Faithhorne represents her as a sculpted bust atop a pedestal on which her sobriquet 'Orinda' is engraved. Both enclosed and framed within a semi-circular niche, the classicized poet wears the earrings, curled hair and low-cut dress of a Restoration court beauty. Modestly, her head is tipped downward, looking not toward the viewer, but toward the title page, where she is designated 'the most deservedly Admired / Mrs. Katherine Philips, / The matchless Orinda'. Embedded within an unsigned preface is a letter Philips had written in 1664 for Cotterell to circulate among her friends as evidence that Marriott's publication of her poems was not her doing. According to the 1667 editor, the letter 'is enough to shew how little she desired the fame of being in print, and how much she was troubled to be so exposed' (a1v). The preface claims authenticity for this edition of Philips's writing by assuring readers that those 'once transformed, or rather deformed Poems . . . are here in some measure restor'd to their native Shape and Beauty, and therefore certainly cannot fail of a welcome reception now, since they wanted it not before, when they appeared in that strange disguise' (A4v).

The folio is an important document in the history of women's literature, for the manner in which that physical object presents Philips to her public shows how attenuated was her status in the seventeenth century – that she was perceived as both a respectable woman and a tantalizing object of the male gaze. In an elegy on Philips printed just before the table of contents, Cowley presents Philips as an adversary of male writers: 'Orinda does our boasting Sex out-do' (l. 76). He praises her poetry, but trivializes it by using conditional verbs when suggesting the possibility of her being celebrated by the god of poetry:

> . . . if Apollo *should* design
> A woman Laureat to make,
> Without dispute he *would* Orinda take
> Though Sappho and the famous Nine
> Stood by, and did repine.
>   (ll. 38–42; emphasis added)

Philo-Philippa, the anonymous female author of the central prefatory poem in the 1667 folio, puts the case differently. Unlike Cowley, who images Sappho and the muses envying Philips's success, she presents Philips as 'the glory of our Sex, envy of men, / Who hath both pleas'd and vex'd with [her] bright Pen' (ll. 9–10).

It is of course not only seventeenth-century men who have been vexed by women's writing. As the feminist philosopher Christine Battersby has argued, Western culture has for centuries assigned 'feminine' creative power to male artists, at the same time holding that women themselves cannot be true creators because they lack 'masculine' energy. Hence it is that critics of both art and literature (for more recent years one might add other fields – politics, for example) have so often treated creative women as unnatural beings, scorning their work as either masculinized or prettified. Battersby's own analysis of women's creativity is not psychological, but cultural and formalist. As she says, our culture has for so long been informed by masculinist traditions that it has been difficult for women to do creative work. Throughout Western history, however, there have been creative women whose work has been misunderstood and thus under-appreciated. What we need to learn, Battersby says, is how to read creative women 'who emerge from a female situation (which needs to be explicated), and who fit into the patterns of patrilineal and matrilineal continuity (whose links have to be exposed)' (Battersby 1989: 231). Having lived and been educated within Western culture, readers of the present volume know a great deal about the patrilineal traditions within and against which Philips wrote. And after some thirty years of work, the new scholarship on women has developed to the point that we can begin to define both 'the female situation' within which Philips found herself and the matrilineal traditions upon which she drew in her poetry. For thanks to scholars such as those whose essays are published in this book, twenty-first-century feminists have an ever-increasing understanding of how women's literature corroborates and challenges male forms. As Battersby says, the task of the feminist critic is to understand 'what is involved in writing [not like a woman, but] *as a woman*: as a person confronting the paradigms of male individuality and female Otherness, defining herself in terms of those paradigms . . . and resisting them' (ibid.: 214).

Philips is a perfect candidate for the kind of study Battersby suggests. Her writing, again to quote Battersby,

> has to be positioned in two different, but overlapping patterns; the matrilineal and patrilineal lines of influence and response that swirl through (and across) the intricate network of relationships out of which we shape our past. A female creator needs to be slotted into the context of male traditions. But to understand what the artist is doing, and the merits or demerits of her work, she will also have to be located in a separate female pattern that, so to speak, runs through the first in a kind of contrapuntal way. (Ibid.: 220–1)

We may begin this study by contrasting one of Philips's late poems – her 'On Retirement' (headed 'Upon Mr. Abraham Cowley's Retirement' in the 1664 octavo and in the folio) – with a poem with which it is printed in the 1663 *Poems, by Several Persons*: Cowley's 'On Orinda's Poems' (printed as a prefatory poem in 1664 and 1667). Although no extant evidence shows which Pindaric ode was written first, which second – or even whether one poet was consciously responding to the other – it seems more than coincidental that each ode comprises five stanzas and that the first stanza of each is 17 lines long. Apparently astonished that a woman could write poetry as well as does Orinda, and apparently also feeling her presence as a threat to male sovereignty, Cowley says Orinda 'Do's Man behind her in Proud Triumph draw, / And Cancel great Apollo's Salick Law' (the law that women cannot inherit power from the Greek god of poetry (ll. 5–6)). Cowley's poem is replete with phrases combining praise of Orinda's physical beauty with praise of her wondrous poetic skill. For example, he writes,

> I must admire to see thy well knit sense
> Thy Numbers gentle, and thy passions high
> Those as thy fore-head smooth, these sparkling as thy eye.
>   'Tis solid, and 'tis manly all,
>   Or rather 'tis Angelical.
>
>   (ll. 47–51)

Her verses, he continues, 'are than Man more strong, and more than Woman sweet' (l. 55). Cowley assures the world that in her poems 'no one touch dost find / Of th' ancient Curse to Woman-kind' (ll. 35–6), and he descends into an extraordinary comparison between her writing and the fertile Countess of Holland's childbearing:

>   Thou bring'st not forth with pain
> It neither travel [travail] is nor labour of thy brain,
>   So easily they from they come
>   And there is so much room
>   In th' unexhausted and unfathom'd Womb.
>   That like the Holland Countess thou mayst bear
> A child for every day of all the fertile year.
>
>   (ll. 37–43)

Cowley concludes by writing of the British queen who was defeated by a Roman army in AD 60, his imagery (as before) drawing on the language of warfare:

>   Ev'n Boadicia's angry Ghost
> Forgets her own misfortune, and disgrace,
>   And to her injur'd Daughters now does boast,
> That Romes o'recome at last, by a woman of her Race.
>
>   (ll. 83–6)

By contrast, in her first four stanzas Philips focuses not on Cowley, but on her own calm indifference to worldly success:

> No other wealth, will I aspire
> But that of Nature to admire,
> Nor envy on a Lawrel will bestow,
> Whilst I have any in my Garden grow.
>   (ll. 47–50)

With quiet deliberation Philips images herself in and yet not of the natural world:

> when my soul her wings does raise,
> Above what mortals fear or praise,
> With Innocent, and quiet Pride, I'le sit
> And see the humble Waves pay tribute to my feet.
>   (ll. 55–8)

Only after she has fully demonstrated her command of the poetic form for which Cowley was by 1663 so well known does Philips turn to her fellow poet, now introducing military imagery into her ode. He, she says,

> Is now Triumphantly retir'd;
> The mighty Cowley this hath done,
> And over [the world] a Parthian Conquest won,
> Which future Ages shall adore,
> And which, in this subdues thee more
> Than either Greek, or Roman ever could before.
>   (ll. 75–80)

Never overtly dispraising Cowley, Philips nonetheless distinguishes between her own triumph and his. His retirement is literal, for in 1663 he had recently retired to Barn Elms in Surrey, some 7 miles southwest of London. In 1663 Philips by contrast was in Dublin enjoying the success of her play *Pompey*. Her retirement, she claims, is one of spiritual self-sufficiency: psychological, not literal, isolation from the everyday world. To put it another way, while Cowley's language rejects Philips from his world, she uses the poetic form of which he is England's master even as she declares herself independent of his power.

In 'The Virgin', a poem first printed in the 1667 folio, Philips enters into an even larger poetic contest, this time involving a host of male writers who had translated and imitated Martial's Epigram 10:47. The first poet to translate the epigram into English was Henry Howard, Earl of Surrey. As William Sessions has noted, Surrey takes as his key Martial's phrase *mens quieta* (the quiet mind) and

> accomplishes a bravura performance of brevity by a powerful use of medial caesura (typically after the fourth syllable). . . . Surrey combines [the classical devices asyndeton, chiasmus, periphrasis, litotes, anaphora and alliteration] to make not only the English

phrase more flowing but to adapt its conception for an English audience, as in line 13, with its chiastic adjectival formula learned from the Italians . . . but Chaucerian in theme: 'The chaste wife wyse, without debate'. (Sessions 1986: 76–7)

Versions of the epigram by writers such as Ben Jonson, Robert Fletcher, Thomas Randolf and Abraham Cowley vary in emphasis and structure – Jonson for example recommending 'No sour, or sullen bed-mate, yet a chaste' (l. 10), and Cowley cautioning 'Let rest, which Nature does to Darkness wed / And not Lust, recommend to thee thy bed' (ll. 28–9). An anonymous poet used Martial's 13-line form to list 'The things that make a Bishops life more fayr' (l. 1) in a poem transcribed in a manuscript now in the Folger Library. His imitation lists 'Unpurchasd Goods, to piety set apart' (l. 3), and also 'Night rapt with Heav'n, and sequesterd from Care / A wife not courtly prancet, but debonaire; / Sleepe that instructs how swift the howers are' (Folger Library MS V.a.125, p. 53, ll. 9–11).

Philips's response to this tradition is to combine Martial's rhetorical form with the genre of the Theophrastan character and to describe what will 'make a Virgin please' (l. 1). One might argue that Philips merely replicates patrilineal traditions, writing a ventriloquist poem in which a male voice outlines the attributes of a virgin who will please him. But since 'The things that make a Virgin please' are characteristics that will appeal to rational men, one could also argue that Philips gives advice that may lead to happiness for a female living in seventeenth-century Britain. Her poem shows how well Philips understood that culture, and her epigram might be called, if not a feminist poem, then a proto-feminist critique of male traditions. Philips's virgin should have 'A Face that's modest, yet serene, / A sober, and yet lively Meen' (ll. 11–12). As Jonson directs his male reader to a life of 'wise simplicity' (l. 13), Philips advocates 'wise lowliness' (l. 15). Margaret Doody has noted that Philips's virgin is not 'a sentimental reflection of the Virgin Mary, but a human being with a sense of her own identity. She is free to think for herself, and to engage in good works and sensible conversation' (Doody 1998). We may also observe that the final four lines of Philips's poem present the virgin as a younger version of the stable dowagers she memorializes in poems such as 'In memory of . . . Mrs. Mary Lloyd'. Of the virgin, Philips writes,

> [Her] equal mind, does alwaies move,
> Neither a foe, nor slave to Love;
> And [her] Religion's strong and plain,
> Not superstitious, nor prophane.
>   (ll. 9–12)

Of Mrs Mary Lloyd,

> And as in Youth she did attract, (for she
> The Verdure had, without the Vanity)

> So she in Age was mild and grave to all,
> Was not morose, but was majestical.
>
> (ll. 81–4)

We see another side of Philips's female imagination in her several celebratory epi-thalamia, each of which differs from the typical male epithalamium of the time by focusing on the bride's happiness. In 'To my dear Sister Mrs. C.P. on her Marriage' Philips alludes to the groom only with pronouns as she writes 'Orinda's wishes for Cassandra's bliss' (l. 8):

> May her Content and Duty be the same,
>
> . . .
>
> May his and her Pleasure and Love be so
> Involv'd and growing that we may not know
> Who most Affection or most Peace engrost.
>
> (ll. 13, 15–17)

Philips never forgets her culture's definition of companionate marriage as a hierar-chical relationship – thus the word 'Duty' in line 13. Nevertheless, she hopes that Cicily's life will be one of shared love and pleasure – that *'they* may count the hours as they pass, / By *their* own Joys, and not by Sun or Glass' (ll. 21–2; emphasis added).

Something of the same 'spin' on marriage appears in 'To the Countess of Thanet, upon her marriage'. Philips begins the poem by asserting that it was Elizabeth Boyle's own choice to marry her second cousin Nicholas Tufton: 'you have found such an illus-trious sphere, / And are resolv'd to fix your glories there' (ll. 9–10). But toward the end of the poem the reader is reminded of the true dynamics of early modern mar-riage when Philips writes,

> . . . may the happy owner of your breast
> Still find his passion with his joys encreas'd;
> Whilst every moment your concern makes known,
> And gives him, too, fresh reason for his own:
>
> . . .
>
> Or if all wishes we in one would give,
> For him, and for the world, Long may you live.
>
> (ll. 41–4, 47–8)

Two of Philips's poems express sympathy for widowed friends: 'To Mrs. Wogan, my honoured friend, on the Death of her Husband' and 'To my dearest friend Mrs. A[nne] Owen, upon her greatest loss'. In each, the poet begins by joining the widow in her grief; in the central and longest part of the poem, she praises the dead spouse in rather formal terms; and she concludes each poem by urging her friend to give over her lamentations. To Mrs Wogan Philips speaks on behalf of a group of (apparently female) friends as she begins, 'Dry up your tears . . . / . . . we must pay our share of Sorrows too' (ll. 1–2) and ends, 'Let's not lose you in whom he still doth Live. / For while you are by Grief excluded thus, / It doth appear your Funeral to us' (ll. 43–5). With Anne Owen she is more intimate, beginning with an extended epic simile presenting the poet's and her friend's sorrow as a pair of ever-growing 'sister rivelets' (l. 1). With the phrase 'Endure thy loss' Philips again urges stoicism, but her conclusion looks forward to a glorious future when the loss will be restored:

> Endure thy loss till Heav'n shall it repay,
> Upon thy last and glorious wedding-day,
> When thou shalt know him more, and quickly find
> Thy love increas'd by being so refin'd,
>   And there possess him without parting fears,
>   As I my friendship free from future tears.
>   (ll. 77–82)

Even more striking is the poem Philips wrote when Cicily Philips's husband died in 1657. This is a ventriloquist poem in the voice of the widow addressing her late husband's funeral monument:

> . . . since my Grief at Length must dy
> (For that's no longer liv'd then I)
> His name can live no way but one,
> In an abiding faithfull Stone.
>   (ll. 9–12)

In a second, somewhat shorter verse paragraph, the widow tells the 'faithful Stone' what it must say to passers-by so 'They may instructed go from thee, / To follow him, and pitty me' (ll. 19–20). Here again Philips validates the wife's grief even while offering consolation by way of human friendship.

In poems such as 'Friendship's Mystery', 'Wiston-Vault', 'Orinda to Lucasia', 'Parting with Lucasia' and 'To Mrs. M. A. upon Absence', Philips does even more to demonstrate women's joy in female friendships. Most often anthologized today is the justly admired 'Friendship's Mystery' in which Philips transforms modes of address and image patterns familiar to readers of John Donne to present her friendship with Lucasia as greater even than his and his beloved's devotion. Unlike Donne, who tells his lady what to think and feel, Philips begins with an invitation to Lucasia to join her in the task of asserting their love:

> Come, my Lucasia, since we see
> That Miracles Mens faith do move,

> By wonder and by prodigy
> To the dull angry world let's prove
> There's a Religion in our Love.
>
> (ll. 1–5)

Having thus echoed Donne's 'The Canonization', Philips moves on to his 'The Sunne Rising'. In contrast to Donne, who proclaims of his lady, 'She's all States, and all Princes, I, / Nothing else is' (ll. 23–4), Orinda and Lucasia claim equality: 'all our Titles [are] shuffled so / Both Princes, and both Subjects too' (ll. 24–5). Reversing the usual pattern of seventeenth-century parting poems in which the male poet consoles his lady, Philips gives Lucasia the dominant voice in her 'Dialogue of Absence 'twixt Lucasia and Orinda'. Here it is the poet who is bereft at parting, Lucasia who offers consolation. By the end of the poem Orinda has learned Lucasia's lesson and the two sing in Chorus that one day, '. . . we shall come where no rude hand shall sever, / And there wee'l meet and part no more for ever' (ll. 25–6).

Before her marriage to James Philips, young Katherine Fowler wrote out and dedicated to Anne Barlow, a neighbour in Seblech, about 2 miles from Picton Castle in Pembrokeshire, two witty poems about marriage and a playful prose 'recipt to cure a Love sick Person who cant obtain the Party desired' (Limbert 1986: 387–8). The prose receipt could be used to 'cure' either a man or a woman whose love is unrequited, but both poems are explicit in treating women's place within seventeenth-century marriage. One is in the voice of a sensible woman who outlines her goals in choosing a husband: 'No blooming youth shall ever make me err / I will the beauty of the mind prefer' (ll. 1–2). The other is a 16-line version of a longer anti-marriage poem located by Margaret Ezell, Claudia Limbert and John O'Neill in a total of seven late seventeenth- and eighteenth-century manuscripts and one printed book, *The Agreeable Variety* (1717). Philips's manuscript poem begins with the couplet 'A marryd state affords but little Ease / The best of husbands are so hard to please'. The printed version, headed 'Ardelia to Cordelia, advising her not to marry', is a 28-line text beginning 'If once you let that Gordian Knot be tyed, / Which turns the Name of Virgin into bride'. The printed poem includes four lines also in Philips's version: her lines 1–4 are lines 7–10 in the printed copy. By contrast, a 58-line manuscript variant headed 'A Satyr against Marriage' in Folger Library MS W.a.135, pp. 72v–73v, and beginning 'Virgin, I cannot but Congratulate, / Your brave desire of living in that State', includes all but two lines from Philips (her lines 11–12 are found in none of the variants treated by Ezell, Limbert and O'Neill). The Folger manuscript version concludes, as does Philips's, with the couplet 'Supress wild nature if she dares Rebell, / There's no such thing as leading Apes in Hell' (ll. 57–8 in the Folger MS; ll. 15–16 in Philips). Shakespeare's Kate in the *Taming of the Shrew* uses the same proverb in her angry complaint to her father: 'I must dance barefoot on [Bianca's] wedding day / And, for your love to her, lead apes in hell' (2.1.36–7), and Beatrice in *Much Ado about Nothing* laughingly overturns conventional wisdom when she predicts that after she dies the devil will say, '"Get you to heaven, Beatrice, get you to heaven; here's no place for you maids." So deliver I up my apes and away to Saint Peter; for the heavens, he shows me where the bachelors sit, and there live we as merry as the day is long' (2.1.45–9). Allying herself with Beatrice over Kate, young Katherine Fowler claims freedom from the proverbial warning that old maids will, for all eternity, lead apes in hell (Tilley 1950: M37).

Limbert and O'Neill (1993) argue that after Philips wrote her 16-line poem it circulated among an ever-widening circle of women readers 'beginning within Philips's circle of intimate friends and extending over time beyond her death to her unknown co-author', a female writer who expanded the short poem into a longer and even more pointed anti-matrimonial poem. They see in this chain of readers, copyists and authors 'a community of women writers known only partly to one another but engaged in a collaborative effort to give literary expressions to the concerns of their sex' (ibid.: 494). To their analysis one might add that just as Philips's final lines overturn an anti-feminist proverb of the time, so too other couplets in her satire and its longer descendants may take their origin in proverbial verses common in early modern women's discourse but not yet catalogued by modern scholars. Rather than thinking in terms of one later writer expanding a text originally authored by Philips, we might imagine this anti-matrimonial satire as an ever-changing text, appropriated by a series of women writers in various times and places, beginning perhaps earlier than Philips and extending perhaps beyond the eighteenth century.

Some of Philips's other poems – 'To the noble Palaemon on his incomparable discourse of Friendship', for example – seem gender-neutral. But in her political poems Philips often uses her culture's notions of womanhood as a way into her subject matter. Once or twice the lack of a poetic tradition of a woman writing political poetry causes trouble. For example, in 'To the Queen on her Arrival' Philips awkwardly conflates the voice of the poet with that of her female muse when she says, 'Let an obscurer Muse, upon her knees, / Present you with such offerings as these' (ll. 13–14). More successful is the poem printed first in the 1664 octavo (and also in the 1667 folio): 'Upon the double murther of K. Charles'. Philips begins by speaking as a reticent woman who knows that politics is not her ken: 'I think not on the State, nor am concern'd / Which way soever that great Helme is turn'd'. But she then claims that the press of the current situation forces her, as it forced Atys, son of Croesus, to break silence. As Atys's voice saved Croesus, her voice will rescue Charles I from a poem by the Fifth Monarchist Vavasor Powell. Scornfully, she asks, 'What noble eye could see, (and careless passe) / The dying Lion kick'd by every asse?' (ll. 9–10). Powell had claimed that Charles deserved to die because he broke all ten of God's commandments (Hageman and Sununu 1994: 129). Rather than counter that charge directly, Philips uses the slyly ironic phrase 'I ne're understood' (l. 29) to allude to her earlier disclaimer 'I think not on the State' (l. 1) and then wins her argument against Powell by referring to Christ's own adherence to God's commandment against murder:

> Christ will be King, but I ne're understood,
> His subjects built his kingdome up with blood,
> (Except his owne) or that he would dispence
> With his commands, though for his own defence.
>
> (ll. 29–32)

Similar in structure is the poem that is perhaps her last, 'To his Grace Gilbert [Sheldon] Lord Arch-Bishop of Canterbury' (in the folio this poem is misdated 10 July 1664 – July being the month after Philips's death). Philips's subject is the publication of the 1664 unauthorized volume, by which means, she says, her Muse has been 'hurry'd from her Cave with wild affright, / And dragg'd malitiously into the light' (ll. 7–8). Philips's hope is that the archbishop will protect her as he has protected the English church. As in the poem countering Vavasor Powell's claims against Charles I, Philips again uses the metaphor of the ship's 'Helm', here to praise Sheldon's leadership of the English church:

> Times curious Eye till now, hath never spy'd
> The Churches Helm so happily supply'd.
> Merit and Providence so fitly met,
> The Worthiest Prelate in the highest Seat.
>
> (ll. 53–6)

From a political perspective, feminist readers may be disappointed in this poem, for we would wish that Philips did not feel the need to seek protection from Sheldon. From an artistic perspective, we may however be delighted, for Philips has done a magnificent job of imaging the plight of a female poet violated by the patriarchal system of buying and selling books. Moreover, if we think of this poem as one by a poet who writes '*as a woman*' (Battersby 1989: 214), we realize how subversive Philips is when she images the archbishop as an androgynous figure: captain at his ship's helm (l. 54), heroic defender brandishing a crosier (l. 25), a male (and Protestant!) Madonna of Mercy with his 'wing' (l. 15) spread comfortingly over the poet/petitioner, 'under which, when she is once retir'd, / She really may come to be inspir'd' (ll. 17–18). Even while praising Sheldon, this poet claims energy from him and daringly ends her poem with words no other poet could (or would) use in quite this way:

> If Noble things can Noble Thoughts infuse,
> Your Life (my Lord) may, ev'n in me, produce
> Such Raptures, that of their rich Fury proud,
> I may, perhaps, dare to proclaim aloud;
> Assur'd, the World that ardour will excuse,
> Applaud the Subject, and forgive the Muse.
>
> (ll. 57–62)

REFERENCES AND FURTHER READING

(1717). *The Agreeable Variety. In two Parts: Containing, First, Discourses, Characters and Poems . . . extracted from many worthy Authors. Consisting, Secondly, Of Letters, Poems, &c. by several Private Persons, on divers Occasions.* London: Printed for the Author, Sold by G. Strahan and others.

Andreadis, Harriette (1999). 'The erotics of female friendship in early modern England.' In Susan Frye and Karen Robertson (eds), *Maids and Mistresses, Cousins and Queens: Women's Alliances in Early Modern England* (pp. 241–58). Oxford: Oxford University Press.

Aubrey, John (1898). *'Brief Lives,' chiefly of Contemporaries set down by John Aubrey, between the Years 1669 & 1696*, vol. 2, ed. Andrew Clark. Oxford: Clarendon Press.

Barash, Carol (1996). *English Women's Poetry, 1649–1714: Politics, Community and Linguistic Authority.* Oxford: Clarendon Press.

Battersby, Christine (1989). *Gender and Genius: Towards a Feminist Aesthetics.* London: Women's Press.

Beal, Peter (1993). *Index of English Literary Manuscripts*, Vol. 2: *1625–1700*. Part 2: *Lee–Wycherley.* London: Mansell.

——(1998). *In Praise of Scribes: Manuscripts and Their Makers in Seventeenth-Century England.* Oxford: Clarendon Press.

Cartwright, William (1651). *Comedies, Tragi-Comedies, With other Poems by Mr. William Cartwright . . . The Ayres and Songs set by Mr. Henry Lawes.* London: Humphrey Mosely. (Wing C709)

Colie, Rosalie L. (1973). *The Resources of Kind: Genre-Theory in the Renaissance*, ed. Barbara K. Lewalski. Berkeley: University of California Press.

Cowley, Abraham (1663). *Poems, by Several Persons.* Dublin: Samuel Dancer. (Wing C6681A)

Donne, John (1968). *The Complete Poems,* ed. John T. Shawcross. New York: New York University Press.

Doody, Margaret A. (1998). 'Gender, literature, and gendering literature in the Restoration.' In Steven N. Zwicker (ed.), *The Cambridge Companion to English Literature, 1650–1740* (pp. 58–81). Cambridge: Cambridge University Press.

Ezell, Margaret J. M. (1987). *The Patriarch's Wife: Literary Evidence and the History of the Family.* Chapel Hill: University of North Carolina Press.

Greer, Germaine (1995). *Slip-shod Sibyls: Recognition, Rejection and the Woman Poet.* London: Viking.

Hageman, Elizabeth H. and Sununu, Andrea (1993). 'New Manuscript Texts of Katherine Philips, the "Matchless Orinda".' *English Manuscript Studies, 1100–1700*, 4, 174–219.

——(1994). ' "More Copies of it abroad than I could have imagin'd": further manuscript texts of Katherine Philips, "the Matchless Orinda".' *English Manuscript Studies, 1100–1700*, 5, 127–69.

Jonson, Ben (1963). *The Complete Poetry,* ed. William B. Hunter. New York: New York University Press.

Limbert, Claudia A. (1986). 'Two poems and a prose receipt: the unpublished juvenilia of Katherine Philips.' *English Literary Renaissance*, 16, 383–90.

Limbert, Claudia A. and O'Neill, John H. (1993). 'Composite authorship: Katherine Philips and an anti-matrimonial satire.' *The Papers of the Bibliographical Society of America*, 87, 487–502.

Philips, Katherine (1662). 'To the Queens Majesty on her Happy Arrival.' London: Henry Herringman. (Wing T1598A)

——(1663). *Poems, by Several Persons.* Dublin: Samuel Dancer. (Wing C6681A: see also Cowley)

——(1664). *Poems by the Incomparable Mrs. K.P.* London: Richard Marriott. (Wing P2032)

——(1667). *Poems by the most deservedly Admired Mrs Katherine Philips, The Matchless Orinda, To which is added Monsieur Corneille's 'Pompey' and 'Horace', Tragedies.* London: Henry Herringman. (Wing P2033)

——(1705). *Letters from Orinda to Poliarchus.* London: Bernard Lintott. Rpt. with one additional letter, 1729.

Radzinowicz, Mary Ann (1990). 'Reading paired poems nowadays.' *LIT: Literature-Interpretation-Theory*, 1, 275–90.

Sessions, William A. (1986). *Henry Howard, Earl of Surrey.* Boston: Twayne.

Shakespeare, William (1992). *The Taming of the Shrew,* ed. Barbara A. Mowat and Paul Wernstine. New York: Washington Square Press.

——(1995). *Much Ado About Nothing*, ed. Barbara A. Mowat and Paul Werstine. New York: Washington Square Press.

Souers, Philip Webster (1931). *The Matchless Orinda.* Cambridge, MA: Harvard University Press.

Swaim, Kathleen (1997). 'Matching the "Matchless Orinda" to her times'. *1650–1850: Ideas, Aesthetics, and Inquiries in the Early Modern Era*, 3, 77–108.

Temple, Sir William (1664). 'Upon the death of Mrs. Catherine Philips.' London: Samuel Speed. (Wing T662C)

Tilley, Morris Palmer (1950). *A Dictionary of the Proverbs in England in the Sixteenth and Seventeenth Centuries: A Collection of the Proverbs Found in English Literature and the Dictionaries of the Period.* Ann Arbor: University of Michigan Press.

Vaughan, Henry (1651). *Olor Iscanus: A Collection of some select Poems, and Translations, formerly written by Mr. Henry Vaughan, Silurist.* London: Humphrey Moseley. (Wing V123)

14

Aphra Behn, *The Rover,*
Part One

Anita Pacheco

Introduction

Aphra Behn's establishment as an important figure in Restoration and early modern
literary studies has been accompanied by a critical debate about the extent to which
her work can be seen as 'proto-feminist' in spirit. This debate has tended to centre,
with good reason, on a particular aspect of her work: her treatment of contemporary
upper-class constructions of masculinity. Behn's plays, especially her comedies, give a
prominent place to the libertine, a popular theatrical type whose single-minded
pursuit of sexual conquests seems to reinforce reductive views of women as little more
than sexual diversions for men. Moreover, it is undeniably the case that Behn portrays
her rakish heroes with at least a degree of indulgence, for their libertinism is more
often than not a signifier of the Tory cause to which Behn herself was committed.
Throughout her dramatic career, but especially during the political conflict of the
Exclusion Crisis (1678–83), Behn, like other Tory dramatists, supported the royalist
cause by turning the libertine, endowed with wit, charisma and virility, into a symbol
of the inherent superiority and right to power of the Stuart ruling elite.

Yet despite Behn's political investment in this upper-class concept of manhood,
the argument that her plays offer simple celebrations of libertine masculinity remains
unconvincing (see, for example, Cotton 1991; Jordan 1972; Zook 1998). Susan Owen
has demonstrated that Behn produced her most conservative plays during the Tory
reaction to the Exclusion Crisis, when it became 'most urgent to give ideological
affirmation to Toryism' (Owen 1996: 27). Yet even in a play of this period, such as *The
City Heiress* (1682), the portrayal of the rake-hero is far from straightforwardly positive.
Tom Wilding has suffered from syphilis, after all, a rather stark reminder that the
libertine lifestyle has consequences (Wiseman 1996: 40). In Susan Wiseman's view,
'this complex political comedy both invites the audience to empathize with the central
male figure and signals his sexual, ethical and economic unreliability' (ibid.: 39).

If Behn could be ambivalent about libertinism even in her most reactionary Tory comedies, it should not surprise us to find a critical perspective on masculine ideals in a pre-Exclusion Crisis play like *The Rover, or the Banished Cavaliers* (1677). As the representatives of the royalist political values signalled in the play's sub-title, the hero Willmore and his exiled comrades are certainly treated favourably. However, Behn's political agenda does not prevent her from offering an astute anatomization not only of libertinism but, more broadly, of elite masculinity. This essay will suggest that Behn's adaptation of her source play, Thomas Killigrew's Interregnum drama *Thomaso, or the Wanderer*, produced a new emphasis on the tensions and instabilities inscribed within upper-class masculine culture. It will examine the way this emphasis shapes two important aspects of the play: the portrayal of the banished cavaliers and the representation of relationships within the patriarchal family.

Honour and Manliness: The Banished Cavaliers

Mark Breitenberg (1996) argues that early modern patriarchy produced a brand of masculinity that was fraught with anxiety:

> Anxiety and masculinity: the terms must be wed if only for the obvious reason that any social system whose premise is the unequal distribution of power and authority always and only sustains itself in constant defense of the privileges of some of its members and by the constraint of others. (Ibid.: 3)

For Breitenberg, it is the patriarchal project of affirming and sustaining the superiority of men over women that makes early modern masculinity inherently anxious.

But, as Breitenberg recognizes, any account of masculinity in this period has to consider as well the complex interaction of gender and class. Not all men in early modern England were equal, and for the male elite it was as important to establish their superiority over lower-class men as over women. Honour was the crucial mechanism in the creation of this hierarchy of manliness. The propertied men who, broadly speaking, comprised the English ruling class identified themselves as 'honourable' men, possessed of a cluster of masculine virtues – strength, courage, martial prowess – that distinguished them from low-born men and (so they claimed) justified their access to power and privilege. There was a problem with honour, though, in so far as its stratifying function also operated *within* the group, drawing distinctions between honourable men, ranking some claims to honour more highly than others. It created a smaller, more exclusive masculine hierarchy characterized by an often ferocious competition for eminence. This upper-class honour culture put a premium on competitive self-assertion, fostered acute sensitivity to affront, and made even comrades potential rivals in the contest for honour and status (Pitt-Rivers 1977: 3–4; James

1986: 310–15). The anxieties built into elite masculinity in early modern England were in large part the kind of homosocial anxieties engendered by the psychology of honour, and they made violent conflict virtually a foregone conclusion.

Both libertinism and the Hobbesian conception of man from which it is often thought to spring have traditionally been associated with the acquisitive values of the emergent bourgeoisie. But this view obscures the continued currency of honour within Restoration ruling-class culture and, indeed, the extent to which the fiercely competitive world of Hobbes's natural man derives not from the mentality of the marketplace but from the psychology of honour. As Keith Thomas argues, 'the obsessive passion of Hobbes's men seems to be not acquisitiveness, but pride. . . . Some of Hobbes's contemporaries may have considered that the most frequent cause of human contention was property, but for Hobbes himself it is "honour and dignity" for which "men are continually in competition"' (Thomas 1965: 190). Likewise, the libertine heroes who populate Restoration drama often adhere to a ruthlessly competitive model of manliness that displaces the mentality of honour to the sexual realm. For libertine heroes like Dorimant and Horner, sexual desire is inseparable from the will to power (Chernaik 1995: 12); what they desire are the sexual conquests that prove their manly prowess and give them dominance over others – over women and, through women, over other men. Hence Richard Braverman's claim that 'rakish types hold fast to the principles and privileges of an honor culture' (Braverman 1995: 152).

Behn's adaptation of Killigrew indicates her interest in exposing the cracks that inevitably appear in the agonistic world of upper-class men. Killigrew's play contains plenty of male rivalry, but on the whole it is the kind of national rivalry predictable in a play about a group of English royalist exiles living in Madrid amid their longstanding political enemies. Behn retains this aspect of Killigrew's play in scenes like Act 2, scene 1, in which Willmore's theft of Angellica Bianca's portrait sparks a brawl between Spanish and English. And throughout Behn's play competition for women defines the interaction between English cavaliers and Spanish dons, most notably between Belvile and Don Pedro, but also between Willmore and Don Antonio.

What Behn adds to the nationalistic, political hostilities she found in Killigrew is a sensitivity to the way such contests in manliness also work to fracture relationships between male characters who are at least nominal comrades and allies. In fact, on the surface at least, the world of *The Rover* seems chillingly devoid of genuine male comradeship. In their calmer moments, Behn's cavaliers can afford the luxury of sentimental displays of royalist camaraderie: 'Yet sir, my friends are gentlemen, and ought to be esteemed for their misfortunes, since they have the glory to suffer with the best of men and kings' (244). This is Belvile in the closing moments of the play; now happily possessed of his elusive object of desire, he can conveniently forget the two recent occasions when, enraged with Willmore for wrecking his elopement, he threatened to kill him.

Jones DeRitter has demonstrated that one of Behn's most significant innovations in adapting *Thomaso* for the Restoration stage was her division of Killigrew's eponymous hero – comprised of equal parts rake and romantic lover – into the two distinct and opposed characters of Willmore and Belvile (DeRitter 1986: 83). This decision had two closely related consequences: by stripping her libertine hero of any vestiges of romantic idealism, Behn foregrounds his disruptive character traits, and places at the centre of the play a male friendship that is conspicuously strained. Indeed, one would be hard pressed to say whether Don Pedro or Willmore represents the more serious obstacle to Belvile's amorous ambitions. Willmore manages to get Belvile arrested in Act 3, scene 4 and to reveal his identity to Pedro in Act 4, scene 2. But the gravest threat he poses is of course to Florinda's chastity.

Willmore's attempted rape of Florinda in Act 3, scene 3 is bound up with the play's carnival setting and its 'suppression of social identity' (Hughes 1996: 208): in seeking to secure the husband of her choice, Florinda abandons the signs of her status as a 'lady of quality' and so looks to the drunken Willmore like an 'errant harlot' (204). But it is also part of the play's portrayal of the libertine as a sexual predator. From his first appearance on stage, Willmore is presented as a potential sexual threat to other men's women. When Belvile requests his assistance in delivering Florinda 'from the threatened violence of her brother', Willmore eagerly assents, anticipating a sexual reward from the woman in question: 'thou knowst there's but one way for a woman to oblige me' (172). This is a moment of comic misunderstanding, stemming from the newly arrived Willmore's ignorance of Belvile's intentions towards Florinda. But it signals nonetheless Willmore's predisposition to violate other men's territorial claims on women; and the play makes it clear that this is a predisposition from which no man is entirely secure. Even at the end of the play, after the confusion surrounding Florinda's identity has been cleared up, Willmore registers in an aside an unaltered desire for sexual dominance over her. Not only is Willmore inclined to encroach on other men's erotic territory; he fully expects other men, his friends included, to do the same thing to him – hence his momentary suspicion, in Act 3, scene 1, that Belvile is his rival in the pursuit of Hellena (197). For Willmore, *all* men are potential sexual competitors, and the bond of friendship offers at best a fragile check on this universal male *agon*.

Willmore likes to present his rapacious sexual conduct as the manifestation of a naturally unstable and transitory sexual instinct:

> I wish I were that dull, that constant thing
> Which thou wouldst have me, and Nature never meant me;
> I must, like cheerful birds, sing in all groves,
> And perch on every bough,
> Billing the next kind she that flies to meet me . . .
>
> (238)

But the play on occasion undermines this simple libertine discourse, suggesting that for Willmore women are less the objects of an innately unruly libido than the terrain on which he proves his manliness. When he discovers Antonio at Angellica's house and promptly attacks him as an interloper, Willmore's ardour for the courtesan has in fact already waned. His metaphor, at once nautical and mercantile, aptly captures Angellica's status as a possession on which he seeks to stamp his ownership: 'How is this! A picaroon going to board my frigate!' (205). The most significant relationship in this sexual triangle is that linking Willmore to Antonio, the rival who is challenging his claim to mastery.

Like other libertine heroes of the Restoration stage, Willmore exhibits a sexuality imbued with the psychology of honour. However much wit and charm Behn bestows upon her rake-hero, she is not averse to revealing the less appealing aspects of the masculinity he embodies. His sexual adventurism is exposed as at least in part a form of competitive self-assertion through which he affirms his masculine power. In this struggle for dominance, women play second fiddle to his male competitors and the boundary separating friends from enemies is blurred.

Yet it would be a mistake to see Willmore as the sole source of conflict within the English camp. His is merely the most extreme expression of a particular brand of honour-driven masculinity embraced to some extent by every member of Behn's group of Englishmen abroad. The Blunt subplot seems designed in part to expose the workings of this miniature honour culture, in particular the violence it generates and the aggressivity latent in its male alliances. Blunt, like Willmore, threatens Florinda with rape, though in his case it is the failure to achieve a sexual conquest that leads to sexual aggression: his humiliation at the hands of Lucetta prompts Blunt to seek revenge 'on one whore for the sins of another' (226). The play's second scene of attempted rape thus represents rape as a crime motivated not by sexual desire but by the urge to punish and humiliate women, which leads Jacqueline Pearson to call it 'the most realistic attempted rape in the drama of the period' (Pearson 1988: 154).

Yet the play also locates Blunt's misogynistic violence in the honour culture he inhabits. As this culture measures manliness in large part by power over women, it encourages fear and loathing of women as potential agents of emasculation. But Blunt's immediate response to his disastrous encounter with Lucetta is not misogyny but self-reproach for having been conceited and complacent enough to believe her flattering lies. He turns violent only *after* he confronts the unpalatable prospect of the mockery and dishonour that await him at the hands of his comrades: 'but my comrades! death and the devil! there's the worst of all . . . but Fred that rogue! and the Colonel, will abuse me beyond all Christian patience' (200). It is the public dimension of his sexual misadventure – the fact that it entails a loss of face before his comrades – that transforms it into an affair of honour demanding the 'satisfaction' of revenge.

Blunt's terror of his comrades turns out to be fully justified. So determined are they to subject him to collective derision that they join forces to break down his door when he refuses them admittance. This episode is another of Behn's inventions; she devotes considerably more time than Killigrew to staging the mockery of the fool. On one level, then, the scene colludes in the humiliation of Blunt, presenting him as a laughable spectacle of failed masculinity. Yet this simple comic project is complicated by the fact that the play has given us access to the motives of the comrades who engineer his disgrace. For example, it is the gentlemanly Belvile who brings the greatest fervour to the shaming of Blunt, acting very much as ringleader, and we know this is because he has a score to settle. Unlike his comrades, impoverished by the expropriations of the Cromwellian government, Blunt remains firmly in possession of his property back home in England. His financial solvency enables him to lend money to his banished friends, which creates problems for Belvile, who clearly feels superior to the 'English boy of thirty' (172) at the same time that he is uncomfortably dependent on him. Lucetta's duping of Blunt provides him with an opportunity to put the foolish country squire firmly in his place. Belvile relishes in particular the prospect of seeing Blunt reduced to poverty:

> he yet ne'er knew the want of money, and 'twill be a great jest to see how simply he will look without it; for my part I'll lend him none, and the rogue knows not how to put on a borrowing face, and ask first; I'll let him see how good 'tis to play our parts whilst I play his. (223)

Belvile's *schadenfreude* illuminates the psychology of a ruling-class male as he struggles to cope with a reduction in status and power that places him at a disadvantage *vis-à-vis* his 'inferiors'. It also enables us to recognize the humiliation of Blunt as a kind of clarification of the masculine pecking order. The enthusiasm with which the cavaliers approach the occasion is a measure of their need to draw the line between winners and losers in the contest for honour. Through the mockery of Blunt's masculine failure, they establish their masculine superiority.

Among the 'winners', the shaming of Blunt produces an atmosphere of almost festive *bonhomie* which extends even to Don Pedro, but the rivalry latent in this masculine hierarchy is not long in making itself felt. As the characters prepare to gang-rape Florinda, once again deprived of her identity as an upper-class virgin, this grotesque expression of male camaraderie rapidly degenerates into an equally grotesque competition in manliness; for even a gang rape, Behn shows us, gives rise to anxiety about the order of precedence: which of them is to have the privilege of going first? Willmore comes up with the solution: 'the longest sword carries her' (231). It is unquestionably unsettling to find gang rape pressed into the service of stage comedy, and at this point we have to ask, with Susan Wiseman, 'precisely what social and cultural work comedy is doing in representing such moments as funny' (Wiseman 1996: 56). One may feel that the phallic joke of the collective drawing of swords trivializes the problem of sexual violence against women by dissolving it in laughter. Or one may feel that once again the comedy can be made to work against the male characters, in this instance exposing and mocking the absurd anatomical anxieties that are part of their obsessive brand of masculinity and help to foster a culture dogged by emulous rivalry.

Behn's portrayal of the homosocial tensions at work among her cavaliers points to the internal instability of early modern patriarchy. Yet the endemic rivalry she dramatizes is clearly not accompanied by the collapse of patriarchy, which remains a force to be reckoned with even in the play's closing moments. Hellena and Florinda may get to marry the men of their choice, but only because they possess the requisite assets of money, status and (first and foremost) virginity. When it comes to controlling women in the interests of upper-class men, Behn's cavaliers show a reasonably united front. Beneath the ethos of competitive one-upmanship lies the solidarity of men joined together by their identity as the patriarchal elite. This patriarchal *esprit de corps* is exposed with particular clarity in the play's scenes of attempted rape. When Florinda relinquishes the signs of her status as a gentlewoman, she enters a world of legalized rape, in which women who lack upper-class male protection or transgress the code of feminine honour are read as by definition sexually consenting. This meaning emerges during the first attempted rape in the gap between Willmore's apparent belief that Florinda is looking for sex and the fact that throughout the scene he has hold of her arm and refuses to release his grip. Why, we ask ourselves, if Willmore thinks Florinda is willing, does he look so suspiciously as if he is forcing her (Pacheco 1998: 327–33)? Later, during the attempted gang rape, all the assembled male characters, irrespective of nationality or position in the hierarchy of honour, join forces to assault the woman whose conduct and appearance identify her as available for their 'diversion' (231). The distinction made here between women 'of quality' who are off limits and low-class women who are up for grabs gives concise expression to the dichotomous definition of womanhood constructed by elite men in order to secure their interests, protecting their own women from the sexual predations of other men and relegating others to a world in which they are easy sexual prey (Pacheco 1998: 335).

Willmore's role as would-be rapist has significant repercussions for the play's representation of libertinism. Throughout the play, Willmore claims to have nothing but contempt for the code of feminine honour: 'Why, what the devil should I do with a virtuous woman? – a sort of ill-natured creatures, that take a pride to torment a lover, virtue is but an infirmity in woman' (214). On this level too the play undermines his libertine discourse, making it clear that Willmore's attitude towards female sexual morality is rather more conventional than he allows. He may prefer promiscuous women in so far as they cater to his need for sexual conquests, but his treatment of Florinda demonstrates his complicity in the patriarchal edict that punishes the sexually wayward woman by denying her the right to refuse her sexual consent. Willmore's extreme machismo, with its tentative grasp of other men's property rights in women, may complicate his relationship to patriarchal imperatives, but both his attitude to rape and his rejection of the prostitute in favour of the upper-class virgin tell us where his allegiances ultimately lie.

Father and Son, Brother and Sister

Relationships among Behn's Spanish male characters are, if anything, even more strained than those of their English counterparts. Here, too, Behn's revision of Killigrew leads to a foregrounding of the instabilities of upper-class masculine culture. In *Thomaso* Serulina (the character that would become Behn's Florinda) is being courted by a wealthy old man but is in love with Thomaso. Because her father is dead, her brother Pedro takes on the role of the anti-comic agent of arranged marriage, even planning to confine Serulina in a monastery until she agrees to the match. Behn altered her sources in significant ways. Most obviously, she invented the character of Hellena, and made the monastery to which Serulina is to be temporarily consigned the life-long imprisonment in a convent which the younger sister is seeking to avoid. More importantly for the purposes of this essay, she decided to transform Killigrew's dead father into an absent father, and to make the relationship between father and son a less than harmonious one. Behn's Don Pedro has a competing plan for his sister's sexual destiny: he wants her to marry not Don Vincentio, the rich old man favoured by their father, but his friend Don Antonio; and he hopes to use their father's absence in Rome to secure his own scheme at the expense of the patriarch's. (See Szilagyi 1998 for a rather different approach to the 'absent father' in the play.)

Behn's reworking of Killigrew's arranged marriage plot produces a representation of the patriarchal family as internally unstable. In Killigrew, patriarchal authority is challenged solely by the rebellious heroine; in Behn, it is undermined initially from within, by the son and heir one would expect to promote and share the father's wishes. Indeed, Pedro first appears on stage in the role of the father's messenger and ally, revealing his own agenda only later in the scene. This has the effect of emphasizing the son's position as his father's rival.

Pedro's motives for violating his filial obligations are never articulated in any detail, though he does tell Florinda: ''tis not my friendship to Antonio which makes me urge this, but love to thee, and hatred to Vincentio' (163). Pedro may be a coercive bully, but the play does not entirely discount his claim to be acting out of sibling loyalty. The opening scene establishes the closeness of the bond between Pedro and Florinda, who have been raised together without their younger, convent-bred sister. Florinda certainly thinks it reasonable to expect that their relationship will take precedence over the relationship between father and son: 'I would not have a man so dear to me as my brother, follow the ill customs of our country, and make a slave of his sister — and sir, my father's will I'm sure you may divert' (160). Pedro's love for his sister does not extend to granting her the freedom to choose her own husband; but it remains possible to interpret his choice of Antonio as a bid for a compromise candidate better able to provide for Florinda's happiness than the aged Vincentio, but also possessed of the wealth and status which the foreign and dispossessed Belvile so singularly lacks.

Yet the play also associates Pedro's plans for his sister's future with his 'hatred to Vincentio'. Coupled with his challenge to his father's authority, this rather cryptic declaration may seem to signal Pedro's predisposition to oppose and defy other men. This view gains credibility when Angellica Bianca informs us of Pedro's difficult relationship with his uncle, the now dead Spanish general who was her keeper: 'Don Pedro! my old gallant's nephew, when his uncle died he left him a vast sum of money; it is he who was so in love with me at Padua, and who used to make the general so jealous' (178). This narrative of erotic rivalry between uncle and nephew is another of Behn's innovations; in Killigrew, the Spanish general is unrelated to Pedro and had an entirely amicable relationship with him; Behn's introduction of a less than wholly affectionate blood tie between the two men reinforces the volatility of male familial bonds and implicates Pedro still further in a code of aggressive masculine emulation. We may accept Angellica's view that Pedro's erotic bid for his uncle's mistress stemmed from the intensity of his desire. Then again, we may read his attempt to steal Angellica as a challenge to the older man's authority, and conclude that Pedro is very much a man of honour, impatient with his inferior position in the patriarchal pecking order, desperate to assert his will over his 'superiors' (see Szilagyi 1998: 445). Certainly Behn's decision to place Pedro and Florinda within a network of familial relations makes conflict look like the inevitable condition of even the most intimate upper-class male relationships. Her invention of the character of Antonio intensifies this impression, for Pedro's friend and chosen brother-in-law is rapidly transformed into his enemy and opponent in two duels (with a third promised at the end of the play).

There is, then, very little to distinguish Behn's Spaniards from her English cavaliers, at least when it comes to their conception of what it means to be a man. As we have seen, their shared values are further exhibited in the attempted gang rape, though Pedro's presence in this scene turns a near-gang rape into a near-incestuous rape. The play's carnival disguises and disruptions of normal behaviour blur several boundaries separating women who are sexually within reach from those who are off limits: not only the boundary dividing gentlewoman from low-class whore but also the boundary dividing sister from sexual partner. As Terry Castle points out, incest provided a convenient symbol in early modern thought for the violation of boundaries effected by carnival masquerade, with its collapsing of crucial cultural distinctions and oppositions, 'its unholy mixing of things meant to stay apart' (80). Yet if this scene's near-incest is bound up with the play's larger interest in carnival confusion, it also enhances its portrayal of the patriarchal family and the brother's role within it.

From the start of the play there is a curious undercurrent in Pedro's attitude to Florinda. His opposition to Belvile as a marriage partner is on one level entirely pragmatic: he refuses to countenance the prospect of a kinship alliance with a man who, although well-born, is also 'banished his country, despised at home, and pitied abroad' (162). Yet the desire to avoid an undesirable match seems insufficient to account for the peculiar quality of Pedro's animosity towards Belvile, which at times smacks of sexual jealousy:

> I know not how dear I am to you, but I wish only to be ranked in your esteem equal with the English Colonel Belvile – why do you frown and blush? is there any guilt belongs to the name of that cavalier? (161)

Pedro apparently feels that Belvile has supplanted him in his sister's affections. He turns the cavalier into yet another rival, and the equivalence he draws between his own relationship with Florinda and her amorous attachment to Belvile is captured in the word 'equal'. The prurient suspicions that follow serve to reinforce the impression that Pedro's fraternal role is at some level entangled with sexual feelings.

The subplot tracing the conflict that erupts between Pedro and Antonio provides further signs of the brother's confused attitude to his sister. When Pedro, in carnival disguise in Act 2, scene 1, witnesses Antonio's decision to buy Angellica Bianca's sexual favours, the discovery of his friend's interest in the prostitute entails a double humiliation: Antonio simultaneously defeats Pedro's hopes 'of the possession of Angellica' (179) and delivers a resounding insult to Florinda and Pedro: having offered his friend the precious gift of his sister's body, Pedro sees him treat that gift with contempt by his pursuit of another woman.

Pedro's response to this double insult is violence; the two friends fight on stage until separated by the English, at which time Pedro challenges Antonio to a duel. In an aside, he tells us that he is fighting on Florinda's behalf, but what the scene stresses are his own muddled erotic and fraternal anxieties: whom is Pedro fighting for – Angellica or Florinda? Throughout this strand of the plot the confusion over which woman is the subject of the quarrel reminds us how precarious is the boundary between the gentlewoman and the prostitute (Hughes 1996: 212). Yet it also works to establish links between Pedro's fraternal protectiveness and his erotic involvement with Angellica, a link underlined by Pedro's disguise. When he challenges Antonio to a duel, he does so in the guise of a frustrated suitor for Florinda's hand. Antonio logically concludes that his opponent must be Belvile; the brother then looks unsettlingly like the lover.

This particular comic confusion recurs throughout this strand of the plot. When Antonio prevails upon Belvile to fight the duel on his behalf, he passes on to the cavalier his own mistaken assumption that the challenger is a rival for Florinda's love. The duel scene, in which Belvile and Pedro (both disguised) meet and fight, drives home the identity of brother and lover, even subjecting Belvile to the tormenting sight of Florinda interceding on behalf of the man he thinks is his 'rival'. The brother who is repeatedly mistaken for a lover goes on, during the attempted gang rape, to mistake his sister for a sexual plaything.

Pedro's disguise is obviously a plot device: for the brother, a strategy that enables him to fight his sister's betrothed without revealing his identity, and for the dramatist, a convenient motor of comic confusion. But disguise can enhance characterization at the same time that it generates stage action, signalling hidden facets of the character that adopts it. Does Pedro's disguise as a sexual rival for Florinda betray his secret erotic life? While Behn's characterization of Pedro gestures consistently at incestuous impulses, these are clearly not the kind of conscious incestuous desires dramatized in Ford's *'Tis Pity She's a Whore* (1630). Rather, Behn's portrayal of Pedro works subtly to suggest the underlying sexual dimension of the fraternal role within the patriarchal family.

Pedro's central role as the opponent of marriage for love clearly allies him, despite his anomalous relation to paternal authority, with a patriarchal kinship system that gave men in this period considerable power over the sexual destinies of their female relations. In early modern England, a society 'in which there were very large numbers of orphans' (Stone 1979: 48), this power often passed from the father to the eldest son and heir. Killigrew's brother and sister are indeed orphans, which accounts for the extent of the power the original Pedro wields over his sister. Behn brought Killigrew's dead father back to life without diminishing Pedro's coercive presence: she wanted him both to challenge patriarchal authority and to embody it.

By the time Behn wrote *The Rover* there was a well-established tradition of stage brothers who use their masculine dominance to make sexual arrangements for their sisters. In Heywood's *A Woman Killed with Kindness* (1603), for example, the character of Sir Charles Mountford gives his sister to his benefactor Sir Francis Acton, using her body to 'pay back all my debt' in 'one rich gift' (scene 10, 124). A comparable exchange of a sister's body is effected by the Colonel in the main plot of Middleton and Rowley's *A Fair Quarrel* (1615–17), a play which heightens the sense of the brutality of such fraternal control by presenting a second coercive sibling relationship in the subplot (Gossett 1992: 437–8). The unpleasant economic and sexual implications of sibling bonds in which the brother has an intimate interest in and control over his sister's sex life were not lost on Jacobean dramatists. *A Fair Quarrel* associates the relationship between brother and sister to that between a pimp and his prostitute; and when Vindice, in *The Revenger's Tragedy* (1605–6), puts on the disguise of Piato and attempts to procure his sister Castiza for Lussurioso, the part he plays exposes the pander-like quality of the fraternal role (Gossett 1992: 453; 447–8).

Critics have also detected an incestuous subtext in such dramatic representations of fraternal power (Shell 1988: 105–9; McCabe 1993: 240–56). The brothers in plays like Heywood's *A Woman Killed with Kindness,* Shakespeare's *Measure for Measure* (1604) and Webster's *The Devil's Law Case* (1623) seek to make sexual use of their sisters' bodies in a manner which Shakespeare's Isabella famously describes as 'a kind of incest' (3.1.138). Jacobean dramatists alert us to the numerous ways in which the patriarchal family could generate a highly sexualized view of the sister: the way a brother's rights of bestowal in his sister might produce a fiercely proprietorial attitude towards her; the way the dependence of family honour on female chastity encouraged an intense and unsavoury interest in the sexuality of female relations. Stage brothers like Vindice in *The Revenger's Tragedy*, Melantius in *The Maid's Tragedy* and Ferdinand in *The Duchess of Malfi* (1613–14) show an interest and involvement in their sisters' sex lives ranging from prurience to derangement (McCabe 1993: 245). Behn's Pedro arguably belongs to this seventeenth-century dramatic exploration of sibling relations within the early modern family. His emotional attachment to Florinda and his apparent concerns for her marital happiness coexist with a view of her as a body to be exchanged, a sexual gift to be given by him to the man of his choice. The play's opening scene makes clear the way Florinda's role in the kinship system produces a sexually charged attitude towards her. Not only is Pedro seeking to make sexual use of his sister; he is also engaging in the favourite fraternal pastime of sexual policing, trying to read her face for clues to her secret erotic life: 'why do you frown and blush? Is there any guilt belongs to the name of that cavalier?' (161). Obsession with the chastity that partly constitutes her value on the marriage market is here inseparable from a fascinated scrutiny of Florinda's sexual feelings.

The intimations of incest that inform Pedro's character and role are part of Behn's searching exploration of upper-class masculinity in *The Rover*. And like her portrayal of the banished cavaliers, they contribute to a representation of patriarchy as simultaneously unstable and resilient. The motif of the brother who resembles a lover comments on Belvile as well as Pedro; as Florinda's perilous progress from maid to wife makes clear, the lover *is* like the brother in so far as he too plays the role of guardian of the woman's chastity. Beneath their competition for control over Florinda's body, brother and lover are joined by a kinship of interests, a shared concern to use women's bodies to guarantee the perpetuation of the patriarchal elite. Ruling-class masculinity in *The Rover* may reveal the deep-seated instability of patriarchal culture, but it also serves to account for its remarkable staying power.

See also DRAMA

REFERENCES AND FURTHER READING

Behn, Aphra (1992). *Oroonoko, The Rover and Other Works*, ed. Janet Todd. London: Penguin Books.

Braverman, Richard (1995). 'The rake's progress revisited: politics and comedy in the Restoration.' In J. Douglas Canfield and Deborah C. Payne (eds), *Cultural Readings of Restoration and Eighteenth-Century Theater* (pp. 141–68). Athens, GA: University of Georgia Press.

Breitenberg, Mark (1996). *Anxious Masculinity in Early Modern England*. Cambridge: Cambridge University Press.

Castle, Terry (1986). *Masquerade and Civilization: The Carnivalesque in Eighteenth-Century English Culture and Fiction*. London: Methuen.

Chernaik, Warren (1995). *Sexual Freedom in Restoration Literature*. Cambridge: Cambridge University Press.

Cotton, Nancy (1991). 'Aphra Behn and the pattern hero.' In Mary Anne Schofield and Cecilia Macheski (eds), *Curtain Calls: British and American Women and the Theater 1660–1820* (pp. 211–19). Athens, OH: Ohio University Press.

DeRitter, Jones (1986). 'The gypsy, *The Rover,* and the wanderer: Aphra Behn's revision of Thomas Killigrew.' *Restoration,* 10, 82–92.

Gossett, Suzanne (1992). 'Sibling power: Middleton and Rowley's *A Fair Quarrel.' Philological Quarterly,* 71, 437–57.

Hobby, Elaine (1999). 'Not stolen object, but her own: Aphra Behn's *Rover* and Thomas Killigrew's *Thomaso.' Women's Writing,* 6, 113–27.

Hughes, Derek (1996). *English Drama 1660–1700.* Oxford: Clarendon Press.

——(2001). *The Theatre of Aphra Behn.* Basingstoke: Palgrave.

James, Mervyn (1986). 'English politics and the concept of honour, 1485–1642.' In *Society, Politics and Culture: Studies in Early Modern England* (pp. 308–415). Cambridge: Cambridge University Press.

Jordan, Robert (1972). 'The extravagant rake in restoration comedy.' In Harold Love (ed.), *Restoration Literature* (pp. 69–90). London: Methuen.

Killigrew, Thomas (1664). *Comedies and Tragedies.* London: H. Herringman.

McCabe, Richard A. (1993). *Incest, Drama and Nature's Law 1550–1700.* Cambridge: Cambridge University Press.

Macpherson, C. B. (1962). *The Political Theory of Possessive Individualism.* Oxford: Clarendon Press.

Munns, Jessica (1998). 'Theatrical culture I: politics and theatre.' In Steven N. Zwicker (ed.), *The Cambridge Companion to English Literature 1650–1740* (pp. 82–103). Cambridge: Cambridge University Press.

Owen, Susan J. (1996). 'Sexual politics and party politics in Behn's drama, 1678–83.' In Janet Todd (ed.), *Aphra Behn Studies* (pp. 15–29). Cambridge: Cambridge University Press.

Pacheco, Anita (1998). 'Rape and the female subject in Aphra Behn's *The Rover.' English Literary History,* 65, 323–45.

Pearson, Jacqueline (1988). *The Prostituted Muse: Images of Women and Women Dramatists 1642–1737.* New York: St Martin's Press.

Pitt-Rivers, Julian (1977). *The Fate of Shechen, or The Politics of Sex: Essays in the Anthropology of the Mediterranean.* Cambridge: Cambridge University Press.

Rosenthal, Laura J. (1996). *Playwrights and Plagiarists in Early Modern England: Gender, Authorship, Literary Property.* Ithaca, NY: Cornell University Press.

Scobie, Brian (ed.) (1985). *A Woman Killed With Kindness.* New Mermaids. London: A. & C. Black.

Shell, Marc (1988). *The End of Kinship: Measure for Measure, Incest, and the Ideal of Universal Siblinghood.* Baltimore, MD: Johns Hopkins University Press.

Stone, Lawrence (1979). *The Family, Sex and Marriage in England 1500–1800.* London: Penguin Books.

Szilagyi, Stephen (1998). 'The sexual politics of Behn's *Rover*: after patriarchy.' *Studies in Philology,* 95, 435–55.

Thomas, Keith (1965). 'The social origins of Hobbes's political thought.' In K. C. Brown (ed.), *Hobbes Studies* (pp. 185–236). Oxford: Blackwell Publishers.

Thompson, Peggy (1996). 'Closure and subversion in Behn's comedies.' In Katherine Quinsey (ed.), *Broken Boundaries: Women and Feminism in Restoration Drama* (pp. 71–88). Lexington: University of Kentucky Press.

Wiseman, S. J. (1996). *Aphra Behn.* Writers and Their Work. Plymouth: Northcote House.

Zook, Melinda (1998). 'Contextualizing Aphra Behn: plays, politics, and party, 1679–1689.' In Hilda L. Smith (ed.), *Women Writers and the Early Modern British Political Tradition* (pp. 75–93). Cambridge: Cambridge University Press.

15

Mary Astell, Critic of the Marriage Contract/Social Contract Analogue

Patricia Springborg

Mary Astell came in at the end of a century dominated by corporatism, patriarchalism and contractarianism. Interlocking but separate, these principles generated a three-cornered debate, in and out of which political theorists moved. It is perhaps anachronistic to term Astell a feminist, but in her age she achieved something signal, and that was to call into question the tissue of legal fictions around which early modern political theory was constructed. The marriage contract, as a juristic formula for the union of two wills, was the cornerstone of corporatism and patriarchalism and the model to which social contract theories were drawn (see Hinton 1967–8; Shanley 1979; Okin 1982). Centuries of canon lawyers who had reflected on the institution of marriage had set this peculiar contract at the heart of the constitution of the state. Contracted by free and equal individuals, marriage necessarily produced asymmetrical power relations as its consequent. The freedom of the parties entering the contract was a condition on which the church insisted, so that coercion represented an impediment to legal marriage. But once transacted the marriage brought into play institutions of family government whose terms were set, defining relations of property, inheritance and power. The family as a corporate body was founded on a union that was deemed sacred, irrevocable and indissoluble, by virtue of the holy vows that provided its sanction. It is not difficult to see how the marriage contract might provide an analogue for the social contract itself.

How is it that a little-known North Country English gentlewoman, who in fact barely qualified for this rank, should have challenged the basis of early modern contractarianism almost at the moment of its birth? These were years in which illiteracy for North Country women, as measured by their ability to sign court documents (admittedly a class-weighted measure), ran at 83 per cent in the 1660s and 1670s and at 72 per cent in the 1680s and 1690s (Cressy 1977, 1980; Perry 1986: 53). Mary Astell combined the career of a Tory political pamphleteer with a deeply philosophical and theological interest that produced her most enduring works. The young woman who, upon her arrival in London, dedicated an edition of her poems to the non-juring former Archbishop of Canterbury, William Sancroft, at the same time petitioning him for financial support (Hill 1986: 183–4), presented herself as a religious thinker. As interlocutor with Bishop John Norris, the Cambridge Platonist, who (as he declared) published their correspondence for the brilliance of her contribution (Astell/Norris, *Letters Concerning the Love of God*, 1695), Mary Astell first impressed her audience as a philosopher and theologian. It was as a religious writer that Astell first challenged John Locke, in response to whom her magnum opus, *The Christian Religion as Profess'd by a Daughter of the Church of England* (1705), was written.

But it was as a political writer that Astell was most celebrated in her lifetime. She was among the first, if not indeed the first, to provide a published critique of Locke's *Two Treatises of Government* (see Springborg 1995, 1996, 1997, 1998a, 1998b). Moreover, her history of the English Civil War, *An Impartial Inquiry into the Causes of Rebellion* (1704), is a trenchant critique of Whig historiography. Her *Reflections upon Marriage*, first printed in 1700, went through five editions, each of a probable print-run of at least 2,500 copies. Her *Serious Proposal to the Ladies, For the Advancement of their True and Greatest Interest* (1694) ran to five editions, attracting the momentary support of Queen Anne for her proposed women's academy, as well as the unsigned criticisms of Swift or Steele in *Tatler*, nos. 32 and 63.

An already established writer known for her support of women's causes, Astell was engaged by her publisher, Richard Wilkin, as a High Church Tory pamphleteer from 1703 to 1709, producing two important contributions to the debate on Occasional Conformity, her exemplary set-piece Tory history of the Great Rebellion and its lessons, and an elegant philosophical response to Anthony Ashley Cooper, the Whiggish third earl of Shaftesbury's *Letter Concerning Enthusiasm*. It is worth reflecting on the reasons a publisher might have had for signing on as a Tory propagandist a woman already renowned for her insistence on women's need for education and her very critical reflections on marriage. Did Richard Wilkin appreciate perhaps the peculiar vulnerability of the Whigs to Astell's assaults? The extension of Hobbesian and Lockean contractarianism to family relations, always the bedrock of state institutions, produced anomalies that cast doubt on the whole argument for social contract. Did Astell intentionally choose marriage as a vehicle to hoist the social contract with its own petard? Perhaps Wilkins understood what so many of her critics failed to appreciate, that Astell's provocation lay less as champion of women's rights and more as powerful pamphleteer for the Tory cause (McCrystal 1992a, 1992b). Speaking of herself in the third person, she expresses genuine surprise that the views of the author of *Reflections upon Marriage* should be thought seditious:

> Far be it from her to stir up Sedition of any sort, none can abhor it more; and she heartily wishes that our Masters wou'd pay their Civil and Ecclesiastical Governors the same Submission, which they themselves extract from their Domestic Subjects. Nor can she imagine how she any way undermines the Masculine Empire, or blows the Trumpet of

Rebellion to the Moiety of Mankind. Is it by exhorting Women, not to expect to have
their own Will in any thing, but to be entirely Submissive, when once they have made
choice of a Lord and Master, tho' he happen not to be so Wise, so Kind, or even so Just
a Governor as was expected? (Astell 1700: 134–5)

The juridical complexity of the marriage contract and its ramifications in the seventeenth century require our attention. For it is the juridical efficacy of the marriage
contract that made it such a handy vehicle, and not simply the fact that it legitimized
the sexual trade in bodies (Pateman 1988, 1989). From remote antiquity the institution of marriage, as the foundation of corporate life, was treated as a strategic social
resource, accorded the full trappings of the law (Finley 1955; Wolff 1944). The
medieval church had long recognized the imperative of reproduction as the justification of marriage as a social institution, granting men and women a surprising degree
of conjugal equality in terms of the rights each could enforce on the other (Sommerville 1995). It was not the official sexual equality within marriage – leaving aside
the question of social practices – on which early modern thinkers focused, but the
asymmetry by means of which marriage became the foundation of corporate property
rights and the vested power of the husband as head of the household.

Overstatement of the divide between medieval and early modern political theorists
suggests a false novelty to the marriage contract/social contract analogue, for certain
features of the institution of marriage had made it inescapable. Among these are the
conviction that marriage was a creation of positive law; distinctions between the contract made between the parties to each other and the separate vows made to God, as
guarantor of the pact; the indissolubility of the marriage bond due to obligations
incurred by these vows which took precedence over the question of how the contract
between the parties to it was honoured; and the corporate micro-society that this combination of contracts and vows created.

The marriage metaphor bespoke corporatism, and mystical body language, but it
also spoke the language of patriarchy. Centuries of Roman civil law, and later canon
law, had utilized the fiction of collectivities as corporations, enjoying the rights and
immunities of individuals (Gierke 1900, 1934). This fiction had been given an affec-
tive dimension in the notion of foundation contracts being in the nature of a marriage between the individuals who comprised them and the representatives who
governed them. Thus the church was seen as both the Bride of Christ and, not inci-
dentally, the mystical body of Christ. And, without any apparent inconsistency,
bishops, since Gratian's Decree (*c*.1140) at least, had been officially deemed to be
'married' to the church (Kantorowicz 1957: 215–21). Mystical body language, generated to account for the special relation of Christ to the church, was later extended
to account for the relation of the monarch to the national church and to the realm.
So when Elizabeth I claimed that the Commons loved her better than a step-dame,
and the Commons referred to her both as natural mother and wedded spouse, this
charming metaphor was not uttered in innocence. James I declared to his parliament

of 1609: '"What God hath conjoined then, let no man separate". I am the husband, and the whole island is my lawful wife; I am the head, and it is my body; I am shepherd, and it is my flock' (cited in Kantorowicz 1957: 223).

The seventeenth century was also a century of explicit patriarchalism, in a manner that we no longer know, just because the structure of the modern family is so different. Attempts to legitimize the whole array of corporate entities, from the crown to religious sects to families, on the model of the grant of power given from God to Adam and then to Noah, and to trace the filiations of that power in genealogies of Noah's sons as they peopled the whole earth, is a project long since abandoned (Schochet 1975). But in some of its more arcane ramifications it occupied some of the greatest minds of the seventeenth and eighteenth centuries.

Biblical patriarchalism, the spirit of strict textual exegesis and the attempts of Protestant reformers to recreate the social relations of the Old Testament, had political ramifications at all levels. Not only did such concerns animate those participatory Puritan sects that tried to recreate the primitive democracy of the ancient Israelites and the civilizations in which they were embedded. It also contributed to the ethos of the emergent nation-state, pulled between the simple patriarchal theocracy of the original Chosen People and the juridical complexity of feudal Christendom.

As patriarchy stands to monarchy, so theocracy stands to absolutism. In the hands of the most explicit patriarchalists of the age, Jean Bodin and Sir Robert Filmer, all the marks of absolutism are present on the strictest terms of biblical fundamentalism. The king *was* the father of his people, the family *was* the state. God's will was absolute and the king's will was too. As we are born into the family, so we are born into the state, and Aristotle's carefully constructed hierarchy of authorities, endorsed by medieval Christendom, which made political, matrimonial, patriarchal and despotic power (the latter the power of a master over slaves) qualitatively different, was conflated to produce one people, one realm and one source of power.

The simplicity of Filmer's construction, one of the most rare and crude examples of genetic argument to receive wide public endorsement, met the early criticism of seventeenth-century thinkers, Astell among them. Perhaps it took the boldness of such argument from sacred history to provoke the deliberately ahistorical rationalism of Locke – although not necessarily of Hobbes, who nowhere openly refutes Filmer, and for whom the fact of conquest in English history always provides a case of contract. Ironically, the explicit simplicity of Filmer's patriarchalism, unparalleled in the previous history of political thought, as Schochet (1975) argues, provoked the very line of argumentation which, in the form of radical liberalism, was to undermine all claims to special entitlement in the distribution of rights, and to right by precedent more generally. But all that lay in the future. The power of genealogical argument, or argument from origins, to the extent that it constituted a mode of religious and political argument in the seventeenth century (a matter on which, for instance, Pocock 1957, 1970, and Sommerville 1986a, 1986b, disagree), was always vulnerable to the criticism that practice proves no title. From the fact that something was once done, nothing strictly follows, or if it follows, it does so only contingently. To make a political precedent out of an historical event involves invoking an authority, if it is not done simply by political fiat. Analytic arguments concerning reasons always triumph over genetic arguments concerning origins, unless the latter are specially assisted in this way.

Political patriarchalism foundered on the additional fact that if it was to fathers that God had given the original grant of power, then either this grant was subversive of kings or kings were subversive of fathers. It fell to Hobbes and Locke to exploit this particular vulnerability and to show that the right of kings was not by nature but by convention: in a word, by contract. In so doing, as Sommerville (1986a: 257–9) has succinctly shown, they resumed a debate about the contractual origins of government, as a principle derived from Roman law, that had been argued almost continuously from medieval times up to Richard Hooker and John Selden, and defended by writers as different as John Pym, William Ames, Robert Mason and the Jesuit Francisco Suarez (Sommerville 1986a: 258–9).

As critics have widely concurred, Locke's version of the marriage contract/social contract, which Astell has specifically in her sights, puts a burden on consent that it was not apt to bear: if a highwayman travelling through a territory was deemed, as Locke suggested (*Second Treatise*, para. 119), by the use of its roads to assent to its form of government, the concept was so overextended as to be meaningless. Right gives way to might, as Astell percipiently remarked: 'And if meer Power gives a Right to Rule, there can be no such thing as Usurpation; but a Highway-Man, so long as he has Strength to force, has also a Right to require our Obedience' (*Reflections upon Marriage* 1700: 149). The image of the highwayman was invoked again by Astell, in *Moderation truly Stated* (80), to make precisely the same argument, although this time with reference to Milton's defence of contract in the *Iconoclastes in Answer to a Book Entitled 'Eikon Basilike'* (1649). It seems very likely that she took it from Locke, with whom she had several scores to settle, believing, as she did, that he had masterminded Lady Damaris Masham's attack on her in two celebrated works (Perry 1986: 91).

Locke, invoking the authority of Aristotle and Cicero, saw property as an extension of personality, the resource in terms of which characteristic human powers and purposes are played out. While he believed hereditable restrictions on persons to be insupportable, his concept of freedom did not extend to the removal of hereditable restrictions on property. Moreover, on these two questions on which he lays so much emphasis – rights of entitlement in one's own person such that one cannot contract into subordination, and rights to property as an extension of personality – women are in effect excluded. Although Locke was concerned to speak of 'parental' as opposed to 'paternal' or 'patriarchal' power, in order to deny father-right or the superior *rights* of the husband over his spouse, at the same time insisting that the wife cannot *consent* to her own subordination, he capitulated to *custom* in both respects. What could not be garnered by natural rights was yielded to men by custom: on the basis of physical superiority.

Astell, in perhaps her finest rhetorical piece, the Appendix to *Reflections upon Marriage*, locates the subordination of women precisely in custom. But custom, she properly argues, yields no right, going on to compare woman's duties as a wife and housekeeper with those of a man who has contracted to raise hogs – something that should not reflect on the status of either of them!

> That the Custom of the World, has put Women, generally speaking, into a State of Subjection, is not denied; but the Right can no more be prov'd from the Fact, than the Predominancy of Vice can justifie it. . . . 'tis certainly no Arrogance in a Woman to conclude, that she was made for the Service of GOD, and that this is her End. Because GOD made all Things for Himself, and a Rational Mind is too noble a Being to be Made for the Sake and Service of any Creature. The Service she at any Time becomes oblig'd to pay a Man, is only a Business by the Bye. Just as it may be any Man's Business and Duty to keep Hogs; he was not made for this, but if he hires himself out to such an Employment, he ought conscientously to perform it. (Astell 1700: 139–40)

It was the great accomplishment of Astell to kick away the chocks supporting the wheels of social contract and liberal democratic theory based on it. It was a ridiculous fiction to maintain, like Locke, that men are born free:

> *If all Men are born free*, how is it that all Women are born slaves? as they must be if the being subjected to the *inconstant, uncertain, unknown, arbitrary Will* of Men, be the *perfect Condition of Slavery*? and if the Essence of Freedom consists, as our Masters say it does, in having a *standing Rule to live by*? And why is Slavery so much condemn'd and strove against in one Case, and so highly applauded and held so necessary and so sacred in another? (Ibid.: 150–1)

The exclusion of half of the human race from the purview of natural right, in the denial to women of property and interests, cast serious doubt on the bold rationalist claim to freedom as a birthright. But to universalize the claim was not to improve its truth. The widely circulated Leveller claim that 'men are born free', sometimes extended to women, had attracted extensive debate (Thomas 1958: 50). Filmer, with uncharacteristic subtlety, alighted on the anomaly in their subsequent argument that it was only by contract that men could be bound. He provided an excellent rebuttal: the contractarians could not have it both ways; either men are born free or they are not, and if they are free they can never be bound. Moreover, Filmer specifically applied his formula to children, whose relation to their parents Hobbes and Locke also construed contractually:

> For if it be allowed that the acts of parents bind the children, then farewell the doctrine of the natural freedom of mankind. Where subjection of children to parents is natural,

there can be no natural freedom. If any reply that not all children shall be bound by their parents' consent but only those under age, it must be considered that in nature there is no nonage. If a man be not born free she doth not assign him any other time when he shall attain his freedom, or if she did then children attaining that age should be discharged of their parents' contract. So that in conclusion, if it be imagined that the people were ever but once free from subjection by nature, it will prove a mere impossibility ever lawfully to introduce any kind of government whatsoever without apparent wrong to a multitude of people. (Filmer 1991: 142)

Such an argument closed off the emancipation of women on the basis of natural right, as Astell was forced to agree. *Reflections upon Marriage* had been occasioned by the scandalous divorce of the Duchess of Mazarin, which Astell made the occasion for a cautionary tale, but not to sanction divorce. Astell defended the customary social order, much as she railed against it. Or else, as Filmer put it,

where there is an equality by nature, there can be no superior power. There every infant at the hour it is born in, hath a like interest with the greatest and wisest man in the world . . . not to speak of women, especially virgins, who by birth have as much natural freedom as any other, and therefore ought not to lose their liberty without their own consent. (Filmer 1991: 142)

Natural right entailed further false inferences, such as freedom of belief, and freedom of the press, both of which Astell opposed. If freedom of belief is a 'natural right', it is subversive of the entire social order. J. Nalson, whom she cited in *An Impartial Inquiry*, had argued that religion was 'the only bond of union, the only maintainer and preserver of those respective duties which are owing from one to another, in those little primitive societies of mankind' that constitute the family. Without it 'neither the obligations of nature, education, or reason, are powerful enough to keep men within the limits of their duty' (Nalson 1678: 13; cited in Thomas 1958: 54).

Astell agreed. Human beings were born into a tissue of networks and obligations, and only the blind could pretend otherwise. Arguments for natural right were but thinly disguised arguments for might and, where might is right, men come up trumps (to paraphrase Hobbes):

Men are possess'd of all Places of Power, Trust and Profit, they make Laws and exercise the Magistracy, not only the sharpest Sword, but even all the Swords and Blunderbusses are theirs, which by the strongest Logic in the World, gives them the best Title to everything they please to claim as their Prerogative; who shall contend with them? Immemorial Prescription is on their side in these parts of the World, Antient Tradition and Modern Usage! (Astell 1700: 173)

Astell stood firm by her philosophical conviction that custom yielded no right. By the same token, she argued on Platonist grounds that, if might is right, rulers cannot press a title to rule in superior wisdom. Subjects ruled by governors whose title to rule is established customarily, obey them customarily, and not for any other reason. The spiritual equality of all believers entitles subjects to keep their own counsel on the question of the duty-worthiness of their governors, passive obedience being the only form of resistance she will concede. What holds for the realm *eo ipso* holds for the family:

> But does it follow that Domestick Governors have more Sense than their Subjects, any more than that other Governors have? We do not find that any Man thinks the worse of his own Understanding because another has superior Power; or concludes himself less capable of a Post of Honour and Authority, because he is not prefer'd to it. How much time would lie on Mens hands, how empty wou'd the Places of Concourse be, and how silent most Companies, did Men forbear to censure their Governors, that is, in effect, to think themselves wiser. Indeed Government would be much more desirable than it is, did it invest the Possessor with a superior Understanding as well as Power. (Ibid.: 148–9)

Astell was no contractarian and no patriarchalist either. The Appendix to *Reflections upon Marriage* is a litany of biblical references affirming the power of women, in answer to the patriarchalists who would argue from the creation of Eve from Adam's rib to her inferiority (ibid.: 151–71). And corporatism features quite importantly in her thought. Not only is Astell quite consistent in maintaining the real constraints imposed on men and women by the institutions and structures into which they are born, but her views accord much more with the widely held perceptions on marriage and the family of her day than those of Hobbes and Locke, which were considered far-fetched and outlandish (Goldie 1978). Astell turned the tables on them:

> Again, if Absolute Sovereignty be not necessary in a State, how comes it to be so in a Family? or if in a Family why not in a State; since no Reason can be alledged for the one that will not hold more strongly for the other? If the Authority of the Husband so far as it extends, is sacred and inalienable, why not of the Prince? The Domestic Sovereign is without Dispute Elected, and the Stipulations and Contract are mutual, is it not then partial in Men to the last degree, to contend for, and practise that Arbitrary Dominion in their Families, which they abhor and exclaim against in the State? For if Arbitrary Power is evil in itself, and an improper Method of Governing Rational and Free Agents it ought not to be Practis'd any where; Nor is it less, but rather more mischievous in Families than in Kingdoms, by how much 100,000 Tyrants are worse than one. (Astell 1700: 149)

In many respects a legacy of medieval society, the High Church Tory view to which Astell subscribed saw society as an elaborate artifice constituted by many-layered juridical institutions and their constituencies. Freedoms, like duties, were yielded

from the specificity of laws, and freedom was not the great space which fills the political vacuum into which men step, or are born, as Hobbes and Locke would have it.
Astell is oftentimes heard extolling the particular genius of the English people for
freedom, in *An Impartial Enquiry* at length, but it is certainly not the freedom of
Locke, whose language she so heavily satirizes. Rather it is the very freedom guaranteed by English common law and customary rights over which the parliamentarians
had so bitterly fought, to the point of extinguishing these very liberties in their zeal
and risking

> The bringing *the Necks* of their Fellow Subjects, *Englishmen*, who *had the Spirit of a Free
> People*! under their own infamous *Yoke*, and *their Feet into* the most reproachful *Chains*;
> becoming themselves the Actors of those Arbitrary and Illegal Actions, which they had
> so loudly, and in great measure, falsely imputed to their Lawful Superiours. And the
> *Freeborn* People of *England*, for all their *Spirit of Honour and Genius to Liberty*, even those
> great *Fore Fathers*, whose *Off-spring we are*, had the *disdain of serving* in the most slavish
> manner and of wearing the heavy and shameful *Yoke* of some of the vilest of their Fellow
> Subjects: Till GOD was pleas'd to restore our Monarch, and with him the Exercise of
> our Religion, and the Liberties of the *English* Nation. (Astell 1704c: 9–10)

The universe, in Astell's view, is governed by a personal God, whose design for
humankind includes the unfolding of history and situated social institutions, as well
as the rights and duties they can command. It is not, Astell believes, a self-regulat-
ing mechanism composed of harmoniously arranged laws, from which divine intervention is absent, as the rationalists and Deists would have it. It is therefore a universe
in which there are specific freedoms and specific constraints, historical rights and historical injustices. The cause of women, like that of all souls, is affected by the outcome
of local struggles against local powers on particular issues. And just as reason is powerless to effect sweeping changes, it is not going to be constrained by any particular
construction placed on it, such as the exclusion of women.
    Astell is scathing against those who would conclude from the mystical-body lan-
guage of Paul in 2 Corinthians, the inferiority of women, noting

> that *the Head* of every *Man is Christ, and that the Head of the Woman is the Man, and
> the Head of Christ is GOD*; It being evident from the Form of Baptism, that there is
> no natural Inferiority among the Divine Persons, but that they are in all things Coequal.
> . . . The relation between the two Sexes is mutual, and the Dependance Reciprocal, both
> of them Depending intirely upon GOD, and upon Him only; which one would
> think is no great Argument of the natural Inferiority of either Sex. (Astell 1700: 140,
> 143)

The very sacredness of marriage, which in the Christian religion, unlike the pagan
religions of antiquity, Islam, or even orthodox Jewry, is a sacrament, and not merely
a special kind of contract, requires that women understand the form of dominion,

irrevocable and absolute, that they enter when they choose it; just as it is incumbent on subjects to understand the obligations they enter into when they swear allegiance to the crown:

> She who Elects a Monarch for Life, who gives him an Authority she cannot recall however he misapply it, who puts her Fortune and Person entirely in his Powers; nay even the very desires of her Heart according to some learned Casuists, so as that it is not lawful to Will or Desire any thing but what he approves and allows; had need be very sure that she does not make a Fool her Head, nor a Vicious Man her Guide and Pattern, she had best stay till she can meet with one who has the Government of his own Passions, and has duly regulated his own desires, since he is to have such an absolute Power over hers. (Ibid.: 32–3)

If only family tyrants were as sensible of their obligations as civil sovereigns, the world would be a different place. A husband can make a great travesty of the trust a woman places in his hands, whereas a woman 'makes a Man the greatest Compliment in the World when she condescends to take him *for Better for worse*' (ibid.: 46). The injustice is a double injury, for it rests on a false inference:

> when we suppose that over which we have Dominion to be made purely for our sakes, we draw a false Conclusion, as he who shou'd say the People were made for the Prince who is set over them, wou'd be thought to be out of his Senses as well as his Politicks. (Ibid.: 50)

Astell subscribes to Platonist notions of the educative function of superiors over inferiors, and the justification for hierarchy in a society geared to achieving the common good. On the uses of Dominion and Divine Order, she has this to say:

> Superiors indeed are too apt to forget the common Priviledges of Mankind; that their inferiors share with them these greatest Benefits and are as capable as themselves of enjoying the supreme Good; that tho' the Order of the World requires an Outward Respect and Obedience from some to others, yet the Mind is free, nothing but Reason can oblige it, 'tis out of the reach of the most absolute Tyrant. Nor will it ever be well either with those who Rule or those in Subjection, even from the Throne to every Private Family, till those in Authority look on themselves as plac'd in that Station for the good and improvement of their Subjects, and not for their own sakes; not as the reward of their Merit, or that they may prosecute their own Desires and fulfil all their Pleasure, but as the Representatives of GOD whom they ought to imitate in the Justice and Equity of their Laws, in doing good and communicating Blessings to all beneath them: By which, and not by following the imperious Dictates of their own will, they become truly Great and Illustrious and Worthily fill their Place. (Ibid.: 48)

But Astell is cynical enough about the uses of power in practice, observing of the subordinate wife:

And if she shew any Refractoriness, there are ways enough to humble her; so that by right or wrong the Husband gains his Will. For Covenants between Husband and Wife, like Laws in an Arbitrary Government, are of little Force, the Will of the Sovereign is all in all. (Ibid.: 39)

Astell's dismay at the injustices that the sacrament of marriage entailed for women in her age – an institution whose prospects for the mutual well-being of both partners she deemed in principle so great – is expressed in the bitterness of her portrait of the Eligible Bachelor (ibid.: 33–5). The conclusion is a dismal one: passive obedience, since resistance is ruled out. Astell is careful to absolve herself of any charges of sedition, feigning 'with an *English* Spirit and Genius, [to] set out upon the Forlorn Hope, meaning no Hurt to any body, nor designing any thing but the publick Good, and to retrieve, if possible, the Native Liberty, the Rights and Privileges of the Subject' (ibid.: 134). It is perhaps an ironic testimony to the triumph of the Whig version of history (Goldie 1978: 6) that Astell's Tory commitment to expose social contract theory for a Whig conspiracy has now dropped from sight, and she is seen instead as a proto-feminist highly critical of marriage as an institution. This seems very far from her intentions as we may infer them from her writings.

See also WOMEN AND WRITING; DEFENCES OF WOMEN

REFERENCES AND FURTHER READING

Astell, Mary (1689). *A Collection of Poems humbly presented and Dedicated to the most Reverand Father in God William by Divine Providence Lord Archbishop of Canterbury etc.* Excerpted in Bridget Hill (ed.) (1986), *The First English Feminist: 'Reflections Upon Marriage' and other Writings by Mary Astell.* Aldershot: Gower/Maurice Temple Smith.
——(1695). *Letters Concerning the Love of God, between the Author of the Proposal to the Ladies and Mr. John Norris.* Published by J. Norris, Rector of Bemerton nr. Sarum.
——(1696–7). *A Serious Proposal to the Ladies for the Advancement of their True and Greatest Interest. Parts I and II.* London.
——(1700). *Reflections Upon Marriage.* London.
——(1704a). *Moderation Truly Stated: Or, a Review of a Late Pamphlet, Entitul'd Moderation on a Vertue. With a Prefatory Discourse to Dr. D'Avenant, Concerning His Late Essays on Peace and War.* London.
——(1704b). *A Fair Way with the Dissenters and their Patrons.* London.
——(1704c). *An Impartial Enquiry into the Causes of Rebellion and Civil War in this Kingdom in an Examination of Dr. Kennett's Sermon, Jan. 31, 1703/4 and Vindication of the Royal Martyr.* London.
——(1705). *The Christian Religion as Profess'd by a Daughter of the Church of England in a Letter to the Right Honourable T.L., C.I.* London.
Ballard, George [1752] (1985). *Memoirs of Several Ladies of Great Britain Who have been Celebrated for their Writings or Skill in the Learned Languages, Arts and Sciences,* ed. Ruth Perry. Detroit, MI: Wayne State University Press.
Cressy, David (1977). 'Literacy in seventeenth-century England: more evidence.' *Journal of Interdisciplinary History,* 8, 141–50.

——(1980). *Literacy and Social Order: Reading the Writing in Tudor and Stuart England*. Cambridge: Cambridge University Press.

Filmer, Robert (1991). *Patriarcha and other Writings*, ed. Johann Sommerville. Cambridge: Cambridge University Press.

Finley, Moses I. (1955). 'Marriage, sale and gift in the Homeric world.' *Revue Internationale des Droits de l'Antiquité*, 3rd series, 2, 167–94.

Gierke, Otto von (1900). *Political Theories of the Middle Ages*, trans. F. W. Maitland. Cambridge: Cambridge University Press.

——(1934). *Natural Law and the Theory of Society 1500–1800*, trans. E. Barker. Cambridge: Cambridge University Press.

Goldie, Mark (1978). 'Tory Political Thought 1689–1714.' Ph.D. dissertation, University of Cambridge.

Hill, Bridget (ed.) (1986). *The First English Feminist: 'Reflections Upon Marriage' and Other Writings by Mary Astell*. Aldershot: Gower Publishing.

Hinton, R. W. K. (1967–8). 'Husbands, fathers and conquerors', 2 parts. *Political Studies*, 15.3, 291–300; 16.1, 55–67.

Kantorowicz, Ernst H. (1957). *The King's Two Bodies: A Study in Medieval Political Theology*. Princeton, NJ: Princeton University Press.

Locke, John (1988). *Two Treatises of Government*, ed. Peter Laslett. Cambridge: Cambridge University Press.

McCrystal, John William (1992a). 'An Inadvertent Feminist: Mary Astell (1666–1731).' M.A. thesis, Department of Political Studies, Auckland University, New Zealand.

——(1992b). 'A lady's calling: Mary Astell's notion of women.' *Political Theory Newsletter*, 4, 156–70.

Masham, Damaris (1696). *A Discourse Concerning the Love of God*. London.

Nalson, J. (1678). *The True Liberty and Dominion of Conscience*, 2nd edn. London.

Okin, Susan Moller (1982). 'Women and the making of the sentimental family.' *Philosophy and Public Affairs*, 11.1, 65–88.

Pateman, Carole (1988). *The Sexual Contract*. Cambridge: Polity Press.

——(1989). 'God hath ordained to man a helper: Hobbes, patriarchy and conjugal Right.' *British Journal of Political Science*, 19, 445–64.

Perry, Ruth (1986). *The Celebrated Mary Astell: An Early English Feminist*. Chicago: University of Chicago Press.

Pocock, J. G. A. (1957). *The Ancient Constitution and the Feudal Law*. Cambridge: Cambridge University Press.

——(1970). 'Time, history and eschatology in the thought of Thomas Hobbes.' In J. H. Elliott and H. G. Koenisberger (eds), *The Diversity of History: Essays in Honour of Sir Herbert Butterfield* (pp. 148–201). London: Routledge and Kegan Paul.

Schochet, G. J. (1975). *Patriarchalism and Political Theory*. Oxford: Blackwell Publishers.

Shanley, Mary Lyndon (1979). 'Marriage contract and social contract in seventeenth-century English political thought.' *Western Political Quarterly*, 32, 79–91.

Sommerville, Johann P. (1986a). 'History and theory: the Norman Conquest in early Stuart political thought.' *Political Studies*, 34, 249–61.

——(1986b). *Politics and Ideology in England 1603–40*. London: Routledge.

——(1991). *Introduction to Sir Robert Filmer, Patriarcha and Other Writings*. Cambridge: Cambridge University Press.

Sommerville, Margaret R. (1995). *Sex and Subjection: Attitudes to Women in Early-Modern Society*. London: Arnold.

Springborg, Patricia (1995). 'Mary Astell (1666–1731), critic of Locke.' *American Political Science Review*, 89, 621–33.

——(ed.) (1996). *Mary Astell (1666–1731): Political Writings*. Cambridge Texts in the History of Political Thought. Cambridge: Cambridge University Press.

——(ed.) (1997). *Mary Astell's A Serious Proposal to the Ladies (1694)*. London: Pickering and Chatto.

——(1998a). 'Astell, Masham and Locke.' In Hilda Smith (ed.), *Women Writers and the Early Modern
British Political Tradition* (pp. 105–25). Cambridge: Cambridge University Press.

——(1998b). 'Mary Astell and John Locke.' In Steven Zwicker (ed.), *The Cambridge Companion to English
Literature, 1650–1750* (pp. 276–306). Cambridge: Cambridge University Press.

Thomas, Keith (1958). 'Women and the Civil War sects.' *Past and Present*, 13, 42–62.

Wolff, H. J. (1944). 'Marriage law and family organization.' *Traditio*, 2, 43–95.

PART THREE
Genres

16

Autobiography

Sheila Ottway

Introduction

Although autobiographical writings have existed at least since classical antiquity, autobiography was only recognized as a literary genre at the end of the eighteenth century. Already in the early modern period, however, there was a burgeoning of auto-biographical writing throughout Western Europe. While very few autobiographical writings are known to have been produced by women in Britain before 1600, in the course of the seventeenth century, as literacy became more widespread, increasingly more women came to write about themselves in autobiographical texts. Such texts may be understood to include not only autobiographies in the most usual sense of the word, that is to say, recollections of an author's life in narrative prose, but also other kinds of personal writings, such as diaries, poems, letters, prophecies, defences and mother's advice books. The common feature of these different kinds of autobio-graphical texts is that they are all written from a first-person point of view. The pre-sentation of the self in these texts is often problematical, on account of the subordinate position of women in early modern society.

For women in early modern Britain, writing about oneself was a potentially trans-gressive activity. The culturally prescribed code of conduct for women demanded of them that they be chaste, silent and obedient, and submissive to patriarchal author-ity as exercised by their fathers, brothers or husbands. The ideal Christian woman was expected to be not only submissive but also self-effacing. Indeed, throughout the sev-enteenth century the word 'self' had distinctly negative connotations for all devout Christians, whether male or female. 'Self' was that part of the human psyche that had to be controlled and repressed before one could be a recipient of divine grace. Conse-quently early modern women had to adopt certain strategies in order to be able to write about themselves at all. Many of their autobiographical writings were not intended for publication, but rather for the exclusive readership of the author herself or her close relatives, or for fellow members of a religious community. Those autobiographical writings by women that did appear in print were usually intended for a specific purpose that exonerated the author from an excessive concern with self, for example in order to set an example to fellow Christians of the way in which God shows his favour to the faithful. A characteristic strategy employed by devout women in early modern times is the portrayal of oneself not so much as an autonomous individual, but as a mouthpiece for God's word. This is particularly conspicuous in the autobiographical writings of female prophets and sectarians of the mid-seventeenth century.

While most of the earliest autobiographical writings by women in early modern Britain were of a religious nature, in the course of the seventeenth century it gradually became more common for women to write about themselves and their own lives in a secular context. Secular autobiographies were rarely published, however, as such texts would generally have met with public disapproval. As a rule, it was considered unseemly and indecorous for women to write about themselves so explicitly. When Margaret Cavendish published her brief secular autobiography (*A True Relation of My Birth, Breeding and Life*) in 1656, she took care to emphasize her excessive bashfulness, evidently in order to preclude any adverse criticism of her audacity in thus making a public display of herself. Lady Ann Fanshawe was able to write about her own life in her largely secular memoirs, written in 1676, because they were intended not for publication but for the exclusive readership of her son; even so, she decided to delete certain passages, evidently because they were too personal. Similarly, Lady Anne Halkett wrote her secular memoirs in 1677–8, but without any desire to have them published.

Both religious and secular autobiographical writings by early modern women often bear witness to the imitation of models. The cultural historian Peter Burke observes that the proliferation of autobiography during the European Renaissance is to a great extent attributable to the increasing availability of ancient models from both Christian and pagan antiquity. According to Burke, the rise of the autobiographical habit can be seen as 'a chain reaction, in which certain texts awoke or restructured perceptions of the self, while these perceptions in turn created a demand for texts of this kind' (Burke 1997: 27). Whereas the imitation of Christ had been an ideal of the later Middle Ages, after the Reformation the accessibility of the Bible, now translated into the vernacular, made available a variety of biblical figures with whom Christians could identify. In the early modern period Christ continued to be a role model for some devout female autobiographers, such as Lady Grace Mildmay. Among the female models provided by the New Testament were the sisters Mary and Martha (see Luke 10.38–42), to whom, for example, Mary Rich, Countess of Warwick compares herself in her spiritual diary. As for role models from classical antiquity, it is noteworthy that in her autobiography Margaret Cavendish compares herself to Ovid, an appropriate model for a writer in exile.

In addition to ancient biblical and classical texts, some more or less contemporary texts could provide models worthy of emulation, for example the various conduct books that were published throughout the early modern period. While sixteenth-century conduct books for women tend to stress the necessity for women to be submissive and devout, seventeenth-century conduct books published in Britain are more concerned with correct behaviour in polite society. For devout Protestants in early modern Britain, the martyrs described in John Foxe's *Acts and Monuments* (commonly known as *The Book of Martyrs*, first published in English in 1563) functioned as eminently suitable role models, inasmuch as they were portrayed as demonstrating their faith and fortitude in the face of extreme affliction. Fictional writings, too, could provide role models for autobiographers. For example, romances, in the form of long narrative poems or prose, were very popular during the later Middle Ages and early modern period. Some women writers emulated romance heroines in their autobiographical writings; thus Mary Carleton portrays herself as a German princess in her account of her trial in London in 1663. Similarly, Dorothy Osborne regularly assumes the role of a romance heroine in her intimate letters to Sir William Temple, written during the early 1650s.

For women in early modern Britain there was thus a range of textual models available for emulation, at least for those women who were able to read and write. It must be emphasized that the textual role models described above were by no means slavishly imitated by women writers; rather, the models were taken as a basis on which the writer concerned could construct or fashion herself in accordance with various other factors, including her social status, her religious conviction, and her individual personality. In their introduction to an anthology entitled *Her Own Life: Autobiographical Writings by Seventeenth-Century Englishwomen*, Graham et al. (1989: 22–4) have identified the following features that are common to autobiographical writings by seventeenth-century Englishwomen: the sharing of a particularly female perspective on experience and self-expression, a high level of awareness of the writing process, and a frequently avowed concern with the truth. An additional common feature of many of these writings is the author's desire to express her dissatisfaction with a certain state of affairs in her life, of which she desires to be disencumbered. In their autobiographical writings women thus take the opportunity to voice their own particular grievances, thereby attempting to evoke the sympathy of the reader. For some women, it would seem that the actual process of writing about personal hardship was in itself therapeutic.

Considering the period 1550–1700 as a whole, it is clear that the practice of autobiographical writing by women gradually increases as a result of more widespread literacy and the spread of print culture. The instability of the political situation in Britain in the 1640s and 1650s resulted in a power vacuum, of which some women writers were able to take advantage. It is precisely in this period that a number of women's autobiographical texts were published, for example An Collins's collection of poems, *Divine Songs and Meditacions* (1653), and Margaret Cavendish's *A True Relation of My Birth, Breeding and Life* (1656). Although Lady Anne Halkett's memoirs were never published in her own lifetime, her vivid recollection of her youth in the 1640s and 1650s in this autobiographical text indicates that this was a period during which women could experience a remarkable degree of empowerment.

Autobiographical writings by early modern women in Britain are difficult to categorize precisely. Of the various sub-genres mentioned already, closer attention is devoted in this chapter to diaries, autobiographical writings in narrative prose, and autobiographical poems. It must be emphasized that autobiographical writings by women of the upper and middle classes predominate here, simply because literacy among women was largely restricted to these social groups, at least up until the middle of the seventeenth century. Also predominant are writings by Protestant women, not surprisingly in view of the success of the Reformation in Britain. Because Englishwomen's writings are the most readily accessible in published form, most of the women writers considered in this chapter are English, rather than Scottish, Irish or Welsh: only one came from a Scottish family (Lady Anne Halkett, née Murray), while one other, an Englishwoman, lived for some time in Ireland (Elizabeth Freke).

Diaries

Diaries may be considered as a form of serial autobiography, consisting of a large number of separate entries, each describing, as a rule, the diarist's activities during a certain day. In the late sixteenth and seventeenth centuries devout Protestants were encouraged to keep a diary as a means of spiritual self-examination. By recording their daily successes or failures in living a godly life, these diarists could ascertain the extent to which they had been granted divine favour, and the likelihood of their eternal salvation. Among the cultural elite such diaries were often written under the supervision of a spiritual adviser, who may have been invited to read and comment on the text.

The earliest known diary by a woman in Britain is that of Lady Margaret Hoby (1571–1633), who kept a diary from 1599 to 1605 (Hoby: 1998). During this period of her life Lady Hoby was living with her third husband, Sir Thomas Hoby, at Hackness in Yorkshire. The earliest entries in Margaret Hoby's diary are brief and repetitive; these entries record the daily pattern of her life, in which private prayer, meditation, spiritual self-examination and the reading of godly texts feature conspicuously. Margaret Hoby was a devout Protestant, whose diary was primarily intended as a record of her spiritual progress. It seems likely that she was prompted to keep a diary by her chaplain, Mr Rhodes, who is frequently mentioned in the earlier part of her diary. The more mundane activities in which Hoby was regularly involved are described summarily throughout her diary; these activities include dyeing, spinning, keeping household accounts and managing servants, as well as visiting friends and relations, and providing medical aid for the local community. In her diary Hoby also records her three journeys to London and back. Although most of the diary entries are bare and factual, it is clear that Hoby interpreted certain occurrences, such as her own experience of physical pain, as punishment justly inflicted by God. There is very little self-reflection in her diary, but the entry for 1 April 1605 shows that she was aware that the habit of keeping a diary could be spiritually beneficial:

> at Night I thought to writt my daies Iournee as before, becaus, in the readinge over some of my former spent time, I funde some profitt might be made of that Course from which, thorow two much neccligence, I had a Longe time dissisted: but they are vnworthye of godes benefittes and especiall fauors that Can finde no time to make a thankfull recorde of them. (Ibid.: 210)

Hoby thus sees the practice of writing in her diary as a religious duty, enabling her to give thanks to God for the favours bestowed upon her in her everyday life. In addition, the practice of reading her diary evidently prompts her to think about how she can best spend her time.

Another English woman who kept a spiritual diary was Mary Rich, Countess of Warwick (1624–78) (Rich 1847). Mary Rich's diary covers the last 12 years of her life, during which time she lived at Leighs in Essex. She was almost certainly prompted to start keeping a diary by her spiritual adviser, Dr Anthony Walker. Like the earlier part of Margaret Hoby's diary, Mary Rich's diary is primarily concerned with the inward life of religious devotion. At the same time, Rich records in her diary her everyday social activities, and mentions events of national significance, such as the great fire of London in 1666, and the Dutch raid on the English fleet in the Medway in 1667. Such dire events are interpreted by Rich as just punishment for the sins of the nation. In the same way, she interprets the death of her only son as God's punishment for her own sins, as is evident in her diary entry for 16 May 1667:

> I kept a private fast, being the day three years upon which my son died. As soon as up, I retired into the garden to meditate; had there large meditations upon the sickness and death of my only child, upon all his sick-bed expressions, and the manner how God was pleased to awaken him, with which thoughts my heart was much affected; and then I began to consider what sins I had committed, that should cause God to call them to remembrance, and slay my son. (Ibid.: 111)

It would seem that by writing her diary Rich attempted to come to terms with misfortune on both a national and a personal level. Her family life was far from happy: she was not only deeply distressed by the death of her son, but also tormented by the verbal abuse vented upon her by her chronically sick husband, who suffered from gout. Mary Rich appears to have borne all her sufferings with fortitude, portraying herself in her diary as a saintly heroine. Her diary bears witness to the overwhelming importance of religious faith to women in early modern Britain, who often had little to hope for in terms of fulfilment as wives and mothers.

The spiritual diary of Elizabeth, Viscountess Mordaunt (d. 1678) covers the years 1656–78 (Mordaunt 1856). This diary is not so much a record of Elizabeth Mordaunt's activities, but rather a collection of prayers and thanksgivings addressed to God, on various occasions in her life. Her entries for the year 1657 are listed in two separate columns with the headings 'To return thanks for' and 'To aske perden for', respectively. This demonstrates how Mordaunt's diary functioned as a kind of ledger, from which she could attempt to assess her spiritual 'credit' and 'debit' in the eyes of God. A number of entries in this diary are in rhyming couplets; in such cases it would seem that Mordaunt made an extra effort to express her heartfelt thanks to God for deliverance from peril, for example from the great fire of London in 1666. There is a memorable entry in Mordaunt's diary following the death of her husband:

> The thoughts of this [i.e. her husband going to heaven] aught to be a Joy to great to admit of any trubble; but so frale is this vile natur of mine, and so powerfuly does Self Loue prevale with me, that this, which ought to be my Joy, is drownd by my greefe. (Ibid.: 180)

In thus denouncing her self-love, Elizabeth Mordaunt shows her awareness of the culturally prescribed need to repress selfish thoughts and desires, and to submit meekly to the will of God. In another entry in her diary, she addresses God, saying that 'I my selfe obhor, and wish to be with thee' (ibid.: 171). Here, too, we may discern the desire for the repression of self, as a necessary step towards spiritual union with the deity.

One of the most remarkable women diarists in early modern Britain was Lady Anne Clifford (1590–1676), who assiduously kept diaries and other records of her family throughout her long life (Clifford 1990). In her earliest diary, known as the Knole diary, covering the years 1616–19, Anne Clifford is preoccupied with her stormy relationship with her first husband, and her attempt to prove herself the rightful heir to her father's lands and titles. There are passages in this diary where Clifford prides herself on her self-determination in the face of patriarchal authority. For example, she records in her diary how on two occasions in January 1617 King James I tried to persuade her to renounce her claims to her late father's estates and titles. On both occasions Clifford stood firm and refused to give in to the king. The Knole diary also testifies to the importance of female friendship at the Stuart court: thus Clifford records how Queen Anne, consort of James I, befriended her and even warned her to beware of the king's deceitfulness. There is some mention in the Knole diary of Anne Clifford's devotional activities, but this diary cannot be classified as a spiritual diary; it is rather a largely secular diary, in which self-celebration is conspicuous. Clifford's last diary was composed in 1676, long after she had inherited the Clifford estates in the far north of England. This is the diary of an old woman anticipating her own death. Each of the entries is followed by a biblical quotation, stressing the author's piety. This diary records Anne Clifford's daily round of receiving guests, tenants and tradesmen, and of dictating letters to her family and friends. Its most striking feature is the frequent recollection of events in Clifford's life that had occurred many years ago to the day, for example the day on which she had stubbornly resisted the authority of King James I, as she recalls in her diary entry for 20 January 1676:

> I remembered how this day was 59 years [since] I went with my first Lord to the Court at Whitehall, where in the inner withdrawing chamber King James desired & urged mee to submitt to the Award which hee would make concerning my Lands of Inheritance, but I absolutely denyed to do so, wherein I was guided by a great Providence of God for the good of mee & mine. (Ibid.: 240)

Clifford's last diary thus functions as a review of the author's past life, in which she recalls her own achievements with pride. At the same time Clifford emphasizes her strong sense of relatedness with her family. It is clear that her sense of identity was very much embedded in her consciousness of the importance of kinship ties and her sense of belonging to an ancient noble family.

Elizabeth Freke (1641–1714) kept a diary throughout her married life and her widowhood, from 1671 to 1714 (Freke 1913). A gentlewoman who had been brought up in the south of England, she lived for much of her life in Ireland after her marriage to her cousin, Percy Freke, in 1671. The marriage was not a success: as we read in the diary, Percy Freke repeatedly abused his wife and squandered her marriage portion. The earliest entries in the diary were clearly made some time after the events concerned, in view of the comments made by the author. For example, Elizabeth Freke recalls her wedding day (14 November 1671) as 'A most dreadfull Raynie day, A presager of all my sorrows & Misfortunes to mee' (ibid.: 21). The diary is a tale of woe, in which we read of the various mishaps that befell the author throughout her adult life: the birth of a stillborn child, her mistreatment at the hands of her husband and sister-in-law, perilous sea journeys between England and Ireland, her disappointment in the behaviour of her son and daughter-in-law, and the accidental death of a grandchild. It is highly appropriate that the diary is given the following sub-title: 'Some few remembrances of my misfortuns which have attended me in my unhappy life since I were marryed'. Like Mary Rich, Freke portrays herself in her diary as a suffering saint, who has to endure the affliction of an abusive husband. In Freke's diary the leitmotif is her unhappiness as a wife and mother, which she continually laments. The practice of keeping such a diary, consisting of a catalogue of misfortunes, may well have been therapeutic, enabling the author to distance herself from her unhappiness.

Autobiographies in Narrative Prose

The earliest women's autobiographies in prose, like the earliest women's diaries, bear witness to the great importance of religious faith in women's lives. Indeed, early modern women's autobiographies were often written primarily as a testimony of religious faith, in order to demonstrate to others the benefits of living a godly life. It is convenient to classify early modern autobiographies as spiritual or secular, although in practice religion played such a significant role in most women's lives that the distinction is not always meaningful. Spiritual autobiographies were written by women in Britain throughout the seventeenth century; in particular, autobiographical writings by women belonging to Nonconformist sects, such as Baptists and Quakers, were important vehicles for the spiritual reassurance of their fellow sectarians. Some spiritual autobiographies follow the pattern of the conversion narrative, in which the author perceives in her past life a moment of 'conversion', or spiritual regeneration, as having been of immense spiritual significance. There is no such paradigm for secular autobiographies, which were first written by women in Britain from the mid-seventeenth century onwards. These secular autobiographies by women were usually private writings, intended for the exclusive readership of their close relatives. In these secular autobiographies there is often an unresolved tension between the urge towards self-celebration and the culturally prescribed need for self-abnegation.

One of the earliest autobiographical texts by a woman in early modern Britain is the account of her life written by Lady Grace Mildmay (1552–1620) expressly for the readership of her daughter and grandchildren (Mildmay 1995). A provincial English Protestant gentlewoman, Grace Mildmay wrote her autobiographical recollections towards the end of her life, shortly after the death of her husband in 1617. It would seem that she wrote an account of her life primarily in order to set herself up as a model of Christian behaviour for her grandchildren. In her autobiography she gives a brief account of her early life, emphasizing the formative influence of her parents and her governess. Mildmay's mother is described as having been 'as an angel of God unto me, when she first put me in mind of Christ Jesus' (ibid.: 28). Such devotion to the memory of one's mother is a conspicuous feature of a number of early modern autobiographies by women. Mildmay remembers her mother's recommendation to her as a child 'that I should carry myself silent and humble in mine own conceit, esteeming others better than myself and only seek to find out mine own defaults and endeavour to reform them' (ibid.: 28). Mildmay thus fully accepted the need for female subordination and self-renunciation. Her mother also played an important role in her upbringing by providing her with several books, including the Bible, *The Imitation of Christ*, attributed to St Thomas à Kempis, and John Foxe's *Acts and Monuments*. Foxe's hagiographical text, with its descriptions of the sufferings of the Protestant martyrs, many of whom were women, may have been especially appealing to women like Grace

Mildmay, who could identify with such exemplary women. It is indeed as a kind of saint that Mildmay on occasion portrays herself in her autobiography, for example in recalling how she personally provided a marriage portion for her daughter, at a time when her husband was in financial difficulty. On other occasions, Mildmay appropriates the words of the biblical psalmist to describe her afflicted state at some moment in the past. While Mildmay's autobiography is ostensibly about herself and her past life, its purpose is to show how God bestows his favour on the faithful. It seems likely that the autobiography was not intended to be an autonomous text, but rather a narrative context for her copious written meditations: a large collection of writings, probably made throughout her adult life, recording her spiritual communing with God. The autobiography and the meditations were intended for the readership of her daughter and grandchildren, both as a memento of herself and for the purpose of their spiritual guidance.

The prose autobiography of Mary Rich, Countess of Warwick (1624–78), written in 1671, with additions made in 1673 and 1674, is structured in the form of a conversion narrative (Rich 1848). As we have seen, Rich also kept a spiritual diary, which clearly served as an *aide-mémoire* for her autobiography. Rich's autobiography contains much information that is largely secular: she presents an account of her parentage, her childhood, her youth, her courtship and her life as a married woman. Whereas Rich's diary is concerned with her day-to-day experiences as a mature woman, in her autobiography, written in her middle age, she looks back on her youth as a time misspent in the pursuit of earthly pleasures. Almost halfway though her autobiography she recalls how at the age of 21 she first became aware of the need for spiritual regeneration. In her own words: 'I did then begin to think of being in earnest for my salvation, and made promises to God of a new life' (ibid.: 17). When, soon afterwards, Rich's young son fell ill, she made a promise to God that if he recovered, she would become 'a new creature' (ibid.: 18). Her son's recovery appears to have been a turning point in her life, after which she did indeed become 'a new creature'. After this critical event she became committed to a godly way of life, to which her rural seclusion contributed. She recalls in her autobiography how she loved to withdraw to her favourite place of meditation, a 'wilderness' in the grounds of her country house,

> that I might there meditate of things of everlasting concernement, and therefore never was with the company but when I could not fairly avoid being so: and indeed it was no wonder to me that I appeared so altered to them, for I was so much changed to myself that I hardly knew myself, and could say with that converted person, 'I am not I'. (Ibid.: 23–4)

Rich thus sees her conversion experience as a transformation of her identity, that is clearly visible to others. This is the pivotal moment in her life as recalled in her autobiography. Her spiritual rebirth gives her the strength to endure various tribulations throughout the rest of her life, notably the death of her son at the age of 20, and the chronic illness and physical decrepitude of her husband, before his death in 1673. In looking back on her life in her autobiography, Rich clearly discerns a pattern: a sinful self becomes transformed, through a conversion experience, into a new, spiritually regenerated self. The pattern is familiar from the *Confessions* of St Augustine of Hippo, with whom Rich may well have identified.

There is a sharp contrast between Rich's autobiography, which was never intended for publication, and the wholly secular autobiography by her contemporary, Margaret Cavendish, Duchess of Newcastle (1623–73). In *A True Relation of My Birth, Breeding, and Life* (1656) Cavendish portrays herself as a devoted royalist and dutiful wife. As mentioned previously, she lays great emphasis on her chastity and her bashfulness. Yet Cavendish's protestations of modesty are hardly convincing, for she makes it plain that one of her chief objectives in life is to become a celebrity, to be raised 'to fame's tower, which is to live by remembrance on [*sic*] after-ages' (Cavendish 1915: 211). Cavendish thus portrays in her autobiography two distinctly different 'selves', one characterized by decorous subordination, the other by unabashed assertivity. Cavendish's paradoxical self-representation in *A True Relation* is typical of women's self-writing of the period, in which one can often discern a tension between the desire to write about oneself as an individual and the need to conform to a culturally pre-scribed pattern of female conduct. In other respects Cavendish's autobiography is exceptional, being the first known secular autobiography written by an English-woman, which was, moreover, published in her own lifetime. While other women autobiographers of the period tend to justify their boldness in writing about them-selves by stressing some kind of divine inspiration, Cavendish portrays herself in her autobiography as a woman of importance in high society. She is clearly proud of her personal achievement of having made a socially advantageous marriage, albeit to a nobleman impoverished by his life in exile. It seems likely that Cavendish's experi-ences in exile, in France and the Low Countries, between 1644 and 1660, strongly influenced her life as a writer, not only as an autobiographer but also as a writer in various other genres. Already in the first half of the seventeenth century a number of Frenchwomen's secular autobiographies had appeared in print, with which Cavendish may well have been familiar. In Britain her autobiography did not inspire imitation; it was to take another century before any other woman in Britain was to write about herself with such candour.

Another royalist woman writer who merits attention as an autobiographer is Lady Anne Halkett (née Murray) (1623–99), who wrote her memoirs during her widow-hood in Scotland during the late 1670s (Halkett 1979). In her memoirs, which were never intended for publication, she gives an account of her past life, devoting much attention to her activities as a supporter of the royalist cause, in England and Scot-land, during the 1640s and 1650s. Halkett clearly takes pride in recollecting how, as a young woman, she had assisted the royalist secret agent Colonel Joseph Bampfield in arranging the escape of the young Duke of York from England in 1648. Her close working relationship with Bampfield soon developed into one of intimacy, and their love affair is of central importance in her memoirs. It was an affair that was fraught with uncertainty, as for several years she did not know whether Bampfield was a widower, as he himself avowed, or whether, as rumour had it, he had a wife still living. In 1653 Anne found out that Bampfield's wife was indeed still alive, and shortly afterwards she effectively broke off their relationship. By this time she was engaged to a Scottish gentleman, Sir James Halkett, whom she married in 1656. In her memoirs Halkett gives a detailed account of her life up until 1656, at which point the narrative breaks off. In recalling her various activities in support of the royalist cause, Halkett clearly indulges in muted self-celebration. At the same time, her memoirs bear witness to her troubled conscience concerning her relationship with Joseph Bampfield. With regard to this relationship, Halkett portrays herself in her memoirs as a young woman torn by inner conflict. This finds expression in a passage in which she describes her reaction on receiving a letter from Bampfield: 'But affter I had dispatched his footboy I began to have great debates with my selfe, and the conflict betwixt love and honor was so great and prevalent that neither would yield to other' (ibid.: 57). Her love for Bampfield clearly conflicted with her sense of honour that inhibited her from having an intimate relationship with a married man. One senses that Halkett was motivated to write her memoirs above all in order to vindicate her conduct as a young woman. Repeatedly she stresses that she had always believed Bampfield to be an honourable man, and that she had acted in good faith in maintaining a relationship with him for several years. While personal issues are clearly of great importance in Halkett's memoirs, at the same time it would seem that her autobiographical narrative was inspired by her keen awareness of having lived through historically stirring times, and by the desire to record for posterity her own role in historical events. The memoirs are, moreover, stylistically accomplished, and make frequent use of naturalistic dialogue. In this respect Halkett's narrative anticipates the genre of the novel.

Among those autobiographical texts produced by women belonging to Nonconformist religious communities, the narrative of Agnes Beaumont (1652–1720) is one of the most dramatic (Beaumont 1992). In this narrative, written in 1674, Beaumont recalls the events that had occurred over a period of several weeks earlier that year, when she had been accused and acquitted of the murder of her father, a yeoman farmer and widower who lived in a small village in Bedfordshire. She had also been accused, at the same time, of having indulged in indecent behaviour with John Bunyan, who was the leader of the Independent Church in Bedfordshire of which she was a devoted member. Beaumont's father had died at home, probably of a heart attack, shortly after a serious quarrel with her: he had not approved of her frequent attendance at Bunyan's church, and had been incensed to hear that she had ridden to a church meeting on the same horse as Bunyan, riding pillion. When his heart attack began he had been alone with her; she had immediately sought help for him, to no avail. Not long after her father's death, Beaumont was accused of his murder by an acquaintance who clearly bore a grudge against her. She was obliged to appear before a coroner and jury, but had no difficulty in convincing them of her innocence. Beaumont recalls all these events in her narrative, which was evidently written for the readership of fellow members of Bunyan's Independent Church. The narrative is above all a testimony of religious faith, intended to demonstrate the way in which God favours the truly faithful by coming to their aid in times of trouble. Beaumont intimates that she had a foreboding of affliction shortly before her father's death, when he had locked her out of the house one night, obliging her to spend the night in a barn:

> It froze vehemently that night, but I felt no cold; the dirt was frozen upon my shoes in the morning. My heart was wonderfully drawn out in prayer, and as I was in prayer, that scripture came with mighty power upon my heart, 'Beloved, think it not strange concerning the fiery trials that are to try you'. (Ibid.: 48–9)

The 'scripture' referred to here is from the New Testament epistle of St Peter (1 Peter 4.12); Beaumont's recollection of these words coming into her mind while she was at prayer testifies to the immense significance of the language of the Bible in everyday life in seventeenth-century England. She subsequently uses the expression 'fiery trials' on several occasions in her narrative, indicating to her readers that the false accusations made against her were intended as a test of her faith. There was in fact a very real 'fiery' threat to a woman in early modern England accused of murdering a husband or father, for if found guilty of this crime of 'petty treason', the penalty was being burned at the stake. Beaumont's success in convincing the coroner and jury of her innocence enables her to set herself up as an example to other Christians, who may be in need of spiritual reassurance under similar circumstances of affliction. Although her narrative was apparently not intended for publication, it was circulated in manuscript among her fellow church members, and was eventually published in 1760. Beaumont's narrative is of special interest because it is one of the earliest autobiographical writings by an ordinary English woman, in which the human drama of everyday life in a small rural community unfolds with remarkable vividness.

Autobiographical Poems

While most women in early modern Britain who wrote about themselves in autobiographical texts did so exclusively in the medium of prose, a few women recorded the events of their own lives in autobiographical poems. These women used the formal constraints of poetry to confer a pattern of significance upon their past lives. For women in early modern Britain such a pattern of significance was usually connected with their religious faith, enabling them to interpret the events of their lives as having occurred within a divinely ordained plan.

An Collins was the author of a collection of religious poems, entitled *Divine Songs and Meditacions*, published in London in 1653, in which her past life plays a significant role (Collins 1996). Nothing is known about An Collins apart from the sketchy details of her life that are given or hinted at in her poems. Among those critics who have commented on Collins's poems there is no consensus of opinion as to her religious affiliation. In view of her familiarity with the Bible it is likely that she was, in any case, a devout Protestant. While none of her poems is overtly autobiographical, several of them are written in the form of a retrospective meditation on her life, enabling her to perceive the way in which God has shown her his special favour. In this respect her collection of poems can be regarded as a kind of spiritual autobiography, written in verse, intended for the readership of fellow Christians. In describing her own experiences, above all the way in which she has been relieved of affliction through the operation of divine grace, Collins sets an example to others, especially those who may be suffering from religious doubt and despair. In her introductory address, 'To the Reader', written in prose, she explains how she has had to endure 'a retired Course of life', evidently on account of some kind of chronic illness or disability. Far from being inhibiting, her physical inactivity has facilitated an 'activity of spirit', bestowed upon her by God, which has prompted her to write poetry. Collins emphasizes that the practice of writing poetry has brought her immense satisfaction. These autobiographical details are elaborated in her introductory 'Preface', written in verse, and in the following poem entitled 'The Discourse'. In her 'Discourse' she describes her unhappiness as a child, possibly referring to her physical infirmity; she points out that in her youth she had had an aptitude for learning, but that she had profited little from this because of her preference for reading 'pleasant histories', that is to say, fictional writings, and 'profane discourse'. Looking back on the pleasures of her youth as 'vanities', Collins recalls the moment at which she experienced spiritual rebirth:

> But all this while, the fumes of vanities
> Did interpose between my soules weak sight,
> And heavenly blisse, devine felicities;
> Vntill that morning starr so matchlesse bright
> The Sun of righteousnesse reveald his light
> Vnto my soule, which sweet refreshing brings,
> Because he coms with healing in his wings.
>
> (Ibid.: 12)

For Collins this moment of climactic significance is clearly a conversion experience. Her reworking of the language of the Bible in this stanza (here she gives a marginal reference to Malachi 4.2) indicates how the scriptures have come to replace the 'profane discourse' of her former reading matter. Indeed, many of Collins's poems are effectively a commentary on a particular biblical text. In another of her autobiographical poems,

'The Winter of my infancy', the Old Testament book of the Song of Songs clearly functions as a subtext: using the distinctive imagery of the Song of Songs, Collins envisages her mind as an enclosed garden, capable of producing 'a fruit most rare', that is to say, her poetry. She uses such biblically inspired metaphorical language to express what has been most important to her in her life: the relief of affliction through divine grace. In writing about herself in this way, giving very few details of the actual circumstances of her life, Collins draws attention not to her individuality, but rather to her exemplarity: what has happened to her, in her experience of spiritual regeneration, can, in principle, happen to anyone who shares her religious faith.

An autobiographical poem that is much more explicit about the circumstances of the author's life is the 'Memorandum' of Martha Moulsworth (1577–1646) (Moulsworth 1995). A narrative poem written in 1632, on the occasion of Moulsworth's fifty-fifth birthday, the 'Memorandum' describes the major events in her past life, recalled by her from the perspective of middle-aged widowhood. With remarkable economy Moulsworth gives an account of her childhood, her upbringing and education, her three marriages, and the deaths of her infant children and her three husbands. In writing her poem on her fifty-fifth birthday she looks back on her past life and takes stock of her present situation, with which she is clearly satisfied. As the middle-class widow of a goldsmith (her third husband), with no children of her own, Moulsworth was evidently left comfortably well-off. She portrays herself in her 'Memorandum' as a Christian for whom eternal life in the hereafter is taken for granted, with no fear of damnation. Although death features conspicuously in the poem, there is a remarkable absence of morbidity. Rather, Moulsworth's confidence in her own resurrection and in that of her three late husbands imbues her 'Memorandum' with cheerful optimism. The poem, discovered only in the 1990s, is of interest because of the harmony that is achieved between its content and formal organization. As Moulsworth points out, the 55 couplets of the poem correspond to the 55 years of her life. The poem can be divided into three parts, each of which corresponds to a part of Moulsworth's life, as virgin, wife and widow, respectively. There is a remarkable sense of balance throughout the poem that is achieved by the exploitation of the rhetorical figure of chiasmus, that is to say, a structure in a text in which elements are repeated in reverse. Chiasmus is displayed in the 'Memorandum' at different levels. Syntactical chiasmus, for example, is clearly discernible in lines 45–6:

> three husbands me, & I haue them enioyde
> Nor I by them, nor them by me annoyde
> (Ibid.: 206)

Here the subject/object reversal pattern of 'husbands'/'me' and 'I'/'them' is reversed in the second line of the couplet: 'I'/'them', 'they'/'me'. The overall effect is to suggest that each of Moulsworth's marriages has been a mutually satisfying arrangement, in which there has been equality between husband and wife. Chiasmus is also used in

Moulsworth's 'Memorandum' at the level of the poem as a whole. Within the obvious tripartite division of her life into spinsterhood, intermittent wifehood and definitive widowhood, there is a finer division of her life into seven stages: unmarried, married, unmarried, married, unmarried, married, unmarried. In this sequence Moulsworth's second marriage is centralized as the pivotal stage of her life; appropriately, it is described in a single line (l. 55) right in the middle of the poem. On either side of this line a structurally symmetric patterning of life phases is discernible. The seven phases in Moulsworth's life are reminiscent of the traditional division of a person's life into seven ages, as described in Shakespeare's *As You like It*. Moulsworth may have perceived this symmetrical pattern as a divinely ordered plan having structured the sequence of events in her life. The overall effect of Moulsworth's 'Memorandum', with its strong emphasis on balance, is to present an image of the author as a rhetorically gifted, level-headed individual. In this respect Moulsworth implicitly challenges stereotypical ideas about women, namely that they display verbal incontinence and emotional volatility.

Conclusion

From the various texts discussed above it is clear that there is considerable diversity in the ways in which women in early modern Britain wrote about themselves and their own lives. The motivation for a woman to write about herself may have been, variously, to facilitate spiritual self-examination, to testify to her religious faith, to set an example to others, to vindicate her conduct in the past, to celebrate her personal achievements, or to leave a lasting record of her life for posterity. For devoutly religious women, such as Mary Rich and An Collins, their autobiographical writings were intended to demonstrate the importance in their lives of a conversion experience. The autobiographical writings of some aristocratic women, such as Anne Clifford and Margaret Cavendish, are concerned hardly or not at all with religion; rather, they reflect the author's pride in her sense of identity as a person of high social status, through blood ties or through marriage. In some women's writings, for example the diary of Elizabeth Freke and the narrative of Agnes Beaumont, a difficult relationship with a husband or father features conspicuously, testifying to the specific problems of women in a patriarchal society.

One senses that for many of these women autobiographers the writing process was a liberating and empowering experience, even if the texts they produced had a very limited readership at the time. Although one can hardly speak of a tradition of women's autobiography in early modern Britain, seeing that most of the women writers concerned were isolated from mainstream literary culture and had no desire to publish their own texts, it is clear that for some women the autobiographical impulse was strongly compelling. It is thanks to the assiduity of these women in recording the events of their own lives, as well as their personal reflections on certain of these events, that we are able to have some idea of how women in early modern Britain experienced their individuality. At the same time, we are made aware of the difficulties that these women faced in negotiating the conflict between a culturally conditioned need for self-effacement and a personal desire for self-assertion.

See also MARGARET CAVENDISH, *A TRUE RELATION OF MY BIRTH, BREEDING AND LIFE*; ANNA TRAPNEL, *ANNA TRAPNEL'S REPORT AND PLEA*; WOMEN'S POETRY 1550–1700

REFERENCES AND FURTHER READING

Benstock, Shari (ed.) (1988). *The Private Self: Theory and Practice of Women's Autobiographical Writings*. London: Routledge.

Beaumont, Agnes (1992). *The Narrative of the Persecutions of Agnes Beaumont*, ed. Vera Camden. East Lansing, MI: Colleagues Press.

Blodgett, Harriet (1989). *Centuries of Female Days: Englishwomen's Private Diaries*. Gloucester: Alan Sutton.

Burke, Peter (1997). 'Representations of the self from Petrarch to Descartes.' In Roy Porter (ed.), *Rewriting the Self: Histories from the Renaissance to the Present* (pp. 17–28). London: Routledge.

Cavendish, Margaret, Duchess of Newcastle (1915). *The Life of the Duke of Newcastle, Memoirs of Her Own Life and Certain Sociable Letters*. London: Dent.

Clifford, Anne (1990). *The Diaries of Lady Anne Clifford*, ed. D. J. H. Clifford. Far Thrupp: Alan Sutton.

Collins, An (1996). *Divine Songs and Meditacions*, ed. Sidney Gottlieb. Tempe, AZ: Medieval and Renaissance Texts and Studies.

Freke, Elizabeth (1913). *Mrs Elizabeth Freke Her Diary 1671 to 1714*, ed. Mary Carbery. Cork: Guy.

Graham, Elspeth, Hinds, Hilary, Hobby, Elaine and Wilcox, Helen (eds) (1989). *Her Own Life: Autobiographical Writings by Seventeenth-Century Englishwomen*. London: Routledge.

Halkett, Anne (1979). *The Memoirs of Anne, Lady Halkett and Ann, Lady Fanshawe*, ed. John Loftis. Oxford: Clarendon Press.

Hoby, Margaret (1998). *The Private Life of an Elizabethan Lady: The Diary of Lady Margaret Hoby 1599–1605*, ed. Joanna Moody. Far Thrupp: Sutton.

Jelinek, Estelle C. (1986). *The Tradition of Women's Autobiography: From Antiquity to the Present*. Boston: Twayne.

Keeble, N. H. (1995). 'Obedient subjects? The loyal self in some later seventeenth-century royalist women's memoirs.' In Gerald Maclean (ed.), *Culture and Society in the Stuart Restoration: Literature, Drama, History* (pp. 201–18). Cambridge: Cambridge University Press.

Mascuch, Michael (1997). *Origins of the Individualist Self: Autobiography and Self-identity in England, 1591–1791*. Cambridge: Polity Press.

Mendelson, Sara Heller (1985). 'Stuart women's diaries and occasional memoirs.' In Mary Prior (ed.), *Women in English Society 1500–1800*. London: Methuen.

Mildmay, Grace (1995). 'Autobiography.' In Linda Pollock (ed.), *With Faith and Physic: The Life of a Tudor Gentlewoman, Lady Grace Mildmay, 1552–1620* (pp. 23–47). New York: St Martin's Press.

Mordaunt, Elizabeth (1856). *The Private Diary of Elizabeth, Viscountess Mordaunt*. Duncairn.

Moulsworth, Martha (1995). 'The Memorandum of Martha Moulsworth.' In Robert C. Evans and Anne C. Little (eds), *'The Muses Females Are': Martha Moulsworth and Other Women Writers of the English Renaissance* (pp. 204–8). West Cornwall: Locust Hill Press.

Rich, Mary (1847). *Memoir of Lady Warwick: Also Her Diary, from AD 1666 to 1672*. London: Religious Tract Society.

——(1848). *Autobiography of Mary Countess of Warwick*, ed. T. Crofton Croker. London: Percy Society.

Sawday, Jonathan (1997). 'Self and selfhood in the seventeenth century.' In Roy Porter (ed.), *Rewriting the Self: Histories from the Renaissance to the Present* (pp. 29–48). London: Routledge.

Smith, Sidonie (1987). *A Poetics of Women's Autobiography: Marginality and the Fictions of Self-Representation*. Bloomington: Indiana University Press.

Stanton, Domna C. (ed.) (1987). *The Female Autograph: Theory and Practice of Autobiography from the Tenth to the Twentieth Century*. Chicago: Chicago University Press.

Wilcox, Helen (1992). 'Private writing and public function: autobiographical texts by Renaissance Englishwomen.' In S. P. Cerasano and Marion Wynne-Davies (eds), *Gloriana's Face: Women, Public and Private, in the English Renaissance* (pp. 47–62). Detroit, MI: Wayne State University Press.

——(ed.) (1996). *Women and Literature in Britain 1500–1700*. Cambridge: Cambridge University Press.

17

Defences of Women

Frances Teague and Rebecca De Haas

Yet she was not produced from Adam's foot, to be his too low inferior; nor from his head to be his superior; but from his side, near his heart, to be his equal: that where he is lord, she may be lady.

Rachel Speght, A Mouzell for Melastomus

Defending Eve

Whether defending Eve or all womankind, a Renaissance writer had to address this argument: since women are descended from Eve, they are morally inferior, which in turn leads them to be socially and intellectually inferior. Controversy over women's nature is by no means new to the Renaissance. Medieval and Renaissance writers knew that the subjugation of women had existed from biblical times. As Betty S. Travitsky argues, 'in the civilizations of the ancient Greeks, Jews, and Romans, the subordinated position of the respectable woman ranged from one of almost complete seclusion . . . to one conferring prestige on certain female roles within the family'. One consequence of their long-term subordination was that women 'came to be identified more and more with the body and temptation'. As a result, 'distrust for women remained an undercurrent of medieval thought' (Travitsky 1989: 3–4).

Yet medieval attitudes toward women began to change in the sixteenth and seventeenth centuries. Increasingly, the argument ran that men and women were equal spiritually, on the basis that 'souls have no sex'. All equality between men and women ended there, however, for 'the doctrine of equal souls did not entitle women to equal participation in the Church's temporal hierarchy' (Mendelson and Crawford 1998: 31). As any scholar of early modern England knows, women were not allowed to minister to the general population. Of course, one reason for this subjection of women is womankind's descent from Eve:

And when the woman saw that the tree was good for food, and that it was pleasant to the eyes, and a tree to be desired to make one wise, she took of the fruit thereof, and did eat, and gave also unto her husband with her; and he did eat. (Genesis 3.6)

Eve, the first woman, ate of the apple first, and then gave the fruit to Adam, causing him to fall. Therefore, Eve's weakness is revisited on the head of every woman. Rachel Speght's defence of women in our epigraph is interesting, because of Eve's identity as the perpetrator of the fall, and thus of womankind's inferiority to man. Speght clearly avows that woman is equal to man because God made woman from Adam's rib, or 'near his heart', so woman is therefore not beneath man, but rather beside him. But even placing woman beside man did not necessarily make them equals. Commentators used the verse 'And the Lord God said, It is not good that man should be alone; I will make him an help meet for him' (Genesis 2.18) to justify female subjugation. Because the woman was only a 'help meet' she was beneath the man in judgement and moral capacity. Therefore, women in early modern England were subservient to the powerful men in their lives, whether fathers, husbands or brothers. This belief in women's subjection to men is an essentialist position with powerful consequences: women were not considered citizens in early modern England. As a result of not being legal citizens, women had no legal rights. A wife could make no legal contract without her husband's consent; she could make no will of her own and could not receive an inheritance to keep for herself (Mendelson and Crawford 1998: 38). To complete the notion that women were the property of the men they married or were related to, records of wife sales exist as well (ibid.: 142).

Because of their supposed moral and social inferiority to men, women were also considered mentally inferior to men. Literacy of any kind was usually limited to 'noble or upper-class families and to occasional religious or professional clerks' (Hull 1982: 2). Girls in these upper-class families might be encouraged to study, but learning was by no means extensive. Margaret More Roper, Sir Thomas More's daughter, is an exceptional example of a learned woman. Most lower-class girls, if taught to read early, went out into service; they were to help provide for the family, not to waste their time studying (Mendelson and Crawford 1998: 90). (One must note here a difference in the modern meaning of the word 'literacy'. Some women in the Renaissance could read, but not write, and are therefore 'literate' in some sense: see Hull 1982: 4). The movement towards having women learn to read was furthered by England's Protestant leaning and the belief that individuals should read scripture for themselves. So women were increasingly taught to read to give them access to the scriptures.

Speght was not the only woman to answer biblically based attacks. An earlier woman who explicitly defended Eve was Aemilia Lanyer, whose book *Salve Deus Rex Judaeorum* (1611, STC 15227–15227.5) included a poem, 'Eve's Apologie in defense of Woman' (for more discussion of Lanyer's defence, see chapter 8, this volume). Another defender of Eve was Margaret Askew Fell Fox, who published a pamphlet entitled *Women's Speaking Justified* (1667, Wing F643), which Moira Ferguson (1980: 114) considers a 'feminist revision of conventional biblical interpretations'. In it, Fox does indeed reinterpret the traditional readings. For example, she says, '[T]he Lord is pleased, when he mentions his Church, to call her by the name of Woman. . . . Thus much may prove that the Church of Christ is a woman, and those that speak against the womans speaking, speak against the Church of Christ' (ibid.: 116). Here Fox implies that if Christ is happy enough to associate woman with his infallible church, then woman cannot be the horrible entity that men have made her out to be. Fox then goes on to discuss famous, faithful women of the Bible, such as 'Mary Magdalen, and Mary the Mother of James, and Salom' (ibid.: 118). Her argument is that God reveals his truths to them, so therefore women cannot be the morally weak beings men conceive them to be.

The controversy over women continues through the Renaissance, well into the seventeenth century. Linda Woodbridge divides the controversy into three sections: 'The Early Tudor Controversy', 'The Elizabethan Controversy' and 'The Jacobean Tragedy to 1620'. She then says: 'defenses outnumber attacks by four to one' (Woodbridge 1984: 44). In the early Tudor period, for example, Edward Gosynhyll's 'The Scole house of Women' (1541?, STC 12104.5) is the only attack. The assaults continue throughout the Elizabethan period, with Thomas Nashe's 'The Anatomie of Absurditie, Contayning a breefe confutation of the slender imputed prayses to feminine perfection' (1589, STC 18364). The controversy diminishes between 1592 and 1615 (Woodbridge 1984: 74), but Joseph Swetnam's publication of *The Arraignment of Lewde, idle, froward, and unconstant women* in 1615 revives it and sparks Rachel Speght's *A Mouzell for Melastomus*, Ester Sowernam's and Joane Sharpe's *Ester hath Hang'd Haman* and Constantia Munda's *The Worming of a Mad Dogge*. Once again, the anti-woman text is outnumbered by the defences of women (one to three).

Thus, from anti-woman invectives, a literary form emerged: the defence of women. The defence of women exists in two literary traditions: the literary catalogues in praise of exemplary women and the more formal polemical defences that characterized the later *querelle des femmes* and are characteristically written by women. In the next section of this essay we shall explore these categories, with particular stress on defences of women written during the period 1500–1700. Our treatment of Mary Astell, like our treatment of Lanyer, is brief, since both writers are thoroughly discussed elsewhere in this volume.

Early Defenders

When scholars speak of the *querelle des femmes* they mean a collection of seventeenth-century texts, discussed below, arising from the 1615 attack by Joseph Swetnam. Yet that moment, when the controversy over women peaked for early modern

Englishwomen, grows from a much longer tradition, just as arguments about whether women most resembled Eve or Mary were many centuries old. Sixteenth-century works defending women are less coherent or influential than those in the Swetnam contretemps. Yet they raise significant theoretical questions, both about how best to defend women and about how such defences should be voiced. Pamela Benson argues that works about women take different forms, each of which has its own conventions that a reader is expected to understand if they are to appreciate the texts fully: Renaissance writers considered the controversy over women 'first in collections of biographical sketches of famous women written in imitation of Boccaccio's, then, in a variety of documents about the education of women, in encomia and defenses of womankind, in dialogues on the nature of women and her place, and in narratives such as the *Orlando Furioso* and *The Faerie Queene*' (Benson 1992: 1–2). We shall concentrate on two traditions: the catalogue and the polemic.

The former is the older European tradition, starting in the late fourteenth century with Boccaccio's *De Mulieribus Claris* (*c*.1370) and Chaucer's *The Legend of Good Women* (*c*.1380). Both of these works list exemplary women, ostensibly to praise the sex, without much consideration of why women face criticism as men's inferiors. The catalogue form is one that worked well for male authors who wished to enter the controversy over women, for it places the author as a kind of judge who gazes at womankind and then selects individual women for his purposes and pleasure. With Christine de Pizan's adaptation, *Livre de la Cité des Dames* (*c*.1407), the encomiastic catalogue has for the first time a female voice and begins to investigate the source of misogyny, reversing the male stance by allowing a woman to serve as the judge. Her conclusions are conservative, for she too isolates women, both by the act of selecting and by her insistence that women cannot compete with men and must withdraw to a city where they will be protected in the contemplative life. Nevertheless, Christine de Pizan is of particular importance, for in her work we hear for the first time a woman's voice defending women.

While male-voiced works continue in the early modern period, increasingly the works either are or purport to be by women. This convention has a double edge. On the one hand, it suggests an acknowledgement that a woman may be able to speak for and defend herself, doing without a masculine protector. On the other hand, the belief that a defence of women is more plausible and convincing when undertaken by a woman implies that men and women are irretrievably separated by gender roles; the only way that a man may defend women is by surrendering his masculine identity and playing a woman. In such a false binary the assumption is that one may defend women only by attacking men. This double-edged quality also affects our understanding of the catalogue tradition, which often influences writing by early modern women. Ostensibly the encomiastic catalogue defends women by providing proof that a woman might be silent, chaste and obedient, contrary to misogynist images of all women as loquacious, lascivious libertines, but it often includes women who are exceptional because they are active, eloquent and independent. Thus the form is inherently inconsistent. Moreover, by mentioning exceptional women only, catalogues may imply that an ordinary female reader falls short in significant ways simply by being ordinary (if any woman reading such works is ordinary in the sixteenth century). Despite these problems the catalogue tradition has great importance because it offers an answer to misogyny and because it provides models of achievement to women who have been repeatedly told that their principal precursor is Eve, who lost paradise. As a form that male and female writers were permitted to use, its popularity helps to account for Brian Ansley's early translation of Christine de Pizan's *City of Ladies* (1521, STC 7271), as well as the many editions of Thomas Heywood's *Gynaikeion, or History of Women* (1624, STC 13326), Charles Gerbier's *Elogium Heroinum* (1651, Wing G583), or Henry Cornelius Agrippa's *Female Pre-eminence* (1670, Wing A784). These works chronicle excellent women in an effort to invoke *auctoritas* for a particular construction of woman; the catalogues' essentialism may help explain why male authors so often employed them.

Such catalogues influenced works by women as well. Later writers such as Bathsua Makin (discussed below) or Rachel Speght in her *Mortalities Memorandum* (1621, STC 23057) include catalogues as central parts of their argument. Such verse works as Diana Primrose's *Chaine of Pearle* (1630, STC 20388) and Mary Fage's *Fames Roule* (1637, STC 10667) show the marks of the catalogue tradition, the former in the way that Primrose lists Queen Elizabeth I's virtues and the latter in her catalogue of anagrams. (Arguably the catalogues also influence Aemilia Lanyer in the string of dedications that opens *Salve Deus Rex Judaeorum*.) For Primrose, the concentration on a single figure and her fragmentation of Queen Elizabeth into a catalogue of allegorical qualities says much about both the hunger early modern women felt for models and the way that a woman constructed her own identity, as well as that of others. For Fage, the catalogue is an end in itself; the multiplication of names and their reworking into anagrams and acrostic verses (420 in all) implicitly establish that writer's skill with language and her refusal of a cloistered life as she reaches out to prominent courtiers. One's evaluation of such works, which today may seem tedious or repetitive, depends on a recognition of the way that they appropriate elements of the catalogue tradition for their own purposes.

While the catalogue is an important form in defences of women, it is not the only one. Another is the polemic, in which the text (often, though not always, an anonymous pamphlet) takes a strong position on a controversy, mocks those opposed to that position, and flamboyantly sets forth the case in favour of that position. Clusters of pamphlets that replied to or decried one another were popular in the sixteenth and seventeenth centuries: inevitably some considered the controversy over women. While the pamphlets of the *querelle des femmes* are the best known of these polemics, they are not the first. In the sixteenth century the 'Maydens of London' answered a misogynist attack on their virtue with a polemic pamphlet, *A Letter Sent by the Maydens of London* (1567, STC 16754.5); Margaret Tyler wrote a mildly polemical defence of women in the preface to her translation of a Spanish romance (1578, STC

18859–18861); and Jane Anger scourged 'the newe surfeit of an olde lover' in *Jane Anger her Protection for vvomen* (1589, STC 644). Tyler uses her own name, while the other works may be by men rather than women, but all three raise the question of how authorship and authority could be gendered.

In *A Letter Sent by the Maydens of London*, which R. J. Fehrenback has edited (Farrell, Hageman and Kinney 1990: 28-47), 'Rose, Jane, Rachell, Sara, Philumias, and Dorothie' write to the 'right wise, sober and discrete Matrons, and Mistresses of London'. These maidservants declare their intention of defending women's liberties; specifically, of defending themselves against a misogynist attack in a pamphlet by the lawyer Edward Hake, 'A Boke Intitled a Mery Metynge of Maydes in London' (1567). Hake's work, written at a time of 'intense attacks and defences' in the controversy over women (ibid.: 31), condemns the unmarried women who worked as servants because they have too much liberty and too little religious devotion. *A Letter* is probably written by a man, another lawyer, posing as the various maidens, not only because it would be unusual for a group of working-class London women to respond to such a pamphlet, but also because *A Letter* uses a sprinkling of Latin and demonstrates a thorough knowledge of the law. The voicing of *A Letter* nonetheless has relevance for a history of defences of women. First of all, the pamphlet suggests that in the mid-sixteenth century the idea of female authorship was plausible. In other words, women were sufficiently literate and articulate that such a pamphlet was not immediately denounced as a hoax. Indeed, Hake's response to the pamphlet seems to have been 'suspiciously disproportionate', suggesting that he feared he had indeed been the target of 'domestic maidservants . . . collaborating on a mocking, humiliating riposte to the pontifications of a moralizing windbag' (ibid.: 30). In the second place, the multiple voices of *A Letter* reflect an interesting cultural assumption that women worked most effectively in groups, i.e. that their strength came from affiliation and collaboration. Not only do the six maidens stand together against their attacker, but they also address themselves to the matrons of London for support. This attitude has particular importance when one turns to the misogynist pamphlets in which a male attacker imagines himself in opposition to a group, even a monstrous regiment, of women. For whoever wrote *A Letter*, whether a lawyer or a group of women, the claims of female gender and affiliation are empowering.

Margaret Tyler translates a Spanish romance as *The Mirrour of Princely Deedes and Knighthood* (1578, reprinted in 1580 and 1599, STC 18859–61), and in her polemical preface she makes both gender and affiliation claims as well. Acknowledging herself to be a woman, she defends her right to translate, if not author, books, while she positions herself socially by announcing that she is a member of the aristocratic Howard household (implicitly affiliating herself both to a noble family and to a Roman Catholic stronghold). Perhaps because she connects herself to a powerful male figure rather than to a network of like-minded women, her preface drew no response that survives, although the work was published three times. The argument she makes is quite interesting because it employs indirection to argue for her right to publish her translation, acknowledging the common arguments against women's writing and then incorporating them into her own defence. She suggests that what society sees as improper in a woman's writing is the interaction between men and women, not the woman author's refusal to remain silent. Turning around the usual state of affairs, she points out that if a woman may experience a man by reading what he has written, or if a man may represent a woman by writing about her, then the relationship that occurs when a woman writes for a male reader can hardly be said to be improper. The ingenious argument is temperately expressed and invokes the modesty topos, for while she defends herself against the charge that it is 'unseemly for a woman' to translate, she also seeks to reassure the reader of her propriety, 'least perhaps understanding of my name and yeares, those mightest be carried into a wrong suspect of my boldnesse and rashnesse' (Ferguson 1980: 56).

Far less temperate is Jane Anger, whose pamphlet *Jane Anger her Protection for vvomen* complains of the treachery of male seducers. As with *A Letter*, *Jane Anger her Protection* was written in answer to a misogynist attack in another (lost) pamphlet. Because *Jane Anger her Protection* uses a female voice, it is often regarded as a landmark for early women writers. A fair amount of scholarly ink has been spilled over the question of whether Jane Anger is, in fact, a woman, but finally this question is not one we can answer. Of far greater importance is the pamphlet's being voiced as a woman's writing because this circumstance implicitly suggests that a woman's identity lends strength to an attack on a man. Anger is a woman. Just as iconography often presented Wrath as a woman carrying a sword, so this pamphlet allegorizes anger in the person of a woman armed with a pen. Further, the pamphlet is presented as the work of one woman who represents and cares for all women. In the conclusion the text declares: 'I have set down unto you (which are of mine own sex) the subtle dealings of untrue meaning men' (Ferguson 1980: 69). Thus the text defends every woman against the seducer who threatens chastity by revealing his secrets. Once shared, knowledge of his technique renders him harmless, a 'noddie' or a 'jade'. In these sixteenth-century polemics, female voice and affiliation become important.

The *Querelle des Femmes*

The *querelle des femmes*, a series of four pamphlets and a play published between 1615 and 1620, started in 1615 with Joseph Swetnam's *The Arraignment of lewd, idle and froward women*, which provoked the three pamphlet defences mentioned earlier: Rachel Speght's *A Mouzell for Melastomus* (1617), Ester Sowernam's and Joane Sharp's *Ester Hath Hang'd Haman* (1617), and Constantia Munda's *The Worming of a Mad Dogge* (1617). One last publication, *Swetnam the Woman-hater Arraigned by Women*, a tragicomedy, appeared in 1620 (Crandall 1969: ix). (Several pamphlets concerned with cross-dressing also appeared in 1620: *Hic Mulier, or the Man Woman*; *Haec Vir, or the Womanish Man*; and *Muld Sacke: or the Apologie of Hic Mulier*. Since these are not really defences, but rather attacks on women, we shall not consider them here.) The first three pamphlets in the *querelle des femmes*, those by Swetnam, Speght and Sowernam, focus on the man–woman dichotomy (particularly on the various interpretations of Adam's rib). Constantia Munda and *Swetnam the Woman-hater*, however, take different approaches. Munda focuses more on the lamentable fact that Swetnam could be published, while *Swetnam the Woman-hater* subordinates the gender debate to a love story.

As we have seen, Swetnam's *Arraignment* revived the polemical pamphlet controversy over women that had been on the wane since 1592. And, as Woodbridge argues, 'during the Swetnam controversy, the debate lost an important element of artistic dishonesty: while earlier defences only pretended to be answering a published attack on women, the defences of Speght, Sowernam, and Munda actually did answer such an attack' (Woodbridge 1984: 110).

Swetnam's *Arraignment*, published under the pseudonym Thomas Tel-troth, 'went through at least ten editions by 1637, and at least six more by 1880', and was 'also translated into Dutch' (ibid.: 81). One has only to read his opening epistles to know that Swetnam is a misogynist; he says that 'men will be persuaded with reason, but women must be answered with silence' (Henderson and McManus 1985: 192). In other words, a man, who possesses reason, is worthy of participating in discussion, whereas a woman, with her essentially irrational nature, is to be ignored. Swetnam's attacks on women grow increasingly virulent; he says women are crooked by nature and worse than animals. The 'crooked by nature' argument, of course, stems from the biblical story that Eve was created from Adam's rib. Then, in a selection borrowed from *The Golden Book of Marcus Aurelius* (Woodbridge 1984: 83), he writes: 'A buck may be enclosed in a Park; a bridle rules a horse; a Wolf may be tied; a Tiger may be tamed, but a froward woman will never be tamed' (Henderson and McManus 1985: 194). Swetnam's aggressive posturing cannot disguise the weakness of his attack. Woodbridge argues that he 'has plundered the formal controversy, carrying off an unsorted booty of the controversy's conventions, arguments, authorities, jests, and exempla' (Woodbridge 1984: 87). Elaine Beilin concurs: 'his attack, lacking wit, skill, polish, and even the rhetorical ingenuity of earlier works, demonstrated how debased the entire genre had become by 1615' (Beilin 1987: 249). Yet although Swetnam came late to the fray, his pamphlets drew strong opposition.

The first published response was Rachel Speght's *A Mouzell for Melastomus*. Speght, the daughter of the minister James Speght (Lewalski 1996: xi), wrote *A Mouzell for Melastomus* in 1616; it was then published in 1617. As we have seen, Speght, like Swetnam, discusses the issue of Adam, Eve and the rib, though she uses the biblical story to establish women's equality rather than their inferiority and crookedness. As Ann Rosalind Jones argues, 'the sharpest focus in Speght's pamphlet is turned upon antiwoman elements in religion' (Haselkorn and Travitsky 1990: 50). Next, Speght attacks Swetnam's argument that St Paul said it is not good to touch a woman. Speght counters that St Paul's stricture resulted from 'the Corinths present necessitie, who were then persecuted by the enemies of the Church' (Lewalski 1996: 16). As Jones notes, Speght seems 'to be aiming . . . at an educated audience seriously interested in biblical interpretation and marriage theory' (Haselkorn and Travitsky 1990: 51).

An interesting side note is Barbara Lewalski's discovery of an annotated copy of Rachel Speght's *Mouzell for Melastomus* in the Beinecke Library (Yale), 'containing some eighty-seven manuscript annotations in a contemporary hand' (Lewalski 1996: 91). The author of these notes could well be Swetnam himself, as Lewalski suggests, particularly given Constantia Munda's report that 'he [Swetnam] was preparing to growl back at Speght' (ibid.). Moreover, the annotator explains that one mistake in Swetnam's pamphlet was a printer's error and 'on at least one occasion, he undertakes to speak for Swetnam' (ibid.). Lewalski does acknowledge that other possible authors exist, such as another polemicist, since the tone 'seems more irate and contemptuous of women' than Swetnam's (ibid.). Though we may never know with certainty who wrote these notes, the likelihood that Swetnam planned a vehement rejoinder suggests that he, like Hake before him, was particularly troubled by a female-voiced response.

Rachel Speght was not the only writer to respond to Swetnam's attack; the next published defender was Ester Sowernam (along with Joane Sharp), who wrote *Ester Hath Hang'd Haman*. While we are certain that Rachel Speght was indeed an actual woman, the name Ester Sowernam is most likely a pseudonym (Shepherd 1985: 86), and a man may well have written the pamphlet. Whatever Sowernam's sex, the voice is gendered female, as Sowernam, like Speght, attacks Swetnam and defends women. Yet her defence includes a sharp critique of Speght: 'When I had likewise run [Speght's pamphlet] over, I did observe that whereas the maid doth many times excuse her tenderness of years, I found it to be true in the slenderness of her answer' (ibid.: 88). Clearly, for Sowernam, Speght's response is inadequate, so she proceeds to write her own. Like Swetnam and Speght, she addresses the rib issue; however, her interpretation differs from Speght, and of course from Swetnam. In her opinion, the woman did receive a crooked rib from man, but she then counters, 'if woman received her crookedness from the rib, and consequently from the man, how doth man excel in crookedness, who hath more of those crooked ribs?' (ibid.: 92). For Sowernam, the account in the Book of Genesis provides evidence of man's moral inferiority. Sowernam continues her argument by giving exempla of zealous, faithful women such as the Virgin Mary, John the Baptist's mother Elizabeth, and Mary Magdalene (ibid.: 97), and important, powerful women in British history, such as Boadicea, Eleanor (wife of Edward I), and the most recent, Queen Elizabeth (ibid.: 100–1). Her use of these examples shows an excellent knowledge not only of the Bible, but also of history, placing the controversy in a specifically English context.

The fourth and last pamphleteer was Constantia Munda. Like Sowernam, Munda's name is a pseudonym; it means 'Moral Constancy' (Shepherd 1985: 126). In addition, Munda, again like Sowernam, does include comments about women's superiority to men. For example, in the introductory poem to Swetnam, she tells him that 'Women [are] the crown, perfection and the means of all men's being, and their well-being' (ll. 40–1), and in the text of her pamphlet she calls women 'the greatest part of the lesser world' (ibid.: 131). But as in Sowernam's case, scholars speculate that the 'she' is indeed a 'he': both Simon Shepherd and Ann Rosalind Jones assert their suspicions (Shepherd 1985: 126; Haselkorn and Travitsky 1990: 58, respectively). Shepherd notes the significance of Munda's references to classical authorities like Juvenal, whom he sees as 'an unlikely author in a woman's education' (Shepherd 1985: 126). Jones, on the other hand, bases her suspicion on the fact that Munda 'is more interested in excluding upstart scribblers like Swetnam from the press than in defending women in any sustained way' (Haselkorn and Travitsky 1990: 58). Indeed, the author does seem excessively concerned with the press; Munda's pamphlet changes to an invective against 'the itching desire of oppressing the press with many sottish and illiterate libels' (Munda, quoted in Shepherd 1985: 130). In addition, Munda seems to be more concerned with a demonstration of learning than with defending women. In the first paragraph alone, the author uses five foreign-language phrases (four Latin and one Italian), all carefully translated. As Jones argues, 'Munda thunders from above', in opposition to Swetnam (Haselkorn and Travitsky 1990: 60). The 'you' in this text is clearly Swetnam, and the author is lecturing him. Moreover, Munda is 'not interested in constructing a persona based on contemporary ideologies of the good woman' (ibid.). The author does not create a sense of 'womanly' identity nor attempt gender identification except for the odd 'we', although the pamphleteer is kinder to Speght than Sowernam was, since she 'uses Speght quite heavily' (Shepherd 1985: 126). Josephine Roberts agrees with Shepherd and Jones, though her contention is that the problem of Munda's gender arises from the way it 'hints at a male writer's mocking the entire process of responding to Swetnam' (Amussen and Seeff 1998: 45–6). The issue of voice becomes one of affiliation: the author uses a female voice not to strengthen the polemic, but to undercut the argument by suggesting the argument itself is foolish.

The Swetnam controversy has one last hurrah with *Swetnam the Woman-hater Arraigned by Women*. Unlike the previous publications, *Swetnam the Woman-hater* is a play, and hence has no authorial voice, nor does it, strictly speaking, arraign Swetnam. The arraignment is placed in a larger story about Lisandro and Leonida, 'the noble lovers whose story is the main plot' (Crandall 1969: 11). The Swetnam character, Misogenos, appears early on in the play, but his trial does not begin until late in Act 3, and it is not until Act 5, scene 2 that the old women call out 'Guiltie, guiltie, guiltie. / Guiltie of Woman-slander, and defamation' (289–90). Then, in the Epilogue, Swetnam enters, muzzled (stage direction) and repents (Crandall 1969: 12). Crandall argues that while the play does 'arraign' Swetnam, 'the major concern of *Swetnam the Woman-hater* is not the man–woman question', but simply having fun at Swetnam's expense (Crandall 1969: 18, 19).

In his introduction to Munda, Shepherd comments that 'by 1621 Swetnam was silent' (Shepherd 1985: 126). And indeed, after the last pamphlet and play, the *querelle des femmes* was over as well, at least in publication. One interesting item to note is that Swetnam's attack drew the largest publishing base. It also drew a large response, spawning three defences and a play that denounced his attack. Of course, these responses complicate the issues of voice and affiliation, both by challenging the assumption that all women think alike and by suggesting that a female voice could write against women. The play presents a different story altogether, especially since the audience was probably more concerned with amusement than with the question of which sex was superior (Crandall 1969: 19). Misogyny has become a figure of fun when Swetnam is muzzled and humiliated. As James I's reign drew to a close, the formal controversy over women seems of less importance than laughter. But perhaps we would do well to interpret the *querelle des femmes* as a 'literary exercise' (Woodbridge 1984: 110) rather than a serious pamphlet war.

The Later Defences

The play *Swetnam the Woman-hater* signals not only the end of the controversy about Swetnam's *Arraignment of . . . Women*, but also the end of the polemic as a line of defence for women. Yet misogyny certainly continued in the seventeenth century, as did a marked rise in literacy among both men and women. Given these factors one can readily understand why defences of women continued to appear. New forms took the place of the invective associated with the polemical pamphlets.

Later in the seventeenth century pamphlets written in defence of women have a very different tone. To some extent one can posit a shift connected to the Civil War and the Commonwealth years, for women in the decades from 1640–60 were far more likely to be engaged in writing, particularly petitions or religious tracts. Even after the Restoration the energetic invective of the earlier pamphlets gave way to more dignified and polished writing. Another probable factor is that such defences, even when the author's identity is disguised, are by women and not men pretending to be women. Unlike the anonymous Jane Anger or Ester Sowernam with their gleeful personal attacks in a woman's voice, later defenders sought a more balanced tone.

A good example is Anna Maria van Schurman's *Amica Dissertatio . . . de Capacite Ingenii Muliebris ad Scienta* (1638), translated into English by Clement Barksdale as *The Learned Maid, or Whether a Maid May Be a Scholar* (1659, Wing S902). In it van Schurman does not examine women's 'essential' nature as earlier defences had done. Rather she appropriates male discourse as she constructs a formal debate on the educability of women. The work itself is, of course, by its very existence proof that a maid may indeed be a scholar. Her use of rhetoric and logic to construct her case for women implies that both genders operate in a world of reasoned ethical arguments. Moreover, she adds to the tradition of affiliation, including a range of letters from learned men and women that testify to her excellence as an individual and as a scholar and that establish her as a participant in a network of worthy people. Her work is not one that could be turned into a mocking play.

Another such defence is the livelier *Essay on the Antient Education of Gentlewomen* (1673, Wing M309) by Bathsua Reginald Makin. She too appropriates the masculine role, even more explicitly, by writing a series of letters purporting to be from men, one opposed to educating women and one in favour. The man who attacks women has the more foolish arguments; indeed his voice blusters and argues by assertion without any substance to his claims. In a nice inversion of earlier pamphlets claiming to be by women though actually written by men, the masculine defender in the pamphlet insists that his praise of women is disinterested, for 'I am a man myself'. Every argument made against educating women is debunked, and in the process the speaker implies that those opposed to such education are unworthy sons and fathers, ignorant of the Bible and the classics, who would be content with a mandrill for a wife. Makin appears (indirectly) on the final page when readers who wish to educate their daughters are urged to send them to Mrs Makin's new school, where they will be taught according to the very latest methods. While this essay plays with voice in a particularly interesting way, developing and complicating the technique found in earlier pamphlets, it also fits into the pattern of introducing the author's affiliations and of cataloguing notable women. Throughout, the essay lists women who have been renowned for their learning in various fields. Among these are a number of women who are associated with Makin: Lucy Hastings, the Dowager Countess of Huntingdon, who had been one of Makin's pupils (as had her children); another pupil, Princess Elizabeth Stuart, daughter of Charles I; Anna Maria van Schurman, epistolary friend of Makin; and so forth.

(An interesting sidelight is that, as a girl, Makin had lived only a few streets away from Rachel Speght, whom she might well have known, since both girls had reputations for exceptional learning. In 1616 Bathsua Reginald's first book appeared, just a year before Speght's 1617 pamphlet defending women from Swetnam's 1615 attack. This work was *Musa Virginea* (STC 20835), a collection of poetry and epigraphs in half a dozen languages demonstrating her learning. The two girls may well have been friends who planned their works as a collective response – one pointing out Swetnam's shortcomings, one demonstrating feminine learning – but this friendship must remain speculation.)

In addition to the pamphlet defences, which principally concerned women's education, women writers began producing verse defences in the later seventeenth century. Such authors include the anonymous author of *The Triumphs of Female Wit* (1683, Wing T2295); Sarah Fyge Egerton, *The Female Advocate* (1686, Wing F56a), and Mary Lee, Lady Chudleigh, *The Ladies Defence* (1701). *The Triumphs of Female Wit* is a work that plays with male and female voices to defend the ability of women to write the Pindaric odes that had become so fashionable in this period. The work begins with an essay, 'The Preface to the Masculine Sex', in which 'The Young Lady' asks the men why women 'should not be thought capable of all the Endowments of humane Nature' (3). She then asserts that she is sure that women 'seem framed . . . with the same Materials too both of Body and Mind as the best composed of you all' (4). In these few brief lines 'The Young Lady' asserts, as did the pamphleteers (specifically Rachel Speght), that women are equal to men since they are made of the same materials. She then goes on to refute the argument that women were stupid and dull: 'the Faculties of our souls are always brisk and sprightful, our Senses quick and intelligent' (4). For 'The Young Lady', women are, at least at this point in the work, clearly equal to men in make-up and in mental capacity.

After the essay, a series of odes follows: 'The Young Lady' writes in favour of women's abilities in her ode, as does a Mr F, while a Mr H writes against women. In her ode, 'The Young Lady' reiterates her belief that women are equal to men; she says 'We've souls as noble, and as fine a Clay' (l. 9). But she then pulls back from her strong argument and says that women have no desire to reign over anything but 'those passions which we find / Too potent for the Mind' (ll. 52–3). Her apology for women is answered by a Mr H, who positions himself against 'The Young Lady' from the beginning. He asks her to 'Stand valiant she, a Parley I desire' (l. 11). His first condescending remark is to inform 'The Young Lady' that ''twas from Jove's Brain alone Minerva came' (l. 17), which implies that a woman has no intelligence save what she receives from a masculine figure. Mr H then asserts that women should not exert their minds; for example, he says 'Knowledge divine you may attain / Without the labour of the Brain' (ll. 80–1). He goes on to say that 'But for the Learning of the Schools, / That can't make Women wise, that makes Men Fools' (ll. 84–5). With both comments, the speaker condescendingly tells 'The Young Lady' not to worry about educating herself and exercising her mental capacity because it will not help her. Besides, she can read the Bible and attain 'knowledge divine' (l. 80), which is all a woman needs. Mr F then responds, and complicates the situation by the curious use of a woman speaker. The speaker in Mr F's ode refutes Mr H's arguments and answers his challenges, specifically his Jove and Minerva example, just as the female pamphleteers addressed Swetnam's arguments. In refuting the example of Jove and Minerva, Mr F counters the argument that men provide women with 'brains' by pointing out that women give men life and therefore 'sense' (ll. 25–6). Mr F's speaker then goes on to say that ''Tis Female Souls shall then appear / The most unsullied, bright and clear' (ll. 97–8); as with Sowernam and Munda, the claim is that women are superior. An interesting note is that Greer et al. (1988: 309) suspect the entire work is by a male author, but it seems just as plausible to argue that the Young Lady is just that: a young lady. One should, however, still be suspicious of the true identities of Messers F and H. (It is worth noting that the tone of the poems is similar to that found in Mary Astell's poetry written in the 1680s.) For the first time, a defence of women is doubly voiced, with both male and female speakers.

Sarah Fyge Egerton published a work also entitled 'The Triumphs of Female Wit' in 1703, although she uses heroic couplets in it and shows no interest in Pindaric odes, which probably removes her from consideration as the author of the earlier work. Egerton also published *The Female Advocate*, which has a polemical tone closer to that of the *querelle des femmes* writers. For example, her poem opens with the epithet 'Blas-

phemous Wretch', immediately engaging in abuse of a masculine attacker. Like Sowernam and Munda, Egerton will clearly refute the argument that women are prideful,
lustful and inconstant. Her argument, like the pamphleteers', addresses the problem
of Eve. For Egerton, as with Sowernam and Munda, Eve is superior to man because

> Woman she had a far nobler Birth
> For when the Dust was purify'd by Heaven,
> Made into Man, and Life unto it given,
> Then the Almighty and All-wise God said,
> That Woman of that Species should be made
> (ll. 27–31)

Since the dust that made man had been purified in the process of making him, woman
was that much better and nobler. Egerton goes on to praise women's constancy, saying
that 'they often men excell' (l. 127). At the end of the poem Egerton laments that
woman has been made the scapegoat, when men themselves have been just as sinful
and 'sharers of Impiety' (p. 23). Thus, defences of Eve continued late in the period.

Chudleigh's *The Ladies Defence* was more influential than either *The Triumphs of
Female Wit* or *The Female Advocate*. Its form is slightly different from the other two;
while *The Triumphs of Female Wit* is a series of Pindaric odes and *The Female Advocate*
is an extended verse argument against women's inferiority, *The Ladies Defence* is a dialogue between Sir John Brute, Sir William Loveall, Melissa and a Parson. Sir John
Brute, the host, is clearly on the side of male superiority; he calls wives 'Furies' (Ezell
1993: l. 16) and congratulates Sir William Loveall's bachelorhood (ibid.: l. 24). The
Parson, by his own admission, teaches the church's doctrine: that the wife is to obey
and please her husband (ibid.: l. 58). Sir William Loveall is the male defender of
women. The main female character, Melissa, is of course the female defender. Again,
this defence of women is doubly voiced. We see Melissa's chagrin from the outset,
when she asks 'Must Men command and we alone obey / As if design'd for Arbitrary
Sway?' (ibid.: l. 64). Already she challenges patriarchal conventions and men's domi-
neering ways. Melissa, like the young lady from *The Triumphs of Female Wit*, argues
for the education of women on the grounds of women's equality. She says that men
think women are happy if they know how 'to Work, to Dance, and Dress . . . As if
we were for nothing else design'd' (ibid.: ll. 545, 547). But if women were not just
designed for 'work, dance and dress', Melissa asserts, then their minds can handle
other thoughts too. While these comments sue for women's equality, she also reminds
men that they are not quite as superior as they think they are. Later in the dialogue
she, like Egerton, reminds men that they are sinful as well, so they must 'live those
Sermons you to others Preach' (ibid.: l. 806).

These verse defences tend to be longer poems and, of necessity, somewhat pro-
grammatic. They certainly point to the prominence of women poets in this period,
such as Aphra Behn and Anne Finch, Countess of Winchilsea, and their form and
approach is much closer to the satiric verse epistles of the eighteenth century than to

the lyrics of the seventeenth. In the later seventeenth century the catalogue form so loved by earlier writers fades away, while the harsh tone of the polemics is softened. Yet the topics discussed in defences of women remain: the guilt of Eve, the relative merits of men and women, and the education of women.

Finally, at the end of the century, Mary Astell writes to defend women in a new way (see chapter 15, this volume, for a full discussion of Astell). Her work attacks as well as defends, urging a rejection of the masculine world and its values. For Astell, at least, the central issue was affiliation with other women. Thus in *A Serious Proposal to the Ladies* she seeks segregation of women from men in an academy that will provide autonomy. Gone is any suggestion that women should study languages like Latin, Greek or Hebrew, attaining masculine skills if they wished to compete in the educational world. Astell refuses to compete, withdrawing instead from a system she regards as inherently unjust. While such arguments are novel, they may suggest a return to the old essentialism and repudiate the playful voicing that implicitly interrogated the construction of gender. And although Astell breaks new ground in defending women, she too considers the same topics as other defences when she remarks that for women a retreat for education 'will be the introducing you into such a *Paradise* as your Mother *Eve* forfeited, . . . Here are no Serpents to deceive you' and 'Men will resent it, to have . . . Women invited to tast of that Tree of Knowledge they have so long unjustly *monopoliz'd*' (*A Serious Proposal to the Ladies*: 67, 87). For women, the best defence against calumny remained education.

See also WOMEN AND WRITING; AEMILIA LANYER, *SALVE DEUS REX JUDAEORUM*; MARY ASTELL, CRITIC OF THE MARRIAGE CONTRACT/SOCIAL CONTRACT ANALOGUE

REFERENCES AND FURTHER READING

Amussen, Susan D. and Seeff, Adele (eds) (1998). *Attending to Early Modern Women*. Newark: University of Delaware Press.

Beilin, Elaine (1987). *Redeeming Eve*. Princeton, NJ: Princeton University Press.

Benson, Pamela Joseph (1992). *The Invention of the Renaissance Woman: The Challenge of Female Independence in the Literature and Thought of Italy and England*. University Park: Pennsylvania State Press.

Bornstein, Diane (1978). *Distaves and Dames: Renaissance Treatises for and about Women*. Delmar, NY: Scholars' Facsimiles and Reprints.

Crandall, Coryll (1969). *Swetnam, The Woman-Hater: The Controversy and The Play*. Lafayette, IN: Purdue University Press.

Ezell, Margaret J. M. (ed.) (1993). *The Poems and Prose of Mary, Lady Chudleigh*. New York: Oxford University Press.

Farrell, Kirby, Hageman, Elizabeth H. and Kinney, Arthur F. (eds) (1990). *Women in the Renaissance: Selections from English Literary Renaissance*. Amherst: University of Massachusetts Press.

Ferguson, Moira (ed.) (1980). *First Feminists*. Bloomington: University of Indiana Press.

Greer, Germaine, Hastings, Susan, Medoff, Jeslyn and Sansone, Melinda (eds) (1988). *Kissing the Rod: An Anthology of Seventeenth-Century Women's Verse*. New York: Farrar Straus Giroux.

Haselkorn, Anne and Travitsky, Betty (eds) (1990). *The Renaissance Englishwoman in Print: Counterbalancing the Canon.* Amherst: University of Massachusetts Press.

Henderson, Katherine and McManus, Barbara (eds) (1985). *Half Humankind.* Urbana: University of Illinois Press.

Hobby, Elaine (1988). *Virtue of Necessity: English Women's Writing 1649–88.* Ann Arbor: University of Michigan Press.

Hull, Suzanne (1982). *Chaste, Silent, and Obedient.* San Marino, CA: Huntington Library.

Kelly, Joan (1982). 'Early feminist theory and Querelle des Femmes.' *Signs,* 8, 4–28.

Kelso, Ruth (1956). *Doctrine for a Lady of the Renaissance.* Urbana: University of Illinois Press.

Lewalski, Barbara (ed.) (1996). *The Polemics and Poems of Rachel Speght.* Oxford: Oxford University Press.

McLeod, Glenda (1991). *Virtue and Venom: Catalogs of Women From Antiquity to the Renaissance.* Ann Arbor: University of Michigan Press.

Mendelson, Sara and Crawford, Patricia (1998). *Women in Early Modern England 1550–1720.* Oxford: Clarendon Press.

Prior, Mary (ed.) (1985). *Women in English Society, 1500–1800.* London: Methuen.

Rogers, Katherine (1966). *The Troublesome Helpmate: A History of Misogyny in Literature.* Seattle: University of Washington Press.

Shepherd, Simon (1985). *Women's Sharp Revenge.* New York: St Martin's Press.

Stenton, Doris Mary (1957). *The English Woman in History.* New York: Macmillan.

Travitsky, Betty (ed.) (1989). *The Paradise of Women.* New York: Columbia University Press.

Utley, Francis Lee (1944). *The Crooked Rib: An Analytical Index to the Argument About Women in English and Scots Literature.* Columbus: Ohio State University Press.

Warnicke, Retha (1983). *Women of the English Renaissance and Reformation.* Westport, CT: Greenwood Press.

Woodbridge, Linda (1984). *Women and the English Renaissance: Literature and the Nature of Womankind: 1540–1620.* Urbana: University of Illinois Press.

18

Prophecy

Elaine Hobby

Elaine Beilin (1987) has demonstrated that writing on religious matters formed a crucial focus for early female literary activity. With the heightening of the social tensions that led to the outbreak of civil war in 1642, however, women, like their male contemporaries, turned in ever greater numbers to composing a particular kind of religious text: prophecies, commenting on the contemporary political scene. In doing so, they drew on God's promise in Acts 2.17–18 (repeating Joel 2.28–9) that in the last days before the most apocalyptic event in human history, Christ's Second Coming, 'I will pour out my Spirit upon all flesh: and your sons and your daughters shall prophesy, and your young men shall see visions, and your old men shall dream dreams: And on my servants and on my handmaidens I will pour out in those days of my Spirit; and they shall prophesy'. The assumption was common that such biblical passages could be applied explicitly to contemporary Britain, and that the individual believer, encouraged by Protestantism to establish a personal relationship with God, might be directly in receipt of the divine Spirit.

In the early modern period a prophecy did not necessarily foretell the future, though it might well do so. Instead, prophecy was understood to be 'divinely inspired utterance' (OED). It was believed that God might communicate directly with individuals, giving them a message to convey to the world, or illuminating to them particularly important or obscure passages in scripture. In the 1640s several learned women alluded to their resultant role as 'handmaidens' (Acts 2.18) when they published works of scriptural exegesis, explaining that God was requiring them to make his meaning clear. Elizabeth Warren's *A Warning-Peece from Heaven* (1649), for instance, advised her reader that God did not want the recently captured king to be executed, demonstrating her case with detailed scriptural evidence. Mary Pope, similarly, proved from the Bible that the king, having been divinely appointed, was not accountable to men (*Behold, Here Is a Word*, 1649); and Elizabeth

Poole appeared before the Council of Officers to explain that just as a wife must not kill her violent husband, so a monarch's people could not execute him (*A Vision*, 1649; extracted in Trill, Chedgzoy and Osborne 1997).

Even someone with such a relatively conservative position might have the prophet's bounden duty to pass on God's words by preaching or through publication. Most of the prophetic writings of the period, however, are written from a more radical perspective, and a substantial minority of those who wrote were women. Phyllis Mack has indeed argued convincingly that women might be thought especially likely to be used by the Lord in this way, since the obedience and self-effacement normally required of them made them especially responsive to divine possession (Mack 1992: 7). In the revolutionary changes Britain was experiencing in its 'great overturning', it seemed entirely possible that the Bible's frequent assertion that God's people are those who have been despised and rejected should be applied specifically to the kinds of people traditionally silenced or ignored (Hill 1972: 41–3, 115–28, 241–7). According to Mack's estimate, more than three hundred women claimed the role of prophet between 1640 and 1660. Due to the close interconnection between church and state in the period, these women were writing not only about religious matters, but also about government policy.

Ecstatic and Visionary Prophets

Lady Eleanor Davies

The most prolific woman prophet of the early modern period was an aristocrat, Lady Eleanor Davies (earlier, Touchett; later, Douglas). As she repeatedly explains in her pamphlets, she was awoken at her house, Englefield in Berkshire, in July 1625, by 'the Heavenly voice descending, speaking as through a trumpet of a most clear sound these words: *Nineteen years and a half to the Judgement, and you as the meek Virgin*' (*Revelations. The Everlasting Gospel*, 1649; reprinted in Salzman 2000; Cope 1995). Between then and her death in 1652, she published more than sixty pamphlets, presenting herself as a re-embodiment of the prophet Daniel, and applying passages from the Bible to events in her own and the country's life. In *Samson's Fall* (1642), for instance, she connected the story of Delilah's betrayal of Samson to the malign influence of the Catholic Queen Henrietta Maria over the king, a matter also much commented upon by other Protestants, who identified Catholicism with royal absolutism. When Archbishop Laud, Charles I's architect of religious reforms loathed by mainstream English Protestants, was executed in January 1645, she excitedly saw this as a clear proof that the judgement day she had been told to expect in her vision nineteen and a half years before had arrived. Later, after Oliver Cromwell's rise to power, she addressed to him *The Benediction* (1651), welcoming him as the overthrower of tyranny, and presenting his name as a rough anagram, 'Howl Rome'. (Those on parliament's side in the civil wars regularly associated Charles I's attempts to take more power into his own hands and to remodel the English church with 'Romish' or Roman Catholic principles.) She declared:

> The Prophet *Joel* as foresaw and others: By whom Decypher'd that Generals Thundring Donative his the Crown and Bended Bowe (*Rev.* 6.). That Seal or Box of Nard opened; as much to say, *O: Cromwel*, Renowned be Victorious so long as Sun Moon continues or livever.
>
> Anagram, *Howl Rome*: And thus with one voice, *come and see*, *O: C:* Conquering and to Conquer went forth. (Reprinted in Salzman 2000; Cope 1995)

As this passage should make clear, the precise meanings of Lady Eleanor's prophecies are difficult to determine: her style is both condensed and elliptical, and her syntax is idiosyncratic. She did, however, attract considerable attention from the state, being imprisoned in the Gatehouse from 1633–5, and then incarcerated as a madwoman in Bedlam (Bethlehem Hospital) in 1636 for vandalizing the altar hanging of Lichfield Cathedral. Transferred from Bedlam to the Tower of London, she was not released until 1640 (Cope 1992: 96). The explanation for how seriously she was taken by the authorities might be found in the accuracy of some of her predictions, which famously included her foretelling both the death of the king's favourite, the Duke of Buckingham, and the demise of her first husband, Sir John Davies, after he had destroyed some of her works. As the punishments she received escalated, however, her writings seem to have less to say about national events, and to become ever more focused on her own identity as a prophet. *Sion's Lamentation* (1649), for instance, uses the death of her young grandson to reflect on the significance of her grief, seeing it as a type of the scriptural laments for Sion. As a grieving grandmother, she is Sion, standing for God's chosen people. Then, in *The Appearance and Presence of the Son of Man* (1650), she uses wordplay on her married names of Davies and Douglas to declare, 'I am A. and O. *alias* Da: and Do:'. This echoes the identification of God with Alpha and Omega, the beginning and the end, in the Book of Revelation (Rev. 1.8; 21.6; 22.13).

The strange syntax and vivid imagery of Lady Eleanor's tracts have prompted some commentators to apply French feminist theories to them, and to see their passionate, anarchic language as a kind of eruption of the semiotic chora through the constraints of the signifying chain. Similar arguments have also been made about other visionary women prophets (Berry and Berg 1981; Ezell 1993: 132–60; see also Hinds 1996: 108–18). The inclination in such interpretations is to see the ecstatic woman prophet as a representative figure, whose words and punishments are typical of the situation of a woman (or the valuation of the feminine) at that time. There is some evidence in Lady Eleanor's story that supports such a view. The account of her trial given in *The Blasphemous Charge* (1651), for instance, indicates that her accusers were particularly offended by the fact that she, a mere woman, had taken it upon herself to interpret the most obscure places in scripture. On the other hand, as Esther Cope's (1992) fine analysis of her life and works makes clear, Lady Eleanor's pamphlets do not really fit the French feminist model. Variations between copies and editions of these prophecies demonstrate clear planning and deliberate purpose: the French-based psychoanalytic model does not really account for the peculiar linguistic features of these texts. There is also a further reason to hesitate over seeing Lady Eleanor's prophecies as somehow typical of their age, however teasingly fascinating they may be in their condensed and excited language. Her high social rank meant that she was able to pay for her pamphlets' printing. Unlike other prophets, she needed to convince no one, and, other than in the recorded opinions of her persecutors, there is no record of what other people of the day made of her words, however much better equipped they might have been than people are today to catch her biblical allusions.

Other ecstatic and visionary prophets

There are though some significant connections between Lady Eleanor's works and those of her contemporaries. She dated her call to prophecy from the experience of a vision, and this kind of ecstatic initiation was also cited by several other women. At the other end of the social spectrum from Lady Eleanor, for instance, was Elinor Channel. Described by Arise Evans, the male prophet who arranged for the transcription and publishing of *A Message from God, (By a Dumb Woman)* (1654; reprinted in Hinds 1996), as simply the wife of 'a very poor man, and hath many small children, three of them very young ones' (1654 edn: 2) she travelled to London from her home in Cranleigh, Surrey, in an attempt to gain a hearing. Awakened in the night by 'a Blow given her upon her heart', she had heard a voice commanding her to take her message to Cromwell. When her husband opposed this scheme, she was struck dumb, 'whereupon your Petitioners Husband seeing her restless condition, consented to let her come to London' (ibid.). Her message, Evans insists in his marginalia, is a call for reconciliation between parliament and the exiled Charles Stuart (the later Charles II), the position Evans himself supported. Read without his commentary, however, it seems more likely that Channel's prophecy was an appeal for peace and for better treatment of poor debtors, two problems also preoccupying other petitioners at that time:

> The sword must be stayed. The world draweth toward an end, and the knots of peace & love must be made in all Christian lands. . . . If a man falls into the hands of a Creditor, if his Creditor be one of Gods servants, he will not take Bodie and Goods; if his *Bodie* pays the *Debt*, his *Heir* shall have the inheritance. (Ibid.: 3–4; italics reversed)

Channel's story is illuminating in several ways. First, it alerts us to the importance of print: God's prophet was duty-bound to spread the word by getting it published. Second, the significance of gender is dramatized, both in Channel's being unable to travel without her husband's permission, though having a means to elicit this, and in Evans's subsequent appropriation of her actions to serve his own political ends. The role of prophet could, to some extent, offset the requirement that a woman obey her husband, but the meanings of her pronouncements, once in the public sphere, were not within her control.

Similar patterns, of prophecy providing some measure of status or temporary autonomy, and of male authorities intervening to limit the significance of their messages, can also be found in the cases of the other best-known visionary prophets of the period. A notable example is Henry Jessey's account of Sarah Wight's trances and revelations, *The Exceeding Riches of Grace Advanced by the Spirit of Grace, in an Empty Nothing Creature*, which was reprinted many times, going through eight editions between 1647 and 1666. It describes a four-year period in which the young Sarah Wight felt driven to suicide attempts. Then, after several weeks of fasting, the 15-year-old girl fell into a trance, and in that state she prophesied, prayed and offered advice and comfort to the long list of people who came to visit her during the two months that followed (extracted in Trill, Chedgzoy and Osborne 1997). She was said to be in constant contact with God, and quoted frequently from the Bible. Jessey commends this '*Empty Nothing Creature*' to his reader, intimating that if even she can be close to God, his atypical Baptist principles, which favoured open church membership, must be in accordance with divine will.

Both Arise Evans and Henry Jessey mention the best-known woman visionary of the period, Anna Trapnel, Evans assuring his reader that in Elinor Channel's message, as interpreted by him, 'you shall find more truth and substance . . . than in all *Hana Trampenels* songs or sayings' (Hinds 1996: 7). Jessey, who unlike Evans was fully in support of radical social change, presents the fact that Wight and Trapnel have simultaneously experienced trances as proof that the last days before Christ's Second Coming have begun (1652 edn: 139). Trapnel, a Fifth Monarchist, who describes herself as a shipwright's daughter from Poplar, London, began to prophesy in 1654, as crisis over the outcome of the years of civil war and experimental democracy loomed. Cromwell had dissolved the short-lived Parliament of Saints, a body expected by radicals such as the Fifth Monarchists to deliver wide-ranging religio-political reforms. At the examination of Vavasor Powell, a leading radical, by the Council of State in January 1654, Trapnel fell into a trance which lasted eleven days and twelve nights, in the course of which, 'being as it were seized by the Lord, she was carried forth in a Spirit of prayer and singing from noon till night' (*Strange and Wonderful Newes from White-Hall*, 1654: 3; reprinted in Trill, Chedgzoy and Osborne 1997). From the appearance of her first visionary utterances, the meaning of Trapnel's prophecies was a matter of heated debate. She was accused of madness, evil and witchcraft by those who opposed her, and regarded by her male supporters as a useful pawn in their arguments over the future of the nation (Smith 1989: 45–53, 86–95). What differentiates Trapnel from Channel and Wight, however, is that she herself intervened in this process of interpretation. The anonymous account given of her prophecy in *Strange and Wonderful Newes* was swiftly followed by her *The Cry of a Stone*, which adds much detail and explanation, putting her prophecies in the context of her own earlier concerns about political developments in the nation. In *Anna Trapnel's Report and Plea* (1654) she presents her trial as a battle of wits, saying of her accuser: 'I saw he indeavoured to catch my words, and to ensnare me, putting his own sense upon them, but the Lord kept me out of his insnarements' (p. 33; extracted in Graham et al. 1989; Otten 1992). The wit she employed is evidenced in her response to the judge's attempt to contain her, in his observation: 'I understand you are not married?' According to her own account, she replied: 'Then having no hinderance, why may not I go where I please, if the Lord so will?' (1654 edn: 26). If Trapnel is unmarried, the judge implies, there is something wrong with her, or else she should behave in ways more suitable to the social role of maid or virgin. Trapnel will have none of it, joyfully defining herself, as so many of her female contemporaries also did, as Christ's bride (*Voice of the King of Saints*, 1658: 1).

Answering back is also a fundamental element in Katherine Evans's and Sarah Cheevers's narrative of their imprisonment by the Inquisition in Malta from 1659–62. Arrested by the Catholic authorities for attempting to spread their Quaker message, in prison they not only argued analytically with their inquisitors about true Christian values, but also took off into periods of ecstatic prophecy, sometimes following the biblical practice of stripping naked to the waist, or casting ashes on their heads, as a sign that their message was transmitted directly from God (*This is a Short Relation*, 1662; extracted in Graham et al. 1989; Garman et al. 1996). When the friars showed Evans (who had left her own children behind in England) a picture of Mary and the baby Jesus, she would not be distracted, if that was their intention, from her purpose: 'I stampt with my foot and said, Cursed be all Images and Image-makers, and all that fall down to worship them' (1662 edn: 38). According to the women's own account, published as part of a campaign to have them freed, and then expanded after their release, their behaviour unnerved the inquisition: 'We were very dreadful [i.e. terrifying] to them', Katherine Evans reflected (*A True Account*, 1663: 229–30). After their release they continued to travel and prophesy, prompting the governor of Tangiers, for instance, to undertake to be guided by them: 'the Governour said, he did lovingly receive our good Instructions and Admonitions, and promised to follow our Counsel' (ibid.: 258).

What is evident from this sample of visionary prophets is both that the role of prophet could give a woman access to an audience for her views, and that the question of her gender was always an issue for those who received her message. A provocative analysis of such concerns can be found in Diane Purkiss's suggestion that these ecstatic writings, which often allude to the writer's long periods of fasting, 'allowed a glimpse of a space in which gendered subjection was confined to the disavowed flesh, while the escaped spirit had freedom' (Purkiss 1992: 158). Although this battle over female identity is of immediate interest to the modern reader, this cannot be the sole focus of an analysis of such texts. These women prophets lived in a culture very different from our own, one where knowledge of Bible stories could be assumed, and where religious and political questions could not be discussed in isolation from one another. To read ecstatic prophecy as if its primary significance lies in a quasi-modern preoccupation with the female body would therefore be a mistake. In order to prompt a more properly historicized approach to such prophecies, then, this chapter will now turn to the far more numerous but less dramatic texts that make up the bulk of women's prophetic writings.

Prophetic Campaigning and the Quaker Legacy

In 1672, as the Society of Friends, or Quakers, set about introducing administrative and disciplinary structures in their movement, they also decided to collect and pre-serve two copies of each text published by their members since their inception in the early 1650s (O'Malley 1982). As a result, we know that between 1650 and 1700 many dozens of women Quakers published pamphlets, and that in the first twenty years of the period the great majority of these works were prophecies. Since no similar action to ensure preservation was taken by any of the other radical religious groups of the period, it is impossible to know how far the literary activities of women Friends were like or unlike those of Baptists, Seekers, or Muggletonians; too much material has simply disappeared. Certainly, of the more than three hundred women prophets active between 1640 and 1660 identified by Phyllis Mack, only about one quarter appear to have left published work (Mack 1992; Hobby 1992).

Many of the published Quaker women's prophecies of the 1650s have two traits in common: they are usually of joint or collective authorship, and they are often written from prison. *The Saints Testimony Finishing through Sufferings* (1655), for instance, both describes the questioning at the Banbury assizes of a group of female and male Friends arrested for their activities, and includes narratives and prophecies written by several of them. The pamphlet shows how integral divinely inspired action is to the identity of Quakers in the period. Believing that God might best be under-stood as a kind of Inner Light that could inspire and guide anyone who turned to its illumination, the *Saints Testimony* Quakers were arrested for trying to deliver their message at church services. According to one of them, Anne Audland, on Sunday 14 January they

> were moved to go to the Steeplehouse [i.e. church], to speak the word of the Lord to Priest and People; and in obedience to the Lord, we went, and stayed till the Priest had done, and then my friend spoke to the Priest, and the rude multitude came and hurried her forth, as the customes of the Heathens is; Then I spoke to the Priest, Man, here see the fruits of thy Ministry, and presently [i.e. immediately] the rude people hurried me forth. (1655 edn: 29)

This kind of behaviour, which must have seemed like deliberate provocation to their opponents, was typical of early Quaker prophecy. Inspired by the Light, the believer must speak, whatever the consequences. Another 1650s multi-authored pamphlet reporting the sufferings of prophets, *The Lambs Defence* (1656), includes a description by Dorothy Waugh of her confrontation with the Mayor of Carlisle after her arrest for prophesying in the marketplace. Before he consigned her to whipping and to wearing the scold's bridle (the traditional punishment for overly talkative women), the mayor had asked her where she had come from. 'Out of *Egypt* where thou lodgest', she proudly reports that she responded (1656 edn: 30; reprinted in Hinds 1996). Since, in the Bible, Egypt is the home of oppressors and evil-doers, she could not have been trying to appease him.

In part, what these confrontations demonstrate is that religious and political ideas in the period were intimately interrelated. In Quaker belief, each person could turn to their Light Within for guidance. This meant not only that the traditional church, with its university-trained ministers, had no monopoly on knowledge of God's will, but also that, in essential ways, all people were equal. As a matter of principle, Quakers refused 'hat honour': they declined, that is, to use conventional marks of subservience to their social superiors, for instance addressing everyone by the familiar 'thou' rather than selectively using the respectful 'you'. Dorothy Waugh was a household servant when she embarked on her travels as a prophet, and she was repeatedly arrested and imprisoned: in Norwich in 1654, in Truro as well as Carlisle in 1655, in New Amsterdam (now called New York) and then Boston in 1657. For her to take on the mantle of the prophet might be biblically justifiable, but it was still socially outrageous. The disruption to social hierarchies manifested in Friends' behaviour also extended to gender relations, the judge in *The Saints Testimony* angrily rebuking one of the arrested women, Sarah Tims, that '*sweeping the house, and washing the dishes was the first point of law to her* (or words to that effect) so sent her back to the Prison, she not being charged with the breach of any Law' (1655 edn: 8).

Another example of the intimate interconnection between religious and social concerns that Quaker prophecies regularly address is the existence of tithes. Throughout the 1650s radicals called for the abolition of this tax, under which everyone was required to pay 10 per cent of their income to the national church. Those who had left the Church of England and formed groups of Quakers, Independents, Seekers and so on, had no desire to support the institution they opposed. Moreover, in 40 per cent of livings, the tithes that were paid ended up in the pockets of local gentry and the universities, who had been ceded the right to collect them as impropriators (Hill 1972: 99). In 1659 Quaker women organized a nationwide petition against tithes, and before its publication it was signed by more than seven thousand women. *These Several Papers was sent to the Parliament* also calls for a range of other social reforms, including an end to the imprisonment of prophets, and the abolition of the privileged university education of the rich (reprinted in Garman et al. 1996; analysed in Gill 2000: 174–218). It is important to note that discussion of these issues was by no means confined to the Quakers. In the 1640s and 1650s the allegiances of individuals and the boundaries between groups shifted constantly, as women and men worked to establish their sense of God's plan for the nation. Amongst the most radical and exciting prophetic texts of the period, and still largely missing from discussions of pamphleteering, are the works of Mary Cary who, like Anna Trapnel, was a Fifth Monarchist. In *A Word in Season* (1647) and *The Resurrection of the Witnesses* (1648), Cary argued strongly that the government should encourage prophecy, whatever religious position it comes from, because open discussion is essential if God's will is to be discovered. In her 1650s pamphlets she offers a series of visions for the nation's future. In *The Little Horns Doom and Downfall* (1651; extracted in Hinds 1996) these include the expectation that

> the time is coming, when this promise shall be fulfilled, and the Saints shall be abundantly filled with the Spirit; and not onely men, but women shall prophesie; not onely aged men, but young men; not only superious [*sic*], but inferiours; not onely those that have University-learning, but those that have it not; even servants and handmaids. (1651 edn: 238)

In her *Twelve Humble Proposals to the Supreme Governours of the Three Nations* (1653) she not only calls for the abolition of tithes and the remodelling of the universities, but urges

> That you seriously and in good earnest lay to heart the condition of the poor, and make it your care to provide for the supply of their wants, and that consideration be had of their Condition before any rich mans case whatsoever be taken into consideration, how neerly so ever related to you, or any of you. (1653 edn: 8)

Cary also proposes the imposition of a national maximum wage, in order to promote redistribution of wealth.

What is clear, then, is that the early collective prophecies of Quaker women (and of other sectaries) are no less than the most visible sign of a wide-ranging movement for change, one that involved much talking and organizing together. It is not surprising, therefore, that many of the same issues and arguments occur again and again in the prophecies they produced. In *Wo to thee City of Oxford* and its companion piece *Wo to thee Town of Cambridge* (1655), Hester Biddle forcefully presents a key Quaker position: the universities are evil places, the breeding grounds of inequity and iniquity, and should be reformed or abolished. Her method of argumentation is typical of the prophecies issued in the period of ferment, as she mobilizes scriptural allusions in her own Bible-like language to threaten the university men with God's wrath if they do not return to the innocent simplicity that governed life in the Garden of Eden before Adam's sin:

> for they that come forth of Oxford and Cambridge, they are such as Isaiah was sent to, to cry woe against, greedy dumb-dogs that never have enough [Isaiah 56.11], and love greeting in the marketplaces, and long prayers in the synagogues and the upper seats

at feasts, and to be called of men, masters [Matthew 23.6–14; Luke 20.46–7]; they are filthy brute beasts which maketh my people to err, therefore the ground is cursed for your sake: thorns and thistles shall it bring forth for your sakes until you return to Adam's first estate [Genesis 3.17–18]. (As edited in Hobby 1991: 165)

A similar rewriting of the Bible is found in Margret Killin's and Barbara Patison's *A Warning from the Lord to the Teachers & People of Plimouth*, where in God's voice the women curse the rich, magistrates, and church ministers or 'hireling priests', as Quakers tended to call them, so as to draw attention to the fact that they were being paid through the hated tithe system:

> If ye had stood in my counsell, ye should have turned many away from the evill of his doings, but because ye have departed out of my counsel, I wil spread dung on your faces [echoing Malachi 2.3], yea I have cast dung on your faces alreadie; and now the false Prophet rides on the beast, but they shall be cast into the Lake, which is prepared for the devill and his angells [alluding to Revelation 19.20; 20.10]. (p. 2)

After the restoration of the monarchy in 1660 persecution of radicals increased, and the rage of many of the prophecies published in 1661 and 1662 is palpable. Biddle curses 'you high and lofty ones! who spendeth God's Creation upon your lusts, and doth not feed the hungry, nor cloath the naked, but they are ready to perish in the streets' (*A Trumpet of the Lord Sounded forth*, 1662: 12; reprinted in Salzman 2000; extracted in Garman et al. 1996). Dorothy White, one of the most prolific Quaker pamphleteers of this period, who in 1659 had tried to intervene directly to prevent the restoration of the monarchy (Reay 1985: 82), published a series of prophecies, declaring that God would overturn the Cavalier Parliament, and calling everyone to rejoice that the Day of the Lord would imminently arrive: 'Yea, the day is at hand, it is at hand' (*A Trumpet of the Lord of Hosts*: 3; reprinted in Garman et al. 1996).

Although it was by no means their sole concern, another major recurrent issue addressed by these prophecies is the position of women. Given the general social requirement that women consider themselves as subordinate to men, and the specific scriptural injunction, 'Let your women keep silence in the churches: . . . and if they will learn any thing, let them ask their husbands at home' (1 Corinthians 14.34–5), the prophets needed repeatedly to justify their speaking out. Merely reiterating that, in these last days, God is pouring out his Spirit upon all flesh (Acts 2.17) could not in itself silence opposition. The terms of the argument for women's right to preach were rehearsed again and again in the 1650s and 1660s, finding their fullest and most entertaining early expression in Priscilla Cotton's and Mary Cole's *To the Priests and People of England* (1655; reprinted in Hinds 1996; Salzman 2000; extracted in Trill, Chedgzoy and Osborne 1997). From their prison cell in Exeter, where they had been incarcerated for prophecy, they explained that Paul's proscription on women's speaking should be read metaphorically, not literally. The 'woman forbidden to speak' is 'weakness whether male or female'; that is, mere human wisdom (1655 edn: 7). Anyone inspired by the Spirit is permitted to speak, 'for the Scriptures do say, that all the Church may prophesie one by one' (ibid.: 7–8, alluding to 1 Corinthians 14.31). The glee with which these prophets play with words and support their case with the Bible's authority is unmissable, as they urge the priests who have had them imprisoned, 'Come down thou therefore that hast built among the stars by thy arts and learning' (ibid.: 5), and advise them that, if they would only turn for guidance to the Light Within, 'you would not need so many Authors, and Books, you would not need to rent [i.e. rend] your heads with studying' (ibid.: 4). This analysis, which was presumably worked out orally in Friends' meetings, had earlier appeared in a pamphlet by Richard Farnworth, *A Woman Forbidden to Speak in the Church* (1654), and in *The Saints Testimony*, and it was to reappear repeatedly, for instance in Sarah Blackborow's *The Just and Equal Balance Discovered* (1660) and in Dorothy White's *A Call from God out of Egypt* (1662). In a more mutedly rational form, with much alternative argumentation based on the activities of named women in the Bible, the justification also makes up part of the case of Margaret Fell's *Women's Speaking Justified* (1666; reprinted in Latt 1979; extracted in Trill, Chedgzoy and Osborne 1997; Otten 1992), and of Elizabeth Bathurst's *The Sayings of Women* (1683; extracted in Garman et al. 1996).

The specific question of women's right to speak at all is not the only element of the traditional female role discussed in these prophecies. As Esther Richey succinctly shows, the figure of the Whore of Babylon, the evil female figure overcome by Christ in the Book of Revelation, was routinely used in Protestant prophecies to represent the Roman Catholic church (Richey 1998: 1–14). In the hands of women prophets, this unmistakably female figure, who has made the inhabitants 'drunk with the wine of her fornication' (Revelation 17.2) and is 'the mother of harlots' (Revelation 17.5), is remade. In Cotton's and Cole's *To the Priests and People of England*, for instance, the whore is the learned men who sit 'as a Queen and Lady over all [echoing Revelation 18.7], and wilt have the pre-eminence, and hast got into the seat of God, the consciences of the people, and what thou sayest must not be contradicted' (ibid.: 6). In Anne Gargill's *A Brief Discovery* (1656), similarly, she is 'your Schools of learning, and your Libraries of Books, and all your compleated subtlety . . . This is the whore that sitteth upon many waters' (1656 edn: 30). In Biddle's *A Warning from the Lord God of Life and Power* (1660) the whore is female, but is not in any sense a sexualized figure. Instead, she serves as an example of the kind of wealthy Cavalier woman who puts her own pleasures before the needs of the poor, with her 'gaudy apparrel, and outstretched neck, with thy face decked with black spots' (1660 edn: 10, alluding to Isaiah 3.16–24).

It is not surprising that these prophecies include such reimaginings of the meanings of gender. The life of a prophet often entailed a woman setting out on her travels to spread God's word, leaving behind her husband and children in her drive to public ministry. Katherine Evans and Sarah Cheevers in Malta, Barbara Blaugdone in Ireland

(*An Account of the Travels*, 1691; extracted in Garman et al. 1996), Joan Vokins in New England and the Caribbean (*God's Mighty Power Magnified*, 1691; extracted in Garman et al. 1996; Graham et al. 1989), all describe the call to abandon their families and follow their sense of God's will, and these examples could be multiplied (see Hobby 2000). Susan Wiseman (1992), analysing prophetical writings by other women of the period, has suggested that these texts show their authors negotiating new and multiple subject positions, and has explored the great variety of 'selves' that appear. Such an unfixing of identity is an understandable product of the startlingly new social activities of the female prophet.

The Autobiographical Imperative

The Protestant imperative for each believer to establish a personal relationship with God has long been recognized as an important spur to the writing of conversion narratives, themselves a key origin of the modern autobiography (Watkins 1972). A good number of Baptist, Congregationalist and Independent women wrote accounts of their journeys to their new faith, examining in the course of their narratives such matters as falling in love, attempts at suicide, and the joys of writing (see Graham et al. (1989) for the examples of An Collins, Sarah Davy, Hannah Allen). Quaker prophecy did not follow the conversion narrative framework, in which the writer's life was examined for signs of God's interventions, and the incidents of a life were arranged into a recognizable pattern (a false assumption of salvation being followed by a period of despair, then, after conversion, by confidence in having been chosen by God); none the less, prophetical pamphlets frequently included autobiographical passages. This seems in part to have been a result of the fact that many of the earliest Quaker prophecies, like *The Saints Testimony* and Priscilla Cotton's and Mary Cole's *To the Priests and People of England*, were written from prison, and include the prophets' accounts of how they came to be incarcerated. Repeatedly in Dorothy White's pamphlets, too, an account is given of the circumstances in which the drive to prophesy arrived, 'as I was passing along the street' (*A Diligent Search*, 1659: 1). In some pamphlets, however, such as Martha Simmons's *A Lamentation for the Lost Sheep* (1655) and Hester Biddle's *The Trumpet of the Lord Sounded forth* (1662), the autobiographical component is much more extensive.

The *Trumpet of the Lord Sounded forth*, written from Newgate prison, warns London, 'this treacherous and backsliding City', to 'repent from the bottom of thine Heart and lead a new Life' (1662 edn: 3; reprinted in Salzman 2000; extracted in Garman et al. 1996). The account of Biddle's own life that is subsequently given works, therefore, to indicate to her reader what kind of 'new Life' is divinely required. In a manner typical of Quaker prophecy, the 'I' who emerges is first placed as part of a wider 'us', as one of God's people who has been misunderstood and persecuted under the regimes of both Cromwell and Charles II: 'we have been a suffering People, and nothing could be found against us, but concerning the worship of our God, which must disannul all unjust Laws made by Man' (1662 edn: 8), she insists. She then tells the story of her realization, shortly after the king's execution in 1649, that the Anglican religion she had been raised in did not coincide with God's will:

> that Faith which I was baptised in, did no good, for all that the Man and Women [i.e. her godparents] had promised, and vowed, I should do, I could not forsake the Pomps and Vanities, and sinful lusts of the Flesh I run into; and they stood alwayes before my eyes. (Ibid.: 15)

Only by joining the Quakers and refusing 'all the unjust Laws made by Man' could she find peace. This, therefore, is the 'new Life' she is proposing to her reader: it is to be a life in which inequity is refused in God's name:

> Oh you high and lofty ones! who spendeth God's Creation upon your lusts, and doth not feed the hungry, nor cloath the naked, but they are ready to perish in the streets; both old and young, lame and blind lyeth in your streets, and at your Masse-house doors, crying for bread, which even melteth my heart, and maketh the soul of the righteous to mourn; did not the Lord make all men and women upon the earth of one mould, why then should there be so much honour and respect unto some men and women, and not unto others, but they are almost naked for want of Cloathing; and almost starved for want of Bread? and are you not all brethren, and under the Government of one King? Oh repent! least the Lord consume you, and be ashamed, and cloath the naked, and feed the hungry, and set the oppressed free. (Ibid.: 12)

Biddle's account of her experiences functions to place herself in her wider community, and to present to the reader an example of the kind of story God can create. The self is examined and used for what it can communicate to others. This is a very different logic from that of the conversion narrative, where the primary impulse is to ascertain, through searching the events of a life, that this individual can be assured of salvation. Where the conversion narrative's central concern is with the individual, autobiographical elements in prophecies act as a particular sign of God's plan for his people. Events in the life of the prophet are as available as any other contemporary incidents to be used for the larger prophetic end. This is the thinking that also informs, for instance, the use of autobiographical narrative in Katherine Evans's and Sarah Cheevers's account of their imprisonment by the Inquisition in Malta, and that causes Dewans Morey to explain in *A True and Faithful Warning from the Lord God* (1665), 'for a sign unto you all have I been made to fast, hunger and pine, to groan, weep and cry' (1665 edn: 1). The Quaker's life is neither more nor less than a 'sign', a unit of meaning used by God, or by God's prophet, to communicate the wider divine plan. This analysis also lay behind the key prophetic actions of Quakers, such as the symbolic act of 'going naked for a sign', where the prophet walked through the streets wearing few or no clothes, 'as testimony to the spiritual nakedness of the world, as a forewarning that all pride would be cast aside at the Last Judgement, and as a symbol of their regenerate nature (Adam and Eve had gone naked before the Fall)' (Reay 1985: 36). It also produced another major development in Quaker publications from the 1670s on, where multiply-authored accounts of the lives of deceased Friends were issued, offering the life of the individual prophet as an exemplum of the story of God's people (Gill 2000: 218–40; 256–64). Though these narratives, such as Joan Vokins's *God's Mighty Power Magnified* and Barbara Blaugdone's *An Account of the Travels* (both 1691; in Garman et al. 1996; Vokins extracted in Graham et al. 1989), lack the expectant fervour of prophetic writings (and, indeed, Rebecca Travers records her own initial hesitation over whether to support the appearance of the account of Alice Curwen's life in *A Relation of the Labour, Travail and Suffering*, 1680, 'there not being much prophecy in it' (sig. A4ʳ)), their origin in the prophetic practice of using the self as a sign is clear.

The Ends of Prophecy

Since it was the social upheavals of the mid-seventeenth century that triggered the outpouring of prophecy, it is not surprising that the new stability imposed after the restoration of the monarchy led to its dying away. From the 1670s onwards Quaker women writers were more likely to compose Epistles and Warnings concerning the proper conduct of young women and maidservants than they were to issue God's prophetic messages on the state of the nation. The Women's Meetings of female Quakers that were established around the country modelled themselves on the advice given in St Paul's Epistle to Titus, where the role of 'aged women' is to 'teach the young women to be sober, to love their husbands, to love their children, To be discrete, chaste, keepers at home, good, obedient to their own husbands, that the word of God be not blasphemed' (Titus 2.4–5; examples of the advice issued by Women's Meetings are given in Garman et al. 1996: 489–533). In the view of the Quaker hierarchy, these were not, after all, the 'last days', when 'your sons and your daughters shall prophesy'. Beyond the structures of the Society of Friends, however, a small number of women continued to insist that they were required by God to speak.

The most striking example of later Restoration female prophecy is the story of a former Baptist, Anne Wentworth, who combined the conversion narrative practice of reviewing a life's events, and the prophetic drive to interpret such incidents as an example of God's plan, in order to present a radical account of the significance of her decision in the early 1670s to leave both her husband and her church. So certain was she of the importance of her revelation that in 1677 she wrote both to the Lord Mayor of London and to Charles II to alert them to the imminent apocalypse (*Calendar of State Papers (Domestic Series)* 1677: 279–80). Given the existence of a number of references in official state papers to Wentworth's claims, it seems likely that the king believed her message might have some bearing on the national tensions building as parliament tried to prevent Charles's Catholic brother James from being next in line to the throne. The visions Wentworth describes in *A Vindication* (1677; extracted in Graham et al. 1989: 180–96) and *The Revelation of Jesus Christ* (1679; in Taft 1997) suggest that the King was mistaken. Wentworth had come to believe that her own suffering at the hands of her 'Hard-hearted Yoak-Fellow', her husband William Wentworth (*A Vindication*: 1), was symbolic of the larger oppression of the godly Zion by evil Babylon. In the great overturning to come, God had promised her that her husband's power over her would cease:

> he has assured me, that the man of earth shall oppress me no more; no more shall I return to be under the hands of the hard-hearted Persecutors, unless he become a new-man, a changed man, a man sensible of the wrong he has done me, with his fierce looks, bitter words, sharp tongue, and cruel usage. And I do further declare, That in the true reason of the case, I have not left my Husband, but he me. (Ibid.: 5)

Once it became clear that Wentworth's message did not concern questions that Charles II cared about, she dropped out of the picture. The last she is heard of in the public record is in her pamphlet *England's Spiritual Pill*, which was probably published in 1680. God has gone so far, she happily informs her reader, as to reinstall her in the house her husband had evicted her from, and he has even sent her the money to pay her rent. God's handmaid has proved to her own satisfaction that she is specially chosen.

Anne Wentworth's pamphlets indicate a continuation of one older tradition of prophecy: for her, as for persecuted Quakers and for Lady Eleanor Davies, prophecy has a material force, one which can be extended into an argument concerning her personal circumstances. Those of Jane Lead, by contrast, indicate another direction for the late seventeenth-century female prophetic voice. By the time of her death in 1704 Lead had published fifteen ecstatic, visionary prophecies, several of which had been translated into German and Dutch, and she had led the Philadelphian Society, a group of Anglicans excitedly awaiting the millennium (Walker 1964: 218–30; McDowell 1998: 167–79). Building especially on the mystical thought of the German philosopher Jakob Böhme (1575–1624), which made extensive use of sexual imagery to conceptualize spiritual matters, she developed a version of Christian theology in which the feminine is of crucial importance. Her prophecies return repeatedly to two female biblical figures. One is the goddess Wisdom, who in Proverbs 8, for instance, is God's companion in creation, and is the source of success and happiness to those who seek her (Proverbs 9). Lead's other female figure is the woman clothed with the sun, who appears in Revelation 12 as a symbol of the church. Powerful and pregnant, she is promised salvation, and her son is destined to rule all nations. It is through following the example of these figures, Lead insists, that redemption can be assured. Her vision is a wholly spiritual one, and her self-presentation that of a 'subordinate Author' led inexorably by God. The dedicatory epistle to her second book, *The Revelation of Revelations* (1683), explains:

> This little Volumn . . . is presented to the publick view, contrary to the intent and purpose of the subordinate Author hereof, who, as I was waiting in my continued course and order, upon the heavenly showring, and to feed, and be refreshed in this all-fruitful and pleasant Pasture, being satisfied here to take my lengths and breadths in all free conference with the Lord, the Spirit, whom I did well know by his inward flaming Body, which at certain times did stir and rise, and then I could hear and distinctly know the Voice of his Mouth, which came as a soft melting *Fire-breath*, and said, *Record what since* October 1679. *hath been seen, heard, tasted and felt, and shun not to declare it, for it hath a peculiar service on Gods behalf to do, though at present hid from thee; only observe and be watchful, and I will certainly follow this at the Heels.* And thus you may perceive under what constraint I am, and by whose Commission these deep and mystical *Revelations* are now to have, and what Souls and Spirits are to be touched and enkindled from the same burning-Ray, which will surely over-shadow the believing. (Sig. A2ᵛ; italics reversed)

Having been melted by God's '*Fire-breath*', Jane Lead could proclaim the eternal power and significance of the feminine (Smith 1979a, 1979b).

In the 1640s, 1650s and early 1660s women possessed by God and required to prophesy could pronounce on the fate of the captured king, on the inequities of the British social system, or on women's right to preach. They might travel the world to spread their message, and boldly confront anyone who tried to silence them. Once the monarchy was firmly re-established, prophecy became an increasingly marginal activity, though the prophets themselves continued to reinterpret and remake the scriptures in highly inventive ways. It is arguable that prophecy is the single most important genre for women in the early modern period: with God's permission, a woman could write, and, for a while at least, could insist on having a hearing. Modern understandings of those times, and of women's role in them, would be much increased by a closer acquaintance with prophecy.

See also RELIGION AND THE CONSTRUCTION OF THE FEMININE; ANNA TRAPNEL, *ANNA TRAPNEL'S REPORT AND PLEA*; AUTOBIOGRAPHY

REFERENCES AND FURTHER READING

Beilin, Elaine (1987). *Redeeming Eve: Women Writers of the English Renaissance*. Princeton, NJ: Princeton University Press.

Berry, Phillipa and Berg, Christine (1981). 'Spiritual whoredom: an essay on female prophets in the seventeenth century.' In Francis Barker et al. (eds), *1642: Literature and Power in the Seventeenth Century* (pp. 37–54). Colchester: Essex University Press.

Braithwaite, William C. (1961). *The Second Period of Quakerism*, 2nd edn. Cambridge: Cambridge University Press.

Cope, Esther S. (1992). *Handmaid of the Holy Spirit: Dame Eleanor Davies, Never Soe Mad a Ladie*. Ann Arbor: University of Michigan Press.

—— (ed.) (1995) *Prophetic Writings of Lady Eleanor Davies*. New York: Oxford University Press.

Crawford, Patricia (1993). *Women and Religion in England 1500–1720*. London: Routledge.

Dailey, Barbara Ritter (1986). 'The visitation of Sarah Wight: holy carnival and the revolution of the saints in civil war London.' *Church History*, 55, 438–55.

Ezell, Margaret J. M. (1993). *Writing Women's Literary History*. Baltimore, MD: Johns Hopkins University Press.

Garman, Mary, et al. (eds) (1996). *Hidden in Plain Sight: Quaker Women's Writings 1650–1700*. Wallingford, PA: Pendle Hill.

Gill, Catie (2000). 'Women in the Quaker community: a literary study.' Unpublished Ph.D. thesis, Loughborough University.

Graham, Elspeth, et al. (eds) (1989). *Her Own Life: Autobiographical Writings by Seventeenth-Century Englishwomen*. London: Routledge.

Hill, Christopher (1972). *The World Turned Upside Down: Radical Ideas During the English Revolution*. London: Temple Hill.

—— (1993). *The English Bible and the Seventeenth-Century Revolution*. London: Penguin Books.

Hinds, Hilary (1996). *God's Englishwomen: Seventeenth-Century Radical Sectarian Writing and Feminist Criticism*. Manchester: Manchester University Press.

Hobby, Elaine (1991). '"Oh Oxford thou art full of filth": the prophetical writings of Hester Biddle, 1629 (?)–1696.' In Susan Sellers (ed.), *Feminist Criticism: Theory and Practice* (pp. 157–69). New York: Harvester Wheatsheaf.

—— (1992). '"Discourse so unsavoury": women's published writings of the 1650s.' In Isobel Grundy and Susan Wiseman (eds), *Women, Writing, History 1640–1740* (pp. 16–32). London: Batsford.

—— (2000). '"Come to live a preaching life": female community in seventeenth-century radical sects.' In Rebecca D'Monté and Nicole Pohl (eds), *Female Communities 1600–1800: Literary Visions and Cultural Realities* (pp. 76–92). London: Macmillan; New York: St Martin's Press.

Latt, David (ed.) (1979). *Women's Speaking Justified* (1667), by Margaret Fell. Los Angeles: Augustan Reprint Society.

Lilley, Kate (1992). 'Blazing worlds: seventeenth-century women's utopian writing.' In Clare Brant and Diane Purkiss (eds), *Women, Texts and Histories 1575–1760* (pp. 102–33). London: Routledge.

McDowell, Paula (1998). *The Women of Grub Street: Press, Politics, and Gender in the London Literary Marketplace 1678–1730*. Oxford: Clarendon Press.

Mack, Phyllis (1992). *Visionary Women: Ecstatic Prophecy in Seventeenth-Century England*. Berkeley: University of California Press.

Matchinske, Megan (1998). *Writing, Gender and State in Early Modern England*. Cambridge: Cambridge University Press.

O'Malley, Thomas (1982). '"Defying the powers and tempering the spirit": a review of Quaker control over their publications 1672–1689.' *Journal of Ecclesiastical History*, 33.

Otten, Charlotte F. (ed.) (1992). *English Women's Voices, 1540–1700*. Miami: Florida International University Press.

Purkiss, Diane (1992). 'Producing the voice, consuming the body: women prophets of the seventeenth century.' In Isobel Grundy and Susan Wiseman (eds), *Women, Writing, History 1640–1740* (pp. 139–58). London: Batsford.

Reay, Barry (1985). *The Quakers and the English Revolution*. London: Temple Smith.

Richey, Esther Gilman (1998). *The Politics of Revelation in the English Renaissance*. Columbia: University of Missouri Press.

Salzman, Paul (ed.) (2000). *Early Modern Women's Writing: An Anthology 1560–1700*. Oxford: Oxford University Press.

Smith, Catherine F. (1979a). 'Jane Lead: the feminist mind and art of a seventeenth-century Protestant mystic.' In Rosemary Ruether and Eleanor McLaughlin (eds), *Women of Spirit: Female Leadership in the Jewish and Christian Traditions* (pp. 185–203). New York: Simon and Schuster.

—— (1979b). 'Jane Lead: mysticism and the woman clothed with the sun.' In Sandra M. Gilbert and Susan Gubar (eds), *Shakespeare's Sisters: Feminist Essays on Women Poets* (pp. 3–18). Bloomington: Indiana University Press.

Smith, Nigel (1989). *Perfection Proclaimed: Language and Literature in English Radical Religion 1640–1660*. Oxford: Clarendon Press.

Taft, Vickie (ed.) (1997). *Anne Wentworth, The Revelation of Jesus Christ* (1679). http://chaucer.library.emory.edu/wwrp/went_web/went_frame.html.

Trevett, Christine (1991). *Women and Quakerism in the Seventeenth Century*. York: Ebor Press.

Trill, Suzanne, Chedgzoy, Kate and Osborne, Melanie (eds) (1997). *Lay By Your Needles Ladies, Take the Pen: Writing Women in England, 1500–1700*. London: Arnold.

Walker, D. P. (1964). *The Decline of Hell: Seventeenth-Century Discussions of Eternal Torment*. London: Routledge and Kegan Paul.

Watkins, Owen (1972). *The Puritan Experience: Studies in Spiritual Autobiography*. London: Routledge and Kegan Paul.

Wiseman, Susan (1992). 'Unsilent instruments and the devil's cushions: authority in seventeenth-century women's prophetic discourse.' In Isobel Armstrong (ed.), *New Feminist Discourses: Critical Essays on Theories and Texts* (pp. 176–96). London: Routledge.

19

Women's Poetry 1550–1700:
'Not Unfit to be Read'

Bronwen Price

Now touching that I hasten to expresse
Concerning these, the ofspring of my mind,
Who though they here appear in homly dresse   80
And as they are my works, I do not find
But ranked with others, they may go behind,
Yet for theyr matter, I suppose they bee
Not worthlesse quite, whilst they with Truth agree.

Indeed I grant that sounder judgments may
(Directed by a greater Light) declare
The ground of Truth more in a Gospel-way,
But who time past with present will compare
Shall find more mysteries unfolded are,
So that they may who have right informacion   90
More plainly shew the path-way to Salvacion.

Yet this cannot prevayl to hinder me
From publishing those Truths I do intend,
As strong perfumes will not concealed be,
And who esteemes the favours of a Freind,
So little, as in silence let them end,
Nor will I therfore only keep in thought,
But tell what God still for my Soule hath wrought.
(Collins 1996: 5–6, ll. 78–98)

These stanzas, taken from 'The Preface' to An Collins's *Divine Songs and Meditacions* (1653), exemplify the complex web of negotiations women writers of the early modern period frequently undertook in order to enter poetic discourse. While claiming that

her work appears 'in homly dresse' (l. 80), the poem enacts a set of rhetorical strategies which reflect considerable subtlety in producing a position from which to speak.
Typically, the poem is framed not only by its explicit sense of religious purpose, but
also its implicit response to seventeenth-century gender ideology in which the ideal
woman was required to be silent, chaste and obedient. Throughout the period women's
entry into the public domain through publication (l. 93) was associated with feminine transgression and particularly promiscuity. Here, however, Collins's literary production, 'the ofspring of my mind' (l. 79), is presented as being the result of an
immaculate conception, the chaste union between the speaker and God. Moreover,
Collins's authorization to speak is asserted through her own apparent lack of authority and autonomy, for it is the ultimate patriarch, God the Father, who 'wrought' in
'my Soule' 'The fruit of intellectuals' (ll. 98, 9) and who thus provides her with a
'firme defensive Tower' (ll. 129–33). This phallic image stands as an emblem of his
'Sov'rain Power' (l. 127) that defines the limits of her agency and sense of identity.
Her subversion of worldly values that conventionally demand women's silence is vin-
dicated by her submission to a higher authority. It is only through being lodged in
these terms that her poem becomes, in Aemilia Lanyer's words, 'not unfit to be read'
(contents page, *Salve Deus Rex Judaeorum*).

Throughout the poem Collins adopts a position of humility and modesty. Such
values are in accordance with the Calvinist tone of her poem. However, by the 1650s
the humility topos was such a feature of women's writing across the religious and
political spectrum that it may also be regarded as a feminized convention. As in other
women's works of the period, the concept of humility is given a notably ambivalent
edge in Collins's poem. The speaker contrasts the inadequacy of her own authorial skill with the 'sounder judgments' of others (ll. 85ff.). Yet this apparent self-
effacement is followed by the self-affirmative, unapologetic declaration of her
intention to publish and refusal to contain her thought by staying silent (ll. 92–8).

Collins emphasizes the significance of her work's matter, albeit couched in negative terms (l. 84), over the manner in which it is presented. Yet the apparent artless-
ness of her verse is a means of shaping a particular self-image. Her self-conscious lack
of 'style', a common component of women's verse during the period, provides a mode
of writing that stands as a code for her innocence and Christian humility. The speaker's
modesty extends to her request for assistance from the reader to supplement her own
writing's deficiencies so as to make it 'fit for some good end' (l. 122). However,
Collins's seeming self-deprecation is also a means of asserting moral authority.
She distinguishes between good and bad readers: those who choose to understand her
'good intent' are 'the humble sort' who 'from small things of worth extract', whereas
those who do not are 'a spider generacion, / Whose natures are of vennom' (ll. 126,
120, 123, 114–15). Collins thus requires her readers to undergo a process of self-
examination by interrogating their own values and motives. She thereby provides
interpretative guidance by demanding complicity with her reading of her work and
its production.

Collins's 'Preface' illustrates the 'discursive instability' that informs much sixteenth- and seventeenth-century women's writing (Belsey 1985: 149). Like many other works by women, Collins's poem troubles conventional gender categories even as it seems to maintain them. Jostling between self-negation and affirmation, it registers the tenuous process of female self-authorization by problematizing the boundaries between speech and silence. If early modern poetry is often characterized by its stylistic self-consciousness and dialogic quality, where innovation derives from its interaction with other sources and voices, women's verse has a peculiar relation to such practices. It invariably responds to 'a shared set of prohibitions and exclusions' (Wall 1993: 338) which reflect 'a consciousness of the masculine control of discourse, in all its areas: genre; interpretation; reading; style; and publication' (Aughterson 1995: 231). Women's entry into poetic discourse, as Collins's example shows, often produces contradictory subject positions which demand a rethinking of, if rarely an outright challenge to, those constraints. Indeed, as Wall argues, 'woman's unstable speaking position is not merely a sign of her culturally circumscribed subject position . . . but also act[s] as a complex form in which a provisional self-authorization is made possible from within cultural restrictions' (Wall 1993: 287).

This utilization of 'discursive instability' manifests itself particularly in the prefaces that almost invariably accompany women's writing of the period. Although first appearing in the same year as Collins's work, Margaret Cavendish's *Poems and Fancies* (1653) could hardly be more different. Cavendish's verse primarily concerns speculations on natural philosophy without any reference to a religious framework. However, the epistles that introduce her verse share Collins's tentative mode of self-authorization. Continually shifting between different positions, the speaker is often most at the foreground when asserting her sense of deficiency. Her authorial identity is most prominent when she requests that it should be wrapped 'up in *silence* as a *Shrowd*' ('The *Poetresses* Petition', l. 6). The title of the last of her nine prefaces, 'An excuse for so much writ upon my Verses', is as ironic as its concluding statement: 'Thus write I much, to hinder all *disgrace*' (l. 10). Indeed, the speaker often strikes conventional feminine postures only to problematize them in the process, justifying her writing by transforming it into a domestic activity, 'Spinning with the braine', which keeps her out of mischief, prevents her from gossiping and ensures that she stays in the privacy of her closet ('An Epistle to Mistris Toppe').

The unstable subject of Cavendish's prefaces indicates the provisionality of feminine self-authorship, while also implicitly dislodging the patterns of sexual difference. Presenting herself as both a writing subject and object of discourse, the speaker expresses a sharp sense of the power relations underlying speaking and writing, while also gently eroding their foundations.

Cavendish's writing is particularly adventurous for the period not only in entering the masculine province of scientific debate, but also because Cavendish took the unusual step of publishing her work and distributing copies to university libraries. Aughterson notes 'that the total publications by women in the early seventeenth century was only 0.5 per cent of the total number of publications in England, a figure which rose to only 1.2 per cent after 1640' (Aughterson 1995: 230). Even at the end of the seventeenth century poetry still tended to be circulated among small coterie groups in manuscript, which was regarded as a more socially privileged activity than publication (Lamb 1990: 10; Jones 1990: 36). While much writing that initially appeared in manuscript eventually found its way into print, manuscript circulation enabled women poets to present their work as being principally for local if not private use in being addressed to an exclusive set of people. Print, however, contained the specific taint of social as well as feminine indecorum.

Wendy Wall explores how the emerging mode of print publication was rhetorically gendered. The female body was used 'as a metaphor for the newly commodified book, both became defined as unruly objects in need of supervision' and helped to establish 'a masculinized notion of authorship' (Wall 1993: 282). Like many women's prefaces of the period, Collins's and Cavendish's reflect an implicit anxiety about the woman writer's own identity being read as unruly through the appearance of her printed text. In line with other women writers, Collins and Cavendish anticipate such criticism by emphasizing the privacy of the writing process. Collins, for example, highlights her physical debility which confined her to her house when producing her poems. Katherine Philips, a close contemporary of Collins and Cavendish, whose poems were printed in an unsolicited edition in 1664, expresses an 'aversion' to publication ('The Preface'). Other women writers, as Wall shows in the case of the earlier poets Isabella Whitney, Mary Sidney, Aemilia Lanyer and Mary Wroth, produce a self-authorizing position through the inscription of their bodily erasure or anticipated death (Wall 1993: 296–340). A rhetoric of corporeal confinement, fragility or absence becomes almost a condition of exposing the female corpus.

Women's poetry not only shapes its modes of self-presentation with a sense of being scripted by its audience, it also participates in shaping and creating audiences. We have already seen how Cavendish's prefaces are acutely aware of reader response. Appearing much earlier than Cavendish's work, Aemilia Lanyer's *Salve Deus Rex Judaeorum* (1611) also addresses a range of readers in its prefatory verse. Unlike the aristocratic Cavendish, Lanyer was on the court's fringes and, at one level, adopts the standard masculine practice of using her poetry to seek patronage. All of her dedicatees are royal or aristocratic, from whom she continually acknowledges her social distance. However, Lanyer is exceptional in targeting her poetry towards a specifically female audience and still more so in directing that audience towards new types of reading practice, ones that will encourage them to read her work against the grain of masculine privilege and identify with her celebration of female honour.

Not all women's poetry of the period is as strategic in its relationship to its audience as Lanyer's, but most does signal a self-consciousness about the relationship between gender and the processes of literary production and reception. However, while much women's writing shares this, there is enormous variety within the types of poetry that women produced. There is little sense that women poets identified themselves as a cohesive group during this period. In addition, while it is important to recognize the particular effects that women's gender has on their poetry, there are also dangers in separating their work from men's writings. This can promote a tendency to treat women's poetry as a separate, homogeneous genre and to overlook both its interventions with common poetic conventions and the poetic practices that men and women of this period share.

It is also important to note the differences between women writers in terms of their class and relation to centres of power, which often have an impact on the kinds of poetry they produce, just as they do with writing by men. Not surprisingly, aristocratic women generally had easier access to education, as well as material support, compared with their less socially privileged counterparts.

As we have seen from the prefaces explored so far, women's writing itself draws attention to the specificity of the conditions under which it was written. It is crucial that we grasp these variations of writing and reading contexts if we are to have a full insight into women's poetry of the period. In order to establish these permutations I have divided the poetry into different periods which mark key social and cultural shifts, but make the proviso that women's poetry itself does not, of course, necessarily fall neatly into historical categories.

1550–1603

The output of poetry by women in the period 1550–1603 was relatively small, though much has been lost. The vast majority of women were illiterate. Most of the extant writing is by courtly women who benefited from the new humanist education and its advocacy of female learning by figures such as Juan Vives and Thomas Elyot in the mid-sixteenth century. The Reformation also helped to promote women's education, but Protestant theology, like humanist concepts of female study, was often employed as a means of regulating boundaries for female conduct: women's literary activity generally was encouraged to be private in form and geared towards the goals of domestic humility and Christian piety. Much women's poetry from this period is indeed religious and Protestant in focus, including prayers (Elizabeth Tyrwhit), psalms (Mary Sidney) and meditations (Ann Lok).

Elizabeth I, an exemplar of the new humanist learning as well as being a figurehead for Protestantism, was the most prominent female figure to write verse during this period and provided an important reference point for later women writers. Elizabeth wrote eight original poems besides numerous translations. Her poetry mainly comprises occasional verse written in response to specific circumstances. Two of her earliest poems were scratched on a window and written on a shutter when Elizabeth was imprisoned in Woodstock in 1554 while her half-sister Mary Tudor was monarch. Her later poem 'The Doubt of Future Foes' (1570) probably refers to the

threat of rebellion posed by Mary Queen of Scots. It opens with a sense of impend-
ing crisis suggested by the fluctuating 'flow' of 'falsehood' and 'ebb' of 'subjects' faith'
(Wynne-Davies 1998: l. 3). It is this sense of an insecure future which 'exiles my
present joy' (l. 1). The image of self-division and internal strife presented
here, however, rapidly gives way to an assertion of monarchic authority and
containment that encompasses time and space. Punctuated by a series of imperatives, uncertainty is replaced by a list of determined punitive action that will follow
sedition.

The authoritative subject position of this poem is untypical of women's poetry of
the period and seems particular to Elizabeth's official role as queen. One of the more
common modes of women's writing at this time was verse translation, especially of
biblical and religious texts. On the surface translation might be regarded as a means
of cloaking a 'female' voice, for here the speaker's words are mediated by those of the
primary source. However, Renaissance texts in general are overtly intertextual and
were not treated as original utterances in the post-Romantic sense. Translation could
also comprise significant innovation as a result of adaptations of style, form and focus
and, as Lamb (1990: 12) argues, 'often embodied active political or personal designs
of their women translators'.

This is certainly true of Mary Sidney's work. Her *Psalmes* (1599) are striking for
their technical prowess, especially their remarkable range of versification. Also of
central importance is the *Psalmes*' use of the English vernacular as an appropriate language in which to praise God through, for example, their manipulation of rhythmic
metre, use of idiomatic terms and extension of vocabulary. The focus placed on the
lyric 'I' and the relationship forged between the speaker and God have a strongly
Protestant cast. As Fisken (1985: 168–72) points out, the psalmist's voice is person-
alized and its internal conflicts dramatized, but, as in other reformist writing, it is
also identified as embodying the general condition of humanity. Its particularities are
representative: thus the first-person speaker of Psalm 131 learns to be supplicant
towards God by observing 'the wained babe' (ll. 5–8), who provides an example of
absolute dependence, humility and faith. In turn, the speaker is presented as typify-
ing the means through which 'Jacobs race' must 'learne' 'such endlesse trust on god
to place' (ll. 9–10).

It is clear that Sidney's *Psalmes* were not simply private expressions of faith, but
had an underlying political function of fostering Protestantism. As numerous critics
have noted, the accompanying dedicatory panegyric to the queen is underscored by
an implicit suggestion that she should represent the reformist cause more forcibly
(Hannay 1985: 149–65). Moreover, Philip Sidney, who died fighting in the service of
Protestantism, is held up as a martyr in both this poem and the following elegy, 'To
the Angell spirit', dedicated to him. While the voice of the *Psalmes* is not feminized,
the subject positions set out in the elegy are complicated by the combination of the
humility topos and a reworking of stock Petrarchan tropes through which Philip is
identified as his sister's muse (Wall 1993: 315–16). The psalms are 'halfe maim'd' (l.

18) both because Philip died before completing them and because of Sidney's deficient artistry compared with his. His death gives birth to her 'wounding lynes of smart' by dissolving 'to Inke' 'the bleeding veines of never dying love' (ll. 81, 79–80) (Lamb 1990: 116–18). But the secretion of her private grief into external text is also subsumed under public duty which authorizes her to continue Philips's authorial and political tasks.

Sidney's *Psalmes* demonstrate how women's devotional verse does not necessarily simply conform to feminine codes of propriety. Because of the interrelation between church and state it sometimes involved entering the public arena and participating in political debates, even if that was in muted terms. Protestantism was promoted by a wide range of women's poetry. For example, Anne Dowriche's huge verse-narrative *The French Historie* (1589) presents a dramatized partisan account of the recent French civil wars. Presented through the voice of a male persona, the poem follows John Foxe's influential *Actes and Monuments* (1563) in highlighting the martyrdom of the reformists. By contrast, Elizabeth Melville, Lady Culross's 'An Godlie Dreame', which was printed first in Scots dialect (1603) and then in English (*c.*1606), traces the internal journey of a representative pilgrim figure culminating in a vision of the 'smuke and flaming fyre most fell' (Greer et al. 1988: l. 258) that looms over all those but God's elect. Commitment to reformism together with the Protestant stress on individual conscience, personal engagement with the Bible and private prayer were means through which women's poetry could be legitimized.

However, not all poetry of the period was specifically religious. As Sidney's poem on her brother testifies, elegy was also an important genre to which women contributed. The learned Elizabeth Cooke Russell wrote epitaphs on her two husbands and other members of her family, some of which appear on tombs in Westminster Abbey (Walker 1996: 60), while her niece, Anne de Vere, wrote four sonnets on her son's death, which were printed in John Soowthern's *Pandora* (1584). The familial context of these elegies makes them appear to be an acceptable poetic genre for women. However, Sidney's elegy reveals that this genre could have a wider set of functions than representing personal grief.

Much more unusual in women's non-religious poetry are Isabella Whitney's two collections of verse. These appeared in cheap pamphlet form, and it is likely that she contributed to other anthologies (Wynne-Davies 1998: 348). Whitney, who was from a non-aristocratic background, is remarkable in being the first English woman to publish secular verse and negotiate a position, albeit tentatively, as a professional writer. Her attempt to appeal to a broad audience is indicated by her deployment of popular genres and use of simple ballad metre and plain diction. As recent commentators have noted, however, the poems are more sophisticated than they initially appear, especially in their formulation of an authorial position. Whitney's first work, *The Copy of a letter by a yonge Gentilwoman to her unconstant Lover* (1567?), was published anonymously and is a verse epistle which draws on the tradition of female complaint established by Ovid's *Heroides*. It is presented as a private correspondence to which the reader gains voyeuristic access. The illusion of intimacy is undercut, however, both by its revision of its Ovidian model, whereby, as Jones reveals, the female complainant is given moral superiority rather than being presented as 'a spectacle of pathos' (Jones 1990: 44–6, 49), and by its accompanying *Admonition to al yong Gentilwomen, and to all other Mayds in general to beware of meenes flattery*. While affirming standard virtues of feminine modesty, the speaker both undoes the masculine rhetoric of seduction which underpins her Ovidian source and identifies herself as an adviser, a role officially the preserve of men.

The hybrid quality of this text and its advisory tone are also important features of Whitney's next volume, *A Sweet Nosegay* (1573). The central body of this work comprises 110 poetic aphorisms 'gathered' from Hugh Plat's pseudo-Senecan prose work, *Flowers of Philosophie* (1572). But it is the apparently extraneous epistolary verses to family members with responses appended to this volume that afford particular interest. These are underwritten by the self-conscious mapping out of an authorial role. Authorship is presented as being a housewifely activity; the 'Juce' of Plat's 'Flowers' is extracted to 'make' the reader 'a conserve' so as to produce spiritual sustenance in the form of 'a soveraigne receypt'. The letters go on to outline the speaker's economic and physical hardship resulting from social misfortune, where writing replaces the domestic duties the authorial persona would otherwise perform had she a husband. Presenting the poems as a 'gift' to family and friends, the letters suggest an intimate mode of address which detracts from their published form, while also justifying it.

By mixing genres and locating established ones in new poetic frameworks, Whitney's verse shows how innovative women's poetry could be in spite of the restrictions which governed their literary production.

1603–1642

James I's succession instigated a period in which an increasingly overt and encompassing form of patriarchy was articulated by official culture. The ideology of patriarchal absolutism advocated by James I's *True Law of Free Monarchies* (1598) presented an image of natural law in which paternal authority was affirmed through a network of interdependent relations between God over the world, king over state and father or husband over the family. Moreover, during the early seventeenth century there was an increase of texts explicitly expressing misogynistic sentiments. Yet, as Lewalski (1993: 2–4) argues, women's writing of this period often troubles theories of patriarchal containment and tends to be more experimental than previously.

Lady Mary Wroth's *Pamphilia to Amphilanthus* (1621) may be regarded as one such work. It is exceptional in being the first Petrarchan sonnet sequence to be written by an English woman, though the last in a line of such sequences to be written in the period. While it is likely that Wroth's poem was written, circulated and revised over a number of years, it first appeared in print appended to her prose pastoral romance *Urania*. Clearly both texts resonate with and rework her uncle Philip Sidney's *Astrophel and Stella* (1591) and *Arcadia* (1590). Indeed, Wroth writes in self-conscious reference to her Sidney heritage. *Pamphilia to Amphilanthus* is also often read as being a dramatization of her affair with and betrayal by her cousin William Herbert. The poem's allusion to Wroth's personal circumstances, though, should also be read in reference to its revision of Petrarchan conventions at a broader level. By 1621 the Petrarchan sonnet was a somewhat outmoded genre, whose codes had already been reworked by numerous male sonneteers. Wroth, however, employs this well-established form in order to place a new, feminized perspective upon it.

In Petrarchan conventions the woman is idealized and idolized, but her 'honour' makes her 'cruel' by demanding that she remain chaste. She is displayed as an erotic other, her physical form dissected into a series of fragmentary images which are matched against her inner coldness. Wroth's poem, though, immediately provides a more complex dynamic than a simple reversal of gender roles. The very names of the lovers signal this: Pamphilia meaning 'the all loving' and Amphilanthus, 'the lover of two', establishes a distinction between feminine fidelity and masculine betrayal. The poem thus converges with the female complaint genre. Moreover, Amphilanthus is not addressed directly, nor does the poem assume a response, focusing instead on Pamphilia's isolation and dark, inner world. Unlike the Petrarchan woman, Amphilanthus is never physically emblazoned, but is emphatically absent. It is this which generates Pamphilia's speech, while also confirming her chastity (Wall 1993: 334–5). There is, indeed, an insistent focus on the speaker's constancy and privacy, imaged in the secluded contexts in which her utterances take place. In this sense, she displays features that comprise feminine virtue. Yet these very attributes are employed as a means of critiquing the public, implicitly masculine world of the court. For example, in sonnet 23 (Wroth 1983: 26) the 'poore vanities' of courtly pastimes are set against her solitary thought when she is 'free from eyes' and so released from being the object of speculation or desire. As Jones reveals, the speaker rejects daylight and its associations with official time and public spectacle, instead identifying herself with night, which both reflects 'my mind destrest / Darke, heavy, sad' (p. 43) and is presented as being a more reliable companion than her beloved (Jones 1990: 146–7).

Near the end of the sequence, however, the tone and focus of the poem shift from the introspective, dispersed songs and sonnets to a formally contained crown of fourteen sonnets, which present an allegorical exploration of the true nature of love. The intricate pattern of the corona demands that the last line of each sonnet is repeated in the first line of the next, so that as Pamphilia attempts to unravel 'this strang labourinth' of love and 'take the thread of love / Which line straite leads unto the soules content' (Wroth 1983: 77, 78), the form troubles its quest, ultimately winding back to the unresolved question with which it begins:

> Soe though in Love I fervently doe burne,
> In this strange labourinth how shall I turne?
>
> (p. 90)

Yet while the effects of love remain to confound the speaker, she underlines her dedication to Platonic ideals in which 'Noe staine is ther butt pure as purist white' (p. 79). The encircling form of the corona thus provides an emblem that lays claim to the speaker's intact virginity. But, as Walker (1996: 188–9) argues, the language of the crown also entails a loss of subjectivity where the speaker's voice is effaced by a male constructed abstract ideal. The corona is thus as much a sign of the entrapment of feminine subjectivity as it is of integrity.

Wroth's poetry highlights the contradictory manoeuvres that underlie the articulation of feminine desire. It uses a rhetoric of femininity to question masculine domains and values, yet also finds itself entangled within that very discourse. Rachel Speght's work is informed by a rather different writing context from Wroth's. The daughter of a learned Calvinist minister, Speght is best known for her outspoken defence of women, *A Mouzell for Melastomus* (1617), written in response to Joseph Swetnam's misogynistic polemic, *Arraignment of Lewd, idle, froward, and unconstant women* (1615). Speght's second printed work was a volume of poetry. The central text, *Mortalities Memorandum* (1621), which comprises a meditative sermon on death, gains most interest when read in the light of the striking 'Dreame' that precedes it. This allegorical dream-vision poem forms part of the same genre as Elizabeth Melville's 'Dreame'. Here, however, the religious message incorporates a justification of female learning and is specifically linked to the author's own quest for knowledge.

The poem explicitly revises the Eve myth and women's traditional relationship to knowledge. The ignorant state in which the speaker begins reduces her to an instinctual being who feels but cannot reason the nature of or cure for 'my maladie' (l. 60). The narrative proceeds by guiding her out of her natural fallen state into '*Eruditions* garden' (l. 100). Entry into this garden reinscribes the events of Eden (Beilin 1987: 111). Here '*Desire*', 'taste' and 'appetite' are linked not to sensuality, but the pursuit of 'True *Knowledge*', which is 'a lawfull avarice' resulting in 'grace' and leading to salvation (ll. 199, 191, 217, 231, 221–2). Underpinning her argument with biblical references, women's knowledge is given divine sanction and, as Beilin (1987: 116) suggests, justifies Speght's 'ministerial role' in the central text.

Aemilia Lanyer's earlier *Salve Deus Rex Judaeorum* ('Hail God, King of the Jews', 1611) also participates in the debate about women. Here, too, women's conventional positioning in relation to knowledge is redefined, but Lanyer goes further than Speght in her poetic innovation and experimentation. Like a number of other works by women poets, Lanyer adopts a mixture of genres. The central work concerning Christ's Passion is framed by an extensive set of prefatory poems dedicated to noble women, already noted, including a celebration of Mary Sidney's work, and concludes with 'The

Description of Cooke-ham', a topographical poem eulogizing Margaret Clifford, Countess of Cumberland, together with an address 'To the doubtfull Reader'.

Arguably pre-dating Ben Jonson's 'To Penshurst', 'Cooke-ham' is often cited as being the first poem in the country-house genre, but its tone is elegiac, for it is a 'Farewell' mourning the loss of 'pleasures past' (ll. 1, 13). Drawing on the classical pastoral tradition, 'Cooke-ham' offers a transient, self-contained paradise, embodying feminine goodness and inhabited by three women: Clifford, her daughter Anne and the speaker. Identified primarily through its Edenic natural setting, it is a place of Christian meditation and chaste companionship. In particular, though, Cookham is defined by Clifford's presence and infused with her Christian qualities (ll. 76–92). When she arrives 'The Walkes put on their summer Liveries, / And all things else did hold like similies', but when she departs her godly spirit goes with her and Cookham enacts a microcosmic Fall, as 'all greene things did make the earth their grave' (ll. 21–2, 196). Her 'grace' combines and emanates a series of virtues: courtesy, nobility, friendship, underpinned by godly grace. In this sense, 'Cooke-ham' exemplifies the image of 'grace' offered in the dedication poems. The volume, then, is bound together by a sense of female community and feminized patronage.

The integration between the various parts of the text does not stop here, however. The main poem *Salve Deus* (51–129) is a lengthy verse meditation on Christ's last days, following St Matthew. What is most striking about this work is the feminized reinscription of those events and, in particular, its defence of biblical women, most notably Eve. It is women who seem to possess a wisdom beyond the reach of men, for it is they who understand the crucial significance of Christ's presence in the world and the blasphemous implications of condemning him to death. In addition, this work is dedicated to Clifford, who is presented as being a 'Deere Spouse of Christ' (l. 1170) and whose own 'blessed Soule' (l. 11) links her to a line of virtuous women from the scriptures. The values presented in the outer poems are thus highlighted by those contained within the central text.

Lanyer's explicitly revisionist feminine perspective, together with her defence of women's virtue through her construction of a female interpretive community, is unusual in women's writing of the time. Initially, women's religious verse of the Caroline period seems less challenging. Imitating Camden's *Annales* (1615 and 1625), Diana Primrose's *A Chain of Pearl* (1630) presents a nostalgic panegyric on Elizabeth I, addressing itself 'To all noble ladies and gentlewomen' in 'honour of our noble sex'. Like Lanyer's work it thus establishes a specifically female framework. Each of the ten stanzas provides a 'pearl' comprising Elizabeth's individual virtues, which together form the entire 'chain' of the poem and an emblem of Elizabeth's integrity. Yet, as Walker (1996: 69) shows, Elizabeth's royal authority is gendered masculine and presents her as an exception to her sex. Women in general are placed outside the public sphere and it is only Elizabeth's feminine virtues, such as prudence and chastity, which demand emulation. However, the text is riddled with contradictions, not only because of its own publication, but also because the first pearl on religion precisely locates the poem within public debate. Primrose's vigorous positioning of Elizabeth as representative of the 'Reformed' 'true religion' of Protestantism (Wynne-Davies 1998: ll. 8, 2, 9), can only be read as a critique of Charles I when the king was married to a French Catholic princess and was progressively shifting the church towards high Anglicanism under the direction of William Laud.

1642–1660

Women poets' interventions in public debates come further to the foreground in the Civil War and republican periods. During this time there was a significant increase of published writing by women across the social spectrum, the majority appearing in the 1650s, when women writers employed a much wider range of genres and topics than previously. While advances in printing, the growth of the literary marketplace and the relaxing of the censorship laws in 1641 were all significant factors in these developments, there is no question that it was the compelling political events and their interconnection with religious controversy that instigated much of this writing.

Appearing in manuscript in the early 1650s, Katherine Philips's royalist poem 'Upon the double murther of K. Charles, in answer to a libellous rime made by V.P.' presents its own outspokenness as forced upon the speaker by extraordinary circumstances. It is the slander uttered by the sectarian preacher Vavasor Powell against the executed Charles I that commits the king's second murder and provides 'a cause / That will excuse the breach of nature's lawes. / Silence were now a Sin' (Philips 1990: 69, ll. 5–7). The speaker is thus commanded to break the 'natural' law of women's silence by honouring the king's memory so that Christian justice may be defended.

Although married to a parliamentarian, Philips's royalist sympathies infuse her work in intricate ways. Her cultivation of a coterie 'society of friends' during the 1650s, together with her poems' thematic focus on private community and sequestered retreats, link her writing with a specifically Cavalier aesthetic found in the work of other royalist poets such as Richard Lovelace. Also significant in this regard is Philips's idealization of Platonic codes. Platonism was developed by Henrietta Maria in the 1630s from the French cult of *préciosité* and was subsequently adopted in Cavalier writing in the 1640s and 1650s to demonstrate loyalty among the defeated and exiled royalists (Thomas in Philips 1990: 7). While Platonism contains a more elaborate function in Philips's verses than simply this, it nonetheless signals the political encoding of her work.

Writing from a different political perspective, Anne Bradstreet, who emigrated to America with her Puritan family in 1630, details the specific events surrounding the Civil War in 'A Dialogue between Old *England* and New, concerning their present troubles. Anno 1642' (1642/3). Elevated in tone and style, the poem presents Old England as a sick, grief-stricken mother explaining the current crisis and its history to her optimistic, forward-looking daughter. While the poem does not demand

Charles's dethronement, it celebrates the parliamentarian cause, with New England condoning the expulsion of 'dark Popery' and 'Prelates', commending the efforts of the Earl of Essex, leader of the parliamentary army, and praising 'thy Commons, who for Common good, / And thine infringed Lawes have boldly stood' (ll. 216, 231, 220–1).

However, the majority of women's writing that appears during the period derives from the radical Protestant sects that emerged from the 1640s. Much of this work is in prose and, where verse is employed, it is often difficult to categorize in conventional generic terms. Anna Trapnel's *The Cry of a Stone* (1654) is one such work. Presented as a prophecy, it begins in prose and concludes with songs, uttered outside Whitehall when Trapnel was allegedly in a 12-day trance. Having been transcribed by witnesses, the written text of *The Cry* is in one sense a communal work and unsettles the boundaries between the oral and the literary. The notion of communal activity underlying Trapnel's prophecy is highlighted by the fact that she speaks on behalf of her sect, the Fifth Monarchists, whose leaders were being tried at the time of her visions. Her work alleges that Cromwell has betrayed the revolutionary cause by announcing himself Lord Protector and retaining the vestiges of monarchic political structures. Closely following the Books of Daniel and Revelation, *The Cry* predicts the imminent Second Coming of Christ, the true Protector, prophesying that 'Antichrist shall fall' (Greer et al. 1988: 178). Its concerns are therefore both immediately politically charged and metaphysical, specific and apocalyptic.

This ambiguity is apparent in the way the speaker is positioned. The spectacle created by Trapnel's visions is highly subversive politically and also in terms of her gender. Her prophetic utterance presents a scene of self-display which could not be more public, addressing itself to all the major institutions: 'the Governors, Army, Churches, Ministry, Universities: And the whole Nation'. Yet Trapnel's prophecies also present her as a mere vessel for God's voice. In this, she has no agency herself but, like the Old Testament prophets, is positioned as God's instrument, moved solely by the divine Spirit to impart his word. Paradoxically, this image conforms with concepts of feminine passivity and obedience, where Trapnel's loquacious body becomes a sign of heightened spirituality and receptiveness to God.

Trapnel's prophecy apparently expresses her subjection to God's will, while also demanding that she dynamically engage in public events. However, not all women's religious poetry of the period participates so directly in political debates. An Collins's *Divine Songs and Meditacions*, mentioned earlier, does not apparently highlight politico-denominational commitment, but takes the form of spiritual autobiography. Employing a wide and often sophisticated range of verse forms which reflect shifts in tone and mood, the poems concentrate on inward self-analysis. There are nonetheless two poems on the Civil War ('A Song composed in time of the Civill Warr, when the wicked did much insult over the godly' and 'Another Song') which are centrally concerned with the need 'Disorders to expell' so that England may be 'fenc'd with unity' and re-established as a godly nation (Collins 1996: 62, l. 64; 63, l. 7). The importance of self-contained tranquillity and spiritual stability is exemplified by the quiet 'inward peace' ('The Discourse', l. 146) of the speaker's current personal existence after a period of physical debility and external strife. By retreating from worldly cares into an internal realm centred on 'Sweet Meditacion and Contemplacion / Of heavenly blis' ('Another Song', ll. 54–5), the speaker may experience a paradise within, for, 'as a garden in my mind enclosed fast / Being to safety so confind from storm and blast' ('Another Song', ll. 26–7).

Rejection of public concerns and spiritual withdrawal devoted to God's worship are central themes of a number of women poets during the period. Like Collins's work, Elizabeth Major's *Honey on the Rod* (1656) offers a type of spiritual autobiography in which the lessons derived from the speaker's life are depicted as a form of moral instruction for the reader. The poems, which comprise the last part of this work, identify the speaker as a sinful child, whose physical suffering is a punishment wrought by God the Father. Yet this disciplining 'Rod' provides 'honey' in teaching her humility, thus leading her towards salvation. The anonymous *Eliza's Babes* (1652), which was written after its (probably royalist) author had fled England in the 1640s (Hobby 1988: 55), foregrounds spiritual rapture rather than physical torture in its depiction of the speaker's devotion to God. The lyric 'I' presents herself as Christ's spouse, her marriage to whom is portrayed as a preferable alternative to earthly wedlock, 'The Virgins-Offering', her poems, being the fruit of this union.

The three poets above present withdrawal into religious devotion as a means of self-containment. Their concentration on introspective self-scrutiny and personal testimony associates their work with Calvinism and ironically justifies its publication. There are, however, other forms of privacy to be found in women's verse of the period.

Along with her political and philosophical work, Bradstreet wrote a significant number of poems that focus on personal and domestic matters, which tend to be associated with a later period of her writing. Together they read as a journal recording specific incidents and immediate personal emotions attached to family life: 'Before the Birth of one of her Children', 'A Letter to her Husband, absent upon Public employment'. Some poems are identified by date alone and interspersed with diary-like entries; the verse 'May 13 1657' relates the speaker's recovery from illness immediately after a journal submission recounting the same event. The style of these poems establishes a new type of feminized poetics which is informal, personal and colloquial, in complete contrast with the highly wrought 'Old England' literariness that underscores Bradstreet's earlier work.

The representation of privacy and retreat takes a different form again in Katherine Philips's poetry. While Philips wrote a number of occasional and philosophical verses, most of her lyric poems concern female friendship and are addressed by 'Orinda' (Philips's pseudonym) to various close associates. Embedded in a discourse of Christian Platonism the poems often contain more complex layers of meanings than are initially apparent. The conventional features of feminine virtue with which the poems identify female friendship are frequently employed as a means of mapping out an autonomous, feminized space set apart from a world implicitly gendered masculine. The 'inocent', 'sacred union' portrayed in 'L'amitié: To Mrs M. Awbrey', for example, offers an interiorized sanctuary in which 'Thy heart locks up my secrets richly set, / And my brest is thy private cabinet' (Philips 1990: 142, ll. 17, 21, 9–10). Operating in a realm unpenetrated by 'the dull world' and its values, the friends are able 'to pitty Kings, and Conquerours despise' (ll. 15, 20).

The creation of an enclosed, elevated domain of love is not unusual in seventeenth-century poetry. It is a common feature of Donne's verse, to which Philips frequently directly alludes. However, Philips's intensely charged sphere of female friendship places a different dimension on this motif. Orinda's Platonic exchanges tend to undo polarities between subject and object in a form that reconfigures the terms of pleasure and desire found in much heterosexual poetry of the period. The rapturous union of souls presented in 'Friendship's Mysterys, to my dearest Lucasia', for instance, depends on an intersubjective, reciprocal merging and mutating of identities:

> Our hearts are doubled by their loss,
>   Here mixture is addition grown;
> We both diffuse, and both engrosse,
>   And we, whose minds are so much one,
>   Never, yet ever, are alone.
>
>   (ll. 11–15)

Self-sacrifice is figured in terms of sensual ecstasy so that the boundaries of body and soul collapse and feminine 'innocence' is rethought (Price 2001: 236–7).

1660–1700

After the Restoration Philips turned her attention to the public domain, writing a number of verses celebrating the return of the royal family. It was her poetry on feminine withdrawal and friendship, however, that was to have a major influence on women's verse of the late seventeenth century, when there was a significant increase in secular writing by women, together with a more self-consciously feminized poetics. Indeed, a number of poets, including Anne Killigrew, Jane Barker, 'Ephelia' and Anne Finch, refer to 'Orinda' directly as a source of inspiration. After the re-establishment of the Church of England only a small amount of poetry by women sectarians (or what became termed 'dissenters') came out. The majority of women poets of the period, and certainly Orinda's followers, were from courtly circles.

While privacy and retreat remain dominant themes in women's poetry, they are put to new uses and given new meanings. Images of feminine virtue linked to pastoral retirement from worldly conflict and corruption pervade Anne Killigrew's small, eclectic, posthumous collection of poems (1685/6). The volume includes 'Upon the saying that my Verses were made by another' in which the speaker defends her own writing and its value through the example set by 'Orinda' (Killigrew 1967: ll. 48–9). Elsewhere, Mary of Modena, to whom Killigrew was a lady-in-waiting, is presented as a model of feminine goodness who legitimates her poetry. In 'To the Queen' Mary's virtuous authority emanates from within, for she 'Erects a Throne i'th' inward Parts' (l. 37). It is this internally autonomous sphere of virtue which forms a protective haven against those who attack the Catholic queen and, in turn, represents a sanctuary for the speaker against 'Vice and Folly' (l. 82).

Killigrew's 'On a Picture Painted by her self, representing two Nimphs of Diana's, one in a posture to Hunt, the other Batheing' offers a rather different version of heroic feminine virtue. By drawing attention to its own role as representation, the poem highlights how the nymph figure is conventionally constructed. Speaking communally as 'We' of *'Diana's* Virgin-Train' (l. 1), the nymphs of Killigrew's picture are not treated as objects of a desiring male gaze, but are awarded agency and desires of their own. While chaste, theirs is a world of self-contained pleasure in which they hunt, chase the wind, bathe and blow their horns. But they will, if necessary, 'strike' their 'Javelins' in self-defence, aggressively attacking 'Whatever does provoke our Hate' (ll. 13–14).

Jane Barker's poetry also redefines feminine types and offers new inscriptions of feminine pleasure. Her verses, which reflect a greater level of formal experimentation than Killigrew's, were initially published in the first part of *Poetical Recreations* (1688) and a number were later revised. *Poetical Recreations* includes an early version of 'A Virgin Life' which 'in chaste verse' describes the 'happy state' of chastity (Greer et al. 1988: ll. 5–6). Although Barker converted to Catholicism shortly before going into exile with the Stuarts, the Virgin Mary does not provide the poem's central model here. Instead, Barker's verse demythologizes virginity's cultural stereotypes of hopeful maid and 'helpless dame' (l. 10). These are revealed to be no more than 'mad conceptions' which 'our sex betray, / And often makes us fling our selves away' (ll. 16, 11–12). Rather, singleness offers release from 'the power, / Of mans, allmost omnipotent amour', for a maidenhead intact 'bears the impress of all good' (ll. 4–5, 23) in providing independence and autonomy. Centring on friendship, good works and religious devotion, this 'lovely state' (l. 15) is characterized by moderation, reason and usefulness. Virginity enables the possibilities of women's identity to be rethought and is not connected with retirement from the world, but with social interaction.

Elsewhere Barker questions women's exclusion from masculine domains. Her anti-pastoral 'An *Invitation* to my Learned Friends at *Cambridge*' (see Barker 1997) satirically portrays women's isolation from the sphere of learning, identifying their confinement through a topography of pastoral retreat. Recasting the Eden myth, the poem explains that 'the Tree of Knowledge' will not grow in this 'cold Clime', for it has been transplanted into an exclusively masculine province, whose inhabitants are the sole beneficiaries of the 'Luxurious Banquets' supplied by its fruits (ll. 42–8).

Barker's is one of a number of poems (and prose pamphlets) of the period advocating female learning. Others include the anonymous 'The Emulation' and Sarah Fyge Egerton's 'The Emulation' (1703).

Egerton enters more directly into public debate than Barker with her *The Female Advocate* (1686, revised 1687). Published anonymously when she was still in her teens, this verse essay provides a defence of women that responds point by point to Robert Gould's misogynistic attack *Love given O're* (1682). Like Lanyer 70 years earlier, Egerton begins her work by reinterpreting the Fall, arguing that Adam was guiltier than Eve, for 'She had the strongest Tempter', whereas 'Man's knowing most, doth make his Sin more large' (Ferguson 1985: ll. 48–9). She continues by reversing traditional categories of gender difference, suggesting that men are degenerate and inconstant, while women are naturally 'pious, chast and true, / Heroick, constant, nay, and modest too' (ll. 191, 237–8), providing historical and mythological examples to support her case.

In her later poem 'The Liberty' Egerton launches a still more aggressive attack on conventional gender divisions. Rather than defending women, she criticizes 'those obsequious Fools' who confine themselves within 'Customs scanty Rules' (Greer et al. 1988: ll.1–2). 'That dreaded Censure' (l. 19) is exposed to be an illusory ogre which hems in its victims through their own belief in its power (ll. 20–1). The speaker herself, though, asserts a defiant independence, satirizing stock feminine employment and flouting conventions by rewriting the terms which govern her existence as a result of her gender:

> My daring Pen, will bolder Sallies make,
> And like myself, an uncheck'd freedom take;
> Not chain'd to the nice Order of my Sex . . .
>   (ll. 43–5)

Yet, while 'Brave', her autonomy, like Killigrew's and Barker's, is 'Secure' in 'Virtue' and 'Innocent delight' (ll. 48–9, 22).

A number of women poets, however, negotiate the libertine poetics associated with the Restoration court. Here, too, gender identity remains a central theme. *Female Poems on several Occasions* (1679) by the anonymous 'Ephelia' includes several verses on the values of female friendship and friendship with men, but the volume also explicitly addresses female sexual desire. Imitating Abraham Cowley's poem of the same name, 'Maidenhead' takes a satiric approach to its subject, identifying it as the 'dull Companion of our active Years, / That chill'st our warm Blood with frozen Fears' (Greer et al. 1988: ll. 15–16). While pinpointing the hypocrisy of sexual codes governing women, however, the poem also reaffirms the stereotyping of virginity that Barker and Egerton later challenge, for only those who are 'Ill-natur'd, Ugly, Peevish, Proud / . . . thy Praises Sing aloud' (ll. 21–2).

Aphra Behn's work goes further. Along with Margaret Cavendish, Behn is the most prolific writer of the period. Although most renowned for her plays and novels, she also wrote a significant amount of verse, which appeared, sometimes unascribed, in miscellanies, some of which she edited; in anthologies of other writers' works, including the second edition of Ephelia's *Female Poems* (1682); and in her own *Poems upon Several Occasions* (1684). As an ardent royalist Behn wrote numerous political poems and panegyrics addressed to members of the court, but the majority of her verses concern sexual love and gender relations, participating in the reworking of classical pastoral tropes that informs much Restoration poetry. Behn's poetry also reflects the influence of her dramatic writing, presenting a range of personae who act out a variety of roles. In some cases the speakers of Behn's poems merely replicate stock positions and reaffirm old fictions. Uttered by a male voice, 'A Counsel' is a complaint to Sylvia about her 'needless Scorn' (Behn 1994: l. 1) and ends with the *carpe diem* motif and an invitation to bed with promises of its pleasures. 'The Surprize', on the other hand, mocks the disdainful Phyllis when she is finally seduced by Strephon:

> Her Cheeks with Blushes cover'd were,
> And tender Sighs her Bosom warm,
> A Softness in her Eyes appear;
> Unusual Pain she feels from ev'ry Charm:
> To Woods and Ecchoes now she cries,
> For Modesty to speak denies.
>
> (ll. 13–18)

However, the different perspectives of the poems jostle with and recast each other. 'To Alexis in Answer to his poems against Fruition' identifies the double-bind underpinning the roles to which women are conventionally assigned, where men's 'inconstancy' is such that they 'love the absent, and the present scorn' (ll. 15–16); whereas 'On a Juniper-Tree, cut down to make Busks' extols reciprocal sexual gratification, presenting its observations from the tree's viewpoint. Gender positions are asserted, reversed and challenged through the dialogue the poems produce with each other so that new perspectives are continually created.

Elsewhere Behn's poems unmask archetypal poses found in poetic fiction. Drawing on a theme introduced by Ovid and exploited by Behn's contemporary, the Earl of Rochester, 'The Disappointment' undoes the conventional roles of courtly love. Chloris's guise of feminine modesty is undermined by erotic desire, signalled by 'her swelling Snowy brest' (l. 37), while Lysander's reverence for the 'Lovely Maid' (l. 78) barely masks his sexual fervour when 'His daring Hand that Altar seiz'd, / Where Gods of Love do sacrifice' (ll. 45–6). Sexual climax, however, gives way to bathetic humiliation when Lysander is 'Unable to perform the Sacrifice' and 'that Fabulous *Priapas*' is revealed to be no more than a fiction which 'Poets feign' (ll. 70, 105–6).

Not only does Behn's poetry dismantle the gender types of pastoral mythology; it also troubles masculine performance in the urban marketplace, where sex is reduced to a matter of commerce. The female speaker of 'To Lysander, on some Verses he writ, and asking more for his Heart then 'twas worth' refuses to be the silent object of male rhetoric. Instead, she supplies a sharp, witty retort to Lysander's bargaining position. Unwilling passively to accept his unfaithful double-dealing, she rewrites the terms of his transaction by answering him 'Trick for Trick' (l. 52), demanding the same sexual liberties he claims for himself.

Behn's verse demonstrates the major changes that had taken place in women's poetry since the mid-sixteenth century. Her poems do not covertly negotiate a space from which to speak, but, in line with the Restoration mode, assert, attack and, on occasion, challenge. What becomes clear in exploring women's poetry of the period is its immense diversity. Not only do women poets imitate the central genres of the period, they often place new perspectives upon them. The female complaint, the Petrarchan sonnet and the tropes of Platonic love and pastoral retirement are all recast within a distinctively feminized poetics, as the works of Wroth, Lanyer, Philips, Killigrew, Barker and Egerton testify. While in general women's poetry tends not to be technically innovative, Sidney's, Lanyer's and Collins's writing reveal that women's verse could be formally experimental. Looking at the period as a whole, it is possible to discern key preoccupations and negotiations that form a link between different writers' work. The rewriting of the Fall; the establishment of feminine communities; the themes of feminine retreat and withdrawal; the use of God's word as a means of authorizing speech; the exploitation and revision of standard codes for feminine virtue are all reiterated in various shapes and forms throughout the sixteenth and seventeenth centuries. However, it is also important to note the ways in which women poets respond to the particular contexts in which they wrote. Frequently veering between conservatism and subversion, women's poetry engages with a specific set of cultural conditions which both formulates their work and is reformulated within their writing. By the end of the seventeenth century women's verse included a much wider range of genres and had generated new ones which were taken up by the next generation of female poets and through which women writers justified their work as 'not unfit to be read'.

See also RELIGION AND THE CONSTRUCTION OF THE FEMININE; WOMEN AND WRITING; ISABELLA WHITNEY, *A SWEET NOSEGAY*; MARY SIDNEY, COUNTESS OF PEMBROKE, *PSALMES*; AEMILIA LANYER, *SALVE DEUS REX JUDAEORUM*; MARY WROTH, *THE COUNTESS OF MONTGOMERY'S URANIA*; ANNA TRAPNEL, *ANNA TRAPNEL'S REPORT AND PLEA*; KATHERINE PHILIPS, *POEMS*; DEFENCES OF WOMEN; PROPHECY

REFERENCES AND FURTHER READING

Aughterson, Kate (ed.) (1995). *Renaissance Woman: A Sourcebook: Constructions of Femininity in England.* London: Routledge.

Barash, Carol (1996). *English Women's Poetry, 1649–1714: Politics, Community and Linguistic Authority.* Oxford: Clarendon Press.

Barker, Jane (1997). *The Galesia Trilogy and Selected Manuscript Poems*, ed. Carol Shiner Wilson. Oxford: Oxford University Press.

Behn, Aphra (1994). *The Poems of Aphra Behn: A Selection*, ed. Janet Todd. London: Pickering.

Beilin, Elaine V. (1987). *Redeeming Eve: Women Writers of the English Renaissance*. Princeton, NJ: Princeton University Press.

Belsey, Catherine (1985). *The Subject of Tragedy: Identity and Difference in Renaissance Drama*. London: Methuen.

Bradstreet, Anne (1980). *The Complete Works of Anne Bradstreet*, ed. Joseph McElrath and Allan Robb. Boston: Twayne.

Cavendish, Margaret, Duchess of Newcastle (1972) [1653]. *Poems and Fancies*, reprinted in facsimile with an introduction by George Parfitt. Menston: Scolar Press.

Collins, An (1996). *Divine Songs and Meditacions*, ed. Sidney Gottlieb. Tempe, AZ: Medieval and Renaissance Texts and Studies.

Ferguson, Moira (ed.) (1985). *First Feminists: British Women Writers 1578–1799*. Bloomington: Indiana University Press.

Fisken, Beth Wynne (1985). 'Mary Sidney's *Psalmes*: education and wisdom.' In Margaret Patterson Hannay (ed.), *Silent But for the Word: Tudor Women as Patrons, Translators, and Writers of Religious Works* (pp. 166–83). Kent, OH: Kent State University Press.

Graham, Elspeth, Hinds, Hilary, Hobby, Elaine and Wilcox, Helen (eds) (1989). *Her Own Life: Autobiographical Writings by Seventeenth-Century Englishwomen*. London: Routledge.

Greer, Germaine, Medoff, Jeslyn, Sansone, Melinda and Hastings, Susan (eds) (1988). *Kissing the Rod: An Anthology of Seventeenth-Century Women's Verse*. London: Virago.

Hageman, Elizabeth H. (1996). 'Women's poetry in early modern Britain.' In Helen Wilcox (ed.), *Women and Literature in Britain, 1500–1700* (pp. 190–208). Cambridge: Cambridge University Press.

Hannay, Margaret P. (1985). '"Doo What Men May Sing": Mary Sidney and the tradition of admonitory dedication.' In Margaret Patterson Hannay (ed.), *Silent But for the Word: Tudor Women as Patrons, Translators, and Writers of Religious Works* (pp. 149–65). Kent, OH: Kent State University Press.

Hobby, Elaine (1988). *Virtue of Necessity: English Women's Writing 1649–88*. London: Virago.

Jones, Ann Rosalind (1990). *The Currency of Eros: Women's Love Lyric in Europe, 1540–1620*. Bloomington: Indiana University Press.

Killigrew, Anne (1967) [1686]. *Poems*, reprinted in facsimile with an introduction by Richard Morton. Gainesville, FL: Scholars' Facsimiles and Reprints.

Lamb, Mary Ellen (1990). *Gender and Authorship in the Sidney Circle*. Madison: University of Wisconsin Press.

Lanyer, Aemilia (1993). *The Poems of Aemilia Lanyer: Salve Deus Rex Judaeorum*, ed. Susanne Woods. New York: Oxford University Press.

Lewalski, Barbara Kiefer (1993). *Writing Women in Jacobean England*. Cambridge, MA: Harvard University Press.

Philips, Katherine (1667). *Poems by the most deservedly Admired Mrs Katherine Philips: the Matchless Orinda*. London: H. Herrigman.

——(1990). *The Collected Works of Katherine Philips, the Matchless Orinda, Vol. I The Poems*, 3 vols, ed. Patrick Thomas. Stump Cross: Stump Cross Press.

Price, Bronwen (1996). 'Playing the "Masculine Part": finding a difference within Behn's poetry.' In Kate Chedgzoy, Melanie Hansen and Suzanne Trill (eds), *Voicing Women: Gender and Sexuality in Early Modern Writing* (pp. 129–52). Keele: Keele University Press; rpt. (1998) Edinburgh: Edinburgh University Press.

——(2001). 'A rhetoric of innocence: the poetry of Katherine Philips, "the Matchless Orinda".' In Ursula Appelt and Barbara Smith (eds), *Write or Be Written: Early Modern Women Poets and Cultural Constraints* (pp. 223–46). Burlington and Aldershot: Ashgate.

Sidney, Mary, Countess of Pembroke (1998). *The Collected Works of Mary Sidney, Countess of Pembroke*, 2 vols, ed. Noel Kinnamon, Margaret Hannay and Michael G. Brennan. Oxford: Clarendon Press.

Speght, Rachel (1996). *The Polemics and Poems of Rachel Speght*, ed. Barbara Kiefer Lewalski. New York: Oxford University Press.

Walker, Kim (1996). *Women Writers of the English Renaissance*. London: Prentice-Hall.

Wall, Wendy (1993). *The Imprint of Gender: Authorship and Publication in the English Renaissance*. Ithaca, NY: Cornell University Press.

Whitney, Isabella (1982). *A Sweet Nosegay (1573) and the Copy of a Letter (1567)*, reprinted with *The Floures of Philosophie (1572)* by Hugh Plat in facsimile with an introduction by Richard J. Panofsky. New York: Scholars' Facsimiles and Reprints.

Wroth, Lady Mary (1983). *The Poems of Lady Mary Wroth*, ed. Josephine A. Roberts. Baton Rouge: Louisiana State University Press.

Wynne-Davies, Marion (ed.) (1998). *Women Poets of the Renaissance*. London: J. M. Dent.

20

Prose Fiction

Paul Salzman

Early modern prose fiction is not so much a genre as a concept. During the period under consideration here, writers produced works in a wide variety of modes and genres, such as the romance or the picaresque, which, for the sake of convenience, are now subsumed under the heading 'prose fiction'. The category of prose fiction is therefore extremely elastic, but however broadly one defines it, it encompasses far fewer works than other early modern forms of writing. On a rough estimate, there were approximately 600 works of prose fiction published in England from 1558 to 1700, including translations and collections of stories (Salzman 1985: 351–78). Of these, only 46 were written by women. While it is generally true that during this period women certainly published and also wrote in far fewer numbers than men, the area of prose fiction offers a greater disparity than a number of other areas (especially religious writing and other non-fictional prose). It is hard to determine exactly why this was the case. Perhaps one reason is that, unlike religious writing, prose fiction was not empowering for women, at least until the Restoration. Indeed, the example of Mary Wroth's *Urania* indicates that a venture into the male-dominated world of prose romance could lead to considerable scandal and opposition.

Until Wroth published *Urania* in 1621 there were no original works of prose fiction written by a woman in England. During the outburst of highly original prose fiction during the Elizabethan period, the only example written by a woman was the translation in 1597 of Marguerite de Navarre's *Heptameron* (a collection of stories rather like Boccaccio's *Decameron*, originally published in French in 1558). Later in the seventeenth century the short story became a form used by a number of women writers, including Margaret Cavendish and Aphra Behn, but the *Heptameron* did not inspire any women writers for a generation after its translation. However, one other sixteenth-century example does exist of a woman's engagement with a dominant form of prose fiction: Margaret Tyler's translation of part of a Spanish chivalric romance, Diego Ortunez de Calahorra's *The Mirror of Princely Deeds and Knighthood* (translation published around 1578). The chivalric romance, with its noble heroes and martial deeds, might seem an especially unlikely genre for a woman to translate. Tyler addresses this issue in her preface:

> Such delivery as I have made I hope thou wilt friendly accept, the rather for that it is a woman's work, though in a story profane and a matter more manlike than becometh my sex. But as for the manliness of the matter, thou knowest that it is not necessary for every trumpeter or drumsler [i.e. drummer] in the war to be a good fighter. (Martin 1997: 19)

Tyler points to the hypocrisy of those who support the notion of a female reader but baulk at the idea of a female writer: 'it is all one for a woman to pen a story as for a man to address his story to a woman' (ibid.: 23). Tyler also offers an argument against those who would confine women's writing to religious matters by noting, ironically, that it would be difficult for her to find an acceptable religious work in Spanish to translate (given that all such works would be Catholic and unsuitable for Protestant English readers). Tina Krontiris (1992) has noted that, in de Calahorra's romance itself, the female characters are far from passive and the narrative offers the reader some critique of double standards; Krontiris argues (though this cannot be proven) that a male translator would have reduced the liberal Spanish attitude towards women that is evident in the romance (ibid.: 59–62).

While Tyler's translation had two further editions, in *c.* 1580 and 1599, and the chivalric romance as a genre remained extremely popular in the seventeenth century (although its readership tended to slip further down the social scale as the century progressed), no women wrote examples of the genre, nor did any woman apart from Tyler translate the numerous Spanish and French examples that appeared in English. The first engagement with the romance form by a woman, albeit in a very different mode of romance, occurred when Mary Wroth wrote *The Countess of Montgomery's Urania*, a work inspired in part by the example of her uncle Sir Philip Sidney's romance, *The Countess of Pembroke's Arcadia*. As *Urania* is the subject of a chapter in this volume, I will only note here that it is a significant achievement by a writer who is only now being acknowledged as a major figure in early modern English literature. Wroth dared to venture into print with a major work of fiction and was duly castigated for her presumption, partly because of her thinly veiled depiction of scandalous incidents which were immediately recognizable to at least some of her readers. Wroth had to write to Buckingham, the influential favourite of King James, apologizing for any offence caused and offering to withdraw from sale and recall from circulation all copies of her romance. Wroth did not publish the lengthy continuation of *Urania*, which survives in manuscript.

In terms of its genre, *Urania* draws upon the adept intersection of pastoral and chivalric romance achieved by Sidney during his revision of the *Arcadia*. Wroth also expands upon the political possibilities of *Arcadia* through her examination of

European states in conflict and through her depiction of real events from Jacobean court life. *Urania* contains, at the same time, a searching and complex depiction of a wide variety of female characters, including two who represent quite different notions of the woman writer: the much-praised and long-suffering Pamphilia, an alter-ego for Wroth herself, and Antissia, a much more assertive writer who is the subject of some criticism by other characters and who eventually suffers from a form of madness. Wroth subjects the whole issue of the relationship between gender and power to searching scrutiny throughout the *Urania*. The manuscript continuation in particular is radical in its attack on male heroism and its examination of the fates of the ageing central characters of the published narrative.

Perhaps Wroth's retreat from publication under the pressure of the scandal caused by *Urania* discouraged women from following her lead. Certainly, no prose fiction by women writers appeared during the next generation, despite the fact that there was a sharp rise in women's writing in non-fictional prose, particularly evident in the religious writing that flourished during the time of the English Civil War. The next work of fiction to be published by a woman was, like Wroth's, related to Sidney's *Arcadia*. Anna Weamys published her *Continuation of Sir Philip Sidney's Arcadia* in 1651. Unlike *Urania*, Weamys's work has a symbiotic relationship with Sidney's romance, and is part of a series of additions and continuations that were spawned by the *Arcadia*, partly because of the hybrid nature of the version of *Arcadia* that circulated in the seventeenth century (where after Sidney's death the incomplete revision of his romance was joined to the last part of an earlier version), partly because *Arcadia* concludes with an invitation to other writers to continue the adventures of the characters and their offspring. Weamys's work is one of three continuations of *Arcadia*, the other two being published much earlier in the seventeenth century, when Sidney's influence was at its height. There were nine editions of *Arcadia* published between 1605 and 1638, but only three further editions appeared in the seventeenth century, the next one in 1655 after Weamys's *Continuation* had been published.

Weamys disguised her identity when she published the *Continuation*, but not her sex: the work is described on the title page as being by 'a young Gentlewoman, Mistress A.W.' (see Weamys 1994: xvi–xxx). Unlike *Urania* this text is prefaced by a number of statements about the author as a female writer. Weamys herself begins with a dedication to two women: Lady Anne and Lady Grace Pierrepoint. In a preface to the reader by the stationer we are told, rather hyperbolically, that 'no other than the lively ghost of Sidney, by a happy transmigration, speaks through the organs of this inspired Minerva' (ibid.: 4). This is followed by five poems praising the work and its author, including a catchy and inspiring call by F. Vaughan to 'Lay by your needles, Ladies, take the pen, / The only difference 'twixt you and men' (ibid.: 11). Vaughan (identified by Patrick Cullen as most likely to be Frances Vaughan; see Weamys 1994: xxvii–xxviii) might be alluding consciously to the common association between pen and penis in this suggestion that sexual difference is eradicable. All the poems offer parallel suggestions that Weamys is able to assume Sidney's prowess, even with a suggestion through the Amazon image in the third poem that Weamys carries Sidney's heroism forward.

Weamys's modern editor, Patrick Cullen, while able to identify her as most probably the daughter of a Dr Weamys who was a clergyman, cannot add any real biographical information to that revealed in the prefatory poems. However, he is able to place her in a suggestive political context by outlining the background of her dedicatees' family, the Pierrepoints of Dorchester, and the literary careers of two men who wrote prefatory poems for the volume: James Howell and Richard Vaughan (ibid.: xxii–xxx). Howell, Vaughan and Henry Pierrepoint were all royalists who came to an accommodation with the commonwealth after the execution of Charles I. While the genre of romance assumed a complicated relationship to the Civil War and its aftermath, taking on overt political dimensions for a number of royalist writers, Weamys does not offer any substantial political comment in her *Continuation*. Rather, as Cullen has argued, she emphasizes the love elements in the romance form (ibid.: lvi–lvii). Unlike Wroth (whom she seems not to have read), Weamys is not really interested in questions of power. Here she needs, I think, to be put in the context of a new kind of romance that was extremely popular in England in the 1650s: the French heroic romance.

The French heroic romance developed during the 1640s and was intimately connected to the literary salon discussion groups known as the *précieuses*, groups which centred on women. Madeleine de Scudéry was a member of such a salon and wrote the three most significant French heroic romances: *Ibrahim* (1641), *Artamène ou le Grand Cyrus* (1649–53) and *Clélie* (1654–60). These romances were extremely popular in England as well as in France and were translated into English during the 1650s; they are immensely long narratives full of intertwining subsidiary stories, usually set in some early historical period and much concerned with issues of love and honour. Scudéry's romances might well have had a particular appeal for female readers (we have a series of fascinating comments about them made by Dorothy Osborne in her letters to William Temple), but in England they were not directly imitated by female writers – indeed, the only substantial English example, *Parthenissa*, was written by Roger Boyle. However, from the 1650s through to the end of the century, French women writers working in a variety of fictional modes were translated into English and had a particularly strong influence on English writers from the 1670s through to the early eighteenth century, as the vogue for the long heroic romance was succeeded by the shorter *nouvelle* (novellas) of various kinds, especially those that concentrated on love stories, often of a particularly racy kind.

It was in the 1650s that the prolific Margaret Cavendish, Duchess of Newcastle, began publishing. Cavendish wrote plays, poetry and works of philosophy and natural history. In the area of prose fiction she concentrated on short (often very short) stories and a fascinating utopian narrative, *The Blazing World* (1666). A substantial number of prose stories form part of the heterogeneous collection Cavendish published in 1656 entitled *Nature's Pictures Drawn By Fancy's Pencil to the Life*. Narratives in verse as well as prose form part of this collection, as does her autobiographical *True Relation of My Birth, Breeding and Life*, which comes at the end of the volume. While the prose stories are quite varied, Elaine Hobby has aptly summed up their central purpose as being to produce 'heroines who by being either sexless or androgynous seek to avoid the traps of romance' (Hobby 1988: 91). Two of the most complex narratives in *Nature's Pictures*, 'Assaulted and Pursued Chastity' and 'The Contract', have been edited by Kate Lilley as part of an edition of Cavendish's fiction which also includes *The Blazing World*. For Lilley, these two stories reflect in part the circumstances of Cavendish's marriage to William Cavendish, Duke of Newcastle, but they also shift the genre of romance (a genre Cavendish says she despises) towards a feminized mode which might empower women (Cavendish 1992: xvii). Lady Deletia, the protagonist of 'The Contract', is involved in two arranged marriages without her own consent. In a surprising plot turn, Deletia is reunited with the duke who spurned his marriage contract with her almost nine years earlier, the denouement occurring via a wonderful court scene in which Deletia argues that, despite the duke having married someone else, his initial contract with her must stand. 'The Contract' has been the subject of a fascinating essay by Victoria Kahn, who argues that Cavendish uses the theme of the marriage contract to offer an alternative notion of the social contract during the interregnum, in order to support continuing allegiance to the exiled Charles II as opposed to accommodation with and consent to Cromwell's government (see Kahn 1997, esp. pp. 528–9). The more elaborate narrative of 'Assaulted and Pursued Chastity' incorporates an imaginary voyage as well as a complex romance plot.

The travel theme is extended in Cavendish's utopian narrative *A Description of a New World, Called The Blazing World*, which was first published in 1666 as part of a scientific treatise, *Observations Upon Experimental Philosophy*, in which Cavendish set out to refute Robert Hooke's *Micrographia* (1665) by arguing that the kind of scientific experiment predicated upon the use of the microscope led to false rather than true knowledge. *The Blazing World* forms part of Cavendish's philosophical argument in so far as it creates an imaginary world in which *her* scientific ideas hold sway, rather than the empirical and experimental science that was exemplified by the Royal Society. In her preface Cavendish defends the use of fancy in a work attached to a scientific treatise, and she offers the imaginary world as a solution to some of the frustrations experienced by ambitious early modern women: 'I am not covetous, but as ambitious as ever any of my sex was, is, or can be; which makes, that though I cannot be *Henry* the Fifth, or *Charles* the Second, yet I endeavour to be *Margaret* the *First*' (Cavendish 1992: 124).

In *The Blazing World* Cavendish creates a remarkable imaginary world joined to our world at the North Pole. A young lady enters the Blazing World and becomes its empress, allowed by her indulgent husband to rule with virtually absolute power. This leads, among other things, to her use of the Blazing World's inhabitants to endorse Cavendish's scientific views. In a wonderful piece of self-conscious (one might even say proto-postmodern) writing, Cavendish herself appears as a character, her soul brought to join the empress's soul as a kind of twinned alter-ego. In this section of the narrative, empress and duchess travel back to our world to visit Newcastle's husband. Kate Lilley has pointed out that an important part of the utopian element in *The Blazing World* is Cavendish's depiction of states which allow certain women to circumvent male authority (ibid.: 122). This freedom is only available to an aristo-cratic figure like the empress or like Cavendish herself – a reflection of Cavendish's considerable investment in social hierarchy. As the narrative of *The Blazing World* unfolds, we move from the empress as a figure who fulfils Cavendish's dreams of entry into the male world of science, to the appearance of Cavendish herself, who, within this utopian setting, is given her due acknowledgement as a writer. This begins with her 'appointment' as the empress's scribe after the empress is advised to pass over a host of famous men, from Aristotle and Plato to Galileo and Hobbes, in favour of 'the Duchess of Newcastle, which although she is not one of the most learned, eloquent, witty and ingenious, yet is she a plain and rational writer, for the principle of her writings, is sense and reason' (ibid.: 181). Not only is Cavendish acknowledged as a legitimate scientific/philosophical figure, but her plays are also accorded a more sym-pathetic reception by the emperor and empress than they received in England: 'I intended them for plays; but the wits of these present times condemned them as inca-pable of being represented or acted, because they were not made up according to the rules of art; though I dare say the descriptions are as good as any they have writ' (ibid.: 220). Indeed, the rulers of the Blazing World announce that they will build a theatre especially to perform Cavendish's plays.

Cavendish's somewhat solipsistic representation of her own ideas and ambitions in *The Blazing World* is not without a certain amount of irony – she makes explicit the fact that this utopian fantasy is indeed a fantasy and that she has had to create out of her imagination a world which will fulfil her ambitions:

> By this poetical description, you may perceive, that my ambition is not only to be Empress, but Authoress of a whole world; and that the worlds I have made, both the Blazing and the other Philosophical World, mentioned in the first part of this descrip-tion, are framed and composed of the most pure, that is, the rational parts of matter, which are the parts of my mind. (Ibid.: 224)

Within the Blazing World the empress rules as, in part, a self-projection of Cavendish, but also as a female ruler of a utopia which allows for an almost complete escape from the patriarchal constraints of the society which Cavendish inhabited. While William Cavendish allowed his wife to be a writer, the emperor of the Blazing World allows the empress to control his society, to wage a foreign war (back in the world in which Cavendish lives), even to change religious practices. All of Cavendish's fiction demon-strates her remarkable inventiveness, but *The Blazing World* is especially rich in im-aginative detail, while at the same time adhering to Cavendish's philosophical and scientific interests.

There is another hiatus between the publication of *The Blazing World* in 1666 and the sharp increase in fiction by English women that began in the 1680s and continued through the eighteenth century. In the 1660s and 1670s, as well as the continuing interest in the French heroic romance, there was a large readership for shorter forms of French prose fiction written by women and translated into English. These *nouvelle* (or novellas) can be seen at their most accomplished in the work of Marie de la Fayette, whose *La Princesse de Clèves* (1678) remains a classic; it was translated into English in 1679. La Fayette's fiction offers a particularly subtle and sophisticated analysis of passion and its effect on her characters. Many other examples of the French *nouvelle* involve a more sensationalist approach, especially the large and popular subgroup that purport to be based upon real, scandalous events (for example, the work of Marie-Catherine Aulnoy and Marie-Catherine Desjardins), particularly involving aristocrats or royalty. Ros Ballaster has traced the influence of what she terms 'amatory fiction' through women's prose fiction from the 1680s to the mid-eighteenth century, at which time the erotic power of such work ran into a moral opposition which branded such women writers as scandalous (Ballaster 1992). Ballaster stresses how this fiction, as well as being written by women, specifically addresses female concerns (ibid.: 66).

Many of these French modes and themes are evident in the fiction of Aphra Behn. Like Mary Wroth and Margaret Cavendish before her, Behn produced work in an impressive range of genres. Unlike Wroth and Cavendish, Behn was a non-aristocratic woman who had to make a living from her writing. Behn took up fiction late in her career, after she had, from the performance of her first play in 1670, become a highly successful dramatist. Her first published work of prose fiction, *Love Letters Between a Nobleman and his Sister*, did not appear until 1684, when Behn's career as a dramatist started to wane, perhaps because of a general decline in theatre audiences in the 1680s.

Love Letters draws on the French 'secret history' *nouvelle* and also on the immense popularity of the narrative told in letters, given European currency by the publication of *Lettres portugaises* (*Portuguese Letters*) in 1669. These purported to be love letters written by a nun; they were translated into English in 1678 as *Five Love Letters from a Nun to a Cavalier*, and were also much imitated. *Love Letters* is a work of fiction, but it is closely based upon real events surrounding the scandalous love affair of Lord Grey and his sister-in-law, Henrietta Berkeley. Grey was involved in the Rye House Plot, an attempt to assassinate Charles II and his brother James in order to clear the way for a Protestant succession to the throne via Charles's illegitimate son, the Duke of Monmouth, as opposed to the succession of the Catholic James. In 1685, after James did succeed to the throne, Grey was involved in the rebellion which led to Monmouth's execution.

The first part of *Love Letters* details the affair of Philander (Grey) and Silvia (Henrietta). Behn adroitly combines the political implications of this theme with the voyeuristic pleasures that arise when the reader is granted access to the interior monologue of Silvia in particular. Behn was especially skilled at erotic description and used this skill to the full in *Love Letters*, as this brief example from one of Silvia's letters demonstrates:

> What though I lay extended on my Bed, undrest, unapprehensive of my fate, my Bosom loose and easie of excess [i.e. access], my Garments ready, thin, and wantonly put on, as if they would with little force submit to the fond straying hand: What then *Philander*, must you take the advantage? Must you be perjur'd because I was tempting? (Todd 1993: 68)

The reader's attitude towards Philander is fundamentally ambiguous: like Silvia herself, we are asked to identify with the erotic charge while protesting at its immorality. As she does so often in her plays, Behn examines an intersection between the erotic and the political. In the case of *Love Letters* this occurs through the reader's knowledge that Philander is 'really' Lord Grey, and this encourages us to take the narrative as essentially 'true'. This titillating notion of access to 'true' events becomes a feature of Behn's prose fiction, most notably *Oroonoko*, which is presented as a true story in which Behn herself was involved. In *Love Letters* Philander and Silvia's story closely follows the details of Grey and Henrietta Berkeley, including the ruse of Henrietta marrying Grey's servant in order to protect Grey from charges of abduction and in order to prevent Henrietta from being 'returned' by the law to her father.

The narrative of this first part of *Love Letters* concludes with Philander's arrest on the charge of treason but, as Grey did in June 1683, Philander escapes. The novel was clearly a great success and Behn quickly followed it up with a sequel, entitled *Love Letters From a Nobleman to his Sister Mixed With the History of their Adventures*, published in 1685. This volume continues the story of Grey and Henrietta Berkeley through the time of their exile on the Continent. In its year of publication the Monmouth rebellion took place, the events of which are incorporated into the third part of the novel, published by Behn in 1687. Grey was captain of Monmouth's cavalry and the third part of Behn's novel, entitled *The Amours of Philander and Sylvia*, covers the rebellion in some detail, concluding with the execution of Monmouth (named Cesario in the novel) and a brief ironic reference to Grey's fate – he confessed his part in the Rye House Plot, was pardoned by James, and turned crown witness against his fellow conspirators.

Behn shifts from the epistolary method of the first part to mainly third-person narration in the third part, with the second a mix of the two. The narrative momentum is maintained, not just by the continued weaving in of political and scandalous events surrounding Grey, Henrietta Berkeley and Monmouth, but through an opening out of the narrative scene, away from the internally focused letters of Philander and Silvia towards a larger geographical setting and a broader range of characters. This also involves an increasing use of purely fictional, erotic incidents.

Combined into a single volume, *Love Letters* remained popular well into the eighteenth century. Its success presumably led to Behn's production of a considerable amount of prose fiction, including her best-known work: *Oroonoko: Or, The Royal Slave*, which she published in 1688. I have already noted that *Oroonoko* purports to be a true account (it is subtitled 'a true history'; Todd 1995: 51), based on Behn's time as a young woman in Surinam. Indeed, the narrative begins with repeated assurances to the reader: 'I was my self an Eye-Witness to a great part, of what you will find here set down; and what I cou'd not be Witness of, I receiv'd from the Mouth of the chief Actor in this History' (ibid.: 57). Until recently, scholars spent a great deal of time fruitlessly trying to decide just how much of *Oroonoko* was based upon 'true' events. Margaret Ferguson offers a more productive account of the complex effects of verisimilitude that form part not only of *Oroonoko* but of Behn's self-presentation in general, in connection with an argument that suggests we pay more attention to Behn's constant games with identity and authenticity (see Ferguson 1998). But there is no doubt that Behn's contemporary readers were encouraged by her to read *Oroonoko* as 'true history', especially given details such as her statement that she presented a native Surinam head-dress for use in Dryden's and Howard's play *The Indian Queen* (1664).

However, *Oroonoko* is a particularly layered narrative, and whatever inspiration might lie in Behn's sojourn in Surinam, the text is extremely artful in what might be termed its moral positioning of narrator and reader. The narrative begins in Surinam with an account of an almost Eden-like environment in which the native Indians walk naked and unashamed and live 'in perfect Tranquillity' (Todd 1995: 60) with the English settlers. However, Behn immediately introduces the whole issue of slavery to complicate this colonial situation. The African slaves used on the sugar plantations of Surinam necessitate a shift in the narrative location to Coromantien in Africa, as Behn outlines the origins of the hero of her tale, the valiant Prince Oroonoko, and his love for Imoinda and rivalry with his grandfather, the King, for her possession. The first third of the narrative unfolds this story, which uses a mixture of romance elements and the exotic, oriental tale, both popular Restoration forms. When Oroonoko is tricked into captivity by a slave trader, the narrative returns to Surinam where his relationship with the narrator begins.

As a prince, Oroonoko is carefully positioned by the narrator as wholly different from the other slaves and we are invited to admire him without reservation. He is utterly truthful, as well as brave, and the narrator is at pains to stress his physical attractions: he is jet black, not rusty brown; he has a roman, not African, nose, and a fine mouth, rather than 'those great turn'd Lips, which are so natural to the rest of the Negroes' (ibid.: 63). Therefore, Oroonoko is quite different from his fellow slaves, and he is different from us only in so far as he is wholly admirable and not given to the vices that so-called Christians exhibit: he does not drink and, significantly, he likes the company of women, spending a lot of time with the narrator and her friends. Even more important is Oroonoko's truthfulness: he does not even understand the concept of duplicity (which is why he is so easily tricked into slavery), and he displays true standards of honour, as opposed to the lack of honour displayed by virtually all the white characters.

The story turns to tragedy when Oroonoko is reunited with Imoinda, who has also been taken into slavery. Unable to trust his friends' promises that he will soon be freed, and with Imoinda pregnant, Oroonoko leads the slaves in revolt. He is, during the conflict, tricked into surrendering with the promise of a pardon, and then is severely punished. He escapes again and kills Imoinda to prevent her and their future child being taken back into slavery. The narrative ends with a disturbing, detailed account of Oroonoko's execution after his recapture.

Oroonoko was Behn's most popular work; as well as being reprinted frequently it was adapted into a successful play in 1696 by Thomas Southerne. *Oroonoko* was translated into French in 1745 and frequently reprinted both in France and in England in the eighteenth century, being taken up as an anti-slavery narrative. In fact, Behn condemns not slavery as such, but the inappropriate enslavement of the noble Oroonoko, although Oroonoko's eloquent speech to his fellow slaves in order to inspire them to revolt certainly provides some material for a general polemic against slavery. On a more subtle level, the narrative leads us again and again to condemn the hypocrisy of most of the white characters, who profess to be Christians but who, as the narrator points out, are quite un-Christian in comparison to the highly moral Oroonoko. There are, once again, several layers of identification offered up to the reader. The story is told to us by the narrator, the apparently reliable 'Mrs A. Behn' of the title-page, instantly recognizable to her contemporaries as a famous playwright: for example, she mentions a 'new Comedy' she has written which celebrates the character of Colonel Martin from *Oroonoko* – this was *The Younger Brother*, posthumously performed in 1696. Yet, as she admits in her opening remarks, she was not a witness to some of the most dramatic events in her narrative, including the execution of Oroonoko (this helps to avoid awkward questions about why she did not take more steps to rescue him from his terrible fate).

The narrator's distinctly possessive attitude towards Oroonoko has been tied to her complex negotiation of the relationship between slavery and the position of women, so that Margaret Ferguson is able to read *Oroonoko* as a narrative which complicates the whole issue of identification through Behn's placement of herself 'between' the two slaves, Imoinda and Oroonoko, and between their story and the reader (Ferguson 1991). Because Ferguson is able to combine postcolonial and feminist perspectives, she teases out a number of important tensions within the narrative of *Oroonoko*, most particularly those that stem from Behn's own ambivalent position: she is, as a white woman and a writer, in a more powerful position than Imoinda, but as a writer who was a woman, she has to negotiate a position of (potential) powerlessness within her own culture. Ferguson tries to overcome the critical (and narrative) erasure of Imoinda, while being conscious of the difficulty of 'assuming' a voice for such a representation of 'the silent figure of the black woman' (ibid.: 173). In Ferguson's reading of the text, the narrator is, in a sense, in competition with Imoinda for the possession of Oroonoko, and Behn's narrative involves 'a representation of an economy in which the white woman's book is born, quite starkly, from the death and silencing of black persons, one of them pregnant' (ibid.: 172).

There are other tensions in the narrative, particularly in what we might now call the colonial politics voiced by the narrator. While I have noted the earlier description of the Indians in Surinam as admirable inhabitants of a kind of Eden, later passages complicate this idea by pointing to the extreme violence of the Indian war captains. Links are made between the self-mutilation practised by the Indian war captains and the mutilation of Oroonoko during his execution, as his limbs are cut off and he is emasculated. The bodies of both the Indians and the Africans are seen as both alien and alluring (at a late point in the narrative we are told that Imoinda's body is 'carv'd in fine Flowers and Birds'; Todd 1995: 92), and this accentuates the female narrator's ambivalent relationship to the body of Oroonoko, who is an object of desire but also, at some level, of condescension on the narrator's part.

Given that *Oroonoko* was published in the year of the Glorious Revolution, when the Catholic James II fled England and was replaced by William of Orange and Mary (who arrived in November of 1688), some readers might well have seen political parallels between James and Oroonoko (see Guffey 1975). Given that Behn dedicated *Oroonoko* to the Catholic Richard Maitland, who went into exile with James, and praised him in the dedication as 'so great a Champion for the Catholick Church' (Todd 1995: 55), the narrative could be seen as a political intervention by Behn (although her exact relationship to Catholicism remains unclear). This is also apparent in the way that the narrator expostulates against the English ceding of Surinam to the Dutch by Charles II in 1667. At this late stage in her career, Behn, an ardent royalist, may well have been prepared to offer more direct political comment. *Oroonoko* also allows her to explore some of the tensions (frequently discussed in the prefaces to her plays) occasioned by being a woman writer. The novel's concluding sentence is a telling combination of modesty and self-assertion. Behn starts by suggesting that she is a poor figure to tell a heroic story; a suggestion that takes us all the way back to Margaret Tyler's discussion of the relationship between women and heroic genres and actions. But then Behn proudly draws attention to her reputation as a prominent writer: 'Thus Dyd this Great Man; worthy of a better Fate, and a more sublime Wit than mine to write his Praise; yet, I hope, the Reputation of my Pen is considerable enough to make his Glorious Name to survive to all ages; with that of the Brave, the Beautiful, and the Constant *Imoinda*' (ibid.: 119).

While *Love Letters* and *Oroonoko* are Behn's two most substantial works of prose fiction, she wrote a number of other novels (or novellas) and short stories, most of them published after her death in 1689. In the same year as *Oroonoko* Behn published another novella, *The Fair Jilt*, and *Agnes de Castro*, a translation of a French novel by J. B. de Brillac. These three works were then issued together as *The Three Histories*. *The Fair Jilt* is a very different narrative from *Oroonoko*, except for Behn's repeated assertions (or her narrator's assertions) that the events are true: 'I do not pretend here to entertain you with a feign'd Story, or any thing piec'd together with Romantick Accidents; but every Circumstance, to a Tittle, is Truth' (Todd 1995: 9). *The Fair Jilt* is notable for its powerful and amoral protagonist Miranda, who dissembles and tricks her way through a story of high melodrama, which involves her marriage to a man claiming to be Prince Tarquin, descendant of the kings of Rome. Miranda always acts on her desires (including at one stage of the narrative her desire for a Friar) and allows nothing to stand in her way. She is, in many respects, rather like a modern anti-heroine, escaping any real punishment for her wicked deeds. Miranda constantly forges new identities for herself and in this respect is also rather like an author-figure; it is significant that, unlike Tarquin, who seems completely sincere (his role was apparently suggested to Behn by an account in *The London Gazette* in 1666 that detailed much of the story, including the dramatic failed execution), Miranda is wholly calculating and is even prepared to poison her sister in order to obtain what she wants. The reader is, ultimately, entirely seduced by the heroine's energy and inventiveness; Miranda's imagination, like her author's, allows her to create a series of identities for herself which enable her to escape social constraints. Significantly, at the end of the narrative Miranda has avoided any unfortunate consequences for her deeds and lives happily (and, we are told, perhaps penitently) in Holland, even receiving the admiration of Tarquin's father, who remains oblivious to her true nature.

Two further novellas by Behn were published in 1689: *The Lucky Mistake* and *The History of the Nun*. The latter is a particularly powerful story in the tragic mode; its protagonist Isabella shares with Miranda an inability to resist the force of her desire, but she is a much more straightforwardly sympathetic character. Isabella's fate is seen by Behn as determined by her premature confinement to a convent, which leaves her unprepared for the force of love when it strikes her. She flees from the convent with Henault, the man she loves, but when he is supposedly killed in battle, she marries Villenoys, a man who had courted her before she took her final vows. Henault turns out not to be dead at all, so to avoid disgrace (and a fall from the comforts of her life with Villenoys to the poverty entailed by life with Henault) she kills him. Then, to avoid the eternal reproaches she expects will follow from Villenoys, she kills him as well, by ingeniously sewing the sack containing Henault's body (which Villenoys agrees to dispose of, believing Henault has died of natural causes) to Villenoys' coat, so that he drowns when he throws the sack into the river. The novella ends with Isabella being found out and executed for her crime. This grisly tale is a fine example of Behn's narrative skills, as she is able both to invest Isabella with considerable sympathy, while exploiting the sensationalist aspects of the narrative.

The rest of Behn's prose fiction consists of short stories in a variety of modes, from tragic to racily comic. For example, 'Memoirs of the Court of the King of Bantam' is highly dramatic farce, set out very much like a play (or at least a potential play), written in imitation of the style of the French writer of burlesque fiction, Paul Scarron. 'The Unfortunate Bride', in contrast, is a melodramatic tragedy. All these works were published posthumously in collections of Behn's work, beginning with *The Histories and Novels Written by the Late Ingenious Mrs Behn*, published in 1698, followed by *Histories, Novels and Translations* in 1700. Behn's versatile approach to fiction is in keeping with her general skill as a writer in pretty well all literary modes available in the Restoration, not just drama and poetry but also translation and editing. Whatever style they might adopt, all of Behn's stories have the assurance of a confident, professional writer.

While French fiction by a range of women writers was translated in large quantities during this period, there are only three other examples of Restoration fiction written by women: the work of Catherine Trotter, Mary Pix and Mary Delarivier Manley. All three writers followed Behn's lead in producing plays as well as fiction; indeed, Pix and Trotter wrote only one novel each, though Manley went on in the early eighteenth century to become notorious as a writer of fiction in the 'scandalous history' mode. Catherine Trotter produced an epistolary novel entitled *Olinda's Adventures* when she was fourteen; it is a witty narrative with a rebellious heroine, described as a coquette by Jane Spencer (1986: 144). Mary Pix published *The Inhumane Cardinal* in 1696. The narrative is set at the time of Pope Innocent X and is a sober tale of the deception of a young girl by the amoral Donna Olimpia, who abets Cardinal Antonio Barbarino in his desire for Melora, the daughter of the French ambassador. Melora is tricked into a false marriage with the cardinal and is poisoned when she contrives to escape with the man who truly loves her. The title page of *The Inhumane Cardinal* proclaims that it is 'Written by a Gentlewoman for the entertainment of the sex', but Pix concludes with a severe piece of moralizing about the necessity to be wary of one's fellow women: 'beware the Insinuations of the designing part of your own Sex' (ibid.: 236). In comparison with Behn's amoral heroines like Miranda, Donna Olimpia is a thinly drawn character with little real energy, although Pix is a dexterous plotter, as befits a dramatist.

Mary Delarivier Manley's work, both as fiction writer and dramatist, really belongs to the eighteenth century. In 1696 Manley had her first two plays performed (*The Lost Lover* and *The Royal Mischief*) and published an autobiographical/travel narrative: *Letters Written by Mrs Manley*. But Manley's great success with fiction came in 1709 with the publication of *The New Atalantis*. Indeed, in the early eighteenth century, a number of women writers produced popular works of prose fiction, the most successful being Eliza Haywood, whose *Love in Excess* (1719/20) was a best-seller. Like Behn, Manley and Haywood suffered from being seen as immoral women and from assaults on their reputations, along with their literary endeavours. Prose fiction seems to have been a particularly risky genre for women throughout the early modern period and beyond it, even though another group of early eighteenth-century women wrote novels specifically designed to be didactic and moral, notably Penelope Aubin, Elizabeth Rowe and Jane Barker (see Ballaster 1992: 32–3).

Looking back over the prose fiction written by women between 1550 and 1700, it is hard to trace specific developments because comparatively few women worked in the genre. What is notable is that the three women who made major contributions to early modern prose fiction were remarkable for their achievements across genres. Between them, Mary Wroth, Margaret Cavendish and Aphra Behn wrote an enormous amount in every literary (and in Cavendish's case, non-literary) mode. In the area of prose fiction, each was a spectacular innovator: Wroth shifted the form of romance to accommodate the lives of her contemporaries and her family and to address the issue of gender; Cavendish married the utopian genre to her scientific writing in *The Blazing World*, and experimented with a wide range of short stories; Behn wrote fiction late in her literary career and produced a diverse range of novellas and short stories. Women therefore may only have written a small percentage of the total amount of early modern fiction, but this triumvirate elevates women's achievement in the form well above the average.

See also MARY WROTH, *THE COUNTESS OF MONTGOMERY'S URANIA*; MARGARET CAVENDISH, *A TRUE RELATION OF MY BIRTH, BREEDING AND LIFE*; APHRA BEHN, *THE ROVER, PART ONE*

REFERENCES AND FURTHER READING

Ballaster, R. (1992). *Seductive Forms: Women's Amatory Fiction from 1684 to 1740*. Oxford: Clarendon Press.

Cavendish, M. (1992). *The Blazing World and Other Writings*, ed. K. Lilley. London: Penguin Books.

Ferguson, M. (1991). 'Juggling the categories of race, class and gender: Aphra Behn's *Oroonoko*.' *Women's Studies*, 19, 159–81.

——(1998). 'The authorial ciphers of Aphra Behn.' In S. N. Zwicker (ed.), *English Literature 1650–1740* (pp. 225–49). Cambridge: Cambridge University Press.

Guffey, G. (1975). 'Aphra Behn's *Oroonoko*: occasion and accomplishment.' In G. Guffey and A. Wright, *Two English Novelists* (pp. 3–41). Los Angeles: W. A. Clark Memorial Library.

Hobby, E. A. (1988). *Virtue of Necessity: English Women's Writing 1649–1688*. London: Virago.

Kahn, V. (1997). 'Margaret Cavendish and the romance of contract.' *Renaissance Quarterly*, 50, 526–66.

Krontiris, T. (1992). *Oppositional Voices: Women as Writers and Translators of Literature in the English Renaissance*. London: Routledge.

Martin, R. (ed.) (1997). *Women Writers in Renaissance England*. London: Longman.

Salzman, P. J. (1985). *English Prose Fiction 1558–1700: A Critical History*. Oxford: Clarendon Press.

Spencer, J. (1986). *The Rise of the Woman Novelist*. Oxford: Blackwell Publishers.

Todd, J. (1993). *The Works of Aphra Behn*, vol. 2. London: William Pickering.

——(1995). *The Works of Aphra Behn*, vol. 3. London: William Pickering.

Weamys, A. (1994). *A Continuation of Sir Philip Sidney's Arcadia*, ed. P. C. Cullen. New York: Oxford University Press.

21

Drama

Sophie Tomlinson

The last two decades of the twentieth century saw an explosion of interest in the early modern female dramatist. The publication of biographies, anthologies of plays and scholarly editions of individual texts allowed a reconsideration of particular authors as something more than literary curiosities, and constituted new fields of study and research. Moreover, this excavation work has been accompanied by efforts to revive the plays written by early modern women as vehicles for performance, both within the professional theatre and the academy.

One result of this focusing of attention on plays by women is the rethinking of the canon of Renaissance and seventeenth-century drama. Students familiar with the work of Shakespeare, Marlowe and Jonson know that these authors wrote plays which were performed in the Elizabethan public theatres, at court and at the universities. The plays of these male dramatists were published only after their performance; in Shakespeare's case, though individual plays were published in quarto form, his drama was not collected in print until 1623, seven years after his death, when his fellow actors John Heminges and Henry Condell published 36 of his plays in the First Folio.

There is no equivalent to the Elizabethan professional playwright among the women who wrote in dramatic genres before 1670. Rather than conforming to the sequence of performance followed by publication, the dramatic writing of Renaissance women inverts this pattern: Mary Sidney, Countess of Pembroke and Elizabeth Cary, Lady Falkland both published their plays as literature, rather than as texts conceived for performance. In publishing drama, these aristocratic women were participating in a coterie literary culture which flourished quite apart from the commercial theatres. Women wrote drama intended for both reading and performance within their families, or within circles defined by kinship and political alliances. So did many male writers, like Sir Philip Sidney, Samuel Daniel and John Milton. Such writing comprises an integral part of the history of drama irrespective of whether it was performed on the public stage.

The political ferment of the English Civil War had important consequences for women's relationship to dramatic discourses. The 18-year closure of the professional theatres meant that amateur enthusiasts were able to make a virtue of necessity with regard to both the performance and composition of drama. In the 1640s the Cavendish sisters wrote a comedy and a pastoral which they presented in a manuscript volume to their father William Cavendish, Earl, and later Duke of Newcastle, one of a new breed of 'Periwig Poets' and a patron of professional writers such as Jonson and James Shirley. Cavendish also fostered the interest in drama of his young wife, Margaret Lucas, whom he married in exile in Paris in 1645. This literary marriage inspired, among diverse publications by Margaret Cavendish, two books of closet dramas, totalling 19 plays, published in 1662 and 1668.

Both Katherine Philips, who translated two plays by the French dramatist Corneille in the 1660s, and Margaret Cavendish were poised on the cusp of a new theatrical organization. In 1660 the Stuart monarchy was re-established in England in the person of Charles II; in the same year two theatre companies were formed in London: the Duke's, under the management of Sir William Davenant, and the King's, under Thomas Killigrew. One of the 'improvements' of the Restoration playhouses sanctioned by the King's patents was the presence of actresses. In his autobiography the actor–playwright Colley Cibber depicts the advent of women on the public stage as a watershed, both in terms of audience attendance and the theatrical representation of women:

> The other Advantage I was speaking of, is, that before the Restoration, no Actresses had ever been seen upon the *English* Stage. The Characters of Women, on former Theatres, were perform'd by Boys, or young Men of the most effeminate Aspect. And what Grace, or Master-strokes of Action can we conceive such ungain Hoydens to have been capable of? This Defect was so well consider'd by *Shakespear*, that in few of his Plays, he has any greater dependance upon the Ladies, than in the Innocence or Simplicity of a *Desdemona*, an *Ophelia*, or in the short Specimen of a fond and virtuous *Portia*. The additional Objects then of real, beautiful Women, could not but draw a proportion of new Admirers to the Theatre. (Cibber 1987: 55)

In fact the sexualized commercial theatre described by Cibber was only one mode of performance in which women participated in mid-seventeenth century England. Both Philips and Cavendish were strongly influenced by the female-oriented royalist culture of the 1630s and 1640s, in which the French Queen Henrietta Maria fostered a tradition of female theatricals. Their writing both emanates from and reflects the new possibilities for women created by an elite court culture which valorized the notion of women's ethical and political voice (Tomlinson 1999).

Not until towards the end of our period do women write drama deliberately designed for professional production. Between 1670 and 1689 Aphra Behn, the 'shee spy' turned female wit, had 19 plays produced on the London stage. One of the by-products of Behn's career was the forging of a public space for the professional woman of letters (Todd 1996b: 4–7). This image of Behn has coloured our view of her as an early feminist writer; in the eyes of Virginia Woolf, Behn earned 'all women' the right 'to speak their minds' (Woolf 1982: 63). Behn's career is perhaps better seen as testimony to her efforts to stay afloat in the commercial worlds of theatre and publishing; rather than consciously setting out to give women a voice, she wrote to make money, mining earlier drama, adapting found materials. Nonetheless, Behn's political partisanship (she was an ardent Tory), her criticism of women's entrapment within marriage, her lively stagecraft and exploitation of theatrical sensuality give her work a compelling immediacy to modern audiences and readers.

This essay will discuss the ways in which drama by early modern women approaches the issues of female voicing and agency, focusing in particular on the language of desire and representations of marriage. It will highlight the literary and theatrical contexts which informed and produced women's dramatic writing. I begin by addressing the range of plays produced under the rubric of tragedy in the period, much of which takes the form of translations; this is followed by a section on forms of comic drama. The essay concludes with a section on Aphra Behn, and the work produced by the second wave of female wits inspired by her example who wrote for the stage in the 1690s.

Translations and Tragedies: 1550–1668

An urge for glory and greatness on the part of the female tragic protagonist characterizes the earliest play in our period, a manuscript translation of Euripides' tragedy *Iphigeneia at Aulis* by Jane, Lady Lumley, written during the mid-1550s. Lumley's play exhibits her knowledge of Erasmus's Latin translation of Euripides' work, and was dedicated to her father, the Earl of Arundel, who paid for her expensive classical education. In the course of the play Iphigeneia comes to accept her destiny, to be sacrificed to the goddess Diana to ensure fair winds for the Grecian fleet on their journey to Troy. Her death thus becomes the means to avenge the Trojans' theft of Helen, a virginal sacrifice righting the disruption of a dynastic marriage. Iphigeneia recognizes that her use value extends beyond her family; she was born not solely for the good of her parents, but 'for the commodite of my countrie', for the state (Purkiss 1998: ll. 808–10). Although she laments her fate, Iphigeneia takes pride in the fact that she will 'save all grece with my deathe' (l. 838). Her resilience wins admiration from the Greek hero, Achilles, who declares, 'Trulie I wonder gretelie at the bouldenes of your minde' (l. 840).

Iphigeneia's heroism emerges as a kind of exceptional maturity, a maturity which encompasses pathos in her wish to heal the fractured relationship of her parents, Agamemnon and Clytemnestra. When Clytemnestra expresses anger at Agamemnon's actions, Iphigeneia's response shows her concern for the propriety of her mother's behaviour: 'Take hede I praye you lest you happen to do that which shall not become you' (ll. 880–1)

Approaching the diversity of texts written under the aegis of drama in the early modern period requires not only that we dispense with the critical privileging of plays intended for public performance, but also that we expand our notion of what constitutes a play by taking on board contemporary conceptions of drama. The spare prose of Lumley's translation (she omitted the lyric odes spoken by Euripides' Chorus) reflects the sixteenth-century view of drama as a source of *sententiae*, or memorable moral maxims.

This overt moralism similarly informs Mary Sidney's *Antonie* (1590, published 1592), a translation of Robert Garnier's neo-classical tragedy *Marc Antoine* (1578). In this version of the story the relationship of the lovers Antony and Cleopatra is scarcely dramatized for the reader. Prior to Cleopatra's embracing of Antony's body in the fifth act, the two characters never meet. The play begins after Antony's cataclysmic loss of the Battle of Actium; rather than unfolding action, successive acts present a series of monologues and duologues voicing the attitudes of various characters to this key event. This approach appears flatly undramatic when compared to the sizzling, erotic liaison which forms the substance of Shakespeare's tragedy, written 16 years later. In the continental genre of historical tragedy which Sidney was promoting, dramatic interaction is subordinated to individual character, and the weight of poeticized plaint and lamentation drives home the moral significance of rulers succumbing to Love's 'firebrand' (Purkiss 1998: Act 2, l. 457), with its disastrous consequences for the stability of the Roman and Egyptian realms.

Repudiating dramatic representation, neo-classical drama conveyed action through reported narrative, employing vivid descriptive writing. One potent example is Dircetus's account of Cleopatra's effortful heaving up of Antony to her monument. This description of the queen's bravery and devotion derives from Plutarch's *Life of Antony* (translated into English by Sir Thomas North in 1579), but in the dramatic text, it is presented as an action watched by the crowd like a play.

> So pitifull a sight was never seene.
> . . .
> The miserable ladie with moist eies,
> With haire which careles on hir forehead hong,
> With brest which blowes had bloudily benumb'd,
> With stooping head, and body down-ward bent,
> Enlast hir in the corde, and with all force
> This life-dead man couragiously uprais'd.
> The bloud with paine into hir face did flowe,
> Hir sinewes stiff, her selfe did breathles grow.
> The people which beneath in flocks beheld,

Assisted her with gesture, speech, desire:
Cride and incourag'd her, and in their soules
Did sweate, and labor, no whit lesse then she,
Who never tir'd in labor, held so long
Help by her women, and hir constant heart,
That *Antony* was drawne into the tombe.

(Act 4, ll. 290–312)

Here the empathizing crowd functions like an inset audience, assisting the reader who must 'suppose' the action of the play ('The Argument', line 29). The description pits Cleopatra's femininity against her constancy and courage, facets of her character which are elsewhere undermined through the play's stress upon her weakness, her fearfulness and her physical vulnerability – when her children bid her farewell in Act 5, Cleopatra faints with grief.

The play's strong demarcation of gender roles circumscribes Cleopatra's heroic identity, bearing out the masculine focus of the title. In part, *Antonie* functions as an example of the negative effects of headstrong female passion. Like the shrewish wife Adriana in Shakespeare's contemporaneous *The Comedy of Errors* (c. 1590), Cleopatra acknowledges the destructiveness of her 'burning jealousie' (Act 2, l. 228) which made her insist on accompanying Antony to battle. She accepts full responsibility for Antony's tragic fall: 'I am sole cause' (Act 2, l. 212). This didacticism is accompanied by a positive stress on Cleopatra's 'wifely faithfulness' (Cerasano and Wynne-Davies 1996: 17). Rather than choosing death as an assertion of her own identity, Cleopatra justifies her wish to follow Antony to death in terms of a seemly conjugal virtue, declaring of him, 'he is my selfe' (Act 2, l. 352). Her absorption in Antony's identity foreshadows the Miltonic ideal of marriage, 'she for God in him'. At the end of the play, Cleopatra achieves her wish to be buried in 'one selfe tombe' (Act 5, l. 175) with Antony, an erotic imaging of death as marriage.

Cleopatra's refusal to pursue her own 'selfe-succour' (Act 2, l. 505) marks her out as a model of political and connubial loyalty, even though she is not legally married to Antony. In this respect she forms a striking contrast to the protagonist of Elizabeth Cary's *Tragedie of Mariam* (1613) who is not content to rest a mere 'propertie' of her husband, King Herod (Purkiss 1998: 1.6.148). Mariam is characterized as a Faustian figure by the Chorus who describe her as a woman of 'vast imaginations' (1.6.147). The play offers a prismatic view of its heroine: she is spoken of as both 'matchles' (5.1.172) and 'high-hearted' (2.3.39). Cary's play debates the question: what is a wife's 'proper selfe'? (3.3.103); does it exist beyond her relationship to her husband?

The action of the play turns on Mariam's inability to conceal her resentment of Herod's murders of her father and grandfather, by means of which he has secured the throne of Judea. Mariam prides herself on her transparency; her inability to dissemble her discontent at Herod's behaviour:

> I know I could inchaine him with a smile:
> And lead him captive with a gentle word,
> I scorne my looke should ever man beguile,
> Or other speech, then meaning to afford.
>
> (3.3.46–9)

Mariam's refusal to employ feminine charm to placate her husband leads to her downfall; Herod orders her execution, falsely led by his sister Salome into a belief that Mariam is unfaithful. Rather than the play endorsing Mariam's resistance to Herod's will, the heroine instead becomes a site 'upon which the value and nature of constancy is debated' (Straznicky 1994: 120). Mariam comes to accept the notion that she is 'by her selfe undone' (3.3.31), and that her 'unbridled speech' (3.3.66) has impacted negatively upon her public image. However, the play's ending, in which the report of Mariam's composure at her execution drives Herod into a frenzy of remorse, retrieves a space for female will; as Straznicky proposes, *The Tragedie of Mariam* reappropriates for the disempowered female the political power of stoic heroism as an effective means of redress' (Straznicky 1994: 124).

The concept of stoicism forms a link between the early closet drama written by Renaissance noblewomen and Katherine Philips's *Pompey* (1663), the first of her two neo-classical tragedies translated from Pierre Corneille. *Pompey* was performed at the new Smock Alley Theatre in Dublin in 1663 before a coterie royalist audience; it was the first heroic play written in rhymed couplets produced on the British stage. Although Philips's family and husband were both Puritan, the friendships she made at the school she attended in London drew her into a cavalier literary milieu. After the English Civil Wars, the beheading of the king and the unsettled period of republican government, Corneille's play glorifying Pompey's death and dramatizing the political cunning of Ptolomy, Caesar and Cleopatra was bound to appeal to a young woman who was an enthusiastic convert to royalism, but whose marriage to Colonel James Philips, a member of parliament for Cardigan in Wales, brought her in touch with the everyday realities of political strife and rebellion. *Pompey* offered Philips the opportunity to debate the virtues of friendship, clemency and reconciliation, notions with strong political resonances in the wake of the Civil Wars and the Restoration. Corneille's elevated portrayal of Cleopatra and Pompey's widow, Cornelia, is a further source of his play's attractiveness to Philips.

Philips's depiction of Cleopatra, and her relationship with Caesar, Pompey's conqueror, draws upon the discourse of neo-Platonic love and the dramatic tradition of the *femme forte* or heroic woman (Maclean 1977). Cleopatra's love for Caesar is inseparable from her ambition to ascend the Egyptian throne usurped by her brother Ptolomy. Her aspiration to be 'the Mistress of the World' is justified by her as a 'Noble Passion', in keeping with her sublime love for Caesar (Thomas 1993: 2.1.76, 83). The monumentalizing aspect of Philips's characterization holds in delicate check the 'shadow of uncertainty' (Carlin 1998: 84) which accrues from Cleopatra's formidable exercise of her political will.

Corneille's drama is centrally concerned with the competing claims of love and honour, nature and reason, private passion and public duty. The self-division to which such tensions give rise animates the figure of Cornelia, who, while she burns to avenge Pompey's murder at the hands of Ptolomy, is compelled to acknowledge Caesar's magnanimity as a Roman victor. Cornelia's 'Romanness' functions simultaneously as an inspirational source of her identity and a constraint upon it; for the duration of the play she must bridle her hatred and deal civilly with the man whom she describes as her 'obliging Enemy' (5.4.10). In Philips's translation 'Romanness' is a quality which unites Caesar and Cornelia across genders, signifying courage and stoical constancy: 'But as a Roman, though my Hate be such, / I must confess, I thee esteem as much' (5.4.68–9). The intensity of Cornelia's conflict spoke powerfully to Philips's female audience; her courage and eloquence are singled out for special praise in the poem addressed 'To the Excellent *Orinda*', written in a female voice and signed by 'Philo-Philippa' or 'the admirer of Philips' (Thomas 1993: ll. 99–104, 125–36).

While Philips's first play received a professional production, it was definitely aimed at a limited public. Philips asked her mentor Sir Charles Cotterell to present copies of the printed *Pompey* to the Duchess of York and King Charles II, 'if you think the King would allow such a Trifle a Place in his closet' (Thomas 1992: 77). Like John Milton in his *Paradise Lost*, Philips was concerned to find 'fit audience . . . though few' for her dramatic translations.

Comic Forms 1620–1671

Broadly conceived, tragic drama by early women writers depicts a tension between women's relationship to the public sphere – the realm of heroic action – and their private, domestic obligations. As a genre concerned with social and sexual relationships, most often in relation to marriage, comedy allows a greater focus on female subjectivity and agency. This section begins with a discussion of two comedies written by aristocratic women in the first half of the seventeenth century: Lady Mary Wroth's pastoral tragicomedy *Love's Victory* (*c.* 1620) and *The Concealed Fancies*, a comedy co-authored by the sisters Lady Jane Cavendish and Lady Elizabeth Brackley (*c.* 1645). Neither of these plays was printed, and each seems intended for an audience who would recognize the autobiographical basis of the plays' characters and relationships (Cerasano and Wynne-Davies 1996: 93–94, 127–30). The plays share a concern with women's experience of love, and the regulation of female desire by the ideology of modesty. Each play approaches this theme in a subtly different manner, a difference I will argue derives both from generic affiliation and shifting cultural fashions.

In Wroth's tragicomedy *Love's Victory*, women occupy 'erotically passive roles' (Cerasano and Wynne-Davies 1998: 241). The heroine Musella feels incapable of expressing her love to the man she desires, Philisses. She declares to her friend Silvesta, a follower of Diana,

> Sometimes I fain would speak, then straight forbear,
> Knowing it most unfitt; thus woe I beare.
>
> SILVESTA
> Indeed a woman to make love is ill.
>   (Cerasano and Wynne-Davies 1996: 3.1.77–9)

The emotional muteness of Wroth's female characters contrasts strongly with the power exerted over the action by the goddess of love, Venus, and her son Cupid. At the start, Venus expresses her displeasure at the waning respect granted her heavenly power by mortals, and she instructs Cupid to 'shun no great cross' (1.1.19) which will breed distress for humans in love. Even without Cupid's interference the characters must contend with significant obstacles to their desire. Chief among these is the destructive parental control exercised by Musella's mother, who insists that her daughter marry the wealthy Rustic, a buffoon insensible to poetry.

Musella's predicament precipitates the play's potentially tragic climax, in which, at her suggestion, she and Philisses go to the temple to make a sacrifice to love. Their voluntary deaths are prevented by the intervention of Silvesta, who, like the Friar in Shakespeare's *Romeo and Juliet*, gives the lovers a potion which only puts them to sleep. Silvesta acts as both 'friend and priest' (5.4.21) by providing the lovers with the apparent 'means to wed [them] to [their] grave[s]' (5.4.58). Musella's and Philisses's willingness to die proves them victors in Venus's trial of their faith; in the final scene they miraculously arise from the altar on which they have been laid for dead, a 'deed' Venus claims to have orchestrated using Silvesta as her 'instrument' (5.7.67, 71). As Rustic has willingly resigned his claim to Musella, she and Philisses are free to marry.

This benign resolution is undoubtedly part of what Barbara Kiefer Lewalski terms, with reference to Wroth's play, 'the idealizing ethos of pastoral' (Lewalski 1993: 307). Wroth's comedy valorizes female agency and autonomy in the figure of Silvesta, whose experience of unrequited love has prompted her commitment to a life of chastity and solitude. Moreover, the play celebrates female amity and generosity in both Silvesta and Musella, who minister unstintingly to their male and female friends. In these respects we may interpret Wroth's play as revealing 'a feminine consciousness at work within seventeenth-century literary and social conventions' (Swift 1989: 173–4).

Wroth's 'feminine consciousness' also reveals the disabling influence upon women of the social convention of dissembling. The obligation for women to play the coy maiden is articulated by the wordly-wise Dalina, who advises, 'rather than too soon

won, be too precise' (3.2.164). In the tryste between Musella and Philisses, facilitated
by Silvesta, the problems women face in communicating authentic feeling are dramatized through a discussion of blushing.

The possibility of Musella blushing is raised by Rustic's arrival on the scene,
a potential witness to the love that Musella and Philisses have privately declared.
Musella wishes Rustic were absent:

> For though that he, poor thing, can little find,
> Yet I shall blush with knowing my own mind.
> Fear and desire, still to keep it hid,
> Will blushing show it when 'tis most forbid.
>   (4.1.125–8)

Musella attributes her anticipated blush to a combination of factors: firstly, her preference for Philisses over Rustic, a knowledge which encompasses sexual desire; secondly, her 'fear' or anxiety about whether her blushing cheeks will betray her desire
to Rustic. While Musella links her body's response to her psychological confusion,
Philisses locates the source of the blush in the body's experience of *jouissance*: 'kind
desire makes you blushing know / That joy takes place, and in your face doth climb /
With leaping hart like lambkins in the prime' (4.1.132–4).

This exchange pinpoints the repressive effect of the Renaissance prohibition upon
women displaying sexual feeling or passion; significantly, it is Philisses who speaks
ingenuously of sexual desire, while Musella expresses that knowledge only in terms
of what is forbidden to women. The trauma that attends the disclosure of female
desire, figured here by Musella's blush, also fuels Wroth's most significant literary
achievement, the sonnet sequence *Pamphilia to Amphilanthus*, appended to her
published prose romance *The Countess of Montgomery's Urania* (1621). The buoyancy
and humour of Wroth's pastoral, with its interludes of song and poetry, offer a respite
from the emotional anguish mapped in the sonnets of the female poet and lover,
Pamphilia.

As its title suggests, the necessity of women dissembling their affection provides
the *raison d'être* for the Cavendish sisters' comedy *The Concealed Fancies*. While Wroth's
comedy suggests the destructive impact of this social convention, this play reveals its
authors' complicity with the notion of femininity as theatrical, representing acting as
a vital strategy in the negotiation of both courtship and marriage (Tomlinson 1999:
74–7).

The embracing of female self-fashioning in *The Concealed Fancies* shows a positive
engagement with the idea of mimesis, and women's histrionic capacity. At one point,
the authors use Cleopatra as a heroic exemplar for their besieged female characters to
imitate:

> I practised [acted] Cleopatra when she was in her captivity, and could they have thought
> me worthy to have adorned their Triumphs I would have performed his [her?] gallant

Tragedy, and so have made myself glorious for time to come. (Cerasano and Wynne-
Davies 1996: 3.4.13–18)

This aspect of the play may be linked to the growing recognition of the art of female
acting discernible in the Caroline drama of Jonson and Shirley, to whom the Duke of
Newcastle acted as patron.

The image of the assertive woman wooer provides a source of comedy in both
Wroth's and the Cavendishes' plays. In Restoration comedy the extrovert 'madcap'
heroine who makes no attempt to disguise her desire for the hero was developed by
dramatists as a response to the wit and élan of the actress Nell Gwynn. What was
judged 'Impudencie' by Cary's and Wroth's generation was rendered titillating and
delightful through changing theatrical conventions, specifically the presence on stage
of a woman who was a match for male wit.

This cultural shift allows us to gauge the innovativeness of Margaret Cavendish,
who as early as 1662 confronts head-on the ideology of feminine modesty which
remained a key element of professional drama. Between 1653 and 1671 Cavendish
sought to create a lasting image of herself through the medium of print. Her
substantial output included two volumes of drama, the bulk of which are comedies,
Playes (1662) and *Plays, Never before Printed* (1668). Cavendish's literary career was
driven by an intense desire for poetic genius and a determination to build, through
her published writings, 'a *Pyramid* of *Fame*' (Greer et al. 1988: 165). She believed
strongly in the educative function of the dramatic poet, whom, like Sir Philip Sidney,
she saw as a divine figure. At the same time, she was sensitive to the limitations
imposed on her writing by her lack of serious education; many of her plays show the
liberating possibilities of women acquiring 'Language [and] Learning' beyond 'what
is native and naturall' (Shaver 1999: 270).

Although they were published during the first decade of the Restoration, most of
Cavendish's plays were written while she and her husband were living in exile in
Holland during the Interregnum (1642–60) when England's public theatres were officially closed. Conceived in what she calls her 'Fancy-Stage', Cavendish's plays were
intended to be recreated in the mind of the reader, either silently or through reading
aloud. While forming a link with the earlier tradition of closet drama discussed above,
Cavendish's choice of genre has an added political valence. As Straznicky writes, 'the
proliferation of closet drama during the Commonwealth is . . . part of an emerging
cultural practice of play-reading which was, for author and reader alike, an act of
political opposition' (Straznicky 1995: 357).

Such opposition might take the form of arguments about modes of speech and
action deemed unacceptable by the Puritan authorities, such as female theatrical
performance. Paradoxically, the closet drama form allowed Cavendish to fantasize a
specific relationship to the public stage, and by extension, to the public arena of social
discourse (Tomlinson 1998). In her play *Natures Three Daughters, Beauty, Love, and Wit*
(1662), Mademoiselle Amor challenges the social convention of feminine coyness by

expressing her desire to the man she loves. She spurns the ancient custom of dissembling for what she calls 'Modern Truth', determining to 'break down Customs Walls' by initiating the courtship (Cavendish 1662: 504). Unusually, Cavendish allots the epilogue to this same character, renamed Lady True-Love, and makes her appeal directly to the audience for sanction:

> O how my heart doth ake when think I do,
> How I a modest Maid a man did woo!
> To be so confident to woo him here,
> Upon the publick Stage to every Ear;
> Men sure will censure me for mad . . .
>
> (527)

In the remainder of the epilogue Lady True-Love proclaims the success of her suit and justifies her representation of the 'wooing part', pleading: 'If you approve my Act pray give't a voice!' Here, actress and female character are compacted in seeking approval of their indiscreet 'action'. The slippage between the public theatre and the theatre of the world produces a stage of subjectivity in which acting functions to authenticate female identity. Moreover, Cavendish effects a shift in sexual ideology; Lady True-Love's wooing may appear 'like a bold immodesty', but she analyses this response to her frankness as a masculine misapprehension. This particular instance of custom-breaking forms a striking contrast with the Cavendish sisters' comedy, where concealing one's fancy distinguishes the sophisticated heroines.

Cavendish escaped many of the constraints imposed upon early modern women by their gender through her happy marriage to a dilettante poet, William Cavendish, and the fact that she remained childless. Her exceptional situation is illustrated by the opinion of one of her characters, Mademoiselle Grand Esprit, who justifies a single life on the grounds that 'marriage is the grave or tomb of Wit' (*Natures Three Daughters*, in Cavendish 1662: 525). This conviction accounts for Cavendish's investigation of female communities in plays such as *The Female Academy* (1662) and *The Convent of Pleasure* (1668). Other plays juxtapose a fast set of gallants and amorous ladies with sober couples drawn together by their inclination to the life of the mind. Her favourable contrasting of a stoical with a libertine lifestyle, associated with the court, distances her drama from the new style of Restoration stage comedy being developed from the mid-1660s, although one of her late plays, *The Sociable Companions, or the Female Wits* (1668), shows a marked affiliation with Restoration drama.

The Sociable Companions has elements in common with Elizabeth Polwhele's *The Frolicks, or The Lawyer Cheated* (1671). While there is no evidence that Polwhele's comedy was ever performed, it was clearly designed for the stage. An old-fashioned tragedy by Polwhele, *The Faithful Virgins*, was acted by the Duke's Company sometime close to 1670. In the Dedication to *The Frolicks*, addressed to Prince Rupert, Polwhele declares: 'I question not but I shall be taxed for writing a play so comical, but those that have ever seen my *Faithful Virgins* and my *Elysium* will justify me a little for writing this' (Milhous and Hume 1977: 57–8).

Like Cavendish, Polwhele claims to write 'by nature, not by art' (ibid.: 58). Her play is made up of rotating plotlines, culminating in a masque which facilitates the stolen marriages of three couples. The heroine Clarabell, attracted to the rake Rightwit, adopts a brisk, no-nonsense approach to the onset of love: 'I'll in, and study how to forget him. If 'twill not be, I'll study how to get him' (2.207–9). Clarabell's gutsy display of initiative is what marks her out as belonging to the new brand of Restoration heroine. She frees Rightwit from prison by impersonating a Puritan Sister to dupe the jailer, earning the admiration of the men: 'A brave wench! She would make an admirable comedian' (4.427–8). Polwhele celebrates her heroine's acting ability; her theatrical impersonation is a less refined form of deceit than the taut, emotional self-concealment practised by later Restoration heroines such as Etherege's Harriet in *The Man of Mode* (1676).

Aphra Behn and the Contestation of Pleasure

> Poets, like States-men, with a little change,
> Pass off old Politicks for new and strange.
> (Prologue to *The Second Part of The Rover*, 1681)

Aphra Behn's success as a playwright hinged upon her shrewd recognition of the entrepreneurial nature of the Restoration theatre. The fact that Behn wrote a sequel to her most popular comedy *The Rover, or The Banished Cavaliers* (1677) indicates the extent to which she was guided by the barometer of audience opinion. Capitalizing upon a current taste for physical comedy typical of the Italian *commedia dell'arte*, she incorporated the character Harlequin into *The Rover* II, and drew upon the Earl of Rochester's exploits as a mountebank to provide a platform for her hero Willmore to demonstrate his delight in performance. Behn also created parts for particular actors, such as the tragedienne Elizabeth Barry, for whom she wrote a series of roles (including the courtesan La Nuche in *The Rover* II) utilizing Barry's capacity for emotive, tempestuous acting.

Feminist criticism of Behn's drama sometimes overlooks what Dawn Lewcock describes as her 'unusually acute feel for the visual opportunities the stage offered to enhance story-telling' (Todd 1996a: 68). More than any female dramatist I have discussed so far, Behn's plays exhibit a three-dimensional theatrical intelligence, fully attuned to the new spatial and visual possibilities of the Restoration theatre. Behn's stagecraft is evident in her use of the two doors on the proscenium stage for exits and entrances, her manipulation of the scenic stage in discovery scenes, and her clever choreographing of action which takes place in simulated darkness.

Her relish for pure theatre finds its fullest expression in *The Emperor of the Moon* (1687), a mixture of satire, spectacle and hilarious farce. Behn's interest in the new science of astronomy, and its offshoot in fantastical voyage literature, informs the plot in which two gallants, Cinthio and Charmante, impersonate the eponymous Emperor and the Prince of Thunderland to woo and win the daughter and niece of the credulous Doctor Baliardo, who has been seduced into a belief in extra-terrestrial life by his reading in natural philosophy. The gallants' courtship of the women is paralleled by the antics of Harlequin and Scaramouche, played by the English comedians Anthony Leigh and Thomas Jevon, as they contend for the hand of Mopsophil, the girls' governess. The piece culminates in a scene which exploits to the full the technical resources of the Dorset Garden Theatre (Spencer 1995: xix). It features a moving zodiac, whose descent is viewed through 'perspectives' or telescopes by the astronomers Galileus and Kepler, earthly interpreters for the Emperor and the Prince. The scene's blend of music, dance, scenic illusion and stage machinery shows Behn's mastery of a theatrical tradition which began much earlier in the century with the Stuart court masques designed by Inigo Jones. However, rather than promoting an idealized vision, Behn's stagecraft exposes Baliardo's absorption in recondite nonsense, and thoroughly undermines his rebuking of his daughter's 'female ignorance' (Spencer 1995: 3.3.10).

Behn's ability to stage the power of erotic attraction made her plays a hot commodity on the Restoration stage. The introduction of women actors made the theme of sexual relationships newly immediate; Behn's particular innovation in her comedies was to amplify and elaborate sexual tension between men and women as a source of theatrical pleasure. For example, in Act 2, scene 2 of *The Rover* I, Behn makes brilliant use of physical gesture and vocal inflection to involve the audience in the passion of the situation. Midway through his railing at the Italian courtesan Angellica Bianca, Willmore pauses to contemplate Angellica's beauty:

> Nay, I will gaze, to let you see my strength.
> *Holds her, looks on her, and pauses and sighs*
> By heaven, bright creature, I would not for the world
> Thy fame were half so fair as is thy face.
> *Turns her away from him*
>
> ANGELLICA (*aside*)
> His words go through me to the very soul.
>
> (2.2.71–4)

As audience, we participate vicariously in Angellica's seduction, yet we are also distanced from it through the onlooking presence of Moretta, Angellica's bawd. Like a female intelligencer, Moretta observes the situation and provides a rational analysis, describing Willmore as a sexual plunderer, 'a no-purchase, no-pay tatter-demalion, and English picaroon' (2.2.161–2). Moretta's realistic, feminist voice pinpoints women's susceptibility to men's romantic acting. Her bitter cursing is a dissonant voice in Behn's comedy, which matches its cavalier hero not to the vulnerable Angellica, but to the tough-minded Hellena, one of whose attractions is her fortune of 300,000 crowns. The comic ending of *The Rover* celebrates the cavalier image of swashbuckling masculinity; indeed, Behn assimilates her heroine to this image, for Hellena ends the play in male garb and is addressed as 'my little rover' (5.1.555).

Jaqueline Pearson (1988: 16) describes Behn's later plays as characterized by a darkening vision 'of society and especially of the options available for women'. The late comedy *The Lucky Chance* (1686) is a striking representation of the ambivalence attending women's life-choices in Behn's society, an ambivalence exacerbated by Behn's alteration of her dramatic source.

The Lucky Chance adapts a plotline from a Caroline comedy, *The Lady of Pleasure* (1635) by James Shirley. Shirley's text delineates what appears a clear moral division between one honourable lady of pleasure, the young widow Celestina, who tests a lord by pretending to be willing to sleep with him, and the lewdly named Aretina Bornwell, who pursues an adulterous affair with a minor courtier. Behn draws upon aspects of both women in constructing the more dominant of her two heroines, Julia Fulbank, unhappily married to a greedy, old City merchant. The opaque aspect of the plot centres upon Julia's relationship with her lover Gayman, who enters the play intent upon cuckolding Sir Cautious Fulbank. The 'lucky chance' of the title allows Gayman to accomplish his desire when he wins at dice against Sir Cautious, who stakes a night of pleasure with his wife against Gayman's £300.

In a reversal of the Shakespearian bedtrick where a woman sleeps with an unwitting man, Gayman takes Sir Cautious's place in Julia's bed to steal what he calls 'his right of love' (Spencer 1995: 5.7.19). Julia appears appalled at the callous deception perpetrated by both her husband and lover, and vows 'to separate for ever from [Sir Cautious's] bed' (5.7.64). Julia's adoption of the moral high ground is made problematic, however, by the earlier anonymous assignation she arranges with Gayman, into which she lures her lover with £500 of her husband's money. When explaining this action to Gayman at the end of the play Julia enlists her accomplice Bredwell to 'witness, for my honour, that I had no design upon his person, but that of trying his constancy' (5.7.189–91).

Here Behn uses the testing alibi of Shirley's Celestina as a means to exonerate Julia from any sexual designs upon Gayman. However, the play allows Julia equally to be seen, like Shirley's Aretina, as procuring her own pleasure. Julia's intrigue is closely modelled on Aretina's adultery both in terms of dramatic orchestration and psychological effect.

In Act 3, scene 4 Behn elaborates Shirley's scripted direction for 'music' (Huebert 1986: 4.1.17) into a baroque masque featuring nymphs and shepherds, song and dance. Gayman is conducted through a marriage-like ritual by Lady Fulbank's maid, Pert, who is disguised as an old woman. In *The Lady of Pleasure* the bawd Decoy similarly acts the part of a loathly lady to Aretina's love-object, Alexander Kickshaw, who believes he has been paid to make love to this 'beldam' (4.1.18). Both Shirley and Behn follow the implied sexual encounter with interrogation scenes in which Aretina and Julia are shocked to discover that they were experienced as physically loathsome rather than desirable. Kickshaw tells Aretina that his lover was 'a she-devil . . . a most insatiable, abominable devil with a tail thus long' (5.2.157–8), while Gayman describes his 'amorous devil' as 'rivelled, lean, and rough: a canvas bag of wooden ladles were a better bedfellow' (4.1.75, 83–4). Julia's response registers her pique at Gayman's insensibility to her presence: ''Slife, after all, to seem deformed, old, ugly –' (4.1.94–5). By contrast, Aretina's reaction conveys her feeling of moral ugliness: ''Tis a false glass; sure, I am more deformed' (5.2.178).

While Shirley's treatment of Aretina's adultery conveys a strong didactic element, he also creates considerable sympathy for her subjective experience. One of the creative reticences of Shirley's play concerns the extent of Sir Thomas Bornwell's knowledge of his wife's affair. By having Aretina's confession to Bornwell occur offstage (5.2.8–13), Shirley leaves open the question of how much, or how little, Aretina chooses to tell him. The ambiguity seems deliberately orchestrated by Shirley to make the audience consider the complexities and ironies of his plot.

In comparison, Behn's dramatic intentions are far less easy to discern. *The Lucky Chance* is split between the conflicting agendas of comedy and political satire. The play's attack on forced marriages is linked to the political corruption of the Whig City merchants who have used their wealth to buy themselves young and beautiful wives. Julia's espousing of the concept of loyalty, and her concern for her honour, present an image of Tory virtue which contrasts with the avarice and hypocrisy of her husband. Coincident with this image, reinscribing her source, Behn portrays Julia as an autonomous sexual agent.

The ambiguities surrounding Julia's intrigue leave the way open for a director and actors to explore differing interpretations of the event. In the 1984 Royal Court production of *The Lucky Chance* directed by Jules Wright, the first encounter between Gayman and Julia was interpreted as 'coitus interruptus; the intent, but not the act' (Wright: personal communication, 1987). The denouement after Gayman's bedtrick emphasizes Julia's horror at her loss of honour, as she addresses Gayman, '"Oh, be gone, be gone, dear robber of my quiet." (*Weeping*).' The performance of Julia's distress by Elizabeth Barry, for whom Behn wrote the part, would have evoked the genre of pathetic tragedy with which Barry was linked by her pitiful playing of the sexually victimized Monimia in Otway's *The Orphan* (1680). This association may have heightened the theatricality of Julia's response, allowing a Restoration audience to read her outrage as a masquerade of feminine virtue.

The Lucky Chance, then, is informed by ideological fracture and discontinuity. Behn draws upon a comic plot which deals overtly with a woman's adultery, but the political dimension of her play requires that her women appear staunch embodiments of marital loyalty.

One may find echoes of Julia's riven identity in Behn's authorial prevarication over her play's 'indecencies' in the preface. Here Behn at once defiantly lays claim to a masculine poetic 'freedom' and ostentatiously pays heed to the 'censuring world' by attempting to prove that her play contains nothing offensive to 'common sense' and 'good manners' (Spencer 1995: 188–91). The 'public voice' of the early modern female dramatist remains constrained by society's expectations of 'woman'.

The Daughters of Behn

For seven years after Behn's death in 1689 no plays by women were performed on the London stage. But the second half of the 1690s saw the careers of three female dramatists established: Catherine Trotter, Mary Pix and Mary Delarivier Manley. Trotter was the author of 'austere and idealistic plays' (Pearson 1988: 169) about which she received literary advice from the dramatist William Congreve. After her marriage to a clergyman in 1708 she stopped writing drama, though she continued to write and publish on philosophical and theological subjects. Notwithstanding the very different moral colouring of her plays, Trotter, together with Pix, penned congratulatory verses to Mrs Manley on her heroic tragedy *The Royal Mischief*, which was produced at the Lincoln's Inn Fields Theatre in April 1696.

Manley's play, with its exotic Eastern setting, is a heady mixture of transgressive female desire, sensational violence and eroticism. *The Royal Mischief* reworks tragic materials familiar from *Othello*, *Antony and Cleopatra* and Cary's *Mariam*: an innocent wife whose virtue is unfairly maligned and who is eventually poisoned, an oriental *femme fatale* whose 'strong desire' and active brain wreak mayhem, and a husband who too readily believes in his wife's infidelity. The theatrical centre of the play is the incestuous coupling between Princess Homais and her elderly husband's nephew, Levan Dadian, the Prince of Colchis.

The Prince's passion for Homais is roused by her accomplices Ismael and the eunuch, Acmat, who represents Homais as driven to delirium by the mere sight of the Prince's picture:

> How often have I seen this lovely Venus,
> Naked, extended in the gaudy bed,
> Her snowy breast all panting with desire,
> With gazing, melting eyes, survey your form,
> And wish in vain 't had life to fill her arms.
> (Morgan 1981: 229)

Manley uses the presence and action of the actress to flesh out the portrait. On Acmat's advice, Homais feigns timidity and shame upon meeting Levan, hiding her eyes from her lover's gaze. The audience takes pleasure in Homais's counterfeit, having heard from her own mouth how difficult it will be 'to conceal desire when every / Atom of [her] trembles with it' (ibid.: 231). Manley even requires her actress to feign an orgasm: as Homais subsides into an erotic swoon after she and Levan kiss, Levan exclaims:

> 'Tis ecstasy and more. What have I done?
> Her heart beats at her lips, and mine flies up
> To meet it. See the roses fade, her swimming
> Eyes give lessening light, and now they dart no more.
> She faints! . . .
>
> (Ibid.: 233–4)

The image of women's sexuality as allied with their histrionic ability is highlighted by Acmat's comment, 'He's caught . . . Her eyes have truer magic than a philtre' (ibid.: 234). Manley heightens the audience's voyeuristic curiosity by having Acmat close the scene upon the couple; they are discovered some time later in a state of post-coital bliss. Such flagrant female self-pleasuring cannot go unpunished, and Homais is killed in her lover's arms by her enraged husband. As Elizabeth Howe comments, Homais's drive, determination, and her frank enjoyment of sex give the impression of her 'having achieved a new female freedom'; however, her lovemaking ultimately 'bring[s] her nothing but failure and death' (Howe 1992: 51).

Mary Pix's career demonstrates an easy shifting back and forth from comedy to tragedy; between 1696 and 1706 she produced six plays in each genre. *The Innocent Mistress* (1697) is a buoyant London comedy which at times approximates a Restoration version of a modern television soap like *Neighbours*. The naivety or sophistication of Pix's characters is gauged by their familiarity with the cultural worlds of the playhouse and music-meetings; it is her valuation of such civilized pursuits that leads the witty Mrs Beauclair to pronounce that 'all virtue does not lie in chastity' (Morgan 1981: 294).

The titular heroine Bellinda has grown up on a diet of plays and romances; her reading has fostered a melodramatic tendency which is amply exercised by the fact that she is in love with a married man, Sir Charles Beauclair. In Sir Charles, Pix provides Bellinda with a soulmate content to act the role of a platonic lover, whose valiant endurance of an arranged marriage to the uncouth Lady Beauclair is rewarded by the return from the Indies of her first husband, Flywife.

Much of the pleasure of Pix's comedy derives from the combination of verve and irony which her characters bring to bear on their chosen roles. Deciding she must part from her lover forever, Bellinda summons Sir Charles for a last farewell, but is stopped in her tracks by his lyrical lamenting, and utters crossly: 'You interrupt me when I just begin' (ibid.: 314). A pair of wily servants trick Squire Barnaby Cheatall into believing he is guilty of murdering his young female ward: 'Kill a pretty lady and cut her to pieces! Oh, horrid!' (ibid.: 301). The libertine, Wildlove, acknowledges the ingenuity of Mrs Beauclair, who dons two different disguises to hunt him out in his rambles: 'Twice in one day, that's hard, i'faith' (ibid.: 307). The easy generosity of Pix's characters is matched by her pliancy in dishing out a comic solution; the non-consummation of Sir Charles's marriage enables his and Bellinda's union, Lady Beauclair's attempt to match her daughter wealthily is foiled, and Mrs Beauclair and Wildlove enter upon a marriage in which she pledges to turn a blind eye to his future indiscretions. Pix's comedy is less challenging than Behn's in its attitudes towards women's social and sexual roles, but her plays are brimful of incident and comic diversion.

Thus, by the end of the seventeenth century, women were writing for the professional stage with considerable dexterity. Although I have concentrated in this final section on work produced for the commercial theatre, other women such as the aristocrat Anne Finch, later Countess of Winchelsea, continued to produce dramatic writing that was not designed for professional production (Cotton 1980: 151–6). The seventeenth century was a period in which women achieved a voice in the domain of the public theatre, as actors, as audience and as authors.

See also WOMEN AND WRITING; ELIZABETH CARY, *THE TRAGEDY OF MARIAM* AND HISTORY; MARGARET CAVENDISH, *A TRUE RELATION OF MY BIRTH, BREEDING AND LIFE*; APHRA BEHN, *THE ROVER, PART ONE*

ACKNOWLEDGEMENTS

I wish to thank my colleagues Janine Barchas and Mark Houlahan for helpful discussions during the writing of this chapter.

REFERENCES AND FURTHER READING

Carlin, C. (1998). *Pierre Corneille Revisited*. New York: Twayne.
Cavendish, M. (1662). *Plays*. London.
Cerasano, S. P. and Wynne-Davies, M. (eds) (1996). *Renaissance Drama by Women: Texts and Documents*. London: Routledge.
——(eds) (1998). *Readings in Renaissance Women's Drama: Criticism, History and Performance 1594–1998*. London: Routledge.
Cibber, C. (1987) [1740]. *An Apology for the Life of Mr. Colley Cibber, Comedian*, ed. J. M. Evans. New York: Garland Publishing.
Cotton, N. (1980). *Women Playwrights in England, c. 1363–1750*. London: Associated University Presses.
Greer, Germaine, Medoff, Jeslyn, Sansone, Melinda and Hastings, Susan (eds) (1988). *Kissing the Rod: An Anthology of Seventeenth-Century Women's Verse*. London: Virago.
Howe, E. (1992). *The First English Actresses: Women and Drama 1660–1700*. Cambridge: Cambridge University Press.

Huebert, R. (ed.) (1986). James Shirley, *The Lady of Pleasure*. Manchester: Manchester University Press.

Lewalski, B. K. (1993). *Writing Women in Jacobean England*. Cambridge, MA: Harvard University Press.

Maclean, I. (1977). *Woman Triumphant: Feminism in French Literature, 1610–52*. Oxford: Clarendon Press.

Milhous, J. and Hume, R. D. (eds) (1977). Elizabeth Polwhele, *The Frolicks or The Lawyer Cheated*. Ithaca, NY: Cornell University Press.

Morgan, F. (ed.) (1981). *The Female Wits: Women Playwrights of the Restoration*. London: Virago.

Pearson, J. (1988). *The Prostituted Muse: Images of Women and Women Dramatists 1642–1737*. Brighton: Harvester Press.

Purkiss, D. (ed.) (1998). *Three Tragedies by Renaissance Women*. London: Penguin Books.

Shaver, A. (ed.) (1999). Margaret Cavendish, *The Convent of Pleasure and Other Plays*. Baltimore, MD: Johns Hopkins University Press.

Spencer, J. (1995). Aphra Behn, *The Rover and Other Plays*. Oxford: Oxford University Press.

Straznicky, M. (1994). '"Profane stoical paradoxes": *The Tragedie of Mariam* and Sidnean closet drama.' *English Literary Renaissance*, 24, 104–34.

——(1995). 'Reading the stage: Margaret Cavendish and Commonwealth closet drama.' *Criticism*, 37, 355–90.

Swift, C. R. (1989). 'Feminine self-definition in Lady Mary Wroth's *Love's Victorie*.' *English Literary Renaissance*, 19, 171–88.

Thomas, P. (ed.) (1990–3). *The Collected Works of Katherine Philips, The Matchless Orinda*, 3 vols. Stump Cross: Stump Cross Books.

——(1992). *The Collected Works of Katherine Philips, The Matchless Orinda, vol. 2, The Letters*. Stump Cross: Stump Cross Books.

——(1993). *The Collected Works of Katherine Philips, The Matchless Orinda, vol. 3, The Translations*, ed. G. Greer and R. Little. Stump Cross: Stump Cross Books.

Todd, J. (ed.) (1996a). *Aphra Behn Studies*. Cambridge: Cambridge University Press.

——(1996b). *The Secret Life of Aphra Behn*. London: André Deutsch.

Tomlinson, S. (1998). 'My brain the stage: Margaret Cavendish and the fantasy of female performance.' In S. P. Cerasano and M. Wynne-Davies (eds), *Readings in Renaissance Women's Drama: Criticism, History and Performance 1594–1998* (pp. 272–92). London: Routledge.

——(1999). 'Too theatrical? Female subjectivity in Caroline and Interregnum drama.' *Women's Writing*, 6, 65–79.

Woolf, V. (1982) [1929]. *A Room of One's Own*. London: Granada Publishing.

PART FOUR
Issues and Debates

22

The Work of Women in the Age of Electronic Reproduction: The Canon, Early Modern Women Writers and the Postmodern Reader

Melinda Alliker Rabb

In all the arts there is a physical component which can no longer be considered or treated as it used to be, which cannot remain unaffected by our modern knowledge and power. . . . We must expect great innovations to transform the entire technique of the arts.

Paul Valery, Pieces sur l'art

What [would] the study of literature look like once the supposition that it consisted of fixed works – of texts, given and completed – was abandoned?

Pierre Machery 1987: 74

In constructing a feminist canon of women's literature . . . do we wish to construct it using the identical categories, hierarchies, and critical values that have determined the existing male canon, even though women were writing in very different genres, under very different historical circumstances?

Margaret Ezell 1993: 63

Feminism, the Canon, and Early Modern Women Writers

A recent edition of Christine de Pizan's *The Book of the City of Ladies* (1405) introduces the text with the following claim:

Although *The Book of the City of Ladies* was written more than half a millennium ago, it is filled with potent observations for our own times. The *querelle des femmes* – the woman question in late fourteenth- and early fifteenth-century France – articulated its arguments in much the same way as today's debate about the equality of women. (de Pizan 1982: xiii–xiv)

Should a reader feel puzzled by such a claim? Can we really be articulating arguments about the equality of women in the same terms as were current in late medieval times? If so, such 'relevance' indicts six intervening centuries of struggle toward progress or change. What kind of ideological circularity can circumscribe us within the same bounds as Christine de Pizan? Perhaps we are misreading her. Do the 'breakthroughs' promised by critical theory, new historicism and textual recovery dissipate into Charles Altieri's conservative caution about the 'profoundly circular' process of canon formation: 'all efforts to escape history are themselves historically determined . . . [W]e cannot escape the problem of judging others' value statements by our own values . . . [W]e have ideas about canons because we learn to think about literature with cultural frameworks that are in part constituted by notions of the canonical' (Altieri 1983: 39, 40, 41). The changes in the academy that characterized the end of the twentieth century, like all change, arouse anxious uncertainties and resistance, as well as militancy and hope. Pizan's purported immediacy for postmodern readers raises broad questions: what is the status of women's writing from the centuries following Pizan? What consequences will attend the rediscovery of texts produced by early modern women? Will Renaissance women finally have a renaissance? Will Restoration women be restored to a newly renovated canon?

After reviewing the interrelated problems of feminism, the canon and early modern women writers, this essay will argue, borrowing and adapting terms from Benjamin's famous essay on mechanical reproduction, that the 'aura' of the traditionally canonized work of art is challenged by electronic reproduction. Along with the challenge come opportunities. The text, from the Latin *texere*, *textus* (to weave, woven like a web or net), is acquiring different possibilities for production and consumption in its new mode. The innovations of print culture (books, photographs, film) caused the 'body of the text' to evolve materially and metaphysically. Now this body/book has been unbound and released into the amorphous space of the virtual. Because theories of textuality are inevitably inseparable from theories of both reading and gender (as Linda Brodky (1989) and others have articulated), circumstances are favourable for reassessing the way in which we experience the work of women. By increasing accessibility and allowing experimental uses of information, e-culture encourages a rethinking of what belongs in a canon of early modern women's writing.

Feminism, as a principal instigator of the canon debates of the last decades, has described repeatedly the limitations and distortions of its own practices. With respect to the canon, feminism has experienced what Teresa de Lauretis (1987: 2) calls 'the tension of a twofold pull in contrary directions'. It attempts to intervene politically and practically in the construction of anthologies, editions, collections of essays, course offerings, syllabuses and other institutional apparatuses that hitherto did not include women; it also seeks a new operative space, a frame of reference, outside the ideology of the patriarchal institution, in which it might be possible to think in new terms not only about sexuality and gender, but about class, race, colonialism, aesthetics and systems of value (ibid.: 26). Feminists have been caught between the need to privilege, as an evaluative category, an author's identity as a woman, and the need not to privilege that category because it essentializes and encourages merely biographical, or exclusively proto-feminist readings of a text. Identity politics and poststructuralism have exerted contradictory influences. The search for 'great' female-authored texts in many ways flies in the face of prevailing tendencies in the academy. The trend in Anglo-American studies, articulated by Louis Montrose in 1989, has been away from (often celebratory) critical analysis of individual authors and toward 'the historical, social, and political conditions and consequences of literary production and reproduction. . . . The writing and reading of texts as well as the processes by which they are circulated and categorized, analysed and taught, are being reconstructed as historically determined and determining modes of cultural work' (Montrose 1989: 15). Yet feminists assert that an author's identity, even 'genius', as a woman must claim significance because, as Nelly Furman states, 'Cultural biases, uncovered in style and content, are similarly present in our hearing or reading habits; interpreting language is no more sexually neutral than language use or the language system itself' (Furman 1978: 184). As long as there are shelves of book-length studies of the canonical 'greats' for every single book-length study of an Elizabethan woman writer, the self-sabotaging terms 'minor' and 'marginal', as defined by Giles Deleuze and Felix Guattari, will remain accurate.

The problem can be stated somewhat differently. Flagging interest in celebrating literary 'genius' has the potential to sanction the reading of texts whose pedigree is less well documented. This circumstance is good for the study of women writers. However, women's writing can seem obscure and unfamiliar to most people whose reading habits have been formed by the very geniuses they now demote. Recovered texts by 'others' are relegated to a cabinet of curiosities but are not fully scrutinized. This circumstance is bad for the study of women writers. Deborah S. Rosenfelt remarks: 'If a hundredth of the amount of careful editorial exposition expended on the works of Shakespeare were devoted to these texts, they would indeed be "readable"' (Rosenfelt 1998: 28). Postmodern culture in general is divided, almost schizophrenically, on the status of feminism. On the one hand, bookstores and course catalogues bear witness to an increasing institutional acceptance of women's studies. Entire sections, indeed entire departments and shops, are devoted to, and capitalize on, the opportunities of this emergent field. On the other hand, such acceptance retains evidence of trendiness and controversy. *Reviving Ophelia* and *In a Different Voice* coexist with *How Feminism Is Ruining Our Young Men* and *Vamps and Tramps*. Film, radio and television, popular music, advertising, fashion, and most 'mainstream culture' continue as usual to objectify and devalue women. Acceptance (or tolerance) is not canonization. No one attacks Shakespeare.

If feminism has multiple ideas of its goals and methods, the idea of 'the canon' also has been complicated by contending views. The traditional canon of English literature (Chaucer, Spenser, Shakespeare, Milton, etc.) has been historicized, analysed and destabilized by dozens of critics as diverse as Barbara Herrnstein Smith, Lillian

Robinson, John Guillory, Annette Kolodny, Henry Louis Gates, Gerald Graff and
Homi Bhabha. Despite a few faithful adherents to unquestioning belief in the
universal 'greatness' of certain texts, most academic discussions of 'the canon' (over
the past twenty years) acknowledge its political origins, its ideological function and
its change over time. Studies by Trevor Ross, Isaac Kramnick, Douglas Patey and
Howard Weinbrot argue that, after the English Civil Wars, rising nationalism
brought a corresponding need for a national literature and heritage. The swelling book
trade, the weakening of aristocratic authority, the rise in literacy, the professionaliza-
tion of authorship and criticism contributed to canon-formation and served what
J. G. A. Pocock calls 'civil virtue'. Kramnick (1998: 4) claims that in the eighteenth
century '[a] national canon formed on the precedent example of the ancient canon
took shape. This canon was necessarily old and carried with it much of the aura of
antiquity: difficulty, rarity, sublimity, and masculinity'. This is the canon of mastery
of men over women descried by Eve Sedgwick in *The Epistemology of the Closet.* Print
capitalism, by the late eighteenth century, had enabled the proliferation of a canon
that included vernacular texts. This English canon encouraged the kind of 'imagined
community' described by Benedict Anderson, in which belief in commonality (language, homeland, culture) becomes a driving force in both politics and the marketplace. Beginning in the nineteenth century, according to Terry Eagleton's analysis of
class and gender in the 'rise' of English literature, the canon functions as a secular
replacement for religious belief; acceptance of it promises to save humankind from
suffering 'in a mechanized society of trashy romances, alienated labour, banal advertisements, and vulgarizing mass media' (Eagleton 1983: 33). In a similar vein,
Raymond Williams sees the category of 'great literature' as the means to power and
influence of a bourgeoisie 'ever eager to find an expression of its values and legitimacy'
(Williams 1977: 29–30).

Most scholars admit the canon's continued complicity in the perpetuation of a
certain ideology of a certain culture at a certain time. During the past several decades
considerable energy has gone into new readings of canonical texts in order to test,
resist or reaffirm them. Shakespeare's women characters and Milton's Eve, for example,
are examined with interest, while once-popular interpretations of works like *The
Tempest* and *Robinson Crusoe* are rejected as racist and colonialist. Once the literary
past is unhinged from a rigid notion of 'the canon', history becomes malleable; new
combinations of newly esteemed texts 'narrate' different cultural plots. Even the term
'canon' defies consensus. For some, it consists of 'the best and brightest' and sets a
standard for measuring artistic excellence. But is the standard measured by authors
or texts, Milton or *Paradise Lost*? For others, it consists of crucial documents in the
history of a culture. For others, it is the mechanism for perpetuating extant structures
of political power, while making challengers to that power invisible. If, in the most
practical terms, the canon is what gets taught, then educational institutions can
document its periodic reformulation. Perhaps the canon may be defined pragmatically

as works, the knowledge of which makes it possible to engage in discourses, critical and theoretical, at a given time in cultural history.

The idea of 'counter-canons' has become familiar as well, as new areas of study (women, ethnic, African-American, postcolonial, gay and lesbian) establish their own lists of essential reading. These counter-canons are, as Lillian Robinson and others have stated, separate but not equal. Yet they have been justified and defended in various ways. While acknowledging 'the politics and ironies of canon-formation', Henry Louis Gates endorses a 'black canon' in terms not uncongenial to a feminist: 'To appropriate our own discourse by using Western critical theory uncritically is to substitute one mode of neocolonialism for another . . . [W]e see no true reflections of our black faces and hear no echoes of our black voices, let us . . . master the canon of critical tradition of Africa and Afro-America' (Gates 1994: 176). The creators of counter-canons, by means of new editions, anthologies and reading lists, insist on a greater variety of kinds of texts, and recapture the reader-function described by Barbara Benedict as 'collaborative participa[tion] in forging literary culture', as distinct from a reader's passive receipt of 'commodified literature . . . [that] trains his or her moral response' (Benedict 1996: 6). A counter-canon can look at a wider variety of kinds of texts, beyond traditional genres, for its materials.

Special status accords not only to *what* we read, but also to *how* we read. Canons and counter-canons of 'literary' texts have been joined in recent decades with canons of both criticism and theory, with their own histories, celebrated figures and 'key' books and essays. The canon enshrines not only texts but the interpretive strategies that reveal the excellence of those texts: 'literary conventions are not in the text waiting to be uncovered, but in fact *precede* the text and make discovery possible in the first place' (Rabinowitz 2000: 262). The list of 'what any educated person should know' (and presumably admire) has become complex and self-conscious. The idea of 'just reading' has come to seem naive. 'Conventions of interpretation' govern most encounters with a text (Richter 2000: 236). Various scholars have assessed the relationship between the canons of criticism and theory and the canon of literature: 'the degree to which the work lends itself to a particular critical theory is responsible for the value we assign it' (Daiches, cited by Rabinowitz 2000: 219); 'In so far as we are taught how to read, what we engage are not texts but paradigms' (Kolodny 1980: 8); 'conflicts of judgment arising from fundamental and perhaps irreconcilable diversity of interest are exhibited in currently charged political debates. . . . [I]nstitutions of evaluative authority will be called upon repeatedly to devise arguments and procedures that validate the community's established tastes and preferences' (Smith 1983: 9, 18). English departments that may no longer require a course in Milton or Shakespeare may require a course in critical theory. At the same time, challenges to the very notion of the canon remain unresolved. How big can a canon be? Is the solution glib: 'simply open the doors to admit the work of talented writers who are not white, or not male, or not European'? (Searle 1994: 83) Or does each addition require a deletion, so that the canon will fit within the parameters of a semester or a career or a lifetime? How can we tell quality from taste, what is good from what is great, genius from popularity, value from marketability? Are we ransacking the past for treasures to 'sell' or are we preserving a precious heritage? To what degree should politics affect the choice of what to read and what to study? To what extent is the power of canonical texts to achieve nation-building, tradition-making and subject-formation desirable or dangerous? In the world outside the academy, will the shifting canon matter?

The relationship of work by early modern women writers to the general debates of feminism and the canon poses special problems. Women's antithetical roles as producers and consumers of texts experience something like a crisis as modern culture develops. Women's potential to participate in mainstream culture increases, but so do the means of excluding them. The formation of an English canon is part of a dialectic, a reaction against the perceived feminization of culture (the levelling effects of rising literacy and consumerism) that 'threaten[s] national, masculine fortitude': women 'were understood . . . to augur polite culture writ large *or* to vitiate the republic of letters' (Kramnick 1998: 40). Recent attempts to recover early modern women's texts, to accurately historicize them, and to appropriately theorize them are further complicated by the advent of electronic text. As we will see, the material conditions of production of the work of early modern women writers have certain parallels to the emerging material conditions of textual production in our own time, and these parallels, however qualified by changes in cultural history, may enable some reconsideration of both canon formation and technologies of reading.

In the 1990s early modern women's writing had gained little acceptance into the traditional canon, despite the (re)visionary injunction 'to include a significant body of works by women' and to develop 'new ways of reading women's literature . . . that will only be possible when women writers take their equal place in the canon with men' (Schweikart 1991: 536). Aphra Behn has the surest claim as cultural capital. The signs of her canonization are abundantly clear, especially during the past decade: critical studies of her work appear both as book-length studies and as chapters and articles; several biographies exist; editions, anthologies, course syllabuses, meetings and conferences testify to her importance today. Of the 267 entries on Behn in the *Bibliography of the Modern Language Association* since 1963, 182 have been written since 1990. The Aphra Behn Society has an annual conference and newsletters; its website has had almost 17,000 visitors since 1997. Behn's claims on the university-based canon are increasingly diverse; points of intersection between her writing and other texts or other areas of study have multiplied. Her career has a history of public recognition and professionalism, notwithstanding the embarrassed scepticism of the Victorians. Its quality is 'provable' by familiar critical paradigms; its subject matter remains in vogue. She worked in conventional genres (comedy, tragedy and lyric verse, for example). Familiar plays and poems by famous men offer ready comparisons. *The Rover* is eminently discussable in relation to Wycherley's *The Country Wife*; 'The

Disappointment' contrasts interestingly with Rochester's 'The Imperfect Enjoyment'. Behn also worked innovatively in experimental genres, particularly in epistolary fiction. *Love Letters Between A Nobleman and His Sister* has become a part of the new explanation of the novel's 'rise' and must be considered along with Richardson's fictions of seduction. Given the importance of novel studies for the past several decades, Behn's pertinence to academic discourse should not be underrated. Further, Behn seems to have written at least one relevant text for almost every new area of enquiry in the academy. Poems like 'To the Fair Clarinda' command the attention of students of gay and lesbian writing and of the history of sexuality. *The Widow Ranter* interests Americanists. *Oroonoko*'s textual nexus of race, class and gender has made it essential reading for feminists and postcolonialists; its combination of old-world and new-world characters and settings attracts transatlantic studies; its representations of slavery, commodification and the body have drawn attention from cultural critics of many kinds. Virginia Woolf may have taken the first post-Victorian step toward the canonization of Behn, but Behn's stature has long surpassed anything envisioned by Woolf.

In addition to the writers before Austen who have already secured places in the university-taught canon (Behn, Montagu, Burney, Wollstonecraft), others rise in stature as 'statistical studies keep revealing the increasing numbers of women writers, and criticism of their work keeps broadening our sense of its scope' (Spencer 1998: 96). Montagu, Burney and Wollstonecraft all were connected to famous men (Alexander Pope and Jonathan Swift; Samuel Johnson; Fuseli, William Godwin and Percy Shelley). Montagu's *Turkish Embassy Letters* are becoming crucial in discussions of orientalism and colonialism. The relationship of Burney's *Evelina* to Austen's *Pride and Prejudice* has ensured a steady readership. Wollstonecraft's *Vindication of the Rights of Woman* has been obviously useful to any discussion of the history of feminism, and to the history of late eighteenth-century politics connected to Edmund Burke's controversial conservatism in *Reflections on the Revolution in France.* Ironically, evidence suggests that the first English canons of the seventeenth and early eighteenth centuries included now-neglected women writers such as Katherine Philips and Delarivier Manley, and did not insist on connecting their personal lives to their work. Behn and Manley, for example, are not always censured for their private affairs (Ezell 1993: 71–8). However, their disappearance during the Victorian era has been very partially reversed. *The Norton Anthology of English Literature* (6th edn, 1993) includes 35 pages (out of 2,518) of women's writing before Aphra Behn. Of Aemilia Lanyer's poem *Salve Deus Rex Judaeorum*, 95 lines are excerpted from almost 2,000. In addition to the 47 pages devoted to *Oroonoko*, there are 8 pages representing women before the Romantic period. In *Chaucer to Spenser: An Anthology of Writings in English 1375–1575* (Blackwell 1999), 19 pages out of 665 represent medieval and early Renaissance women's texts. In *Restoration Drama: An Anthology* (Blackwell 2000), two plays (by Aphra Behn and Susannah Centlivre) constitute 78 of 814 pages. This imbalance is particularly striking because women's contributions to the theatre in the late seventeenth century have been critically recognized (Pearson 1988; Backscheider 1993). *The Norton Anthology of Writing by Women* is hardly an improvement. Examples before 1800 constitute a mere 172 pages out of 2,390. Traditional anthologies of early modern literature represent women's writing as minor and marginal. At colleges and universities, reading lists increasingly include some examples of women writers, but their inclusion depends on availability and on the willingness of instructors to negotiate still unfamiliar material. The list of names is growing, but to non-specialists most remain ciphers: Aemilia Lanyer, Anne Askew, Lady Mary Wroth, Elizabeth Cary, Katherine Parr, Margaret Fell, Anna Trapnel, Mary Evans, Sarah Cheevers, Sarah Davys, Lady Eleanor Davies, Margaret Cavendish, Aphra Behn, Katherine Philips, Bathsua Makin, Mary Pix, Catherine Trotter, Sarah Egerton, Elizabeth Elstob, Mary Chudleigh, Delarivier Manley, Eliza Haywood, Mary Astell, Jane Barker, Lady Mary Wortley Montagu, Susannah Centlivre. The list of women who wrote from mid- to late-eighteenth century has also enlarged: Frances Sheridan, Ann Radcliffe, Sarah Fielding, Charlotte Charke, Sarah Scott, Charlotte Lennox, Anna Laetitia Barbauld, Hester Thrale, Elizabeth Inchbald and Mary Robinson now have some readers, the fiction writers claiming the most attention. In the sometimes fickle atmosphere of the academic institution, however, the initial difficulty of some writing by early modern women may encourage their continued neglect in the face of the attractions of other newly available fields, such as postcolonialism and transatlantic studies. The Modern Language Association has just published a collection of essays in its 'Approaches to Teaching' series on early modern women writers. Yet despite the outpouring of critical work on early modern women writers, the concepts of 'genius' and 'seminality', so fundamental to the canon, remain masculine.

Feminists have attempted several solutions to the canon problem. Alternative readings of canonical male-authored texts have exposed patriarchal assumptions, analysed constructions of gender and reassessed representations of women. New readings of better-known women writers have focused on the political possibilities of their work. Women whose principal fame was their relationship to a famous man (as sister, daughter, wife or mistress) have been afforded a more independent claim to scholarly attention. Efforts have been made to add women to the male canon, to mainstream, for example, Behn with Rochester and Dryden, Montagu with Pope, Lennox with Sterne, or Wollstonecraft with Burke. Ann Messenger's (1999) *His and Hers* is a recent example of such pairing. Susanne Fendler's (1997) collection, *Feminist Contributions to the Literary Canon*, is organized around examples of a woman preceding a man in some innovative textual production – such as Elizabeth Justice's *Amelia*, which pre-dates Henry Fielding's novel of the same name.

Equally strenuous efforts have been made to establish a counter-canon and an alternative tradition. Recovery of lesser-known texts has widened and enriched the ground on which to position the idea of the woman writer. Numerous anthologies have appeared in the last twenty years, beginning with Germaine Greer et al.'s *Kissing the Rod* and Betsy Travitsky's *A Paradise of Women*, and continuing in volumes edited by

Jane Spencer, Bridget Hill, Roger Lonsdale, Janet Todd, Fidelis Morgan, and others. The Pickering Women's Classics series, the Virago Press's 'Mothers of the Novel' series, volumes from Oxford and Broadview Press, have been in the vanguard of increasing numbers of new individual and serial editions (including *Women Writers in English, 1350–1850*, edited by Susanne Woods and Elizabeth Hageman, and *The Early Modern Englishwoman: A Facsimile Library of Essential Works*, edited by Betsy Travitsky and Patrick Cullen). Elaine Showalter imagined a 'coherent . . . female literary history' and a 'gynocriticism' with which to appreciate it. More recently, Janet Clare endorses this idea with respect to early modern women: 'The writings of women, whether religious, popular, humanist, or courtly, had in the mid-sixteenth to early seventeenth century at least one common aspect: women writers represented in their work an alternative culture which ran alongside the dominant culture' (Clare 1998: 37).

But the process of separatism is tricky. Women are automatically underdogs. In appraising newly available texts for teaching, Mary Thomas Crane invokes the old disturbing questions: 'Are translations and polemical tracts sufficiently "literary" . . . Are these writers really worth teaching?' (Crane 1998: 945). While it is possible to canonize an underdog as a martyr or a saint, we should remember that most male writers are canonized as heroes. Further, the canon, as the product of print/consumer culture, has not escaped the pressures of commodification. Its purported 'transcendent values' are objectified in the marketplace. 'The good' becomes 'the goods', and, like all desirable products, it can be possessed, circulated and consumed. From this perspective the canon is already feminized in ways that parallel Lévi-Strauss's model of the exchange of women by men. Judith Fetterley's caution about the 'immasculation' of women, even as they work on women writers, is apt:

> [Women suffer] not simply the powerlessness which derives from not seeing one's experience articulated, clarified, and legitimized in art, but more significantly, the powerlessness which results from the endless division of self against self, the consequence of the invocation to identify as male while being reminded that to be male – to be universal – is to be *not female*. . . . [T]he cultural reality is not the emasculation of men by women, but the immasculation of women by men. As readers, teachers, and scholars, women are taught to think as men, to identify with a male point of view, and to accept as normal and legitimate a male system of values, one of whose central principles is misogyny. (Fetterley 1991: 493, 497)

Within its institutional framework the recovery and study of work by women has proceeded with certain assumptions that we may now be ready to question, so that we may rethink the vexed issue of early women's writing and the canon. What do we read and how do we read it? We read what is materially accessible and we employ the critical and theoretical skills that characterize our moment in history. We speak of the cultural work that texts 'do', and we must speak as well of what we 'do' to texts.

Given the power of metaphor, what residual questions arise from the implied materiality or animation of texts that both act and are acted upon? Margaret Ezell is a strong proponent of re-evaluating the way we read early modern women writers: 'if the current model of women's literary history now offers a coherent narrative of women's literary lives for the last 250 years, what was happening before 1700 and why is it not a part of this narrative?' (Ezell 1993: 2). Important early feminist criticism, and much of what followed (Elaine Showalter's *A Literature of Their Own*, Sandra Gilbert's and Susan Gubar's *Madwoman In the Attic*, Hélène Cixous's 'Laugh of the Medusa' are cases in point) embraced Virginia Woolf's now-discredited assumptions in *A Room of One's Own* that 'nothing is known about women before the eighteenth century', that Aphra Behn's professionalism liberated women, that the demise of Shakespeare's fictive sister Judith represented accurately the inevitable fate of women with literary aspirations – loneliness, parental cruelty, sexual abuse and the suicide's unmarked grave. Sanctioned by Woolf's views, the novel, widely accepted as a uniquely feminine genre, has dominated criticism. The prevailing pinnacle of success has been the nineteenth-century novelist. Ezell, Elaine Hobby, Isobel Armstrong, Virginia Blain and others have argued that the lines of continuity between nineteenth- and twentieth-century writers can 'strangle those women who lived and wrote in centuries when the technology and the ethos of authorship were significantly different' (Ezell 1993: 65). Before the middle of the eighteenth century many women published, and according to Patricia Crawford's catalogue of 300 publications, fewer than 60 concealed their names. But many important texts by women were written without being conventionally published. Their subject matter is not about 'popular' feminine issues (as imagined by later generations) such as love, marriage and family, but about religion and politics. Conventional generic categories, such as comedy, tragedy and poetic 'kinds', accommodate only some of their forms of writing. The majority of women's writing is in letters, journals, diaries, poems, stories, self-writing, prophecy, religious tracts (both conservative and radical), political pamphlets, drama for both theatre and coterie, translation, propaganda, history, hymns, criticism, periodical essay, narrative fiction and biography (Hobby 1998). As Margaret Ezell states:

> There are two basic problems with the current literary history of female authorship and the resulting canon of women's literature. First, . . . 'the canon' was formed before we knew the extent of women's writing in the Renaissance and Restoration. Second, the canon has been constructed in general using the definition of literary hierarchies found in the male canon – poetry, drama, fiction, and belles lettres – and . . . privileges some forms over others, the novel being depicted as a uniquely 'feminine' form. (Ezell 1993: 41)

Early modern women appear not feminist enough, not professional enough, not plentiful enough, not middle class enough. They look instead like a sequence of eccentric aristocrats, sectarian radicals and brazen demireps, like so many slippery stepping stones on the path to Jane Austen.

Attempts to establish a counter-canon have not yet emancipated the work of women from the powerfully restrictive intellectual systems that govern postmodern interpretive communities. In the rush to expand pluralistic and democratic learning, we can be reductive and indiscriminate in applying paradigms of difference, too ready to enter a text already in possession of the knowledge we are looking for, such as the subversion of patriarchy (or colonial domination, or commodification of text and body, or the fear and objectification of the 'other'). We have sought themes of female education, courtship, seduction, marriage and childbirth, organized in plots of happy wedding endings or tragic deaths of heroines. Our prevailing evaluative categories often conflict with the demands of texts by early modern women. Current interest in the founding of the modern subject, which encourages the kind of unified discourse that is allied to bourgeois patriarchy, devalues texts in which a multiplicity of subject positions seems initially confusing. (Rosenfelt's discussion of prophecy is a case in point.) Work that is finished and unified is valued more than work that is fragmentary, amorphous, nonce, enigmatic or seemingly incomplete (such as letters, diaries, narrative experiments), despite a willingness to prize these qualities in, say, Laurence Sterne or James Joyce. Print capitalism measures success in our 'publish or perish' world, thus obscuring the value of manuscript culture which was so vital to early modern women (and men) during the sixteenth, seventeenth and early eighteenth centuries. Being the best at something is generally accepted as more important than being the first at something. Generic forms rank above non-generic ones. (Non-generic forms reveal great gender bias. In the Public Record Office personal letters by women have been catalogued dismissively as 'gossip about private friends' while gossipy letters by men are labelled more eruditely as 'private news': see Rosenfelt 1998: 27.) 'Literary representation' is assumed to transform experience, while 'historical documents' are downgraded (perhaps decreasingly so) as unprocessed chunks of reality. Linda Woodbridge's metaphor for the canon – 'a stable of fine horses' – alludes to this problem: 'we may habitually analyze the thoroughbred literary documents safe in their stalls according to recognized conventions, rhetorical devices', but 'the cart-horse texts outside the stable' suffer neglect or mishandling (Woodbridge 1998: 58). Work that participates in systems of representation that are considered not overly topical with respect to a particular party, religion or class, are accorded more prestige than those that seem narrowly sectarian (such as Quaker writings or Baptist conversion narratives). Competition and commercial success (a factor in the canonization of Aphra Behn) are esteemed over communal, non-competitive practices. The work of an identifiable 'author' is prized more highly than anonymous or collaboratively written works, in which attribution may be uncertain. (Women writers, singly or in groups, may be catalogued under the name of a male relation or under the name of the one male member of their group.) Modern esteem for the individual has removed the possibility of canonizing a group, even though many works by early modern women may be best evaluated this way: court coteries, Quaker women, English nuns, amatory writers, correspondents, prophets, and manuscript circles may achieve different stature when single works are understood interactively or as part of a combined effect. 'Recent interest . . . constructs women's writing very narrowly, searching as it does for the nearest female equivalent of men, "readable" writers of the genres constructed by a male literary criticism . . . [T]he chimerical search for proto-feminist "good" writers avoids questioning the very notions of genre, "readability", and "good writing" which attention to the full range of women's writing must confront' (Woodbridge 1998: 56). Both the Victorian construction of a female tradition characterized by modesty, virtue and domesticity, and the modern one predicated on anger and resistance, are too limited: 'What both of these visions of the past have not been able to see or to bring into the general discussion are those early women writers whose lives and work lie outside traditional definitions and categories, both social – women's proper sphere – and literary – what constitutes our definition of literature itself' (Ezell 1993: 130–1).

The Work of Women in the Age of Electronic Reproduction

What will be possible in the twenty-first century? Stanley Fish's 'vexed question of where the text ends and the reader begins' may find different answers as computers expand our interpretive strategies and make the text 'virtual'. Without insisting on absolute parallels, it is possible to imagine how the experience of 'e-culture', with respect to new practices in the exchange of communication, might alter habitual reading (and writing) practices both subtly and radically. The alterations effected by the 'virtual' world of computers entail the loss of some aspects of modern writer/reader/text relations, but they also open up differences that, in various ways, approximate more closely writer/reader/text relations of the early modern period. Since the advent of print culture in the seventeenth century (and its later variation in the nineteenth-century printing of film), no intervening revolution in communication has occurred of the magnitude of the recent advent of the worldwide web. We now are being forced to reconsider the mechanisms that translate speech and thought into other modes of discourse and to rethink their various consequences. Whereas Walter Benjamin described the acceleration with which print could be reproduced in order to keep pace with speech, electronic reproduction functions at far greater speed and with the simultaneous multiplicity of 'split' or 'layered' screens/pages. Problems of authenticity, authority, value and transmission challenge notions of identity and exchange. Benjamin writes of the 'emancipation of the work of art' from its ritual-ized 'aura': 'During long periods of history, the mode of human sense perception changes with humanity's entire mode of existence. The manner in which human sense perception is organized, the medium in which it is accomplished, is determined not only by nature but by historical circumstances as well' (Benjamin 1969: 222). While there is some irony inherent in approaching a discussion of the emancipation of reading early modern women's writing through this initial invocation of male-authored texts and technologies, feminism has often manoeuvred, purposefully and unapologetically, through the conditions that provoked its 'rise'. If readers are able to embrace the viability of an unfamiliar category like 'animals that from a distance look like flies' (from Foucault's famous Chinese encyclopedia entry in *The Order of Things*), they should be able to accept some reclassification of literature by women.

In his discussion of the historical analysis of discourse, Foucault acknowledges the need to 'study not only the expressive value of and formal transformations of discourse, but its mode of existence: the modification and variations, within any culture, of modes of circulation, valorization, attribution, and appropriation' (Foucault 1977: 137). Such a view intersects conveniently with the textual theory of D. F. McKenzie, who defines bibliography as a 'sociology of texts' whose practices are governed by a 'non-elitist, non-canonical, non-generic, all-inclusive principle' (McKenzie 1986: 5). The text 'may be much more of a social product than we have been used to thinking it, so that an author's specific verbal intentions may be more important at one point, broader social concerns may matter at another' (McKenzie 1976: 18). This approach to texts is capacious enough to accommodate early modern women's writing: 'to enable the discovery of any possible relationship between any one text and any other text – whenever, wherever, and in whatever form' (ibid.: 51). Textual form can be highly significant. McKenzie cites the example of Joyce's *Ulysses* in which the physical form of the book and printed text are highly symbiotic: any change would result in loss of meaning. But he also represents the opposing view of text as open and indeterminate:

> Whatever its metamorphoses, the physical forms of any text, and the intentions they serve, are relative to a specific time, place and person. This creates a problem only if we want meaning to be absolute and immutable. In fact, change and adaptation are a condition of survival, just as the creative application of texts is a condition of their being read at all. (McKenzie 1986: 50)

The social and technical transmission of non-book texts, including their perceived meanings, control by institutions, and social effects, participates in a history 'of cultural change, whether in mass civilization or minority culture' (ibid.: 5).

Until very recently scholarship avoided the full range of early modern textual production. The 'public sphere', while empowering certain kinds of literature, devalues texts produced outside of the marketplace of printed matter. Fuller representation would have to include records of religious societies, documents in State Papers Domestic, diaries, journals, manuals of practical information, and the three popular (and overlapping) types of manuscript exchange: manuscript books, loose sheets (for miscellanies and commonplace books) and correspondence. Carol Barash and Margaret Ezell have begun to investigate the qualities of women's manuscript circulation and correspondence networks. They point out that women's reluctance to appear in print does not simply prove the constricting inhibitions of feminine modesty but manifests 'a much more general, and much older, attitude about writing, printing, and readership' (Ezell 1987: 65), one that influenced John Donne, Ben Jonson and John Wilmot, Earl of Rochester, as well as Mary Wroth, Jane Barker, Anne Finch and Katherine Philips. Many authors preferred manuscript circulation because it afforded them greater control over their work, or because it allowed a more assertive expression of personal belief, one that would need to be moderated in print. (On the challenging question of 'how . . . we know what was written' and who wrote it, see McKenzie (1976: 16) and Ezell (1987: 62–100).) But manuscripts also allowed for collaboration and emendation, as friends rewrote and imitated one another's work in 'networks along which manuscripts and letters travelled' (Barash 1996: 2). Published and manuscript versions of the same poem might circulate concurrently, one fixed and one changeable: 'these two kinds of literary production, in turn, suggest different relationships among author, poetry, and communities of reception' (ibid.: 8). This dynamic of textual production was not confined by class, religion or faction to court-based coteries, but included Quakers as well as royalists, spiritual narratives as well as poems on friendship, titillation as well as edification. Further, the more communal nature of writing corresponds with the phenomenon of concurrent printing in the seventeenth century (McKenzie 1976: 20). Several printers and publishers might be involved in the production of a single edition. In such cases, communal interests (such as giving work to poor printers) override deference for the author and 'the insistence on scrupulous proof correction to define the true word' (ibid.: 53). Not until the eighteenth century do prevailing practices change, and printers like Benjamin Tonson mark the 'emergence of a discernible textual tradition notably different from that of the Elizabethan era [with] new and respectful attitudes toward authorship which led to the *Act for the Encouragement of Learning* in 1709' (ibid.).

The work of early modern women writers occurs during this complex transition between manuscript culture and print culture when the text may be 'much more of a social product than we have been used to thinking it' (Ezell 1987: 18). Recapturing the full dynamic of these overlapping phenomena is ongoing: the recovery of material, as well as the analysis of the meanings of the different communities of production and reception, go against the assumptions of print culture. But until we come to terms with it, we cannot surmise the direction a women's canon will take. The profound effects of print culture and the literary marketplace have lasted for, and have significantly defined, four centuries of modernity. The age of electronic reproduction, somewhat ironically, may allow us a closer approximation of reading pre-print culture material than has hitherto been possible. The encoders of the *Women Writers Project* at Brown University believe that 'the electronic archive seemed like the ideal successor to the physical archive, since it promised to overcome the problems of inaccessibility and scarcity which had rendered women's writing invisible for so long' (http:\\www.wwp.brown.edu). But it is not merely the visibility of women's writing that is at stake, but the new perceptual opportunity offered by detaching it from the fixed systems of valuation and comprehension belonging to conventions of the book and the book trade. If there exists what Nancy K. Miller calls a 'female signature', what material and immaterial forms can that signing take in order to make perceptible the florid or confident or cramped movements of a woman's hand? In 'Fashioning a Female Canon' Elizabeth Eger asks: 'Are there perhaps new structures which could challenge old modes of representation, encourage a more playful approach? The development of computer technology has already started to affect women's studies, publication on the internet avoiding the commercial strictures of more conventional publication' (Eger 1999: 212). The attempt to reimagine the transition period between manuscript and print is not simply a call to recover manuscripts (although recovery is important) but to recover and revitalize ways of responding to the written word, to inhabit 'a new cultural space for the study, preparation, and transmission of texts' and to recognize that 'the roots of these activities as practised today lie in . . . manuscript traditions, and the humanist recovery and study of classical texts' (Flanders 1997: 130).

In print culture, writing is not fully realized until it is a published text. It is difficult to imagine a canonical work not bound between covers and circumscribed by introduction, notes, glossary and index, a demarcation begun by the eighteenth-century editions of Shakespeare and Johnson's *Lives of the Poets*. In *Women in Print Culture* Kathryn Shevelow calls for 'a more encompassing view of writing as a broadly cultural process implicating the entire field of linguistic representation' (Shevelow 1989: 19). Both manuscript and electronic cultures tolerate and value other parameters of what constitutes a text. They loosen up our notions of reading. They disrupt comfortable readerly encounters with a stable work fixed in regular lines and indentations, on uniform sheets, between covers. They defamiliarize the text, making it 'textual' again, in keeping with Victor Shklovsky's injunction that art must alter the process of perception as an aesthetic end in itself, making 'the stone stony' (Shklovsky 1965: 12). Both realize the literal meaning of text as 'something woven'; they allow for the rearranging and merging of the threads of language of which they are composed. Both permit continual changes and copies. Both tolerate variations in the appearance of the text which may vary by handwriting, formatting or software. Both encourage the 'coterie' experience. Correspondence through e-mail (and on-line 'chats') has become an integral part of postmodern life, has made many people into 'writing subjects' in ways that resemble exchanges of letters centuries ago, when irregularities in spelling were tolerated, copies could be made or shared with others than the intended recipient, replies could be sent on the original document, and trivia intermixed with urgent matters. In both manuscript and electronic texts, sight or visual transcription (paper/screen) supersedes sound or voice (talk/telephone/

recording). Both traverse the boundary between public and private, between communal and individual authorship, between collaboration and competition, between for profit and not-for-profit, between patterns of circulation inside and outside of the marketplace. Manuscript circles, 'zines', and chat-rooms demur from the notion of commercial viability as the hallmark of literary activity. The idea of a network configures experience very differently than concepts like 'central' and 'marginal'. One does not progress linearly along a continuum when circulating or surfing back and forth along the interconnecting threads of a fabric of words. The metaphor that comes to mind was once applied by John Chamberlain to Mary Wroth's *Urania*: '[the writer] takes great libertie or rather license . . . and thinks she daunces in a net' (Wroth, *Poems*: 36).

Just as the letter has been viewed as a feminine space (Terry Eagleton (1983) views the letter's folded enclosure as an erotic metaphor for secrecy and private pleasure in *The Rape of Clarissa*), claims have been made for the gendering of virtual text. Unlike the place of writing envisioned by Woolf, a room where the writing woman achieves autonomy through isolation (but where she also could be locked away like Clarissa in her closet), the virtual world has no walls. Unlike the printed text, which Laurence Sterne (among others) envisioned as a living body to be possessed, used and sold (the caged starling in *A Sentimental Journey* circulates from Lord A to Lord B to Lord C and so on), electronic text resists embodiment. Traditional ideas about the book encourage one kind of gendering: belief in the desirability of a pure and uncorrupted text, a flawless edition that circulates among men until worn out and in need of replacement, feminizes the object of circulation and eroticizes the experience of reading as one of possession, control and pleasure. Certainly women writers during the emergent years of print culture were aware of an association between prostitution and the buying and selling of books. In *The Rover* II.i., author and whore are implicitly conflated: A. B. (Aphra Behn/Angellica Bianca) is represented by a material image displayed in the public square (a frontispiece/an advertisement) proving she is for sale (see Todd 1989: 1–10). New ideas about the 'virtual' gender the text differently. In 'The Body Encoded' Julia Flanders argues that virtuality, while freeing the feminized text from the strictures of a 'body', also approximates the feminine condition in more salutary ways. In one sense, to be 'virtual' is to occupy the feminine cultural position of being secondary, 'almost', or 'endowed with a power or virtue without formal entitlement'. But, in another sense, 'the loss of the body is a severance of the bonds between the sign and the signified, the loss of a referent which was never really there to begin with' (Flanders 1997: 128). Because 'our understanding of textuality originates in the same philosophical crux as our ideas of physicality and representation' (ibid.: 127), encoded text has many potential ramifications. It invites a re-imaging of the place, form, organization and authorship of information; it encourages readerly/writerly experimentation outside conventional systems of representation and exchange. While it is possible to speculate about arguments on behalf of the gender neutrality of the electronic environment (men who would not buy women's books might access them through the web), the hardware itself does not prevent (and may encourage) behaviours we recognize as constructed along gender lines. Flanders concludes that 'there is nothing intrinsic, then, about the electronic medium that guarantees a radical departure from the habits of thought fostered by the culture of the book . . . [T]he medium will not do this work for us . . . the medium is only an instrument of our methodology, and remains limited by our conceptual horizons' (ibid.: 141).

What new methodologies of the virtual can we conceptualize and deploy with respect to early modern women's position in the traditional canon or in a counter-canon? The concept of a database provides a starting point, or more precisely, provides a vantage point from which to examine the philosophical underpinnings that long have governed reading and representation. A database, for example, differs fundamentally from an anthology, in which the editor's selections predetermine the reader's options and encourage normative response and consensus. Anthologies have exerted powerful canonical influence since the late seventeenth century (Benedict 1996: 4–6). After reviewing recent editions of early modern women, Eger articulates a compelling possibility: 'Perhaps we can look forward to a time, sooner rather than later, in which it will be possible to "pick your own" anthologies from a freely accessible database of poetry' (Eger 1999: 212). Several databases are in varying stages of availability and financial stability. They include *The Brown University Women Writers Project* (currently a 200-text database which includes *Renaissance Women On-line*); *The Orlando Project: An Integrated History of Women's Writing in the British Isles* (mostly nineteenth- and twentieth-century texts, sponsored by the Social Sciences and Research Councils of Canada); *The Perdita Project* (400 sixteenth- and seventeenth-century manuscript compilations, sponsored by Nottingham Trent University); *The Emory Women Writers Resource Project* (50 texts from the seventeenth to the nineteenth centuries). *The Women Writers Project* began as an anthology, in response to immediate teaching needs and to frustration with the *Norton Anthology of Literature by Women*. The original founders created a 'wish list' that would become a resource for students and faculty wishing to access material before 1800. But the Project transformed itself dramatically from an anthology into a database dedicated more broadly to the long-term recovery of works by early women writers. The website explains: 'The emphasis was clearly on accessibility, especially for teaching, requiring diplomatic editions of specific copies; the priority was on accurate transcription rather than on scholarly apparatus, footnotes, critical introductions, et al., which would delay the availability of the material. The most compelling motivation has been getting the texts into electronic circulation in the virtual world.' The anthology often serves an ulterior purpose: to demonstrate periodicity, to mark out an evolutionary narrative in which the earliest example leads to the later ones, to show linking themes or forms that would allow one writer to be discussed in relation to another in the collection. The database can allow the reader independently to form connections, create categories, test and experiment with critical paradigms, to look for pattern in what at first appears quirkiness, to ascertain meaning in combinations of words that at first appear impenetrable, especially when 'we are dealing with a group of non-canonical writers – for instance women – whose texts have not necessarily been a formative part of our expectations about textual meaning' (Flanders 1997: 134). Let me briefly suggest some kinds of experimentation, based on my own limited use of the database. These modest experiments are not intended as general conclusions. At present, manuscripts are in one database (Perdita) and published works on another (WWP), and no website yet transfers information between others, or has come close to completing its encoding. Yet, even with these disclaimers, I believe it is appropriate to speculate about a possible direction of future efforts to change or develop the canon of early modern women writers.

The new electronic medium can explore language with great pliancy: words – singly, in phrases, or in variable proximity to other words – can be viewed in a variety of ways: chronologically, by author, by variants, by frequency. These options are tantalizing to poststructuralist readers. If women writers are supposed to be specialists in the topic of love, for example, it is easy to discover how often the word appears in their work, or which writers use it (or variants of it) most often, or in which texts 'holy love' is discussed, or erotic love, or married love. If one wished to make an anthology of one's own on, say, women and nature, the database would reveal the text in which these (and related) words occur. It would reveal that of 4,500 'hits', 2,400 occur in a single text by Margaret Cavendish. This work could be scrutinized and placed in relationship to others. Or do women more frequently write about death? or children? or household matters? or politics? In Brown's database, they write 'death' twice as often as 'love', 'father' twice as often as 'mother' – and far less frequently write 'child' or 'baby' (most of these examples occur in midwifery manuals), or 'marry' or 'wed'. Religious or potentially religious terms ('god', 'heaven', 'love', 'pride', 'church', etc.) far exceed domestic ones. In fact, the database exposes the disjunction between middle-class critical vocabulary and early modern women's words in the example of 'domestic', which is used only 128 times, all examples dated after 1735 and most after 1790. Of course, these examples are far more speculative than scientific, but speculation can be revealing.

Another option for bringing women's writing into the canon of early modern literature could be realized by searching for interconnections to the male-authored canon. Because encoded text makes women's words visible in various formats, it would be possible to search a database for texts that share a religious controversy or political debate: works on the commonwealth or on divorce contemporaneous with Milton, for example. Further, it may be more appropriate to judge women writers as communities, to replace the kind of hero-worship accorded to individual authors with respect for the kind of achievement that results from interaction or collaboration. Electronic texts permit simultaneous enquiry into any combination of works. If the work of, say, Quaker women, or prophets, or amatory writers, could be analysed according to the linguistic codes that were shared by each discrete subset, the features of their distinctive modes of representation might open up. They might be understood as crucial players in cultural history, as innovators of distinctive speech acts, and therefore valued. Finally, electronic text has great potential for teaching the rising generations of students, whose conventions of interpretation remain relatively unformed, how (not merely what) to read. The availability of women's writing is revolutionized by electronic texts. Faculty who trained in Shakespeare, Sidney, Wycherley, Dryden and Richardson may have difficulty at first in teaching Lanyer, Wroth and Behn. But many who have ventured into 'new' material discover how readily students accept it. We gain esteem for the things we feel we understand – 'what we love, others will love', Helen Vendler (2000: 31) cannily observes. Teachers can change the canon by changing syllabuses. Even the most self-conscious scholar, one who relentlessly examines the motives for 'loving' certain critical paradigms more than others, must choose a technology of reading and assign meaning to a text. Reader by reader (as Austen revolutionizes English society couple by couple), a new kind of canon will emerge.

   The idea of the canon connotes stability, but the scene of reading is always shifting. In the seventeenth and eighteenth centuries it might be at coffee-houses or tea-tables, in market square, garden or private chamber, just as now it might be in library, school, subway or workstation. Any text can be rendered vulnerable by the wrong context. Delarivier Manley's autobiographical *Adventures of Rivella* is in part about the perils that attend a woman writer's elevation to fame. Manley wrote this account of her life when she learned that two male contemporaries were planning to 'immortalize' her in a volume for which advertisements were already circulating. Her *New Atalantis* had won a place in the early eighteenth-century canon (this is the text with which Pope ensures the immortality of Belinda's lock). It was read, according to report, everywhere, along with a separately published 'key'. Manley had public recognition and political influence. *Rivella*'s ironic self-history demonstrates the reasons why even the most popular woman's work (rivalling Defoe's *Robinson Crusoe* in circulation and respect) has trouble belonging in a canon. Rivella never speaks directly; in fact, she is entirely absent from the text. Instead, two male characters, Lovemore and D'Aumont, discuss her life and her writing. But they misrepresent her person and misread her texts. Her political satire is transformed by them into a discourse on love; an attack on the Whigs is construed as an invitation to erotic pleasure. Manley is self-conscious about the way in which a woman's writing is produced and consumed. Rivella is silenced and displaced from her own narrative; she is worshipped for the wrong reasons. The men walk in a garden, praising her work, without consulting the actual text. And yet the ultimate irony is that the two men who misunderstand her are her own fictional creations. Several conflicting reading paradigms are superimposed on the same narrative. D'Aumont and Lovemore experience the text as a body. It does things to them and they do things to it. By the end, they are in a state of high sexual excitation as they imagine Rivella naked on a flower-strewn bed. But the inadequacy of their way of valuing her is clear. She is to be contemplated (like other early modern women writers) fully dressed in the fabric of her words, or even better, completely disembodied in a state of virtuality.

See also WOMEN AND WRITING

REFERENCES AND FURTHER READING

Altieri, Charles (1983). 'The idea and ideal of a literary canon.' *Critical Inquiry*, 10: 1, 37–60.

Backscheider, Paula (1993). *Spectacular Politics: Theatrical Power and Mass Culture in Early Modern England.* Baltimore, MD: Johns Hopkins University Press.

Barash, Carol (1996). *English Women's Poetry, 1649–1714: Politics, Community, and Linguistic Authority.* Oxford: Clarendon Press.

Benedict, Barbara M. (1996). *Making the Modern Reader: Cultural Mediation in Early Modern Literary Anthologies.* Princeton, NJ: Princeton University Press.

Benjamin, Walter (1969). *Illuminations*, ed. Hannah Arendt, trans. Harry Zohn. New York: Schoken Books.

Bennett, Tony (1987). 'Texts in history: the determinations of readings and their texts.' In Derek Attridge, Geoff Bennington and Robert Young (eds), *Post-Structuralism and the Question of History* (pp. 63–81). Cambridge: Cambridge University Press.

Brodky, Linda (1989). 'On the subjects of class and gender in "The Literary Letters".' *College English*, 51: 2, 125–6.

Clare, Janet (1998). 'Transgressing boundaries: women's writing in the Renaissance and Reformation.' In Marion Shaw (ed.), *An Introduction to Women's Writing from the Middle Ages to the Present Day* (pp. 37–64). New York: Prentice-Hall.

Crane, Mary Thomas (1998). 'Women and the early modern canon: recent editions of works by English women, 1500–1660.' *Renaissance Quarterly*, 51, 942–56.

Crawford, Patricia (1985). 'Women's published writings, 1600–1700.' In Mary Prior (ed.), *Women in English Society 1600–1800* (pp. 211–82). London: Methuen.

De Lauretis, Teresa (1987). *Technologies of Gender: Essays on Theory, Film, and Fiction.* Bloomington: Indiana University Press.

De Pizan, Christine (1982). *The Book of the City of Ladies*, trans. Earl Jeffrey Richards. New York: Persea Books.

Eagleton, Terry (1983). *Literary Theory.* Minneapolis: University of Minnesota Press.

Eger, Elizabeth (1999). 'Fashioning a female canon: eighteenth-century women poets and the politics of the anthology.' In Isobel Armstrong (ed.), *Women's Poetry in the Enlightenment: The Making of a Canon, 1730–1820* (pp. 201–15). London and New York: Macmillan and St Martin's Press.

Ezell, Margaret (1987). *The Patriarch's Wife: Literary Evidence and the History of the Family.* Chapel Hill: University of North Carolina Press.

——(1993). *Writing Women's Literary History.* Baltimore, MD: Johns Hopkins University Press.

Fendler, Susanne (ed.) (1997). *Feminist Contributions to the Literary Canon.* Lewiston, NY and Lampeter, Wales: Edwin Mellen.

Fetterley, Judith (1991). 'Introduction: on the politics of reading.' In Robyn R. Warhol and Diane Price Herndl (eds), *Feminisms: An Anthology of Literary Theory and Criticism* (pp. 492–508). New Brunswick, NJ: Rutgers University Press.

Flanders, Julia (1997). 'The body encoded: questions of gender and the electronic text.' In Kathryn Sutherland (ed.), *Electronic Text: Investigations in Method and Theory* (pp. 127–43). Oxford: Clarendon Press.

Foucault, Michel (1977). 'What is an author?' In Sherry Simon and Donald F. Bouchard (eds and trans.), *Language, Counter-Memory, Practice* (pp. 113–38). Ithaca, NY: Cornell University Press.

Furman, Nelly (1978). 'The study of women and language.' *Signs: Journal of Women in Culture and Society*, 4, 182–5.

Gates, Henry Louis (1994). 'Canon-formation, literary history, and the Afro-American tradition: from the seen to the told.' In David H. Richter (ed.), *Falling Into Theory: Conflicting Views on Reading Literature* (pp. 172–80). Boston: St Martin's Press.

Guillory, John (1993). *Cultural Capital: The Problem of Literary Canon Formation.* Chicago and London: University of Chicago Press.

Haselkorn, Anne M. and Travitsky, Betty S. (eds) (1990). *The Renaissance Englishwoman in Print: Counterbalancing the Canon.* Amherst: University of Massachusetts Press.

Hobby, Elaine (1988). *Virtue of Necessity: English Women's Writing 1649–1688.* Ann Arbor: University of Michigan Press.

——(1998). 'Usurping authority over the man: women's writing 1630–89.' In Marion Shaw (ed.), *An Introduction to Women's Writing from the Middle Ages to the Present Day* (pp. 65–93). New York: Prentice-Hall.

Kolodny, Annette (1980). 'Dancing through the minefield: some observations on the theory, practice, and politics of a feminist literary criticism.' *Feminist Studies*, 6, 1–25.

Kramnick, Jonathan Brody (1998). *Making the English Canon: Print Capitalism and the Cultural Past, 1700–1800.* Cambridge: Cambridge University Press.

Machery, Pierre (1987). *Post-Structuralism and the Question of History*, ed. Derek Attridge, Robert Young and Geoff Bennington. Cambridge: Cambridge University Press.

McKenzie, D. F. (1976). *The London Book Trade in the Later Seventeenth Century.* London: Sandars Lectures.

——(1986). *Bibliography and the Sociology of Texts: The Panizzi Lectures 1995.* London: The British Library.

Messenger, Ann (1999). *His and Hers: Essays in Restoration and Eighteenth-Century Literature.* Lexington: University of Kentucky Press.

Montrose, Louis A. (1989). 'Professing the Renaissance: the poetics and politics of culture.' In H. Avram Veeser (ed.), *The New Historicism* (pp. 15–36). New York: Routledge.

Pearson, Jacqueline (1988). *The Prostituted Muse: Images of Women and Women Dramatists 1642–1737.* New York: St Martin's Press.

Rabinowitz, Peter (2000). 'Actual reader and authorial reader.' In David Richter (ed.), *Falling Into Theory: Conflicting Views on Reading Literature*, 2nd edn. Boston: St Martin's Press.

Richter, David H. (2000). 'How we read: interpretive communities and literary meaning.' In David Richter (ed.), *Falling Into Theory: Conflicting Views on Reading Literature*, 2nd edn (pp. 235–52). Boston: St Martin's Press.

Rosenfelt, Deborah S. (1998). 'The politics of bibliography: women's studies and the literary canon.' In Joan Hartman and Ellen Messer-Davidow (eds), *Women in Print: Opportunities for Women's Studies Research in Language and Literature* (pp. 11–35). New York: Modern Language Association of America.

Ross, Trevor (1998). *The Making of the English Canon From the Middle Ages to the Late Eighteenth Century.* Montreal: McGill-Queens University Press.

Schweikart, Patrocino (1991). 'Reading ourselves: toward a feminist theory of reading.' In Robyn R. Warhol and Diane Price Herndl (eds), *Feminisms: An Anthology of Literary Theory and Criticism* (pp. 525–50). New Brunswick, NJ: Rutgers University Press.

Searle, John (1994). 'Storm over the university.' In David Richter (ed.), *Falling Into Theory: Conflicting Views on Reading Literature* (pp. 83–7). Boston: St Martin's Press.

Shevelow, Kathryn (1989). *Women in Print Culture: The Construction of Femininity in the Early Periodical.* London: Routledge.

Shklovsky, Victor (1965). 'Art as technique.' In Lee T. Lemon and Marion Reis (trans.), *Russian Formalist Criticism: Four Essays* (pp. 3–24). Lincoln: University of Nebraska Press.

Smith, Barbara Herrnstein (1983). 'Contingencies of value.' *Critical Inquiry*, 10, 1–36.

Spencer, Jane (1998). ' "Public view": women's writing, 1689–1789.' In Marion Shaw (ed.), *An Introduction to Women's Writing from the Middle Ages to the Present Day* (pp. 94–121). New York: Prentice-Hall.

Todd, Janet (1989). *The Sign of Angellica: Women, Writing, and Fiction 1660–1800.* New York: Columbia University Press.

Vendler, Helen (2000). 'What we have loved, others will love.' In David Richter (ed.), *Falling Into Theory: Conflicting Views on Reading Literature*, 2nd edn (pp. 31–40). Boston: St Martin's Press.

Weinbrot, Howard (1993). *Britania's Issue: The Rise of British Literature From Dryden to Ossian.* Cambridge: Cambridge University Press.

Williams, Raymond (1977). 'Literature in society.' In Hilda Schiff (ed.), *Contemporary Approaches to English Studies* (pp. 24–37). New York: Barnes and Noble.

Woodbridge, Linda (1998). 'Dark ladies: women, social history, and English Renaissance literature.' In Viviana Comensoli and Paul Stevens (eds), *Discontinuities: New Essays on Renaissance Literature and Criticism* (pp. 52–71). Toronto: University of Toronto Press.

23
Feminist Historiography
Margo Hendricks

The choice of narrative implies that behind the vicissitudes of every narrative there are a set of *a priori* values – regarding time and materiality – that will emerge naturally from the 'natural' mode of narration.

Kearns 1997: 121

The historian's decision to write about one facet of human experience and not another gives that aspect permanence and significance. For history represents a people's, a society's, a culture's way of remembering itself. Jacob Burckhardt described history to his nineteenth-century readers as 'the record of what one age finds worthy of note in another'. The recorded is saved, and conversely, the unrecorded is lost.

Zinsser 1993: 117

Lorenzo: I shall answer that better to the commonwealth than you can the getting up of the Negro's belly. The Moor is with child by you, Lancelot.
Lancelot: It is much that the Moor should be more than reason, but if she be less than an honest woman, she is indeed more than I took her for.

The Merchant of Venice, 3.5.35–40

The Problem of History

Since the publication of Jacob Burckhardt's *Civilization of the Renaissance in Italy* (1860) modern historiography about Renaissance cultures has been shaped by Burckhardt's insistence on the importance of the individual to these cultures. Apart from a few aristocratic females, women seemed to have played virtually no role in the 'civilizing' of cultures that (for Burckhardt) marks the 'Renaissance'. Furthermore, given the aims of 'traditional historiography', women as a group appeared to have only a tangential connection to the events and relations of power that produced 'History', with a few notable exceptions like Elizabeth I and Mary Stuart. For academic women interested in writing about ordinary ('common') women's lives, the place of such women in the grand narrative of 'English History' was a rather contested one. First, these historians faced the difficult challenge of proving that there was a history to tell, and that its telling required new methodologies. Second, because the majority of historians in the academy were male, any woman seeking to write women's history was likely to face criticism for wanting to deal with such supposedly trivial issues. Thus these early women historians often either acquiesced in the rules of traditional historiography – telling the story of major events, peoples, civilizations and ideas – or broke from the ranks and suffered marginalization and/or trivialization for their insistence on researching 'women's' histories.

The publication of Alice Clark's *Working Life of Women in the Seventeenth Century* (1919, reprinted 1982) marked a major turning point for the study of women's history. For the first time, the historian's concern with women as a group intruded itself into the telling of 'English History' and, by extension, into the question of historiography itself. Clark's book made the study of working-class English women's lives a legitimate and necessary component of labour historiography. Clark's book was followed by studies such as Carroll Camden's *The Elizabethan Woman* (1952), Ruth Kelso's *Doctrine for the Lady of the Renaissance* (1956) and Lawrence Stone's *The Family, Sex, and Marriage in England 1500–1800* (1977). These studies increased awareness of women's lives in Renaissance and early modern England, yet none represented itself as 'feminist historiography'. Not until Joan Kelly asked 'Did Women Have a Renaissance?' did the problem of historiography become a feminist concern to scholars of Renaissance cultures. Kelly's essay, first published in 1977 (and reprinted in 1984), served as a clarion call for feminist historians (literary as well as social or cultural) to rethink their assumptions about the period called the Renaissance (Kelly 1984).

As Kelly argues, 'one of the tasks of women's history is to call into question' the accepted view of women's equality with men during the Renaissance (ibid.: 19). Furthermore, as she aptly demonstrates, the Italian Renaissance worked to foster a 'new division between personal and public life . . . and with that division the modern relation of the sexes made its appearance' (ibid.: 47). Since then historians have redefined the theoretical and historical tapestry of Renaissance and early modern cultures. Women's lives have been solidly woven into the narrative fabric of history – economic, political, social/cultural, intellectual and artistic. Historians of literature, culture, politics, philosophy and economics no longer ignore the role of women in helping to shape the contours of Renaissance English history.

Insisting that women's lives and activities were critical to Renaissance and early modern English social formations and their histories worth telling, feminist social historians helped to redraw the boundaries of historiography, thus prompting feminist scholars to reconsider not only their political relationship to the telling of history but women's role in making history. This 'second wave' of feminist historiography includes such works as Susan Amussen's *An Ordered Society: Gender and Class in Early*

Modern England (1988), Keith Wrightson's *English Society 1580–1680* (1982), Margaret R. Sommerville's *Sex and Subjection: Attitudes to Women in Early-Modern Society* (1995), Martin Ingram's *Church Courts, Sex and Marriage in England, 1570–1640* (1987) and Anthony Fletcher's *Gender, Sex and Subordination in England 1500–1800* (1997). It has engineered a shift in the imperatives guiding historiography concerned with early modern English history. Hence, while it is possible to write a history of early modern England without 'attending to women', it is difficult to imagine that such a study will be accepted without some form of criticism.

Feminist and radical historiography, in its attempt to address Kelly's provocative (at the time) question, 'Did Women have a Renaissance?', has fundamentally altered what constitutes normative historiography. Moreover, in tracing the history of labouring women, unruly women, women writers, mystics, rebellious women, as well as wives, mothers, daughters, sisters, whores, courtesans, tribades and 'spinsters', feminist cultural, social and literary historians have facilitated historicist approaches to literary texts and have broadened the basis of evidence that constitutes sites of discursive engagement. For example, Elaine Hobby's *Virtue of Necessity: English Women's Writing 1649–88* (1989) and Margaret Ezell's *Writing Women's Literary History* (1994) prompted a similar project in literary studies. Seeking to ' "re-vision" women's literary past and to reveal some of the assumptions embedded in the current model of feminist historiography concerning the connections between gender and modes of literary production and about historical conditions of authorship', these two very different works challenged traditional assumptions about our ability to 'recover' a past or a 'women's tradition' (Ezell 1994: 5–6).

We now take for granted the publication of anthologies such as *Kissing the Rod* (1989) and *Renaissance Drama by Women* (1996). Critical anthologies such as *Early Women Writers: 1600–1720* (1998), *Re-writing the Renaissance* (1986), *Women, 'Race', and Writing in the Early Modern Period* (1994), *Feminist Readings of Early Modern Culture* (1996), *A Feminist Companion to Shakespeare* (2000), *Maids and Mistresses, Cousins and Queens* (1998) and *Rereading Aphra Behn* (1993) have forever changed the theoretical and intellectual landscape of Renaissance Studies. Editions of texts written by Renaissance and early modern women writers are no longer on the 'unavailable list'. We now have access to the collected works of Aphra Behn, Mary Wroth and Mary Sidney; individual editions of works such as Aemilia Lanyer's *Salve Deus Rex Judaeorum*, Elizabeth Cary's *The Tragedy of Mariam* and Anna Weamys's *A Continuation of Sir Philip Sidney's 'Arcadia'* (published under the auspices of the Women Writers Project at Brown University) have expanded our literary horizons and made us acutely aware of the contributions Renaissance women made to 'the Renaissance'. Recent technological innovations helped to generate Brown University's 'Renaissance Women Online' – a resource that continues to place more texts by women in the hands of students and scholars alike.

Like Joan Kelly's ground-breaking query, these timely interventions have triggered, among feminist scholars of Renaissance culture, a rethinking of theoretical and historical methodologies. Women's literary practices did not reside in a single genre, but rather emerged in a myriad of forms. And, importantly, authorial voice was not one of feminine singularity among pre-1700 women writers but one as varied as the experiences of the women writing. In particular, Margaret Ezell's *Writing Women's Literary History*, while not the only work to critique modern historiographical assumptions about pre-1700 women, was one of the few studies to interrogate a branch of feminist historiography and its relationship to the past. Since these pioneering studies, revisionary literary histories are being written that resist prescriptive categorization of women writers into 'feminist' or 'non-feminist' camps. Significantly, gender studies, queer studies and cultural studies have effectively redefined the terms of literary historiography.

Questions about the relationship between gendered identities and sexual identities and about the role of race and colonialism in the construction of history have begun to redefine the practice of cultural historiography. Similarly, since the publication of Alan Bray's *Homosexuality in Renaissance England* (1982), the complex (and often problematic) place of sexuality in Renaissance and early modern English culture has made us crucially aware of the significance of erotic desire not only in the lives of men but also in the lives of women. Women's challenges to patriarchal ideologies regarding female sexuality have been explored in feminist literary studies such as Susan Zimmerman's *Erotic Politics: Desire on the Renaissance Stage* (1992) and Ferguson's, Quilligan's and Vickers's *Re-Writing the Renaissance* (1986). Similarly, attention to the discourses of 'race' and colonialism in Renaissance English literary culture has grown by leaps and bounds. Within these studies women are of especial interest given the social constraints imposed by imperialist and colonialist social formations.

Yet in all that is 'new' it is intriguing that feminist historiography continues to reflect an unconscious complicity in positing a portrait of early modern English culture that is singularly homogeneous and white. In other words, it is both ironic and troubling that, despite the current critical engagement with ethnicity and race in early modern English studies, the histories of non-European (and even some European) women residing in England (especially in the larger towns and cities) remain untold or under-told. Did all immigrant women so easily assimilate into English culture as to erase their 'ethnic' presence in the nation? While the personal history of Aemilia Lanyer provides some insight into one immigrant family's assimilation, Lanyer's musician family moved in social circles unavailable to the thousands of women settling in England. What about those women fleeing persecution, or seeking a better socio-economic existence, or forcibly brought to England? Where do these women fit in the historical paradigm of early modern English culture? How do we 're-vision' their histories, to use Margaret Ezell's chosen term?

Renaissance London, in its own way, was as diverse in its population as the Venetian world represented in *The Merchant of Venice*. Yet we know little of that England. Who are the immigrant women who resided outside the city, in Spitalfields, Moorfields, in Southwark? Who are the ethnic women who worked in the 'stews' and brothels of Renaissance London? What place do these immigrant women have in our 'read-ings' of Shakespeare's women? While much has been done on 'blackness' of late, our sight has been directed at the manor house and not the 'public' house. In other words, we've studied the master's house, not the servant's.

Over the course of the past five to ten years new voices have confronted these prob-lems in feminist historiography and scholarship. The year 1992, the quincentenary of Columbus's voyage to the Americas, proved especially significant in terms of a reap-praisal of Renaissance culture. 'New World studies', postcolonial studies and 'ethnic studies' renewed interest in the dynamics of colonialism and imperialism. Feminists of colour began to question the grand narratives of feminist theory and historio-graphy, which not only generalized or essentialized 'women' according to a single paradigm but also seemed to elide non-European and non-white feminist issues from those grand narratives. In an astute commentary on the critical and theoretical prac-tices of Western feminism, Chandra Talpade Mohanty writes: 'Western feminists who sometimes cast third world women in terms of "ourselves undressed" (Michelle Rosaldo's [1980] term), all construct themselves as the normative referent in such a binary [first world/third world] analytic' (Mohanty 1991: 56). The problem, in Mohanty's view, is that this positions women as 'somehow socially constituted as a homogeneous group prior to the process of analysis' (ibid.).

Women, 'Race' and Writing in the Early Modern Period (Hendricks and Parker 1994) was an epistemological attempt to redress some of the problematic issues noted by Mohanty. A collection of essays written by women scholars and reflective of the interdisciplinarity of contemporary feminist scholarship, *Women, 'Race' and Writing* marked a sea-change for feminist historiography; Woman suddenly became women, and Women became women individuated by ethnicity. A new generation of feminist historians of early modern culture has begun cogently to interrogate the universal woman model and to outline ways of illuminating women's heterogeneity in terms of ethnicity, class and sexuality in sixteenth- and seventeenth-century England. The ten-dency to speak of women in universal terms has not entirely disappeared, however. In part, the epistemological difficulty inheres in the terms of the debate; women across the globe and temporalities, regardless of class, ethnicity, education and sexuality, do share a common set of experiences. But the elision of fundamental differences born of cultural and economic specificity that accompanies the subsuming of all women under the category Woman not only marginalizes those differences but occludes the privilege that accrues to some women as a result of their affiliation with a colonial or imperial power.

With the publication of Ania Loomba's *Race, Gender, and Renaissance Drama* (1989) and more recently of Kim Hall's *Things of Darkness: Economies of Race and Gender in Early Modern England* (1996), with its excellent attention to the 'archive', we may now have a theoretical and/or historiographical paradigm for bridging the 'gap' between literary history, cultural studies and social historiography. As Hall illustrates, within the epistemology and historiography of Renaissance Studies (whether literary, historical or visual), non-European women play an important role in the definition(s) of the category of Woman. Hall, in particular, has shown us how to investigate the gender and ethnic contours of Shakespeare's England without sacrificing theoretical concerns. The women of Shakespeare's plays have ethnic and racial identities that are drawn not just from the imagination; these representations are indicative of the complex and multi-ethnic environs that foster that imagination.

These scholarly and historiographical developments make clear that Renaissance and early modern England was neither ethnically homogeneous nor inexorably heterosexual. Ironically, much of this work has been undertaken by literary historians; many social and political historians dealing with Renaissance and early modern England continue to represent sixteenth- and seventeenth-century England as if none of this new historiography exists. In other words, issues of race, sexuality, ethnicity and immigration are curiously absent from these historians' publications. This absence, in turn, engenders a curious interpretive window for literary and cultural historians interested in investigating, for example, the English context for play texts such as *Othello*, *Titus Andronicus*, *The White Devil* or *The Merchant of Venice*, or for proclamations such as Elizabeth I's authorization of the 'deportation of negars, negroes, and blackamoores' from England. Was there 'just cause' for Elizabeth's action? Was there a significantly large population of people of African ancestry in England, and were a large number of these individuals becoming a 'drain' on society? Was the visit of the Moroccan ambassador to Elizabeth I's court the only possible context for Shakespeare's *Othello* and *The Merchant of Venice*, or were there a number of mixed marriages or sexual unions (like that suggested between Lancelot Gobbo and the Moorish female in *The Merchant of Venice*) evident in the London boroughs for the playwright to draw upon?

Similar questions can be asked, and perhaps more fruitfully answered, about the influx of other European non-aristocratic women into England, especially Dutch, Flemish, Spanish, German, Italian and eastern European women. Was there extensive migration of labouring women from these areas? Were these women single or married? What types of labour activities did they engage in, especially if they were not attached to a household? Did women who were not attached to households become assimilated into English culture, and if so, how? Did any of these women become involved in the sex trade in London? If so, did ethnic and national enclaves develop? What place did gypsy women have in this world? Is it possible to reconstruct these histories? And if so, what type of historiography is required? Do historians (social, political, literary, economic and cultural) have the requisite tools and theories to discover/uncover these histories?

I must confess that, other than raising the questions, I can only suggest possible ways of beginning to 'balance' our historical enquiries into women's lives in Renaissance England. Perhaps the most important way is one advocated by social historians: archival investigations. If there are evidentiary materials that can provide answers to my questions, these materials are not going to be found easily, nor are they necessarily easily comprehensible. We may have to redefine the parameters of our expectations and perceptions of what constitutes 'factual evidence' and 'truths' about Renaissance societies and their cultural practices. We may have to exercise a 'necessary suspension of disbelief' in order to practise a feminist historiography that acknowledges not only the diversity of women in Renaissance and early modern England but also the politics of patriarchal historiography when dealing with these women.

The first step, however, is a traditional one: into the archives. There is a wealth of unexamined materials awaiting the intrepid cultural detective. Feminist historiography has not yet begun to exhaust the rich archival materials residing in major libraries and resources such as the Bodleian and British Libraries, the Public Records Office, the London Metropolitan Records Office, and local and county archives throughout England. We cannot, however, go into these archives looking for the 'usual suspects'. We must begin to read these documents with an air of defamiliarization – as if we were coming to Renaissance English history for the first time. This does not mean that we project some vision of 'objectivity' onto our endeavours: far from it, for 'objectivity', like 'truth', has always been the bane of women's histories and feminist historiography. Rather, we must read archival materials with the expectation that they will conceal as much as they reveal, and our task is to account for both.

To illustrate this point I want to focus on two accounts dealing with women's lives that have not yet made their way into the scope of feminist historiography dealing with Renaissance and early modern England. The first discussion focuses on an incident brought to my attention by Kim Hall concerning the activities of Sir Francis Drake during his travels in the Pacific. The second account seeks to highlight some of the intriguing histories extant in the archives. Both accounts are intended to serve as an indication of the possibilities for feminist historiography and its aims.

A Matter of History/Historiography

> The Negress Maria stared unblinkingly at the retreating white sails of the English ship, her belly slightly swollen against the thin linen shift the English captain preferred her to wear. To her right stood the Mandingo, to her left the Bambara. Her own people no more than the shadowy image associated with the faint whisper of remembered voices in a language she no longer used. Don Francisco had called her María, but that was not her name. The Anglo Captain had called her Mary each time he had taken her to his bed, though in her tears and passion she had whispered her true name. When she could no longer see the white spectre of the English ship, she turned and looked to the bare encampment the English had left on the barren island. She vowed that the niño in her womb would leave this island and seek the land of his father.

The above account of the Negress Maria is a fictional 'narrative' based on a historical account describing an event that took place in 1577–8 (Nuttall 1967). In 1577 Francis Drake sailed along the coast of Central America, near Panama, towards

Guatulco. On the way, he captured a Spanish vessel bound for Lima. On board the ship was a gentleman named Don Francisco de Zarate. Drake held the Don for three days, showing de Zarate 'much favour' and giving him 'the poop to sleep in' (Nuttall 1967: 31). De Zarate travelled with a black woman, apparently his mistress. According to John Drake's report, Drake 'took from Don Francisco a negress named Maria, and the pilot of said ship' (ibid.). Drake continued his journey to Guatulco where he released Don Francisco and the other hostages he had taken before reaching Guatulco. After replenishing his vessel, Drake 'set sail with men of [his] own nation only, the said negress Maria, a negro whom they had taken at Païta, and another they took at Guatulco, besides one they had brought with them from England' (ibid.). From Guatulco, Francis Drake sailed westward, eventually reaching the Indian Ocean. Reaching the Moluccas islands, Drake 'took in a supply of meat and provisions and lightened their ship by reducing their company to sixty men' (ibid.: 32). From the Moluccas the ship sailed north until it reached an uninhabited island, where, because of contrary winds, it remained for approximately six weeks. When the ship departed three people were left behind: 'the two negroes and the negress Maria, to found a settlement' (ibid.). In his generosity, the Englishman Drake left the three 'rice, seeds and means of making fire' (ibid.).

According to the accounts used by Zelia Nuttall (which form the basis of my discussion), Maria was the mistress of a Spanish nobleman (Zarate) and, when he is captured and held for ransom by Francis Drake, made part of the ransom payment (apparently at the insistence of Drake). A pregnant Maria is abandoned by Drake some few months later, along with two male slaves, on a deserted island in the Indian Ocean. Maria was by no means the only woman of African ancestry to have been abducted from her homeland, nor was she the first to become (whether by force or choice) the sexual partner of a European. On the contrary, like Maria, thousands of young women forcibly taken from Africa's west coast became subject to sexual exploitation and rape by European sailors. Some, in recognition of the limited power that might become available to them, became the mistresses of European men such as Zarate or Francis Drake.

The story of the Negress Maria occurs in two Renaissance narratives: Francis Fletcher's *The World Encompassed* (1628) and John Drake's testimony to an inquisition court in Lima, Peru. My 'version' of the Negress Maria's situation is a deliberate attempt, on my part, to minimize the Anglo-Spanish conflict and emphasize the undocumented details of an African woman forcibly taken from her family, community and homeland. Such an intrusion, and a fictive one at that, is a direct response to the historian Zelia Nuttall's handling of the incident, which gives no significance either to Drake's appropriation of the slave woman or to the fact that he kept her on board his ship for months, and then left her, and two male 'negroes', on an 'uninhabited' island. Granted Nuttall's edition was published in 1967; yet the type of historiography practised by Nuttall remains intact even now. Published in 1995, reprinted in 1997, John Cummins's *Francis Drake: Lives of a Hero* reproduces the 'historicity' of Nuttall's account, along with his own masculine interpretation. As

Cummins writes, 'Drake retained from Zarate's ship a good-looking black girl called María, "which was afterward gotten with child between the captain and his men pirats, and sett on a small iland to take her adventure"' (Cummins 1995: 111). The very next sentence, ironically, is 'Drake's business with the Spanish was now almost done' (ibid.). Cummins's 'business' with Maria, however, was not yet 'done'. Later in the chapter he returns to her story. This time, however, Cummins's language lacks the inflection of familiarity that marks his earlier account: 'When they sailed on 12 December they left behind the black woman María, now pregnant, and two negroes, "to start a population"' (ibid.: 121).

The historiography exemplified in Cummins's celebratory biography of Francis Drake and in Nuttall's translation of the Spanish documents and her editing of the English accounts dealing with Drake's abduction and abandonment of Maria is the mode of historiography that feminists need to challenge. Cummins's description of Maria as 'good-looking' serves to trivialize and, seemingly, justify Drake's taking her from the Spanish ship. We need to resist reaffirming with our silence this problematic exemplum of Renaissance English heroism. Feminist historiography engaged in critiques of patriarchal exploitation of women cannot ignore this example of one of the more extreme forms of that exploitation.

Eighty years after Drake abandoned Maria, Richard Ligon composed his *A True and Exact History of the Iland of Barbadoes* (1657), creating titillating images of women of African ancestry as part of English imperial attitudes towards women in English colonial space. While Ligon's experiences and actions differ radically from Drake's, Ligon too finds himself drawn to the 'dark' body of the African woman. Ligon's story, however, is told in his own words. Confined at Upper Bench Prison, Ligon decided to write an account of his 1647 journey from England to the Caribbean island of Barbados. Ligon's *A True and Exact History of the Iland of Barbadoes* is far more than just a travel diary, however. In his text, Ligon offers his readers an ethnographic, topographical and social portrait of places and peoples he found along the way. One of the more interesting segments of Ligon's account concerns his adventures on the Cape Verde island of St Jago. Like most ethnographers, Ligon is concerned to set down in as detailed a fashion as possible all that he sees so that anyone reading the narrative will gain as accurate a likeness of the inhabitants, customs and social relations on the island as his words can convey.

In his description of Vagado, the Portuguese Governor of St Jago, for example, Ligon writes: 'though he were the chiefe Commander of the Iland: yet by his port and house he kept he was more like a Hermite then a Governour. His familie consisting of a Mollotto of his own getting, three Negroes, a Fidler, and a Wench' (Ligon 1657: 11). When invited to dine at Vagado's house, Ligon continues his profile of the governor's household, dwelling at length on the physical appearance of the governor's black mistress. In the course of his account Ligon reveals to the modern reader a side of seventeenth-century English history that was, until recently, rarely investigated within the context of early modern English literature.

As he concludes his description of Vagado's household, Ligon finally comes to the one figure conspicuously absent from the earlier details of the Padre's hospitality, the female presence which marks domestic space. Until this point, it is not clear whether Vagado's mistress was present during the dinner or whether she joins the group at precisely the moment Ligon indicates in his narrative. Regardless, the presence of this woman apparently so affected Ligon that he felt compelled to include a detailed exposition of her person and manner, and of his attempts to engage her in polite conversation. The passage begins with Ligon declaring the woman to be a 'Negro of the greatest beautie and majestie together: that ever I saw in one woman. Her stature large, and excellently shaped, well favoured, full eyed, and admirably graced' (ibid.: 12). From his description, the woman's garments clearly denote her privileged status, for she is adorned in costly fabrics and materials. Richly attired in buskins of silk, a mantle of 'purple silk', 'pearls' and 'large pendants', Vagado's mistress stands before Ligon, 'the rarest black Swanne' (ibid.).

Ligon's description of Vagado's mistress conveys the same erotic register as Cummins's remarks on the attractiveness of Drake's Maria. Because these women are registered narratively merely as sites of erotic pleasure, their subjectivity remains an enigma in the historical narratives crafted in celebration of early modern colonization. Given the general perception of women as primarily breeding sites, it is intriguing to note that rarely is there any mention made of the offspring generated by these momentary sexual encounters, especially those in England. What about the children of second- and third-generation relations of miscegenation? How did they fare in a cultural climate in which increasingly blackness was linked to slavery? As social historians of American slavery have shown, when English colonial slave codes began to figure lineage in terms of skin colour, mandating that '"Mulatto" children . . . born of slave mothers, were categorized as slaves irrespective of their fathers' social status', the aim was not only to confront the disruptive sexual dynamics of a new social formation but, more importantly, to shore up the rifts accruing to patriarchal property relations (Beckles 1989: 133). The question we may want to ask is whether these new 'Europeans' disturbed or undermined patriarchal ideologies about racial identity in Renaissance and early modern England as well.

In 1555, when John Lok returned from Africa accompanied by five Africans, London's total population was approximately a quarter of a million. Of this number an estimated five thousand inhabitants were 'aliens'. This figure is misleading as it only represents the 'registered alien' population and thus fails to account for those 'undocumented aliens' that have plagued governments since the inception of the modern nation-state. The complexity of immigration into England is not by any means new; rather, as Laura Hunt Yungblut demonstrates in *Strangers Settled Here Amongst Us* (1996), xenophobia has long plagued England's perceptions of itself. Throughout the sixteenth century, surveys, legislation and royal proclamations became recurring reactions to increasing immigration and its attendant problems. As Yungblut illustrates, an influx of Italians, Germans, Dutch, French and Mediterranean peoples provides insight into the effect immigration had on native English people. Yet people of African ancestry are routinely ignored as a contributor to this documented history of immigration.

Yungblut, for example, directs our attention to a 1567 London survey on immigrants to England:

> By Easter (March 30) 1567, authorities found 3,324 aliens in London, the liberties, and Westminster. The point of the survey was clear, since the aliens were questioned primarily about nationality and length of residence in England. Of these immigrants, 156 had come in the past twelve to twenty-four months, and 232 had arrived within the last year. A survey dated December 15 of that same year reported 3,758 aliens in London and the adjoining liberties, with 1,059 of them citing a length of residence of one year or less. (Yungblut 1996: 21)

In the footnote where she provides the source for her citation, Yungblut remarks: 'interestingly, two "blackmores" were [reported] living in London at the time of this survey' (ibid.: 134). Yungblut's comment is significant not just because it provides some 'evidence' of a black presence; it is also important for its revelation that these 'blackmores' were clearly viewed as part of the foreign-born immigrant population in London.

Yungblut's decision to relegate the 'two blackmores' to a footnote rather than include them in her general discussion of ethnic immigrants into England sadly reflects the tendency by most historians to marginalize the place of blacks in England's history. Even more problematic is the fact that Yungblut's book was published in 1996 — nearly a quarter of a century after James Walvin's *Black and White: The Negro and English Society 1555–1945* and Folarin Shyllon's *Black People in Britain, 1553–1833*; over a decade after Peter Fryer's *Staying Power: The History of Black People in Britain* and Nigel File's and Chris Power's anthology, *Black Settlers in Britain, 1555–1958*; and fewer than four years after the anthology *Essays on the History of Blacks in Britain*, edited by Jagdish S. Gundara and Ian Duffield. What is missing in Yungblut's analysis (and most of the recent social histories of sixteenth- and seventeenth-century England) is an acknowledgement that a small group of historians have made us very much aware of Renaissance and early modern England's black immigrant population. Yungblut's oversight is indicative of the degree to which race and ethnicity truly do not register on historians' methodological and intellectual radar.

Despite the work of Walvin, Fryer, Shyllon, File and Power, and Gundara and Duffield, academics such as Anthony Appiah and Ivan Hannaford can still make sweeping generalizations about the question of an African presence in Renaissance and early modern England. The idea that sixteenth- and seventeenth-century England lacked a sufficiently large population of African/English to warrant anxiety about race continues to influence the theoretical and historical analysis of race. So endemic is this assumption to traditional historiography, that I have often jested that perhaps it is time we literary critics who work on race temporarily abandon the 'literary' (i.e. the texts of Shakespeare and company) and expand our archival efforts on behalf of the Renaissance and early modern English/Africans who are denied a presence in the world in which they lived. My point here is that historiographers have been shown a path for such investigations; they need only follow it.

Given the increased presence of scholarly discourse about the significance of race and colonialism to Renaissance and early modern English literary culture, it is surprising that a concomitant discussion is not taking place among social and cultural historians about the presence of non-Europeans residing in English cities and towns, especially London. The histories of these individuals are intricately interwoven into the history of England's ethnic diversity and, if one looks closely, residing in the very archives that social and cultural historians privilege. One such individual is Martin Francis, an African/Englishman whose name appears in public records. I discovered Francis by accident during a recent visit to the London Metropolitan Archives. As I perused a reference book filled with cases selected from the *Middlesex Sessions Registers* (in search of references to gypsies and courtesans for another project) I came across a brief account of a complaint filed by Francis against Katherine Hutchins. The case, recorded on 21 October 1658, was both a find and a puzzle. According to the accusation, Hutchins, along with Elizabeth Simpson and Mary Biggins, pretended 'to make a marriage between the said Martin Francis (a Blackmoore) and the said Elizabeth Simpson; thereby defrauding him of seventeen pounds in money' (Middlesex County Sessions of Peace Roll, 1658: 1189/117, 281). The full entry in the Sessions book also suggests that this was not the first time the three women had undertaken such a pretence.

The record of Martin Francis's complaint is significant for two reasons. The brief entry serves as further 'proof' of the presence and assimilation of people of African ancestry into early modern English culture. Second, the entry is complete enough to give us some insight as to the degree of assimilation on the part of individuals like Francis. Francis clearly understood that he had recourse to English law when the agreed-upon marriage failed to occur. Moreover, he was apparently financially sound enough to be the target of a marriage scam, suggesting that perhaps money and not colour might have carried greater weight within the communities where English/Africans resided. What remains a puzzle are the same queries that we should ask about 80 per cent of England's population during the period: where did Francis earn his income (his trade is not indicated in the Sessions entry); what was the final disposition of the case? Did Martin Francis eventually marry? How and when did he arrive in England, or was he native born? Were his parents native born, or immigrants? Martin Francis appears on very few historical radars in the renewed attention to matters of race in Renaissance and early modern English culture. One reason is that records such as the *Middlesex Sessions Registers* are generally not among the archival starting points for the study of the African presence in England. Another, and more troubling explanation, is the pervasiveness of assumptions about the size of the English/African population in sixteenth- and seventeenth-century England.

Martin Francis has shown us that English/Africans did not have a propensity for celibacy, nor were they isolated into a single ethnic community. While some English/Africans probably married among themselves, others often married or became sexually involved with non-black English men and women. In other words, English/Africans most likely lived the same lives as their peers whatever their social status. The Martin Francis case warrants further investigation (as does the case of Drake's Maria) by feminist historians. These cases document the place of ethnic women and men as part of the English social fabric; Elizabeth Simpson and Katherine Hutchins exploit a man for money; that he happens to be a 'blackamoore' appears not terribly significant if we recognize that the parentheses that surround the term in the Sessions Roll may be there solely to distinguish this Martin Francis from another man of the same name. In addition, as the document indicates later, this is not the first time the two women have been brought before the courts on this type of charge.

My own interest in this case is generated by the obvious interactions between peoples of different ethnic groups within the communities of London, and by the fact that the women appeared to exploit brilliantly a major patriarchal institution that circumscribed women's agency. The activities of women such as Hutchins and Simpson lead me to wonder how many immigrant women, including those of African ancestry, may have used similar ploys to survive in Renaissance and early modern London? Were Hutchins and Simpson preying on some anxiety of Martin Francis related to his presence in London, or did they merely see a victim? Interestingly, there is no indication in the Sessions Roll account of Francis's age, occupation, and whether he had been previously married. Such information would make Hutchins's and Simpson's deception even more intriguing matters for historical study, especially in the light of George Best's observations about the offspring produced by such 'mingling' (in Hakluyt 1903–5: 1589–90).

Instances such as these ought to serve as prompts for greater scrutiny of archival materials by social, political and cultural historians interested in the lives of women in Renaissance and early modern England. Furthermore, literary historians writing about issues of race and ethnicity must begin to expand the categories of textual analysis on the topic; that is, these scholars must begin to look beyond the literary text. The type of cross-fertilization I am suggesting here is reflected in works such as Hall's *Things of Darkness* and Imtiaz Habib's *Shakespeare and Race: Postcolonial Praxis in the Early Modern Period* (1998). In both studies, woman becomes a decentred category of analysis, and ethnicity is as much a paradigm as sex. Importantly, as a result of the increasing significance of postcolonial theories to the study of the past, ethnicity becomes a dynamic force in the study of gender relations in Renaissance and early modern England. What has to happen, in my view, is that as we use the term 'ethnic' in our historiographical practices we must begin to include women of African ancestry in the definition of what constitutes ethnicity. English-African women need to be viewed under the same microscopic conditions as their English-Italian or English-Irish counterparts, especially if these women were born in England.

As always, there are an infinite number of questions which dance at the edge of cultural criticism, especially of the sort I attempt here. The most pressing ones include: how do feminist scholars of early modern English culture understand the immigrant woman's position in a world which symbolically exploits her 'otherness' as a literary and cultural foundation for the construction of a particular form of womanhood at the same time as it literally conceals her presence in Renaissance England? How do we 'discover' this archived history in the light of this concealment? Moreover, what are the dynamics between these women and other immigrant women? I believe answering these queries may shed epistemological light on the literary representation of immigrant women in Renaissance and early modern England. To what degree does the behaviour of women such as Elizabeth Simpson and Katherine Hutchins speak to the problems facing indigenous English women in cosmopolitan London? How many Negress Marias find their way to London, pregnant by some Englishman or another European male? Do they link up with the Katherine Hutchinses and Elizabeth Simpsons to survive in a city that affords them an opportunity to 'disappear' into its communities and archives?

Feminist historiography has as its theoretical and political obligation the imperative to redress traditional historiography's gendered oversights. Feminist historians of Renaissance and early modern English culture also have the added imperative of redefining the parameters of feminist historiography so that it is truly representative of 'women's histories'. In essence, feminist historiography cannot afford to generate totalizing narratives about women's existence in Renaissance and early modern England, particularly when a number of these women were from diverse ethnic and social backgrounds. It is important that feminist social historians take the lead in reshaping and redefining the categories of analysis in modern historiography. Literary historians have brought the non-English female body from obscurity to visibility in their readings of Renaissance and early modern literary texts. It is time social and cultural historians incorporate that visibility into their own historiographical methods and investigations.

Ernst Breisach (1994: 410) writes: 'no other endeavour fits as well as history does with the peculiar needs of human beings, to whom the temporality of life allots the roles of emigrants from the past, inhabitants of the present, and immigrants into the future'. If there is one major task remaining for feminist historiography it is the positing of how best to undertake this project. And, without question, uncovering the complex and diverse history of Renaissance and early modern England affords feminist historiography a continuing opportunity to demonstrate Breisach's postulation. In the university settings of England, the United States and member nations of the English Commonwealth, feminist social, literary and cultural historians should not sit complacently and assume that someone else will take up the task of writing and interpreting the histories of immigrant women, of ethnic women, of women involved in the sex trade, or migratory women. Alice Clark's *Working Life of Women in the Seventeenth Century* should not stand as the *sine qua non* of research on labouring women in Renaissance and early modern England. Nor should aristocratic, middle-class and poor women be collapsed into the general category of 'Renaissance or Early Modern Woman'. Finally, we should not wait for (nor expect) these accounts to be written by someone who 'identifies' with one or any of these categories. Having accepted the wisdom of a feminist revision of history, we must continue practising what we preach.

REFERENCES AND FURTHER READING

Amussen, Susan (1988). *An Ordered Society: Gender and Class in Early Modern England.* New York: Columbia University Press.

Beckles, Hilary M. (1989). *Natural Rebels: A Social History of Enslaved Black Women in Barbados.* London: Zed Books; New Brunswick, NJ: Rutgers University Press.

Bray, Alan (1982). *Homosexuality in Renaissance England.* London: Gay Men's Press.

Breisach, Ernst (1994). *Historiography: Ancient, Medieval, and Modern*, 2nd edn. Chicago: University of Chicago Press.

Clark, Alice (1982) [1919]. *Working Life of Women in the Seventeenth Century.* London: Routledge and Kegan Paul.

Cummins, John (1995). *Francis Drake: Lives of a Hero.* New York: St Martin's Press.

Ezell, Margaret J. M. (1987). *The Patriarch's Wife: Literary Evidence and the History of the Family.* Chapel Hill: University of North Carolina Press.

——(1994). *Writing Women's Literary History.* Baltimore, MD: Johns Hopkins University Press.

Ferguson, Margaret, Quilligan, Maureen and Vickers, Nancy (eds) (1986). *Re-Writing the Renaissance: The Discourses of Sexual Difference in Early Modern Europe.* Chicago: University of Chicago Press.

File, Nigel and Power, Chris (1981). *Black Settlers in Britain, 1555–1958.* London: Heinemann.

Fletcher, Anthony (1997). *Gender, Sex and Subordination in England 1500–1800.* New Haven, CT: Yale University Press.

Fryer, Peter (1984). *Staying Power: The History of Blacks in Britain.* London: Pluto Press.

Gundara, Jagdish S. and Duffield, Ian (eds) (1992). *Essays on the History of Blacks in Britain: From Roman Times to the Mid-Twentieth Century.* Aldershot: Avebury.

Habib, Imtiaz (1998). *Shakespeare and Race: Postcolonial Praxis in the Early Modern Period.* Lanham, NY: University Press of America.

Hakluyt, Richard (1903–5). *The Principal Navigations, Voyages, Traffiques & Discoveries of the English Nation (1600)*, 12 vols, ed. Walter Raleigh. Glasgow: James Maclehose and Sons.

Hall, Kim F. (1996). *Things of Darkness: Economies of Race and Gender in Early Modern England.* Ithaca, NY: Cornell University Press.

Hendricks, Margo and Parker, Patricia (eds) (1994). *Women, 'Race' and Writing in the Early Modern Period.* London: Routledge.

Hobby, Elaine (1989). *Virtue of Necessity: English Women's Writing 1649–88.* Ann Arbor: University of Michigan Press.

Ingram, Martin (1987). *Church Courts, Sex and Marriage in England, 1570–1640.* Cambridge: Cambridge University Press.

Kearns, Katherine (1997). *Psychoanalysis, Historiography, and Feminist Theory: The Search for Critical Method.* Cambridge: Cambridge University Press.

Kelly, Joan (1984). *Women, History and Theory: The Essays of Joan Kelly.* Chicago: University of Chicago Press.

Ligon, Richard (1657). *A True and Exact History of the Iland of Barbadoes.* London.

Loomba, Ania (1989). *Race, Gender, and Renaissance Drama.* Manchester: Manchester University Press.

Maclean, Ian (1980). *The Renaissance Notion of Woman: A Study in the Fortunes of Scholasticism and Medical Science in European Intellectual Life.* Cambridge: Cambridge University Press.

Middlesex County Sessions of Peace Roll, 1189/117 (1658). London: Metropolitan Archives.

Mohanty, Chandra Talpade (1991). 'Under western eyes: feminist scholarship and colonialist discourses.' In Chandra Talpade Mohanty, Ann Russo and Lourdes Torres (eds), *Third World Women and the Politics of Feminism* (pp. 51–86). Bloomington: Indiana University Press.

Nuttall, Zelia (ed. and trans.) (1967). *New Light On Drake: A Collection of Documents Relating to His Voyage of Circumnavigation 1577–1580.* Reproduced by permission of the Hakluyt Society from the edition originally published by the Society in 1914. Nendeln/Liechtenstein: Kraus Reprint.

Orlin, Lena Cowan (1994). *Private Matters and Public Culture in Post-Reformation England.* Ithaca, NY: Cornell University Press.

Shakespeare, William (1988). *The Merchant of Venice.* In Stanley Wells and Gary Taylor (eds), *The Complete Works of William Shakespeare.* Oxford: Oxford University Press.

Shyllon, Folarin (1977). *Black People in Britain 1555–1833.* London, New York and Ibadan: The Institute of Race Relations, London by Oxford University Press.

Sommerville, Margaret R. (1995). *Sex and Subjection: Attitudes to Women in Early-Modern Society.* London: Arnold.

White, Hayden (1978). *Tropics of Discourse: Essays in Cultural Criticism.* Baltimore, MD: Johns Hopkins University Press.

——(1987). *The Content of the Form: Narrative Discourse and Historical Representation.* Baltimore, MD: Johns Hopkins University Press.

Wrightson, Keith (1982). *English Society 1580–1680.* New Brunswick, NJ: Rutgers University Press.

Yungblut, Laura Hunt (1996). *Strangers Settled Here Amongst Us: Policies, Perceptions, and the Presence of Aliens in Elizabethan England.* London: Routledge.

Zimmerman, Susan (ed.) (1992). *Erotic Politics: Desire on the Renaissance Stage.* New York: Routledge.

Zinsser, Judith P. (1993). *History and Feminism: A Glass Half Full.* New York: Twayne Publishers.

Index